CW00798047

THE BRITISH WAY OF WAR

THE BRITISH WAY OF WAR

JULIAN CORBETT
and the
BATTLE FOR A
NATIONAL STRATEGY

ANDREW LAMBERT

YALE UNIVERSITY PRESS
NEW HAVEN AND LONDON

For information about this and other Yale University Press publications, please contact:
U.S. Office: sales.press@yale.edu   yalebooks.com
Europe Office: sales@yaleup.co.uk   yalebooks.co.uk

Set in Minion Pro by IDSUK (DataConnection) Ltd
Printed in Great Britain by TJ Books, Padstow, Cornwall

Library of Congress Control Number: 2021944149

ISBN 978-0-300-25073-2

A catalogue record for this book is available from the British Library.

10 9 8 7 6 5 4 3 2 1

For Zohra, always and forever

CONTENTS

Introduction

On 31 May 1920 two of the most original minds ever applied to the development of national strategy met over dinner in a spacious Knightsbridge apartment. The apartment belonged to Sir Julian Corbett (1854–1922), official historian of British grand strategy in the First World War, and creator of national strategic doctrine.[1] His guests brought the war in the Middle East to his dinner table, one of them making a profound impression upon him, as he recorded in his diary:

> Hedjaz Lawrence & Ernest Richmond[2] to dinner. Very interesting talk on his experiences & on art of war generally, on which his views are original, & much in accord with mine. Spoke highly of Wemyss & Allenby, but of very few others. His horror of waste of life soldiers' strategy involves needlessly. Very learned on medieval castles, esp. those in Syria on which we had much fraternising talk. Also of abortive Alexandretta project, which he regretted & and vainly urged.[3]

It is significant that Corbett did not slip into the populist 'Lawrence of Arabia', preferring the more specific regional connection. Ernest Richmond was the third son of Corbett's best friend, artist Sir William Richmond, and brother of Admiral Sir Herbert, who projected an amphibious offensive in the Gulf of Alexandretta that would have been far more effective in securing British interests than the disastrous Gallipoli operation.[4]

Corbett's epigrammatic note reflected a conversation that took place at two distinct levels. When Lawrence and he discussed wartime operations and strategy the two men were on common ground. As naval commander-in-chief in the Red Sea, Vice-Admiral Sir Rosslyn Wemyss and his squadron had been the base from which Lawrence's campaign had operated, supplying arms, money, fire support and hot baths, all of which Lawrence greatly valued. Wemyss became First Sea Lord at the end of 1917, helping to win the war, and then, with Corbett's assistance, secure the future of Britain's seapower empire at Versailles. Corbett shared Lawrence's judgement of Wemyss, and Field Marshal Lord Allenby, who led the conquest of Palestine, Jerusalem and Damascus in 1917–18. Corbett had known Wemyss for over a decade, working very closely with him in 1918 and 1919, and was exceptionally well informed on the higher direction of the war in the Middle East.

The sentence 'His horror of waste of life soldiers' strategy involves needlessly' recorded a profound meeting of minds. Corbett had spent four years contesting the War Office's obsession with the idea of a 'decisive theatre' in which a complex global conflict might be won by mere weight of numbers. Lawrence's campaign, sea-based, fast-paced and largely conducted by locally raised forces, had been the absolute antithesis of the Western Front. It was, as Corbett recognised, a properly British strategy. Little wonder Lawrence emerged from the war as the one truly admirable hero, dressed in white, scarcely a British life lost in his battles, and determined to settle a debt of honour to the Arabs. Ultimately these two great romantics, students of chivalry and castles, fine printing and elegant prose, were grappling with the consequences of a catastrophe that had wrecked their world. There was an undertone of deep emotion, prompted by the human cost and the sheer folly involved. Corbett had argued there was a better way before 1914; Lawrence had demonstrated that he had been right. Tragically, Corbett died before he could write Lawrence's campaign into the Official History of the war: the development of his thinking on that subject, clearly foreshadowed in volume III of *Naval Operations*, faltered in the minds of lesser men.

Lawrence understood seapower, describing how Wemyss's forces had moved the Sherifian army by sea, kept it supplied, and enabled it to outflank a larger Turkish force at Wejh, which had been driven from the coast by naval bombardment before the Arabs arrived. Corbett highlighted it as 'a most interesting case of the value of command of the sea as a factor in shore operations against an enemy depending entirely on land communications for his maintenance'. The vital Hedjaz railway was cut from the base secured by the Navy at Wejh. Lawrence's praise for Wemyss and the fleet was unreserved.[5]

*

This book is an intellectual biography of Sir Julian Corbett and his concept of a distinctive 'British way of waging war',[6] a limited maritime method, focused on economic pressure, that proved effective in limited and unlimited conflict, one that addressed British needs rather than copying 'continental' methods that used mass conscript armies in restricted geographical contexts, seeking victory by knockout blow. Corbett recognised that practical strategy was a unique, contingent response to specific circumstances. There was no ideal method of waging war, supporting peace, or balancing the costs and risks of security policy. He believed the strategy would be developed by digesting past practice and strategic theory into a living doctrine to inform the decisions of political leaders, and the advice of military professionals. He stressed that the ultimate responsibility lay with statesmen, not soldiers, or sailors.

The only previous biography was published forty years ago.[7] Professor Schurman's assessment emphasised merit unrewarded and hopes unfulfilled, mistaking Corbett's wry self-deprecating irony for despair, more concerned with the problems Corbett faced than his achievement. The book was influenced by Brian Tunstall, his university tutor, and Corbett's posthumous son-in-law, who viewed Corbett's career through the lens of his own unhappy experience as an inter-war naval educator, and controlled access to Corbett's archive.

The negative cast of Schurman's text was encouraged by existing work on the Royal Navy's war planning in the Fisher era. In 1960 Professor Arthur Marder focused on the personal and political quarrel between Admiral Lord Charles Beresford and Fisher, rather than policy disputes. Marder ignored the educational and doctrinal functions, and relevance of the Ballard Committee War Plans of 1907, which included Corbett's theoretical preface 'Some Principles of Naval Warfare'.[8] These opinions were echoed by his friend Lieutenant Commander Peter Kemp, Head of the Admiralty Historical Section: who dismissed them as outdated, irrelevant and 'almost juvenile'.[9] This judgement was seriously flawed.

Fisher had tasked Captain George Ballard, the Navy's leading strategist, and Captain Edmond Slade, the director of the Naval War Course, to examine the operational and strategic issues of an Anglo-German conflict for the Naval Intelligence Division (NID), which, with the War Course, formed the core of Fisher's planning process.[10] The plans reflected the new realities of European Great Power politics, the Anglo-French and impending Anglo-Russian Ententes which focused British strategic concerns on Germany, prompting the creation of a powerful Home Fleet in the Thames Estuary. Furthermore Kemp's critique was profoundly ahistorical, criticising Ballard for not anticipating the naval situation in 1914.[11] In 1907 Germany had only a single primitive submarine, and only four such craft by 1909. In 1907 the German battlefleet was less than half the strength of the British, and had no answer to Fisher's larger, faster and more heavily armed 'Dreadnoughts'. Kemp's comments about mine warfare were equally inaccurate. The Royal Navy had access to the Japanese experience of mine-fields and minesweeping in the Russo-Japanese War, 1904–5.[12] Ultimately Fisher intended the plans, endorsed by Fisher and Admiral Sir Arthur Wilson, the leading fleet commander of the era, to disseminate current doctrine to the service.

Marder had noted Ballard's focus on economic warfare, delivered through a distant blockade. That Corbett addressed the mechanics of blockading the Scotland–Norway gap in his preface indicates a familiarity with the central themes of the document. His contribution contained early sketches of his legal and strategic justification for Ballard's new 'distant blockade', ideas developed in the subsequent essay 'Private Property'.[13] These plans also emphasised the possibility of an offensive into the Baltic to complete the economic blockade of Germany. The French could control the eastern Baltic from the otherwise empty bases of their Russian ally, leaving the western Baltic and North Sea to the Royal Navy.[14] These were hardly 'juvenile' options in early 1907, when the Entente partners outnum-bered Germany in modern battleships by three to one; the ratio Clausewitz thought necessary for a successful offensive.

A decade later Marder concluded Corbett 'had little influence' on the wartime Royal Navy, with *Some Principles of Maritime Strategy* as 'not nearly as influential as Corbett would have liked'.[15] Schurman concurred, claiming that the war ended his educational role and demonstrated the limits of his influence.[16] These closely linked claims seriously underesti-mate Corbett's pre-war consequence and wartime impact, mistaking modest irony for a confession of irrelevance. This flawed assessment would be developed by Marder's most ardent critics.

In 2013, 'revisionist' historian Nicholas Lambert dismissed Corbett as a mere 'pen for hire', who 'misunderstood the changed world of the twentieth century around him', and therefore 'lacked the strategic relevance to enter the inner sanctum of Edwardian naval strategy'.[17] Any interest such assertions might have engendered was quashed by the failure to address the context in which Corbett operated, and the misreading of familiar documents.[18] Corbett was a 'False Prophet' because he did not anticipate, and validate discredited 'revisionist' arguments about economic warfare.

Corbett was never a 'pen for hire'; he turned down many invitations to write to order.[19] These were his opinions. He worked for the Royal Navy because he loved the service, had a powerful sense of duty, and enjoyed the challenge. If the Navy asked the questions, Corbett cherished the intellectual independence to think for himself. That independence flowed from a global investment portfolio and extensive London property, managed with his elder brother, an MP who worked in the City of London.[20] The assertion that Corbett did not understand the nature of modern finance is absurd. Not only was he personally enmeshed in global finance, but he attended Naval War Course lectures on the relevant issues, including international law and world shipping, often dining with the speakers. He would commission two of them to write War Course textbooks in 1913.[21] Furthermore, *Some Principles of Maritime Strategy*, his 1911 exposition of national strategic doctrine, clearly differentiated between modern economic warfare and sailing-age blockades, stressing that 'commerce prevention' would enable Britain 'to do that which really brings wars to an end – that is, to exert pressure on the citizens and their collective life'. 'Wars', he noted:

are not decided exclusively by military and naval forces. Finance is scarcely less important. When other things are equal it is the longest purse that wins. ... Anything, therefore, which we are able to achieve towards crippling our enemy's finance is a direct step to his overthrow, and the most effective means we can employ to this end against a maritime state is to deny him the resources of seaborne trade.

No government would miss an opportunity to undermine the 'financial position on which the continued vigour of those armed forces so largely depends'. Corbett emphasised economic war as the prime deterrent, depending on the right to capture private property at sea.[22] Not only was Corbett well aware of the latest thinking on economic warfare but he also understood that the primary function of British strategy was to deter other powers from damaging British interests.[23] There was nothing 'secret' about the broad lines of British thinking on economic warfare in 1914 because 'secret' plans have no deterrent value.

Corbett was equally well informed about communication technologies and the strategic uses the Royal Navy was making of them. He attended Charles Tilston Bright's interminable War Course lectures on submarine telegraph cables, and Rear Admiral Sir Henry Jackson's account of long-range wireless, while his friend Captain Herbert Richmond wrote to him while conducting strategic wireless trials at the Cape of Good Hope in 1907–8. Nor was he unaware of modern gunnery technology: he discussed the issues with Percy Scott and translated Frederic Dreyer's gunnery paper into English. He visited warships, both at sea and under construction, along with the new floating dock at Portsmouth, while his beloved eldest nephew was a pioneer aviator, an early casualty over the Western Front. Finally, his thinking reflected a progressive liberal assessment of the evolution of the Empire.

The outbreak of war did not end Corbett's effort to energise the Navy's intellectual processes, merely redirecting his energies to present-minded tasks: strategy papers, propaganda and analytical narratives. In the first major war for which Britain compiled an Official History, Corbett was chosen to direct the project. He ensured the history would be an educational/doctrinal asset, focused on the strategic and grand strategic level, restricting the vastly expanded Army to the operational and tactical levels. In addition, he advised on strategy, directed the Historical Section of the Committee of Imperial Defence, linked to the Admiralty Historical Section, wrote Cabinet and Admiralty memoranda, including critical input into the development of the War Cabinet, wrote sophisticated propaganda to support British maritime belligerent rights policy, recorded the war at sea as it happened for the Naval Staff, prepared the ground for British success in the 'Naval Battle of Paris' of 1919, the 'decisive' engagement that secured British seapower for another generation, and dominated the committee that shaped British policy on a League of Nations.

Every aspect of his wartime career reflected a profound anxiety to ensure that post-war Britain returned to the sound strategy of limited maritime warfare, which he had explained in an officially sanctioned doctrine primer of 1911. The Official History analysed the war as the basis for future naval education and doctrine development.[24] A belated knighthood in spring 1917 recognised the importance of his contribution. Corbett found himself recording the mistakes of an immature naval command structure and a misguided First Lord of the Admiralty who, along with his Cabinet colleagues, changed the strategy of a unique global sea empire. He took control of the Official History project to ensure future generations would recognise the 'continental commitment' as an aberration, entirely unrelated to British practice, serving military ambition, rather than national interests. From that vantage point he would link and explain grand strategy and naval operations, the higher aspects of the conflict. Elsewhere he explained British policy to uncertain Americans, to counter the insidious threat of 'freedom of the seas'. In the process he became a public figure, attacked by old opponents and feared by those whose reputations were exposed to his forensic analysis. Winston Churchill and David Beatty, men with big egos and patchy war records, contested his Official History, but Corbett won those battles. However, such distractions took their toll: Corbett's sudden death left the strategic argument unfinished. Deprived of his guiding hand, memories of the war became focused on tactics, bloodshed and sacrifice in Europe, rather than the success of global maritime strategy that enabled the empire to evolve into a 'sea commonwealth' behind the aegis of a global Navy, the basis of Britain's distinctive strategy of limited maritime/economic war.

The last three decades have changed the world and our understanding of Corbett; new evidence, new contexts and new scholars have revived his reputation and vindicated his arguments.[25] Today his work occupies a central place in the history of strategic thought.[26] It is also the basis of a unique national approach to strategy.

*

On 13 February 1913 Corbett discussed his ideas with Colonel Hubert Foster, Lecturer in Military History at Sydney University, 'a believer in my strategy'.[27] The casual claim to authorship of a distinct strategy, in a cryptic diary entry is critical. It is also highly unusual. Corbett was well aware that he had created something new and specific, that he was a strategic thinker, a theorist of war, and that his ideas were recognised as such across the empire and commonwealth, by soldiers as well as sailors. Four years later he would describe that strategy as the 'British way' in another diary. He did not make the claim in public because the resulting furore would have damaged the case he was making, and the policy of those, including 'Jacky' Fisher and Foster, who agreed with him. Not only was Corbett innately modest, but he was also highly unusual among pre-1918 strategists; a liberal civilian with no military experience, that civilian status was a critical asset: it helped him avoid the military obsession with tactics and battle that limited the value of much nineteenth-century writing. He preferred to focus on the political dimension of conflict. Corbett's experience of local and national politics, and his travels, along with the literature, culture and social anxieties of the late Victorian era, shaped his thinking before he became a strategist. He read John Robert Seeley's assessment of the future of the British Empire two decades before Clausewitz provided him with a theoretical framework to approach that agenda. Nor was it an accident that his most important intellectual follower, Admiral Sir Herbert Richmond, was the son of his best friend, a prominent artist. Corbett knew many of the leading men of the age, statesmen, authors, artists, publishers, soldiers and only latterly admirals. Understanding the man and his world is critical to understanding his thinking.

Corbett's legal expertise provided the forensic skills to exploit the conceptual weakness of contemporary literature on strategy and policy, while his own arguments displayed uncommon clarity of thought and expression. He castigated special pleading, self-interest and lazy assumptions. In addition he addressed the evolution of international law as it affected maritime belligerent rights, which determined the ability of dominant naval powers to control the movement of neutral merchant vessels on the high seas in wartime. This was of critical importance to British strategy, which relied on economic warfare. In 1907 he explained the Admiralty's position on the forthcoming Second Hague Conference and how the law had impacted on the strategy of a global maritime war between 1756 and 1763. The views of powerful maritime neutrals had been significant in several wars, the Armed Neutrality projects of 1780 and 1801 posed serious challenges to British power, while American hostility, dating back to the War of 1812, would hamper the application of economic warfare in any future conflict with a European power. He contrasted the powerful synergy of law and strategy between 1756 and 1763 with the position of the current Lord Chancellor, who advocated abandoning strategic advantage to secure international concord.[28] Working alongside naval planners, he emphasised the need to settle the legal position before the next war because that position would have a massive impact on Britain's strategic options. In 1911 a shift in the legal position compromised Admiralty strategy. The issue became pressing after war broke out, requiring legal arguments, propaganda and policy briefs to sustain sea power.

Corbett explained how the unique methods that had sustained the state and built a global seapower empire remained critical to the strategic doctrine of the Edwardian era. He introduced historical scholarship and legal expertise into the education of the Royal Navy, influenced national policy and war planning, and produced a body of literature that transformed the writing of history and strategy. Yet, for much of the past century, Corbett's reputation has been a battleground between the proponents of total war, on land and latterly in the air, and those who think a limited maritime strategy has been and remains the best model to address Britain's peculiar needs.

The difference between Corbett's subtle, sophisticated elucidation of his theme and the grandstanding journalese of Basil Liddell Hart's 'British Way in Warfare' was at heart a question of method: the argument was Corbett's, passed on by his friend Herbert Richmond, who recognised the limitations of the advocate.[29] Unlike Liddell Hart, Corbett had the intellectual power and literary skill to construct a durable argument, one that could not be refuted by those who disagreed at a visceral level. His 'British way' has stood the test of time.

In 1972 Professor Sir Michael Howard's *The Continental Commitment* provided historical precedent for the Cold War primacy of NATO in national security policy, reducing global interests to a diminutive 'out of area' issue, and rewriting the past to align with current practice.[30] His attack on maritime strategy used Liddell Hart's 1931 essay as a 'straw man', and reduced Corbett to a cipher. His book helped persuade British historians to take a European view of British strategy, dominated by Army operations, and ignore Corbett. Reading backwards from the specific short-term needs of 1972 to validate Army General Staff calls for a continental role between 1905 and 1914 was ahistorical. Howard shaped a strategic canon that ignored Corbett and emphasised Clausewitz, despite Corbett's brilliant development of the Prussian text to address British needs.

Howard's argument influenced the most important study of the 'British way', David French's *The British Way in Warfare, 1688–2000* of 1990. French only engaged with Corbett in the introduction, and then briefly. When he cited Corbett's emphasis on the contrast between the British and German methods he excluded the critical clause, 'which too many writers both at home and abroad quietly assume to have no existence'.[31] French followed Howard in attributing the 'British way' to Basil Liddell Hart's 1931 lecture.[32] Corbett's strategic histories ranging from the sixteenth century to 1916 were ignored. Fortunately the tide turned. In 2013, Sir Hew Strachan noted:

'The real originator of a distinctively British approach to strategy was Julian Corbett.'[33] He goes on to explain:

> Strategic thought requires a capacity to interrogate strategic practice, to reflect on the experience of the application of theory, and to do so in a way which produces ideas which are applicable beyond historical boundaries in terms of widening our understanding of war and its utility. Such an approach embodies the possibility of change, not just the straitjacket of continuity. Britain has made such a contribution, its most original author was . . . Julian Corbett.[34]

Critically, Corbett's understanding evolved across twenty-five years, it was never reduced to dogmatic checklists, and his judgements were qualified – something he stressed by adding the word *Some* to the title of his core text *Principles of Maritime Strategy*. He wanted strategy to become a living process in the minds of his students, senior officers and the statesmen who must direct the use of force in war. As Beatrice Heuser noted, strategy – the link between political aims and the use or threat of force – is not a science.[35] Strachan described it as a 'profoundly practical business': an art to be mastered by study and practice, one that develops the intuitive judgement to meet unforeseen futures and new situations, not a process or rule.[36] The central focus of modern strategy has been the link between land battles and the political objectives of organised polities.[37] This approach is intimately connected to tactics, not least in the work of Clausewitz, who has far more to say about defending mountain passes than the political nature of conflict.

Clausewitz's famous aphorism that war is a continuation of policy by other means only appeared novel in the context of an autocratic military power. No-one in Britain in 1830 would have considered civilian control of war novel. For the previous 150 years, elected ministers, not monarchs or generals, had settled strategy. The key issue in strategy is to understand the political outcomes those battles and campaigns were intended to achieve. The classically educated British elite had long been familiar with Thucydides' discussion of strategy, in which 'the business of the general' included naval and combined operations, including the catastrophic expedition to Sicily, directed by the people.[38] The Athenian strategic model of economic warfare and amphibious power projection to obtain strategic advantage by location, resources or money was essentially identical to that of Britain. Athens

10

exploited the asymmetry of maritime power to counter larger and more powerful terrestrial states, adopting a maritime identity, culture and strategy to support that policy, while using the democracy that had voted to make Athens maritime, and directed those wars, as a weapon.[39] Not only is strategy a practical subject but its remit extends far beyond the use of force.

Corbett's strategy met contemporary British needs – not those of other states or other ages – advancing theoretical understanding of war was only a tangential benefit. His critical outputs promulgated doctrine, not strategic theory. He recognised that British aims in Europe were necessarily limited, Britain had no desire to become a European power, with all the political social and economic implications of such a programme, even to secure the invasion ports of the Scheldt estuary and the Flemish coast.[40] While the argument that the changing balance of power in the early twentieth century compelled Britain to take a more active role in Europe is sound, the assumption that this must necessarily involve deploying a large army is not.[41] Britain could not impose order on the Continent without risking the empire that alone made it a great power, and the command of the sea that kept the islands secure. While Heuser suggests that 'only the British had the geographic luxury of not having to think about' mass conscript armies before 1914, Corbett knew that such thoughts were a commonplace in social conservative circles, influenced by German agendas, popularised by the Army General Staff and the right-wing press.[42] He demonstrated that Britain had relied on limited maritime strategy, even in European total wars, using economic warfare and small military forces to support allies. This option flowed from the fact that British aims in continental wars were limited and essentially negative. This option was only available to Britain, which was both an insular power *and* possessed a dominant navy.

Corbett, a man of his age, his class and the imperial world of Edwardian Britain, became a strategist in a rapidly evolving context. He joined the debate with France and Russia the primary threats; after 1900 they were replaced by Imperial Germany, whose ambition to become a world power could only be achieved through European hegemony. Despite the changing threat, Corbett focused on the core issue: how to protect the British Empire as it evolved into a 'sea commonwealth' of nations. To meet that need, Corbett recovered a 'British way' from past practice, practice he refracted through strategic theory and delivered in officially sanctioned lectures and texts for policymakers and naval officers. His thinking developed through the systematic examination of past practice as precedent. In the process he transformed naval history into a modern discipline, focused on service education, but grounded in academic professionalism. Above all he explained how a unique seapower great power functioned in a world of continental military challengers.

Corbett made explicit something that Clausewitz had left implicit – that strategy was a unique national construct, where 'strategical' principles meet specific contexts. Liberal ideology shaped his response to the problem of war, separating him from conservative thinkers, uniformed or otherwise. His maritime strategy provided a British/imperial alternative to continental warfare, linked to progressive politics, while exploiting Britain's global power, rather than exposing its military weakness. His genius lay in using the ideas and language of German theory to explain that system, while illustrating his argument from British experience in limited and unlimited conflict. His work influenced sea officers, statesmen and a wide constituency of intellectuals and opinion-formers, none more so than Admiral Lord Fisher. Their friendship reflected shared progressive, democratic values – Fisher being the more radical of the two. Fisher prompted, read and applied much of Corbett's work on history, strategy and international law. He used Corbett's arguments to shape strategy and influence decision-makers, including King Edward VII.[43] Corbett supported Fisher when they agreed; but he would not compromise. As Jon Sumida suggested, his methods raised the standard of debate in Edwardian England, forcing Fisher's critics to raise their game.[44]

Edwardian Britain needed a strategy to deter war, and strategists who understood deterrence. Here Corbett and Fisher were as one. Fisher loathed violence and understood that Britain had no interests that would be advanced by a major European war. Deterrence was central to his policy, using fleets and press leaks to coerce Germany, focusing on German weaknesses. Critically, its dependence on Swedish iron ore in a prolonged conflict made the Baltic central. He encouraged Corbett to refine the legal and strategic cases for an attack on the German war economy. Neither Fisher nor Corbett had any desire for war, but they understood that only a credible threat would deter. This required a national maritime strategy that integrated all elements of strength, including mail steamers, telegraph cables and financial markets to secure sea control. The basic security task was to exploit that control to attack the enemy by economic and amphibious means, while supporting allies and attacking the enemy's economy. Fisher urged the statesmen to adopt a national programme, promising significant savings, but the Liberal governments of 1906 to 1914 allowed the services to pursue divergent strategies. The resulting tensions compromised the development of wartime strategy.

Some Principles of Maritime Strategy reduced those ideas to doctrine, explaining the strengths and weaknesses of the British imperial state, and the 'way of war' needed to secure it into the future. Three years later Corbett was obliged to explain how the grand strategy of a unique global maritime empire had ended up being defined by the commitment of a small army to a short section of the Franco-Belgian frontier. Little wonder he commended T.E. Lawrence's methods: using local forces, naval support and economic input, as an alternative to British conscripts. While his forensic mind processed and analysed information, a broader intellectual engagement and progressive politics inflected his arguments. The wider worlds of Julian Corbett remain essential to understanding the man, and his ideas: they are also the occasion for the unconscionable length of this book.

CHAPTER 1

Victorian Empire

In March 1921, having reached an age when childhood memories become especially precious, Julian Corbett and his wife Edith walked to No. 148 Kennington Road, just south of the Thames, close by the Oval, the home of Surrey Cricket Club. Corbett and two of his siblings, Charlie and Ada, had been born there, before the family moved out in 1856. The house was in a sad state, no longer suitable for a gentleman, 'ruinous and shabby – garden neglected and kitchen garden gone'. He took some photographs and they walked back to their apartment in Kensington.[1]

Julian Stafford Corbett was born on Sunday, 12 November 1854, at the family home, also known as Walcott House. It was an auspicious arrival: the family was on the cusp of significant economic success. His father, architect Charles James Corbett, had moved to London from Croft in Lincolnshire in the late 1840s. He became a property developer, creating dedicated office space in London, then something of novelty, before moving into suburban development. Charles married Elizabeth Stafford in 1852: Julian was their second son. Elder brother Charles would be the most important of his siblings, although sister Ada, the third child, and three more brothers were close. He was christened at Lambeth Church on Friday, 2 February 1855; his godparents included Manchester businessman David Alexander, his future father-in-law. Social ties and family connections bound the newly wealthy middle classes, as ancient lineage had shaped the aristocracy.

By 1861 Charles Corbett was seriously rich, prompting a move to Imber Court at Thames Ditton, close by Hampton Court Palace. A large, rambling structure, mostly built in the eighteenth century, Imber gave the Corbetts a prominent position in local society, easy access to the River Thames, extensive grounds and a sense of history. Corbett would begin his literary career in the attic. The Corbett children moved effortlessly into the wealthy elite, sharing assumptions of progress and privilege common to their class. Their liberal views, and decidedly Liberal politics, appear to have been a birth-right. Charles James Corbett had been named for Charles James Fox.

The family also owned Woodgate, a country estate near Hayward's Heath in East Sussex. It offered a base for hunting, shooting and fishing, sports that all the Corbett boys enjoyed; Corbett often visited, creating gardens and mixing in local society. Later he acquired his own country retreat.

His parents were endlessly curious – and highly sociable. They enjoyed museums, art galleries, walking in Hyde Park, the Crystal Palace at Sydenham, attending public events, and entertaining. They visited relatives in Lincolnshire, the Alexanders in Manchester, and from the 1860s enjoyed continental travel. This family-centred social life made a lasting impression. Elizabeth Corbett was at the heart of this world, a woman of intelligence, character and musical taste. Julian may have been her favourite, he carried her family name. Elizabeth survived her husband, who died in 1882, by a decade. Julian did not marry during her lifetime, and chose a wife from within the extended family circle. His daughter would be named in her memory.

While Corbett's first biographer was struck by the apparent indolence of his siblings, wealthy families had little need to work before 1914. Elder brother Charles, who inherited their father's drive and ambition, ran the family finances, extensive property and stock portfolios from the City of London, while Julian looked after the Imber Court estate. The family unit began to fragment after their mother's death, but the younger brothers remained independently wealthy. They never settled to anything of conse-quence, because they never had to. Herbert, 'Bertie', was a global traveller – a passion that Julian shared – and he spent much of his life abroad. Frank planned the ponds they laboured to create at Woodgate, while Edward, 'Tod', a passionate yachtsman, possessed a fine but chaotic mind. Sister Ada married a barrister, W.H.C. Wilson: their son Denys Corbett Wilson (1882–1915) spent much of his adult life in Ireland, following the same outdoor pursuits as his uncle. A pioneer airman, Denys was the first to cross the Irish Sea.[2] An advocate of the monoplane, he was an early casualty of the First World War. Corbett's nervous breakdown reflected a deep emotional attachment to the young airman he had watched flying from Hendon before the war.[3] In later years Ada lived near Corbett in Knightsbridge, main-taining the family tradition of regular social gatherings.

In 1869, Julian followed elder brother Charles to Marlborough College, where all five Corbett boys were educated. This relatively new public school, founded in 1843 by Church of England clergymen, was intended to educate sons of the Church, with the sons of laymen subsidising clerical pupils. After early problems the college was saved by two able masters, trained by Thomas Arnold at Rugby, where piety, rigorous academic standards founded on Latin and mathematics, and outdoor exercise, equipped pupils for middle-class careers. The second of these Rugby men, George Bradley (headmaster 1858–70), was in post when Corbett arrived. Bradley's enthusiasm for military history may have influenced Corbett. Recent pupils included artist-entrepreneur and socialist William Morris and Field Marshal Sir Henry Wilson, while Hallam, 2nd Lord Tennyson, son of the Poet Laureate, was a contemporary and a lifelong friend.[4] Hallam followed Corbett to Trinity College Cambridge, and was also admitted to the bar. Having dedicated half his life to his father, Hallam spent the rest serving the empire. Like Corbett he was 'devoted beyond the call of duty'.[5] Bradley specialised in teaching logical precision, through Latin grammar, and placing boys at university. Although the Corbett boys only attended from the age of 14, treating the college as a university crammer, Corbett retained enough institutional pride to note the presence of fourteen old Marlburians on Francis Young husband's 1904 Tibet expedition.[6] The brief period at Marlborough mattered: Victorian public schools consciously inculcated specific values and ideals. As Colonel Charles à Court Repington observed of his near contemporary childhood:

> the history and glories of England, enshrined in the traditions of countless families, sank unconsciously and without schooling into our youthful minds, and remained there imperishably engraved upon the tablets of our hearts. We learnt to believe that the English were the salt of the earth, and England the first and greatest country in the world. Thus England became the real and true love of our lives.[7]

Corbett's mental world would be shaped by the late Victorian age, and the experiences of his formative years. This was particularly evident in the romantic medievalism that both he and William Morris encountered in Marlborough's gothic revival chapel, amply reinforced at Cambridge, where medieval mores and gothic architecture lent an ageless resonance to contemporary messages of duty, service and patriotism. He found a kindred spirit in poet Henry Newbolt, product of Clifton, another newly made medieval romantic school, which acquired a great headmaster from

Marlborough. Marlborough tended to confirm the liberal elitism of a newly prosperous family. Corbett was, first and foremost, an English gentleman; he happened to possess a brilliant mind, which he used in the service of his family, and his country. The public schools, bastions of the chivalric revival, obsessed with honour, gentility and moral quality, implied that war and violence were more gentlemanly than trade or industry. That ideology had an obvious allure for impressionable young men.

It did not matter that the Corbett family had only just arrived at gentility; although *nouveau*, they were *riche* enough to make the transition. In his brilliant evocation of the lost age that shaped Corbett, Mark Girouard emphasised mental and material influences exemplified by an obsession with Arthurian romance, expressed in Tennyson's *Idylls of the King* and William Morris's designs. Both had powerful Marlborough connections.[8] The intense, chivalric chapels at Marlborough and Clifton echoed a lost age, when armoured heroes lived for ever, alongside beautiful consorts. This heady mix of fact, fantasy, high culture and more than a hint of high church, shaped a class, and a generation: 'the mixture of sport and public service seemed to epitomise the ideal of the English gentleman; patriotism was virtually exalted as a religion'.[9] The leisured classes acquired their vocation at school; Corbett's career was profoundly shaped by this experience. His delight in the hunting field, on active service in the Sudan, and on naval manoeuvres, had deep roots in his formative years. With no economic pressure to work, he found a public career in national service, working himself into an early grave.

By the time Bradley left Marlborough in 1870 the college had established a reputation for academic excellence and progressive Christian principles. Such schools helped middle-class families preserve their social distance from the offspring of office workers and shopkeepers, equipping their sons for university and imperial opportunities as soldiers, civil servants, clerics and missionaries. The new headmaster was Frederic William Farrar (1831–1903), philologist, and honorary chaplain to the queen. Farrar modernised the curriculum, introducing courses on English literature.[10] Farrar matriculated from Trinity College Cambridge, which may have influenced Charles James Corbett's decision to shift his university preference.

Although elder brother Charles entered New College, Oxford, their father soon realised that a bastion of high church Tory politics had little to offer a progressive Liberal family. Julian and his younger brothers went to Cambridge.

It was a mark of their father's ambition, and practicality, that Julian read law at Trinity, later joining the Middle Temple with his elder brother. The railway made it possible to combine academic and legal educations. Admitted as a pensioner to Trinity on 18 February 1873, Corbett studied the Law Tripos, taking a first-class degree in 1876. After a slow start in the first year he was consistently in the first class thereafter,[11] although high grades were not the most important things he acquired. His tutor, classical scholar and founder of the British School at Athens, Sir Richard Claverhouse Jebb (1841–1905), was a major figure in the college, and later Conservative MP for the university. Widely travelled and well connected, Jebb was a role model for his students. He counted Sir Leslie Stephen, historians John Robert Seeley and Edward Augustus Freeman, as well as Tennyson, among his friends, and involved his students in his active social life.[12] As the younger Corbett brothers followed Julian to Cambridge it appears their father was satisfied.

Corbett blended easily into a quasi-aristocratic student body at Cambridge. He disliked boisterous 'Town versus Gown' riots, archaic rituals and the almost universal lack of interest in music. While the architectural wonders of the town were a lifelong delight,[13] he found the surrounding flat, damp Fenland countryside depressingly dull. His slight build, a family trait, equipped him to cox rowing eights, finding some success on the river. After graduating in 1877 Corbett abandoned rowing for hunting, shooting and fishing, but retained a deep affection for the university. He acquired a Master's degree in 1880, returning to Cambridge four decades later as the Lees Knowles lecturer and, to his great delight, became an Honorary Fellow of Trinity in 1920. Cambridge placed Corbett at the heart of the establishment: his fellow students included future leaders in politics, law, science and finance.

Corbett also studied under Sidney Colvin, the Slade Professor of Fine Art at Cambridge. Felix Slade's 1871 bequest had established a School of Art in London and chairs at Oxford and Cambridge, all of a liberal tendency. Celebrated Olympian artist Edward Poynter gave the opening lectures in London in 1871 while John Ruskin served in Oxford. Corbett may have met artist Sir William Blake Richmond (1842–1921), Ruskin's successor at Oxford, at this time. The ebullient, bearded Richmond, a leading portrait painter, moved in high society, travelled with Gladstone and knew the great German historian of Rome, Theodor Mommsen, while Bismarck, Charles Darwin, William Morris, Holman Hunt, Robert Louis Stevenson, Robert

Browning and archaeologist Arthur Evans were among his sitters. His stock-in-trade was the transformation of society beauties into glamorous goddesses, often paired with Byronic images of young noblemen, but his passion was classical figure work. A 'fine decorative classical painter, firmly opposed to all modern painting', Richmond became a lifelong friend, introducing Corbett to the light and culture of Italy.[14] Corbett shared his taste for pre-Raphaelite and Olympian work, attended London exhibitions, and acquired some of Richmond's work.[15] Corbett frequented Richmond's home, Beavor Lodge, an old riverside house in Hammersmith, near William Morris's Kelmscott, 'a favourite retreat for artists, academics, and political figures'.[16] (It was demolished in the 1920s to make way for the A4.) Corbett supported Richmond's protests against modernist art.[17] This connection also linked Corbett to Sir William's son Herbert, his most important intellectual follower.

The bookplate that Corbett created, but never used, suggests a frustrated man of action, anxious to serve. While he may have re-drawn the figures from other sources, including Albrecht Dürer and Edward Burne-Jones, the design is the work of an accomplished amateur. A knight on a quest, the twin themes of wisdom and ignorance, and the motto on his lance are all worthy of reflection. The Corbett/corvus connection reworked the family coat of arms and employed the family motto, 'God feeds the Ravens', although it is not clear that he was entitled to use them. The choice of post-nominal honours, Cambridge and the Middle Temple, was suitably gentlemanly.[18] The drawing may have been a wry response to his knighthood in 1918. Contemporary bookplates were often allusive, prone to punning combinations of image and word, hinting at underlying ideas and values that separated the owner from other readers. Owls and bats, crows and chivalry offer ample scope for psychoanalysis, but Corbett remained a late Victorian romantic, even if his thoroughly modern skills were directed by an altogether different ideology. The bookplates were printed and applied by his widow, as a mark of ownership, when his library was lent to two major national collections.

While Cambridge equipped Corbett to master the legal profession and to operate in the higher reaches of academic life, his interests did not develop into a fascination with pure intellectual enquiry. His mind took a more practical turn, largely through his legal education: Charles and Julian were admitted to the Middle Temple on 12 October 1874, and called to the bar on 13 June 1877.[19] Corbett later 'took up literary work; [and] subsequently interested himself in problems of naval strategy'.[20] Forty years later Corbett renewed his acquaintance with one of the eminent men from his Chambers, Robert Finlay, 1st Viscount Finlay (1842–1929), Lloyd George's Lord Chancellor from 1916 to 1919, and a member of the International Court of Arbitration at The Hague. Meeting at a literary dinner, he told Finlay 'how much I had learned from him that helped writing history'.[21] Noted for 'scholarship rather than oratory', Finlay's courtroom method was 'systematic, precise, direct, fair, and courteous'. The Chambers at No. 5 King's Bench Walk were those of John Charles Day, later a High Court judge, primarily focused on Chancery, Admiralty and patent law. It was no coincidence that Finlay, like Corbett, was a Liberal with political ambitions, taking a seat in the Commons in 1885, becoming a Liberal Unionist.[22]

While brother Charles administered the family's investments and business interests, Julian gave up the bar in 1882, after his father's death, because it was a tedious occupation. It was not that Corbett disliked the law – its rigour and precision, standards of evidence and ability to address larger issues made it both endlessly fascinating and essential to his subsequent career – but the lot of a junior barrister, tramping around the country circuits, was an 'irksome' distraction from his real interests, and lacked the appropriate gravity of purpose for a Marlborough man. Then as now, legal training and experience did not necessarily lead to long-term legal careers. Many leading men in late Victorian public life had legal careers that segued into public office, politics, journalism or literature. While Corbett turned to administering the Imber estate with some relief, the law remained central to his self-image, a thoroughly practical temper for his intellectual attainments. The credentials Barrister at Law and LL.M. implied accuracy and integrity.

This combination of an academic and practical legal education shaped Corbett's intellectual evolution. He was not an academic historian: while the past provided precedent and example, his primary concern lay in the present. He remained an advocate, well aware that history was a debate without end, one in which judgements were a long time coming, and always open to a retrial. The arguments he wanted to win did not concern dead men and past centuries, but current policy choices.[23]

These arguments were shaped by his experience of the wider world. Already familiar with Europe, Corbett visited India in 1877–8, North America in 1880 and Algeria in 1890, recording the experience in elegantly composed letters that revealed an eye for detail, and the undercurrents of local politics and society. Preparation for his Indian tour included acquiring an impressive grasp of Indian history from the Mughals to the Mutiny. Travelling on Peninsular & Oriental Company mail steamers filled with imperial soldiers, administrators and merchants made this a journey within and about the empire.[24] The impact of such effortless superiority, slicing through the Egyptian desert at Suez, skirting the harsh coasts of the Red Sea, coaling at Aden, and heading across the Indian Ocean, on a young man fresh from university, his head filled with ideals of service, must not be underestimated. The maritime strategist of 1911 may have begun his journey thirty-four years earlier.

Leaving Britain aboard the P&O liner *Australia* on 11 October 1877, Julian and Charles reached Malta on the 23rd.[25] Corbett used the seven-hour run ashore to see as much of Valetta as he could, couching his description of the majestic eighteenth-century fortifications of the Knights Hospitaller in military-technical terms. The British fleet that dominated the Mediterranean was nowhere to be seen; most of the ships were moored in Besika Bay, to counter a Russian advance into Turkey.[26] A week later the brothers arrived at Suez, where the shore was altogether less scenic:

> of all the dilapidated, dirty, fusty, smelly places under the great heaven this must be the worst. The streets are narrow uneven donkey tracks crowded with ragged Arabs and Pariah dogs in force, flanked with mud houses with shutters and doors mouldering from neglect. Here and there a gaudy French Bazaar, or tobacco shop with its divans of rotten wood crowded with picturesque forms in bright rags enlivened the scene.

Corbett had a lifelong dislike of noisy, crowded places.[27]

Arriving at Bombay (Mumbai) on 9 November, he was impressed by the western gateway to British India. The six-month itinerary ranged across India from Bombay to Delhi by way of princely Jaipur, the Deccan and Lahore. At Lahore, the northernmost point of their journey, the brothers encountered the Army camped close to the tribal frontier. They were not impressed by the vulgar language young officers directed at their native servants. Corbett thought this was matter of class, describing one young fellow as having the manners and language of 'a bargee'.[28] Older, more experienced officers spoke favourably of their men and native people in general. The letters also reveal a cigarette addiction that led to a succession of dental, pulmonary, bronchial and heart problems, contributing to his early death.

Already well informed about the glories of the Mughal Empire and its architectural masterpieces, Corbett was too excited to write when he arrived at Agra. Having composed himself and inspected the obvious sights, the Taj Mahal and the Red Fort, he expanded on 'the el dorado of civilisation. The magnificence is all that I expected, the taste, the beauty, the art far more.'[29] At Cawnpore and Lucknow, recently sanctified by British blood, he heard how civilisation and valour had defeated barbaric savagery, restating Britain's right to rule. Corbett's descriptive power and cultural assumptions shaped a striking passage about the relief of Lucknow by General Sir Colin Campbell:

> In the suburbs every garden, every palace, mosque & tomb has some story to tell of the successive reliefs. One high walled garden there was with only one small door. Sir Colin's men came & found 2000 sepoys holding it. He made one little narrow breach, they show you still, and the 93rd went in. He placed his guns before the gate that none should escape and waited. In two hours the 93rd came out, and 2000 sepoys lay in a lake of blood with not a bullet mark amongst them. They were bayoneted every man. This is the sort of plain tale that Lucknow tells, a tale of fierce, speedy, ruthless revenge for great crimes, a salient but eloquent record of the superiority of Europe over Asia, with no attempt to throw a sickly halo of priggishness over godless but glorious acts.

The city was 'a melancholy exhibition of the depth of depravity to which native taste may be brought by contact with Europe. . . . The Buildings . . . represent the union of the most florid Hindoo art with British architecture at a time when British architecture was at its lowest ebb. . . . The whole city might have been designed by the architect of a travelling menagerie or the builder of the Lord Mayor's Coach.' The ghastly effect was heightened by a florid mix of colours.[30]

The brothers travelled from the foothills of the Himalayas down the Ganges, overwhelmed by the scale, intensity and sheer mass of humanity they encountered at Benares. Public displays of absolute faith, cremation and ritual purification stunned Corbett's restrained English senses. Arriving at Calcutta (Kolkata), capital of British India, the brothers spent a few days touring the sights. Corbett recognised its strategic importance, 'in every way to be worthy of its position as the capital of the Indian Empire'. The great merchant ships moored on the Hooghly had the same visual impact 'as a line of battle ship on the Imber'. Yet 'the actual sights of Calcutta are not great. We have been reduced to the Zoo & the Botanical Gardens, the latter being far the prettiest I know, but rather too far from the city. Such a collection of orchids.'[31] He sent home a case of orchids for the family hothouse. The following day the brothers took passage to Madras (Chennai) on the P&O steamship *Khedive*, arriving on the 11th.[32] Their overland expedition traced the late eighteenth-century Mysore Wars, which ended with the overthrow of Tipu Sultan in 1799. Arriving at Mysore on the 19th, Corbett knew all about Haider Ali, Tipu and Arthur Wellesley, the Duke of Wellington. A visit to Sri Lanka on the P&O *Ceylon* prompted reflections on the connection between land and sea, a critical issue for any analyst of British imperial power.[33] With a great artificial harbour then under construction he observed, 'Ceylon is very unfortunate in its harbours. Trincomalee which they say is the finest harbour in the world is so placed that it is next to useless for trade and is used entirely as a naval Station & Colombo is equally out of the way except for trade with the Continent.'[34]

While he may have acquired such strategic insights in conversation, their presence in a letter home suggests a serious engagement with the maritime imperial issues of the Indian Ocean. Returning to Bombay, the brothers joined the crowded, noisy homebound P&O steamer *Poona*, forming a friendship with Julia Margaret Cameron, pioneer photographer and friend of Lord Tennyson.[35] When the *Poona* stopped to coal at superheated Aden, Corbett did not go ashore, joining Mrs Cameron on a visit to HMS *Undaunted*, where they were 'entertained most hospitably by the Captain' at afternoon tea. The old wooden steam frigate, flagship of the East Indies Station, the last of her kind on active duty, would be paid off in December.[36] Corbett did not comment on the contrast between the obsolete warship and the iron passenger liner, but he did spend a few hours on a British wooden warship in full commission. The brothers disembarked at Suez, taking the train through Egypt to Alexandria. There they joined the P&O *Ceylon*, and enjoyed a race with an Austrian Lloyd steamer that left the harbour at the same time. Now a long way ahead of schedule, the captain elected to kill time by steaming slowly past Crete, providing passengers with a fine view of Mount Ida, before passing Navarino, Zante and Kefalonia; these classical locations were as familiar to men of Corbett's education as the British Empire, while comparisons between different ages shaped the Victorian debate about Britain's future prospects. They disembarked at Brindisi, the railhead for a transcontinental journey home.

Corbett's letters captured the experience of empire. Consciously crafted to be savoured, read and re-read over and again, they have the worn, creased, edge-turned shabbiness of a popular resource. He wrote about people, British, Indian and otherwise, and places visited, often comparing them with images captured in art and photographs, while connecting history, empire, the sea, art and culture in a mature, elegant prose. They may be Victorian ephemera, but they enhanced the understanding of a sophisti-cated and well-travelled family. His mastery of language conveyed the consequence of these encounters. Above all, this was the work of a man at ease with his pen, aware of his literary powers.

The brothers had toured a very British India, newly imperial, and increas-ingly self-satisfied. If the scale and splendour were overwhelming, Corbett recognised a looming problem. If the capital moved to Delhi, a project under discussion during the visit, the British would join the long list of land empires to hold sway on the sub-continent, trading the maritime commercial margin-ality, symbolised by Fort William at Calcutta, that had enabled them to conquer without threatening the core of Indian society, for a new Mughal Empire of soldiers and emperors. The implications for Indian society were obvious. Corbett's attention was drawn to the local, not the imperial: he sketched Indian people, animals and places, not European incomers, or their works. He was troubled by evidence that dishonesty and bad government had demoralised the people, leaving them irresponsible and weak. He despised vulgar, boorish aspects of British rule, above all the abuse of the local people. He concluded that British rule in a climate that rendered everyone lethargic depended on a steady turnover of men to maintain the appearance of effort-less superiority, something unique, and wholly British. This vision of an empire in flux would endure, although his interests moved from terrestrial rule to an oceanic commonwealth. The voyage to India exemplified the global needs of the seapower state and shaped a literary output suffused with impe-rial themes, Viking conflicts, Tudor expansion and imagined bastions of outlying Englishness in exotic lands. If Corbett read India as a man of his time, he recognised the fragility of British rule amidst the vast populations of the sub-continent – a bloody lesson soaked into the sand at Cawnpore. His Britain was far larger, and far more important, than the British Isles. The sea route that linked Britain to India, through the Mediterranean, the Suez Canal and the Red Sea, emphasised the global nature of British power, stitched together by the people and mails travelling on steamships, and submarine telegraph cables that followed the same routes. These technologies enabled London to reinforce slender garrisons from other imperial outposts. Having travelled in the footsteps of Clive, Wellington and the heroes of the Mutiny, developing their legacy would be the task of his mature years.[37] Travelling the imperial ocean routes ensured Corbett's imperialism was anything but 'absent-minded'.[38]

Corbett would not have been surprised by Professor John Robert Seeley's bestselling 1883 study of the empire, which contrasted Britain's sea empire with the continental cohesion of Russia and America:

> Between them, equally vast, but not as continuous, with the ocean flowing through it in every direction, lies, like a world-Venice, with the sea for streets, Greater Britain.[39]

Seeley, Regius Professor of History at Cambridge in Corbett's time, called for a larger, more coherent British seapower state to compete with the emerging continental superpowers. While the message that a Greater Britain based on oceanic power was the only safeguard for the future was widely consumed, the far-sighted warning that any serious commitment to Europe would endanger the empire was ignored.[40] Seeley's concern had been to prevent the fall of the British Empire.[41] He saw the past as a 'school of [contemporary] statesman-ship'.[42] Corbett may have heard the original lectures at Cambridge; Jebb and Seeley were friends. He was not alone: Seeley impacted many seapower thinkers and statesmen. Both Captain Alfred Thayer Mahan USN and Corbett consulted his work in the 1880s.[43] In 1884, future Foreign Secretary Sir Edward Grey (1862–1933) was struck by the argument. In 1892–4, Grey and Foreign Secretary/Prime Minister Lord Rosebery used Seeley's ideas to settle strategic priorities while upholding Liberal domestic policies.[44]

In 1879 Corbett visited North America with brothers Charles and Bertie and Cambridge contemporary, family friend and near neighbour at Woodgate Maurice Macmillan (1853–1936), scion of the publishing firm.[45] Between July and November they took in much of the continent, from Boston, New York, Washington and Philadelphia, moving to Lake Champlain and the Hudson Valley, the Niagara Falls, and west to Chicago, St Louis, Kansas City,

Denver and the Rocky Mountains, adding Nashville, Charleston and Richmond in the southern states, and ending in Canada, for a week split between Toronto, Kingston, Montreal and Quebec. The rapid itinerary exploited the rail network, offering a *tour d'horizon* of a new world and rapidly growing nations. Like many British visitors, Corbett found much to dislike: Americans could be over-familiar, unrelentingly and unthinkingly patriotic, lacking humour and aesthetic sensibilities. Worst of all, they were ruled by money and a form of mob democracy intimately linked to corruption and sectarianism. The young travellers made a familiar connection with the worst excesses of the French Revolution, and recognised the impact of Irish immigrants on American politics.[46] At this remove it is hard to appreciate the revulsion that American politics prompted in Victorian Britain, a revulsion that delayed the extension of the franchise, unifying Tories and Liberals against radical change. Predictably Corbett found Brahmin Boston, Harvard and the new Museum of Fine Arts more agreeable than brash, pushy New York. He enjoyed the West, contrasting simple frontier manners with the absurd affectation to be found in Britain and on America's east coast. The West would be the only part of America that he revisited in later years, in a short story. He was appalled by the well-nigh universal tobacco-chewing and spitting habits of the American male. Canada had merits, superior buildings and a greater sense of permanence, but everything seemed slow after America. He loved the majestic scenery, if it could be separated from rampant consumerism. Quebec combined a great river with ancient buildings: he cannot have been unaware of the history that lay beneath his feet, the heroes of Britain, France and Canada who fought over the city, or the lasting effect of those events on the Dominion. Thirty years later Corbett would revisit Quebec, the central location of one of his greatest books.

North America provided a powerful contrast to the imperial splendour of India. Americans did not defer, nor were they especially mysterious: the best of them were as open and accessible as the latest novel. Travel may have broadened Corbett's mind, but it also confirmed prejudices and reinforced comfortable assumptions of innate superiority in power, politics, manners and culture. While it was a Liberal article of faith that there was room for improvement at home, he saw nothing to recommend. The tension in his travel was obvious; while he sought the great outdoors, taking a sportsman's interest in the chase and applying an artist's perspective to the scenery, high culture remained important. Yet nothing in his travels would be wasted.

In the 1880s, Corbett continued to travel, visiting Norway to fish, sketch and enjoy the majestic scenery. That experience provided rich descriptive passages for his first novel, reinforced by a deep immersion in the dynamic field of Norse and Icelandic literature, and an ability to create human drama with complex characters. Norway was also the occasion for a court case: he sued an agent who misrepresented the stretch of river that he had hired.[47] There was more to Corbett's Norway than fishing. He also discussed literature with Henrik Ibsen, whom he greatly admired. Nor was he alone in making the journey to a country that offered a sense of shared history.[48]

By contrast, Italy indulged his artistic sensibilities and he enjoyed the company of a rich, varied collection of British and other expatriates, the chance to exercise his linguistic talents, and ramble about the ancient world. Latterly he did so in the company of Mark Twain, another author he appreciated.[49] As they sat amidst the ruins of the Forum, their conversation shifted effortlessly from Twain's western experiences to the most powerful of ancient cities, past and present merging into a survey of all human experience. Perhaps they reflected on Edward Gibbon's moment of present-minded historical inspiration in the same space.

Corbett honed his literary skills, crafting descriptions of places and people that could be worked into publications, and evolved an elegant, economic prose style, capable of sustaining long, complex narrative passages, switching to thick analytical overview, and illustrated with striking word-pictures of pre-Raphaelite clarity. The lure of literature led him to stop taking briefs in 1882. Running Imber Court was hardly a full-time occupation for a man of his expertise and aptitude, while a full programme of country sports left ample time for literary work.

Among the many influences that shaped Corbett's thinking, Matthew Arnold's Victorian Humanist Hellenism was critical. Arnold's *Culture and Anarchy* essays contrasted the intellectual freedom and liberty of classical Greece with the religious rigour of the Old Testament to assess the state of the nation. Arnold's ancient Greeks were proto-Victorians, modern thinkers.[50] This approach, shared by John Ruskin, made Hellenism a living force in contemporary thought. For Arnold, Hellas was 'hardly less important to mankind than Judea'.[51] This was a radical position in an age still dominated by religion and confessional controversy. Corbett would develop this theme in his controversial essay 'Jezebel'.[52]

Other influences included historian and social reformer John Richard Green, whose widow would be a lifelong friend, novelist Robert Louis Stevenson, and the Olympian artists Richmond, Burne-Jones and Poynter, who worked history, myth and metaphor for an increasingly self-conscious Victorian audience. He helped run Richmond's National Coal Smoke Abatement Society for decades, addressing the physical aspect of John Ruskin's 'Storm Cloud of the Nineteenth Century'.[53] In a dramatic illustrated lecture the unstable sage, social reformer and art critic exploited meteorological evidence to evoke the inner malaise and moral pollution of a godless age. His clouds, external symbols, could be read at every level from the prosaic to the divine. Ruskin's work was especially affecting for elite liberals.

There was something of a doom foretold in these links: an obsession with decline and fall, a search for precedent and portent amid the signs and symbols of past and present. J.M.W. Turner and Ruskin had foreseen the doom of Britain's sea empires in those of Carthage and Venice, while George Grote attributed the end of Athenian greatness to a similar loss of inner vitality: when the people were no longer prepared to strive and sacrifice, they lay down before the latest conqueror.[54] Arnold agreed the danger was internal disunity, not external aggression. Classical culture provided lessons and metaphors to address the looming decline of Victorian Britain. There was a specific place for seapower in that process: highlighted in Arnold's father's edition of Thucydides, in George Grote's *History of Greece* and Ruskin's *Stones of Venice*. In a private reflection, Arnold explained the core of *Culture and Anarchy*:

> I have a conviction that there is a real, an almost imminent danger of England losing immeasurably in all ways, of declining into a sort of great Holland, for want of what I must still call ideas, for want of perceiving how the world is going and must go, and preparing herself accordingly.[55]

This was a metaphor of immense power. Arnold understood the peculiar decline of seapower empires; he knew Athens and Carthage, and studied contemporary Holland. As a son of Thomas Arnold, who left Rugby School to become the Regius Professor of History at Oxford, he understood Britain had far more in common with Athens than Rome. Arnold's elitism, social and hereditary, reflected a powerful strain in Victorian liberalism, imbibed by the *arriviste* Corbett clan, newly established on the secure uplands of significant wealth. If Arnold's ideas made the elite anxious, they also provided the liberal intelligentsia with purpose. By the time Corbett joined the debate, Arnold had become alarmist, and despondent. 'The Nadir of Liberalism' of 1886, in the heavyweight Liberal monthly *The Nineteenth Century*, hoped the defeat of Gladstone's Irish Home Rule Bill would create a new political alignment of aristocratic Whigs and moderate Tories under Lord Hartington and the Marquess of Salisbury, to save the nation from levelling democracy. At this point Arnold reconnected with James Anthony Froude, an old friend from Oxford, who spoke on the Tory side of the debate. Froude continued to warn of impending doom into the 1890s, making the defeat of Philip II's Habsburg world-empire an exemplary tale for British audiences.[56] How far Froude's work influenced popular campaigns like 'The Truth about the Navy' and the agitation that split the Liberal party over the naval estimates in 1893 is hard to gauge, but the connection with Corbett's writing is obvious.

The search for exemplary pasts continued throughout Corbett's formative years. Deeply affected by Arnold, he avoided the hectoring prophetic language and outright alarmism of Thomas Carlyle's anti-democratic 'Great man' solution. Carlyle's ideas were too simple, and Corbett had no interest in populism. Yet rather than sliding into Froude's darkening Toryism, or Arnold's Liberal despair, he tried to understand how the empire worked as a political/strategic entity, systematising those insights to prepare for the future. Addressing those in positions of power and influence, he soon discovered that his message required a medium with greater expository power than fiction or essays, however elegantly executed.

Don Schurman dismissed Corbett's literary output as a failure, marred by an inability to delineate character, and lacking originality.[57] While that judgement provided a useful narrative device, which Schurman used to propel Corbett into historical writing, it misunderstood the context and purpose of Corbett's fiction, and ignored its commercial success. Corbett had no trouble marketing his writing, in any format, but he did not care about money – being independently wealthy he rejected invitations to write to order. His fiction reflected his interests and developed his experience. Self-deprecatory asides and innate modesty should not be mistaken for confessions of inadequacy or failure. From the start, Corbett was well aware of his abilities and expected to be paid the proper rate for his work. Publishing four novels with leading London houses was hardly a failure, more a useful stage in the intellectual and technical development of an author confident that he had important things to say to his contemporaries.[58]

Late nineteenth-century British fiction sustained professional authors, editors and journals. The novel, as a magazine serial or hardcover publication, was the dominant literary form, with realistic tales of romance, crime and violence, then as now, the most marketable. Readers preferred happy endings and simple tales. Distraction and amusement were more important than intellectual stimulation. Novels that engaged with the rapidly changing world helped readers address the scientific, theological, political and technical developments that had replaced the comfortable world of Jane Austen with the grim realities of an urban underclass. In this market, social realism registered more powerfully than Corbett's elitist dreamscapes. Cheap editions crowded the railway bookstands, reaching mass audiences by the mid-1890s.[59] Although his works appeared in this format, Corbett lacked the commercial power of his friend Conan Doyle.[60]

The Victorian novel was not overtly intellectual, yet ideas distinguish the enduring classics of Victorian fiction. George Eliot and Thomas Hardy worked on grand themes and elevated their readers. Lord Acton, austere master of the historical past, was a devotee of Eliot's work.[61] In an age that dismissed 'professionals' as self-aggrandising place-hunters, Corbett dropped his legal qualifications when publishing fiction. As the century wore on, the pessimism of Arnold, Ruskin and Froude seeped into fiction, notably that of Rider Haggard, Robert Louis Stevenson and Hardy.[62] Corbett, who admired Stevenson, shared their retrogressive, degenerative view of the human condition. His first two novels lamented lost ages of adventure and, describing the Vikings as 'White Zulus', reworked the metaphor of the 'noble savage', linking the fury of the Northmen who destroyed Ethelred's unready kingdom to the onslaught of Cetshawayo's *impi* at Isandlwana in 1879.

As such links suggest, Corbett's literary concerns were present-minded, even if his settings were not. He wrote for those who shared his interests, his education, and his concern for the future, well aware that this was not a large audience. He took the same approach with non-fiction, ignoring the mass market to address naval officers, statesmen and academics.

Corbett knew little of the working class, occasionally betraying a telling combination of fear and loathing: Jacobins, Fenians and the unenlightened masses were a looming threat to his privileged world. He combined romantic notions with a sophisticated grasp of high culture, politics and world history. Consciously intellectual in a market dominated by aesthetics, romance and the comedy of manners, he was not alone in moving between fiction and history; a generation earlier Froude had used a variety of literary forms to address his political and social concerns.

Corbett's literary career spanned the decade that separated the deaths of his parents, ending in 1892 when the death of his mother broke up the family home at Imber Court. It was a suitable intellectual pursuit for his spare hours, one of many lives that filled his schedule. His earliest extant diary, from 1890, retails a hectic schedule of social, sporting and political activity, writing was an evening and rainy day alternative to the domesticity of the wife and family he had yet to acquire. There was nothing of the freezing garret or the struggling artist. Living in a large house, with staff, ample funds, a stable of horses and a shooting estate at his disposal, Corbett could indulge his passion for travel, and enjoy the intellectual, social and political life of London, only a short train journey away. His close family network offered all the emotional support he needed, and a rich source of inspiration. Gudrun in *Asgard*, the Queen Mother in *Kophetua XIII* and 'Jezebel' – strong, sophisticated, positive female characters – were all, at least in part, based on his mother.

His writing engaged with major contemporary themes. A concern for Britain's place in the world linked his fiction and journalism with later historical/strategic texts. The shift away from fiction was not driven by lack of ability, or inadequate rewards. Literary work paid £1 a page, rather better than history: the *English Men of Action* series earned £100 for a 200-page book, while academic and official writing did not pay at all.

Working at the higher end of the popular entertainment spectrum, Corbett soon discovered that financial rewards were limited by the fickle taste of an ephemeral market.[63] Subscription libraries shaped the form and content of novels. Many publishers ran house magazines, edited by retained authors, to test and promote new works, spreading production costs by reusing the type from the serial to print the book. Corbett's novels appeared in this format, then as hardback editions and finally in paperback form. This demonstrated their success.

Predictably, Corbett entered the world of Victorian publishing through a friend, Malcolm Macmillan (1852–89), cousin of Frederick and Maurice, and another old Marlburian. Malcolm passed Corbett's manuscript to Fred, who specialised in fiction, without naming the author. The press readers were positive, and Fred decided to take a risk, although he was not certain if there was much demand for Norse stories.[64] An astute businessman, Fred kept the Macmillan list, 'solid and sound' rather than experimental and ambitious: he had no interest in racy or salacious material. He published several authors from Corbett's social circle.[65]

The Fall of Asgard: A Tale of St. Olaf's Days appeared in the spring of 1886. Drawing on Norwegian history, mythology and the Icelandic sagas, Corbett juxtaposed the hero, and his equally heroic mother, the last leaders of the pagan faith, with King Olaf, the real-life warrior saint who forced his people to accept baptism at the point of a spear. Corbett's preface advised readers which of the characters were real, and which imagined. Rather than a simple story of good and evil, Corbett offered balance: both men were brave, and righteous, but progress and 'civilisation' triumphed. The pagan hero was reconciled to his king and the new faith, if only temporarily. While most characters were well drawn, his villain was less successful: too complex and uncertain to be compelling, and too far removed from the historical original. It seems Corbett had little experience of evil, while his faith, like that of Matthew Arnold, was an element of English culture, a binding agent for a diffuse stratified society, rather than an overt expression of belief, the Church of England being, in essence, 'a great national society for the promotion of goodness'.[66] In the 1890s he occasionally preached the lesson in Thames Ditton Church, including one on chivalry, but otherwise only mentioned church-going on Christmas Day.[67] His extant letters and diaries do not mention religion.

Reviewers were largely positive; *Punch* was amused,[68] while *The Academy* noted 'passages of great beauty and power ... with the true spirit of poetry'.[69] The *Contemporary Review* found the story too painful for modern tastes, too powerful to be entertainment, reminding the reviewer of 'the pathetic clinging to a vanishing belief that mirrored the feelings of our own age', the ebbing of Christian faith. This had been Corbett's intent.[70] Such notices paled into relative insignificance beside the belated, but positive judgement of John St Loe Strachey in the *Spectator*.[71] Strachey included a substantial sample of Corbett's elegant prose, although he feared the consciously archaic style would deter readers. Even so the Viking age possessed an enduring interest for Englishmen.[72] Few would challenge Strachey's largely positive judgement, especially at this remove. Such attention from one of London's leading reviewers would have gratified any first-time novelist: any long notice in the *Spectator* was a success. Well received and a modest commercial success, Corbett's book revealed characteristic traits. Ships, the sea and war prompted his best writing: he had an artist's eye for detail, recreating Nordic vistas from his travels. Although immersed in the Viking age, he found a new approach, their submission to the Christian God. He could create and sustain compelling characters, although the heroes were more convincing than the villains, his matrons than his maidens. An enquiry about translation rights from Christiania (modern Oslo) suggests at least one Norwegian was impressed.[73]

For his second novel Corbett turned to more familiar sea-rovers, Elizabethan privateers. Once again he set the story in a solid factual context, weaving invented characters into historical events, including locations such as the university, while tracing the Reformation and the career of Francis Drake. This time he wrote in the first person, offering the fictive memoir of Jasper Festing, a Cambridge-educated man of action, with something of the author about him. Abandoning a professional life for oceanic adventure, the slave trade and privateering hinted at a path not taken. Perhaps Corbett's ambition for a life of imperial action had been frustrated by paternal pressure. Macmillan published *For God and Gold* in 1887, the cover embossed with a Tudor galleon. They hoped to build on the success of *Asgard*. The reviews began well,[74] while the *Athenaeum* made the obvious comparison with Charles Kingsley's *Westward Ho!*, and not unfavourably.[75] Once again there was no romance and few female characters. Life had not equipped Corbett for that. While he could write persuasive female characters, his relationship with them was familial rather than amorous.[76] Having anticipated much from the author of *Asgard*, the *Westminster Review* was disappointed, noting: 'the best part is the portrait of Francis Drake; his character is drawn with great power and distinctiveness'.[77] In sum, the book was too cerebral, with little action, lacked even a frisson of romance, and was dominated by a historical figure, rather than his fictional foil.

In 1888–9 Corbett, still unsure of his voice and his audience, dabbled with more commercial writing, perhaps testing his skills. He tried short essays for younger readers, working with travelling companion Maurice Macmillan, now a director of the firm.[78] If 'Smiling Ford' lacks the depth and suspense of a great ghost story, it moved along nicely, with powerful descriptive passages.[79] He also tried the children's market in 1889.[80] He ended the year working on 'Jezebel', rehabilitating the infamous Tyrian princess by exploring Matthew Arnold's themes.[81] Portrayed in the Old Testament as a sorceress, heretic and harlot, Jezebel was reworked to stress the power of Phoenician civilisation. Corbett's description of Tyre as a port, meeting place of cultures, centre of power and source of the civilising impulse was a striking endorsement of the critical role Phoenician seafaring and trade played in the creation of the classical world. His heroine was a martyr to the cause of light and reason, fated to see the Kingdom of Ahab rise to glory then, in his death and that of their eldest son, fall into the hands of fanatics and their violent faith. Jezebel, her work destroyed, was murdered by religious zealots; the mental world of Judaism closed, traducing her memory. In a brilliantly suggestive closing paragraph Corbett begged the question how history might have turned out had Ahab and Jezebel brought the civilisation of Phoenicia to bear on the stern faith of Judea, and 'unthwarted by the spirit of Israel, Greece had worked out the destinies of mankind alone'.[82] This homage to *Culture and Anarchy* must have been prompted by Matthew Arnold's death in April. The essay was illustrated by brilliant artist-designers Charles Ricketts and Charles Shannon, devotees of French symbolism. The elegant woodcut letter T that opened the essay reworked the wounded lioness from an Assyrian wall relief in the British Museum, while Ricketts' naked figure of the Tyrian goddess Astarté referenced classical models. Jezebel on her throne awaiting death owed a debt to Tenniel's *Alice in Wonderland*. Shannon's writhing naked fanatics on Mount Carmel, prostrated before a Golden Calf and Jezebel's Ivory Palace, more Tower of Babel than residence, shared the brazen nudity of Astarté, with the clothed figures of Ahab and Jezebel occupying the foreground. The combination of a serious intellectual challenge to religious orthodoxy and strikingly human figures met resistance. Given Corbett's taste for Olympian art, a genre dominated by nudes, stylised backdrops and wisps of clothing, it is highly unlikely he was shocked. Strachey dismissed Corbett's essay as 'a somewhat grotesque attempt to whitewash the wife of Ahab' and derided the 'clever, affected and ugly' illustrations.[83] On this occasion Strachey missed the mark; Corbett's historical base was secure, his argument no more than a textual critique, stressing the superior cultural attainments of polytheistic Tyre over the fanatic monotheists of the mountains, and Strachey's judgement of the illustrations was simply outdated.

While the unthinking hostility of religious zealots was unwelcome, although hardly unexpected, Corbett must have hoped for a better outcome from his next novel. *Kophetua XIII* began with a commission from Walter Sichel, who became a lifelong friend, for a ten-part serial on the subject of love for the Swan Sonneschein monthly *Time* in January 1888.[84] Corbett's friend, the author Mrs Molesworth, thought him 'far too humble about your books'.[85] *Kophetua* appeared in 1889 and would be reprinted in Britain and America before the year was out. The obvious point of contact for a contemporary audience was Edward Burne-Jones' masterpiece *King Cophetua and the Beggar Maid*, the culmination of a career-long engagement with Tennyson's poem of 1842, itself based on a medieval ballad. The picture secured Burne-Jones a European reputation and was widely reproduced.[86] Corbett's book exploited three distinct literary traditions: medieval ballads, the political speculation of Thomas More's *Utopia*, and the Victorian fascination with exotic travel, in this case a recent book by Friedrich Gerhard Rohlfs (1831–96), a German explorer of Morocco. Corbett situated his story in a wider engagement with the Renaissance, travel and history. Setting his imagined world in a real geographical location consciously blurred the lines between fact and fiction in a travel tale he claimed to have found on a library shelf. Where More had written about 'nowhere', Corbett named his imaginary kingdom Oneiria, 'dreamland': his intended audience, limited to those with at least a smattering of Greek, would recognise the joke and the link with other imagined worlds. He made no concessions to the tastes of the masses or, one suspects, the hopes of his publishers. Corbett wrote for his own intellectual pleasure.[87]

Corbett's kingdom had been founded by a well-travelled, self-effacing Elizabethan Englishman in the valley of the River Draa in the Anti-Atlas of southern Morocco, an area where Rohlfs reported rich soil and superior men.[88] It had been destroyed in the age of the French Revolution by jihadi Moroccan tribesmen, as reported by a contemporary traveller. Within the imagined exoticism of a Renaissance kingdom Corbett played out an allegory of manners and mores, which reads like a satire on the imploding politics of the contemporary Liberal party, ripped apart by Irish Home Rule. The book addressed the prospect of revolutionary change, represented by the internal *sans-culottes*, leading to destruction at the hands of an external foe. His jihadi savages may be read as violent nationalists, the internal enemy their English supporters. Corbett, like many Liberals, did not share Gladstone's assessment of Ireland, or favour sweeping concessions. In a revealing line Corbett observed: 'The lofty ideals of romantic youth were withered and trodden underfoot.'[89] There is no evidence of grand passion in his life or his writing.

Kophetua is self-indulgent, with too many insider jokes and too rigid a view of society and class, and none of the characters has the power to fascinate or enchant. While critics recognised key influences, including *Utopia*, Sir Francis Bacon's 'New Atlantis' and *Gulliver's Travels*, Strachey noted the similarity with Robert Louis Stevenson's *Prince Otto*. Disclaiming any imputation of plagiarism, he used the link to praise Stevenson for completing his book in one volume rather than Corbett's pair. Tales of fantasy should not be overly drawn out. Ultimately he damned the book with faint praise: the second volume moved slowly and was not especially interesting, yet those who preferred 'intellectual flavour' to 'mere narrative excitement' would not be disappointed. In sum, too clever by half, cerebral sophistication being a poor substitute for solid amusement.[90] Corbett, an intellectual masquerading as a popular novelist, might be better advised to try another format. Five months later, Strachey's condemnation of 'Jezebel' added religion to the subjects he ought to leave alone.

Modern analysts treat *Kophetua* as a Ruritanian fantasy, for much the same reason that More's *Utopia* is generally viewed as an ideal society, rather than an improved, defiantly insular England.[91] Such judgements ignore Corbett's wider output and his social conscience. There was nothing trifling or comic about Julian Corbett. His concerns were serious and pressing, and his novels all sold three editions, including colonial paperbacks.[92]

Strachey had penned the final word on Corbett's literary endeavours in September 1886: 'Historical novels receive rather a cold welcome in England at present. Critics complain that they are wearisome, and recommend the authors to write history instead.'[93] The recent emergence of a professional historical consciousness, as Strachey understood, offered an opportunity. Joining the strategic debate, Corbett charted a course for Britain and the empire that avoided the twin threats of impending decline and rising militarism. He looked to history to inform the great contemporary debates. He was never a historian for the sake of history, or money.

By 1889 the obvious tension between Corbett's intellectual and political interests and the unsatisfactory business of writing middlebrow novels had run its course. More ambitious and complex than most, his work had not changed the world. His final novel, *A Business in Great Waters*, dealt with British support for French Chouan rebels in the 1790s, exploiting a range of historical sources on the British intervention, alongside Frederick Marryat's novel *Frank Mildmay*.[94] War, the sea and history were his themes. To market the new book Corbett enlisted a literary agent.[95] William Morris Colles founded the Author's Syndicate, Ltd in 1890, representing many authors, including H.G. Wells, Thomas Hardy, Lord Bryce, Arnold Bennett and J.M. Barrie.[96] Colles dealt with publishing, editorial input, serial and translation rights, copyright and accounts. The relationship ended acrimoniously in 1917. Colles consistently mistook Corbett's concern over contract terms for a focus on money.[97]

Responses to *A Business in Great Waters* were familiar. Strachey complained Corbett had 'hardly made himself quite a master of the difficult art of narrative architecture', although the 'exhilarating' vigour and drive of individual episodes made 'capital reading for the holiday season'.[98] If Corbett wanted to write for a mass audience, he needed to go back to basics and get a grip on storylines and structure. Instead, his fictional career ended with a perfectly good book that did not advance his agendas or his literary craft. His clever, elegant and thought-provoking fiction was better suited to the elite circles in which he moved than the mass audiences that sustained the genre. Corbett sacrificed entertainment for ideas, to debate the state of the nation. Life had not equipped him to deliver Dickens's social realism, or Tolstoy's soul-stirring understanding of war and the struggle for survival. Writing from personal experience, he produced clever, well-crafted books that were desperately short of romance. Still searching for purpose and meaning, Corbett tried writing for the theatre. In 1891 he submitted *The Deserters*, which was judged 'very brightly written – but is of too slight a texture, I fear, to bid for popularity'.[99] He could not match the artistry of his Norwegian friend. For Corbett the world of fiction was fading, in tempo with the life of his mother. After her death he handled the sale of Imber Court, married, moved to central London and found his vocation.[100]

CHAPTER 2

Making Waves

Corbett found his vocation in the changing mental world of the 1890s. Realising his literary talents were better suited to another genre, Fred Macmillan invited him to write for the series *English Men of Action* when he completed *Kophetua XIII* in March 1888. These small-format 200-page biographies followed the success of *English Men of Letters*, the series edited by Liberal politician John Morley. Offered a choice between George Monk, 1st Duke of Albemarle and Nelson, Corbett chose the relatively unknown Civil War and Restoration general, leaving Nelson to naval historian John Knox Laughton.[1] The fee was a flat £100. Series editor Mowbray Morris required a narrative 'rather than an analysis or criticism, and above all abjure Mr Seeley's dictum that history has no business being entertaining'. Spelling should follow Macaulay's popular *History of England*, and delivery in six months would be appreciated.[2]

Although he was only expected to provide an elegant *résumé* of older texts, gilded with a few striking phrases about heroism, Corbett took the job seriously, turning to leading expert Samuel Rawson Gardiner, who suggested he consult the archives and fellow scholar Charles Firth.[3] The first draft was ready in late December, although the academic turn resulted in an over-long, unnecessarily original, thoroughly referenced manuscript.[4] Faced with 250 pages, Morris compromised on 210 or 215, telling Corbett to cut long quotes and most references. The task was completed within a week.[5] The intellectual synergy between legal work and history was obvious, exploiting Corbett's capacity for detailed, precise thinking and archival research.

Corbett wrote history for contemporary Britain, following Froude and his contemporaries, delivering sophisticated arguments about policy, strategy and empire. He would develop intellectually coherent arguments by sustained application to the singular problem of recovering and codifying British strategy. His thinking would be shaped by the newly professional academic discipline of history, and philosophical approaches to war and conflict. Initially his audience was restricted to an elite group that shared his university education, political engagement and intellectual curiosity, men of influence and power. Later he found another audience among service professionals, and reconciled the two groups in the definitive Corbett text *England in the Seven Years' War* of 1907, the model for subsequent books.

Monk focused on the Civil War, reducing the Commonwealth and Restoration era, when Monk became Duke of Albemarle, to a matter of academic interest. Having engaged deeply with his subject and the wider military and naval contexts, Corbett provided clear, consistent judgements, while his delivery suggested an author at ease with his work. Of Monk's pacification of the Highlands he observed: 'It is a campaign of the highest interest and well repays the laborious task of piecing it together from the obscure and confused notices that are extant.' He enjoyed the forensic analysis of sources and cross-examining the witnesses. Reconstructing Monk's professional reading demonstrated his mastery of seventeenth-century military theory, while this connection between text and thought would recur throughout Corbett's work. He would craft texts to be used by professionals, much as Monk had used the Duc de Rohan's *Perfect Captaine*.[6] He explained the ease with which his subject had changed sides by arguing that Monk, first and foremost a patriot and a professional soldier, lacked political ambition.[7]

By contrast Corbett the High Victorian disapproved of Monk's lax morals, and those of Charles II, reserving particular scorn for Monk's lowly marriage. Mrs Ratsford, 'neither pretty nor well bred', had entertained Monk while he was imprisoned in the Tower; at her husband's death she was with child, and Monk married her. In the process a 'farrier's daughter' became a duchess. In Corbett's world 'Great Men' did not marry camp followers, although he implied an exception might be made if they were pretty.[8] The innocence and prudery of such judgements may explain why his fiction misfired with the mass audience. He simply did not understand how the other three-quarters lived: it may have been a blessing that he turned down Nelson. Corbett never wrote with or about passion: letters to his wife, Edith, were thoughtful, considerate, and occasionally apologetic, reflecting an unconscious assumption of superiority on grounds of gender and age. They reduce Edith to a shadowy presence, defined by her husband, and her children. They, not she, were the focus of Corbett's tightly buttoned devotion.

Despite pressure to trim his references, Corbett cited new evidence and launched into scholarly controversy.[9] His sea battles were dynamic and exciting, but he made the past live with a proper concern for accuracy. His incisive analysis addressed complex events that still divided contemporary opinion. While occasional literary flourishes might mislead the unwary, *Monk* remained the standard biography for many decades. If Macmillan hoped Corbett's literary craft would catch the mass market, *Monk* made his reputation as a historian.

Corbett sent copies to the Marquess of Bath, Field Marshal Lord Wolseley and Samuel Rawson Gardiner. Bath and Wolseley were delighted;[10] Gardiner offered two minor corrections, while the assumption that Corbett read the *English Historical Review*, house journal of the academic profession, suggests he considered him a fellow scholar.[11] Reviews were positive. Strachey's *Spectator* declared Corbett's 'lively biography' might expand popular under-standing of a man but vaguely remembered, accepting the account verbatim, picking out the major themes, apolitical professionalism, courage, skill and dedication. Monk, 'desirous as a soldier to obey the civil power ... could not endure a military despotism' and disbanded the Parliamentarian Army once the king had been restored, consistent with British practice.[12] Yet the way ahead remained uncertain. While Macmillan signed Corbett up to write another *Men of Action*, on Sir Francis Drake, Corbett was also pondering a political career, visiting Algeria and writing for the theatre.

In mid-January 1890 Corbett spoke at a Liberal meeting in East Grinstead, celebrating Gladstone's 80th birthday, dining with brother Charlie and Captain Brand RN. The branch chairman 'pressed me again to stand for the division.'[13] Yet much of his time was occupied researching Drake, including a visit to Captain Pilkington of the Blue Anchor liner SS *Murrumbidgee*, on the Australia run, who helped him plot Drake's course through the Indonesian archipelago.[14] Pilkington would be consulted again in April 1893 'to get sea-matters right' for the novel *A Business in Great Waters*.[15] The British Library, Public Record Office and London Library provided more conventional sources.

When Macmillan agreed to wait for *Drake*, Corbett set off for Algeria, accompanied by his brother Frank on 16 February. They crossed France by train and took a rough passage from Marseilles to Algiers on the steamer *Kleber*, arriving at Algiers on the 19th. They toured the city, sketched, visited the mosque, the old fort and the 'pirate harbour', activities that proved useful when Corbett wrote about the Mediterranean a decade later. The hotter parts of the day were devoted to *Drake*. The brothers took the train south on 12 March. Reaching the end of the line they went out with some French cavalry officers for a 'Glorious ride' near Leghourat and 'saw Sahara like a sea'. Dining under the stars on lamb and couscous, they spent the night in the Arab camp. While local food and culture were a revelation, and eating without cutlery a novelty, the hard Arab saddles proved a sore trial for English posteriors. They rode on, thankfully in French saddles, an armed escort reminding them that France's grip on the region was tenuous. Corbett realised that the French were universally loathed, while the Spahi officers were 'desperately stupid' and tiresome. By 3 April the brothers were back in Algiers. Departing on the 7th they were back at Imber Court on the 19th after '[o]ne of the most interesting and enjoyable tours ever made'. Having seen French imperialism up close, Corbett was not impressed: the contrast with India made him 'proud of being English'.[16]

The next day he was back at work. Having reached the Cadiz expedition of 1587, he found the standard account, Froude's *History of England*, 'very inadequate and inaccurate'.[17] A week later he began the Armada, working laboriously through Fernandez Duro's Spanish naval history, dictionary in hand.[18] A month's work on the Armada revealed serious defects in almost all existing accounts, which ignored the initial English sortie south to intercept the Armada. Later he excused the eminent Catholic scholar John Lingard from this criticism.[19]

On 14 May, Corbett attended the Gala Dinner of the Royal Literary Fund as the guest of George Macmillan. The charity event raised funds to support indigent authors and included a speech from a famous author. Corbett would patronise the event for the rest of his life: he greatly enjoyed the company of fellow intellectuals and had the funds to be charitable.[20] Suitably inspired he planned a fishing trip to Scotland with fox-hunting neighbour Clinton Dawkins, Private Secretary to the Chancellor of the Exchequer.[21] Having concluded his account of the pivotal battle off Gravelines, he departed for Loch Rannoch, and a week of beautiful weather, fishing, drawing, social calls and debating the issues of the day with Dawkins, who brought a wealth of political and commercial insight to the loch. Corbett's sporting life was far more than the pursuit of vermin, or the taking of fish: it was a vital part of his world, an opportunity to meet his peers on neutral ground, free from political rancour. A prominent atheist,

Dawkins moved into banking in 1899, becoming a partner in J.P. Morgan's London branch.

Suitably refreshed, Corbett completed *Drake* on 7 July in a state of nervous exhaustion, compounded by an invitation from Lewis 'Lulu' Harcourt, to stand at the coming general election.[22] The Ipswich Liberal Association enquired if he would stand, an offer he discussed with Harcourt on the 22nd. In mid-August, Corbett joined Sir Alexander Stephen's 268-ton steam yacht *Nerissa* at Dartmouth for a cruise along the Cornish coast, including a visit to Lady Elliot-Drake, a noted authority on family history, at Buckland Abbey. Page proofs, shooting and pond-digging at Woodgate occupied the next two months. By late November he was drafting a family play and consulting a doctor about his throat.

Drake was a transitional work. While Corbett remained a literary conjuror, seeking impact through style and artifice, evidence and analysis assumed a greater role. Occasional romantic flourishes of dubious veracity included describing the hero as 'dead like a sick girl of an inglorious death', or putting his orders in a (non-existent) pocket, while the *Revenge* was 'gilded with the romance of war'.[23] *Drake* remained a popular history, one the publisher hoped to sell in large quantities, following a formula, limited in size and focused on accessibility. This may explain why he described Tudor warships as battleships, cruisers and gunboats, rather than galleons, brigantines and flyboats.[24]

Despite these constraints, Corbett paraded his evidence and overran his allowance for a second time. He had used original material at Buckland Abbey, Hatfield House and the British Museum, alongside contemporary texts and modern documentary collections from the Historical Manuscripts Commission, the Hakluyt and Camden societies, and Spanish material. Corbett shared Froude's view that Drake had changed the course of world history. The West Indies raid of 1585 halted Spain's attempt to become 'a new Roman Empire', a theme echoed when he quoted Leopold von Ranke's portentous line that 'the fortune of mankind hung in the balance' when the Armada sailed.[25] England's deepest fear in 1585, a single universal empire, alien in culture and faith, dominating Europe, remained the same in 1890. The example of continental Rome defeating maritime Carthage and assuming the dominion of the world had shaped Elizabethan conscious-ness, as Raleigh made clear. Linking Drake's raid and Philip II's recovery of Antwerp, the lynchpin of the regional economy, in the same year set up a 'last great battle in the west'.[26] Such portentous Arthurian overtones, from Sir Thomas Malory's *Morte d'Arthur* or Tennyson's *Idylls of the King*, reflected Corbett's enduring romanticism. He sustained the David and Goliath theme from the opening argument to the last lines. Nor could he resist attempting to improve Raleigh's immortal account of the loss of the *Revenge*, and the devastating storm that scattered the Spanish fleet the following day.

Drake reached a market fascinated by naval power, linking the tercentenary of the Armada in 1888 with the Naval Defence Act of 1889, doubling the size of the Navy. No longer would Drake be consigned to the shadows, a pirate chief of doubtful repute, isolated from naval glory by the informality of Tudor naval service and the ample supply of paladins provided by more recent wars. Froude had begun the process in the early 1850s, celebrating Drake as a 'Forgotten Naval Worthy'. Corbett shared his romantic thrill and national purpose, linking Drake to Nelson and the case for a larger Navy.[27] He incorporated the latest strategic ideas, introducing Admiral Philip Colomb's concept of 'Command of the Sea' and the strategic value of sea power to a wider public. He acquired Colomb's article on Tudor naval history on 23 June 1890, a year before it appeared as a chapter in *Naval Warfare: Its Ruling Principles and Practice Historically Treated*.[28] Corbett popularised the Admiral's ideas as he absorbed them.

Having already mastered seventeenth-century military practice, Corbett assessed the striking development of late sixteenth-century naval power and set it in the national context. His claim that Drake had penetrated the secret of maritime strategy by 1587 appeared under the page header 'ADVANCE IN NAVAL STRATEGY'.[29] He had Drake recognise: 'the tremendous weapon a powerful fleet would be in the hands of the power that used it against an enemy's trade ... he was the pioneer of this strategic revolution'.

Corbett had recognised the critical role of economic warfare and was never 'disdainful of trade activity'.[30] If the strategic argument was premature and present-minded, exaggerating Drake's sagacity, he had identified the direction of travel, using modern ideas to analyse the Spanish War for modern audiences. He identified the dawn of English sea power in the failure of the great bank at Seville and the associated collapse of the Spanish king's credit. Linking trade, credit and politics was hardly a novelty for a politically active Liberal who lived on the proceeds of international finance and went fishing with Clinton Dawkins. Corbett's contention that Drake was 'beginning to dimly grasp that the command of the sea was the first object for a naval power to aim at' echoed Colomb: 'The "Command of the Sea," was henceforth to be understood as the aim of naval war.'[31] Corbett recognised the importance of bases to maintaining command. Drake believed holding the Azores would enable English ships to annihilate Spain's Atlantic trade and win the war through economic pressure. Corbett pushed the evidence further than a cautious academic because the point had tremendous contemporary significance. While Drake developed a sea control strategy, Philip II had no concept of sea power, only sea transport for land forces.[32]

Elsewhere, Corbett, who had fallen under Drake's spell half a decade before, indulged his hero. He was anxious to exonerate him for beheading the treacherous Thomas Doughty on a desolate Patagonian beach in 1578, troubled by the obvious parallels between Julian Corbett, Jasper Festing and the Iago-like creature that emerged from his research. Doughty, a Cambridge-educated lawyer, had studied at the Temple, his eloquence and intermittent military career deceiving several men of action. While Corbett had no evidence for his claim that Lord Burghley sent Doughty to thwart the expedition and thus preserve peace with Spain, Doughty was a dangerous man with an agenda. Occasionally the novelist stepped into the story: echoing For Gold and God he had Drake swagger into the Temple to address 'spirited young barristers weary of their briefless existence and eager to embark their younger son's portions in a romantic adventure.'[33]

Corbett's account of the Armada campaign exceeded even his hero's immodest claims and excused him abandoning the night watch, which nearly caused a disaster. Objectivity gave way to literary flourishes, heightening the impression of English success and Spanish despair.[34] He had Drake adopt the 'line-ahead' battle tactics of a later era. Corbett had read far too deeply into the events of 1588 to be ignorant of the circling gunnery tactics employed by Tudor race-built galleons. The use of Monk to link Drake with Nelson was predictable, but the Commonwealth soldier had a far better claim to be the originator of linear tactics. The passage where Drake waited for the Armada to wreck was pure invention.[35] It conveyed the grandeur of a looming tragedy in the absence of a suitable quotation. Elsewhere Corbett denigrated the judgement, conduct and reputation of Lord Howard of Effingham, allowing his subject to occupy centre stage, even inferring Drake was in command.[36] In similar vein, he praised the 'flower of Spanish chivalry' for their heroic, if futile, resistance.[37] While the phrase came from Froissart, the intention was to add some honour, and a dash of romance, to a savage struggle for survival on a stormy sea.

After the Armada, the dramatic climax of the book, Corbett faced an obvious problem. Drake's last years appeared to be a succession of failures: the Portugal campaign of 1589 and the last raid to the West Indies were normally passed over quickly, any blame offloaded onto lesser men. Corbett took a different approach, stressing their strategic potential and Drake's forward thinking. Having already reinvented Drake as the precursor of Nelson, he tried to make him a proto-Marlborough. In 1589 Drake and Sir John Norreys set out to destroy the shattered remnants of the Armada, but the expedition became enmeshed in an attempt to overthrow Spanish rule in Portugal and secure a base at Lisbon. This policy was ruined by the queen's 'womanly craving for peace', limited resources and delayed departure. There were not enough troops, and many were new-raised men. Norreys could not attack Lisbon, and the expedition returned decimated by sickness. Corbett covered the catastrophe by stressing the strategic benefits, including significant damage to Spanish resources. Norreys' march through Portugal became a precursor of Wellington's, his troops passing Torres Vedras, site of the duke's Iberian bastion.[38] Despite the failure to take Lisbon, Corbett carefully avoided the word defeat: Drake retained 'complete command of the sea' and planned a 'great blow'. He was holding station off the Azores to intercept Spanish trade when a gale sent his ships back to Plymouth. For Corbett, the eclipse of Drake's reputation after 1589 was unwarranted, citing Lisbon veteran Sir Roger Williams, who told the queen the attack had done her more real service than all the men and money poured into the Netherlands.[39] Corbett had chosen his position in the strategic contest between continental intervention and maritime pressure. The development of Spanish strategy in the 1590s, when they seized a base in Brittany to support another Armada, prompted Drake's recall. With Drake on his death-bed the pathos rose to a crescendo. With England's David gone, the Spanish Goliath, though sorely wounded, 'arose again dogged and huge and terrible still'.[40]

Corbett revived Drake's reputation by placing his actions in a recognisably maritime strategic context. Sir Francis used combined operations to destroy hostile naval resources, ships and ports, and secured command of the sea that achieved decisive effect through economic warfare. These ideas would dominate Corbett's intellectual life.

Corbett had used an engaging popular history, connected to Charles Kingsley's *Westward Ho!*, another creative text shaped by Froude's *Forgotten Worthies*, to spread the navalist message.[41] He had updated Froude's account, part of a national prose epic that linked the ages of Elizabeth and Nelson with the late Victorian empire. Contemporary strategic concerns were blended with ideas from *For God and Gold* and expressed in romantic fashion. These contradictions would not be fully resolved for another decade, and continued to shape Corbett's thinking and writing, albeit in subtler ways, for the rest of his life. While waiting for the reviews, Corbett worked on a play and read Ibsen's *Hedda Gabler*, which he saw in London on 23 April, the first performance in English.[42]

Critical responses to *Drake* were consistent, noting an authorial voice tinged with romance, something that affected his handling of evidence. The *Athenaeum* struck first. Although unsigned, as almost all popular reviews were, the notice was evidently the work of a historian familiar with Spanish sources. The most likely candidate, Martin Hume, wrote on sixteenth-century Spain.[43] He attacked Corbett's handling of the evidence; relegating Lord Howard to a secondary role in 1588 was not warranted by the documents, while Drake's visit to the Temple and 'line-ahead' tactics in 1588 were pure invention. 'We fear that Mr Corbett's historical instincts have been demoralised by a course of novel-writing, and that he is occasionally led to confuse imagination with evidence.' Yet such criticism paled before the central problem. The suggestion that Burghley had inspired Doughty's treachery was unfounded; he demanded Corbett publish his sources. A condescending conclusion dismissed the book as 'well adapted to the wants of the casual reader, whose taste, cloyed by a surfeit of sensation novels or newspapers, cannot relish a wholesome diet without an undue amount of seasoning', it 'must not be taken quite seriously'.[44] Corbett was deeply hurt, because the judgement was correct. The review helped make him a great historian. Nor was it alone: other reviews followed similar lines.[45] Others again rejected Drake as a precursor of Nelson, preferring the pirate identity that had prevailed for the last two centuries.[46] The *Westminster Review* dismissed it as the work of 'a romance writer; rather than the work of a "sober chronicler".'[47] Fred Macmillan or Mowbray Morris might have written those lines to explain the objects of the series.

These reviews prompted a series of articles that earned Corbett a reputation as a historian. He enjoyed the cut and thrust of intellectual exchange,
while the monthly and quarterly formats were ideal for elegantly constructed
briefs, packed with evidence, coolly controlled and precisely delivered. He
would have been pleased when his old friend Hallam Tennyson reported
his father and all the family had read *Drake*, 'liked it much', and invited him
to visit.[48]

January 1891 found him in London to discuss standing for East
Grinstead with Sir William and 'Lulu' Harcourt, who managed the Liberal
election machine. Lulu, he noted, was 'very good at extracting promises of
action but I don't mean to act'.[49] After a fortnight on the hunting field the
promise that the party would pay any expenses persuaded him to reconsider. Then he set off for Rome, where he mixed sightseeing and sitting for
his portrait with work on the play.

The year 1891 was an important one. Corbett began reading Alfred
Thayer Mahan's *The Influence of Sea Power upon History, 1660–1782* on
9 February, noting the discussion of Monk's campaigns.[50] In late November
he read Colonel George Sydenham Clarke's *Fortification: Its Past
Achievements, Recent Developments, and Future Progress*.[51] Mahan and
Clarke would influence his mature writing, as exemplars and foils.

With the play complete, Corbett and a family party visited the Royal
Naval Exhibition at Chelsea in November, Corbett returning for a second
time with Edith Rosa Alexander, his future wife.[52] He proposed an article on
Doughty to Samuel Rawson Gardiner, editor of the prestigious *English
Historical Review*. This would be the ideal response to his critics.[53] Work
was interrupted by Ascot week in early June, the highlight of social and
racing calendar, which he spent at the Army Staff College, Camberley.
Soldiers were a familiar feature of his social world, and Camberley was no
great distance from Imber Court. The one-time cox of a Trinity racing eight
enjoyed Henley week in July, while political activity focused on supporting
Thomas Brassey, the Liberal candidate for the local seat.[54]

Not content with Ascot and Henley, Corbett joined the steam yacht
Morven at Southampton in late July.[55] On 1 August they anchored off
Portsmouth, watching the 'torpedo gun vessels *Sea Gull* and *Gossamer*
return from manoeuvres'. The voyage took them across the Channel to Le
Havre, and along the French coast to Cherbourg, the epicentre of nineteenth-
century invasion scares, where they remained for two days. A rough passage

through the Alderney Race brought *Morven* to Guernsey, and after a five-day stopover the yacht headed for Dartmouth, coasting to Falmouth. Corbett remained at Penrose, the country estate of the Rogers family just outside the Cornish town of Helston, for a month, attending a society wedding in the picturesque fishing village of Cadgwith. Sailing to Plymouth the fortress enthusiast rode round the defences with 'the Colonel', probably his friend John Richardson of the Royal Artillery. Returning to Woodgate on 23 September, Corbett departed for a week fishing and shooting in Wales.

Later he visited Tennyson, finding the aged poet 'well & hearty. Lot of talk with him principally about dialects, spent rest of day with Hallam T & his wife. He advised me to return to *Monk* & write more important work about the Restoration.'[56] The plasticity of his thinking at this stage is striking.

Having spent three months of the year travelling, finishing a play and toying with a political career, he read the key text on sea power theory and began his response to the Doughty doubters. Hallam Tennyson secured an introduction to James Knowles, editor of the high-profile periodical *The Nineteenth Century*, but it came to nothing. Instead he chased the unsettling memory of Thomas Doughty through the library of the Middle Temple, and left his play *The Deserters* at the Garrick Theatre.[57] The inclination to historical work was encouraged when he discovered Gardiner had referenced *Monk* in his latest history.[58] As the year ended he began drafting a novel and an article.[59]

The early 1890s witnessed a striking shift in public engagement with the Navy: demands to enlarge the fleet led by the new Navy League, the growth of foreign fleets and the epochal books of Alfred Thayer Mahan created a market for naval history. By 1893 France and Russia, the second- and third-largest naval powers, were allies, providing a solid base for scaremongering. The challenge fell hardest on the Liberal party, already weakened by a bitter split over Irish Home Rule and ideologically averse to increased defence spending. The Spencer Naval Programme in 1893 and Prime Minister Gladstone's resignation were predictable outcomes of effective campaigning by the admirals, City leaders and navalist writers, Corbett's *Men of Action* taking a minor role.

Despite the critics, Corbett's short study remained the basis of popular writing on Drake for the next sixty years, years in which academics eroded his florid claims, reducing the hero to an exceptionally talented sea-rover, driven by religious and national fervour.[60] Popular interest remained strong, and the Armada anniversary in 1988 made him famous all over again. Corbett maintained his interest in Drake, who remained his favourite subject.[61]

Another author inspired by Corbett's text, Clifton-educated romantic poet Henry Newbolt, published 'Drake's Drum' in the *St James's Gazette* in January 1896, transforming a few scraps of West Country folklore into an Arthurian romance. Newbolt's once and future sea-king sleeps under the ocean, a Viking chief carousing in a briny Valhalla, waiting to be summoned by the famous drum at Buckland. Newbolt's mythic construct appealed to a nation grown anxious about the future, the rising tide of naval armaments threatening to outstrip Britain's efforts. Newbolt published *Admirals All*, including 'Drake's Drum', in October 1897. It sold four editions in two weeks. The two men formed an enduring friendship. Newbolt's poetic shaping of a naval heroism drew strength from Corbett's work; it would be the high-water mark for Sir Francis: his popularity faded at the turn of the century, overwhelmed by Nelson's centenary and Trafalgar.[62] Corbett helped persuade the First Lord of the Admiralty to name a suitably impressive warship for his hero. Although Lord Goschen feared the public would confuse the ship with a gunboat named after wildfowl, HMS *Drake* was the largest and fastest armoured cruiser afloat, built to destroy sea-raiders. His name also graced a naval barracks at Devonport, incongruously affixed to a great pile of stone. As Corbett emphasised, Drake and Nelson belonged at sea, representing the nation abroad.

Although *Drake* concluded Corbett's career in popular history his growing reputation led publishers to solicit more hack work. In 1899 Macmillan, having published the first two volumes of John Fortescue's massive *History of the British Army*, invited Corbett to write a companion work on the Royal Navy.[63] With William Laird Clowes' seven-volume work already in production, he saw no possibility of a financial return for his friends, or himself. Fred offered £1,000 for the project in February 1912, but Corbett declined.[64] It would have been a thankless, laborious task, wholly antithetical to his concern that naval history should inform the analysis of national strategy, rather than merely record events. When Mowbray Morris requested another *Men of Action* in 1901, on Prince Rupert, or Admiral Sir John Norris, at the standard £100 fee, Corbett demurred. He earned twice that for 'magazine work', did not need the money and had no interest in hack work.[65] Morris took the rebuff in good part: 'When a man can write such a volume as your *Drake* – and *Monk* is only, I think, less good because the theme is less fine – he owes his position to his own wits, and not to any editor or publisher.'[66] By then *Drake* had been reprinted three times; four more printings would follow by 1911. As there were no royalties Macmillan took the profits.

Monk and *Drake* introduced Corbett to historical writing, and other historians. Reviewers exposed significant weaknesses in his methodology, prompting him to develop as a historian. At the same time his literary ambitions remained alive, a novel, a play and a stint as a war correspondent separated *Drake* from *Drake and the Tudor Navy*: it would be in this half-formed state that Corbett found his voice, and his audience.

CHAPTER 3

Finding an Audience

Unsettled by the criticism of *Drake* and the illness and death of his mother, who bound him to Imber Court and the life of a local worthy, and reluctant to step up from local politics to a national role in the House of Commons, Corbett spent much of the early 1890s abroad. Having exhausted his literary impulse he found a new challenge in naval history and the oceanic realities of British and imperial identity. Although insulated from the obvious pressures of life, Corbett shared the sense of service and duty that inspired so many of his peers. He began writing as a pleasant distraction for wet days, lonely evenings and long voyages, by 1890 it had become central to his sense of self, although discreetly hidden behind the suitably Corinthian disclaimer, 'Barrister at Law'.

His final novel, *A Business in Great Waters*, was a dead-end, but a series of Drake articles deepened his engagement with archives and scholarship. He wrote them for heavyweight history and public policy journals, the *English Historical Review* and *The Nineteenth Century*.[1] Rejected by the top tier, they appeared in the decidedly middlebrow *Macmillan's Magazine*.[2] Relegated from headline feature to filler, 'The Tragedy of Mr Thomas Doughty: His Relations with Sir Francis Drake' finally appeared in August 1893.[3] Blissfully unaware he was entering a snake-pit of venomous egocentricity, Corbett lambasted the very people he hoped to impress:

> Of all the minor passions the bias of the average professor of history in favour of the uninteresting is the most obstinate. There is nothing to compare with it, unless it be the opposite bias of the historical novelist, but as that is usually classed with the manias the comparison is perhaps hardly decent.[4]

Perhaps there was a middle way.

'Our First Ambassadors to Russia' examined Anglo-Russian relations in the sixteenth century, rescuing 'a story full of adventure and romance' from the shadow of Drake's exploits.[5] Prompted by worsening Anglo-Russian tensions, it exploited the strangeness that lurks at the edge of the known world.[6] Corbett lamented the end of a 300-year-old friendship forged across the frozen north in the age of Edward VI and Ivan the Terrible in terms more Liberal than imperialist, dismissing the Crimea as 'the most bloody and ill-advised war'.[7] Written over Christmas 1891, the manuscript was sent to Morris in January 1892.[8] Corbett began a third essay, 'The Sancho Panza of Madagascar', in February. Responding to the French occupation of Madagascar he examined a quixotic English plan to occupy the island of 1637, one with an engaging cast of characters. Courtier Endymion Porter, prompted by tales of Elizabethan enterprise, persuaded the grandee connoisseur Earl of Arundel to support an insular imperial alternative to joining the Thirty Years' War. Corbett's intellectual range was reflected by a reference to van Dyck's portrait of Arundel, which represented him pointing to the island, as a putative governor. While the original picture was on display at Arundel Castle, seat of the dukes of Norfolk, there was a contemporary print in the British Museum.[9] Parliament cancelled the project and Corbett's message was anything but imperialist; 'the world is wide; we can heartily wish our neighbours God-speed, and hope they were not going to fry'.[10] Despite solid research, Corbett's essays remained closer to *For God and Gold* than the incisive academic model he would employ a decade later.

Corbett's interest in contemporary defence issues developed around 1890, perhaps prompted by a request from his friend Colonel John B. Richardson RA to research the history of coast defences.[11] Suitably inspired, Corbett read George Sydenham Clarke's *Fortification*. Clarke stressed the importance of establishing 'principles' and separating them from the 'morass' of detail.[12] In June 1892 he visited Richardson, then commandant of the artillery range at Shoeburyness, to watch gun trials, and attended his lecture 'Coast Artillery Practice' at the Royal United Services Institute (RUSI) a year later.[13] This friendship may also have sparked an interest in the origins of Richardson's rank. While in Rome in spring 1891 Corbett collected Italian Renaissance military texts, which informed 'The Colonel and his Command', published in the *American Historical Review* five years later.[14] More significant was the introduction he provided for Thomas Taylor's *Running the Blockade*, a narrative of economic warfare in the American Civil War.[15]

By early 1893, Corbett accepted that his dream of writing for the theatre had failed; his work lacked the common touch. Elizabeth Corbett died after a long illness on 6 May 1893.[16] Shortly afterwards John Laughton encouraged Corbett to join the Navy Records Society (NRS), established on 13 June at the Royal United Services Institute. The NRS became the central pillar of his life, providing a sense of purpose and regular contact with naval officers, statesmen, journalists and historians.[17] The NRS served as an unofficial historical section for the Naval Intelligence Division (NID), the Admiralty's equally unofficial war planning centre. Laughton and the Director of Naval Intelligence (DNI), his old friend and shipmate Captain Cyprian Bridge, shaped the NRS to provide edited archival materials to inform naval education. Although supported by statesmen, journalists and authors, the Admiralty dominated the programme. Meetings were held at the RUSI, Britain's leading defence forum, a hundred yards from the Admiralty. The NRS would address key contemporary concerns through history. Laughton edited its first published volumes, using the Armada campaign to demonstrate how the Navy defended the country, just as the Army challenged that age-old reality.[18] Down to 1914, forty-five volumes appeared, ranging across grand strategy, fleet tactics, blockade and naval culture. As a councillor, Corbett mixed with men who made policy and influenced public opinion. The NRS offered him the chance to contribute.

Within a month Corbett was discussing a project.[19] He suggested a volume of documents covering the Spanish War after the Armada, to follow Laughton's opening volume, or a volume on the Medway Raid of 1667. Laughton discouraged the Dutch Wars project, keeping that task for Samuel Rawson Gardiner, the NRS funding transcripts of Dutch material. He urged Corbett to begin with the Tudor era and proposed meeting at the Public Record Office.[20] Laughton's *Armada* demonstrated how historical scholarship could inform contemporary naval policy and strategy, and Laughton urged Corbett to take on the war before the Armada, between 1585 and 1587. Corbett agreed, but the NRS Council, anxious not to overload members with Tudor material, delayed publication. Laughton advised him to follow his research methods and use the archival transcriber who had worked on the Armada papers. Critically, Laughton treated Corbett as a fellow expert, discussing arcane sources and ongoing debates.[21] He also observed that work on this period would support Corbett's planned second book on Drake.[22] This is the first evidence for the project.

The shared sense of purpose proved infectious: Laughton helped Corbett evolve from a romantic novelist into a historian for the Navy. Corbett dropped Tennyson's idea of a book based on Monk in favour of an archival study of the Tudor Navy centred on Drake. Ironically, Corbett's 1894 diary has literally nothing to say about the NRS. He was busy with other literary work, and waiting on the society's first publication. In the interval he travelled to Rome for two months, where he met William Richmond. Newly released from familial tasks, he had time to consider his options – whether in local or national politics, or a greater commitment to writing, genres and subjects as yet undecided.

Once the novel (*A Business in Great Waters*) had been delivered to Methuen on 30 December 1894, Corbett 'resolved to begin Drake & began to read and sort old notes'.[23] The relationship with Laughton quickly matured into one of mutual regard, Corbett's mastery of procedure and drafting became a key asset for Laughton's management of the NRS, and the wider development of naval history.[24] The intellectual rigour of archival history, as practised by Gardiner, Laughton and other leading scholars, proved attractive to a man of Corbett's legal training and historical interests, while the purpose of the new body connected him with policymakers debating national strategy after Mahan's *The Influence of Sea Power* had made the case for studying strategic history. This would be a worthy intellectual challenge, one that linked ideas and action through policy and strategy.[25] Laughton referred him to a wealth of evidence while the NRS funded transcripts.

Work on these projects was halted in the spring of 1896 when Corbett sailed to Egypt to act as a war correspondent in the Sudan for the *Pall Mall Gazette* and *Daily Graphic*. In Cairo he dined with Clinton Dawkins, and lunched with Dawkins' Balliol contemporary, diplomat Rennell Rodd, biographer of Tudor heroes, navalist poet and NRS member. They discussed Drake and diplomacy.[26] He spent two months in the desert, but there was little to report: the Army was busy with the logistical foundations for the 1898 campaign. Corbett formed close relationships with fellow reporter Arthur Conan Doyle, and Army Intelligence Chief Sir Reginald Wingate.[27] He sketched for the *Graphic* and wrote a Kiplingesque poem, 'Dongolay', for the *Pall Mall Gazette*, his only published verse. Having seen the British Empire at war on a distant frontier, met a wide range of soldiers, diplomats, statesmen and fellow journalists, ridden a camel and travelled down the

Nile to Wadi Halfa, the correspondents retreated north when it became clear that nothing would happen for a long time.

Corbett had already completed the manuscript of *Drake and the Tudor Navy* down to 1588, deputing his literary agent to find a publisher.[28] He spent June 1896 writing up the Armada. Despite a hectic round of socialising, hunting and visiting, Corbett completed the manuscript by the end of the year. He started 1897 with an extended visit to Italy and France, accompanied by brother Tod, and occasionally Edith, his future wife. The trip included three days in Venice. He also discovered a hitherto unknown manuscript by Petruccio Ubaldino, a Florentine humanist, in the Medici archives at Florence. The first 'official' historian of the Armada, Ubaldino had produced an Italian text for Lord Howard. The new document, an unpublished second version, included new material supplied by Drake.[29] He worked this material into the text before delivery to Longman in May 1897.

Visiting Cambridge to vote on university matters, Corbett photographed the Anthony Roll of Henry VIII's ships, to illustrate the book. By mid-June proofs for both *Drake* and the *Spanish War* demanded attention, as he began collating the Ubaldino material in the British Library.[30] The proofs were completed on a fishing trip to Scotland. The sheets followed in November and were complete by mid-December. At the same time he helped the NRS address the chaos caused by editorial incompetence.[31] In the interval, Edith accepted Corbett's belated proposal. The accumulated tension made him ill, and a doctor was called.[32] He would not be the last.

Drake and the Tudor Navy examined the emergence of a unique seapower state, linking the agendas of Laughton and Mahan to debates about world power and empire in an age of uncertainty. While Laughton and Gardiner influenced his handling of evidence, the intellectual method was original. Corbett located naval affairs in national policy, dramatic passages of combat were thoroughly contextualised, by examining the development of national aims by Queen Elizabeth and her ministers. Extracting larger patterns from past events would be his greatest contribution. Although specific aspects of his work have been challenged, much of the analysis remains.

Corbett did not follow the whiggish habit of using the past to set up the present. For him the age of Drake was not the dawn of the British empire, but a first step in developing a national strategy to prevent Europe falling under the dominion of a single, over-mighty power, to ensure the security of the British Isles. He stressed that sea power alone was not a decisive strategic instrument, especially in the days of Queen Elizabeth, despite ample evidence that English naval operations had damaged Spanish power.[33]

Drake examined the aggressive commercial expansion of England outside Europe, supported by the progressive party at court, led by the Earl of Leicester and Sir Francis Walsingham. Expansion was both an economic imperative, given the collapse of the old Antwerp staple, and a strategic necessity – once Philip II moved to crush the Dutch Revolt. With the finest army in Europe only a day's sail from Kent and Essex, close to the invasion ports of northern Flanders, the English state had good reason to be alarmed. That this Catholic army was being used to suppress Protestants, by a monarch who combined an intimate knowledge of England and its Navy with the leadership of the Counter-Reformation, compelled Elizabeth's government to respond. The threat hastened construction of a seapower state, relying on the asymmetric strategic and economic advantages of sea control. The partnership between royal authority and commercial enterprise supplied most of the wealth, and many of the ships required to meet the greatest danger. If the policy roots and naval infrastructure could be traced back to 1545, when Henry VIII faced a French invasion, 1588 vindicated the choices made by father and daughter. Corbett indulged his antiquarian bent by tracing the evolution of naval materiel, explaining how the galleys and round ships of 1545 had evolved into galleons by 1588.

If Drake was the poster-boy of Tudor power, the fleet was commanded by the queen's cousin Lord Howard of Effingham, who possessed both the queen's confidence and the social rank to lead men of all stations.[34] Corbett frequently exaggerated Drake's proto-Mahanian insights, and the relative perfection of the tools at his disposal, analysis that stressed current affairs over the historical record. He missed the key point that Drake's Caribbean raiding had not prompted Philip II to declare war, it was English military intervention in the Low Countries. Placing English garrisons in Flushing and other 'Cautionary Towns' on the Scheldt estuary in 1585 denied an enemy army easy access to the North Sea from newly recovered Antwerp, a recurring theme in an English/British way of war. He recognised the oversight two years later.[35] England's defensive move was reinforced when Drake's 1587 raid on Cadiz wrecked Spanish invasion shipping.

Published by Longman in February 1898 in two octavo volumes at 35 shillings (£1.75), the book was a big step up from *A Business*, which retailed at 6 shillings (30 pence), reflecting very different audiences. Corbett paid close attention to the contractual side of every book deal, pushing for better terms and additional advertising.[36] Delegating the task to an agent enabled him to preserve a personal relationship with the publisher. The front covers were embossed with Drake's arms, a powerful maritime device consciously echoing Mahan's similarly decorated 'Sea Power' texts.

Reviewers immediately placed Corbett in the front rank of naval historians: the more acute connected his book with the growing body of present-minded writing that emerged in Mahan's wake. In the *Graphic*, navalist author H.W. Wilson suggested that the life of Drake and development of naval technology might have been kept separate, but Corbett's 'consummate skill':

> places its author amongst the first living English historians, and this without bestowing excessive praise. There is a fullness of research which is monumental, a philosophic amplitude of view, and, though the style does not attain the dignity and force of Froude,[37] a clear and spirited manner of narration.[38]

Not only had Corbett replaced Froude, lately Regius Professor at Oxford, but *The Times* naval correspondent and NRS councillor James Thursfield[39] considered his work 'of the same order of naval literature as the classical volumes of Captain Mahan'. This was high praise, from Mahan's chief cheerleader in the British press. Thursfield's lengthy review linked Corbett's emphasis on Drake as the 'first champion' to Mahan's use of Nelson as the 'embodiment' of British sea power. Thorough research and a broad assessment of the international context enabled Corbett to emphasise the 'essential principles of naval warfare'.[40] Longman quickly deployed the Mahan reference as advertising copy.[41] A month later Thursfield reinforced the message, contrasting William Laird Clowes' 'laborious' multi-volume *The Royal Navy: A History from the Earliest Times to the Present* with the strategic insight provided by Corbett and Mahan, who made the facts 'yield all their teaching'.[42]

Laughton's review for the *English Historical Review* in July 1898 marked a significant shift in the naval historical firmament. Having declared the book 'a standard work on the history of the rise of England as a maritime power', he dismissed the 'rather exaggerated' idea that Drake alone was the 'creator and inspiration' of the new navy. Sir Francis lacked administrative expertise and he did not make the significant tactical contribution that Corbett implied; furthermore 'line ahead' was not the basic formation in 1588.[43] Laughton, by now almost 70, was handing the torch to a new generation. A cheap edition appeared in October 1899.[44]

Corbett's book was overly biographical, and indulgent of his hero's weaknesses, conflating plunder and strategy. Ultimately it was the skilful use of all forms of national strength, not least the finances so carefully managed by the queen, that enabled the Elizabethan state to weather the storm. Modern scholarship has reconfigured Elizabethan foreign policy, transformed Corbett's assessment of the failed 1589 attack on Lisbon, and demolished Drake's proto-Nelsonic credentials.[45] Yet it would be wrong to judge the book by the scholarly standards of another age: Corbett wrote for an audience that expected 'lessons' for contemporary consumption.

The linked NRS volume, the *Spanish War, 1585–1587*, which appeared five months later, completed his transformation from London literary man to research scholar. That year the NRS Council included two former First Lords, a former First Sea Lord, two eminent naval constructors, the leading historical geographer, two imperial strategists called Clarke (both Royal Engineers), Admiral Philip Colomb, former naval officer and now Chichele Professor of History at Oxford Montagu Burrows, the Hydrographer of the Navy and Corbett. His introduction to the *Spanish War* addressed their concerns, individually and jointly, emphasising the contemporary naval situation.

Specifically designed as the precursor to Laughton's *Defeat of the Spanish Armada* of 1894, Corbett linked his work to archival publications by the Hakluyt and Camden societies, the Royal Commission on Historical Manuscripts and Michael Oppenheim's study *Naval Administration*, assuming readers had access to them all.[46] Material from Fernandez Duro's Spanish naval history reinforced his argument.[47] Addressing the quasi-war before the declaration of hostilities, Drake's 1585–6 West Indies voyage, operations on the Spanish coast in 1587, and naval administration, Corbett stressed the reactive nature of English operations. Philip II had excluded his Caribbean empire from Anglo-Spanish trade treaties, to preserve economic monopolies, enabling England to attack without declaring war. When Philip seized English merchant ships in the ports of Old Spain, the English sought redress in New Spain. Drake went to the West Indies to limit Spanish naval power, which reached alarming proportions following the absorption of Portugal in 1580. The campaign was 'a thoroughly well-conceived, if ambitious, design to destroy the sources of Spanish transatlantic commerce and ruin her colonial empire'.[48] Although the results were less impressive than had been hoped, the voyage had a profound impact across Europe, where the prospect of Spanish hegemony, financed by American bullion, alarmed many, including Dutch rebels and his Holiness in Rome.

Sir Francis Walsingham dispatched the 1587 raid to the coast of Spain after uncovering intelligence of the 'Enterprise of England'. The pre-emptive strike prevented shipping, dispersed in ports from Galicia to Sicily, assembling and victualling for war.[49] Drake's dispatches downplayed the impact of 'singeing of the King of Spain's beard' at Cadiz to emphasise the strategic dislocation created by cutting Spain's maritime communications. Holding station off Cape St Vincent and dominating the adjacent sea lanes paralysed the movement of Spanish ships, men, cannon and stores for many weeks, preventing an Armada in 1587. Corbett claimed it was 'the first example of true naval strategy in the modern sense'.[50] Drake had exploited information acquired at Cadiz to extend his campaign, emphasising the long-term impact of intelligence-led sea control over the transient glory of battle. The English fleet held station in the mouth of the Tagus, the obvious base for an Armada, defying Spanish commander Santa Cruz to fight. Drake even considered an amphibious assault on Fort St Julian.[51] When his hold on Cape St Vincent was finally broken, by storms and desertion, intelligence enabled Drake to intercept a fabulous prize off the Azores. The *San Felipe*, homebound from the Indian Ocean, carried the richest cargo yet taken by the English, including spices, specie and documents that helped promote Indian trade.[52] Corbett emphasised, 'how a small well-handled fleet, carrying a compact landing force and acting on a nicely timed offensive, may paralyse the mobilisation of an overwhelming force'.[53] The contemporary relevance of his line was obvious. In a single campaign Drake had disorganised a pan-European invasion project, taken a fabulous prize, and made Spain fear for the communications and bullion flows that funded the entire Counter-Reformation. When Drake reached Plymouth the Spanish, unaware that he had left their waters, were desperately trying to protect an incoming treasure fleet.[54] This was the type of detailed work required to establish the 'scientific' credibility of the past and attract the attention of technically minded sailors. However, both the *Spanish War* and *Drake and the Tudor Navy* contained outbursts of florid prose.

The *English Historical Review* took the *Spanish War* seriously. Oxford professor Frederick York Powell noted the romantic prose but commended Corbett's 'clear introduction and helpful notes' along with his larger themes, resistance to a proto 'world-empire', 'sound and intelligent strategy' and the recovery of Drake's reputation. On the last point he issued a magisterial judgement: 'The ridiculous ignorance that sneers at Drake as a greedy and bloodthirsty pirate making war for private ends should not survive the perusal of this volume.' Delighted by the range and richness of the documents, Powell enjoyed Corbett's mastery of the Elizabethan names for the various sizes of cannon, and the ships that carried them, warning against the tendency to switch into modern terms like battleship and cruiser, apparently unaware that his primary audience was uniformed and professional.[55]

Fresh from this triumph Corbett dined with the Royal Literary Fund, where he discussed the subject of his next book – the last years of the Spanish War – with James Thursfield, who provided an astute *précis* for readers of *The Times*: 'Though this part of the history has never been written in any completeness, its value to a modern student of strategy is higher than that of the earlier and better-known campaigns when Spain was weak at sea.'[56]

The NRS and historical writing had provided Corbett's life with a purpose, linking scholarship to the Navy's growing need for education and doctrine. He had become a significant naval authority, but that was not the end of his journey. Progressive Liberal views continued to shape his response to an age of uncertainty for the empire and strategy.

In January 1899, Corbett was 'pressed' to stand as the Liberal candidate for a by-election at Epsom. He declined.[57] Instead on 7 February 1899 the 44-year-old Barrister at Law married 28-year-old Edith Alexander at St Mary Abbott, Kensington.[58] Corbett had known Edith, the daughter of his godfather, all her life, and the happy event followed a prolonged courtship dating back almost a decade. After a reception for 150 guests at the Royal Palace Hotel the newlyweds left for Egypt. On their return they moved into a large apartment at 3 Hans Crescent in Knightsbridge.

The other major event of the year, the Second Anglo-Boer War, began eight months later. Corbett responded to the initial run of British defeats in the *Daily News*, noting: 'Law students are taught that there is nothing so misleading as a legal maxim. The same is true of military maxims. Only the most finished masters of the Art can handle them with safety.' Anticipating his most controversial strategic principle, he chided another correspondent for repeating the old maxim of seeking out the enemy army when it was 'better to force it to come to you'. Furthermore, the wisdom of Jomini and Napoleon was 'not contained in bald maxims'.[59] This attempt to educate readers of a decidedly Liberal newspaper in the realities of war revealed Corbett's intellectual journey from romantic novelist to strategic analyst. He did not mention Clausewitz.

Responding to criticism of his new books, he emphasised that naval success was only part of the skilful balancing of power and money that enabled the Elizabethan state to weather the storm. He needed better tools to analyse the higher direction of war. He wrote *The Successors of Drake* without a contract, belatedly settling a new agreement with Longman on 5 February 1900, citing 'private reasons' for the decision. Even so he secured an improved royalty deal.[60] He delivered the manuscript a week later, and read proofs in the week of Paardeberg and the Relief of Ladysmith. Despite such distractions, the work was finished within a month, the index occupied another two weeks. On 2 May he attended the Royal Literary Fund dinner, walking home to Knightsbridge with Mark Twain. He spent July in Ireland, probably visiting his sister and her son.[61] The single octavo volume was published on 13 October 1900, priced at 1 guinea (£1.05).

Corbett followed the new book by canvassing East Grinstead for brother Charlie, who would be defeated in the Conservative 'Khaki' election triumph.[62] The choice reflected the belated recognition that he was not cut out for front-line politics. Charlie, made of sterner stuff, entered the House in the Liberal 'landslide' of 1906. It is unlikely Corbett would have made an impression in a House of Commons packed with brilliant lawyers and powerful orators. Innate modesty, diminutive stature and limited personal ambition may have restricted him to an occasional well-regarded speech to an empty House – a waste of his talent.

The new book appeared in a uniform binding, Drake's arms again gracing the front to stress the looming presence of the dead hero, while his most important successor, the Earl of Essex, occupied the frontispiece. Following Laughton's criticism, *Successors* treated English strategy as maritime, not naval. Corbett's preface shared the national jubilation prompted by the relief of Mafeking, arguing that studying naval and military activity in isolation 'would not be history' and consciously linking his book with

Seeley's *The Growth of English Policy*, 'the highest and most recent of English authorities'.[63] He countered Seeley's triumphal version of the Elizabethan era, stressing weakness and danger in the face of an overwhelming Spanish threat, and treating the 1596 Cadiz raid as an 'irretrievable miscarriage' in an age of splendid failures. The inability to exploit maritime power gave the subject 'deep and living interest'.[64] England did not dominate the seas when Elizabeth died. 'For defensive war a navy may suffice alone; but how fruitless, how costly and long drawn out a war must be that for lack of an adequate army is condemned to the defensive is the great lesson we have to learn in the failure of Drake's successors.' Corbett doubted 'we have learnt it yet'.[65] His prediction proved prescient in 1914. War broke Spanish naval power and loosened Madrid's grip on the Low Countries, but it did not create a sea empire. Corbett thought the queen's refusal to invest national resources in an overseas empire mistaken – a judgement modern scholarship would reverse. Without an army or the funds to build one, Tudor England had no business speculating on the long term. His ideal English army would be a small, professional, mobile force, a 'projectile to be fired by the Navy', reflecting the agendas of contemporary generals John Maurice and Lord Wolseley as well as the Earl of Essex. In a book dominated by the projection of sixteenth-century sea power Corbett argued that Essex understood the strategic value of overseas bases for short-range fleets, especially Lisbon, but overestimated England's ability to hold them.[66] Without the experience or endurance for sustained long-range operations the Tudor fleet could not maintain an economic war. Sixteenth-century naval operations were closer to those of Mediterranean galleys than Nelson's fleet, making advanced bases essential for effective offensive campaigns. Base-centric warfare determined the English response to the Spanish landing in Brittany, and the savage treatment of Irish 'rebels' at Kinsale.[67]

Essex wanted to seize the initiative, meeting the menace of another Armada by crushing the Spanish fleet, occupying key bases and blockading the coast. Critically, the blockade would be self-funding. The missing element was a professional army to seize and hold bases. Essex rejected indecisive continental campaigning in the Low Countries in favour of Drake's plan to secure Lisbon in 1589. England had no vital interests inland and should not waste men and money aiding allies.[68] Essex had challenged vested interests: the prospect of cutting ties between the landed aristocracy and local militia frightened the establishment, as it would in Corbett's day.

For Corbett, the last years of the Spanish War emphasised 'the limitation of maritime power' rather than its strength, while the 'real importance of maritime power is its influence on military operations'.[69] English aims were constantly thwarted by the lack of a professional army, and the consequent failure of combined operations.[70] After Drake the key figures were soldiers: Essex, a Trinity man, became Corbett's hero. Despite his ultimate failure, and dramatic end, Essex was the most capable and committed of Elizabeth's entourage, a man of learning, conviction and courage, with the insight to grasp an as yet impossible future.[71] By contrast Corbett dismissed Raleigh, the hero of his own writings, and no seaman. *Successors* used analytical concepts from contemporary strategic writing.[72] British strategy was 'maritime' rather than 'naval', emphasising the interdependence of the two services. Corbett stressed the 'real importance' of Trafalgar 'was what it afterwards enabled Wellington to do'.[73] Compelling parallels ensured service audiences grasped the lesson.

Corbett's argument would be reinforced in the 1950s when Essex's argument for holding Cadiz was rediscovered by a scholar familiar with his work.[74] Essex claimed that holding Lisbon and Cadiz with a professional army would enable the Navy to maintain an effective blockade of the Iberian coast, cutting trade with the Indies and the Baltic, weakening the Spanish fleet, bankrupting the state and humbling its pretension to European hegemony.[75] Essex's account of the Cadiz operation, intended to secure a hearing for this strategy and the related policy paper, had been suppressed by Robert Cecil.[76]

Successors advanced Corbett's strategic thinking, recognising Essex's plans as presaging later practice – and doing so before engaging with Clausewitz. Corbett had mastered English strategy through an archival study of a relatively brief historical period, using analytical tools provided by Mahan, Colomb and General Sir John Maurice. He recognised that the higher direction of war was a political issue, while contests between military and naval methods within the political leadership would persist in the following centuries, a core theme for his long-term analysis of national policy. Essex understood that as England had to command the sea, for security, it would be wise to use that command for offensive strategies, primarily through economic blockade, deploying a small professional army from the sea to seize critical bases and burn hostile fleets. Drake had advanced a similar concept of bases and economic warfare: his final voyage to the West Indies was intended to occupy Panama, and cut the flow of bullion to Spain.[77]

Corbett emphasised how Essex's connection with Drake enabled him to understand the critical role of oceanic landfalls and the Straits of Gibraltar in exercising command of the sea.[78] The cost of the 1596 Cadiz raid prevented any follow-up; men and money were desperately needed in Ireland. Another Spanish invasion was rumoured in 1597, although the Spanish target was Brest, prompting Essex to invest his remaining credit, personal and financial, in another amphibious campaign. The campaign would begin with a grand raid, destroying the Spanish fleet at Ferrol, then seize the Azorean island of Terceira as a base to intercept the Indies treasure fleets, an offensive 'maritime' strategy. In the event, unseasonal storms, limited land forces and Essex's lack of naval experience handed control of national policy to his bitter rival Robert Cecil.

Corbett included contemporary references: the failure of multi-ethnic Spanish imperial navies implied that a Franco-Russian alliance would be equally ineffective. His discussion of ship design might appear superfluous, if the contemporary relevance of superior ships was not so obvious.[79] The Tudor navy was not the modern Royal Navy, only the seed from which it would grow, but it provided useful experience. That said, book learning was no guarantee of success; the instinct for the offensive was, he noted, 'rare in a soldier made from books'.[80] Essex was an exception. Although widely read, he retained experienced soldiers to develop his thinking. He also commissioned expert analysis of Thucydides and Livy, historians of great conflicts between seapower states and continental military states.[81] Essex, a student of leadership, knew how to put on John Keegan's 'mask of command' to ensure he was seen at the head of the army, or the fleet, ensuring due prominence in written accounts.[82] The search for fame had a purpose: the 1596 campaign had been a massive gamble; success might hand Essex control of national policy and the opportunity to wage offensive maritime war. His rival Robert Cecil, and Cecil's father, Lord Burghley, took a different view. The Cecils saw no reason to defeat Spain only for France to assume its place as England's most dangerous enemy. The Cecils focused on pacifying Ireland and improving national defences, the 'primary points were to keep the Queen's dominions safe and to ensure that no single power could threaten them by dominating Europe'.[83]

Overt digressions into contemporary strategy, the Boer War and other epochs of naval history were counterbalanced by a scholarly appendix analysing manuscript sources for the Cadiz raid. These included British

Library Sloane MS 1303, 1, which Essex had created for publication to secure popular support for his vision of national strategy.[84]

Early reviews stressed the 'great historical value' of a book that revised Seeley, challenged the assumption that Raleigh had been a significant figure in the war at sea, and highlighted comparisons between Elizabethan and Victorian standards of power.[85] The *Scotsman* declared, 'there is not a dull page in the volume'.[86] The *Standard* emphasised the 'fresh and suggestive' strategic core of Corbett's approach, citing the justly famous passage on the link between maritime and military operations, focusing on soldiers like Essex, Vere, Mountjoy and Raleigh, rather than sailors.[87] In *The Times* Thursfield greeted *Successors* as the sequel to *Drake and the Tudor Navy*, which established Corbett as 'one of the few English writers of our time who are entitled to take rank with Captain Mahan as authorities on naval warfare and naval history'. He stressed Corbett's conclusions: 1588 had revived Spanish sea power, while Drake's successors failed because they 'could not or would not understand the essential limitations of maritime warfare and its true relation to concomitant military operations'.[88] The conservative *Pall Mall Gazette* applauded his literary skill and his argument for an efficient Army.[89] Tudor specialist Albert Frederick Pollard's notice in the *English Historical Review* suggested that Corbett's partiality for Essex led him to overlook his failure in Ireland, preferring the 'War Party' to Robert Cecil, whose views were inadequately represented. That said, he praised the academic and analytical rigour.[90]

Corbett recycled off-cuts from the book as magazine articles, including a compelling study of Robert Cecil's use of censorship to control the official version of the capture of Cadiz in 1596, skilfully deflating the claims of court rivals Essex and Raleigh.[91] Laughton assessed Corbett's three Tudor books in the magisterial *Edinburgh Review*: they had placed him 'high on the list of modern historians', restored Drake to history, largely shorn of legendary accretions, extended the work of Mahan and Colomb, and vindicated the strategic principles of battlefleet-based sea control. 'He deserves and has the warm gratitude of every student of naval history.'[92]

Today the *Drake* texts are more often consulted by historians than strategists: Corbett had used strategy to analyse events, but it remained eccentric to the historical core of his work. This approach would change in the new century, a development foreshadowed in the links he made between the age of Elizabeth, the Fashoda crisis, the Boer War and the threat to floating trade from French and Russian armoured cruisers. His audience was acutely aware of the didactic value to be drawn from the past. As he traced the faltering early steps of English sea power he ensured his readers understood the contemporary importance of maintaining naval mastery. These books mark a distinct phase in Corbett's intellectual career. They addressed a cultured, politically aware audience, including the councillors of the NRS. Soon he would acquire another audience: naval officers undergoing professional military education, a student body that inspired him to develop a new language to convey his ideas. This process began within two years of *Successors*, tracing the evolution of a British 'way of war' through historical case studies of national strategy.

Drake and *Successors* shifted the focus of naval history from ships and battle to the interplay of national strategy, policy and operations, even if their biographical focus harked back to the hero-centred histories of Thomas Carlyle. Equipping Sir Francis with Mahanian insight and Nelsonic leadership, as Garrett Mattingly observed, stretched the bounds of credulity.[93] Furthermore, Corbett had yet to grasp all the complexities, and limits, of the higher direction of war. Despite those weaknesses he had demonstrated critical assets for a great historian: forensic insight, judgement, the ability to pose new questions, and a fine prose style, in his case honed by legal practice and literature. Although imperfect, focused on leading men and prone to digress on technical issues best addressed in another format, these books were the foundation of Corbett's career, inasmuch as they examined the foundation of English sea power. With the support of NRS councillor George Sydenham Clarke, his next step would be more certain. Corbett would be the strategist of empire, not its poet.

Corbett recognised the critical importance of detailed archival research to uncover the making of policy and strategy. Titanic figures like Nelson, who appears as a shadowy 'super Drake' in the early books, would have to be examined, alongside the statesmen of victory: William III, Marlborough and the Pitts replacing the cautious queen who looked to preserve, rather than expand the state, an approach at odds with Corbett's convictions, and the realities of global power in 1900. Those convictions were obvious in both *Drake* books: he supported a progressive empire having seen how it made a difference in distant Sudan – an experience that proved useful when discussing land operations.

Corbett's development as a historian was not shaped by the new academic practices. Independent wealth and alternative intellectual approaches, including the law and a focus on contemporary issues, made Corbett a very different scholar from his university peers.[94] His present-minded lectures and monographs taught naval professionals to see strategy and policy in context, highlighting the need for a systematic understanding of the British 'way of war' the better to debate with statesmen and soldiers.

CHAPTER 4

Politics and Policy

Alongside his historical output Corbett joined contemporary debates about the future of the empire, domestic reform, and British security needs in an increasingly militarised world. After 1902 he focused on teaching strategy to naval officers, informing statesmen and shaping national doctrine. His uneasiness about the future was widely shared. The Boer War disasters of Black Week in 1899 shook the foundations of Victorian complacency, prompting the remarkable transformation of British power that provided the opportunity for him to serve. That his work remains important a century later is a useful by-product, testament to an uncommon intellectual engagement.

Having visited Canada, Egypt, India, Aden and Sri Lanka, and seen the Army at war in the Sudan, Corbett understood national strategy in the broader context of imperial development, which he would discuss in the Liberal *Monthly Review* and Sidney and Beatrice Webb's progressive Coefficients think-tank. Politics and culture shaped his argument that maritime strategy was the key to national and imperial security, the defence of trade and global influence.

Corbett's teaching would be dominated by 'the deflection of strategy by politics', and his politics were Liberal Imperialist, powerfully predisposed to seapower as culture and identity, an amalgam of democracy, progress, free trade, self-determination and the rule of law, including at sea.[1] Here he parted company with most contemporary strategists, uniformed social conservatives who sought a solution for their anxieties in short aggressive wars, a 'German way' where 'decisive' victories averted the destabilising, democratising social consequences of prolonged conflict. Romantic ideals imbibed at Marlborough and Cambridge inclined him to look for heroic leaders, in war and politics.[2] He found a suitable figure in the radical Admiral Sir John 'Jacky' Fisher, who used dreadnoughts and deterrence to avoid war and conscription. He recognised Fisher's intuitive understanding of a 'British way'. In politics Corbett preferred steady progress, widening the domestic franchise to include women, and moving towards an imperial commonwealth of self-governing nations, unified by the sea. These views were underpinned by a conviction that Britain and the empire were forces for good in an uncertain world. Not given to dramatic intellectual shifts his logical, analytical mind demanded evidence, and recognised the other side of every argument. This was the crowning glory of his strategic thought. Not for him the self-absorbed conviction of Jomini, or Mahan, let alone those doctrinaire followers of foreign systems and alien concepts who drove the British Army towards conscription, and the Royal Navy to worship 'decisive battle'. Among such men his friend Admiral Sir Reginald Custance was typical; a closed mental world, unwillingness to reflect, and absolute certainty secured an innately conservative intellect against Corbett's arguments. Corbett ensured their friendship survived the disagreement.

Corbett had considered a political career in the 1890s, but stood aside, supporting fellow navalist author Thomas, later 2nd Earl Brassey. Brassey, a founding councillor of the NRS, became a leading figure in Liberal Imperialism, a colonial governor and supporter of imperial federation.[3] Corbett chose a similar path. He did not share the Liberal 'passion for upholding the rights of oppressed ethnic minorities' in Central Europe, ignoring Mitteleuropa to focus on Britain's oceanic empire.[4] His 'sea commonwealth' concept evolved alongside his understanding of the historical processes that had created and sustained the empire. Not only was the imperial future the greatest problem facing Britain, but it was one that Britain, the Dominions and colonies could resolve. Corbett never discussed Ireland, the issue that had split his party. His predominantly Tory naval audience, which included many Anglo-Irish officers, made the subject especially difficult.[5]

Politically he was aligned with the Liberal Imperialists, including Herbert Henry Asquith, Richard Burdon Haldane and Sir Edward Grey, who had supported Lord Rosebery, and lamented his resignation.[6] The 'Limps' focused on pragmatic progress and increased efficiency, opposed imperial tariff reform, and sought links with other reforming groups. Their political programme had a significant impact on the 1906–16 Liberal governments. Corbett knew these men socially; contacts increased after his brother Charles entered in Parliament in 1906, and Corbett became a Coefficient.[7] The Liberal Imperialists combined a preference for naval power and opposition to continental entanglement with a desire for efficiency. They wanted better defence, not bigger, and definitely not a system dominated by Tory soldiers.[8]

By 1890 the problem had become rather more complex as the naval leadership, increasingly drawn from the social elite, became more Conservative, and many, dismayed by Liberal policies on Ireland, were won over by Lord Salisbury's 1889 Naval Defence Act. The enduring hostility of Cobdenite internationalists, 'Little Englanders' and the Irish nationalists, who kept the Liberals in office, allowed the Conservatives to become the party of empire, union and Navy.[9] Gladstone's Liberals lacked credibility on strategy. Although the Spencer Programme and Rosebery's premiership of 1894–5 were driven by domestic politics as much as international events, they restored Liberal credibility, and cross-party consensus, on defence. Yet naval expenditure and empire remained divisive for Liberals: Rosebery's leadership rival Sir William Harcourt consistently opposed Admiralty spending, as did his son Lewis, a Cabinet minister from 1906. Corbett remained in Rosebery's camp. Never an advocate of 'bloated' armaments, he understood that the empire depended on command of the sea, a command that must never become overbearing, yet must remain strong enough to sustain a system of deterrence based on prestige.

Corbett's thinking evolved across the 1890s, a decade when defence featured prominently in public life. At the higher end of the spectrum were texts like *The Navy and Nation* of 1897, the collected essays of Royal Engineer Colonel George Sydenham Clarke and naval correspondent James Thursfield. They used Mahan's 'Sea Power' argument to analyse growing tensions between Britain and the Franco-Russian Dual Alliance. Liberal Imperialists Haldane and Asquith relied on Thursfield to draft statements on naval policy.[10] Conservative leader Arthur Balfour also sought their assistance. Both authors were recruited by Jacky Fisher, who managed the career of Thursfield's naval son, while discreetly supplying official and unofficial material to inform articles in *The Times*. Fisher valued Clarke's political skills – he had run Lord Hartington's Defence Co-Ordination Committee in the late 1880s – and his opposition to the narrow-minded agendas of the Army. Fisher also encouraged Thursfield to recruit Corbett as a *Times* special correspondent, while Haldane and Fisher worked together on the 1902 overhaul of naval education.[11]

In the mid-1890s Clarke, Thursfield and Corbett were all councillors of the NRS.[12] Clarke and Thursfield failed to grasp the limited relevance of

Mahan's battle-focused continental model of sea power for a global oceanic empire that depended on maritime communications. Mahan's ideas met the needs of continental Russia, Germany and especially the United States, but not a British maritime empire. Corbett would part company with Mahan and his British disciples.

The 1889 Naval Defence Act and the 1893 Spencer Programme ensured no realistic combination of powers could challenge British sea control. Furthermore it soon became clear that the prime cause of concern, the Franco-Russian alliance, had been created to restrain German ambition in Europe, rather than to attack the British Empire. Paris and St Petersburg consistently failed to cooperate during imperial stand-offs with Britain, lest Germany exploit the opportunity. Seapower and the European military balance enabled Britain to conduct the Second Boer War (1899–1902) in relative freedom. While a war with France or Russia could be waged at sea, and in the empire, where Britain was supreme, the Liberals opposed engaging in a European conflict. Rosebery's desire 'to obtain the full advantage of the insular position with which providence has endowed us', avoiding entanglement with Germany or France, satisfied neither of the European power blocs. The price of that freedom was the costly, party-splitting Spencer Programme.[13] Liberal Imperialists believed European hostility had been created by British colonial acquisitions in Africa and Asia, which were transforming Britain into a continental power. When Sir Edward Grey considered accommodating Russia by concessions in the Mediterranean or Persia in 1895, he launched a debate that culminated with Corbett's *England in the Mediterranean* of 1904. By 1902, Grey favoured closer relations with France, to counter German ambitions. As Foreign Secretary after 1906 he used secret defence discussions to sustain an Entente with France that kept Europe in balance: anything more risked splitting his party, and the country.[14]

In opposition Liberal Imperialists demanded Army reform, in office they proved strikingly ineffective, unable to breach the entrenched positions of the second service, a failure of political leadership that fractured defence policy just as Balfour and Clarke's Committee of Imperial Defence (CID) was trying to adopt a single, essentially maritime, national strategy. After 1906 the Liberals would use inter-service rivalry to cut defence spending, which reduced national strategy to partisan squabbling.[15] While the consequences of this abnegation of responsibility are familiar, the causation has been forgotten.

In November 1901, Fisher advised Thursfield that Britain should back France and Russia if they were attacked by Germany, seizing the German fleet and colonies. 'England has plenty of fight in her; let her be true to herself, keep the United States on her side, and she will give opponents plenty of wire to bite.' Furthermore:

> personally I've always been an enthusiastic advocate for friendship or alliance with France. They never have & never will interfere with our trade, it's not their line, & really we have no clashing of vital interests. Newfoundland might be settled in 5 minutes, but we have not been politic towards them. The Germans are our natural enemies every-where! We ought to unite with France and Russia.[16]

In 1902 Thursfield resolved the Liberal search for a politically compatible naval advisor, linking Haldane and Fisher; Sir John described the politician as 'quite splendid'.[17] Fisher was equally pleased with the looming Anglo-French Entente.[18] He manoeuvred Clarke into the critical post of Secretary to the new CID, telling Thursfield: 'one secret line to say I hope I've arranged a permanent billet for Clarke suited to his great ability & his special apti-tudes. The King has been a wonderful man in all this business, he rivals the Tudors!'[19] Such hints were intended to inform newspaper coverage, and ensure Fisher became First Naval Lord. Fisher was also courting radical elements in the Tory party, led by the Chamberlains.[20]

Haldane called a conference of civilian defence experts and politicians at the Palace Hotel in February 1903. It concluded the rising German navy made it essential to have a fleet and naval base in the North Sea.[21] In 1904 Haldane declared his support for 'the "Policy of the Blue-Water School" ... the true principle of naval and imperial defence. Not only was the Navy a great source of economy to us ... but it was really the principle instrument by which our Empire had been made a great Empire.'[22] These strategic initi-atives dominated Fisher's Admiralty in 1904–5. Fisher persuaded Haldane of the merits of scrapping obsolete ships, and reforming officer education while Second Sea Lord in 1902, and Haldane lauded Fisher's Admiralty policy before the Liberals took office. Grey and Haldane accepted the two-power standard, excluding the United States, although they hoped the Entente would limit naval armaments.[23] Nor was Haldane alone in wishing he had a Fisher for the Army. There were no Liberal soldiers, let alone any with radical ideas. The Liberals had no interest in a continental army, only an efficient mobile force for use outside Europe. While Haldane created that force, he could not force the Army General Staff to recognise political primacy, in part because the diplomacy of the Entente led Britain to make ambiguous statements about possible military assistance, which compromised Liberal opposition to a continental army. To square the circle the Liberals kept the British Expeditionary Force (BEF) too small to be of strategic consequence, further alienating the Unionist/conscriptionist military leadership. While the Liberal ministers of 1906–14 shared Fisher's strategic judgement that the proper defence for a global empire was maritime, political weakness and diplomatic need obliged them to compromise with a deeply hostile Army. Such expediency sufficed in peacetime, but it was cruelly exposed by the decision to declare war in 1914.

Corbett's view of the European situation mirrored Fisher's: he detested Imperial Germany, and imperial Germans.

> I regard the Germans as the most savage of recently civilised people – with two prominent characteristics of savages still maintained – suspicion and envy – to say nothing of their tolerance of petty restraints and a military government. A parallel between Masais or Zulus and Prussians might be fruitful of instruction. Suspicion and readiness to take offence is the mark of every middle class German you meet travelling and envy the note of all their journalism.[24]

The operative word was 'recently'.

Such views informed the new Liberal *Monthly Review*, edited by Corbett's friend Henry Newbolt. Although primarily a journal of culture and the arts, Newbolt recruited a striking group of contributors on politics, empire and economics, including Sir Edward Grey, who wrote in support of free trade,[25] Lieutenant Carlyon Bellairs RN, later an MP and a Coefficient, John Colomb, the grand old man of British maritime strategy, imperial novelist Erskine Childers and historian John Holland Rose, to work alongside art critic Roger Fry and Winston Churchill.[26] Haldane provided an article on educational reform.[27] Corbett, who knew them all, produced sixteen essays for the *Monthly*. They reflected his Liberal views, and secured his appointment as lecturer to the Naval War Course. His subjects ranged across Edwardian defence: imperial cohesion, invasion, naval education, national strategy, political control, conscription and Army reserves. The essays are critical to understanding the wider context of Corbett's strategic thought and his connection with Jacky Fisher.

Corbett began by teaching the 'Little Englanders' to love the empire so that a reunified Liberal party could oversee the evolution of empire towards a 'sea commonwealth'. Offering the essay to Newbolt in July 1900 he noted it had been read by 'one or two real Liberals who are keen to see us out of the Little England slough'.[28] Progressive imperialism would be a major theme in all his subsequent writing.[29] 'The Paradox of Empire' opened the first issue of the *Monthly Review* in September.[30] It was greeted with enthusiasm by his friend Thomas Brassey, later 2nd Earl Brassey, editor of *Brassey's Naval Annual* from 1892.[31] He had published 'Great Britain as a Sea Power' in the influential *The Nineteenth Century* in July 1898, arguing the Army should be configured for offensive operations in the colonial sphere, to seize or destroy enemy cruiser bases, while deprecating the mania for building forts in Britain that would only be useful if the Royal Navy had been defeated.[32] It is likely the two men had discussed the subject.

Corbett began by conciliating empire-phobic 'Little Englanders', before claiming the expansion of the British Empire served the interests of progress. Liberal opposition to empire was illogical, an issue of faith and sentiment, not reason. This was his paradox, and his target. Liberty had been highly aggressive, and few Liberals opposed its spread by force. Even Gladstone opposed the idea that peace was the 'first interest of England'. Corbett noted that the war in South Africa, waged against a nation 'where liberty had grown corrupt', had been supported by Australia, the most liberal part of the empire. For Corbett the British Empire was the ultimate expression of autonomous government, the very antithesis of military despotism, using the concept of a commonwealth to distinguish the British version from Napoleon's universal military rule, backed by a discussion of Caesar's subversion of the Republican Constitution from a key Liberal text, James Bryce's *Holy Roman Empire* of 1866.[33] Confusing the British Empire with the Caesarist military model flowed from the false assumption that all empires were identical. There were two distinct types of empire, the British version was an organic compound ruled by law. Imperial Russia, the Liberal bogey, was a modern Roman Empire, while the United States had emerged from a failed attempt to impose the 'Roman' model. British Liberalism having triumphed in the 1770s, there was no need to fear its return. The British Empire was a 'democratic autonomous commonwealth'.[34]

In a second unsigned essay, 'The Little Englander' of 1901, Corbett explained these doctrinaire opponents of empire to fellow Liberals. 'Little Englanders' feared empire would undermine liberty and progress at home, disenfranchise the masses and stultify political life, allowing the elite to accumulate wealth and privilege.[35] Their political tradition, an important element of modern Liberalism, had been compromised by a distorted perception of imperialism: 'a serious obstacle to right thinking' about 'the gravest problem of the new Empire' – that is, future relations between the mother country and the Federations.[36] The 'spontaneous enthusiasm' with which the colonies had provided military assistance in 1899 changed the nature of the empire, earning them a voice in the reorganisation of the whole: 'We have fought our first Imperial war, and the Empire can never be the same again.' It should evolve into a multi-polar structure.[37]

Corbett's answer was a liberal empire of free trade, where political power was shared and expansion unrestricted. Reform would 'keep the body politic sweet and sound', spreading wealth ever more widely. If England fell behind in this process the colonies could look elsewhere for leadership, to Australia's more inclusive suffrage. Ultimately mutual respect would build a stronger empire, not customs unions, or federation. Progressive domestic agendas held the key to future imperial cohesion. If 'Little Englanders' and 'Liberal Imperialists' combined, they could liberalise the empire as England had been liberalised. For Corbett, responsible government was the key to a liberal, progressive empire. If the Liberal government of 1906 to 1914 echoed elements of Corbett's agenda, it would fail the critical test – Ireland.

Having cast aside his anonymity, Corbett produced three essays on 'Education in the Navy' in 1902, essays that secured Fisher's support. Corbett beat on Drake's drum with help from Lieutenant Herbert Richmond and Admiral William Henderson, key contributors to the Fisher–Selborne scheme.[38] Richmond, son of his old friend Sir William, serving on the flag-ship of the Channel Fleet, provided practical experience and much of the argument.[39] While his naval friends were 'terribly afraid of being caught in communication with the Press', Corbett's civilian status risked reducing the impact of the argument, yet when Newbolt insisted on signed articles Corbett gave way.[40] Richmond checked the text before publication.[41]

Corbett argued that the system created in the age of sail was no longer effective. Naval education and training required early experience of respon-sibility, sails only distracted midshipmen from steam-powered careers. The old system should be replaced by one that equipped officers with the essential technical and military capabilities, but 'above all foster his nerve'. Taking boys from public schools at 15 would not answer: the schools were weak on science and vocational studies, ill-adapted to fostering a thirst for knowledge, over-valued Latin, and promoted the cult of team sport. The current syllabus at HMS *Britannia* stifled interest by avoiding practical knowledge and experience while 'naval history – on which the higher knowledge of the art ultimately depends' – was at best 'elementary', not even an exam subject.[42] HMS *Britannia* had become a third-rate public school with an outdated, counter-productive curriculum and too much team sport. Requiring Latin while devaluing naval history was an absurd way to select future admirals.

The education provided on board warships, dominated by the ship's routines, was no better. Instructors were unable to impart much knowledge, especially to the less able. Technical instruction was rather better, because it was real, although inadequate, a failing proved by exam results and the poor performance of midshipmen sent afloat for the annual manoeuvres. It was a pretence based on unsound principles.[43] Naval education was critical to the imperial defence, but the current system would not produce suitable leaders for peace or war. The Admiralty Board was complacent. This polemic might have precluded any official connection with the Navy, but with Fisher as Second Naval Lord, Corbett was safe. Some senior officers were irritated by the first education essay, but the other two were better received.[44] Corbett advised making every officer a seaman, 'the foundation of success', one who could obey, and take command. He must be competent to use modern technologies but, above all, a British sea officer needed instinct, character and knowledge, in that order. The problem was that education could not be conducted at sea, or training on land. Cadets should be caught young, at the age of 12 or 13, to avoid public schools and 'the taint of games'.[45] After four years continuous, coordinated education, they would join a ship at roughly the same age as they did now, but with core skills, both theoretical and practical, in place. They would be useful, and acquire leadership experience across the next three years. Team games should be replaced by boat sailing and practical seamanship, focusing young minds on duty. Successful midshipmen could be rewarded with advanced promotion, or a place on the annual manoeuvres. Corbett also criticised excessive reliance on maths-based subjects for promotion; other aspects of naval leadership should be recognised.

New lieutenants would be 23 or 24, and mature enough for a revised Greenwich Course. However, 'it must be a true war course, concerned with broad principles of naval art, tactics, strategy, and naval history, together with international Law', with 'lectures aimed at fostering original thought' and weekly seminars. Non-specialist officers would find opportunities to shine, and self-education would be encouraged.[46] Corbett dismissed foreign models: 'let our system be our own', based on seamanship above all else. 'Here has been our advantage over all other nations, and so long as we foster it, it will remain an advantage that no-one can overtake.'[47] Having exposed the intellectual incoherence of the existing system, and demolished a succession of flawed enquiries that had created the current system, the ground was cleared for Fisher's reforms.

'Lord Selborne's Critics' of July 1902 observed that the country loved the Navy but did not understand it. The 'Selborne scheme' had made Fisher famous, and moving from Second Naval Lord to commander-in-chief at Portsmouth enabled him to execute the measure. Backing Fisher against his critics added to Selborne's 'growing reputation as a statesman.'[48] Corbett dismissed senior officers' laments for the old system as a funeral dirge; the debate was over and they should hold their peace.[49] Corbett counter-attacked, his preferred method, demolishing the case against combining command and engineering education. At this point he was invited to lecture to the Naval War Course. A month after that invitation Corbett produced the final naval education essay.[50] The subject had never been taken seriously, being examined at the level of 'anti-fouling compositions or the pattern of a cable-holder'. Elegant irony highlighted naval indifference across the past thirty years, creating a system precisely the opposite of what had been recommended. He traced the absence of any system to the fact that no-one had individual responsibility for naval education.[51] Six months later the Admiralty recruited Alfred Ewing, Head of the Engineering School at Cambridge, to become the First Director of Naval Education, his task was to ensure the 'Selborne scheme' worked. Both Ewing and Corbett recognised Admiral Sir Reginald Custance as the intellectual core of conservative resistance.[52]

Newbolt did not take Corbett's proposal for an essay on Anglo-American links, the wartime security of Britain's vital Atlantic shipping and the future of the English-speaking world.[53] Instead he published 'Lord Selborne's Memorandum I & II', which hailed the 'great and pregnant reform' as 'the product of no ordinary minds'.[54] This was a complete system, using modern methods and 'hands on' experience to produce probationary officers ready to serve when they joined the fleet.[55] Part III addressed secondary provision. Rather than repeating primary education at Greenwich, which did nothing to prepare officers for war, they should be mastering their profession afloat.[56] The academic curriculum was too ambitious, and lacked textbooks, while education at sea was failing.[57] Fisher asked Newbolt for more articles, while Corbett thanked him for printing work considered 'too serious for most editors'.[58] On 8 July 1903 Selborne commended the public discussion of naval education in the House of Lords, citing the *Monthly Review*. Corbett was delighted, but attributed his success to Fisher's input.[59]

The educational reform project ended with a dinner at the Athenaeum in November 1903: Corbett joined Prince Louis of Battenberg, the DNI, James Thursfield, Sir William and Lieutenant Herbert Richmond, Sir William White, Director of Naval Construction, and James Ewing. Fisher was absent in Portsmouth. The setting reflected shared social, professional and cultural values.[60] Prince Louis had approved Corbett's appointment to lecture at Greenwich the previous year.

By this time Corbett's focus had shifted to War Office reform, although his essay would fall victim to the growing chaos within Balfour's Tory government, shattered by Joseph Chamberlain's dramatic resignation.[61] Corbett, like other Liberals, had a special disdain for the renegade radical advocate of tariff preference, and taxes on food, the opinions of 'a retired suburban grocer'.[62] Free trade remained the unifying Liberal totem. The essay appeared in October 1903. It reflected Corbett's deepening connection with George Sydenham Clarke and Jacky Fisher – the service experts on Lord Esher's War Office Reform Committee. While the Boer War demonstrated Imperial Unity, fostering a shared pride in the idea that had earned the admiration of the world, Lord Elgin's Commission on the current state of the Militia and Yeomanry suggested Britain no longer had the power or the prestige to protect the empire. The essay was a failure, packed with clumsy allegories and endless references to bodies, disease and doctors.[63] Corbett opposed colonial navies as unnecessary: 'had we not a single self-governing colony we must still, for the sake of our shores and our commerce, maintain a navy as great as we do. Their protection does not add to our burden: the conditions of their contribution diminish our strength to bear it.'[64] This was Corbett's least satisfactory *Monthly Review* essay.

His response to the Esher reforms, using information from George Clarke, marked a return to form.[65] Corbett considered the War Office re-organisation, signed into law by the king on 6 February 1904, as 'one of the greatest administrative reforms of our time'. The new system was an integrated whole and should not be unpicked in detail. He demolished Spenser Wilkinson's claim, in the *Quarterly Review*, that boards were incompetent to conduct war.[66] Both services had been run by boards for centuries, with great success, notably between 1702 and 1713, a period Corbett was studying.[67] British strategy was uniquely maritime and global:

> The study of national policy and the preparation of strategical plans can only be adequately done, in a sea-girt country above all, in close and well-adjusted consultation with Ministers and seamen; and therefore it is best done by a body [the CID] where all are represented.

This process must continue after the outbreak of war: 'This is the teaching of plain history and experience.' The prime minister must chair 'the new Committee of [Imperial] Defence'. To judge these reforms in the context of the Army alone reflected the continentalism that was already distorting Army thinking. Critically, the new system was the same as that in use in Germany, 'not that the unintelligent and slavish appeal to German practice should ever be allowed to influence our own system'; our mental processes and strategic needs were 'so different from theirs'.[68]

Corbett echoed Clarke's hope that the CID would become 'a thinking department, a "great general staff" in which all the elements of war, diplomatic, financial, naval and military, are brought in contact ... under direct and close control of the responsible Ministers of the Crown'.[69] Civilian control was a Liberal article of faith. Corbett hoped the reformed Army and the CID would generate a coherent national strategy, one that would be adopted by the Cabinet. That he read the reforms through a maritime lens, and stressed the unique nature of British needs, only reinforced his case. Corbett endorsed Clarke's desire for a permanent coordinating body with a powerful secretariat, trying to sell a Tory defence measure to a deeply suspicious Liberal audience by reinforcing Clarke's agenda with insights drawn from his own work.

Clarke was delighted, providing Corbett with 'material for at least two more articles: 'What I have done he describes as a good beginning, but I must modify it a bit, after what he has told me.' Clarke also admitted his long-term agenda: 'economy, great reductions in army expenditure and many things too long to write'.[70] 'Queen Anne's Defence Committee', a striking combination of academic research and present-minded purpose, provided the CID with a precedent.[71] Corbett's purpose was to persuade Liberals with legal backgrounds, notably Asquith and Haldane. The War of the Spanish Succession, the first global war, had been waged with allies and won by a board. The evidence came from his book *England in the Mediterranean*. The old council had been 'a true Committee of Defence ... co-ordinating the other theatres of war, in the Mediterranean, the Peninsula, the West Indies, and the Atlantic, where everything depended on a nice adjustment of diplomatic and military action with the all important operations of the fleet'.[72] A secret inner group conducted sensitive business, avoiding the need for written orders, while consulting service experts. This model enabled Marlborough to direct the strategy and diplomacy of the campaign in north-west Europe, and run the wider war. This was an 'elastic board closely resembling our new conception of a Committee of Defence, and its special concern was ... that world-wide arena where success depended wholly and primarily on the handling of sea power, and its sagacious co-ordination with the military and political factors'. He ended with a rhetorical question: 'Can we do better than begin where the men of Queen Anne left off?'[73] This was the gospel of Sir George Clarke, delivered through historical analogy and legal precedent.

Corbett also assessed the reorganisation of the Volunteers, a politically sensitive subject excluded from the Esher Committee's remit. The Duke of Norfolk's Committee raised a fundamental question. Were they 'a regular or an irregular force ... to be confined to passive defence or available also for active defence'?[74] With 250,000 paid third-line regulars under War Office control, Esher had recommended cuts. Corbett emphasised the political risk of an over-mighty military. The Volunteers should revert to their original status or be reduced; their continued existence was evidence of 'the incalculable, irrepressible eccentricity of the British genius for war'.[75] Confusion between Militia and Volunteers would be resolved by Haldane in 1906, along Liberal lines, and largely to Corbett's satisfaction.

Corbett condemned a failure of imagination that devalued the process:

the persistent heresy of regarding military and naval strategy as two different subjects that can be dealt with apart, of refusing to see them

broadly as mere branches of the great art of war, two branches so intimately intertwined that one can never be treated apart from the other,
and least of all when we are dealing with the fundamental problems of
Insular or Imperial Defence.

Lord Elgin's Commission had treated the Navy as 'a negligible quantity',
because it had no authority to consider wider strategic issues.[76] Corbett
condemned the 'heart-breaking' insistence of commissioners and witnesses
to adopt service positions, rather than addressing the need for a combined
effort. These themes had been evolving since 1900 and reflected Clarke's
influence. While he did not know the answer, Corbett suggested 'a rigid
refusal to regard naval and military strategy separately serves at once to
clear the fog and to reveal a plain line leading to a wholly different conclusion from that to which the majority of Commissioners perversely hurried'.[77]
A few years later he would use the Norfolk Commission evidence to analyse
invasions and raids, an increasingly important issue as the decade unfolded.
Bemused by the assumption that Britain might lose command of the sea
and face an invasion in a matter of weeks, Corbett noted the greatly increased
power of torpedo-armed flotillas meant losing command of sea did not
mean another power would gain it, and certainly not in a matter of weeks.
Referencing the ongoing Russo-Japanese War and Trafalgar linked the essay
to his War Course lectures. The assumption that an invasion was relatively
easy, and might happen soon after the outbreak of war, ignored the Admiralty
submission, because it relied on invasion to justify conscription. Britain
needed enough troops at home to deal with raids and ensure an invasion
force would be so large as to ensure interception at sea. In an echo of the last
'Great War', Corbett argued there would be plenty of time to train a home
defence army in wartime, secure behind the fleet and the flotilla. Dismissing
the 'bolt from the blue' scenario – popular with alarmist novelists and
conscriptionist soldiers – as 'insane' inferred that those who advanced it
were similarly afflicted. Invasion was no more likely than an earthquake in
London. He wondered if any masters of war, by inference the German
General Staff, would risk an enterprise that made the defenders' task so easy.
Napoleon never did. Britain needed a more efficient auxiliary army and the
capacity to counter-attack, issues the Elgin Commission had ignored.

Ultimately Corbett hoped the flawed report would be referred to the
CID, 'where soldiers and sailors sit side by side'.[78] This essay was 'a good

opportunity of preaching the gospel of Greenwich and Geo. Clarke – which they both want crammed in – that all our mistakes are due to neglecting to treat Naval and Military strategy as one'.[79] The obvious intellectual synergy between book, lectures and essays was the use of historical examples to analyse contemporary issues. He had reason to be pleased with the results.[80]

Elsewhere, 'A Russian Privateer in the Mediterranean' addressed the contemporary debate on maritime international law by highlighting appalling brutality by privateers in order to support Britain's continued adhesion to the Declaration of Paris of 1856, while also warning that conceding the immunity of private property would undermine British power.[81] This was Corbett's Liberal/strategic position for the forthcoming Second Hague Conference.[82] Belligerent rights became a persistent theme of his work.

In the summer of 1903 Corbett's naval engagement reached new levels. He spent three weeks with the fleet on the annual manoeuvres. Fisher secured the opportunity through Thursfield, who had Corbett appointed a special correspondent of the 'Thunderer'.[83] Living at sea and discussing the manoeuvres with some of the Navy's brightest officers heightened a romantic engagement he shared with his editor:

> It was the most gorgeous time I ever had. The battle of the Azores was enough to make a journalist sing. A bard would have filled the skies with music. You ought to have been there. But it was not only the battle. It was everything. My opinion of the Navy has risen to the highest. Indeed I wonder what on earth ever made me find fault with it. A little bare navy leaven injected into the army would settle the whole difficulty – army corps and all. It is just that their profession is the absorbing interest of the sailor's life. But old hands tell me there has been a striking growth of this feeling in the last few years. If it can be traced to any one thing it is the exuberant stirring of the Jack-fish spirit. The lusty living wind 'blows from The Straits' – so far as I can judge it.

The 'Jack-fish', a former Mediterranean commander-in-chief, was already the central figure in Corbett's naval world. Stunned by 'the indescribable experience Heaven has let me have these last three weeks', he wrote for *The Times*, his unsigned contributions were reworked for the *Monthly* once the Admiralty had published the final report.[84] He judged these extensive manoeuvres, 'the most interesting, instructive, and successful' to date.[85]

Furthermore, he credited his friends in the Naval Intelligence Division for making them far more realistic than Army exercises. Two fleets were striving for command of the sea; one comprised two or more allied forces (French and Russian). The (British) force was divided, part blockaded in Madeira, the other heading south from the United Kingdom; once combined they would be superior to the enemy. Sir Arthur Wilson, commanding the 'British' force, defeated Allied commander Sir Compton Domvile, but umpire Admiral Sir Lewis Beaumont awarded the prize to Domvile. Corbett disagreed, Wilson's 'bold and masterly tactics' would have secured command, he had more ships, and more coal. Corbett attributed Beaumont's verdict to the dubious concept of local command of the sea. One side had command of the Channel, the other of the Mediterranean approaches. In such circumstances only 'local control' existed, a third category – 'temporary or special control' – should be used when a belligerent was able to use the sea for some special purpose, moving an army, relieving a fortress or escorting a convoy without seeking local control. Corbett argued that 'the technical expressions of naval strategy' must be standardised to be useful.[86] Weakness of terminology rendered the umpire's decision 'misleading, ambiguous and unscientific'. 'Command of the Sea' only existed when one side had forced the other battlefleet from the sea, and it ceased to be a factor in the conflict. Wilson won the exercise by relieving Beresford's fleet, and preventing the enemy from maintaining local control. This experience informed *England in the Mediterranean*, as history helped transform argument into strategic principle.

Newbolt's editorship of the *Monthly* ended in the autumn of 1904, and with it Corbett's contributions. The journal had been resolutely Liberal, which did not suit the Conservative John Murray. Also, sales had fallen.[87] The *Review* helped Corbett develop into a sophisticated critic of contemporary defence policy, British intellectual anxieties, fears of impending imperial decline and loss of economic vitality. He could see the growing economic power of Imperial Germany being translated into naval might, and an overseas empire that challenged British dominion.

These millennial concerns coalesced around the notion of 'national efficiency', the need to improve health, economic competitiveness and security. The assumption that the solution lay in cross-party debate, bringing the best minds of Conservative, Liberal and Socialist parties into contact with academics, defence experts and philosophers, attracted the intelligentsia. In 1902 social reformers, Fabian leaders and historians of local government

Sidney and Beatrice Webb used the growing synergy between imperial development, defence and their concern with social reform and economic efficiency to create a suitable cross-party debating group, where the 'best men' would discuss the major issues of the age outside political allegiances. The 'Coefficients' dining club exchanged ideas over dinner, on a regular, if infrequent basis, stimulating rather than deciding.[88] Webb's ideal solution can be inferred from the presence of three directors of the London School of Economics (LSE) in the small group.

The initial members were the Webbs, H.G. Wells, Sir Edward Grey, Richard Burdon Haldane, economist William Hewins (1865–1931), philosopher Bertrand Russell, Conservative politician and journalist Leopold Amery (1873–1955), financier Sir Clinton Dawkins (1859–1905), former naval officer and Conservative MP Lieutenant Carlyon Bellairs (1871–1955), Germanophobe *National Review* editor Leopold Maxse (1864–1932), the New Zealand High Commissioner in London William Pember Reeves and geographer Sir Halford Mackinder. The experience impacted Mackinder's thinking: he switched from a Liberal Imperialist to a Conservative Tariff Reformer before delivering his striking paper 'The Geographical Pivot of History' in early 1904. Each member had been chosen for their expertise, although in the field of defence Bellairs was a relative lightweight.[89] The membership evolved; Bertrand Russell was the first to leave, while Dawkins died. Later, Lord Milner, George Bernard Shaw, Michael Sadler, Henry Newbolt and Corbett joined.

The Coefficients were never going to reach a verdict: the purpose was discussion, not resolution. Sidney Webb's position was typical; he disagreed with Amery and Maxse over imperial preference but saw the empire as the critical unit for discussion.[90] When free trade became a major political issue the Coefficients mirrored a divided country. When Hewins and Mackinder moved into the Tariff Reform camp, Webb adopted a free trade stance, to retain a degree of balance.[91] Corbett joined in late 1905 when the group discussed the results of their deliberations. While the invitation may have reflected Newbolt's advice, or the death of his friend Dawkins, it established Corbett among the Edwardian intelligentsia. He stressed the distinction between different forms of imperialism and considered the British model a force for progress. He attended the twenty-first meeting, in December 1905, as one of three guests, along with George Sydenham Clarke and George Bernard Shaw. Newbolt, who may have invited them, spoke on 'A Possible First Step to Revolution'. With the expansion of the group to twenty-five,

Corbett became a full member before the twenty-third meeting on 19 February 1906. Fellow new boys included Lord Robert Cecil, Liberal MP Charles Masterman, Lord Milner, *Times* defence correspondent Charles à Court Repington and Josiah Wedgwood.

Dinners were held at St Ermin's Hotel, Westminster. Most diners lived within walking distance, with Wells the obvious exception. The twenty-third meeting began with Wells expounding on 'The Higher Stage in Education', which may have been a rewarding evening for Corbett. Wells argued that there were three stages in education: training in the means of expression, elaboration of knowledge, which he associated with history and geography, and then the higher points of view, philosophy, politics and aesthetics. Wells deplored the lack of a 'wide theoretical outlook' in those holding responsible positions, while the inability to discuss major issues in a philosophical way 'militated against any really great efficiency in the nation at large'. The meeting concluded that 'the responsible classes in England were incapable of a broad intellectuality', but differed strongly as to the solution and the object of such discussions. The clarity and force of Corbett's exposition of theoretical education in the 'Green Pamphlet' only months later may owe something to this meeting.

Corbett spoke at the twenty-fourth meeting on 'The Economic Mean in National Defence', a powerful case for a two-power fleet and a small, efficient Army, in essence a thoroughly referenced update of the classic Liberal position. He warned that if Britain went too far in acquiring military strength the results would be counter-productive:

> while a two power standard of naval strength was accepted by the nations of world as a fair defensive standard for England, a three power standard, even if built with a defensive object, would be regarded as having an offensive one. Much more would a strong fleet and a great army be regarded as menace to Europe, since a fleet is not an offensive weapon in itself, but a strong fleet and a strong army is a most formidable aggressive force.

Germany, he inferred, was acquiring such a combination. The paper reflected his work on the War Course. It was discussed by Haldane, Milner, Amery, Newbolt, Hewins, Birchenough, Mackinder and Hugh Smith. In a debate conditioned by the assumption that 'owing to mechanical innovations, a modern war is of such brief duration that there is no time for the effectual training of an army', some considered using tariff reform to develop the population of the Dominions against future Russian or American challenges. To meet the more pressing problem of a European war they concluded Britain needed a body of men 'to some extent acquainted with elements of the military profession'.[92] Perhaps Haldane's Territorials.

Corbett attended Garvin's 'The Labour Party and its Future', the last paper recorded in printed minutes, on 18 June 1906. Garvin's declaration that Britain was 'not an Empire but a Sea League' doubtless struck a chord, the corollary that 'in England nationalism means imperialism because we have forfeited our agriculture' only emphasised another agenda shared by Fisher, Garvin and Corbett, and opposition to conscription. The cheerleader on that issue, former Army officer Charles Repington, was not present.

If minutes were taken at subsequent meetings they were not printed, possibly a reflection of deepening divisions. In November 1907 Corbett spoke on invasion; the possibility that Repington, the conscriptionist cheerleader, might attend was 'a stronger temptation to trail my coat'. He looked to Newbolt for support.[93] The Coefficients began to drift apart as their agendas polarised: the Webbs lost what little interest they had ever possessed in empire and defence, while Mackinder left the LSE to work for Milner and his version of the future. Corbett's reference to the group as 'old' suggests he realised it had outlived its usefulness. It was no accident that Sidney Webb was not present for Corbett's paper. Webb's presentation on the Poor Law was reasonably well attended, but imperially minded diners were concerned by the cost of social reform.[94] The Coefficients petered out in the summer of 1909.[95] Their discussions revealed a striking unity of purpose, despite fundamental rifts over policy, extending Corbett's networks and honing his debating skills in the era's most ambitious forum. In the company of so many able lawyers his logic met robust Socialist and Conservative counterblasts. He joined the Coefficients before writing the powerful naval essays of 1907, which demonstrated his mastery of controversy, and the strength of his opinions. Above all it helped him refine his concept of a future Britain as the centre of an increasingly autonomous commonwealth of states, bound together by a shared dependence on the oceans, an Imperial Navy, and a distinctive 'British way of war'.

CHAPTER 5

England in the Mediterranean

Corbett's histories began as an attempt to analyse the development of English naval power. *Drake and the Tudor Navy* had voyaged around the world, touched on all aspects of Elizabethan maritime enterprise, from tactics, naval architecture and flag signals to trade and exploration. *Successors* demonstrated that it was essential to locate naval activity in the context of national policy, that war involved all national forces, not a single service. As he moved into the seventeenth, let alone the eighteenth and nineteenth centuries, the subject would only become more complex, more universal, and more relevant. His response to this challenge would be shaped by new roles, as an opinion former, academic historian and Naval War Course lecturer. These audiences were unified by his focus on a core theme, the nature of national strategy across three centuries, the key to understanding the importance of maritime power for contemporary Britain. He would study the shaping and application of strategy, the interface of political decision-making and military capability, his leading characters would be admirals, generals and statesmen. By 1904 Corbett had become a public intellectual.

No sooner was he committed to the Navy than Corbett found himself discussing the higher direction of policy and strategy with a soldier. George Sydenham Clarke recognised British and imperial defence must be maritime, directed by statesmen, but advised by service experts. Between 1885 and 1907 he worked for increased defence coordination under civilian direction.[1] There are obvious links between the joint-service theme of the essay collection Clarke published with James Thursfield in 1897, Thomas Brassey's essay 'Great Britain as a Sea Power' of 1898, and the evolution of Corbett's thinking in *England in the Mediterranean: A Study of the Rise and Influence of British Power within the Straits, 1603–1713*.[2]

In 1900 Clarke was a disappointed man. The failure of yet another high-powered committee to impose order and purpose on the War Office led him to resign his commission and become a colonial governor. Before sailing for Melbourne that summer, he discussed defence issues with Corbett, a fellow NRS councillor, and suggested a subject for his next book. 'PS Turn over in your mind "The naval history of the Mediterranean"; it is a grand subject & worthy of your pen.'[3] While Clarke imagined a comprehensive narrative from Sphacteria to Navarino, he recognised Corbett's ability to develop 'a new idea to take the naval history of a sea & to fix its tremendous importance in the history of the world'.[4] His choice of sea had been prompted by journalist William Laird Clowes' claim that Britain's position within the straits was indefensible and should be abandoned. Clarke's counter-blast left Clowes' reputation in tatters.[5] He hoped Corbett would complete the rout, anticipating a comprehensive assessment of the political impact of naval power to inform future policy. This present-minded agenda collided with Laughton's logical suggestion that Corbett advance chronologically to the Commonwealth Navy and Robert Blake, building on Samuel Rawson Gardiner's work and the NRS's First Dutch War transcripts.[6]

These ideas would be linked by new opportunities. In August 1902 Corbett was invited to lecture on history to the Naval War Course, a new programme for senior officers at the Royal Naval College, Greenwich. The invitation reflected his status as a naval writer. Course director Captain Henry May suggested:

> Within reason I would prefer that you should choose your subject. It ought, however, to be so far modern that some lessons applicable to the present day warfare should be deducible from it.[7]

The lectures began later that year, running alongside the Ford lectures that Corbett was giving at Oxford, a course of at least six lectures, normally given in Michaelmas and Hilary terms. The lectures had been inaugurated by Samuel Gardiner in 1896–7, followed by academic heavyweights Frederic Maitland, Adolphus William Ward and Charles Firth. Firth, an NRS councillor in 1902, may have made the invitation in person.[8] The Ford lectures brought Corbett into the academic history community, alongside his roles in contemporary public debate and defence education. Corbett linked the two opportunities by focusing on seventeenth-century England in Clarke's Mediterranean. Some, although by no means all the chapters, would be delivered as lectures. Corbett also took also public engagements: on 23 May

1903 he discussed Drake's discovery of Cape Horn at the Royal Geographical Society, commemorating the tercentenary of Queen Elizabeth.[9]

Despite such distractions, Corbett had completed his manuscript by March 1903 before opening negotiations with Charles Longman. Dissatisfied with the proffered royalty, he penned a rare assessment of his commercial value and the state of the art. 'Since the publication of those books [*Drake* and *Successors*] my standing as naval writer has risen, – as I have been appointed as lecturer both at Greenwich & Oxford, & have been otherwise recognised as an authority by the Admiralty.' Furthermore 'the demand for naval history is for the reasons above mentioned greatly on the increase', and 'the book will have had, through my lectures, the best kind of advertisement at no cost to you before it comes out'. Hoping to broaden the audience, he suggested a cheaper format, 'within the purchasing powers of junior naval officers', would sell better. Originally he had added '& undergraduates', but expunged the thought.[10] Longman objected that he had yet to clear his costs on the two previous books, 'indeed, but for the considerations you mention, namely that the study of naval history is likely to increase and that your reputation is increasing I should not have been encouraged to take up the book at all'.[11] Unimpressed, Corbett blamed any losses on the failure to advertise well-reviewed books, suggesting Longman might return the manuscript. A contract with an improved royalty was signed on 1 May.[12]

England in the Mediterranean assumed the primary strategic threat facing the British Empire came from the Franco-Russian alliance. Despite Corbett's long-standing aversion to Imperial Germany, there is no hint of a German naval threat.[13] France and Russia remained the obvious enemy, and the book focused on the theatre where they were most likely to strike. The rise of French naval power in the region was a key theme; he linked the emergence of a corsair base at Bizerta in the seventeenth century to 'the latest French ideas'.[14] Modern Bizerta was a torpedo boat and cruiser station. Defending merchant shipping against seventeenth-century 'pirates' or modern warships required 'systematic cruising in the open sea'.[15]

While 'in some measure' a continuation of the Drake series, the focus of *England in the Mediterranean* was restricted, to avoid the 'repellent' method of bulky narrative, where readers quickly lost any 'sense of continuity, failing to seize any underlying principles and sink bewildered into a chaos of facts'. The inference that grand narratives, especially Laird Clowes' ponderous series, were poor resources for educating naval officers and statesmen owed something to Thursfield's review of *Drake and the Tudor Navy*.[16] Examining a century of naval activity in support of war and diplomacy, combating North African corsairing and curbing the hegemonic ambitions of Bourbon France, enabled Corbett to emphasise strategy and policy, lessons learnt and enduring relevance. *Mediterranean* focused on the diplomatic impact of naval activity, and the relative, even absolute unimportance of fleet battle. Placing naval activity in the widest context emphasised the impact of sea power, and brought it to the attention of other historians. Although the three Anglo-Dutch Wars (1652–74) dominated seventeenth-century naval history, Corbett focused on the Mediterranean because it was part of a larger, more consequential history that illustrated 'higher naval strategy'.[17] He linked Britain with 'the greatest empires of the past', precedents for the evolution of a seapower empire, and explained why the Mediterranean Fleet 'stands today in the eyes of Europe as the symbol and measure of British power'. Sea power as deterrent would be a core theme.[18] The preface located his work in history and public policy: Gardiner, Firth and Laughton were thanked, but George Clarke had inspired the book.[19] This forward-looking study examined the rise of a seapower empire in a form calculated to engage Edwardian decision-makers, senior naval officers or Oxford men entering public service.

Corbett opened with a striking literary flourish, and an emphatic state-ment of intent. He demanded attention by boldly linking the irruption of England into the Mediterranean with the rise of Russia as the two great events of seventeenth-century European history. If the opening contained florid passages redolent of *A Business in Great Waters*, later sections were couched in the spare, economical style of his mature work. The focus on high policy prompted the use of footnotes to address important if tangen-tial points, a discussion of tactics was relegated to an appendix.[20] For illus-trations he replaced the portrait- and ship-rich approach of the *Drake* texts with three images: a contemporary view of English Tangier by Wenceslaus Hollar; a contemporary map of Gibraltar; and, in the place of honour, the frontispiece, a costly new folding coloured map. Good maps were critical for students of strategy, not mere amusements for the curious.

To emphasise the shift from Elizabethan marauding to command of the sea Corbett noted Raleigh's final Orinoco voyage had been sacrificed to the needs of the Mediterranean, and the important role of great London merchant houses in securing a British presence in the inland sea.[21] The link between political context and official instructions shaped his assessment of operations. Following Laughton's suggestion, he stressed the Commonwealth had created a truly professional standing fleet of specialist warships for extended operations far from England. He also allowed Blake some of the credit, despite his preference for Monk. These soldier-admirals, men of discipline and subordination, replaced sailor-admirals still wedded to the 'false but profitable game of commerce destruction'.[22]

The first twelve chapters contrasted the diplomatic possibilities of sea power with the economic and political weaknesses that prevented it taking effect before 1650. Corbett hit his stride in 1650, when Robert Blake's Commonwealth battle squadron took control of the Straits of Gibraltar, tracing the evolution of the fleet as the 'symbol of English power', and the key to wrecking French designs. This fleet made England significant in Europe, crushed the last Royalist squadron, and browbeat Spain and Portugal into complying with English demands.

Having long since accepted Mahan's argument that commerce raiding was indecisive, Corbett contended there had been a 'revolution' in strategy under the Commonwealth. The Navy had not entered the Mediterranean merely to defend trade; English merchant ships had hitherto defended themselves.[23]

> For the first time the protection of the mercantile marine came to be regarded almost as the chief end for which the regular navy existed, and the whole of naval strategy underwent a profound modification in English thought. … We forget that so soon as the mercantile marine became a recognised burden on the navy, the main lines of commerce became also the main lines of naval strategy, and the crossing of the trade routes its focal points. Thus, although strategists, for the purposes of commending their views to the public and Treasury, naturally write in terms of commerce, we must never forget that what they were really aiming at was the command of the sea by the domination of the great trade routes and the acquisition of focal points as naval stations.[24]

Sea control was the chosen instrument for a state that sought strategic impact through the control of commerce. There could be no going back: the City of London's interests required protection whoever directed the state. His argument that the Navy served the City, and the City funded the fleet echoed John Colomb.[25]

Sea control not only defended British trade, but it also allowed Britain to cut that of an enemy, to break their economic power. This required British cruisers to prevent neutral ships carrying enemy goods.[26] This issue was as important in 1904 and it had been in 1651, only now it was shaped by international conventions as well as naval power.

While Corbett argued there was no need for battle while a superior British fleet held station, everything depended on securing a suitable local base.[27] Blake and Cromwell discussed taking Gibraltar, but events elsewhere restricted the English to stores depot at Tetuan, on the Moroccan coast.[28] Placing a fleet in the Mediterranean made Commonwealth England a major player in European politics. It overawed France, forced Spain to concede, and secured English shipping from corsair attacks. Cromwell deserved great credit for making England respected and feared: he would share the strategic plaudits with William III and Marlborough; three professional soldiers.

Corbett did not disguise the fact that France remained the enemy, and would still be frustrated by a powerful fleet holding the Straits of Gibraltar. In the second volume he noted that Louis XIV had responded to the English occupation of Tangier by building the Languedoc canal: 'securing interior lines by means of a ship canal anticipated the very latest expedients of naval strategy'.[29] Of the 'strategic' canals in existence in 1903, Suez and the aborted Panama canal were French projects, although the Kiel Canal would assume greater significance in the following years. English naval power, based at Tangier, secured impressive results and French efforts faltered. Corbett treated the troubled history of the fortress and cruiser station as the harbinger of a greater future. He argued that Louis XIV worked with the English opposition to ensure Tangier was abandoned. By 1681 Louis' canal was ready, while Toulon had been doubled in size and fortified. When Parliament obliged Charles II to abandon Tangier in 1684, it handed control of the Mediterranean to France. Corbett saw the following decade as the zenith of a Bourbon drive for universal monarchy. When the English fleet returned, the project collapsed.[30] Although England secured control of the Channel at Barfleur–La Hougue in 1692, the 1693 Smyrna Convoy disaster brought the commercial needs of the City of London to the centre of William III's grand strategy. Recognising Louis XIV needed to control the Mediterranean to defeat Spain and Savoy before concentrating his resources against England, Holland and the Holy Roman Empire, William dispatched the main fleet to the Mediterranean in 1694. The French fleet scuttled back into Toulon, Barcelona was saved and Mediterranean neutrals, from the Pope to the Barbary corsairs, changed their tune. When French sailors were sent overland from Toulon to crew the ships at Brest so many deserted that the navy effectively collapsed.

With peace restored, statesmen prepared for the long-anticipated death of the last Habsburg king of Spain. To secure the vital role of English sea power in the Mediterranean, William III demanded the island of Minorca, with the great naval harbour at Port Mahon, as its share of any settlement. Rather than hand this strategic prize to England, Louis XIV, Corbett argued, preferred Spain should be given to a Bavarian prince. The ability of sea power to thwart continental military hegemony was obvious, and relevant:

> From the point of view of the higher naval strategy no war has more illu-
> minating instruction for our own time than that of the Spanish Succession.
> In many respects the conditions and objects of naval power closely
> resemble those which exist today. It was a war to prevent the dangerous
> preponderance of an ambitious and powerful military state; it was also a
> war for the freedom of commerce: and the one element against which no
> continental power had an equal card to play was the British navy.[31]

William III understood English sea power would only be truly effective against France with a secure base inside the straits, therefore it was essential to focus on securing this primary objective. Having laid out the main lines of strategy as a Spanish war loomed, the king died, entrusting the war to Marlborough, who shared his insight, and exceeded his military talents. William, like Essex, saw Cadiz, or perhaps Gibraltar, as the key strategic position, far more important than oceanic or Caribbean projects. Corbett contrasted the insight and acumen of leading soldiers with Admiral Sir George Rooke's inability to see the big picture. When Marlborough took control of the war in 1702, he recognised Cadiz as the ideal base for a combined arms assault on Toulon, the operation he believed would settle the conflict. Such concepts were wholly alien to Rooke, who botched the attack on Cadiz. His destruction of a French squadron at Vigo was useful, but hardly compensated for the failure to secure Cadiz or Gibraltar. In chapter XXX, 'Marlborough and the Navy', Corbett focused on the higher direction of war, using Queen Anne's 'Secret Committee' as a proxy for George Clarke's 'Committee of Imperial Defence', which met for the first time on 18 December

1902.[32] He stressed that the Home and Mediterranean fleets were flexible elements of a single fleet, to be combined or divided to meet the movements of the French, making his book 'interesting and instructive' for 'the modern student'.[33] Such combinations featured in the 1903 manoeuvres, which he had attended, while it was unnecessary to remind a contemporary audience that his 'modern students' attended the Naval War Course. Despite Rooke's failure, the presence of an English fleet paralysed French strategy in the Mediterranean, and secured the Portuguese alliance, along with the critical base at Lisbon. Portugal enabled the allies to open a land front against Bourbon Spain, the fleet linking campaigns, and wrecking French logistics.

In 1704 Marlborough exploited the strategic mobility of sea power to plan his master stroke, linking the march to Blenheim with a naval deployment that would paralyse France all along the Mediterranean littoral. As he developed this theme, Corbett began writing about strategy in passages effectively divorced from any historical context, sketching 'principles' that would acquire more substance in 1911:

> To the sailor the aim of naval strategy must always seem to be the command of the sea. To the soldiers and the statesman it is only the means to an end. For them the end must always be the furtherance or the hindrance of military operations ashore, or the protection or destruction of sea-borne commerce; for by these means alone can governments and populations be crushed into submission.

He thought military methods were the best option, when resources permitted, being 'preferable to the more lengthy blockade'. Therefore 'bigoted adherence' to the primacy of command of the sea 'may become pedantry and ruin the higher strategy of the campaign'.[34] This was Rooke's error, one he shared with the contemporary 'blue-water' school, who would not have found this skilfully administered lesson particularly agreeable. The ability to develop historical examples to enduring principles reflected Corbett's emergence as a strategist. It is also offered an insight into the ideas of his naval colleagues. The enemy was France, with or without Russia: the French fleets had to be kept apart by a force based at Gibraltar, where large dry docks were in progress to maintain armoured cruiser squadrons. A short war would only be possible with continental military allies, otherwise Britain must rely on the blockade.

Corbett used Marlborough and his naval brother George Churchill to represent a strategic system, rather than assess the more fluid reality of their actual views. He had them impose a coherent, strikingly modern strategy on the English/British war effort, an approach ideally suited to his new naval audience. That contemporary academics did not challenge this sleight of hand demonstrates how skilfully Corbett delivered strategic thought through historical examples. That lessons took precedence over evidence became obvious when later generations retraced his work in the archives. Those who dispute his judgements, and the validity of his overall argument, ignore the context. Corbett did not write for Edwardian historians, let alone their modern successors. His academic contemporaries understood what he was doing and considered him as a major contributor to the discipline. Charles Firth, Regius Professor at Oxford, referred to his 'standard books'. It should be no surprise that John Hattendorf, another historian with a naval audience, provided the best critique of Corbett's Marlborough-centric account of the War of the Spanish Succession.[35]

In 1704 Rooke had secret orders to link up with the Duke of Savoy and destroy Toulon, but if the French fleet escaped it must be pursued and destroyed. The admiral preferred the latter task. While waiting in the straits for news of the French fleet, Rooke captured Gibraltar, an operation of no great difficulty. Corbett developed his wider theme by noting that Rooke's fleet had watered and prepared for the attack in Tangier Bay, a profoundly symbolic location.[36] Rooke secured his prize by defeating the French fleet in battle at Velez Malaga, and leaving enough ships on station over the winter to break the Franco-Spanish siege by driving off a French squadron sent to assist the assault. After that, Louis XIV abandoned his battlefleet, although Marlborough's grand design to seize Toulon would remain incomplete. As Gibraltar could not service the fleet, Admiral Leake and General Stanhope, an impressive soldier-statesman, seized Minorca in 1708. The long-coveted deep-water facilities of Port Mahon enabled British fleets to over-winter in the Mediterranean. Corbett argued that Leake provided 'a lasting example of sagacious naval judgement for all time', and he lambasted other historians for failing to mention the naval role in the capture of the island base.[37] Such failings mattered because they could mislead his naval students. The taking of Minorca prompted the Pope to change sides. Retaining Port Mahon and Gibraltar were Britain's primary demands at the peace. Despite France's best efforts, and the bitter recriminations of the Dutch, they were secured by the Treaty of Utrecht of 1713, making Britain a major European power. This was:

> the greatest achievement that British naval strategy can show ... it proved that with a dominant sea power well placed within the Straits her [France's] Mediterranean frontier was useless to her for offence, and that neither for her nor for any other power could the dream of the Roman Empire be revived.

The defeat of Louis XIV's universal monarchy was 'the greatest political fact of the seventeenth century'.

Command of the Mediterranean enabled Britain to support a European 'balance of power', essential for a small, weak seapower state, a modern Carthage, facing the continental hegemonic ambitions of Bourbon France. Despite the importance accorded to world empires, and the apparent stability of the European state system in 1903, British power in the Mediterranean remained a critical balance for global politics, one best understood through historical study, shaped by strategic principles.[38] Corbett had delivered a compelling strategic argument through a historical case study. War Course students took copious notes, one noting: 'Opens with idea that from Eliz to Wm III strategy set by soldiers because sailors so tied up in tactics and ship handling – eg oppose over-wintering in the Med. Want to lay up ships over winter etc.'[39] Henry May would have been delighted, little wonder he extended and enlarged Corbett's appointment.

The *Mediterranean* found reviewers predisposed to sea power themes; most were familiar with Corbett's work. The *Athenaeum* praised the novelty of his treatment of Tangier, along with his 'strategical' and political approach. It highlighted the power of the fleet.[40] The *Speaker* thought this 'unique study' would teach the English that they acquired a commanding position in Europe through the power of the fleet.[41] After the weeklies and month-lies, Laughton had the last word in the *Edinburgh Review*. After some characteristic criticism of details, including Corbett's overestimation of George Monk, he dutifully followed the narrative, picked out the key arguments, and linked them to George Clarke's robust demolition of Laird Clowes, 'scuttle' thesis. It was, he concluded 'a work which goes far to remove from our literature the reproach of having no naval history ... thanks to him [Corbett], the bearing of our naval power on our national history can be traced from the accession of Elizabeth to the death of Anne.'[42]

Contemporaries rated *Mediterranean* highly because it spoke directly to their strategic dilemmas. In early 1904 George Clarke returned to England to join Jacky Fisher on Lord Esher's Committee to reorganise the Army. By May he had taken office as the first Secretary of the CID, the inter-departmental civil-military strategic coordinating body. While most expected the new organisation would be merely advisory, Clarke wanted a joint service defence staff to impose his own, maritime, concept of British strategy. Corbett's *Monthly Review* article 'Queen Anne's Defence Committee' argued that a highly successful war had been directed by a flexible board not unlike Clarke's CID. That the old committee included a man named George Clarke did not harm his argument, while stressing it had focused 'primarily on the handling of sea power' echoed the aims of the new committee. Corbett concluded with a question: 'Can we do better than begin where the men of Queen Anne left off?'[43] Fourteen years later a short memo developed from this paper would earn him a knighthood.

England in the Mediterranean would be overtaken by events. As 1904 drew to a close, the Anglo-French Entente and the Russo-Japanese War shifted the strategic focus towards the rising naval power of Imperial Germany, Admiral Sir John Fisher began his transformational term as First Sea Lord in October. Nothing would ever be the same again, least of all England's position in the Mediterranean. Yet the book had a critical role in the evolution of historical and strategic writing, exerting a profound influence over those who followed. Reprinted in a cheaper format in 1907, a third edition would be required by 1917.[44]

Corbett's text emphasised the context of naval history, incorporating diplomatic, political and military history, while strategic theory provided the analytical core. Among those to feel the effect of this new scholarship, Lieutenant, later Admiral Sir Herbert Richmond, naval officer and historian, took as his subject Britain's next major war in the Mediterranean.[45] In the 1930s Richmond advised George Macaulay Trevelyan, working on the reign of Queen Anne, to consult Corbett's book for strategic analysis. The Regius Professor at Cambridge followed the judgements of 'England's great naval historian' without demur.[46] At the same time Richmond coached the polemicist Basil Liddell Hart as he developed a 'British Way in Warfare' of 1931, using Corbett's work.[47] John Ehrman examined William III's Mediterranean strategy a generation later, acknowledging his 'indebtedness' to Corbett, who had covered so much of the ground.[48] Ehrman disputed some of Corbett's conclusions, and exploited additional evidence, but the older text endured.[49]

Mediterranean emphasises the historiographical reality that the past is a foreign country. It reflects the assumptions of an Edwardian intellectual, from the durability of British imperial power to the centrality of Europe in world affairs, assumptions that have long since faded. Yet those assumptions and the audiences that shared them are critical to understanding a book that retains much of its original power for those who examine the sixteenth and seventeenth centuries, or the emerging twenty-first.[50]

Although Corbett chose to leave the main theatre of the Dutch wars out of *England in the Mediterranean*, this was not a question of lack of interest. His early War Course lectures had included the subject, while his mastery of the material was evident in the strategic overview of the Third Anglo-Dutch War that he produced to accompany the NRS's publication of contemporary tapestry cartoons belonging to the Earl of Dartmouth.[51] In the late spring of 1907 he assessed the art of the Willem Van de Veldes, father and son.[52] Although he consulted leading art historians in Britain and Holland, his assessment of the artists has long since been overtaken.[53] The remaining 35 pages are a master class in the concise exposition of intricate political and strategic issues, and the analysis of complex battles involving up to 200 warships. The paper also examined the role of William III, once again highlighting the Dutch stadholder's grasp of grand strategy, of which he was 'a master as King of England'.[54] Although the Dutch suffered a tactical defeat at Sole Bay they kept command of the sea in dispute, heartening their despondent countrymen. Elsewhere Corbett demonstrated how the English used an army to pin the Dutch on the defensive, and praised the tactical skill Michiel de Ruyter used to deny the more powerful Anglo-French fleet an occasion to land those troops. The Dutch, he concluded, fought for national independence, a higher cause than the English, where the unpopular French alliance made the country anxious for peace. Charles II gave way because, Corbett concluded, 'The truth is the heart of the country was not in the war, and the Dutch were fighting in exalted religious fervour for all they held most dear.'[55] There remained something of the Victorian novelist in Corbett to the very end.

CHAPTER 6

The Naval War Course

Corbett's career reached a critical point in 1902 when he began lecturing to the Royal Navy War Course. This provided him with an audience to address, in books as well as lectures, constant connection with the Navy's strategic leadership, and access to the best and brightest minds in the service. For the next twelve years he gave ten to twelve lectures to each Naval War Course, usually two a year, repeating lectures at other locations for officers unable to attend the full course. This was his only significant teaching experience: he never held a university post. Every book he wrote after 1902 was shaped by that audience – naval officers with time to think about strategy, policy and operations. His evolving strategic thinking explained the nature and purpose of national/imperial strategy, emphasising the wider political, economic and military contexts in which the Navy would operate in wartime. His work addressed critical challenges to the primacy of naval power in British strategy, including the continental ambitions of the British Army and the naval dreams of the German Kaiser. Both his teaching and his strategic thought responded to a constantly changing War Course syllabus, and the wishes of successive directors of Naval Intelligence (DNIs).

The War Course was a response to the same challenges that prompted the foundation of the NRS and involved many of the same individuals. In June 1900 DNI Captain Reginald Custance advised the Admiralty Board to establish a Naval Strategy course at the Royal Naval College, Greenwich (RNC).[1] This intervention followed an embarrassing question in the House of Commons, which elicited the inaccurate response that naval officers were not taught strategy.[2] Custance may have discussed these issues with Fisher, who also claimed responsibility for the course, when they were at the Admiralty in the mid-1890s. The two men fell out spectacularly in 1901 when Fisher secured reinforcements for his Mediterranean Fleet, overturning Custance's strategic assessment.[3] His role in creating a War

Course was limited. Custance, who was not given to bragging, had a better claim.[4]

In 1902 one of Custance's deputies, Captain Prince Louis of Battenberg, advised Fisher, now Second Sea Lord and responsible for education, that the NID should become a War Staff, linked to the new War Course. Prince Louis believed Custance had replicated the Great German General Staff by adding a third division for 'Defence', or war planning, to the existing NID functions of 'Mobilisation' and 'Foreign Intelligence'.[5] The War Course would be directed by the NID, and integral to Admiralty war planning.

College Captain Henry May's initial course integrated the history lectures he had been delivering since 1898 with the concept of 'the American Naval War College but altered to suit the different conditions under which the work was to be carried out'.[6] In September the Admiralty outlined the elements of the course:

1. Prepare a plan of operations under existing conditions.
2. Attack and defence of fortified places.
3. Lines of communication, coal supplies in operations.
4. British and foreign trade routes.
5. Tactical questions.
6. Naval history 'one or more naval campaigns being selected for special study'.
7. International law.

Students would also study steam, navigation, naval architecture and languages.

Nor was this merely a training exercise: 'the work of the class in the subjects under 1, 2, 3 & 5 of the War Course are to be forwarded for the information of their Lordships at the end of the session'. Analysis by the War Course would obviate the need for a large Admiralty staff. Consequently foreign officers would not be admitted. Two days later fundamental changes were promulgated affecting the work and working conditions for captains attending the course. First 'naval strategy and other technical subjects connected therewith will be compulsory', reflecting foreign experience with strategy courses which had 'hitherto not formed part of the usual curriculum'. When the Treasury agreed to allow students full pay, at a cost of £2,400 per annum for twenty-five captains and commanders, the Admiralty could order officers to attend.[7]

Henry May delivered the initial eight-month course while continuing as College Captain.[8] The original plan proved to be overloaded, allowing little or no time for the essential element of 'self-education', while conflating training and technical elements with intellectual study. To address this classic professional military education failing, 'practical' elements, including navigation and naval architecture, were dropped. The new programme required a public launch, which *The Times* provided in early 1902. The author, probably James Thursfield, personally close to both Custance and Battenberg, used inside information. He linked the course to Mahan and the United States Naval War College, Newport, regretting the failure of Greenwich to meet the aims set in 1873, which he attributed to the dominance of mathematics. The new course would promote fresh thinking. The choice of a course rather than a college was deliberate.

> Our own experience of colleges has been so pitiful that we prefer development along the lines of a naval war course, in which the students are the equals of the lecturer, as together they explore, with the aid of Intelligence Department reports and other publications, the lessons of history, commerce, and strategy.

The Times referenced the German origins of modern military education, citing Moltke's definition of strategy as 'the art of applying the available means to the desired end'. As Britain currently lagged behind all the 'great maritime nations' in theoretical study the Admiralty deserved some credit for making a start. The ongoing Boer War had highlighted the consequences of ignorance.[9] Thus, the course would need more lecturers. May had recruited civilians and fellow officers to widen the programme. Captain Reginald Tupper, lately of the NID, lectured on the Spanish–American War of 1898 and directed war games on the first two courses.[10] Lectures on naval and military cooperation were provided by Lieutenant Colonel E.S. May RA, Professor of Military Art and History at Camberley, who was advised by his namesake that he could hardly pitch his lectures too low as naval officers knew virtually nothing about strategy.[11] Many scholars have failed to see that this was a joke. In September 1902 Henry May approached Corbett. The naval history offering on the first course had been rather 'antiquarian'; May needed a strategic focus. He offered £5 per one-hour lecture, of which there would be between four and eight. As May knew little more of Corbett than that he had 'made a study of naval history,'[12] it seems he had been advised by Custance, who knew Corbett through the NRS, the NID's unofficial Historical Section. In 1902 the two men were working together on an edition of eighteenth-century tactical instructions for naval use.[13] NRS publications, which reflected NID input, were key resources for the War Course, with Corbett shaping his lectures to address contemporary needs. The link between the NRS and the War Course was reinforced when Henry May joined the NRS Council in 1903.

Corbett accepted without hesitation, and May began to refine his concept.

> With regard to the subject we had last year a series of lectures on tactics from Mr Hannay[14] bringing in the galley period & they may probably be repeated with some modifications this autumn – so that I should prefer that you should take up a subject in which strategy came in more. As Mahan has so well shewn politics will greatly affect any future struggle for sea power & it is distinctly necessary to remind naval officers that expediency and strategy are not always in accordance. An Admiral may have the force on the spot but may be restrained by political considerations from striking at the right time and place. Generally speaking the faults, failures & decadence of nations & their commanders are insufficiently considered, so that the difficulties likely to beset one in the present day are minimised.[15]

Corbett summarised this brief as 'the deflection of strategy by politics', a theme that would shape the rest of his career.[16] The other function of his work, as his 1903 lecture notes stressed, was 'to direct & assist private study', with a focus on strategy.[17] He hit that target; Captain Reginald Bacon reported the second War Course was:

> chiefly useful in causing senior officers to 'think', and to bring them face to face with an appreciation of the vastness of the problems that war would create .... sudden inspiration could not be relied on to solve war problems, and he was made to realise the need for constant study and thought if he was to acquit himself with credit in the Great Ordeal. The appreciation of these facts was of even greater value to the individual than the actual instruction provided by the course.[18]

Having attended Corbett's first lectures in October 1902, May declared he had 'in a sense joined the Greenwich Staff', and should pay his respects to Fisher, the Second Sea Lord, whose brief included Greenwich.[19] Already closely linked to the thinking Navy, joining the War Course staff was a small step.[20]

The War Course was launched just as Esher, Fisher and Clarke tried to impose a coherent 'Imperial' strategy with the necessary central planning organisation on the British Empire, a maritime strategy that avoided the risk of competing service-based models.[21] Clarke had been supplying Corbett with evidence for his *Monthly Review* essays, exerting considerable influence on his thinking between 1900 and 1904.[22] In 1900 Corbett had thanked Clarke for the argument that 'the real importance of maritime power is its influence on military operations'.[23] In 1902 Clarke's stress on grand strategy rather than naval operations led to *England in the Mediterranean*, along with Corbett's initial War Course and Ford lectures, with credit going to Clarke for the central theme of how a relatively small naval presence had influenced a major theatre across a substantial period of time. Corbett's book chimed with current strategic concerns, reflected in Mediterranean-focused war games.

In June 1903 May reported that twenty-nine officers had attended the second War Course (October 1902–June 1903) and thirty-two had taken the first course. Yet only ten completed the programme, although several more gained some benefit. The rapidly expanding Edwardian Navy needed more officers afloat; many were frequently withdrawn for career-enhancing commands. May praised the history lectures by Corbett and captains Anson and Tupper, hoping more officers would volunteer. Recognising the urgent need to examine the issue of maritime commerce in war, he hoped the Camperdown Committee, on which new DNI Battenberg was serving, would provide suitable speakers. Tupper, the committee secretary, would devote much of his career to trade defence.[24]

The Admiral Superintendent praised May's 'care and skill', urging the Admiralty to ensure all officers attended, and suggested external lectures should be more accessible. Prince Louis minuted that attendance would be 'practically obligatory', First Sea Lord Admiral Lord Walter Kerr agreeing to divide the course into two shorter blocs. Replacing the long course with two four-month courses would require Treasury approval for a dozen additional lectures, raising the cost of speakers from £400 to £550.[25] Support from Kerr, Battenberg and the First Lord, Lord Selborne, reflected high-level commitment to education, and secured Treasury sanction.[26] The War Course had become a fixture. Training tasks were dropped. The course director was required to classify officers within each rank for the First Lord's Private Office to help determine promotion and appointments. On 21 August the Admiralty publicised the revised course in the usual newspapers and asked for volunteers.[27]

In early 1904 May devised a three-week course on strategy and fleet tactics for admirals, 'mainly intended to initiate these officers into the methods of studying strategy and tactics in use at Greenwich'. They also had the benefit of three lectures on international law: Corbett's lectures on the American Revolution posed the question: 'Can we draw any useful lessons from the failures?' Corbett worked with May to define the concept of 'Command of the Sea'. While May joked that admirals' lectures were only laid on 'because naval officers needed keeping awake', he secured Treasury consent to put those attending on full pay.[28]

Henry May died suddenly in May 1904, leaving a settled programme for his successor, course graduate Captain Edmond Slade.[29] Unusually well-read, with a serious interest in the Franco-Prussian War and German military thought, Slade proved an ideal foil for Corbett's project to capture the strategic logic of a distinctive 'British way'. He took May's seat at the NRS Council *ex officio*.[30] Six months later Fisher's radical reform programme hastened the pace of change. Fisher provided Slade with two naval assistants and additional funding for external speakers.[31] Slade tried to increase the audience for key lectures, including Corbett's, by advertising in *The Times* and the service clubs.[32]

Predictably, Fisher had another agenda: he wanted the War Course to help develop policy, war plans and strategy through the intelligent analysis of pressing issues, many reflecting the shift of strategic focus from France to Germany. Corbett had been drawn into Fisher's orbit by his *Monthly Review* articles on educational reform, and was briefed on the wider reform agenda at Portsmouth in July 1903.[33] He joined Fisher's unofficial strategy group just as the War Course took a turn towards 'staff and planning' functions. Not only was the DNI overloaded with routine business but Fisher wanted an alternate source of strategy, plans and concepts. The additional lectures Fisher and DNI Captain Charles Ottley requested were historical case studies delivering strategic analysis. Slade lectured on strategic theory. The additional lectures increased Corbett's role in the War Course at a critical point in his intellectual development. His mastery of British experience provided the evidence to illuminate strategic 'lessons', while his recent introduction to the strategic thought of Carl von Clausewitz provided theoretical concepts that could transform history into a coherent system.

The synergy between the War Course and Admiralty planning became obvious in May 1905, when Fisher asked Corbett to comment on draft war plans. The response was 'a long and strong letter ... concerning the condition of strategical study in the Navy as revealed by the amateurish rubbish that appeared in official Admiralty papers. It ended in my being instructed to try to teach sea strategy at the War College.' Fisher applauded Corbett's honesty.[34] The initiative was supported by DNI Ottley, another advocate of combined maritime strategy.

Corbett's 1905–6 lecture course, delivered at Greenwich and the Army Staff College, Camberley, was developed into the book *England in the Seven Years' War: A Study in Combined Strategy*, 'history on the large scale with military principles guiding the selection'.[35] This overtly Clausewitzian study of the 'British way' at its zenith carefully integrated the political, diplomatic, naval and military elements that shaped contemporary strategy in a 'luminous' book that delighted Fisher. This was a teaching text for senior officers, Corbett occasionally forcing 'events into a posthumously conceived historical pattern'.[36] He did this with such skill that few historians have noticed.[37] He was, after all, a lawyer by training, an advocate of considerable literary power. Within a year the students were using his ideas in exercises.[38]

In 1905 the War Course left Greenwich, and by January 1906 Corbett was lecturing at Devonport:

> We are much better installed than at Greenwich – 'with every modern convenience'. Round me is raging a most interesting war game to test what we could do in case of having to take up arms with France – but this in confidence. We are fast becoming something like a general staff.[39]

This was no accident. While Fisher opposed the creation of a formal naval staff, which might restrict his freedom of action, or expose his ideas to critics, he needed a quasi-official body to address the strategic problems created by the shift of focus to face Germany in the North Sea, the Army General Staff's rejection of maritime strategy, and the insubordinate nonsense of Admiral Sir Charles Beresford. In May 1906 Fisher asked Corbett if he would be interested in a 'scheme for the extension of the Naval

War College at Portsmouth'.[40] He was fishing for press coverage. Corbett obliged, hoping it would become the basis of an effective war planning system: 'I am entirely at your service if there is anything I can do to support or further your scheme.' In 1912 Fisher endorsed this letter: 'Julian Corbett the best naval writer there is. This is written in 1906 and yet there are some people writing in 1912 that Sir John Fisher did not care a d . . . n about a war college or educating naval officers in strategy!'[41] This should dispose of the old canard that Corbett was insignificant and unappreciated.

Slade provided notes on the origin and function of the War Course, stressing the growth of the student body. It had been settled that the course would be taught at Portsmouth, with short lecture programmes at other ports. Links with Camberley included joint combined operations staff exercises every spring: 'There are thus 40 or 50 officers of each service thrown together with a definite war problem before them to consider and discuss. The result is a very considerable modification of previously conceived ideas, and a much broader view of the whole subject on the part of everybody concerned.' When they discussed the course, Slade stressed:

> we are not copying the German Admiral Staff or General Staff – but . . . the development is going on[,] on lines which are quite constitutional, so to speak, and quite in accordance with our traditions. That is to say we are not trying to evolve a brand new department which is going to revolutionise the whole Navy & teach everybody their work, but that we are merely providing a means of assisting the officer in our Admiralty scheme who holds the analogous position to that of the Chief of the Staff in a military sense, namely the First Sea Lord, by establishing a board of officers whose business it is to consider and thrash out systematically all sorts of war problems, quite independently and unhampered by the routine work of an Admiralty department such as the N.I.D.

The War College would support and enhance existing institutions. Under the direction of the DNI it could conduct war games and exercises based on the latest intelligence, a task quite distinct from the educational role. 'It is important I think to emphasise the fact that the work of the two departments, the NID & the War College, can and should proceed on absolutely parallel lines each helping & feeding the other.'[42] This link was emphasised by the career of NID star Captain George Ballard, top student and 'VG indeed' on the sixth War Course (March–June 1906). Ballard heard Corbett's lectures on the Seven Years' War, exposure reflected in his thinking.

Slade's notes informed two articles Corbett wrote for *The Times*, arguing that the course addressed the Navy's 'most serious problem': how to study war at a time of rapid technological change. Developed by officers, not civilians, it examined strategy 'as a reasoned system, as a scientific study', providing the language and concepts for discussions with statesmen and framing orders. That it took so long to start, and had been conducted in a less than systematic manner, reflected the national character. The first two courses, attended by fifty-eight captains and commanders, had a positive impact on the 1903 annual manoeuvres, while the short course increased the number attending, and included flag officers. In 1904–5 more than 150 officers completed the course, including 20 admirals.

A second major reorganisation followed the introduction of the nucleus crew system: the flag officers' course was rolled into the main programme when the War Course moved to Portsmouth. This reflected the increased size and complexity of war games, especially the strategic exercise – which could only be housed at Portsmouth or Devonport. Corbett also stressed combined staff exercises with Camberley, to establish unity of action between the services. The course would broaden naval officers' horizons, ensuring they recognised 'the political and military' context in which they operated: 'Naval history is studied almost entirely from this point of view – the deflection of naval strategy by politics, and its domination by the military necessities of the case.' It only remained to engage the Foreign Office to complete the process.[43]

Four days later Corbett turned to the future. The War Course only prepared officers for high command: other staff functions, war plans and intelligence, were handled by the NID. 'From the first it was recognised that a General Staff of the Continental pattern was not to be thought of for the Navy.' Overwhelmed by day-to-day business, the NID delegated the writing of draft war plans to the course: 'there is today no machinery at the Admiralty or elsewhere for the preparation of plans of campaign ... it has to be done by the First Sea Lord himself'. The War Course filled that capability gap without becoming a War Staff, merely a sub-department of the NID. Adding a few more staff would release the course director to superintend a dedicated planning team for the First Sea Lord, in concert with the DNI. The War Course would test new ideas and concepts through syndicate work and war games. This organic growth would give the Navy 'the advantages of a General Staff, with none of the objections which have so long held us back', enabling the First Sea Lord to present 'properly prepared' plans to the CID.[44]

Delighted by such fine support for his preferred alternative to a 'General Staff', Fisher confirmed that the War Course and the NID were the twin pillars of his war planning.[45] The *Manchester Guardian* considered Corbett a 'good authority': 'We have more faith in the "war course" than in a few extra big guns or a larger "size" in battleships.' The Devonport-based *Western Mercury* reprised his argument, with a substantial quote.[46] In November the course moved to Portsmouth, staff nominally appointed to HMS *Terpsichore*, an old cruiser used for experimental duties.[47] On 1 July 1907 it became the Royal Naval War College.[48]

Coincident with the move, Corbett and Slade produced 'Strategic Terms and Definitions used in Lectures on Naval History', the first course text. Conceived as a *résumé* of strategic ideas and concepts, common terms and concepts to simplify teaching, the 'Green Pamphlet' became far more than a list. Corbett subtly infused it with his ideas, stressing the critical importance of lines of communication and the relative unimportance of battle. The enemy should be forced to give battle by threats to vital communications. This was an early draft of national doctrine. The strategic focus having shifted to Germany, the college was studying German Baltic trade routes, the obvious target. In 1908 three captains, all course graduates, were employed on the task.[49] Hugh Watson observed:

> my study of the German Navy has been a close one, extending over three years, first at the War College; then visiting German, Dutch, Danish, and Swedish naval centres; at the Intelligence Department of the Admiralty; and subsequently as naval Attaché in Berlin.[50]

The Baltic focus of Fisher's planning explains why Corbett emphasised the relevance of blockade: dominating the enclosed sea would hit Germany hard.

Fisher also persuaded Corbett to write the introduction to the 1907 Ballard Committee War Plans, an attempt to think through the nature of a major war in the light of the latest experience, not least the Russo-Japanese War. The Admiralty had detailed two officers to compile an operational history, while Corbett's lectures occupied a prominent place in the curriculum.[51] Fisher asked Corbett to discuss general strategic principles, which would 'add most materially' to the 'educational value' of the plans.[52] A few days later Fisher declared his 'epitome of the Art of Naval War' would be 'the Bible of the War Course'.[53] Corbett completed the introduction, 'Some Principles of Naval Warfare', in April 1907, a critical stage in the evolution of the ultimate 'Bible of the War Course'.

Corbett wrote this strategic primer in 1907, alongside three essays defending aspects of Fisher's policy: Fisher considered the first, 'Recent Attacks on the Admiralty', his greatest contribution.[54] Corbett also challenged the anti-Fisher 'Syndicate of Discontent', defending the dreadnought concept in the main military forum, the RUSI.[55] It was a bold move, developing an argument that could defeat the obscurantists without unduly offending thin-skinned admirals.[56] Three months later 'The Capture of Private Property at Sea' set out the Admiralty case for the Second Hague Peace Conference in the influential *The Nineteenth Century and After*.[57]

The War College offered students intellectual and practical approaches to professional military education. Lectures and essays flowed into tactical and strategic exercises, exploiting lessons learnt. Attendance was restricted to admirals, captains and promising commanders. Essay questions reflected current concerns, the DNI circulating student responses throughout the service. Fisher's engagement was obvious in March and June 1907: 'What are the treaties dealing with the Baltic and the entrances thereto? What is the present political situation in that sea and how might it affect us?'[58] In October 1906 and January 1907, the emphasis shifted: 'If Germany attempts to close the Baltic in war with Great Britain how would it affect neutrals? What is the probable line of action? What were the rights of Denmark, and when and how were they given up?' In spring 1908: 'Discuss the best method of making use of the *Invincible* type of heavy cruisers in the case of a war with Germany. Which fleet should they be attached to, or should they act independently, and, if the latter, where?', along with 'How could we best support Denmark/Belgium should her neutrality be threatened by Germany?' These open questions offered ample scope for legal, geographical and strategic arguments, while the last question anticipated the development of Fisher's grand strategy in 1914–15. Similarly, in autumn 1908 and spring 1909: 'Give a short account of the construction of the Kaiser Wilhelm Canal and its proposed alterations. How will this affect German strategy?' Geo-strategic analyst Halford Mackinder had lectured these students on the topography of the German and Danish coasts.[59]

The 'Green Pamphlet' of November 1906 was one of many college hand-outs reproduced from typescript by the Gestetner Cyclostyle process: revised 'Green Pamphlets' appeared in January 1909 and 1911.[60] The college had a standing order for NRS volumes and other relevant publications. When Corbett launched the Cambridge University Press 'Naval and Military Series' to address the intellectual needs of the service colleges in 1913, taking on the 'herculean' task of general editor, he received a suitably encouraging letter from the First Lord's Naval Secretary – War College alumnus David Beatty.[61] Among the authors commissioned was Captain Herbert Richmond, whose April–May 1911 War Course lectures formed the basis of *The Navy in the War of 1739–48*.[62]

The War Course/College dominated Corbett's intellectual life after 1902. He tailored his lectures to meet the demands of professional military education, frequently setting his own work aside to address hot topics like invasion and international law, which informed War College lectures, articles and NID submissions to CID enquiries. Corbett usually repeated his lectures at Devonport, Chatham or Sheerness, ensuring a large body of officers, of both services, had access.[63] His work was highly regarded: he received a gentlemanly rate of 10 guineas (£10.50) per lecture, military historian John Fortescue only received £5, while prominent lawyers settled for £10. Corbett's fees accounted for 40 per cent of the external lecturer budget.[64]

When Slade succeeded Charles Ottley as DNI in August 1907, Ottley having replaced George Clarke at the CID, he thanked Corbett: 'without the assistance of your historical knowledge and deep reading I should not have been able to make it half the success that I feel it has been'. A close personal and intellectual relationship, built on shared interests in strategic thought, British and German, ensured they kept in touch.[65] As DNI, Slade asked his friend to develop the Admiralty case for the 1907 Invasion Inquiry. He kept a close watch on the college, adding his name to the revised edition of the 'Green Pamphlet' to ensure it was recognised as an official document. This mattered because it criticised some aspects of Fisher's policy, demanding more cruisers to protect oceanic commerce. Nor was Slade impressed by his successors.[66]

Between you & I Lowry has not got a real grasp of the principles, although he is better than he was. He has a lot to learn yet. He gave me his lectures to read that he is going to deliver to the next course. I had to criticise some of his statements. . . . I don't know what to say about the strategy at the War College now, it is certainly not on a satisfactory footing, but as I said this morning I noticed a considerable advance since I last talked to them about it.[67]

Even so, Lowry's sudden replacement by Rear Admiral Lewis Bayly came as a complete surprise: 'an able man, but a crank. He is a nephew of Chinese Gordon and has many of his uncle's idiosyncrasies. I do not think he is a well read man. . . . He is not conspicuous for his tact.'[68] If Bayly regarded his two-year appointment as 'a very dull time', he proved a useful sounding board for Corbett.[69] Slade maintained his interest in the War College, along with his desire for an Admiralty Staff, after taking command of the East Indies Station in 1909.

> The function of the War College is not the preparation of war plans, but the investigation of war problems, on which the plans can be based. In order that the problem should be properly set, it is necessary that the conditions should be strictly limited & the question should always be formulated by the Admiralty; when the problem has been solved with one set of candidates it ought to be re-examined with a different set of candidates, not as a consequence from the past problem, but as an entirely new one.[70]

The War College essays were still circulated to the fleet, but neither they nor the course director impressed Slade: 'I shall be very sorry indeed to see the War College become a narrow school of paper tactics and that is what I am afraid it is tending to.'[71] Bayly's appointment reflected Fisher's need for a new set of war plans in 1909.[72] By 1910, Slade saw Bayly 'coming round at last to see the importance of having a little education in the theory of war. He was most contemptuous about it when he started.'[73] This conversion had been Corbett's work.

Despite complaining he had become a 'hidebound bureaucrat', Corbett's enthusiasm and commitment never slackened.[74] The critical impact of the course on his strategic thinking can be traced in the spring of 1911, when he combined completing *Some Principles* with lecturing to the sixteenth course. By 1911 the War Course had been running for eight years, providing higher education for senior officers with a core naval staff on short-term postings and outside experts. The work was driven by real needs and examined real scenarios, adding intellectual rigour and a national strategic focus to the salty professionalism of rising officers. Furthermore Sir Arthur Wilson's Admiralty took the results seriously, having recently appointed Rear Admiral Sir Henry Jackson FRS as course director. One of the sharpest minds in Fisher's technology group, a critical contributor to the development of wireless, Jackson's innate modesty disguised a highly capable leader. He became Chief of the Admiralty War Staff in 1913–14, and an effective if low-profile First Sea Lord in 1915–16. The War College had prepared him to conduct war at sea with economy and effect. When Arthur Marder criticised his lack of energy and aggression[75] he mistook an intelligent Corbettian strategy, forcing the enemy to take risks, for passivity.[76]

Jackson was the first director to be spared Slade's criticism. His first course, the sixteenth, ran between 6 March and 29 June 1911. He lectured on strategy, preparation for war, cruisers, the development of modern warships and tactics. Lectures were given every morning at 9.30 and, on some days, at 10.40, leaving the rest of the day free for strategic exercises, private study, syndicate work and preparation. Course staff lectured on engineering, the operational and tactical side of the Russo-Japanese War, foreign naval developments, intelligence and submarine cables. Visiting officers discussed submarines, aircraft, Courts Martial, minelayers and naval hygiene. Wider themes were covered by external speakers: Alexander Pearce Higgins LLD provided twelve lectures on maritime international law. Douglas Owen examined the merchant shipping system in wartime, stop and search, national economies, food supply and finance in ten lectures. Corbett's twelve lectures addressed the strategy of the Russo-Japanese War, combined operations, and the naval war after Trafalgar.[77] Students and core staff spent the first week of April at Camberley, participating in a joint Naval and Military staff exercise before taking Easter leave.

Jackson provided a concise, critical analysis of students, rating them against their peers. Two admirals stood out: Vice Admiral Sir Stanley Colville and Rear Admiral Frederick Tudor Hamilton – 'very attentive and keen experienced officers'. Fifth-placed Rear Admiral David Beatty was 'smart and able, apt to be rash in conclusions'. Charles Dundas brought up the rear, being merely 'steady and attentive'. Among the captains, Alfred Chatfield was top, 'First class, v.g. and very clever in explanation'; Henry

Chatterton brought up the rear, second class, 'rather flighty and too talkative'. The two marines were only seconds, but the two soldiers were both firsts; one provided a good lecture on discipline. Four officers had been redeployed before taking a significant part in the course.[78]

At the beginning of the course Jackson circulated essay questions, inviting each syndicate to select a topic and decide whether to complete the task together, in smaller groups, or as individuals. On this occasion the papers were not printed for circulation, possibly for security reasons.

R. N. WAR COLLEGE, PORTSMOUTH, Spring Session 1911
Proposed Subjects for Essays

Section A.

1. Discuss the question of the fortification of the mouth of the Scheldt, considering its bearing, if any, on the traditional policy of Great Britain with regard to the Low Countries, and its effect on our policy as a belligerent in the narrow seas, the various attitudes of Holland being taken into consideration.

2. Discuss the proposed ratification of the Declaration of London, considering the causes which led to the Conference of 1908–9, and the advantages or disadvantages which might accrue therefrom to Great Britain as a belligerent or neutral.

B.

3. Discuss the question of the use and necessary defences of Ports as designated in recent papers, vis: War Anchorages. Temporary Naval Bases, Defended Mercantile Ports, Coaling Stations, Ports of Refuge.

4. Discuss the question of Commerce attack by Great Britain, with special reference to the general scheme of operations, visit and search of neutrals by ships and destroyers, prize crews etc.

5. Discuss the position of the Orkneys and Shetlands in a possible war with Germany, considering present and proposed communications, fortifications etc, and the possibility of a portion being seized by Germany.

6. Discuss the question of Colonial Navies and the trend of their development, and how they should be used in conjunction with our fleet for training purposes and in war.

C.

7. What effect if any are Submarines and Air craft likely to have in the near future on British Naval Strategy and Tactics?

8. Discuss the question of the best type of Conning Tower for battle-ships in connection with the arrangements for Control of Fire.

9. Discuss the use of Mine Layers and Mine Sweepers as an integral portion of the fleet in war, and their probable effect on the move-ment of the fleet.[79]

These essays, the only written work students submitted, were a significant element in their assessment. If the absence of a Baltic question reflected Fisher's retirement, the subjects provide a compelling demonstration of the Admiralty's clarity of thought and focus on the strategic, legal and diplomatic issues that would shape future conflicts. The Scheldt was a live issue: Dutch plans to build a new fort at Flushing, and the strategic role of the Scheldt, would be debated at the CID in May 1911. First Sea Lord Arthur Wilson concluded the fort would make no appreciable difference to strategic conditions, and that Britain had no right to interfere.[80] Question 7 disposes of old assumptions that the Navy was unprepared for the new technology, or that Corbett was unaware of such things. He attended submarine demonstrations for the War Course, and watched his nephew fly from Hendon.

These subjects were of the utmost contemporary interest, while student responses were informed by recent experience, notably the Russo-Japanese War. This context ensured Corbett's 'history' was relevant and forward looking, part of a course that prepared senior officers for the next war. In 1910 he reduced this experience to order in a doctrine primer that set out the principles of strategy through Clausewitzian analysis of British experience. This work had far greater impact on his audience than has hitherto been acknowledged, his original biographer mistaking wry, self-deprecatory humour for serious concern.[81] Corbett influenced the men who mattered. For David Beatty the course proved highly significant, as an intellectual stimulus and an opportune meeting with Alfred Chatfield, his flag captain or Chief of Staff for the rest of his career.[82] Beatty chose Chatfield to lead a flag staff; he took ship-handling and man management skills for granted. Fresh from the War Course, Beatty turned down a sea appointment he considered useless as a preparation for war. Although by repute a bold huntsman with a zest for speed, Beatty was anything but an unthinking fire-eater. An educated, reflective officer, widely read and suitably instructed, Beatty took a serious interest in naval history, while his comprehension of Clausewitz reflected both Corbett's War Course tuition and personal experience of combat.[83] His paper on the attributes of a good cruiser captain was drawn, almost verbatim, from Corbett's *The Campaign of Trafalgar*.[84]

On the next course, September to December 1911, the star student was future First Sea Lord Rosslyn Wemyss, who, Jackson noted, possessed a 'strong personality and has a good grasp of strategical situations'. Former Berlin naval attaché Captain Philip Dumas was 'very good at strategical research, and exercise work', while Richard Phillimore was 'very good at policy'. In early 1913 the college moved closer to the core of imperial strategy, the course director noting:

> In future officers who are considered particularly suitable for Assistant Secretaries Committee of Imperial Defence should be noted. This to include officers on staff. They must be Commanders, preferably with sea time or just promoted. One will not probably be required till 1914. Cmdr [Kenneth] Dewar would probably be suitable.

Dewar was retained on the College staff, perhaps pending an opening. The spring 1912 course, suffused with Corbett's ideas, was:

> notable for the good discussions they took part in & for the excellent essays they wrote – not quite so keen on tactical games & strategical games as some of the other classes previously – but what they did required very little if any criticism. They all seemed to grasp sound strategical principles. The flag officers frequently assisted me in preparing schemes & researches for the Admiralty Staff, working together for a week with one staff officer to produce a combined opinion on the matter in question. This is worthwhile carrying out in future during the last 2 months of the course when not doing strategical games.

Martyn Jerram was the best admiral, challenging Marder's dismissive treatment.[85] The autumn course starred another maligned admiral: Robert Arbuthnot, 'very good indeed. Has done exceedingly well, he has a great grasp of strategy & is very clear'. Both men were appointed to major commands after demonstrating exceptional ability at sea, on the war game floor and in debate.[86]

The integration of the War Course into Admiralty planning and organisation had been Fisher's alternative to the creation of an Admiralty War Staff, a measure that attracted the support of politicians who read across from foreign military practice. Fisher had no intention of creating a Chief of Staff to coordinate planning: that would weaken his grip on the Admiralty, which was responsible for all aspects of naval policy, including strategy, personnel and construction. A plan to combine a War Staff with peacetime policy responsibilities had been sketched by Prince Louis in early 1902. It would be the basis of the post-1917 system, which combined the posts of Chief of Staff and First Sea Lord.[87] Anxious to protect his radical strategic ideas from civilian scrutiny Fisher used the War Course to develop key elements of his strategic thinking, connecting the Baltic, the Danish Straits and the concept of deterrence.

With Fisher's term as First Sea Lord approaching an end, First Lord of the Admiralty Reginald McKenna accepted the inevitable, consulting the CID Secretariat, Charles Ottley and Maurice Hankey, on the way ahead. As he prepared to leave office in October 1909, Fisher set up the Navy War Council, which had the authority to summon the President of the War College when necessary.[88] He designed this system for his designated successor Arthur Wilson, who had no interest in a War Staff, and was unlikely to have accepted the post if one had existed. Slade considered it a farce, while Ottley, Corbett and Hankey favoured a dedicated Naval Staff acting under the direct authority of the Admiralty. Despite being fobbed off by Fisher, Ottley pressed on, outlining Corbett's next book.

It is submitted that the sole object of the instruction in strategy should be to throw into high relief the fundamental principles on which all sound strategy must be based. Although numerous military works on this subject exist in every language it is believed that there is no single naval treatise which could be used as a text book of strategy. These principles are of course to be found diffused through pages of writers such as Mahan, Colomb, Etc etc., but none of these have published works sufficiently concise to serve as handbooks.

In dealing with strategy therefore the Admiralty will have to trust to the discretion of the lecturer. Some guidance might be given him, however, as to the methods to be pursued. ... There is reason to believe that the discussion of current strategy at both the Naval

War College and the military Staff College have led to unfortunate results.

The principles of strategy can, however, be illustrated by history, or by the elucidation of imaginary problems.

The general principles of Imperial strategy, contained in various memoranda and Minutes of the Committee of Imperial Defence should be included in this part of the War Course.

Other subjects, notably logistics, intelligence, mobilisation and coast defence, would be taught from Admiralty and CID memoranda. Staff duties were still being developed.[89]

In August 1911 Winston Churchill took office as First Lord of the Admiralty, tasked with creating an Admiralty Staff. Ottley's concept was the obvious model. In October Churchill stressed preparation for war required:

> education in the naval principles of strategy, which all historians agree to be permanent in their general application, it may perhaps be roughly estimated that a year's special course of study at the War College would answer the purpose. There is no text book at present which could be taken as the standard for such a course, but the subject is fully treated by Mahan, Colomb, Corbett and others in a manner which would suffice, if properly handled, until an authorised text book has been compiled from the material which may be extracted from their works.[90]

Corbett had already written the necessary 'text book', *Some Principles of Maritime Strategy*.[91] Churchill's Admiralty War Staff, established in January 1912, was compromised by inadequate manpower and badly led. Captain Ernest Troubridge, the first Chief of Staff, was chosen because he would follow Winston's lead. While Churchill claimed the Staff would sift, develop and apply 'the results of history and experiment ... preserving them as a general stock of reasoned opinion available as an aid and as a guide for all who are called upon to determine, in peace or war, the naval policy of the country', this was not a true staff organisation. Nor did it become one until late 1917.[92]

Having created a Staff, the Admiralty needed trained Staff Officers. The obvious solution was run a Staff Course at the War College, sharing key elements including Corbett's lectures, while course director Jackson recruited additional staff. The new course catered for commanders, lieutenant commanders and lieutenants. Between 1912 and 1914, thirty-six Staff Officers were trained, including Bertram Ramsay. In 1912 Commander K.G.B. Dewar criticised the projected curriculum, rehearsing familiar arguments about the value of history for naval education:

> Any attempt to make Officers learn up historical periods or campaigns should be discouraged, the naval Officer cannot spare the time to study history for the sake of history.
>
> He can however be taught to apply its teachings to modern problems and to get his facts as he requires them. The study of a past war should merely be viewed as a commentary on the possibilities of the future. Historical teaching should be combined with tactical and strategical instruction. The study of blockade strategy, tactical formations, commerce protection etc. should always be accompanied by brief historical investigations. . . .
>
> Lectures on history can be very easily overdone, nearly everything that can be said in a lecture can be found in books, and it is better to teach the student to use books, as they are available when he leaves the College. Historical teaching if properly applied will do much to guard Officers from that mire of technical materialism into which they always sink after long peace, they should learn from history that human nature is always the same and that it is the human factor that wins wars.

He feared the Admiralty had set out again:

> on the old Chinese road where the whole object of historical teaching is sacrificed to feats of incoherent memorialisation. What a delightfully simple but ineffective way of teaching history.
>
> It is considered most important that the methods of teaching history to naval Officers and what they are to be taught should be decided by naval Officers. Historians are good servants but bad masters.[93]

College Captain Richard Webb summarised Dewar's analysis: 'Naval History should be taught not as an exact and continuous subject, but as a means of illustrating by actual examples therefrom how various operations should be undertaken.' As this method was already in use, history provision 'might be left to Mr. Corbett'.

The Staff Course prepared officers to plan, coordinate and structure the increasingly complex, interlocked operations that would dominate future wars. Trainee Staff Officers joined War Course exercises, as Staff Officers for the admirals. It was no coincidence that modern staff work reached the Grand Fleet in mid-1917, under the leadership of War Course graduates Beatty, Osmond de Brock, a protégé of Prince Louis, and Chatfield. The staff system improved markedly when War College star Rosslyn Wemyss became deputy First Sea Lord, and took the title Chief of Staff seriously.

The War Course brought the concepts, ideas and methods of modern war to the Royal Navy in the Edwardian age, Corbett's strategic system was at its heart. Between the first short course in 1902 and the last pre-war intake of 1914, 616 officers attended, and most completed the course.[94] The creation of an effective Admiralty Staff in 1917–18 justified the entire pre-war War Course. Most of the men selected for the course had career prospects, Lieutenant Rooke (1907–8) was an exception, rated 'Hopeless, wants in ordinary intelligence.'[95] Students followed a topical course that emphasised the diplomatic, technological and strategic context of naval activity, in peace and war, with Corbett's history/strategy lectures the largest external element, although by no means the only one. The programme fed directly into Admiralty thinking, through student essays and planning projects like the Ballard Committee. Course staff developed war plans, and shaped careers. The belated addition of a linked Staff Course provided the Navy with a nucleus of trained Staff Officers just in time for a war that witnessed an exponential expansion of demand for such work.

The War Course developed planning and doctrine, provided a common resource of knowledge and ideas, drafted critical war plans, introduced Staff training and built command teams, notably that of Beatty, Chatfield and de Brock. Close contact with DNI, the Admiralty and the Army Staff College kept the teaching fresh and responsive. Outstanding officers, including Beatty, Wemyss, Bacon, Chatfield, de Brock, Ballard, Pound and Ramsay, acquired key skills and insights as they prepared for high command.

Corbett's work was widely recognised: in June 1914, Fisher, Churchill, Jackson and War Course director Alexander Bethell pressed for him to be knighted.[96] His course text *Some Principles* remained a snapshot of an evolving national strategic doctrine, not the summary of a closed process. Corbett's dissatisfaction with the book was that of a man seeking certainty when everything was in flux. Had he produced the book four years earlier it would have been very different: had he been able to revisit it in 1914, or 1920, the results would have been startling. *Some Principles* was the opening essay of an endless debate, created to introduce students to a higher and more effective way of thinking about war, hence his insistence on starting the book with a discussion of theory. Nor was it intended to stand alone: *Some Principles* remains the analytical guide to his mature case studies, the *Seven Years' War*, *Trafalgar*, *Russo-Japanese War* and *Naval Operations*. Taken together they provide the intellectual core of a 'British way' that shaped naval education, policy and strategy between 1902 and 1922. Corbett's analysis of British strategy reflected his engagement with a range of remarkable men, Custance and Clarke, Fisher, Prince Louis, Jackson, Slade, Ballard and even Lewis Bayly, who deepened his understanding, and a constantly changing audience that demanded attention. Corbett's elegant, incisive approach, and quasi-religious commitment to the service, ensured the results exceeded expectation. The issues were immediate, political and pressing. Beresford's bluster and the Army's continental obsessions threatened his liberal-progressive worldview with a protectionist empire and a continental army. He responded with elegant essays, sophisticated histories and engaging lectures that sustained the 'British way' while peace lasted.

Working with the Navy made him a better strategist, because it gave him real problems to solve. Strategic texts like *Some Principles* must be studied in context, unique to their time and their audience. Only exceptional examples, like Corbett's book, retain value for other times, and other audiences. Corbett wrote *Some Principles* for the War Course, and a wider debate about national/ imperial strategy, which is why he was anxious to keep it up to date.

The War Course closed at the outbreak of war, releasing Corbett for other tasks, but when it resumed in 1919 he would be summoned. His teaching and texts shaped British strategic thinking, despite the objections of continentalist soldiers and materiel-minded sailors. Seen in its proper setting, as the jewel of the War Course and the culmination of an educational transformation, *Some Principles* assumes a significance far beyond the paltry sales and carping criticisms.

The reputation of the Naval War Course/College still suffers from the pioneer judgements of Arthur J. Marder in the first volume of *From the Dreadnought to Scapa Flow*. Marder ignored the pre-1900 history and strategy courses run at Greenwich and seriously underestimated the War Course audience, which he restricted to commanders and captains. From

1904, admirals were a key part of the audience, both for their own benefit and for the encouragement their presence gave to lower ranks. Furthermore the course was a full-pay appointment: attendance was compulsory.[97] Like much of Marder's analysis, the approach is vitiated by undue reliance on isolated voices of discontent, notably that of Kenneth Dewar and Alfred Chatfield.[98] Chatfield's dismissive approach to Corbett and the course is easily understood after reading the splenetic rant he penned after reading volume III of Corbett's *Naval Operations*.[99] The course equipped him to be a great First Sea Lord. Even Dewar admitted 'the hours were short and the leave generous, which gave one opportunities for thought and study'.

Career-long self-education is, as all service educators understand, critical to preparing for an unpredictable future. Overcrowded courses crammed with endless lectures, exercises, directed study and delivery might be easy to administer, control and assess, generating comfortingly rigorous numerical scores, but they are a poor substitute for intelligent programmes which encourage students to develop. War Course student reports reflected far more than 'results': delivered by an officer of unquestioned professional expertise, it rated men as 'first class' because they had the character to lead, the ability to inspire, the judgement to get it right, and the dedication to see it through. Intellectual skills have little utility in command without character; leadership, teamwork, powers of expression and decision. Men who acquired a combination of new ideas from horizon-broadening lectures, personal study and contact with fellow officers of various ranks, went on to think about their profession in new and more coherent ways. They adopted a common language in which to express their ideas and communicate with colleagues, soldiers and statesmen who shared their concerns. The War Course was no place for hidebound thinking, narrow and prescriptive approaches or closed minds.

Furthermore, Marder's treatment of the course seriously undervalued Fisher's role: he adopted and extended the course to provide strategic education and war planning functions, using it to address key problems that emerged during his period in office. His higher education programme addressed international law, the changing strategic situations and the development of national strategy. He set the questions and appointed key staff, including Corbett. The War Course ensured the Navy's best men had worked on real problems in an atmosphere conducive to study and reflection. When war came they still had much to learn, but they were far better equipped to do so, and better able to express their understanding, because of their time on the War Course. That Corbett's strategic concepts survived such temporary aberrations as the latter stages of the First World War and the longer, if less bloody, era of the Cold War to reappear in the late twentieth century as the basis of British strategy should come as no surprise.

CHAPTER 7

Strategy, Culture and History

Corbett's evolution from literary historian to strategic analyst was shaped by changing circumstances and new challenges. While the War Course provided him with an audience, a bitter rivalry between the services over the direction of national strategy gave his work a specific focus. He became a strategist at a time when the debate had stretched far beyond the defence sector, polarising domestic politics, impacting diplomacy and challenging core assumptions about the future of the empire. Strategy was too important to be left to the parochial concerns of admirals and generals: it must be settled by statesmen. Corbett created a systematic explanation of the way Britain had waged war as a guide to thinking about the future. The maritime strategy he recommended was national, not naval, tailored to the needs and resources of the Edwardian empire. It emphasised the combined action of both services, integrating other resources within a national policy, settled by the Cabinet. His public output was targeted at statesmen as well as warriors.

Corbett used strategic theory to analyse the history of Britain at war, transforming the random, contingent events of the past into coherent patterns that could inform policy choices. This approach was influenced by fellow NRS councillors, men involved in making strategy, including Admiral Philip Colomb, DNI Captain Cyprian Bridge, Lieutenant General Sir Andrew Clarke RE, Inspector General of Fortifications, his namesake George Sydenham Clarke, another Royal Engineer with a grasp of imperial defence, Earl Spencer, the First Lord of the Admiralty and Captain Alfred T. Mahan USN, the NRS's famous overseas member.[1] Where Mahan's advocacy of seapower as strategy had focused naval thinking at the service level, Corbett became a historian, and then a strategist, for the nation. He would replace the fixed naval models of Colomb and Mahan by developing Clausewitz's sophisticated, fluid arguments.

By 1900, at the latest, Corbett recognised the outline of a unique 'British way' that integrated Army and Navy under civilian direction, to secure maritime/economic advantage, and prevent the creation of a single continental hegemon. He recognised that national strategies were unique, and contingent. Work on the second volume of *England in the Mediterranean*, which coincided with his debut as naval educator and an Oxford lecturer, reinforced the strategic focus. Thereafter his key texts were historical case studies exploring the 'British way' as maritime strategy and limited war. This experience secured and shaped his wartime roles as strategic advisor, propagandist and historian, along with post-war efforts to emphasise the anomalous nature of the methods used in 1914–18. This intellectual development was driven by his work on the War Course and linked Admiralty tasks, work with an urgent national purpose. Corbett analysed British experience to develop and disseminate a national doctrine that integrated politics, history, law and strategic theory. By 1902 Corbett had secured the support of two key imperial strategists, George Sydenham Clarke and Sir John Fisher.

At this time strategic theory was largely driven by service agendas, focused on war planning and produced by men in uniform. It was a contested space, one where civilians played a marginal role. Today we understand that strategy, as the art of using national resources to achieve political ends, is at least as important in peace, underpinning deterrence and diplomacy, as it is in war. It is not the province of individual armed services; the necessary matching of aims to assets, balancing risk against opportunity, is most effectively settled at the national level, by civilian governments advised by service professionals. Corbett recovered this model, which had been the essence of British practice for centuries. It was also consistent with his progressive Liberal political convictions. His 'British way' was far more than a contribution to professional military literature, it was directed at the national level.

Strategic texts of the nineteenth century reflected the total character and extended duration of the Revolutionary and Napoleonic wars, which saw the emergence of individual battles as 'decisive', and a romantic obsession with genius that elevated the mechanistic military ideas of the Enlightenment to a new plane. These discussions assumed that strategy had a universal validity. Swiss Staff Officer Antoine Henri Jomini, heir to the Enlightenment tradition, had served both Napoleon and the Tsar. His programmatic model had considerable influence in Britain and the United States, as well as

France and Russia, despite their strikingly divergent political and strategic experiences. Jomini's texts supported programmatic training, teaching officers to follow a prevailing doctrine and obey orders. Mahan consciously followed Jomini when he took strategy to sea. By contrast, Jomini's contemporary Prussian General Carl von Clausewitz focused on educating decision-makers who, he assumed, would be soldiers rather than civilians.

Clausewitz's *On War* reflected the distinctive geography, resources and interests of an essentially landlocked Central European state whose great-power status depended on the army. Rapid, 'decisive' Prussian victories in 1866 and 1870–1 encouraged many soldiers to treat German methods as universally applicable, generating international interest in Clausewitz. German operational and strategic practice emphasised a short-range, high tempo approach to war, focused on battle, which reflected Prussia/Germany's position in Central Europe, limited human resources and the reality that a prolonged war would favour larger, more populous powers.[2] Without defensible borders Germany depended on the field army to conduct short-range offensives into familiar and favourable territory, compensating for the lack of strategic depth and limited resources. This would avoid the 'nightmare' of a prolonged war of attrition against more numerous and better resourced enemies. Consequently German generals:

> rarely thought about the highest realm of war: politics, coalition warfare, strategy, economics, logistics (or at least any long-term, sustained logistics), which they believed were unimportant since they intended to terminate the war victoriously within weeks.[3]

Military doctrine focused on the tactical, not the strategic level, with naval war playing 'only a minor role'.[4] Operational success and diplomatic outcomes become conflated in a system that had lost touch with reality. This method was dominated by aggression, rather than reason.[5]

Late nineteenth-century proponents of a distinctive 'German way of war' distorted Clausewitz into an exponent of absolute war, a nation in arms mobilised and wielded by a military elite more concerned with social status and political power than strategic logic. After 1871 the German Empire had the most powerful army and economy in Europe, reversing the situation that prevailed when Clausewitz wrote. When works by the leading exponent of a 'German way', General Colmar von der Goltz, appeared in

English, readers ignored the irrelevance of his arguments to the political system and strategic needs of a global maritime empire ruled by democratically elected politicians, seduced by a model that promised short, successful wars. The Great German General Staff planned and directed wars in a system where political power remained in the hands of an emperor and ministers he had appointed. Myths of a German 'genius for war' deluded late nineteenth-century British soldiers, and are still confusing twenty-first-century Americans.

Operational excellence in 1870 had secured the German Army a level of political autonomy that distorted the new state. While it remains an open question whether soldiers or statesmen took Germany to war in 1914, the decision was shaped by cultural and political anxieties, seeking world-power status to suppress political opposition and preserve social privilege. The relevance of those anxieties to British Army officers, many of them social conservatives and opponents of Irish Home Rule, should be obvious. It helped them to ignore the absolute irrelevance of the 'German way' to British needs. Ironically, German doctrine had acquired Jominian rigidity by 1914.[6]

Alien strategic ideas were not restricted to the Army. Mahan's *The Influence of Sea Power upon History, 1660–1783* of 1890 was greeted with something approaching religious veneration by a nation and Navy that had ruled the seas for two hundred years without a strategic primer. That Mahan's work, developed from Jomini, had been designed to educate a continental power, not a maritime empire, made it more relevant to Imperial Germany and Tsarist Russia than Britain. Mahan's focus on decisive battle helped British soldiers grasp naval strategy, but ignored the wider maritime dimension. Admiral Sir John Fisher, who understood the need for a national maritime strategy based on British experience, supported Corbett's work. The two men shared political values and global perspectives. If Corbett captured the 'British way', Fisher had set the task. They understood that strategy was contingent, as von der Goltz observed:

> Whoever writes on strategy and tactics ought not in his theory to neglect the point of view of his own people. He should give us a national strategy, a national tactics.[7]

Goltz explicitly rejected attempts to universalise strategy, and 'lessons' from the experience of other states. Yet his habit of scaling up tactical methods into strategy highlighted the defining weakness of contemporary German military thought. British soldiers managed to ignore Goltz's warning, and repeated his error.

The strategic culture of a state is unique, reflecting location, politics, economics, geography, population, history and other variables. Once understood it may inform, but not determine, strategic choice. Pioneer military historian Hans Delbrück stressed the need to see the history of war as an integral part of cultural history:

> For the art of war is an art like painting, architecture, or pedagogy, and the entire cultural existence of peoples is determined to a high degree by the military organisations, which in turn are closely related to the technique of warfare, tactics, and strategy. All these things have mutual influence on one another.[8]

Most strategic thinking reflects the reality that man is a terrestrial creature, but states and empires that depend on control of the sea for security and prosperity necessarily develop appropriate sea-focused strategies. Corbett wrote for the last maritime great power, the British Empire between 1900 and 1922. Yet even in Britain terrestrial assumptions remained potent, not least because the British Army studied war and strategy through continental texts, French and increasingly German, that emphasised high tempo mass army campaigns to overthrow nations in such 'decisive' battles as Austerlitz or Sedan. To meet the danger inherent in such 'continental' thinking, Fisher encouraged Corbett to capture and process the strategic experience of the British Empire into a contemporary doctrine.

British strategic thinking had lacked an institutional locus before the establishment of the Army Staff College at Camberley, shortly after the Crimean War. It remained in thrall to Jomini into the 1880s. Military debate tended to focus on tactical and operational issues. Few officers aspired to strategic insight, while statesmen focused on reducing the services' budgets. Cultures shaped by anti-intellectualism and deference further restricted curiosity. Many Army officers ignored Camberley, while the post-1873 Royal Naval College, Greenwich, provided a more restricted programme, dominated by scientific attainment. Philip Colomb's *Naval Warfare* of 1891, based on college lectures, was the only relevant output.[9] Colomb treated war as a process, untroubled by contact with theory, or the free play of the intellect, paying little attention to the Army or political direction. Few contemporary discussions ventured into strategy and policy.

In 1890 Britain was a global maritime power with no European commitments, while the armed forces were controlled by a political system that combined parliamentary democracy, civilian control and public accountability. As an insular/imperial power relying on sea communications Britain depended on a dominant fleet: it did not need a large field army. The Royal Navy was the 'Senior Service'. In the last major European conflict, in 1870–1, Britain had demanded the belligerents respect the neutrality of Belgium, and remained neutral. It used diplomacy to help balance the European system, while naval deterrence secured the wider empire against French and Russian threats. Britain's primary weapon was economic attrition, the German 'nightmare'. This method had been effective, even in the total wars of the French Revolution and empire. It underpinned a century of effective deterrence, avoiding the social, economic and political costs of conscription. No army, or armies, could protect this distinctive polity.

British policy in Europe since the sixteenth century had focused on the coast of Flanders, the obvious base for an invasion. Sea power, diplomacy, money and, where possible, a small expeditionary army, were the tools of a 'British way'. Britain did not need a conscript army because the country and the capital city were secured by the Navy. Despite those realities, many British soldiers favoured a 'German way', detaching war from the political dimension, confusing battlefield proficiency with strategy. Such methods were irrelevant to British needs and a profound threat to a national culture and identity shaped by progressive liberal values. Fortunately there were more sophisticated minds in the British Army, and their work formed the basis of Corbett's examination of national strategy. Frederick Maurice and G.F.R. Henderson introduced him to the work of Clausewitz, whose analytical framework helped him transform British experience into strategic doctrine. Maurice, Henderson and General Lord Wolseley recognised the irrelevance of continental 'ways of war' to British conditions. Wolseley, as commander-in-chief, understood that in a war with France or Russia British troops would strike naval targets, like Cherbourg or Sevastopol.[10] Another voice challenging the relevance of 'German' military thinking was Captain, later Admiral Philip Colomb.[11] In the 1880s Colomb lectured on tactics and strategy at the Royal Naval College Greenwich, bringing him into contact with John Laughton, the pioneer of naval history as an educational resource.[12]

This connection may have encouraged Colomb to lecture at the Royal United Services Institute on blockade and convoy in 1887, with historical precedent providing a prologue to a contemporary lecture. His essay 'The Naval Defence of the United Kingdom' of May 1888 polarised opinion and opened the debate on a 'British way', just before the massive naval programmes in 1889 and 1893 emphasised the Navy's primacy in national security.

After the humiliations of the Second Anglo-Boer War, many soldiers looked to continental methods to reconstruct their professional standards. While foreign military methods, including structured staff systems, planning and tactical methods, were useful, foreign strategies were not. Strategy was necessarily national, shaped by fixed realities, from geography and population to economic and industrial resources, political practice and the level of dependence on maritime trade. Nor was German influence restricted to the Army; many British intellectuals saw the Hohenzollern empire as bastion of progress in science, philosophy and history.[13] They mistook the technocratic veneer for a deeper reality. Corbett, who detested Imperial Germany, saw no reason to emulate a continental power.

Insular Britain did not need a mass army, or plans for a large-scale land campaigns: sea control provided the time and space to think and prepare a limited maritime response, secure the seas, seize hostile possessions, and shut down enemy economies. The Boer War and the rising threat of Imperial Germany challenged these old-established realities. Consequently Corbett joined a debate that veered between outright emulation of continental models and unthinking British exceptionalism. He used intellectual rigour and logic to challenge the parochial tribalism that had hitherto dominated such debates. His 'British way' was a synthesis of many elements, including continental military theory, British experience, domestic politics, technology and the ongoing evolution of the British Empire. Sound strategy would inform policy responses to a broad range of complex problems.

Corbett's strategic development was shaped by his progressive Liberal values, elite education, travel, legal experience, family wealth and service ethic. His imperial thinking can be traced back to the 1880s, and the arguments of John Robert Seeley, James Anthony Froude and the Colomb brothers. In 1891 he integrated those arguments with Mahan's *Sea Power* strategy.[14] The comfortable assumptions of late Victorian Liberalism, small defence, disengagement from Europe and a focus on domestic issues – the political concerns of William Ewart Gladstone – were shattered by the Irish Home Rule crisis.

Many defence-minded Liberals joined the Conservative and Unionist party, leaving a Liberal rump that lacked credibility on defence. The Conservatives exploited that vulnerability with the Naval Defence Act of 1889, providing a new Navy with major infrastructure upgrades across the empire in a single measure, funded by renegotiating the interest rate on the National Debt. The Naval Defence Act was completed in 1893, leading a nervous Liberal Cabinet to adopt the similarly ambitious Spencer Programme, which ended Prime Minister Gladstone's career. Corbett a Liberal Imperialist, approved the programme; Lord Rosebery was his preferred leader.[15]

The British debate acquired a sharper focus when a new phase of imperial and economic competition began in the 1890s. Much of the rhetoric focused on moral, social and genetic decline, obsessively re-examining the end of older empires for portents and precedents.[16] Liberal thinking was constrained by the pursuit of increased political participation, raising serious concerns about the quality of national decision-making in a democratic age.[17] At the heart of the debate lay the rising tide of European armaments and alliances, and the desperate expectation that future wars would be won quickly, by 'decisive' battles.[18] By 1894 Europe had been divided into two armed camps, the German, Austro-Hungarian and Italian Triple Alliance and a Franco-Russian Dual Alliance, the latter sparking a revival of the 'Two Power' naval standard. A Franco-Russian alliance remained the greatest threat to British security, both powers rebuilding their navies as part of a global naval expansion that included the United States, Japan, Germany and Latin American powers. The sudden expansion of global war fleets put Britain's global communications at risk, challenging the comfortable assumption of naval superiority. Homogeneous new fleets of British battleships, cruisers and destroyers faced a Franco-Russian challenge that combined fleet warfare with cruiser attacks on oceanic trade and imperial outposts. The Army would assist, protecting India and vital bases, while amphibious operations seized hostile naval stations and colonies. The British worldview focused on preserving peace in Europe as the empire evolved into a commonwealth linked by oceans and culture, rather than power. Peace in Europe would prevent any great power from seizing the Low Countries and threatening Britain's insular security.

Clarke and Fisher drew Corbett into this debate, to capture British strategy from past practice and articulate it for a rising generation of officers and statesmen. Corbett contributed to these debates at many levels, from

Monthly Review essays on empire, decline and defence, to history books and War Course lectures. He recognised that a unique maritime great power could not follow continental military models. While men lived on the land, as he famously observed, it was not necessary to attack them there. Command of the sea, essential for the security of the British Isles, most of the empire and the domestic food supply, would enable effective economic warfare; not the random plundering of Drake, but the sustained pressure created by the Orders in Council after Trafalgar.

British writing on strategy before the 1890s was limited and largely derivative. The standard work remained General Sir Edward Hamley's *The Operations of War: Explained and Illustrated* of 1866, updated but essentially unchanged.[19] Hamley echoed Jomini and continental methods.[20] He ignored global warfare, amphibious campaigns and the Royal Navy – a striking omission for a text intended to instruct future leaders of an Army that needed to cross the sea before it could fight.[21] Hamley restricted his attention to wars after 1793, as more relevant to his audience.[22] Naval references were restricted to the use of the sea as a base, and a cursory acknowledgement of the distinctive character of British strategy. While he recognised the central importance of command of the sea, Hamley did not make it a national priority or a military target.[23] He ignored Copenhagen and Lisbon in 1807, Walcheren in 1809 and Sevastopol, where combined operations secured or reinforced command of the sea. This omission restricted the horizons of soldiers who had to think outside the continental box. It is significant that George Clarke credited Hamley with starting the methodical treatment of war in Britain and establishing the necessary language for a national debate.[24] Clarke remained a disciple of Jominian thinkers, Hamley and Mahan, convinced that command of the sea must be secured in battle, and on this point he parted company with Corbett.

If Hamley made scant reference to the sea, naval texts tended to ignore events on land. This oversight mattered little while the Army recognised its primary function in a major war was to help secure naval mastery. After the Franco-Prussian War, a small group of military intellectuals pushed for reforms to improve mobilisation, to facilitate attacks on hostile naval bases. In 1895 their leader, General Lord Wolseley, observed that in a war with France the Army would capture Brest.[25] Corbett was aware of Wolseley's output long before he began writing about strategy, sending him a copy of *Monk* in 1889.[26]

Corbett was influenced by a wide range of contemporary defence intellectuals and journalists, including John and Philip Colomb, Mahan, John Laughton and George Clarke, but as he recognised their limitations, he stopped referencing their work.[27] The men he continued citing were soldiers, Clausewitz, Major General Sir John Frederick Maurice (1841–1912) and Colonel George Francis Robert Henderson (1854–1903). He developed their ideas and exploited their authority to overcome khaki resistance to his 'British way'. Maurice, a brilliant essayist and a fine soldier, became part of Wolseley's clique, serving in several imperial campaigns.[28] In 1875–7 he worked in the Army Intelligence Department, monitoring the Russo-Turkish conflict and preparing for a Russian war. He influenced the decision to bring Indian troops to Malta and move the fleet to Istanbul. In 1882 he contributed to Wolseley's brilliant use of sea power to shift his base of operations from Alexandria to Ismailia, setting up the battle at Tel-el-Kebir. Corbett's intellectual debt to Maurice, a soldier who understood imperial defence, amphibious strategy and command of the sea, was obvious. Furthermore, Maurice was a progressive Liberal. Wolseley deemed him 'the ablest student of war we have'.[29]

Corbett considered Maurice's account of the 1882 Egyptian campaign the model British Official History. It addressed the wider public, whose support was critical if the army was to be reformed, 'rather than his brother officers'.

> I believe that the fate of the next expedition which leaves the shores of England may be most seriously affected by my success or failure in bringing home to the great body of our people the experiences of the 1882 campaign.
>
> The duties of an official historian writing for a country under a constitutional and parliamentary government like that of England are not the same as those of a German historian.[30]

In 1885 Maurice became Professor of Military Art and History at Camberley (1885–92), an appointment linked to the creation of an expeditionary force by Wolseley and Sir Henry Brackenbury, the Director of Military Intelligence. These reforms also addressed the defence of imperial coaling stations 'so that the fleet could rely on them, instead of having to defend them'. There was an obvious synergy with the ideas of Sir John Colomb and the practical output of Lieutenant General Sir Andrew Clarke RE, Inspector General of Fortifications.[31] Maurice stressed 'the paramount importance to a soldier of the careful study of past campaigns'.[32] He also cited Thomas Arnold's opinion that an officer would 'acquire a much better knowledge of history by the close and intimate study of one particular section of it, as a preliminary to all his reading'.[33] The paraphrase of Clausewitz may have been deliberate.

In 1885 Maurice emphasised the centrality of European concerns over Indian/imperial issues, stressed the maritime nature of British strategy and the need for an efficient amphibious army of 70,000 to complete the work of the fleet: 'our best means of defending India is to act where our amphibious strength can be exerted most effectually'.[34] This force could be sustained at great distances by Britain's immense mercantile fleet, enabling Britain to exercise a 'potent military influence' over European powers.[35] Wolseley also favoured a 70,000-man expeditionary force, two army corps and a cavalry division, which should determine the structure of the Army. The current disjointed roster of regiments, batteries and squadrons must be reorganised for this role – the germ of a British expeditionary force – because deploying maritime power against Russia's most vulnerable points, 'her seaboard, fleet, and commerce, and perhaps the sensitive lines of communication through Persia', would counter overland advances against India. The echo of older 'balance of power' postures was significant.[36]

Maurice's concept of national strategy influenced Corbett in the 1890s, a catalyst for his shift to the combined arms model, emphasising the role of Tudor soldiers like Essex in strategic decision-making.[37] It helped Corbett grasp how the unique, specific character of British strategy – seapower and amphibious operations – helped to maintain the European balance. Corbett's Seven Years' War shaped an expeditionary force like the one Maurice and Wolseley desired in the changed context of an Anglo-French Entente.

While professor at Camberley, Maurice met Captain G.F.R. Henderson, then an instructor at Sandhurst, and persuaded Wolseley that Henderson should succeed him.[38] Henderson removed Hamley from the curriculum and developed Maurice's approach to national strategy.[39] He taught his students to solve problems, linking map exercises and staff rides to reading and writing, and influenced able students, including Henry Rawlinson and Edmund Allenby.[40] It is possible that he and Corbett met – Corbett visited the college during Ascot week in 1894.[41]

Reading Mahan in 1894 extended Henderson's intellectual horizons.[42] He recognised Mahan had improved naval theory, the core of British strategy.[43] By the time he left Camberley to join Lord Roberts' staff in South Africa in 1899, Henderson was developing an synthetic overview of British strategy, and the doctrine of a unique global power. He emphasised the greater relevance of military practice in the American Civil War and the British invasion of Egypt over the Franco-Prussian War.[44] 'Both conflicts had been influenced by sea power, and hence were of "very special value" to British soldiers.'[45]

Between 1885 and 1899, Maurice and Henderson introduced Clausewitz to thoughtful officers at Camberley, and to a wider public through essays on 'War' in successive editions of the *Encyclopaedia Britannica*.[46] Corbett acquired the 1873 edition of Clausewitz around 1904, and began using the Prussian theorist just as his name came into common use in defence journalism.[47] Henderson adjusted Clausewitz's arguments to British needs, skilfully paraphrasing key concepts to avoid upsetting anti-intellectual audiences, making more use of his ideas than his name. He only named the Prussian when questioning his relevance.[48]

Henderson's *Encyclopaedia Britannica* essays engaged with the maritime core of British strategy, drawing new insights from Mahan and exemplary campaigns. The essays informed anglophone, rather than British, audiences about the nature of war beyond the continental paradigm, focusing on seapower, amateur soldiers and imperial conflict.[49] He observed that fortifications had fundamentally different roles in British and continental strategies, because strategy was a contingent national construct.[50]

Returning home after his health failed in South Africa, Henderson became the Official Historian of the war, a task that remained incomplete at his death in 1904. When Maurice took over he discovered that Henderson's incisive enquiry into the political and strategic origins of the conflict had been blocked by embarrassed soldiers and statesmen; without that, he feared the text would not justify the cost of publication, having 'little educative effect'.[51] Corbett discovered incisive enquiries were no more welcome in naval circles.

Henderson stressed that a navy acting alone was not all-powerful; even Britain, the most maritime of empires, needed an efficient army to 'complete the ruin of the enemy's fleet' and 'prevent its resuscitation'. In strategic terms, a dominant navy without an army 'can hardly force a hostile Power to seek terms'. Naval power relied on economic exhaustion to secure success, 'but exhaustion, unless accelerated by crushing blows, is an exceedingly slow process'.[52] Corbett reworked the point in *Some Principles*: 'great issues between nations at war have always been decided ... either by what your army can do against the enemy's territory and national life or else by the fear of what the fleet makes it possible for your army to do'.[53]

Henderson accepted economic blockade as the primary tool of seapower:

> There is no great power, and few small ones, to whom the loss of its sea-borne trade would be other than a most deadly blow: and there is no great power that is not far more vulnerable than when Great Britain, single handed, held her own against a European coalition. Colonies, commercial ports, dockyards, coaling stations, are so many hostages to fortune ... to fall as prey to the Power that is supreme at sea and can strike hard on land.

These attributes were essential to effective deterrence.[54] Sea power occupied a higher rank in the globalised economy of 1900 than it had in the era when it enabled Britain to defy Napoleon. If this was high praise from a British soldier, Henderson recognised that purely naval wars would be protracted, and 'antagonistic to the interests of the civilised world'. The Armed Neutrality of 1801 cast a long shadow, another argument Corbett would employ in the *Seven Years' War* and *Some Principles*. Henderson also stressed that a small army had great value for a seapower: 'an army supported by an invincible navy possesses a strength which is out of all proportion to its size', and that this was 'the secret of England's strength', before developing the contemporary point: 'Let it be remembered that the English army of 1808 was almost as small, compared with that of France, as it is today'.[55] Not only was the 'amphibious power of a great maritime state', if intelligently used, a 'most formidable menace' to even the greatest of military powers, but it was a far more terrible weapon now than it had been in Napoleon's day, because the 'substitution of steam for sails has given a force based upon the sea a mobility which has been hitherto unknown'. He valued surprise, the 'bolt from the blue', anticipating amphibious operations to enhance Britain's strategic position.[56] Furthermore, he had a specific target in mind. For centuries English/British policy in Europe had focused on the profound strategic threat posed by Antwerp and the Scheldt estuary in the hands of a pan-European hegemonic power. Northern Flanders dominated British policy in Europe, while imperial strategy focused on the defence of India: these concerns should shape the British Army. Because Britain was an amphibious power, British troops 'took more battleships than colours, and almost as many naval arsenals as land fortresses', prompting Henderson's 'great maxim that the naval strength of the enemy should be the first objective of the forces of a maritime power, both by land and sea'. So important was this point that he repeated it five pages later.[57] Corbett made this phrase a central pillar of his theory.[58]

Beyond imperial campaigning, Henderson examined the diversionary effect of peripheral campaigns and amphibious threats, and the impact of a small British force in Europe. Once seapower had been secured, he expected that the issue of any war would be settled in a major land battle, where 'even one or two army corps might turn the scales'.[59] This line offered some encouragement to 'continentalist' thinking. He applauded Mahan's geostrategic argument that railways were inferior strategic resources to rivers and oceans, being easily destroyed, of limited carrying capacity, and revealing the axis of possible operations to an intelligent enemy.[60] Strategic surprise from the sea had 'the very greatest value in war'.[61] With seapower an obvious vector for military genius: 'some great captain of the future may use the sea to further his purpose and surprise his adversary'.[62] There is an echo of that argument in the Fisher/Corbett Baltic plan of 1914.

Henderson argued that any future conflict with another great power would be 'a fierce, and possibly prolonged, conflict for the command of the sea: for it is absolutely certain that to-day, as in the day of Napoleon, the maritime supremacy of Great Britain must be the objective of its enemies'. In this maritime conflict the Army would capture positions on the seaboard, 'commanding or threatening the trade routes'. Amphibious operations would be facilitated by technology:

> Steam and electricity [the cable telegraph] have wrought great changes in the warfare of the sea, but it would be unwise in the extreme to imagine that in any future conflict the navy will be able to dispense with the help of the army in breaking down the enemy's resistance, in destroying his bases and supply deports, in cutting his communications, in mastering strategical [a term that Corbett adopted from Henderson or von Caemmerer] positions, and in protecting trade routes.

Consequently, 'The first necessity of imperial defence, so far as the army is concerned, is the maintenance of at least three army corps of regulars, ready to render immediate support when the navy asks for it.' They would 'follow the steps of Wellington, or attack another Sebastopol', to enhance Britain's command of the sea.[63] He ended by demanding the statesmen who directed the empire acquire an education that equipped them for their responsibilities, lamenting that: 'history, as taught in English Universities, took no notice of so trivial, though so practical, a subject as Imperial defence'.[64] Corbett was suitably inspired.

Henderson had a significant influence on national strategy in the Edwardian era: notably on Lord Esher, Corbett and the Haldane reforms that created the British Expeditionary Force and the Territorial Army. How far Corbett followed Henderson or how far the two men developed in parallel is hard to assess. In 1900 Henderson learnt hard lessons about incoherent strategy in South Africa, while Corbett approached the subject from a historical perspective in *The Successors of Drake*, his first joint service text. That synergy of ideas can be traced in Corbett's line: 'For defensive war a navy may suffice alone; but how fruitless, how costly and long drawn out a war must be that for lack of an adequate army is condemned to the defensive is the great lesson we have to learn in the failure of Drake's successors'. He doubted the lesson had been learnt.[65] This synergy reflected a shared agenda, rather than intellectual exchange. Neither man referenced the other, both were developing strategic and political ideas drawn from Maurice, Mahan, Clausewitz and Seeley for the British context. Both put command of the sea at the centre of their systems, with the combined action of army and navy the key to success. They resisted the unthinking, irrelevant 'Germanism' that came to dominate Army agendas after 1902.[66] Lord Esher, architect of higher defence coordination, lamented that Henderson's early death had deprived Britain of a Chief of Staff who understood the strategy of a global maritime empire. Although Henderson's lowly rank and social status made that thought visionary, it was shared by Wolseley, who had exploited sea control to secure strategic advantage on several occasions.[67] Corbett developed Henderson's argument that maritime power was central to a coherent imperial strategy, and cited him to demonstrate that some British soldiers understood war. However, Henry Wilson also recognised Henderson's influence: 'so brilliant a lecturer and so profound a thinker on military subjects'.[68] Henderson's Staff College rides to the Franco-Prussian battlefields shaped his continental obsessions.[69]

Henderson's early death left an intellectual void, one that Corbett filled. Corbett and Henderson had developed a 'British way' at roughly the same time, with Corbett only citing Henderson's posthumous text *The Science of War* of 1905.[70] Corbett would have been struck by the intellectual synergy, finding powerful support for his concept of British strategy as limited and maritime: Henderson was a logical alternative to the General Staff's continental-conscriptionist agenda, promoted by Repington of *The Times*, and Henry Spenser Wilkinson, a conservative advocate of General Staff and German agendas, writing in the *Morning Post*. While Henderson provided powerful arguments for a national maritime strategy, the key breakthrough was Corbett's willingness to 'develop' Clausewitz, following the arguments of General Rudolf von Caemmerer, which also appeared in English in 1905.[71]

Another soldier who addressed national strategy from a maritime perspective in 1905 was Colonel Charles Callwell RA, an outstanding Staff College student influenced by Maurice. Callwell served in India, Afghanistan and South Africa, at the Intelligence Branch, and in key naval bases at Sheerness, Devonport, Cork, Dover and Malta. His maritime theme began with *The Effect of Maritime Command on Land Campaigns since Waterloo* of 1897.[72] Having returned to the War Office in 1903 to work on imperial defence, Callwell linked Corbett, Maurice and Henderson in *Military Operations and Maritime Preponderance: Their Relations and Interdependence*, quoting *England in the Mediterranean* to emphasise the interdependence of land and sea operations, and the reality that, where possible, military operations were 'always preferable to the lengthy blockade'.[73] Callwell realised Corbett, no longer of 'the "Blue-water School"', understood that in a maritime nation the 'navy and its army must go hand in hand', adopting Corbett's argument that command of the sea was merely a means to an end, an end that must be secured on land.[74] Although there is no evidence that they met, the convergence of their thinking is significant. Callwell's public declaration of faith in a global/maritime strategy may have hindered his career. He was passed over for promotion in 1907 and retired to become a professional author. In the same year Henry Wilson became commandant and focused Camberley on continental operations, ending Corbett's lectures on maritime limited war, as Royal Marine Colonel George Aston left the staff. Aston's work on strategy and amphibious warfare would reach a wider audience before the outbreak of war, but it no longer interested the Army General Staff.[75] Despite the apparent synergy of their maritime thinking Corbett never mentioned Callwell; his textbooks were overtaken by Henderson's essays and Corbett's deeper engagement with German thought.

Stunning victories at Sadowa in 1866 and Sedan in 1870 brought German writing about war into British intellectual life, part of a wider fascination with all things German. This powerful progressive nation, with impressive scientific, economic and cultural resources, was linked to Britain by blood, history and a shared distrust of France. The 'German way' made strategic theory, war planning by a General Staff and mass conscript armies the acme of modern military professionalism, and brought Clausewitz's *On War* to wider attention. Clausewitz's theory was at once solidly grounded in past experience and systematically developed for modern use. His philosophical approach extracted patterns from the past, avoiding the mindless empiricism that characterised so much anglophone writing.[76] An English translation by Colonel J.J. Graham appeared in 1873; it found few buyers, but they included Maurice and Henderson, who brought it to Corbett's attention. Clausewitz helped Corbett integrate history and theory in military education. Strategic and operational concepts drawn from historical understanding would inform the critical output, sound doctrine.

Corbett began using German strategic writing around the turn of the century, after the First Naval Law of 1897 had exposed the Kaiser's desire for world power and naval might.[77] German strategic thought provided a suitable theoretical structure to organise the practical ideas of the Colomb brothers, enhance Mahan's programmatic Jominian structure, and develop the strategic template of Maurice and Henderson, who had recognised the limits of German practice in British conditions. The three Englishmen had understood that a British 'way' must place practical concerns above elegant theories.

Access to German thought had been eased by the translation of military histories, tactical manuals and strategic arguments, by specialist publishers targeting military readers.[78] The translations influenced British thinking, few recognising the inherent danger of reading across from a continental military power to a global maritime empire. German strategic thought was different: it rejected Western European Positivism, along with any attempt to link the natural sciences and human affairs, condemning 'all formal principles for military theory, and persistently stressed the overriding importance of free circumstantial study, historical change and moral force'.[79] By 1900 German thinking reflected the reality that the Second Reich had moved from a European status quo power to one obsessed with 'world power or decline'.[80] This dangerous combination of anxiety and ambition was fuelled by the anglophobic output of historian Heinrich von Treitschke.[81] Treitschke and his followers, who included Alfred Tirpitz and Friedrich von Bernhardi, thought war with England inevitable. Bernhardi's 1911 text *Germany and the Next War* startled many readers, not least Corbett. In 1914 Lord Bryce, a Liberal Germanophile was astonished by the:

> amazing doctrines proclaimed there, which strike at the root of all international morality, as well as of all international law, and which threaten a return to the primitive savagery when every tribe was wont to plunder and massacre its neighbours.

Bernhardi's views were:

> mainly based on the teachings of the famous professor of history, Heinrich von Treitschke. To readers in other countries – and, I trust, to most readers in Germany also – they will appear to be an outburst of militarism run mad, the product of a brain intoxicated by the love of war and by overweening national vanity. They would have deserved little notice, much less refutation, but for one deplorable fact – viz., that action has recently been taken by the Government of a great nation (though, as we hope and trust, without the approval of that nation) which is consonant with them, and seems to imply a belief in their soundness.[82]

The original proponent of such views, and perhaps the single most influential voice in late nineteenth-century strategy, was Colmar von der Goltz (1843–1916). Experience of the French 'People's War' in 1871 persuaded him that Germany needed a 'Nation in Arms', total national mobilisation. A militarist, Social Darwinist and ultra-nationalist, Goltz believed war to be inevitable, and good for society. He enjoyed the terrible beauty of battlefield carnage, sharing Arthur Schopenhauer's argument that the world was the product of blind, insatiable, malignant, metaphysical will. He predicted a final struggle between Germany and England for world power. In 1914 he practised what he preached: as military Governor of Belgium he executed unarmed civilians in reprisal for guerrilla activity. Goltz's key text appeared in English as *The Nation in Arms* in 1887, with a second English edition in 1906. While he recognised England was different, primarily a maritime state, 'with all its interests dependent upon and bound up with the sea', Goltz argued that it would need to upgrade its military forces 'or it will gradually sink both in power and in its influence upon the Continent'.[83] That British soldiers read Goltz is certain: many accepted his advice. While sea power was a major advantage in war, even if the fleet was not directly engaged in land battles, he dismissed amphibious warfare under modern European conditions. His contemptuous references to the abortive French expedition to the Baltic in 1870 shaped the British General Staff's rejection of Fisher's Baltic plans both before and during the First World War.[84] Had the soldiers read further they might have encountered Goltz's admission that Germany would face serious strategic consequences if it lost command of the Baltic, a point Corbett developed in *England in the Seven Years' War*.[85]

Ultimately *The Nation in Arms* was a passionate plea for a return to a pre-modern Germany, where militarised aristocrats led armies of hardy peasants, securing an empire of the sword in decisive battle, even if the glory proved transitory.[86] It may have been the single most dangerous book of the age, the cutting edge of Treitschke's vision of German world domination. Anglophobe and bellicose, arrogant and contemptuous, yet dominated by a profound anxiety that the modern world was sapping German vitality. The book proved all too influential, and not just in Germany. Successive editions made the tactical offensive and 'decisive battle' the antidote to the military caste's loss of prestige and the rise of democracy, a clarion call for industrialised blood-letting to purify the nation of the ills of modernity. Not that Goltz was alone – such thoughts echoed across the Continent in the early twentieth century – but he was the first to give them a voice. Between 1880 and 1914 he was more widely read than Clausewitz, and far more influential. His impact in Britain can be traced in demands for compulsory training, quasi-military youth movements and conscription,[87] the new General Staff's growing obsession with decisive battle, and their rejection of Britain's strategic experience.

In 1904 Corbett began making systematic use of German theory, probably at Slade's suggestion, acquiring Clausewitz and the 1896 translation of Goltz's *The Conduct of War*, marking passages on maritime issues with a characteristic faint pencil line. Here he encountered an acute intellect, thoroughly immersed in contemporary conflicts, able to express ideas that could only be extracted from Mahan by prolonged labour.[88]

Between two opponents of approximately equal strength victory will finally fall to the one who remains master of the seas. The latter will exhaust the financial resources of the other by destroying his commerce and interrupting all transmarine intercourse, thus undermining his military power also.[89]

Furthermore, Goltz recognised the distinctive character of British strategy: the desire 'to destroy the cradle of the Russian Navy in the Black Sea' justified the massive operation at Sevastopol.[90] His explanation of how Germany would lose the world war reflected a willingness to bring everything to ruin, rather than accept decline. Echoes of *Götterdämmerung*'s cleansing flood were obvious – anything but democracy and mediocrity. Goltz's cavalier treatment of Clausewitz, widely criticised by fellow Germans, did not endear him to Corbett. It was Goltz who transformed Clausewitz into Basil Liddell Hart's 'Mahdi of Mass'.[91]

While Goltz railed against the modern world, Lieutenant General Rudolf von Caemmerer (1845–1911), another veteran of 1870–1, military educator, historian and student of military thought, helped Corbett analyse Clausewitz.[92] Published in 1905, *The Development of Strategical Sciences during the Nineteenth Century* dismissed Jomini as 'only an able staff officer', who tried to reduce the work of Napoleon, 'a great artist of wonderful penetration', to a system, only to render it rigid, fixed and permanent, just as the world began to change. While this static model appealed to a certain type of military mind, Clausewitz's system had 'the enormous advantage' of the '*capacity for further development*'.[93] Corbett used this quality to distinguish his argument from Mahan's static Jominian model, and contest the General Staff's 'German way'. The English edition of Caemmerer appeared just as the War Course began teaching strategy as a distinct subject; both Corbett and War Course director Edmond Slade acquired copies.[94]

Caemmerer considered Clausewitz 'the most prominent theorist', the 'real philosopher of war', who had provided spiritual training for the Prussian armies of 1866 and 1870–1. Much of his analysis would have registered with Corbett, notably his portrait of Clausewitz, a cultured soldier with 'a comprehensive and thorough knowledge of Military History'.[95] Caemmerer noted Clausewitz's declaration that his book was intended to 'iron out many creases in the heads of strategists and statesmen, and at least to show the object of actions and the real point to be aimed at'.[96] Clausewitz wanted to guide the self-education of future leaders, not accompany them into battle. His stress on moral forces and the play of chance over geometrical forms released the Prussian army from artificiality, and stressed the political purpose of war. *Some Principles* had the same purpose, because there were all too many intellectual creases in Edwardian England.

Corbett realised Caemmerer's error in rejecting Hans Delbrück's argument that Clausewitz had intended to develop a theory of limited war. Caemmerer accepted that Clausewitz meant to develop both forms, divided by the political object, but still believed defeating the enemy army was the universal key to success, citing Clausewitz's 1830–1 plan for a limited war with France.[97] Corbett noted this passage in 1911, and brought it to Hankey's attention in 1914.[98] Critically, Clausewitz believed that British strategy in an unlimited continental war in 1830–1 would 'threaten the extended French coastline, in order to detain there considerably stronger forces of the enemy', while limited war could advance larger political aims.[99] This was the conceptual basis of the Fisher–Corbett Baltic plans of 1914.

Caemmerer believed that the final development of *On War* would have emphasised the unlimited/limited contrast, replacing book 7 on attacks without a view to a great decision with one on attack with a limited object.

> The moment this change is made, the whole book is a perfect production, an absolutely finished and harmonious structure, and a theory of war for statesmen and Generals, in conformity with the scientific knowledge and experience of 1830.

It seems Corbett agreed. Caemmerer's Clausewitz was a practical soldier, focused on the present, and, as Delbrück observed, primarily a military writer, only secondarily a historian.[100] Corbett recognised the synergy with his own work, emphasising limited and defensive maritime war as 'Britain's traditional way of war'.[101] Not only was *England in the Seven Years' War* of 1907 a Clausewitzian text, but the Clausewitz in question was Caemmerer's, not Goltz's.[102] Caemmerer's disagreement with von der Goltz on the value of defence was profound; he argued that parrying a blow and counter-attacking were critical elements of defence, satisfied Russia had defeated Napoleon in 1812 by defending.[103]

Clausewitz and Caemmerer equipped Corbett to master the Edwardian defence debate. He was not persuaded by Mahan, Jomini or Goltz.

Clausewitz's rejection of war as a mechanism, elevating chance and contingency into 'friction', nowhere more than at sea, and where the enemy always had agency, appealed to his legal mind. Clausewitz equipped Corbett to recognise the different strategic cultures of Britain and Germany could share a common theoretical root, which transformed his thinking between 1904 and 1907. In 1904, *England in the Mediterranean* used history to address a contemporary debate; in 1907, *England in the Seven Years' War* employed a single conflict as a Clausewitzian case study to establish a generic strategic model, a 'British way' to inform future decisions. At first glance both books appear to be histories, but their intellectual rationales were profoundly different.

CHAPTER 8

Shaping the 'British Way'

Corbett developed his argument amidst a deepening crisis in national strategy, prompted by the attempt to impose order on long-established maritime assumptions, improve inter-service cohesion, and reduce costs after the Second Anglo-Boer War. Before 1900, the assumptions underlying an unwritten British strategy were maritime and imperial, tempered by the needs of home defence, little changed from the Napoleonic conflict that Victorians called 'the Great War'. While aspects of that strategy had been considered by Maurice and Henderson there was no synthetic overview to shape the education of both services, influence national policy and support decision-making in the event of war. The bitter experience of tactical defeat in the Boer War had renewed military interest in continental models. Reading translated German texts without a thorough immersion in national strategic experience led many British soldiers to conflate professionalism with mass conscript armies and military control of national strategy. It is not clear if the soldiers understood how profoundly these methods would change the nation.

For centuries Britain had limited military operations to naval targets, in Flanders, Portugal, the Danish Narrows and the Mediterranean, within a strategy that combined sea control, economic warfare and financial support for allies. It did not create mass armies or engage continental powers in 'decisive' battle. This approach had not failed, and Edwardian Britain remained a global maritime power, the economy dominated by trade and capital flows. Having no intention of attacking another great power, it did not need detailed war plans like those produced by the Great German General Staff and its French counterpart. When the old consensus broke down in 1905, following the Anglo-French Entente and the First Moroccan Crisis, Corbett responded to the challenge by restating old realities in modern strategic terms. He did not invent a 'British way'; he recovered it from past practice, using Clausewitzian theory to provide the intellectual coherence needed to debate with continental alternatives.

The strategic debate began when Prime Minister Arthur Balfour attempted to reduce the cost of national strategy after the Boer War, using Lord Esher's War Office Committee to impose long-overdue reforms, and the CID to develop an essentially maritime security policy. He appointed Admiral Sir John Fisher First Sea Lord in late 1904 to overhaul and economise the Navy; both Esher and Fisher expected to find most of their savings from the Army budget. Fisher's reforms, which attacked entrenched privilege through standardised initial training for officers, including Naval Engineers and Royal Marines, alarmed the Conservative right.[1] Prompted by Admiral Lord Charles Beresford, embittered by his failure to become First Sea Lord, Conservatives in Parliament, the Army and the Navy challenged Fisher's reforms, including the iconic all-big-gun battleship HMS *Dreadnought*, and the shift of resources from distant seas to home waters. The constant sniping of Beresford and his 'Syndicate of Discontent' in Parliament and Tory journals undermined the Navy's credibility without offering a coherent alternative. The controversy distracted attention from the General Staff's attempts to enlarge the Army, initially in order to address ridiculous fears of invasion, and then for the diplomatic role of sustaining the 1904 Anglo-French Entente. The Entente made Germany the obvious military planning target, and raised the possibility that the next war would open with another rapid German defeat of France, as in 1870, before sea power could take effect. Contemptuous references to the French fleet in the Baltic during that conflict, and erroneous assessments of the impact of Britain's Baltic Fleet in the Crimean War enabled the General Staff to argue that only the rapid commitment of an army to Europe could sustain the national interest. Previous strategic thinking, for wars with France and Russia, necessarily reflected the need for limited maritime strategies, with small expeditionary armies.

The Liberal governments of Sir Henry Campbell-Bannerman and Herbert Asquith from 1906 effectively sidelined the CID, which they disliked on ideological grounds, fearing the 'experts' might take control. They refused to settle national strategy or choose between the services, exploiting War Office plans for continental operations to maintain Anglo-French relations without creating a suitable army or making a commitment to act, changing the Entente into an alliance.[2] While the Liberals instinctively favoured small defence budgets and the Navy, their failure to choose a grand strategy created a crisis in August 1914.[3]

The idea of reducing national strategy to doctrine to shape the policies and programmes of the services can be traced to George Clarke. Despite his military career, Clarke was a maritime strategist with extensive imperial service. While Corbett supported Clarke's plan for the CID to direct national strategy, their strategic concepts would be separated by distinctly different cultural assumptions and political ideologies. Clarke's self-aggrandising programme would be defeated by vested interests and political weakness, and he returned to colonial government. That it came so close to success reflected his considerable powers of organisation, and the support of Esher, Balfour and, initially, Fisher. Corbett created the essential doctrine primer, the 'Green Pamphlet' of 1906, and Clarke was quick to approve, but he had already lost the battle to make the CID the national strategic centre. By 1916 he no longer recognised his own ideas, because Corbett had infused them with progressive Liberal values, and aligned them with the radical thinking of Jacky Fisher. Clarke's project addressed the persistent inability of the British state to treat defence planning as anything other than a cost-saving exercise, impacted by vested interests.

Between 1902 and 1914 successive governments evaded their responsibility to establish national strategy, to avoid political problems and exploit the diplomatic benefits of an Anglo-French Entente, without the slightest intention of creating the military capacity to meet the implied commitment. Defence coordination had been discussed for three decades after the Franco-Prussian War, but it required the salutary shock of the Boer War to galvanise the state into action. After several high-profile enquiries, Balfour had established the CID in late 1902, transforming a dysfunctional Cabinet Defence Committee into a mechanism for strategic direction. Balfour considered Britain 'pre-eminently a great Naval, Indian and Colonial Power'.[4] This satisfied the Admiralty. The CID would meet regularly: the political and professional heads of the armed forces, the Foreign Secretary and the prime minister were the core members.

Balfour's primary concern was to reduce defence spending, with a semblance of strategic logic. The primacy of maritime strategy informed the work of the War Office Reconstruction, or Esher, Committee that sat over the winter of 1903–4, re-shaping military administration along lines similar to the Admiralty. The committee consisted of Reginald Brett 2nd Viscount

Esher, George Clarke, who detested the War Office, and Admiral Sir John Fisher, commander-in-chief at Portsmouth. They persuaded Balfour to adopt Fisher's proposal that the CID have a permanent naval and military staff, removing the higher direction of war from the service ministries. In May 1904 the CID acquired a secretariat: Esher and Fisher persuaded Clarke the post would be one of power and influence. War Office objections were ignored.[5] Fisher expected the CID to enshrine naval primacy in strategy, while the Army took significant cuts, becoming 'a projectile to be fired by the Navy'. Balfour's use of the CID to restrict the Army to imperial defence and sea control missions met bitter opposition from soldiers at the War Office. As Nicholas d'Ombrain observed: 'One influential group, centred mainly in the Operations and Intelligence branches, were firmly of the opinion that the Army was receiving less and less of its fair share of responsibility for the maintenance of national and imperial defence.'[6] A continental strategy would change that.

Anticipating the fall of Balfour's government, in 1905 the Admiralty moved to secure its dominance of British defence policy just as the Russo-Japanese War removed the need to focus on the North-West Frontier and the First Moroccan Crisis shifted attention to Europe. Clarke and the Admiralty agreed that Army reinforcements designed for India should be available for combined operations against Germany, establishing a CID sub-committee to develop suitable plans, with executive authority. Aware they were about to be railroaded into a subordinate amphibious role, the soldiers refused to join the sub-committee. They invented a home defence mission, which lacked credibility, given the Royal Navy had more than twice the strength of the German fleet. Refusing to cooperate with the CID undermined the principle of civilian primacy, a profoundly dangerous step in a liberal democracy, one that ministers should have resisted. Similarly unconstitutional ideas, and many of the same men, were prominent when the 'Curragh Mutiny' sabotaged the policy of a democratically elected government.

Status anxiety and a confused sense of professionalism led the soldiers to advocate continental-style mass conscript armies, effectively an alternative national strategy. Britain had long since rejected these ideas, on constitutional, strategic and economic grounds. Mass armies were unnecessary for home defence, ill-suited to imperial roles, and a threat to civil authority. Field Marshal Lord Roberts was persuaded to resign from the CID by officers on the General Staff, Henry Wilson and Sir William Nicholson, and campaign publicly for a conscript home defence force.[7] The 'continental' agenda would be supported by social conservatives across the decade between the creation of the CID and the outbreak of war.

The Entente necessarily encouraged more structured military planning, to meet the novel possibility of operating on the Continent alongside a major ally. In August 1905 George Clarke prompted Balfour to ask how quickly the War Office could move two Army corps to Belgium.[8] The General Staff war-gamed using a British force to secure Belgium against a German attempt to outflank French positions on the Meuse. Conveniently concluding that this force saved the French, this option became the basis of military policy. In August 1914 it became national strategy. Many soldiers had expected Germany to attack France in 1905, but Fisher sent the Channel Fleet into the Baltic and Germany backed down.[9] By contrast Germany did not see the contemptibly small British Army as a threat.

In August 1905 the CID set up the Combined Operations Sub-Committee to study landing on the German coast. After a five-week delay – apparently there was no-one at the War Office over the summer, despite the crisis – the soldiers bluntly rejected combined operations and called for the army to be sent to France. Clarke, Esher and Fisher rejected the idea of the Army linking up with the French. Certain the French would be defeated, Fisher did not want the Army caught up in the disaster.[10] The General Staff refused to cooperate with the Admiralty on amphibious operations, asserting that naval plans were outdated and unrealistic. This was patently false.[11] Repington, the War Office's unofficial intermediary, encouraged the French to reject the Admiralty model, and oppose Baltic operations.[12] Clarke, Esher and Fisher urged Balfour to convene the sub-committee and force the solders to cooperate, to impose a maritime strategy. Balfour's calculated inaction condemned the CID to strategic irrelevance.[13] Fisher felt betrayed, withdrawing his support from the CID over the winter of 1905–6 and refusing to cooperate with War Office continental policy. Political weakness crushed Clarke's vision of a combined service General Staff, reducing the CID to an impotent office of routine.

The opening of Anglo-French military talks in December 1905 implied military support might be provided in the event of war. With Russia gravely weakened by defeat and revolution, France, vulnerable to German pressure, urged the new Liberal government to provide more concrete assurances. The talks became 'official' on 15 January 1906, but Foreign Secretary Grey, who wanted to preserve peace by balancing France and Germany through the period of Russian recovery, and Secretary of State for War Richard Haldane kept them from Cabinet colleagues.

In December 1905 Director of Military Operations (DMO) James Grierson, DNI Ottley and Captain George Ballard of the NID examined a possible war with Germany over Morocco, just as the Algeciras Conference was assembling under the guns of Britain's combined Atlantic and Mediterranean fleets. Grierson insisted on deploying the Army to Antwerp within a month, arguing the obvious *casus belli* would be a German violation of Belgian neutrality.[14] Grierson's insistence on Belgium would prevent the British becoming entangled in French strategy, and remained consistent with the diplomatic and strategic focus on Flanders and the Scheldt, keeping the Army linked to the Navy, not the French. Recognising the importance of public opinion, Grierson presciently reasoned that defending Belgium would be a more popular *casus belli* than aiding France. In April 1907, Prime Minister Campbell-Bannerman doubted the public would approve of British troops being sent to the Continent; Grey agreed, but felt it essential to prevent 'Antwerp, and the Belgian Channel ports falling into the hands of a hostile Great Power'.[15] Russian weakness ensured France accepted the British decision.

Haldane's development of an expeditionary force capable of deploying quickly to Europe led hitherto recalcitrant soldiers to accept reductions and reforms. It also encouraged them to project a 'military' national strategy, leading, inexorably, to a mass conscript army.[16] The ultimate object was military primacy in defence.[17] This approach turned a temporary meeting of minds with the obvious enemy into the basis of national strategy and defence policy. The influence of the 'German way' on this development is hard to quantify but impossible to ignore. Esher was not convinced: he took military advice from General Sir John French, an advocate of combined strategy, while Field Marshal Kitchener was equally averse to being subordinated to the French.

Between May 1906 and August 1910, the military conversations lost their diplomatic impetus. Russia's revival reduced French anxieties, allowing successive prime ministers to block closer military links, and use defence cuts to fund social reform. Campbell-Bannerman treated the talks as a temporary measure for specific circumstances.[18] National strategy remained business as usual, built around maritime power. New DMO Spencer Ewart (1906–10) retained Grierson's plans to deploy the BEF to Belgium, reducing Anglo-French military conversations to a discussion of rail movements and logistics.

While Esher accepted the need to secure Antwerp, he opposed any suggestion of placing the Army under French command, knowing it would infuriate both Fisher and King Edward. Fisher dismissed the idea of a continental mission for the British Army as idiotic folly, blowing up a CID meeting in November 1909 by declaring the Germans would take care to wipe out the BEF. He feared Haldane's projected Ministry of Defence would give national strategy a continental focus and degrade the Navy.[19]

The Cabinet's reluctance to resolve the issue resulted in a complete mismatch between the Army's 'continental' policy, which lacked strategic substance, and the Royal Navy's global power, which had blocked German aggression in 1905–6. Policy and strategy suffered. Britain no longer had a security policy. Deeply frustrated, Clarke left the CID in July 1907; it was only a clearing house for practical issues that might arise in the event of a war, the nature of which it had no power to discuss, let alone determine. He was replaced by former DNI Charles Ottley, who made no attempt to settle policy, or take sides in the bitter arguments that followed. In 1909 the CID effectively allowed the War Office to sit 'in judgement on the Admiralty in the Beresford enquiry', but never challenged the strategic role of a continental army, allowing the General Staff to replace Grierson's plan to secure the Belgian coast with one that linked up with the French. When Esher protested the Staff fobbed him off with blatant lies.[20] The government, more concerned to hide the military aspects of the Entente from their own backbenchers, remained silent.

Shortly after Fisher's retirement, Henry Wilson took over as DMO. A cunning and obsessive operator of deeply ingrained Ulster Unionist and social conservative views, Wilson's enthusiasm for conscription was political as well as military, hoping a 'nation in arms' would preserve domestic political order, and prevent Irish Home Rule. Above and beyond his rejection of civilian direction, and the policy of the elected government, Wilson dismissed the Navy as a strategic asset. He saw the Navy as the defence force for the United Kingdom and Empire, releasing the Army to join a climactic land battle shortly after the outbreak of war. In his dreams, British troops made a significant contribution.[21] In 1927 maritime strategist Charles Callwell revealed the scale of Wilson's delusion by publishing his diaries.[22]

The death of Edward VII shifted the political balance: George V did not intervene in political and diplomatic decision-making. Prime Minister Asquith's profound lack of interest in strategy meant the full CID only met three times in 1910, to ratify the technical work of sub-committees. Forced to act by the Agadir Crisis, he assembled the CID on 23 August 1911 to secure political and diplomatic objects. He had no intention of adopting a continental strategy.[23] Henry Wilson's proposal to deploy the BEF to France would support diplomacy, but lacked strategic substance. Only four divisions were earmarked for a continental role – a policy that remained in place until August 1914. Wilson supported his argument by deliberately understating Russian army manpower. Admiral Sir Arthur Wilson's memorandum was restricted to naval means by the refusal of the Army to cooperate.[24] Asquith prevaricated, leaving Britain with two strategies, based on separate services, denying the Navy the essential military strike force. This was pure political opportunism, avoiding difficult decisions. The Entente helped prevent war for a decade, at minimum political and economic cost, but when it failed, Britain was left without a coherent grand strategy.

The Cabinet remained split over a continental role down to the outbreak of war; four ministers resigned over the decision for war.[25] Where Grierson's plan to secure the Flanders ports and Antwerp, flanking any German advance into France, served British aims, Wilson's served Army ambition. Wilson's obsession with a short war reinforced the problem. He did not criticise French plans to attack with a numerically inferior army.[26] His support for the Curragh Mutiny revealed a profound contempt for civilian government and, when Asquith and his Cabinet gave way, they emboldened the conservative soldiers to press for action in August 1914, backed by political and media allies. Britain went to war in 1914 without a strategy; the government neither challenged the continental notions advanced by the soldiers nor provided the resources to make them credible. British policy, as the Kaiser famously observed, was 'contemptible'.[27] Whatever it was, it was not a British strategy, and it bore no relation to Corbett's work.

The status of the CID was further reduced when Ottley resigned in early 1912. His deputy, Royal Marine Colonel Maurice Hankey, secured the reversion by assuring Esher of his fundamental opposition to a continental policy. Once in post, Hankey blocked Esher's demands to discuss the military policy of the Entente, lest the resulting controversy prompt the government to abolish the committee.

By 1913–14 British strategy had reached a fundamental impasse. Esher's minority report on the Invasion Inquiry condemned the government's position, but was withheld to help Asquith resolve the Irish Home Rule crisis. Esher opposed the soldiers' strategy, and the French alliance some of them favoured, warning Asquith that the soldiers 'were entirely engrossed with the idea of fighting the Germans on the Meuse, and are ready to sacrifice anything to this idea'. He recognised that the Admiralty was using the possibility of an invasion to detain two divisions in the United Kingdom, for amphibious operations. He favoured a dominant navy supported by a small professional army, on eighteenth-century lines.[28] There are obvious parallels with Corbett's *England in the Seven Years' War*, the classic case study of British maritime strategy.[29] It is unlikely the government would have survived a public discussion of Entente military arrangements, backbench Liberal MPs would have been horrified by the exposure of links with France. Later, Hankey claimed he had not realised what the soldiers were doing, even in late July 1914, despite Corbett and Esher having pointed it out to him in strikingly simple terms.[30] Hankey may have deluded himself, believing that no Liberal government would dare adopt the soldiers' policy.

Ultimately, as Esher and others recognised, the under-resourced continental option was a strategic disaster in waiting. War exposed the absurdity of espousing a European role with 'the small professional army of an island empire built upon sea power'.[31] While it had helped sustain the Entente, a four-division BEF had no power to deter Germany. This mattered because Britain, perhaps the ultimate satiated power, was especially anxious to preserve peace. The Navy had deterred Germany in September 1905, while the capacity to do so in future would have been enhanced by adding a military strike force, and adopting a maritime strategy based on economic warfare and coastal power projection, in line with British strategic experience.

Corbett's engagement with national as opposed to naval strategic theory began in 1900, while his concept of a distinctive 'British way' took shape in 1903–4, after he began lecturing to the Naval War Course and taking policy cues from George Clarke. Having explained the limits of naval strategy in 1900 it appears he acquired *On War* in 1904, along with Goltz's *Conduct of War*, and the publications of Caemmerer and Henderson in 1905. These texts equipped him to analyse national strategy, contextualising naval operations, as the struggle between the services deepened. This critical period of intellectual development can be traced in his *England in the Mediterranean* of 1904, which recognised British strategic exceptionalism, and *England in the Seven Years' War* of 1907, which demonstrated how the 'British way' worked, using Clausewitzian theory. Clausewitz's belated recognition of limited war as a political choice, which had prompted him to shift from a theoretical 'Absolute War' to a real world 'Unlimited–Limited' dichotomy proved critical. This conceptual breakthrough, and the incomplete nature of *On War*, left ample opportunity for development, as Caemmerer argued. *On War* had not hitherto featured in anglophone naval thought.

In his initial contributions to the Naval War Course, Corbett used contemporary arguments, primarily supplied by George Clarke. To establish intellectual credibility he located lectures on applied history for naval professionals in the academic tradition, while analysing contemporary political and strategic issues for the *Monthly Review*, work that attracted the support of Jacky Fisher. Corbett recognised that conscription and continental warfare would undermine core aspects of national identity, including liberal democracy and civilian primacy, while maritime warfare was integral to the structure of modern Britain. The 'British way' was not an 'original' argument, but a sophisticated development of existing work, refined through historical research and a broad engagement with contemporary domestic and imperial politics. It was only truly relevant to the Edwardian empire.[32] Mahan's *The Influence of Sea Power upon History 1660–1783* had been a publishing phenomenon, with multiple editions and many translations, but *Some Principles of Maritime Strategy* took almost a decade to sell 1,500 copies. It was neither a universal text, nor a replacement for Mahan.

From the outset, Corbett located his arguments in British experience, linking Clausewitz's ideas with those of Sir Francis Bacon, godfather of empirical Enlightenment science, to provide an English endorsement for German theory and emphasise Britain's distinctive strategic requirements. 'It is much to be regretted that Clausewitz did not see with Bacon's eyes and work out the full comprehensiveness of his doctrine [of limited war].'[33] Corbett followed Maurice and Henderson in rejecting the prevailing obsession with German methods. He detested the underlying ideology and endorsed Caemmerer's criticism of Goltz for rejecting Clausewitz's stress on the superiority of defence over attack. Goltz's false argument sustained his claim that wars would be short, inspiring the 'offensive' approach that dominated military thought before 1914.[34]

In the summer of 1905, Corbett told Fisher, then First Sea Lord, that the draft Admiralty plans he had been shown were amateurish rubbish, prompting an increase in the War Course's strategic content. DNI Charles Ottley explained that the Navy needed a strategic education, without discussing current strategic concepts, which were 'essentially of a secret character'. He delegated this task to Corbett, a civilian, who would be supervised by War Course director Edmond Slade. Slade and Corbett radically enhanced the Navy's intellectual armoury, introducing Clausewitz and the higher level of strategy to ensure that officers were equipped to debate strategy and policy with soldiers and statesmen at the CID. Corbett would analyse naval operations in the context of national strategy. Fisher, Ottley and Slade shaped Corbett's development from an empirical analyst of the 'British way' into a classical strategist, albeit one dominated by the pedagogic demands of a specific audience. He taught 'sound principles' that equipped naval officers to think and act strategically.[35] He did not, as some have argued, try to teach them their business: he taught them how to work with soldiers and statesmen in a national context, employing standard strategic terms and logical thought. He used Clausewitz's system to render British experience coherent, in case studies and a doctrine primer that illustrated strategic principles.

Corbett introduced the historical case studies with five lectures:

1. Need of a theory or Science of Strategy to co-ordinate Strategical Principles into a Logical Order
2. The System of Clausewitz
3–4. The Essentials of a True Naval Defensive
5. Limited and Unlimited War.

The course concluded with lectures on 'Means of Controlling the Enemy's Strategy' and varying types of blockade, a critical strategic concern between 1900 and 1914.[36] The new course began at Devonport in November 1905, shortly before Corbett delivered Clausewitzian lectures on the Seven Years' War at the Army Staff College, Camberley: Commandant Henry Rawlinson, a student of G.F.R. Henderson, was receptive.[37] He suggested 'The functions of the Army in relation to gaining Command of the Sea, and in bringing war with a Continental power to a successful conclusion', paraphrasing Henderson's last essay. These lectures evolved into *England in the Seven*

Years' War: A Study in Combined Strategy.[38] Corbett stressed they would 'treat mainly of how we can confine enemy's strategy if we are working with an ally as in 7 years war. Also gave my definition of naval strategy & said any army against navy talk the most improvident expenditure of national force for a weak military power.'[39] Rawlinson was delighted:

> I quite agree to laying before the students at this College both sides of any question, still at the same time I think it hardly advisable to demonstrate to them the uselessness in European war of Naval and Military co-operation.
>
> We fully realize that so far as the British Empire is concerned in European war where Naval objectives in the first instance must be para-mount, and it seems almost probable that it may be necessary to call on the Army to co-operate in order to completely attain these objectives moreover, even when the enemy's Naval bases have been captured or destroyed, we think that the employment of land forces will be obliga-tory, in order to bring our opponent, whoever he may be, to complete submission, even though these armies may not be wholly composed of British troops.
>
> What are your views on these matters?[40]

This was Henderson's argument. Corbett's lectures were successful.[41]

Clausewitz's conceptual framework helped Corbett to identify the core elements of British practice, he replaced Prussian history with British material, material developed for this purpose. Critically he followed Clausewitz in creating a system with the 'capacity for further development', elegantly exploiting a text dominated by total war on the continent of Europe to explain limited maritime global war.[42] These insights emerged from War Course and Staff College teaching, working with Edmond Slade, and engaging with a German admiral.

Rear Admiral Kurt von Maltzahn, director of the German naval academy, published 'What Lessons has General von Clausewitz's Work "*On War*" for the Naval Officer?' in the official journal *Marine Rundschau* in June 1905. The essay made extensive use of Alfred von Schlieffen's introduction to the current fifth German edition of *On War*. Schlieffen, Chief of the Great German General Staff, was the highest authority. Translated by the NID, and cyclostyled for the Naval War Course in March 1906, the essay was soon in Corbett's hands.[43] Corbett's marginalia contest many of the admiral's arguments, the same method he used when responding to Fisher's critics. Maltzahn reckoned books 1, 2 and 8 essential. His reading of *On War* took 'decisive' battle and the offensive operational emphasis of the contemporary 'German way' to sea, arguing that Britain would be defeated if it lost command of the sea in battle. Corbett rejected Schlieffen's emphasis on the importance of destroying the enemy's forces, and Maltzahn's claim that Nelson belonged to the 'decisive battle' school.[44] Yet Schlieffen's argument that Clausewitz's theory was 'founded on war experience' provided an essential pedagogic tool, one Corbett linked to Maltzahn's explicit attempt to persuade naval officers to use *On War*. The admiral argued that naval officers must view war from the highest perspective, and recognise that general principles could be transferred between war on land and sea. Providing 'a common mental training' for both arms was now essential as imperial conflicts involving both services were becoming more common, even for Germany. It was far more useful in the British context.

Corbett adopted Maltzahn's argument that blockade was an alternative to the military occupation of territory, forcing an enemy 'to make peace, through the injury done to his commerce, his industries, and his financial position'. Maltzahn replaced Clausewitz's occupation of a nation's territory with the occupation of sea communications, 'on which its life depends'. He did so because naval warfare was 'an imperfect form of war', one where victory in battle led only to the enemy's frontier, not the occupation of his territory and the imposition of peace, relying on such indirect methods as blockade and coastal raids.

> Only where a superior army enables the victor in the naval fighting to carry on a land war, or where the loser on account of the great susceptibility of his interests at sea, is forced to conclude peace, will the course of the war be otherwise.

This passage, which Corbett marked, may be the origin of his argument 'Since men live upon the land . . .'.[45]

Clausewitz's ideas could be developed for navies, 'if they are looked at from the highest standpoint'.[46] This is precisely what Corbett did, taking his cue from Caemmerer's stress on the open-ended nature of *On War*. Maltzahn's essay can be traced in *Some Principles*, where Corbett stressed:

the gradual elucidation of the theory of war ... has been almost entirely the work of soldiers, but so admirable is the work they have done, and so philosophical the method they have adopted, that a very natural tendency has arisen to assume that their broad-based conclusions are of universal application.

While Corbett followed Maltzahn in adapting core aspects of military theory, he concluded 'the country we have to travel is radically different'.[47]

Maltzahn adapted Clausewitz's stress on the tactical superiority of the defensive for the weaker side at sea: 'he who adopts it need not go far from his reserves and his harbours of retreat, whereby he runs less risks in action, and retains, in a naval sense "the advantage of position".[48] He thought Clausewitz's failure to discuss naval aspects of the Revolutionary and Napoleonic wars understandable, as a continental soldier only saw its effect on land. Corbett disagreed, noting 'Jomini appreciated it', before posing the question: 'How else was naval success ever decisive?'[49]

Maltzahn developed Clausewitz's limited war plan against France of 1830, from book 8 of On War, which noted that British amphibious power could draw off French troops, as 'a perfect example of the advantage which the command of the sea has to the aggressor, to whom the sea serves as a base'. This argument was especially potent in the British context. Then the admiral lost his grip, claiming seapower, secure communications and lines of retreat enabled the British Army to play an 'important part, really greater than its numbers warranted' in the Napoleonic wars, especially in Iberia, crediting that campaign with 'deciding Napoleon's destiny'. This misreading of Mahan provoked a rebuttal: 'Quite untrue. Her object was to deprive him of a province & to make a diversion. Here Maltzahn assumes destruction of forces is the only end of war!'[50]

While he stressed the utility of Clausewitz's theory at sea, Maltzahn offered no general theory of his own, using specific examples to encourage German naval officers to think for themselves. Corbett would develop Maltzahn's essay, and some of his methods, for the British context. In 1908 Longman, Corbett's publisher, produced an English edition of Maltzahn's Naval Warfare of 1905.[51] Maltzahn, a follower of Mahan and the geopolitical theorist and German imperialist Friedrich Ratzel, condemned British policy in the Napoleonic wars as the self-interested pursuit of its own interests, bound up with its status as 'the Sea Power that ruled the world', reflecting contemporary German agendas and Treitschke's mix of fear and envy. Little wonder that Corbett treated the opinions of contemporary Germans with caution. Maltzahn's essay, printed on 30 March 1906, had a significant impact on the 'Green Pamphlet', which appeared seven months later.[52]

The success of Corbett's strategy lectures prompted Fisher to add a planning role to the educational mission, as Corbett explained in *The Times*. Both functions were tied to the dissemination of national doctrine. Critically, Corbett did not work in a vacuum, nor did he invent new ways of thinking about war, strategy and sea power. He applied precision and logic to contemporary arguments, too often the province of passion and special pleading, shaping a system that addressed the security needs of a global maritime empire in an age of uncertainty, and enhanced the intellectual equipment of a dynamic, changing navy in an age of anxiety. Standing outside service tribalism, focused on national and imperial issues, he adapted distinctive strategic traditions to serve the agendas of Clarke, Fisher and, beyond them, a Liberal Cabinet with little understanding of, or interest in, war. Corbett's lectures and texts were present-minded. He used history to recover British strategy, not to explain the past. Nor did he design a strategic system of universal applicability, historical insight was a by-product of his 'textbooks'.[53]

Corbett crafted the 'Green Pamphlet', the first national strategic doctrine primer, alongside *England in the Seven Years' War*, which began life as lecture series on the War Course and at Camberley. These Clausewitzian texts were also liberal; war remained a policy choice, not Colmar von der Goltz's nihilistic explosion of violence in pursuit of 'world power or ruin'.

Corbett's War Course handout 'Strategical Terms and Definitions Used in Lectures on Naval History' placed naval operations in the context of national policy. It criticised Mahan and others who treated naval strategy as a distinct branch of knowledge. Maltzahn's 1905 Clausewitz essay had helped Corbett recognise that when officers from continental navies took military theory to sea, they navalised the argument without assessing whether it was 'quite permissible to transfer general principles from one kind of warfare and apply them to the other'. Mahan would cite the Alpine campaigns of the Archduke Charles in *Naval Strategy*, for no better reason than they were favourites of Jomini. While Jomini's and Clausewitz's assumptions about the centrality of battle and decision were applicable to the naval needs of military powers they were irrelevant to those of maritime states, which depended on sea control.[54] While the vital interests of maritime powers were exposed to a naval threat from continental states, there was very little maritime powers could do at sea to threaten the vital interests of continental powers. This asymmetry, the central problem of the French wars, had been resolved by blockading French naval bases. In 1906 the dynamics were different: Germany was badly placed to attack British maritime communications.

Corbett wasted no time setting out his key argument. 'The study for officers is the art of war, specialising in Naval Strategy', which 'does not exist as a separate branch of knowledge. It is only a section of a division of the art of war', which demanded a broad examination of war as a form of political intercourse, adopted after diplomacy had failed. A general theory of war equipped students to comprehend the role of naval operations, and to counter the Army's 'continental' arguments. Corbett paraphrased Clausewitz's dictum that war was only a continuation of politics.[55] He did not need to name the source; he was lecturing these officers on 'The System of Clausewitz'.

The 'Green Pamphlet' differentiated between the 'immediate object', the purpose of any operation, and the 'ulterior object', which was 'a step to the end of the campaign or war'. These distinctions were reflected in a division between minor and major strategies; he stressed that every operation should be planned with reference to both. Corbett's 'minor strategy' covered the modern operational level of war. Major strategy, a branch of statesman-ship, involved the 'whole resources of the nation for war; not only the Army and Navy, but also diplomacy and the commercial and financial position'. The 'deflection of strategy by politics', a key Corbett phrase, was not 'a disease' but 'a vital factor in every strategical problem', and the deflection worked in both directions. It was part of Clausewitz's 'friction of war'. The example he offered, Britain's refusal to send a fleet into the Baltic during the Seven Years' War, to avoid diplomatic complications with Russia, had striking contemporary resonance, and was explained in his history lectures. The operational level could be naval, military or combined, but it should not be studied from a purely naval perspective. Naval commanders had to take into account the implications of their actions for the government. Once again he used an example from the Seven Years' War.[56]

In the section 'Nature of Object', Corbett challenged the simple assump-tion that offensive operations were preferable, highlighting Admiral Togo's use of defensive tactics to sustain an offensive strategy in the Russo-Japanese War (1904–5). Following Clausewitz, he noted that while the offensive provided a moral advantage, the defensive was the stronger form of war, a reality emphasised at sea by the introduction of mines and torpedoes. He stressed the option of seizing a defensive position and forcing the enemy to counter-attack, or withdraw. He followed Caemmerer in treating defence as actively waiting to counter-attack, not remaining passive. The counter-stroke was the main strength of the defensive, both strategically and tactically. In a critical point that distinguished global/imperial strategy from European military operations, Corbett noted how acting defensively in secondary theatres allowed forces to be massed for an attack in a primary theatre: balancing force levels between theatres had become a key concern of Fisher's Admiralty.

Corbett expanded Clausewitz's treatment of offensive operations with a defensive purpose in books 6 and 7 of *On War*. Diversions could be used to confuse the enemy's strategy, relying on 'suddenness and mobility', qualities exemplified by combined operations.[57] Citing General Sir John Ardagh's classification of invasions, incursions and raids from the 1904 Royal Commission on Reserve Forces demonstrated the benefit of engaging with contemporary defence debates.

Corbett introduced his students to limited and unlimited war in round-about fashion, under the heading 'Nature of Ulterior Object'. He used the Spanish–American War, a standard War Course subject, and the Franco-Prussian War, the source of so much recent German strategic theory, to highlight the distinction. He linked the essentially defensive strategy of the United States Navy in 1898 with that in the Russo-Japanese War, when Japan achieved the strategic objects by naval defence.[58]

The tone and balance of the text demonstrate that Corbett was preparing his students for a new strategic context – war with Germany – where the majority of naval operations would necessarily be defensive, even if the overall strategy was offensive. The nature of any war, limited or unlimited, offensive or defensive, would be settled at the political level, before 'strategy has to decide on the system of operations'. These would reflect the theatre, resources at hand and objectives. Having distinguished between interior and exterior lines of operation, Corbett emphasised his own contribution, dropping the phrase 'Maritime Strategy' into a discussion of 'Lines of Communication'.

In Land Strategy the great majority of problems are problems of communication, Maritime Strategy has never been regarded as hinging on communications, but probably it does so even more than Land Strategy, as ... they are the main preoccupation of Naval operations.[59]

Not only was this the first time the word 'maritime' appeared in the text, it was a critical stage in the development of Corbett's thinking, one that took him beyond Mahan, Maltzahn and other military thinkers at sea. The maritime descriptor reflected the reality that sea communications were essential for navies, commerce and the strategic movement of armies, not just in the British experience but also in the latest naval conflicts, those of 1894, 1898 and 1904–5. This was a very different concept of strategy from that conveyed by the restrictive term 'naval', one addressed to the national level. Few contemporaries recognised its significance.

The clarity and precision of Corbett's legally inflected language suggests that his use of the contingent term 'probably' reflected an unwillingness to push his ideas too far, at this stage, while encouraging audience feedback, especially from Slade.

Corbett ensured students recognised that securing 'lines of passage and communication' dominated maritime strategy. Trade routes were critical to national strategy because they provided the resources to wage war. He dismissed the analogy between command of the sea and the occupation of territory as 'not safe'. Command of the sea meant 'the control of communications in which the belligerents were adversely concerned'. The ulterior object was not command of the sea, a relatively useless prize, although it could be the immediate strategic object. Instead he advanced a new definition of naval strategy, one based on the 'functions of the fleet'.

1. The preventing or securing of alliances
2. The protection or destruction of commerce
3. The furtherance of military operations ashore.

Furthermore command of the sea, which secured the ability to exercise those roles, only existed in wartime, when asserted against a hostile power. Control of communications was the basis for offensive operations, by land or sea, therefore 'naval strategy is mainly a question of communications'. To prove this contentious thesis Corbett provided inductive and deductive evidence, obliging critics to follow a similarly rigorous methodology. The Barrister at Law wanted to improve the logic and rigour of student responses. The new argument lent weight to a discussion of command, which could be general, local or temporary, using illustrations from the Russo-Japanese War. The loose phrase 'command of the sea' must be replaced by 'control of passage and communications'. Officers should recognise that temporary or local control could secure strategic ends without battle.[60] This was a direct challenge to the battle-centred naval strategy of Philip Colomb, Mahan, and their British followers, including his friend Reginald Custance. He anticipated a hostile response from those who accepted this comfortable old maxim.

Packed with original, challenging arguments, the section 'The Peculiarities of Maritime Communications' stressed that while the land communications of belligerents ran in opposite directions, away from the front line, and only met at the point of contact, the reverse was true at sea, where the lines of communication of both belligerents ran in parallel, if they were not essentially the same. He offered a contemporary example:

> in the case of a war with Germany, the object of which lay in the Eastern Mediterranean, or in America, or South Africa, our respective lines of communication would be identical.[61]

This example, which could only be used in a restricted text, would reappear in the closely related essay 'Some Principles of Naval Warfare', which introduced the Ballard Committee War Plans of 1907, emphasising the context in which the 'Green Pamphlet' was read.

Failure to recognise this reality lay at the root of 'much strategical error and confusion, caused by applying principles from land warfare to the sea without allowing for' this key difference. Striking an enemy's land communications almost always exposed your own to a counter-stroke: at sea, where the lines were the same, securing your own communications necessarily meant cutting those of the enemy. Therefore the obvious opening move for a dominant naval power was to take control of communications, challenging the enemy to contest that control in battle. 'The true maxim is "The primary object of the fleet is to secure communications, and if the enemy's fleet is in a position to render them unsafe it must be put out of action".' Almost all major naval actions had been fought over the control of communications, for trade or war. Having unsettled his audience, Corbett provided some comfort: in nine cases out of ten the old maxim of seeking out the enemy fleet was a sound principle. Despising maxims as an excuse to avoid thinking, his purpose was to set up a crushing riposte. Inferior fleets were usually found inside impregnable bases, consequently it was 'better strategy to make the enemy come to you than to go to him and seek a decision on his own ground'.[62]

The 'Green Pamphlet' assumed the Navy was preparing for a war with Germany; so did the war games, essays and linked planning exercise led by Slade, Captain George Ballard and Captain Maurice Hankey Royal Marine Artillery (RMA). As the small High Seas Fleet could not challenge Britain's control of oceanic communications, Corbett prepared the Navy for a conflict where the enemy fleet would not come out to be destroyed, while overtly offensive operations were likely to be counter-productive. Germany did not have any vital lines of communication, outside the Baltic. The Royal Navy could conduct a blockade from distant positions, although it might push into the Baltic, bringing the enemy to battle in the one theatre where they depended on maritime communications. To support his point he cited the Anglo-Dutch Wars of the seventeenth century, where 'our geographical position placed us astride Dutch trade communications, and they were forced to seek a decision against our fleet'.[63] He used Admiral Rooke's seizure of Gibraltar in 1704, which brought the French fleet to battle, to explain the logic of occupying Copenhagen and blockading the Baltic. Corbett subtly brought his audience into line with Jacky Fisher's strategic vision, which informed the Ballard Committee War Plans, along with his own work on the Seven Years' War and, within a matter of weeks, shaped three major public essays.[64]

Slade showed the 'Notes' to Custance, who treated them as a dangerous effusion from Fisher's Admiralty, to be contested and countered. Disliking the source, Custance ignored the pedagogic message. He:

considered them as being very dangerous, as they would be inclined to prevent men from getting a proper knowledge of the subject. He looked on them as affording men, who were not inclined to work, an excuse for going no deeper than learning the terms & definitions by heart.

Anxious to keep Sir Reginald on board, Slade tried to meet his objections:

I see his point, but I think he has exaggerated it and, as I pointed out to him, it was absolutely necessary, before doing anything else, to fix the terminology, as the looseness with which men talked about strategy was one of the great hindrances to the proper appreciation of what it meant.[65]

That Custance did not recognise the primary purpose of the exercise suggests his had been a cursory reading. He preferred the linear thinking of Philip Colomb and Mahan, and objected to a civilian, even one he knew and valued, teaching strategy to the Navy. This was a typical reaction to civilian commentators but Corbett, as Custance knew, was far more than a commentator. The Navy would never understand war and strategy until it went beyond the closed systems of Colomb and Mahan and mastered the Clausewitzian language required to debate with the Army. Ancient maxims, as Corbett demonstrated, were no substitute for logical argument and standardised terminology when debating with soldiers and advising the civilian leadership. Mahan, who remained a Jominian deductive thinker, recognised that 'Corbett relies mainly on Clausewitz'.[66] This insight flowed from his reading of the *Seven Years' War* while completing *Naval Strategy*.[67] For Mahan, strategy, like faith, was not open to question.[68]

While the handout did not please Custance and the 'Syndicate of Discontent', it was applauded by those in power. Fisher requested an extended version, 'an epitome of the art of war' (modern doctrine), as part of a major strategic exercise. Clarke, as Secretary of the CID, read and approved it as a national strategy primer. Clarke's subsequent argument that it misled the Navy was silenced by a reminder of his original judgement.[69]

In 1909, Corbett and War Course director Lewis Bayly revised 'Notes on Strategy'. The presentation changed from epigrammatic to literary, although most of the examples remained unchanged, because Corbett's examination of maritime strategy in total war remained incomplete.[70] While he left out a challenging passage suggesting that 'seek and destroy' was not always the best option, Corbett justified his insistence on studying the defensive.

> The bulk of our naval history is the story of how we have been baffled and thwarted by our enemies assuming the defensive at sea in support of their offensive on land. We have seldom succeeded in treating this attitude with success, and it is only by studying the defensive we can hope to do so.[71]

His targets were Custance, the 'Syndicate', and Bayly, a highly aggressive thinker, men who needed reminding that war has two sides. The new version had two sections, the second opening with 'Naval Strategy as a Question of Passage and Communications', and he had the confidence to drop the contingent 'probably'. The blockade section included new material on commercial blockades and the legal issues of notification, newly codified at the Second Hague Conference. To encourage readers to recognise the importance of blockade he noted that it was one among many subsidiary operations, including landings, feints and attacks on trade that might induce an enemy to risk battle.[72]

'Concentration', a new heading, challenged Mahan's insistence on a single fleet. Clausewitz provided authority for the alternative, using the articulated dispersal of force to contain the enemy, balancing control of communications with readiness for battle. The passage came from Corbett's forthcoming *Trafalgar* study. A single fleet was unlikely to locate the enemy, something Mahan learnt while providing strategic advice during the Spanish–American War. The 1906 conclusion was reworded to emphasise that fighting in home waters was more likely to ensure the complete defeat of the enemy.[73] This was a direct challenge to the 'seek and destroy' notions of Custance and his allies.

The 1909 text reinforced Corbett's case for a maritime strategy: after the Ballard Committee, British war planning pulled back from the German coast, requiring more reflective men than Custance or Sturdee, and better guides to the future than Mahan. While Clausewitz remained Corbett's main authority, all references to Germany were removed: the identity of the current threat was no mystery.

The 'Green Pamphlet' flowed from Corbett's idea of using the Seven Years' War as a strategic template. It should be read alongside his 1907 articles, the Ballard Committee preface and *England in the Seven Years' War: A Study in Combined Strategy*. The 1909 revision reflected the fluid nature of strategic doctrine, always responding to new challenges, and fresh insights.

In 1911 Corbett took his strategic argument into the public domain, using the book format to add examples to reinforce the argument. While he had a wider audience in view, one which included statesmen, his primary target remained the 'German way', condemning Goltz's 'blind adherence to the principle of overthrow', which would 'turn the art of war into mere bludgeon play'. Not only did Caemmerer provide the voice of reason, but Clausewitz had been too practical a soldier for such absurd propositions; circumstances would not always require unlimited war. Corbett understood that British strategy was limited and maritime, but remained relevant to unlimited continental conflicts, as part of an alliance seeking to overthrow a common enemy, as he demonstrated in *The Campaign of Trafalgar*.[74] Furthermore, the crude barbarism of Goltz's absolute war would provide ample justification for a comprehensive system of economic warfare, an argument he would develop as the First World War lurched ever closer to Goltz's horrific vision.[75]

In 1911 Corbett publicly repudiated the unthinking extremism of Goltz and Bernhardi to discredit their British followers. He attacked German hymns to 'total war', 'decisive battle' and Social Darwinism because they had appeared in English and were widely cited by British authors. These ideas were irrelevant to British needs, and out of step with British practice.

If Corbett's argument that the defensive might be preferable at sea, even for Britain, put him at odds with other commentators, the observation that wars between major powers could remain limited was effectively unique. While contemporary strategists expected wars would inevitably escalate to the unlimited, Corbett provided persuasive evidence to the contrary from the Napoleonic and Russo-Japanese wars. Fisher aside, no-one paid any attention. Instead his authority as an interpreter of Clausewitz was challenged by Spenser Wilkinson, who denied the validity of maritime strategy and limited war, attacking Fisher's Admiralty, and Corbett, its leading intellectual. In the process Wilkinson exposed his own limitations. His attack appeared in the staunchly Unionist, pro-Beresford *Morning Post* in 1909. He echoed Goltz's contention that there was no rational basis for the idea that war could be limited, citing Mahan, Maltzahn and other continental theorists to support his claim that limited war was no longer relevant.[76] A year later Wilkinson called on his countrymen to accept that all future wars would be total, not limited.[77] Nor was he alone: in the *Edinburgh Review* Major Pope-Hennessey also rejected limited war. Deeply frustrated, Corbett wrote, 'I have never suggested it applied to war with Germany' on his copy of the review.[78]

Misreading Clausewitz seems to have been a common failing of Edwardian journalists. In 1913 James Thursfield opened his primer *Naval Warfare* by citing Clausewitz's famous dictum about war and politics, before denying the limitation of war aims would affect the nature of the conflict, because the only sure way of obtaining any object was 'to destroy his armed forces', pointedly rejecting Corbett's limited war argument. Little wonder Corbett called it a 'shilling shocker'.[79] Wilkinson, Thursfield and many others, succumbed to the common delusion that Britain's role in any future European war would inevitably escalate to the unlimited. As Britain had never waged unlimited war, even when allied to powers that did, and all modern conflicts, including that with Napoleon, ended with diplomatic settlements rather than absolute destruction, the rationale for such apocalyptic thinking came from millennial anxieties about 'Decline' and the politics of social change, rather than strategic theory. Corbett realised that contemporary German advocates of 'absolute' war were nihilistic extremists: Clausewitz and Caemmerer were better guides to the reality of war, and the need for a 'British way'.

CHAPTER 9

'Radiant with the Genius of a Maritime State'

ENGLAND IN THE SEVEN YEARS' WAR

Corbett's fourth major book, *England in the Seven Years' War*, reflected the intellectual demands of defence education, the deepening rift between the services and his mastery of Clausewitz.[1] It became the model for all subsequent texts. Writing and lecturing to a demanding, present-minded audience had shifted the focus of his work from history to strategy and doctrine, an approach already evident in the second volume of *England in the Mediterranean*, where the War of the Spanish Succession became the first example of a recognisable 'British way'. Fisher's appointment as First Sea Lord in October 1904 brought Corbett into the centre of naval policy, engaged in the Navy's response to the strategic challenges posed by the First Moroccan Crisis and the subsequent breakdown in relations between the Admiralty and the Army General Staff over national strategy. He would have known that Fisher had deterred Germany by sending the Channel Fleet to the Baltic, while the General Staff merely dreamt of fighting alongside the French.

The Moroccan Crisis made the German threat explicit, and increased the tempo of war preparations, requiring additional strategy lectures for the War Course, the 'Green Pamphlet', and Corbett's introduction to the Ballard Committee War Plans of 1907, the year in which he produced three major essays supporting Fisher's policies and his new book. This dynamic context shaped a historical case study that doubled as an explanation of Fisher's expansive strategic thinking. Despite being written to inspire statesmen, educate the Navy, and challenge the assumptions of continental soldiers and admirals obsessed with 'decisive battle', the *Seven Years' War* remains the standard strategic narrative of the conflict.

The book took three years to complete, 'owing to the interruption of lecturing to War Course, Admiralty memos & inspired articles & the production of my "Fighting Instructions"', another quasi-official project.[2] He began work during the Moroccan Crisis, when Fisher and Edward VII used the Channel Fleet to counter German pressure on France. He had been summoned by Fisher and DNI Charles Ottley in May that year, to help the Admiralty respond to a War Office memorandum, based on von der Goltz's work, that asserted the inability of a French fleet in the Baltic to influence the Franco-Prussian War proved that the Royal Navy would be equally impotent in 1905.[3] Ottley used Mahan's line that Britain's geographical position, a great break-water positioned across the maritime approaches to Germany, made economic warfare effective: 'the blockade of the German ports to-day would <u>sever an artery</u>, essential, it seems to me, to the financial existence of Germany'. Ottley, Fisher and Corbett saw the Entente as the key to the peace and stability of Europe while Russia remained weak.[4] When Corbett emphasised how amphibious operations in the Baltic could bolster the new diplomatic align-ment, Ottley noted the Anglo-French Entente had removed the Russian threat to India, and opened the Baltic to British combined operations, using troops previously earmarked to reinforce the Raj, something suggested by George Clarke at the CID. Ottley thought nothing less 'would be worthy of our tradi-tions, or would be acceptable to France'.[5] This conversation secured the Baltic a prominent role in Corbett's profoundly amphibious *Seven Years' War*.

Corbett also consulted George Clarke, who indicated that he and the CID were keen to promote expeditionary warfare, the key to an effective maritime strategy. Alongside practical concerns about landing craft and transports, Clarke recognised the need for specialist fire-support warships.[6] These were obvious lessons from the Russo-Japanese War, a conflict Corbett was already teaching at the War Course.[7] The new General Staff, anxious not to exchange the continental certainties of defending India for a supporting role in amphibious operations, hastened to reposition their deployable force to Belgium, a strategy that offered diplomatic benefits in Paris, but precious little military consequence.[8]

The risk that Germany's hegemonic ambitions might trigger a European war prompted Corbett to base his new lecture course on the ultimate example of British strategy, a war that maintained the balance of power in Europe, and greatly expanded the empire, a model he expected Britain would follow in such a conflict. His *Seven Years' War* would emphasise the skilful use of naval and amphibious power in a limited conflict: seizing French colonies and destroying the French economy had preserved the European balance, extended the empire and, critically, kept French troops out of Flanders, without Britain having to raise a large continental army. Sustaining the expository focus on strategic leadership, developed in *England in the Mediterranean* through Cromwell, William III and Marlborough, he focused on William Pitt the Elder, Earl of Chatham. Pitt's reputation stood at its apogee; he was widely regarded as a statesman of genius who defeated France, built an empire and might have averted American independence. As Richard Middleton observed, Corbett's assessment of Pitt reflected William Lecky's *A History of England in the Eighteenth Century*, a text that he owned. Lecky was a fine model, a serious scholar, and a delightful prose stylist.[9] Corbett echoed Lecky's judgement that Pitt's 'greatness [as a war minister] was beyond question, and almost beyond comprehension'.[10] Corbett's version of Pitt was a model for future British statesmen, who would require a strategic education if they were going to keep control of a future war. In 1914 uneducated politicians handed control to the soldiers.

Corbett's engagement with national strategy widened in the summer of 1905, when Slade detailed him to lecture at the Army Staff College, Camberley.[11] Sending a civilian historian rather than a naval officer kept the discussion at the national level, while Corbett's growing mastery of strategic theory equipped him to debate the subject with educated soldiers. Slade and Corbett recognised that Britain's limited maritime strategy was intellectually consistent, and fundamentally different. There was an obvious synergy between Fisher's attempt to dominate British strategy through the CID and Slade's and Corbett's work on the theoretical basis of his argument. The 'sound ideas' Corbett would advance at Camberley were consistent with Fisher's thinking.

In July 1905 Fisher stressed his primary purpose was deterrence:

PRIVATE With great difficulty, I've got our Channel Fleet up the Baltic and cruising in North Sea. 'Our drill ground should be our battle ground.' Don't repeat that phrase, but I've taken means to have it whispered in the German Emperor's ear! The next move on the naval board will make you hold your breath when it comes! So get your heart set for a shock!!!

He invited Corbett to an event on 8 August, to celebrate his promotion to Admiral of the Fleet, which kept him on the active list, and potentially at the Admiralty, for another five years.[12] Now secure in office Fisher would continue his campaign to dominate national strategy, relying on Corbett for strategic insight and policy papers.

Corbett gave his first Seven Years' War lectures to the second Naval War Course of 1905, and soon afterwards at Camberley. Where existing texts on naval strategy, by Mahan and Philip Colomb, provided closed systems and prescriptive action points, which did not encourage debate or development, Corbett openly challenging his audience, and the received wisdom of the most eminent men in the field, men who had the priceless advantage of sharing a uniform with their students. He found some relief in a joke: 'My strategy lectures are very uphill work. I had no idea when I undertook it how difficult it was to present theory in a digestible form to the unused organs of naval officers.'[13] Henry Newbolt recognised the irony, unlike later commentators. In truth Corbett had no concerns, the following January he told his wife an 'interested' audience made the lectures 'a success'; despite the subject being the 'dryest & most difficult, I can rest content'. Furthermore, the lectures had an immediate impact: one of 'the principles I had been laying down is already in use in the war game', he felt them 'more important than ever.'[14] Three months later the new material was thoroughly bedded in: 'The lectures continue to go very well – better in fact than they ever have before & I am more of an oracle – which is bad for me you will say.'[15] Corbett had established his mature method.

These lectures were delivered against the backdrop of heightened international tension; rumours of war informed his discussions with course director Edmond Slade. Slade favoured using small military forces to loiter off the German coast, or secure Antwerp in the event of a German violation of Belgian neutrality, holding the flank of a German advance into France.[16] Ottley and Ballard at the NID told him that the War Office was dismissive of such ideas, claiming naval operations in the Baltic had exercised little effect on the Crimean War – a fundamental misrepresentation. Not only had the Army conflated the Crimean campaign, a grand raid designed to destroy a Russian naval base, with the wider war, but they ignored the decisive role of economic warfare and the strategic threat the Navy posed to St Petersburg in the spring of 1856.[17] That an unusually well-read, strategically aware sailor like Slade had to go back to the library for evidence revealed the scale of Corbett's task. The Navy desperately needed strategic narratives that contextualised the role of naval power in every significant British conflict to counter the soldiers' continental approach. Slade's query prompted him to consider the Baltic campaigns of 1854 and 1855, but he never found the time to bring the subject under control. When Slade edited

Corbett's 'Green Pamphlet' doctrine primer, he suggested 'it would certainly be advisable to put in something about the possibility of influencing land operations by the action of Sea Power'.[18]

Lecturing to naval and military audiences developed the analytical thrust of Corbett's text. Initial research revealed existing secondary sources were imperfect, and often unreliable, defeating his original plan to produce a strategic analysis. Furthermore, the decision to focus on grand strategy required a mastery of the European and diplomatic aspects of the conflict, to contextualise his 'British' strategy. He reverted to the dense narrative approach of *Successors*.

In the autumn of 1906 Corbett outlined these tensions to Newbolt, hoping for advice, or at least some sympathy.

> I have got it on too big a scale – too much detail and I am almost in despair – I meant it to be just a strategical commentary on the war – and then you find strategy turns on such minute details or that your predecessors are wrong in their facts and then there's the facts to do as well as the commentary. I have a file of MS [manuscripts] and have not taken Quebec yet.

He feared critics would condemn it as 'absolutely unreadable for excess of matter and of technicalities. But I plough along labouring heavily'.[19] Corbett the essayist looked for elegant solutions to encapsulate complexities, but the lawyer recognised the need for precision, and the historian demanded rigour. Newbolt's response was encouraging, but Corbett remained anxious:

> what haunts me always is that you are not enforcing upon the reader's attention the points which are important, and that in the effect after abstraction you are not making the narrative clear. I fancy though it is in my case chiefly due to that great difficulty of keeping the topography fixed and clear in the reader's mind – I doubt if it is really possible. Naval and military history I expect must be read in front of a map and yet one is always trying to paint the picture as well as tell the story.

Maps had become an obsession.[20] Soon he would be distracted from this war by preparations for the next. From his holiday retreat in Littlehampton he was:

assisting at a staff ride – a landing here – and then the manoeuvres on
the Downs above Chichester. It was very beautiful but war is such a game
of hide and seek now that you see very little. Still a fair eye for country an
inquisitive mind and a bicycle enabled me to see a great deal.[21]

Perhaps the historian of Wolfe and Quebec picked up some useful points
on the South Downs.

The demands of Admiralty work, lecturing, shaping a syllabus for
Dartmouth and countering the anti-Fisher vitriol flowing from the pens of
Reginald Custance, Sir William White and the lesser luminaries of the
'Syndicate of Discontent' frequently dragged Corbett away from the book.
In November 1906 he declined an invitation to write a tercentenary paper
on the settlement of Jamestown for the *American Historical Review*, 'so
much occupied with official work for the Admiralty that I am obliged to
relinquish all magazine work'.[22] By December he feared these delays would
leave the book 'like a French battleship that is usually obsolete before she
gets herself launched'.[23]

Corbett's book demonstrated how effective a limited maritime strategy
could be in a future European conflict. He noted how Lord Anson had
completely overhauled the Navy, an obvious analogy with Fisher.[24] After
completing the draft in July 1907 Corbett spent August and September at
the family's newly acquired country house, correcting proofs, interrupted
by a visit to Lady Elliot-Drake at Buckland Abbey.[25] Stopham Manor, in
West Sussex, was an impressive old house, ideal for a Tudor romantic.[26] It
was fortunate he was able to finish the work before returning to London,
where Slade, newly installed as DNI, co-opted him onto the team preparing
the Admiralty's submission to the CID sub-committee on invasion. What
little time this left for research and writing was taken up editing the
NRS volume *Fighting Instructions*. At least these tasks 'prepared the
ground for writing on the American Independence and Great Wars. Slade
proposed my beginning at once a book on invasions but at present I think
it best to deal with it as a continuation of my general naval history'.[27] Corbett
anticipated continuing the historical case studies, the American War
providing a negative reflection of the Seven Years' conflict, while the 'Great
War', an unlimited conflict, would be the ultimate test of national strategy.
This programme would be overtaken by events, Clausewitzian 'friction',
that diverted his intellectual effort. Corbett lectured to the War Course on

invasion in late 1907 and early 1908, and also spoke to the Coefficients on the subject.

Wrapping up the project Corbett was:

> Still 'fed up' with my book – just finishing my index and remembering all the things I ought to have said or said better and which it is now too late to say. Doubtless you know that hollow feeling. It is just the same as when your fly comes back from a 40 pounder fish.

Such comments suggest he had been drained and deflated by the endless demands of lecturing, writing and advising.[28]

England in the Seven Years' War: A Study in Combined Strategy was the first book to fully reflect Corbett's experience lecturing to the service colleges. It used Clausewitzian theory to elucidate the principles of British strategy, principles demonstrated through the detailed analysis of a successful maritime conflict. No British author had previously attempted 'to write history on the large scale with military principles guiding the selection method'.[29] He harmonised political, diplomatic, naval and military activity into a strategic template for students, senior officers and statesmen: Fisher would cite it for the rest of his life, because it provided theoretical and historical support for his own thinking. Corbett showed how a distinctive 'British way' had secured the interests of a unique global seapower empire. It shattered the assumptions that strategy was a universal possession, and that the best strategic thinking came from Germany.

Corbett followed Clausewitz in developing doctrine drawn from history as the basis for strategic education, because history remained the ultimate realty, the acid test of theory, fad or formula. Furthermore, the use of history to develop strategy was not a closed process. Corbett, like Clausewitz, revised and refined his ideas through historical research and contemporary examples. Strategy was an evolving body of ideas, not Jomini's fixed system. While Corbett provided a template to develop contemporary strategy he reminded his audiences of the role of chance in human affairs, Clausewitzian 'friction'.[30] Within a year students were using his ideas because they aided war planning. This was no accident, as he noted, 'we are fast becoming something like a General Staff'.[31]

When the book appeared in mid-November 1907, Corbett's credits included 'Lecturer in History to the Royal Naval War College' alongside the usual LL.M. He had moved on from the episodic strategic overview of *England in the Mediterranean* to a study of grand strategy in action. It was a finely honed weapon for an increasingly bitter war over the soul of national strategy. Little wonder Jacky Fisher loved it.

Ultimately Corbett's book defined the unique, specific maritime context that shaped British strategy, and his own response to strategic theory. From the outset two things were abundantly clear: the Seven Years' War had been 'maritime', and could only be understood by starting from 'the naval side rather than from the military, as is more commonly done'. Despite numerous 'brilliant actions' on the Continent, and the paucity of sea battles, it was 'luminously informing' on the strategic use of the fleet and amphibious warfare. For Britain the German war was a 'subordinate campaign', while the Army formed 'an integral part of the maritime force with which it was primarily carried on'.[32]

Although this was a Clausewitzian text, the Prussian theorist was not named, to avoid startling naval and civilian audiences. Corbett apologised for offering a strategic analysis, claiming he only did so because the true greatness of his characters became clear as they struggled with 'the inexorable laws of strategy'. To ensure such concerns were seen in their proper context he thanked Slade and his War Course students for their encouragement and support.[33] Emphasising his debt to Richard Waddington's multivolume diplomatic history *La Guerre de Sept Ans* and Lord Bute's papers, owned by the Marquis of Lansdowne, reminded academics that this was a serious work of scholarship.[34] He thought academic endorsement might justify his contentious ideas.

The book was also about the possibility of war with Germany.[35] Corbett balanced competing imperial and continental concerns at a critical point in the development of empire, the danger of a German drive for European hegemony having replaced, or perhaps replicated, the menace of the Bourbon 'Family Compact'. However, the analogy should not be pushed too far: the Franco-Spanish axis had far more power outside Europe than Germany, and rather less within it. Across the past sixty years historians have overrated the importance of Europe in British policy at the expense of the imperial commercial project. Brendan Simms' argument that Britain was tied to Europe by power politics and security is important, but those concerns were fundamentally negative. Britain needed Europe to be balanced, stable and at peace throughout the nineteenth century, in order that it could advance the dynamic sector of the economy, which lay beyond

Europe, and for which the British state configured its strategic instruments: ships, bases and deployable military formations. Had Europe been the epicentre of British policy, as Simms contends, the sustained preference of ministers between 1714 and 1815 for naval power and infrastructure over the Army would have been foolish. Naval power justified the only British garrisons in Europe, at Gibraltar and Minorca, while strategic engagement with Europe was limited to preventing France from using the Low Countries as an invasion base. Ultimately, as Corbett stressed, the national character was averse to continental warfare.[36] The balance to be struck between the competing concerns of Europe and empire had exercised British intellectuals, statesmen and strategists throughout the nineteenth century. Corbett and Fisher understood that the empire made Britain a great power. A major war in Europe would, John Seeley predicted, draw British troops and resources out of the empire, hastening its decline and fall.[37] Britain needed an oceanic empire to sustain the seapower state, and fund the costly naval instrument that secured global trade. Everything depended on the Navy.

While he did not anticipate the imminent end of empire Corbett was at one with Fisher in thinking Britain had no reason to attack another great power. The Boer War offered a salutary reminder of the fiscal consequences of conflict, emphasising the need for a coherent national strategy that provided an effective deterrent. Britain needed to signal intent rather than wage war, but coherent signalling would be impossible if the services marched to different strategic tunes, especially if only one of them was British.

Corbett's contemporary perspective shaped his treatment of the vexed question of why Britain allowed the old Austrian alliance, bedrock of national strategy since 1688, to collapse in the 1750s. Britain's primary continental security concern had long been to neutralise the Scheldt estuary, in the Austrian Netherlands, the obvious point from which to launch an invasion. After 1648 alliances between Spain and, later, Austria, the Dutch Republic and Britain had kept the Scheldt closed to commercial and military shipping. However, Dutch neutrality and Austrian disinterest had undermined a position recently secured by costly colonial concessions to France at the Treaty of Aix-la-Chapelle in 1748. While Corbett's academic contemporaries suggested Britain should have made more effort to keep Austria as an ally:

> to see the matter thus is to see it with Continental eyes, and to miss the
> essence of the British attitude. The whole purpose of the negotiations

was to confine the threatening war to the theatres beyond the sea where lay our special objects and our peculiar strength. Our controlling aim was to ensure that we should not be drawn into a European struggle and forced to fight for our ends where our power was weakest. To purchase the Austrian alliance at the price of sending a serious military force into the very cockpit of Europe was to ensure the consequences which it was the sole object of the alliance to prevent. Moreover, it was to offer a price which the instinct of the country had determined not to pay. The spirit with which the people of a country go into a war is as much an element of strategical calculation as its army or its navy. For a maritime and Colonial war with France the people of this country were eager and resolute, but of Continental wars they had had enough.[38]

Contemporary Britain was equally unwilling to wage continental war, a point he developed from Mahan's focus on national character.[39]

Having created a book for 'those who seek insight into the higher princi-ples of the Art of War', Corbett chose the example best suited to a 'maritime power'. If the materiel of naval war had fundamentally changed since 1756, the functions of a fleet remained a proper study for statesmen, sailors, diplo-mats and soldiers.[40] He defined the national effort as major strategy, reducing the action of individual services, Army and Navy, to minor strategy (the modern operational level), demonstrating how naval concerns were constantly deflected by military and diplomatic considerations. Naval battles, he argued, were the product of strategic combination, not unthinking tactical aggression, distancing himself from Mahan's focus on securing command of the sea in battle, which reduced naval thought 'to feel its sole concern was fighting, and had forgotten the art of making war'.[41] This line was addressed to narrow-minded men like Reginald Custance, who took Mahan's theories to the extreme. Britain won major wars without defeating the enemy fleet, leaving it quietly in harbour where it posed no threat.

Corbett's book illuminated contemporary strategy, demolished uniformed pedants in both services, and highlighted the critical role of capable civilian direction by addressing old issues that remained equally important in the Edwardian era – invasion, continental wars, 'decisive battle', economic warfare and advanced ship design. His argument aligned with key elements of Fisher's policy, the book having informed the essays that had appeared earlier in the same year.

Hoping readers would understand how 'the men of the age struggled against the inexorable laws of strategy', Corbett began by examining the strategic role of the fleet, for 'those who seek insight into the higher principles of the Art of War', countering ingrained resistance to lessons from the age of sail with the observation that 'history alone' enabled statesmen, sailors, soldiers and diplomats to master the art, including the 'deflecting influences of military or diplomatic considerations'. This was not mere naval strategy, studied on a chart, but grand strategy, laid out on the fourteen excellent maps he persuaded Longman to provide. Maps focused attention on the higher direction of war: there were no pictures. He undermined the 'decisive battle' school by observing that battle was the supreme, but not the only function of navies. They were more often brought about by 'interference with the enemy's military and diplomatic arrangements' than naval activity.[42] *England in the Mediterranean* had demonstrated that England secured command of the sea by diplomatic and military, rather than naval activity, sustaining his argument that it was not necessary to destroy an inferior fleet that did not interfere with British strategy. He provided another powerful critique of Mahan: 'of late years the world has become so deeply impressed with the efficacy of sea power that we are inclined to forget how impotent it is of itself to decide a war against great Continental states, how tedious is the pressure of naval action unless it be nicely co-ordinated with military and diplomatic pressure', complete with a suitable Nelson quote.[43] Not only did this lesson of history remain valid, but relying on the 'tedious ... pressure' of economic blockade would create problems with neutrals. Those problems would be legal and diplomatic, rather than naval.

In the Seven Years' War, Britain assumed command without a battle – France made no challenge – using the fleet for higher strategic purposes, containing the French fleets until they attempted an invasion of the United Kingdom in 1759. He credited this strategic insight to Pitt the Elder, a 'true War Minister with almost undisturbed control of army, navy and diplomacy'. In a provocative passage he dismissed Philip Colomb's insistence on securing sea control in battle before attempting to exploit it as 'pedantic'. Pitt, he observed, exploited sea control to strip away France's colonial and economic resources without a battle, 'goading her into a desperate attempt at invasion, to deliver her fleets into his hands'. Having taught sailors to see the war beyond the battle, he disabused the soldiers of the continental notion that they were significant. Pitt exploited the national preference for the sea service to secure power and direct a war 'radiant with the Genius of a maritime state'.[44] As a maritime imperial power Britain demonstrated a deep-rooted aversion to armies, conscription and European warfare in the eighteenth century – and nothing had changed.

Corbett constantly stressed the interplay of diplomacy, military and naval activity, and the strategic principles that emerged. 'The dominant note of English foreign policy from time immemorial had been to prevent either France or Spain securing naval stations beyond the Strait of Dover', in a word Flanders. By 1754 Austria was losing interest in the distant province, and the Dutch would only act if France attacked Britain.[45] Although the security of Flanders mattered far more than that of Canada, India or Hanover, this was only true as a negative: Britain had no desire to rule European territory.

Corbett's discussion of the invasion panic that followed the outbreak of war in early 1756 was a critique of recent alarms sparked by Lord Roberts and Charles Repington. Both were 'unwarrantable, almost unaccountable, but none the less a thing, a real factor in the strategical problem'. The resulting distortion of strategy into unnecessary defensive measures had been 'well-punished' in 1756.[46] In reality France, denied any other means of harming Britain, adopted a false strategy, planning to invade Britain without a fleet to secure the passage. Obsessed by these preparations the Cabinet massed too many battleships, and too many soldiers in the Channel, enabling France to open the war by seizing Minorca, intended to be a diversion. In strategic terms Minorca was a mere bargaining chip that obliged Britain to secure a counterweight.[47]

He used continental endorsements to emphasise Britain's distinctive strategy. Frederick of Prussia urging amphibious diversions to draw French troops away from Central Europe: his status as a master strategist made this a telling blow in favour of a 'British way'. Such operations were necessary because Britain would not send a fleet to assist Frederick in the Baltic, to avoid annoying the Scandinavian powers, united by a treaty of neutrality, on whose goodwill the critical supply of timber and naval stores depended.[48] At this point Pitt became minister, imposing an imperial maritime strategy. Using British money to hire mercenaries, Prussia kept France engaged in Europe while the British home army raided French naval bases, transforming static defence into a targeted maritime offensive. Pitt established the Home Fleet, or Western Squadron, as the basis of British strategy, providing security against invasion, covering the flow of merchant shipping in and out of the Channel, while securing the movement of armies to attack Canada and the West Indies. 'It may be said that no defensive disposition is perfect unless it threatens or conceals an attack.' Pitt achieved this end, confusing the French and assisting the allied armies in Germany. This was the primary purpose of the amphibious raid on Rochfort.[49] In the spring of 1758 minor actions in the Bay of Biscay and off Cartagena wrecked French attempts to reinforce Canada, actions Corbett used to criticise continentalism and 'decisive' battle. Louisbourg fell later that year.[50] Landing troops at Saint-Malo to support the German campaign also aided trade defence by burning the privateer shipping of two Breton ports.[51]

At this point Corbett unleashed Clausewitz. The impending fall of Canada forced France to see that it had lost the limited/maritime war, and could only recover its colonies through an unlimited counter-stroke, invading Britain.[52] Attempting to concentrate for this operation brought French fleets to destruction at Lagos and Quiberon, battles that gave Pitt a platform for peace. In the interval he seized Belle Isle as a *quid pro quo* for Minorca. Pitt resigned when the Cabinet blocked his plans for a pre-emptive attack on Spain, which intelligence had revealed was actively preparing for war. Having reached the culminating point of victory in a limited war, the Duke of Bedford, a former First Lord of the Admiralty, observed that it would be 'unnatural' to drive France entirely from the seas, while humbling Spain would make all maritime powers fear a British trade monopoly. It 'would be as dangerous for us to grasp at as it was for Louis XIV when he aspired to be the arbiter of Europe, and might likely produce a grand alliance against us'. Peace on such terms would not endure, and a durable peace would not be built by needlessly humiliating great powers with long memories.[53] Consequently the Cabinet continued Pitt's war against France, seizing Martinique, while allowing Spain to bring home the annual Plate Fleet, and prepare for war.

Spain did join France, but the war ended with the seizure of Havana and Manila, brilliant grand strategic strokes designed by Lord Anson, and executed by experienced professionals. Lord Bute's anxious search for peace ran alongside Choiseul's projected invasion of Britain, blocked by the Royal Navy and Spanish procrastination. The fall of Havana forced France to accept peace, but the terms proved unpopular at home. Within months Bute had been driven from office by an innately maritime public that demanded altogether more tangible rewards from a long war.

Corbett concluded by making a case for improved, powerful and clearly defined warship types, implying a synergy between Lord Anson's new designs and Fisher's, reusing the argument of Admiral Sir Thomas Hardy from the *Dreadnought* essay.[54] Chapter and essay were written together, a compelling case of intellectual cross-fertilisation between history, strategy and policy. He addressed commerce warfare, another contemporary concern, dismissing French cruiser operations as annoying diversions which, like their *jeune école* successors, were incapable of challenging British sea control.[55] While the French captured numerous merchant ships, they had little success against convoyed traffic, while the value of individual prizes, mainly coasters and other small craft, was low. These small vessels had been taken by privateers, a method of war outlawed in 1856. Critically, French cruisers:

> did very little to injure our credit, and that is the main strategic value of commerce destruction. Money was freely obtainable, at least until the end of Pitt's administration, and then any tightness was entirely due to mistrust of Bute's capacity. On the other hand the credit of France was effectively destroyed, and her finances reduced to the direst straits.
>
> The truth seems to be that the bulk of our commerce was so great that the mere pelagic operations of our enemy, though they absorbed in the end almost the whole of her vitality at sea, could not make a sufficient percentage impression to produce any real warlike advantage. . . . They may produce inconvenience, but cannot paralyse finance. To injure credit to such an extent as to amount to a real consideration of war, operations against trade must be systematically carried on by land and seas till its main sources and the possibility of transit are practically destroyed. Then, and only then, can it become a material factor in securing the ultimate object – a favourable peace. That, at least, is the moral of the Seven Years' War.[56]

The *Seven Years' War* was crafted to engage serving officers and statesmen: academic historians and a wider public were included, but Corbett's methods were not calculated to appeal to those who studied history for its own sake, or enjoyed the evocative lyricism of Francis Parkman.[57] He was not writing for money, or fame, his was a national task, one that provided quiet satisfaction. The esteem of literary friends, fellow strategists and academics was recognition enough. The responses of Richard Haldane, Secretary of State for War, and Charles Firth, Regius Professor of History at Oxford, are compelling. Corbett sent a copy to Haldane, a fellow Liberal Imperialist and Coefficient, to remind him that British strategy was maritime, the Army's primary role being expeditionary warfare to help secure command of the sea and colonial conquests for diplomatic balancing at the peace. Haldane 'read through from cover to cover' and discussed it with his military advisors, adopting the core argument that 'has an especial bearing on the problems with which, as you know, we are engaged in the Defence Committee at the present moment'. Haldane's BEF followed Corbett's case for an amphibious strike force, limited in size, but high in quality. Haldane recognised the difficulty of imposing a unified approach on two services compelled to battle each other for their budgets. He valued Corbett's historical base, the 'concrete' evidence that supported his theoretical case, and the literary skill that held the attention of a discerning audience. Not only did the 'sublime moments' in naval history, like Quiberon, have to be worked for, but they also had to be worked up with literary skill. Corbett's book, the outstanding exposition of the British strategic model, reinforced Haldane's determination to keep the Army under political control, and restricted to an expeditionary role.[58]

Corbett had known Charles Firth since the late 1880s. Firth provided a powerful academic endorsement for the NRS, serving on its council from 1893, and hosted Corbett's Ford lectures, a key component of *England in the Mediterranean*. He understood the context in which Corbett operated, and judged the book a 'standard' that should 'be on every historian's bookshelves': 'but the main thing is the new conception of the strategy of the whole war, and of the relative importance of events which your narrative brings out. That, I think, will exert a lasting influence.' He hoped the clarity of Corbett's exposition would enable sailors, soldiers and statesmen to benefit. Firth lamented his Oxford history lectures were ignored, he had turned to English literature to secure an audience.[59]

Admiral Sir William May was 'very complimentary', but Reginald Custance told anyone who would listen that Corbett misunderstood Clausewitz's limited and unlimited war dichotomy. Custance, like many contemporary critics, conflated the practical concept of 'unlimited war' with Clausewitz's theoretical 'absolute war'. Corbett explained the difference to Custance a few days later, before discussing the mutually agreeable subject of eighteenth-century signalling and fleet tactics.[60] Anxious that such remarks might damage the credibility of the War Course, Corbett informed Captain Osmond de Brock, Deputy DNI, that Custance was wrong. Custance's error was shared by, and perhaps originated with, Spenser Wilkinson, who followed modern German authors in reading Clausewitz as an apostle of extremes. Corbett's source was Colmar von der Goltz, and he condemned Wilkinson for 'trying to substitute continental theorists in place of our own experience'.[61]

Wilkinson's naval ideas were dominated by 'decisive battle', and Slade attributed them to Custance, deriding: 'theories and ideas which have long since been given up'.[62] Meeting Corbett at a Navy League dinner two months later, Wilkinson made 'a sort of apology for his article, but was quite senile'.[63] Corbett asked Newbolt to explain to Custance that:

> 'facts' are not history, but only its dry bones and that no one but an histo-rian can hope to put flesh on them. I know he looks upon me as a traitor because I listened reverently to all he had to say, before performing the painful duty of shewing he was as incapable of drawing historical conclusions as I was of commanding a fleet. ... With all his regard for history he cannot see in it a profession as difficult, complex and absorbing as his own and that it does not begin and end with facts any more than his began and ends with guns.[64]

Corbett's critics failed to comprehend that national strategies are unique and contingent, determining the total effort of an entire state, rather than serving the self-interest of individual armed forces. While Custance actu-ally believed wars could be won at sea, by forcing battle on reluctant enemies, Wilkinson assumed Britain was a 'normal' great power, and therefore required a mass conscript army for 'decisive' land battles in Europe. Such arguments lent a flimsy plausibility to continental arguments.

Leading American historian George Louis Beer provided an altogether more agreeable assessment in the *New York Times*. Beer, a prominent member of the American 'Imperial' School, was more inclined to British perspectives in history and current affairs than the majority of his countrymen.[65] He rated Corbett 'among the select few of Clio's numerous band', despite writing for naval officers who were 'mainly interested in those subjects that are most profitable to the students of the art of war, especially that branch waged upon water'. Corbett had treated naval, military and diplomatic activity in such detail as to largely replace the latest biography of Pitt. Beer highlighted a few inaccuracies, mostly in the field of colonial history, while his claim that

Corbett had ignored the importance of economic power in deciding conflicts was unfounded. Despite the nit-picking, Beer awarded the book 'the highest praise', and linked the methodology with that of Seeley.[66] Corbett acquired Beer's latest book and requested details of the issues that needed attention. Beer repeated his sincere appreciation of 'the high quality of your work' and sent an article on the British colonial system.[67]

The *Spectator* recognised that Corbett had produced the first comprehensive view of a conflict normally studied in distinct European, American and Asian compartments, connecting the threads of Pitt's strategy. Pitt's emphasis on the combined and harmonious effort of Navy and Army was amplified, rather than his strategic insight. It was 'a book of great moment, and deserves the attention, not merely of the naval officers to whom it was originally addressed, but of all serious students of government'.[68] *English Historical Review* critic Charles Atkinson (1874–1964) rated Corbett a master of the naval history, praising 'his powers of vivid and vigorous narrative'. Fellow NRS councillor Atkinson already knew Corbett and his work.[69] He recognised the purpose of the text: 'as the sub-title shows it is quite as much a contribution to strategical theory as to history'. He was less indulgent of the consequences, believing Corbett had, on occasion, been unnecessarily contentious, notably when challenging received wisdom on seapower and battle. He was not persuaded of the relative unimportance of battle, deploying arguments current among the 'offensive' and 'decisive battle' military school to dispute Clausewitz's maxim about the superiority of the defensive. Among the impressive range of archival sources he picked out the correspondence between the Sardinian envoys in London and Paris, Prime Minister Bute's intermediaries in the peace process, which refuted the charge that Bute had abandoned Frederick of Prussia.[70] Canadian Dominion Archivist Arthur G. Doughty, an expert on the North American side of the war, declared it the best guide to the conflict.[71]

However, the most important responses were those of Fisher, Slade and the strategic community. They were positive and unanimous. Fisher reported that James Thursfield had told him it was 'one of the best things he had ever read, and that he believed a review worthy of the book would appear in the TIMES', adding, 'I feel infinitely grateful to you for your public service (as well as your private help) which I earnestly hope some day may get its fit reward'.[72] This would be Fisher's favourite book: in February 1915 he sought a new 'Pitt' to direct the war.[73]

The *Seven Years' War* offered a convenient *résumé* of the 'British way', something other navies recognised, using it as a strategic template for contemporary war games. In the United States Mahan and fellow naval thinker Admiral Bradley Fiske realised the significance of Corbett's achievement. By 1911 the *Seven Years' War* was on the reading list of the Naval War College at Newport, along with *Some Principles*. The spring 1911 version of War Plan Orange, a war with Japan, cited a strategic principle from the book, while Mahan recognised Corbett's 'British way' would integrate naval, military and diplomatic action.[74] It may be no accident that the American naval school 'first laid emphasis upon the importance of doctrine' in 1912.[75] In Britain, Admiralty Chief of Staff Doveton Sturdee used material from the *Seven Years' War* to illustrate a 1913 paper on cruiser operations. His text, circulated to British cruiser captains, followed the NRS model, combining extracts from existing studies with a series of doctrinal 'lessons learnt'.[76] Sturdee's paper demonstrates that Corbett's work, and that of the NRS, were driven by the Navy, focused through the NID and War Staff.

Despite its present-minded focus, the book still occupies a prominent place in the historiography of the conflict. Richard Middleton recognised it as a 'classic study', demonstrating 'how Pitt achieved victory by a military and naval strategy that was co-ordinated to the last detail', quoting a key passage that defined the 'British way'.

> Pitt's system is a most brilliant lesson of the way in which the weak army of a strong naval power can be used, and of how mere superiority at sea can be made to thwart continental ... strategy and upset their moral balance.[77]

Middleton recognised Corbett's connection with the War Course, that he wrote for an audience that had superior systems for centralised control: steam and the telegraph cable.[78] This, he implied, encouraged Corbett to push his argument beyond the evidence, crediting mid-eighteenth-century statesmen with twentieth-century strategic thinking to engage his students. He made the war deliver lessons for an age of strategic thought, and advanced technology. This was a text of its time, and its audience.

Daniel Baugh's superb *The Global Seven Years' War* of 2011 criticises some didactic passages written for naval students, and refined for the CID Invasion Inquiry of 1907.[79] He also takes issue with older academic standards, not least the much-lauded work of Richard Pares.[80] While historians will read Baugh, students of war and strategy will find Corbett's *Seven Years' War* a masterly text, one that has much to say about the ideas of the dreadnought age in which it was created, and an exemplary Clausewitzian assessment of a major conflict. Melding the worlds of Whitehall and the flagship, mastering the correspondence, the context and aims of the directing minds on land and sea, Corbett demonstrated that wars are fluid and reactive, waged and determined by men – not scientific theory. The more realistic the aims, and the more effectively they harness the power of the state, the more likely it is they will succeed. Created for the statesmen, sailors and soldiers of 1907, Corbett's *Seven Years' War* has continuing relevance.

CHAPTER 10

Policy, Strategy and International Law

Alongside *England in the Seven Years' War*, Corbett produced three high-profile public essays and a memorandum for the CID Invasion Inquiry, texts that reinforced his case for a 'British way'. These texts argued that national strategy was maritime/economic, the Navy was the 'Senior Service' and Fisher's policy had secured peace with economy. They placed Corbett at the heart of decision-making in a great power anxious about 'decline', the dissolution of empire, not least the future of Ireland, increasing democratisation, and the looming threat of a major European war, sparked by the ambitions of Imperial Germany. Corbett based his arguments on a sophisticated appreciation of past practice. He addressed the men in power, and they listened. Unlike Mahan, who used the essay format as an economic opportunity, financial independence gave Corbett the luxury of choice. He accepted challenging commissions that dealt with issues of pressing national concern, including partisan attacks on Fisher's policy that damaged the Navy's credibility. The negative, diffuse arguments of the anti-Fisher 'Syndicate of Discontent' had unsettled the political class, and a wider public that took British seapower for granted. He believed the 'Syndicate' risked weakening the prestige that sustained British deterrence, handing the direction of national strategy to a 'continental' Army General Staff.

These high-quality outputs targeted the best minds of the day, but they were ephemera, to be reworked in more durable formats. Shorn of polemical packaging, the 1907 essays, the preface to the Ballard Committee War Plans, and his memoranda for the CID Invasion Inquiry joined the 'Green Pamphlet' and became *Some Principles*, a powerful statement of national strategic doctrine.

Corbett the essayist preferred the counter-attack. Before joining a major public debate he mastered his brief, précised existing arguments, exposing logical flaws and evidentiary failings. Every essay had identifiable targets, a familiar approach for a courtroom lawyer. He was not a controversialist, rarely returning to a subject once he had published. Essays were the dominant medium of contemporary debate, and Corbett's addressed specific audiences, officers, statesmen or intellectuals. As a 'Coefficient' he debated the future of Britain and the empire with an elite group, establishing the national and imperial contexts of strategy, and honing his debating skills.

Corbett and Fisher understood Britain would gain nothing from a major conflict; they abhorred war, opposing the idea of a mass conscript army as politically unsound, strategically unnecessary, un-English and uneconomic. Appreciating the brilliance of Corbett's work, Fisher persuaded him to support his policy through public advocacy, work that deepened his engagement with the evolving grand strategy of a unique maritime empire.

Corbett's first major contribution to the debate on Fisher's reforms, 'Recent Attacks on the Admiralty', appeared in February 1907.[1] The dramatic burst of activity that followed Fisher's appointment as First Sea Lord had raised significant opposition amongst older officers. The opposition acquired a figurehead when Fisher's promotion to Admiral of the Fleet enabled him to remain in office for another five years, ending Lord Charles Beresford's hopes. The intellectual leader of the 'Syndicate of Discontent', Rear Admiral Sir Reginald Custance, already hated Fisher.[2] Backed by Sir William White, architect of the 'pre-dreadnought' fleet,[3] and pro-Army elements in the Conservative party, the Syndicate cited Mahan as their authority when criticising strategic redistribution, turbine-powered dreadnought capital ships, submarines, the wholesale scrapping of obsolete warships, the sale of obsolete stores and, above all, a new officer education system that challenged elite privilege. Common entry for all naval officers challenged the social prestige of seaman officers. The Syndicate wanted to remove Fisher and the Liberal government.

Meanwhile the new Liberal government included a strong contingent of economising radicals, including Winston Churchill and David Lloyd George, who opposed defence spending as an article of faith. Fisher had to persuade the new Cabinet that Admiralty policy was both sound and economical. Conceding the Syndicate's demand for a public enquiry would damage the Admiralty's credibility, providing an excuse to reduce funding. Fisher's contemptuous response to his critics proved counter-productive. On Trafalgar Day 1906 Lord Esher advised him 'Mahan, and Custance and Co ... should be *answered* and argued with. Not by you personally, but by people properly coached to do it.'[4]

Fisher's stable of supportive journalists lacked the intellectual capacity and public stature to deal with Syndicate heavyweights Custance and White, who published under easily penetrated pen-names in leading Tory journals, *Blackwood's Magazine* and the *Spectator*. These essays were reprinted in book form; White's were introduced by St John Loe Strachey, editor of the *Spectator*. Corbett thought White and Strachey were bogus patriots trying to score political points. Strachey repeated Beresford's jibe that Fisher was not 'a great blue-water sailor', before blaming the Liberal government for his actions.[5] Corbett marked up some of White's arguments, noting that Fisher was not the first strong First Sea Lord to dominate a board, and stressing he, and not the Board collectively, was the responsible senior naval advisor to the government. He emphasised the importance of secrecy in key aspects of naval policy, celebrated the success of Fisher's new designs, and observed that strategic redistributions had been a commonplace of past experience.[6] Custance, an experienced senior officer, posed more problems: his arguments appeared plausible, and he was a friend.[7] Yet the task was relatively straightforward for, as Edmond Slade later observed:

> Custance as a rule generally has his facts in good order, but he almost invariably seems to draw wrong deductions from those facts. I quite remember forming the same opinion of him quite 12 years ago, when I used to have long discussions with him on tactical subjects. Even then he always seemed to me to enter the argument in a perfectly confused state of mind as regards the facts which he produced. He would bring them all up good, bad or indifferent, but when it came to deducing some conclusions I generally found he had already done that, quite independently, or even in spite of the facts which he had himself brought up.[8]

Custance, like Mahan, remained a deductive analyst who made up his mind before examining the evidence, an easy target for an inductive lawyer.

'Recent Attacks' began as a riposte to a 'Syndicate' essay by retired Admiral Sir Cyprian Bridge for the influential *The Nineteenth Century and After* in late 1906.[9] Bridge condemned Fisher for leaking information to tame journalists, creating an appetite for endless sensation in an area of public policy that required calm reflection. The former DNI savaged Archibald Hurd's partisan ori-Fisher contribution – it had backfired. Yet Sir Cyprian's real targets were *Dreadnought*, *Invincible* and the nucleus crew system, which

Hurd celebrated without providing a coherent rationale. Bridge demanded the Admiralty defend its policies in Parliament, rather than relying on 'irresponsible and unprofessional writers' unable to explain basic concepts.[10] Such feeble advocacy suggested the Admiralty had something to hide. With the public perplexed, the best solution would be a public enquiry into the Admiralty. Fisher had to respond: few among the political class were unaware that he worked the press. Corbett was the obvious candidate, his demolition of Bridge's Trafalgar essay in 1905 had delighted Fisher, while his literary 'bludgeon' had developed a compelling case for the Naval War Course.[11]

Having secured the right of reply to Bridge's ten-page philippic, Fisher persuaded Corbett to accept the challenge. Jacky demanded twenty pages, not the fifteen proffered by editor Sir James Knowles, and provided Corbett with the services of his shorthand writer Mr Phillips and DNI Ottley. He added some Fisherite flattery: 'I think you are doing a most patriotic thing in so kindly undertaking this task, and it will, I am convinced, be of immense national service.'[12] Admiralty material and Fisher's input enabled Corbett to produce a draft in little more than week. Fisher approved: 'Couldn't be better! ... it is *just* the thing "to meet the present distress", as St. Paul would say!'[13]

Corbett's clear, direct style masked a subtle argument. He contrasted the self-indulgent nit-picking of irresponsible critics, antediluvian admirals, and the partisan Conservative press with the coherence of Admiralty policy and strategy before reducing the Syndicate to irrelevance by demonstrating how Fisher's programme worked, with the mighty *Dreadnought* at its apogee. The Syndicate had no alternative policy, attacking mere details: this must stop 'before further harm is done, and we become a laughing-stock to the world'.[14] Nor did Corbett pull his punches: the Syndicate were irresponsible, partisan and dangerous, attempting to overthrow a dynamic, progressive Admiralty Board to gratify petty objections to essential changes, in particular the Selborne scheme's assault on entrenched privilege.

The enthusiastic press response sharpened Fisher's instinct to go in for the kill. He wanted to annihilate his opponents, weaponising withering logic:

> what a paper you could give us on Fleet distribution, Protection of Commerce, Entry and Training, Dockyard Policy! Won't you be tempted? Are you going to keep that talent wrapped up in the napkin of criminal modesty? Won't you let me tell Knowles of these other shots in your locker?[15]

Corbett demurred, and Fisher accepted this, with regret.[16] He retailed the plaudits of the First Lord, Lord Tweedmouth, the Prince of Wales, Hurd and Thursfield. All agreed the effect had 'been immense'.[17] Fisher reused 'Recent Attacks' in November 1907, sending former First Lord Cawdor a copy, with a key passage highlighted: 'a crowd of little or anonymous men begin to cry an alarm, and demand that the machine shall be stopped and opened up for all the world to see what work is doing. Such folly would be ludicrous were it not our own, and so full of peril. Can they not see?'[18] Fisher also sent the essay to his friend the king for good measure.

Corbett disagreed with aspects of Fisher's policy and did not disguise the fact. He shared Slade's preference for a Staff and recognised that Fisher's vindictive methods were splitting the service. Yet there was no alternative: Custance, the brightest of the Syndicate, was dogmatic, narrow-minded and impervious to logical argument. In the short term Fisher was the future, but there were promising men among the rising generation, including Prince Louis and John Jellicoe.

Where 'Recent Attacks' emphasised skilled advocacy, in the manner of the naval education essays, 'The Strategical Value of Speed' relied on historical sources and logic.[19] Naval opinion was deeply divided over the merits of Fisher's epochal capital ships *Dreadnought* and *Invincible*. These ships combined an all-big-gun armament, large size and turbine power plants that provided high sustained sea speed, enhancing strategic mobility. For the Syndicate they were an error: Custance pointedly used the pen-name 'Barfleur', a small battleship he had commanded.[20] Corbett's research had convinced him that larger, faster ships were superior; the arguments used by Mahan and Custance were one-sided and illogical, and he took the opportunity to teach the Navy to think as rigorously as it manoeuvred.

This time Corbett addressed his audience in person, speaking at the Royal United Services Institute, the leading British Defence forum on 6 March 1907, shortly after 'Recent Attacks' was published. Reading an announcement of the lecture on 2 January Fisher offered his support, including 'some <u>serious</u> papers' from the Admiralty and the fleet.[21] The prestigious venue on Whitehall normally hosted flag officers and field marshals, not cultured literary types. Acutely aware that he was a civilian in a service controversy, Corbett emphasised logic and coherence. 'The Strategical Value of Speed' dismissed critics who had failed to state the core issue, advancing the impeccable logic of a French author who demonstrated that, independent of all other factors, speed was strategically desirable. He focused on strategy; analysing the tactical consequences of the trade-off between speed, protection and firepower was beyond his 'power'. Yet, for all his *faux* diffidence, and the omission of 'Barfleur' from his paper, the critique was precise and unsparing. Custance's argument collapsed under logical analysis, his one-sided examples mere window dressing for a flawed concept. Britain's advantageous global position was best served by big, fast ships, using the empire's superior refuelling facilities. Consequently speed was more important than radius. This logic applied equally to home and imperial defence. Forcing rival powers to sacrifice range for speed made imperial defence easier. Then he demolished the 'historical' case for moderate size, countering Mahan and Custance's selective use of history with stronger examples: Admiral Sir Thomas Hardy, Nelson's right-hand man, a proto-Fisherite First Sea Lord, had built big battleships and cruisers, scrapping small, obsolete types. Having dealt a mortal blow to the case for moderate size Corbett insisted the question must be 'worked out by a competent authority' with an 'open mind', a requirement that excluded 'Barfleur'.[22]

Corbett concluded that 'a policy of high speed seems to be distinctly one method of improving our geographical conditions'. The case against speed had ignored 'the ascertained rules of strategical discussion', introducing 'personal and accidental factors' in place of system and logic, a sound assessment of Custance's visceral hatred of Fisher.[23] Not content with the past as precedent, Corbett addressed the impact of technology:

> Torpedoes, wireless telegraphy, and submarines have produced changes of strategical conditions – not fundamental, perhaps, but very important, and the chief importance is that they practically destroy the old system of blockade ... close blockade ... is now impossible.

He challenged Mahan's claim that the Russo-Japanese War had supported the case against speed, stressing the effect of local conditions off Port Arthur.[24] Furthermore it was unsound to base an argument on a single example. Mahan's observations, published in the *RUSI Journal* four months earlier, should not be treated as gospel. Corbett was equally unsparing on the issue of defensive strategy: advocates of moderate speed indulged the 'characteristic disease of contemporary strategy', ignoring past practice and future prospects for a simple mantra, folded into a Jominian obsession with concentration. He made excellent use of Kempenfelt's letters, published by the NRS in the *Barham Papers*.[25] This material would reach Fisher's opponents: Bridge, Custance, Mahan and White were all NRS members.

Corbett concluded by returning to the critics' hallowed ground, the better to deflate their claims. Having demolished Mahan's argument he magnanimously excluded the American from criticism, blaming 'somewhat loose reading' by his followers, a category he implied included Custance. Speed was essential to the defensive and the offensive, not only had France consistently avoided the decisive engagements so hallowed by Custance, by superior speed under sail, but speed was equally important to defensive warfare, something that 'Admiralty staffs' had recognised.[26] Speed would enable *Invincible* to catch any oceanic raider – an argument reused in the preface to the Ballard Committee plans.

Arguments from this paper reappeared in *Some Principles*, notably the critical importance of logic, avoiding simplistic dogma and special cases. Corbett dissected the contemporary obsession with 'offensive' warfare, a shibboleth almost as prevalent among sea officers as soldiers, emphasising that it had always been necessary to defend in some areas in order to mass for an attack elsewhere. He linked the paper to his examination of the legal aspects of modern economic warfare, emphasising how new technology had altered the strategic realities, ending close blockades. These insights reflected his work on the conceptual element of Ballard Committee War Plans in 1907, and the 'Green Pamphlet', which prepared the service for the open or distant blockade of 1914.

In the subsequent discussion most officers approved Corbett's method-ology, and his conclusions on speed and the *Dreadnought*. They remained unhappy about the mass scrapping of obsolete tonnage. Corbett admitted 'Barfleur' had been his target and extended his discussion to include the tactical perspective. Custance argued that a faster fleet could be countered by turning away, but Corbett observed that simply turning the enemy off course in this way might be a major strategic advantage. He concluded by stressing the distinctive spheres of expertise of historians and naval officers, along with the relative merits of historical examples and recent experience. Examples from the past were more valuable, because they were more numerous.[27]

This was an impressive performance by a man confident of his status in the debate, ready to meet his opponents in the open field. The 'Syndicate' had been defeated on their chosen ground. Fisher thought it 'splendid', drawing Corbett ever deeper into his Admiralty. Sending the latest Cabinet brief on policy and expenditure, he added: 'I would be glad to see you on a very secret matter about some war plans to which I think you could add most materially in their educational value.' Fisher persuaded Corbett to write a preface for the Ballard Committee plans with a combination of patriotic appeal and flattery: 'you will be doing the Navy a lasting service by giving us in the proposed preface an epitome of the art of Naval War'.[28] Fisher wanted to unite the service behind his policy by promulgating a suitable doctrine, and Corbett was the man to produce it. With the plans already complete Fisher was in a hurry: Corbett delivered within a month.[29] Obliged to work from existing resources, including Fisher's notes, 'Some Principles of Naval Warfare' contains much that can be traced to previous projects, not least the first two public essays of 1907 and the 'Green Pamphlet', completed in early 1907.[30]

Captain George Ballard's War Plans Committee began work late in 1906, developing an initial paper by Slade on how Britain might respond to a German occupation of Belgium or the Netherlands. Ballard quickly abandoned a close blockade, advocating a distant economic blockade as the best way to put pressure on Germany. He did not consider a German invasion of France because, unlike the security of Belgium, this was not *casus belli* under existing diplomatic agreements.

For the past sixty years the Ballard Committee plans have been dismissed as outdated and irrelevant, views that can be traced back to Lieutenant Commander Peter Kemp's bizarre comment that they were 'almost juvenile'.[31] These plans were created by the Navy's leading strategist, guided by the director of the Naval War Course, on a committee tasked to examine operational and strategic issues for the NID and the Board. The War Course was a central element of Fisher's planning process, while the structure had been established by Prince Louis, as DNI between 1902 and 1904. Furthermore, Fisher understood how to delegate and use a Staff.[32] Kemp's argument was profoundly ahistorical, claiming plans completed in early 1907 should have anticipated the situation prevailing in 1914. In 1907 Germany had one submarine, and only four by 1909,[33] while the German battlefleet was less than half the strength of the British, with new dreadnoughts providing major strategic and tactical advantages that would last for close on five years. Elsewhere the Royal Navy had learnt many lessons about contemporary minesweeping from Japanese operations off Port Arthur in 1904.[34] Ultimately Fisher intended the plans, and Corbett's preface, to serve an educational function, disseminating doctrine to the service, along with the opinions of Fisher and Admiral Sir Arthur Wilson.

Kemp's profoundly misleading analysis has been widely followed, notably by his friend Arthur Marder. Marder placed far too much emphasis on a covering note that claimed the plans were:

> not in any way to be considered as those definitely adopted, but are valuable and instructive because illustrative of the variety of considerations governing the formation of War Plans.[35]

As Ruddock Mackay demonstrated, Fisher added the disclaimer before sending the plans to Beresford, the Commander-in-Chief Channel Fleet, and removed Wilson's comments. The plans were a guide to current Admiralty thinking and the range of possibilities that might be considered. The first lesson of maritime operations was that nothing survived contact with oceans and weather, let alone the enemy. Unable to grasp their purpose Beresford's Chief of Staff, Doveton Sturdee, urged him to demand detailed plans, which he could criticise to undermine Fisher's authority. The Admiralty could not produce a naval 'Schlieffen Plan', even if one were possible, because the Cabinet, not the Admiralty, would determine if Britain went to war and how a war would be waged. As it was blindingly obvious that Britain had no interest in starting a war with Germany, any plans would need to be flexible. Consequently Ballard and Slade provided a guide to current thinking for those who might have to conduct a war; Corbett provided the doctrinal context.

A historian of great men, focused on the personal clash between Beresford and Fisher, Marder overlooked the plan's educational function, although he did recognise the focus on economic warfare, delivered through a distant blockade. That Corbett addressed the mechanics of blockading the Scotland–Norway gap in his preface suggests Slade briefed him on elements of document, even if he was not allowed to see it. The Ballard plans abandoned close blockade as the basis of economic warfare and downplayed the possibility of amphibious operations against the short, difficult German North Sea coast in the face of mines and torpedo boats. Instead the new realities of the Entente were emphasised, offensive work in the Baltic should be coordinated with the French. They could blockade Germany's eastern Baltic ports from the otherwise empty bases of their Russian ally, leaving the western Baltic and North Sea to the Royal Navy.[36] Hardly a 'juvenile' assessment in early 1907, when the Entente partners outnumbered Germany in modern battleships by three to one; the ratio Clausewitz thought necessary for a successful offensive. Corbett saw Ballard's distant blockade linking cruiser control of the Northern Approaches to fleet battle. The preface also contained early sketches of his legal and strategic justification for the new method, another issue raised by Ballard, which he developed in the essay 'Private Property'.[37]

Intended for a wider audience than the war plans, Corbett's preface followed the 'literary' model of the essays, and toned down the intellectual rigour of the 'Green Pamphlet'. He began by deploying Clausewitz's limited–unlimited dichotomy as the key to war planning, although he did not name the Prussian theorist, citing the less alarming words of Raimondo Montecuccoli on the purpose of war, from another text on his bookshelf.[38] Command of the sea allowed a belligerent to choose between limited and unlimited war, a reality emphasised in the Russo-Japanese conflict, on which he was lecturing to the War Course.

The second section began with Corbett's classic definition: 'Command of the sea means nothing but control of maritime lines of passage and communication.' While such command was never absolute, it provided the base for an effective strategy, dominated by the capture of private property, a measure he proceeded to justify. 'To demand of a maritime power that it should surrender the right of controlling communications at sea is no more reasonable than to demand of a military power that it should surrender the right of controlling the enemy's road and railways.'[39] Logic and brevity were essential to achieving the expository effect he sought.

Command was exercised by cruisers and flotilla craft, not battlefleets, the function of the battlefleet was merely to control hostile battlefleets. If the enemy did not have a battlefleet, Britain would redeploy resources to enhance the application of command of the sea. Having smashed the false idol of Mahanian navalists, he stressed that battlefleets were a deterrent, a 'deflection of pure naval strategy'.[40] The concept of deflection enabled him to explain that Mahan focused on a military state using a battlefleet Navy, not a seapower state defending the maritime communications of a world empire. Mahan's analysis was correct for the United States, or Imperial Germany, but not the United Kingdom, a point von der Goltz might have echoed.[41] Once again Corbett's purpose was critical, he did not believe in 'naval strategy': strategy was national, linking armed forces, economic power and diplomatic effort, and he wanted his readers, in this case admirals, to understand that using the fleet to deter war was far more important than conducting naval operations.

The third section addressed the fluid state of capital ship design; the size, speed and above all firepower of the *Invincible* type called into question the functions of battleships and cruisers. Corbett found ample precedent for cruisers capable of lying in the line of battle, and capital ships capable of cruiser work. The new ships gave the battlefleet 'a vast increase in reach and effective mobility', especially useful for a superior fleet pursuing a weaker foe. They avoided the need to build a faster battlefleet and were 'the expression of the most cherished and distinctive aspiration of our greatest masters of the art, to which no adequate expression was ever given before. It is the very type that ... Hawke and Nelson sighed for, but never obtained.'[42] The argument could have been strengthened by referencing Britain's immense battlefleet superiority in 1907, but that risked prompting 'Syndicate' criticism.

Having lauded Fisher's prize creation, in all probability after personal discussion, Corbett savaged his failure to maintain a cruiser fleet to exercise command. *Invincible* was not a substitute for cruiser numbers, only a supplement, another argument based on discussions with Slade.[43] Twice Corbett expanded on the idea of a sea-control force combining *Invincibles* and scout cruisers, possibly an early version of Fisher's 'Fleet Unit' concept. Having discussed the North Sea with Fisher, Corbett recommended patrolling with 'ocean destroyers' and *Invincibles*, holding back the main fleet 'for the supreme moments of battle decision'.[44] Fisher was preparing to direct a centrally controlled strategy by wireless from Whitehall. The battleship discussion was more explicitly pro-*Dreadnought* than the RUSI lecture, although they shared key arguments. *Dreadnought* was the ultimate expression of tactics, massing more heavy guns in one ship and shortening the battle line improved flexibility. Once again he stressed that speed was more important than radius for Britain. The cruiser's primary role was exercising command of the sea, fleet scouting was secondary; powerful armoured units like the *Invincibles* were required to push through hostile scouting forces and obtain intelligence. Much wartime cruising could be conducted by armed merchant vessels, but in a war against Germany the Scotland–Norway gap would need modern cruisers, including *Invincibles,* to intercept hostile armed liners that were faster than existing cruisers. Flotillas were more powerful and consequential than they had been in the age of sail, and he expected they would escort the battlefleet at night.[45]

In 'Obtaining a Decision', Corbett observed that destroying the enemy fleet, the obvious naval target, might be have to be sacrificed to wider political or strategic demands. Furthermore, he expected fleets would wait on their own coasts to conserve the fuel supplies of their short-ranged flotilla craft, unless there were compelling strategic reasons to take the offensive. He replaced the old mantra of 'seek and destroy' with a more intelligent update:

> The first aim in a naval war plan is to devise some means of forcing the enemy's fleet to expose itself to being struck by your own, and that in waters as unfavourable to him as possible.

As a statement of doctrine for the peculiar circumstances of a war with Germany this was deceptively simple, and strategically brilliant. This was how the Grand Fleet was used in the First World War. Corbett backed his argument with a Baltic example, linking his strategic thought to Fisher's Baltic-focused strategy.[46] This *Dreadnought*-era doctrine was necessarily different to that which had gone before. Unlike Mahan he acknowledged the impact of technology: 'the real teaching of history – is that the old maxims were based on strategical conditions several of which have passed away'. The most consequential change was the end of close naval and economic blockade, the obvious means of forcing the enemy to accept battle.[47]

In a secret document Corbett could discuss Germany as the planning target, driving home his argument with potential operations against the High Seas Fleet, views that reflected War Course exercises, conversations with Ottley, Slade, Fisher and, in all probability, Ballard. Nowhere was this more obvious than in the section on using wireless to ambush the German fleet, the subject of contemporary Admiralty planning.[48]

'Peace Preparations' emphasised the need for higher levels of readiness in the machine age, citing General Gross von Schwarzhoff's claim that the German Army could mobilise in thirteen days. Fisher had met Schwarzhoff at the Hague Conference in 1899 and retained a vivid impression of the highly rated German soldier. Corbett stressed that thirteen hours would be too long for the Royal Navy to secure the North Sea, but Fisher's Home Fleet and strategic rebalancing, a stroke of genius, enabled Britain to be ready at very short notice. The 'Distribution of the fleet' pointedly redefined Mahan's shibboleth of concentration as 'distributing your fleet so as to insure the greatest number of strategical combinations that there is any likelihood of your requiring.'[49] He urged intelligent application. Massing all the Navy's best ships in the North Sea would be uneconomical, and 'an intolerable threat likely to cause more political trouble than the menace of the fleet (to Germany) itself could ever allay.'[50] Corbett saw that Fisher's Home Fleet was an elegant solution to current strategic needs, one that avoided alarming Germany, or weakening the wider imperial position. Located in the North Sea, and close to the Baltic, it could familiarise itself with the theatre or, in Fisher's terms, 'let your drill ground be your battle ground.'[51] It was commanded by the admirals who would lead the main fleet in war. British strategic concentration looked very different to Mahan's massed battlefleet.

> We can never be certain. Even in apparently so simple a case as threatened war with Germany the call might be in the North Sea or at the head of the Adriatic, and even further afield in the Near East or in some colonial sphere. So we stretch the chain of our linked fleets so that it may reach from the Baltic to Alexandria and onward in thinner strength till it couples up with Japan.[52]

The synergy between this model and the events of August–September 1914 is obvious, Corbett would capture this fluid 'Imperial Concentration' in volume I of *Naval Operations*.[53] Fittingly, Corbett ended with 'Personnel', highlighting the superior maritime aptitude of British men, and the importance of the Selborne scheme in bringing the officer corps into the twentieth century. Peacetime manpower must be adequate to meet the first shock of war, with mobilisation capacity to sustain the effort. Fisher's nucleus crews kept the fleet ready for action without massing too many men in home waters. After 'a long period of peace' too many men and ships were scattered across the globe supporting diplomacy, forgetting that: 'Our power of controlling the seas and securing our Imperial interests depends on our command of the great lines of Imperial communications, and the first essential to such command, as all history and theory shows, is to keep a firm hold on the home ends.' Nucleus crews and the Home Fleet had achieved this, 'against a main fleet known to be ready to strike and able strike hard'.[54]

Corbett retained a few polemical asides from his other 1907 texts, aimed at Custance and Beresford, but Slade insisted they should be removed and, following a discussion of the function of cruisers, approved the text.[55] Corbett sent the handwritten manuscript to Fisher, who realised his organic, occasionally inchoate ideas had been transformed into a coherent statement of strategic doctrine for a global empire in the cable and wireless age, situating the detailed, specific and necessarily time-limited plans of the Ballard Committee in a powerful, evolving doctrinal continuum that served Britain's strategic needs. It differed from Corbett's other outputs of this period only in being more explicit and precise, a benefit of restricted circulation. It provided senior officers with a guide to the concepts that informed Admiralty planning, and the thinking of the man who would direct their movements by wireless, to ambush the High Seas Fleet. Corbett's elegant exposition situated operations in the wider strategic context.

The plans were sent to Sir Arthur Wilson, who would command the Home Fleet in the event of war: he saw no need to comment on Corbett's preface. While this has been treated as a demonstration of the irrelevance of the plans, this is demonstrably false.[56] Wilson was content; he chose to highlight a different concern: fighting alongside France 'would be more serious than if we were at war with Germany alone, because although Germany would be unable to injure us directly, the discredit of the defeat of our allies would fall on us, and we should be bound to put forth our full national strength, and, if necessary, exhaust all our resources in their defence'.[57] Britain might be obliged to sacrifice its gains to remove the enemy from the critical strategic region of northern Flanders, as it had in 1748. This historical commonplace was a feature of Corbett's work, most obviously in the *Seven Years' War*. Fisher agreed it would be better to fight alone, and rely on crushing the German economy.[58] The synergy of opinion between the two admirals around the themes of Corbett's forthcoming book was not accidental. They had anticipated the events of 1914.

The target for the new work was obvious. A week after the RUSI lecture Corbett addressed the Naval War Course at Portsmouth, and joined Slade in an attempt to recruit Captain Doveton Sturdee, Beresford's Chief of Staff and a key member of the 'Syndicate': 'if we get him we get the whole service that has not been with us'.[59] Those hopes were disappointed by Sturdee's stupidity and self-regard. That Corbett saw himself, and was seen by others, as part of Fisher's team is significant. Yet when Fisher solicited another essay in defence of the *Dreadnought* in June 1908 Corbett refused: he had lost too many naval friends by openly espousing Fisher's cause. He preferred rewriting a paper on fire control by Commander Frederick Dreyer, who had ignored all evidence and argument.[60]

By the spring of 1907 Corbett's mastery of national strategy, strategic theory and recent experience, notably the campaigns of 1898 and 1904–5, had equipped him to shape a coherent approach to strategic doctrine. With the core arguments in place he would reinforce his expertise, improve his delivery and establish his methodology in naval and academic practice.

The preface to the Ballard War Plans was circulated on 1 May as 'Some Principles of Naval Warfare'. Although Corbett requested his work appear anonymously, he could not disguise his views. Their appearance in an official document was 'resented by Beresford and Custance'.[61] This was hardly surprising: Beresford had received the plans as Commander-in-Chief Channel Fleet, and Corbett's anonymity would not survive Custance's inspection. Key passages drawn from his latest essays made the connection obvious. The stress on logic and clarity of thought was pure Corbett. Defeated and humiliated, the Syndicate sought fresh talismen, finding them in the unlikely forms of an old field marshal and a disreputable journalist.

Refining the instruments of national strategy returned Corbett to the vexed question of maritime belligerent rights, the basis of economic warfare. How would modern blockades work, and could they be used without alienating powerful neutrals, especially the United States? Leaving the issue in a state of flux risked compromising war planning, and diplomacy, while the new Liberal government posed a serious threat to sea power strategy. Prominent Cabinet ministers, including the Lord Chancellor, the senior lawyer, were openly hostile to the Admiralty's position. If their views prevailed seapower would be disarmed. Such views were especially dangerous because they coincided with the narrow-minded, battle-fixated views of Custance and others, who resolutely ignored the role of economic warfare in conflicts with continental powers. Weakening economic warfare would empower the 'continental' argument of the Army General Staff.

Under modern conditions an open blockade was the only viable method, but it lacked a solid legal justification. Corbett's opposition to the 'Little Englander' wing of his own party made the task of crafting one all the more rewarding. He had examined the legal basis of blockade position in 1896, arguing that only the power to blockade, and capture outlying territory, gave 'England, in spite of her military weakness, so commanding a position in Europe'.[62] In 1896 the obvious enemy was France, whose overseas colonies would be useful diplomatic counters. In 1907 Germany was evidently preparing to win a war in Europe, without reference to its handful of unprofitable colonies, or extensive seaborne commerce. This reality informed 'The Capture of Private Property at Sea', the second Fisher-inspired essay in *The Nineteenth Century and After*. It provided the necessary intellectual rigour to support Admiralty opposition to further limitation of maritime belligerent rights at the Second Hague Peace Conference.[63]

Corbett's target was the Lord Chancellor, Lord Loreburn (Robert Threshie Reid, 1846–1923). Loreburn and Corbett took diametrically opposed positions on many issues, including female suffrage, which Loreburn resolutely opposed. The long-serving Liberal MP and barrister, an avowed pacifist internationalist, rejected the 'Little Englander' label. Loreburn distrusted France, seeking better relations with Germany, and actively undermined government policy during the Agadir Crisis of 1911 through the *Manchester Guardian*.[64] Prime Minister Campbell-Bannerman appointed Loreburn in 1906 to balance the Liberal Imperialists in his Cabinet and keep Richard Haldane off the Woolsack. Loreburn condemned British policy on maritime rights in his *Capture at Sea* of 1905.[65] In the build-up to the Second Hague Conference, Loreburn publicly championed the immunity of private property, a long-standing American demand. The Foreign Office and the Admiralty dismissed this as 'peace at any price'.

Corbett's arguments were national and strategic rather than legal: abolition would serve the interests of continental military powers, which had always sought to restrict the economic impact of sea power. Germany would benefit from increased immunity: Professor Perels' German maritime law textbook noted how Britain resisted 'all movements for reforming the laws of maritime warfare *in the interests of the great military states*'.[66] Corbett rejected the Liberal internationalist position that Britain, with the world's largest maritime commerce, had most to gain by the abolition of capture. Britain's absolute dependence on seaborne supplies obliged it to provide adequate naval security. He demolished the apparently 'idealistic' freedom-of-private-property position by demonstrating that it had been created and promoted by self-interested continental aggressors. Loreburn's insufferable self-righteousness prompted a suitably deflating joke, using Sir William Harcourt's judgements to undermine his position.

Far from resisting progress the British had gone too far, conceding 'Free Ships – Free Goods' in the Declaration of Paris of 1856, which allowed enemy property to travel safely on neutral ships, a self-inflicted injury that weakened national strategy. To separate the immunity of private property from the concept of free ships making free goods, Corbett cited international law, where the right to take or destroy enemy property was universally accepted as a legitimate means of coercing hostile states. Any restraints on war adopted on land were for operational convenience, to maintain discipline, or avoid guerrilla activity: they did not prevent the occupation of territory to coerce the enemy into submission. Citing German practice in the Franco-Prussian War of 1870–1 helped readers understand the contemporary relevance of this argument. The right to capture private property at sea was the key to national security in war, and the basis of deterrence: it was the only thing that made sea power effective. Sea battles did not win wars, they only secured command of the sea, which 'means nothing less than control of communications': the offensive utility of command was an economic blockade that could bring the enemy to terms. It was also the best strategy for forcing an inferior fleet to fight. Loreburn's argument would disarm Britain. His confusion about contraband and local blockades prompted the observation that there was no moral distinction between close or open blockades. He was directed to read the correspondence of his eighteenth-century predecessor Lord Hardwicke, who understood the synergy between British policy and legal practice. Corbett also cited Mahan's *War of 1812*, a noted foreign analysis that supported the British position. Mahan offered equally effective testimony against the argument that land transport would render blockades ineffective. Not only had war at sea had been humanised, as Loreburn admitted, by the abolition of privateering, but blockades were the ultimate humane strategy. No-one was obliged to send their commercial property to sea, unless they wished to make a profit. If they did, they were taking an insurable risk. Finally, Corbett dismissed the claim that prize money might warp the judgement of naval officers as insulting in the last degree.

Corbett enjoyed savaging the pomposity of Loreburn and his kind, men armoured against the realities of a dangerous world by Cobdenite mantras, unwilling to see the iron fist behind Imperial Germany's emollient words at the latest conference. The exercise was both timely, and timeless. It proved successful, but he would have to return to the subject in 1911, and again in 1916, when President Woodrow Wilson, who combined Loreburn's beliefs with a visceral hatred of Britain, tried to make 'freedom of the seas' a founding principle of a 'League of Nations'. Wilson's aims were no more idealistic than those of Imperial Germany. He wanted to disarm a powerful economic rival, without having to fight, to make the world safe for the expansion of American commerce and capital.

Fisher sent Corbett's text to the king, Cabinet ministers, journalists, and an American delegate heading for the Hague Conference.

> I am ashamed at not having sooner congratulated you on your article. It has already done splendid service with Choate, who is going to be American Chief Delegate at the Hague. But all the world is going to be against us so I hear![67]

In the event Choate stuck to his official brief, pressing for the very changes the British wished to avoid.[68] Fisher's estimation of the paper led him to persuade James Knowles to let Mahan to reprint it in *Some Neglected Aspects of War*.[69] Mahan, who rarely commended his peers, praised Corbett: 'so well and favourably known for the series of works on naval subjects'.[70]

Corbett reused key arguments from 'Capture' in *Some Principles*, but shifted his focus from attacking Loreburn to establishing correct principles and demolishing common fallacies that ranged from the extreme 'blue-water' argument that victory in naval battle could win a war, to Liberal 'Free Seas' dogma that would permit enemy trade in wartime. For Corbett, economic warfare was the primary instrument of maritime strategy against continental states. It gave Britain, perhaps uniquely, the capacity to make truly limited war. By securing command of the sea a dominant navy could 'exert direct military pressure upon the national life of our enemy ashore': stopping maritime commerce equated with the conquest of territory. Corbett also invested this strategy with a moral quality: 'commerce prevention' caused less human suffering than any other form of war, closer to legal action than a military operation. He laid the foundations for 'distant' economic warfare in the First World War:

> Admit of the principle of tactical or close blockade, and as between belligerents you cannot condemn the principle of strategical or distant

blockade. Except in their effect upon neutrals, there is no juridical difference between the two.[71]

The exception was revealing: the 'neutrals' he had in mind were American.

Reinforcing his argument that the right of seizure at sea was analogous to that of requisition and contribution on land, Corbett claimed it would be wrong to deny sea powers the same right. Wars were ended by the ability to 'exert pressure on the citizens and their collective life', citing von der Goltz's line that peace could only be imposed by making 'the enemy's country feel the burdens of war with such weight that the desire for peace will prevail'. Without the right to capture private property there would be little purpose to naval activity beyond defence against invasion. Indeed, the general tenor of war, if all similar rights were denied, would be reduced to a 'purely legal procedure'. Not only was the world unready for such a change, but it would deprive those seeking to preserve the peace, the British, of their primary deterrent. A nation's financial sinews were an essential strategic resource, and therefore a valid target: the threat to cut them was a key restraint.[72] The synergy between Corbett's elegantly phrased essay and Fisher's blood-curdling phrases at the first Hague Conference in 1899 reflected a shared agenda.[73]

Economic warfare, including capturing the private property of enemy civilians, was, and had long been, Britain's basic strategic weapon: 'indeed such pressure may be the only means of forcing the decision we seek'. To limit it without applying equal constraint to operations on land would be absurd; significant changes to the legal rights of belligerents on one element would make war more, not less, likely. In 1911 he did not oppose the as-yet unratified Declaration of London, which the Admiralty had accepted.[74] The ultimate role of economic warfare in *Some Principles* was to provide an alternative 'British way' to the 'continental' strategy favoured by the Army General Staff. Only economic warfare could turn naval dominance into strategic consequence in Europe.

In August 1914, Britain and other belligerents began the war by adhering to the stipulations of the unratified Declaration of London. However, London was only waiting for German violations of international law to justify more aggressive approaches to economic warfare. This retaliatory principle had been clear in 1856, when Britain signed the Declaration of Paris to undermine American strategy, which relied on privateering. The government expected any state that went to war with Britain would resort to privateering, or another illegal method, vitiating existing agreements and justifying a more severe belligerent rights programme. The problem was that the Hague and London agreements left the status of economic warfare uncertain, and with that the validity of maritime strategy – just as the Army General Staff offered a plausible alternative. To address this problem, Corbett commissioned international lawyer Alexander Pearce Higgins, a War Course lecturer, to produce a suitable textbook in 1913.

The Army had reopened an old line of attack in 1906, reviving the invasion bogey, despite ample evidence that naval defence had worked well for centuries. At the national level, the challenge was to strike a balance between maintaining command of sea, which would make an invasion all but impossible, using land defences to ensure an invader would have to send a large and unwieldy force, with artillery and horses, thereby ensuring interception at sea, while deploying a powerful counter-attacking capability to destroy the bases from which invasions might be launched. In 1903 the CID dismissed the possibility of a French invasion: it did not need to be insured against. The War Office disagreed: in 1905 Field Marshal Lord Roberts resigned from the CID to support the National Service League's call for an enquiry.[75]

The league's demand for compulsory military training was an attempt to create a conscript army by stealth. As such continental military arguments had little appeal for Liberals of any stripe, Roberts joined forces with a journalist favoured by the War Office, former army officer Charles Repington, military correspondent of *The Times*.[76] The General Staff wanted something more than Haldane's BEF, a small amphibious strike force. In June 1907 Roberts abused his seat in the House of Lords to cast doubt on the Navy's ability to prevent an invasion. George Clarke, then stepping down as Secretary of the CID, mocked such invasion nonsense in *The Times* on 5 October 1907, Fisher, for whom the issue was both an unwelcome diversion and a potential opening for his naval opponents, was anxious to avoid further discussion. He had lost faith in Clarke when he opposed *Dreadnought*.[77]

Arthur Balfour agreed to assemble a sub-committee of the CID to hear Roberts, Repington, wealthy volunteer soldier Lord Lovat and Conservative politician Leopold Amery, better known as the 'bolt from the blue' or 'blue funk' school. Fisher passed Roberts' paper to Slade, now DNI, to frame a rebuttal. While Slade recognised the need to meet the Army halfway, by recognising the possibility of small-scale raids, Fisher remained adamant that nothing could get through, concerned any concession would undermine the logic of his Home Fleet.

The sub-committee was chaired by Chancellor of the Exchequer Herbert Asquith, with Sir Edward Grey, Lloyd George, Haldane, Lord Crewe and Lord Tweedmouth the interested ministers. The professional members were Fisher, Slade and successive chiefs of the Imperial General Staff, Sir Neville Lyttleton and Sir William Nicholson, Sir John French, Director of Military Operations (DMO), and Charles Ottley, now Secretary of the CID.

The issue became public as Corbett wrote the Quiberon section of *England in the Seven Years' War*, a striking strategic analogue. A letter linking the book with the invasion debate prompted Fisher to call for a *Nineteenth Century* essay on the theme, to demolish Roberts and his allies 'who are simply putty in Repington's hands'. The whole thing was a fraud because 'there was not a blessed word of the British Navy – our now permanent, fully manned North Sea [Home] Fleet'. An article on the subject would promote Corbett's book, and explain the Navy's case. The answer to Repington's mass of German statistics was obvious: having ignored the inconvenient Home Fleet left him exposed to a Corbettian counter-attack. Fisher's secretary would show him the 'Invasion Print' prepared for the enquiry. Aware that Corbett might refuse, Fisher provided an obvious line of retreat. 'I think you would trot this out so beautifully and effectively. But don't you bother to answer or even consider this proposal as to the *Nineteenth Century* unless the idea rushes at you.'[78]

Initially Corbett was unwilling, but Slade explained the strategic case in July: the Home Fleet would engage the enemy until the Channel Fleet arrived to finish the battle.[79] Slade had the War Course war game this scenario, and plans for a strategic ambush, exploiting wireless direction. It is likely Corbett was aware of this 'secret' work before starting his Admiralty brief. Fisher handed the task of countering Repington to Slade and Corbett in November. He was still hoping to quash the enquiry but as Esher and Haldane, both sympathetic to the Admiralty position, observed, he needed to win the argument, not damn his opponents. Roberts had already escalated the situation by calling Beresford and Custance, serving officers from the Channel Fleet, along with retired Admiral Bridge and the Prince of Wales as witnesses.[80] Giving Charlie an official platform to attack the Admiralty would, as Roberts must have known, destroy the discipline of the entire service. The enquiry met on 28 November and spent two days listening to Roberts' and Repington's prepared draft, which Fisher immediately sent to Corbett.[81] The bulky paper contained nothing new: invasion remained a stalking horse for conscription, although Repington's agenda may have been more overtly political. Corbett and Slade realised that the problem, like most other strategic questions, required the Army and the Navy to act together.

Corbett addressed Fisher's greatest concern, the possible summoning of Beresford, by pointing out that this would give the CID the power to direct naval operations. When the meeting resumed on 12 December, to cross-examine Roberts and Repington, Lord Tweedmouth's zeal got the better of his discretion and he exchanged heated words with Roberts, despite Slade's best efforts to keep the peace. War Office witnesses declared Repington's assessment of German transport capabilities highly optimistic, while Slade exposed his limited understanding of naval operations, and double counting of German warships.

Working closely with Captain Philip Colomb, son of the late admiral, Corbett produced a twenty-three-page typescript drawing on his own work, Édouard Desbrière's magisterial *Projets et Débarquements*, recently compiled for the French War Ministry, and fresh archival research by Colomb on the French invasion threat of 1744. 'Invasion 1744' proved critical. It dealt with a 'bolt from the blue', much like the imaginary case developed by Roberts and Repington, with France massing troops near the Flemish ports before declaring war. Once the British recognised the danger they focused the fleet on destroying the invasion shipping, only a storm saved the French from annihilation. Corbett's contribution was to demonstrate why Roberts' ideas were unsound. The strategic principle was simple: in such situations the role of the British battlefleet was to support cruiser and flotilla attacks on inva-sion shipping, ignoring the enemy battlefleet, whether it was acting as a close escort, or a distraction. Placing a cruiser screen in the North Sea would compel the Germans to deploy their battlefleet as a close escort. Encumbered by slow transports the fleet would be easy prey for the superior British fleet. In a point clearly addressed to the 'Syndicate', he reached higher, demon-strating how Mahan's continental fixation with 'decisive battle' had distracted British naval thought from national principles. The point had been empha-sised in recent years by the enhanced defensive power of torpedo-armed flotillas. Then he parted company with Fisher: a powerful defending army was essential, it would oblige Germany to send 70,000–100,000 men, making the convoy easy to locate. The new Territorial Army would be adequate.[82] This neatly integrated the Admiralty position with government policy, and may have been based on conversations with Haldane.

Corbett's paper, enthusiastically adopted by most of the CID, provided the basis for a sound decision. Haldane considered it: 'one of the most important state papers' that he had ever seen. Several members declared they had not known 'what the naval side of the question was before'. Sir John French was convinced it had defeated the conscriptionists.[83] Although Fisher and Tweedmouth persisted with the line that not even a dinghy could reach Britain, Corbett and Slade prevailed. On 14 February Slade persuaded Nicholson that the question could only be resolved at the level of principles.[84] As Admiral Sir William May observed, Corbett had 'lifted whole controversy out of a rut of mere of detail'.[85] Once Asquith recognised 'command of the sea' was the key, Roberts had lost the argument and the General Staff backed away, although Sir William Nicholson, like Fisher, persisted in his minority view.[86] By March 1908 the issue was settled; the final report appeared in October. It was, as Slade observed, 'practically' Corbett's 'original paper'.[87] He had demolished a ponderous mass of facts and figures with intellectual rigour and strategic logic, presented in a form that appealed to a committee of lawyers.

Yet Liberal Prime Minister Campbell-Bannerman and Chancellor of the Exchequer Asquith awarded the Admiralty no prizes. Instead, much as Fisher had feared, they claimed Britain's naval expenditure was excessive, as naval supremacy was 'completely assured'. Pressure from his radical followers prompted Asquith, installed as premier in April 1908, to replace the blustering Tweedmouth with former Treasury Secretary Reginald McKenna.[88] While German naval construction made it impossible to cut the naval budget, politicians chose to blame Fisher, the most economical First Sea Lord for decades.

Fisher's aim in 1907 had been to demolish the Army's strategic arguments and impose a maritime strategy, famously encapsulated in his 'projectile' argument. He did not want a home defence army, especially one composed of Territorials: he wanted 70,000 deployable front-line troops whose mere presence would tie down German forces by being at hand, possibly afloat on board transports, ready for ambitious offensive operations, including 'Copenhagening' the High Seas Fleet. In May 1908, opposition leader Balfour, who remained a central figure at the CID, stressed the utility of the enquiry: sound naval deployments made a 'bolt from the blue' impossible. Roberts was let down gently: being a national treasure had its advantages. Although much has been made of the enquiry, the conclusions could have been drafted before it met: no peacetime Liberal government would touch conscription, while Fisher and Nicholson were old enemies, incapable of moderation, as Haldane advised Corbett in June 1908.[89]

By this time the General Staff had adopted the Entente military agreement to sustain their claim to shape national strategy, to the consternation of the majority of Liberal ministers and MPs, who only discovered their existence in August 1914. Fisher, like Arthur Wilson, recognised the conversations as 'the thin end of the invidious wedge of our taking part in continental war as apart from coastal military operations in pure concert with the Navy'.[90]

Never one to waste good material, Corbett reused enquiry research for 'invasion Lectures for the War Course'.[91] They were attended by soldiers as well as sailors. In late January 1908 Colonel (later General) Sir Stanley Maude attended the invasion lectures at Devonport, noting 'Very good and interesting, as they always are; but I think he is a little too sure that England cannot be invaded without the sea being permanently in the hands of the enemy'.[92] While Maude did not want to believe what he was hearing, Corbett left him little choice.

Corbett's work on the Invasion Inquiry also informed two more books, *The Campaign of Trafalgar* and *Some Principles* of 1911, where he provided the strategic doctrine of 'Defence against Invasion' in chapter 4, part 3.[93] He built on the 'Invasion 1744' typescript and the Admiralty brief. The range and quality of Corbett's work for the Navy, as teacher, advocate and advisor between 1902 and 1910 would enable him to produce *Some Principles* quickly. Most of what he needed to say had already been tested and refined.

In a little over twelve months, Corbett had completed a major strategic study that explained national strategy to senior officers, demonstrating why it differed from that of continental military powers, while his development of Clausewitz undermined the Army's continental arguments. He also produced a guide to strategic doctrine in the preface of the Ballard Committee War Plans, and robust defences of Admiralty policy on education, strategy, ship design, international law and invasion. The ideas that underpinned these projects necessarily overlapped and interpenetrated his continuing literary and lecturing work, enhancing his ability to establish national strategy and maintain naval primacy in national security planning.

It had been a hard year:

I could do no work for myself except in so far as the Fighting instructions & invasion work prepared the ground for writing on the American
Independence and Great wars. Slade proposed my beginning at once a
book on invasions but at present I think it best to deal with it in a continuation of my general naval history.[94]

CHAPTER 11

Imperial Pageantry
QUEBEC 1908

After his contribution to the critical debates of 1907 Corbett had an opportunity to witness the politics of Edwardian imperial defence in action. He attended a major imperial event, the 1908 Quebec Tercentenary, tasked by the DNI with assessing local support for a Dominion Navy. Within months of publishing *England in the Seven Years' War* he arrived at the pivot point of that conflict aboard a British battleship. The great fortress and port on the St Lawrence River that had witnessed the triumph of the 'British way' over continental methods now stood at the centre of a debate about the future of the empire.

The ultimate purpose of Corbett's work was the long-term security of the empire as it evolved into a progressive 'Sea Commonwealth', linked by mutual dependence on the ocean and the preservation of peace. First developed in the *Monthly Review* essays, Corbett's imperial vision had been shaped by John Seeley, Lord Bryce, Lord Rosebery and latterly George Clarke, along with personal experience of empire and political conviction.

After 1902 imperial defence became a battleground for competing strategic agendas. Military failures in South Africa had prompted public scrutiny, while the staggering costs of the conflict increased the pressure for economy. After the problems of the military system had been exposed by Lord Elgin's Commission, Lord Esher persuaded King Edward and Conservative Prime Minister Arthur Balfour to address the central weakness: the incoherence of the War Office and the lack of a modern staff system. An exponent of maritime strategy, Esher selected two men of like mind and similar energy for his committee: Fisher, who would rebuild the Navy, and George Clarke, who would lead the CID, the civil–military coordinating body, to link the reformed War Office and the Admiralty, the Foreign, India and Colonial offices, harnessing the military resources of the empire that had proved so effective in South Africa. Critically, the CID gave the Dominions a voice.[1] Corbett had been involved from the start, promoting Clarke's agenda in the press, and at the War Course.

Esher's largely pre-determined Army reforms were enacted by Orders in Council, without serious debate in Parliament. Having reformed the War Office and created a General Staff on continental lines, Esher was shocked to find that his creature refused to take direction. In March 1907 the War Office submission to the Colonial Conference, 'The Strategical Conditions of the Empire from a Military Point of View', openly challenged the assumption that British strategy was maritime. A cursory discussion of the importance of sea control for imperial security, the defence of trade and the mutual support of the empire's constituent parts was followed by the assertion that 'naval supremacy is powerless, unaided, to bring a great war to a successful conclusion'. Furthermore, the British Empire, 'with its vast land frontiers and continental responsibilities is confronted by dangers against which a naval force can offer it little, if any assistance'.[2] Any 'threat' to the 'vast frontiers', those of Canada and India, had been removed by improved Anglo-American relations and the desperate weakness of Russia. In truth, the soldiers were using this argument to harness the military forces of the empire for an imperial army that would be used in a major European war. The claim that the Navy was 'powerless' to end a war with a great power failed the test of history. The Crimean War had been settled by economic blockade and limited amphibious operations, and Russia remained vulnerable to similar strategies in 1907. Germany was equally anxious about the economic impact of naval operations in the Baltic, the appearance of Arthur Wilson's Channel Fleet off Germany's Baltic coast eighteen months earlier prompted Berlin to step back from the brink of war. It also prompted Germany and Russia, members of opposing alliance blocs, to sign the Treaty of Björko in 1907, attempting to deny the Baltic to non-riparian navies. While the project emphasised the strategic importance of the enclosed sea, it collapsed when Denmark refused to join.

Britain did not need a grand army, because it had no intention of starting a major war, and neither Britain nor the Dominions would raise large conscript forces in peacetime. Short of war all that could be done was to establish common structures and methods to ensure effective cooperation in a conflict. In strategic terms, this hypothetical Army, as a war-fighting instrument or a deterrent, was no substitute for a Navy that dominated the world ocean and imperial communications. To advance their case the General Staff consistently misrepresented the Navy as tied to the defence of the United Kingdom, the trade routes and empire, while refusing to plan for combined operations. Corbett had seen the latest Admiralty war plans against Germany: they relied on an expeditionary army to secure the Danish Narrows, enabling the Navy to complete the blockade.[3]

The development of what Doug Delaney has called 'the imperial army project' after 1902 deliberately challenged the long-established primacy of maritime strategy, raising important questions about the relationship between Britain and the self-governing Dominions, and the naval needs of empire. The outbreak of war in 1914 was not inevitable, nor was Britain obligated to defend France, as opposed to Belgium, and there was no precedent for military mobilisation on the scale adopted when war was declared. Corbett was not alone in recognising the threat to progressive politics at home and free trade abroad, but he overestimated the Cabinet's ability to resist pressure from the Army.

After 1906 the growing rift between the War Office and the Admiralty, the ministerial failure to use the CID as a central strategic directing body, and ministers' refusal to create a coherent foreign and defence policy left imperial strategy in limbo. The limited impact of Corbett's masterly Admiralty invasion memorandum of 1907 reflected this malaise. Although he had demolished the military argument, reasserting the central role of maritime strategy, the verdict of the Invasion Inquiry had been an emollient compromise, one that allowed the Army to continue the argument.[4] The refusal to settle national and imperial defence policy at Cabinet level avoided a battle with profoundly hostile Conservative soldiers, and facilitated budgetary restraint, at the cost of strategic coherence.[5]

This was the unsatisfactory background to Corbett's attendance at the Quebec Tercentenary Pageant of July 1908, as the guest and agent of the Royal Navy. Well aware of Corbett's imperial ideas, the DNI, his friend Edmond Slade, asked him to assess Canadian opinion on a Dominion Navy. Both men recognised that integrated imperial defence structures emanating from the War Office were shaping Canadian Permanent Force and Militia organisations. The Admiralty hoped for similar local support, in men, money, bases or ships. Corbett took the commission because it aligned with his 'Sea Commonwealth' approach; he loved going to sea with the fleet, enjoyed a well-organised pageant, and had just published a major book centred on Quebec. Civilian status, academic reputation and service connections would facilitate discreet discussions at the highest level, while Slade trusted his political judgement.

The Quebec Pageant would be the culmination of a four-year campaign, directed from London. Governor General Earl Grey had been sent to Canada in 1904 with instructions to encourage engagement with imperial naval needs. The message fell on deaf, and far from disinterested ears. The politically powerful province of Quebec, the base of Liberal Premier Wilfrid Laurier, was profoundly opposed to imperial projects, sending troops abroad, or paying for warships. The Quebecois Minister of the Marine and Fisheries, who presided over a department noted for mismanagement or worse, showed no interest in expanding a fishery protection service into a fleet. When Grey increased the pressure in the spring of 1908, exploiting West Coast concerns about Japan and the cruise of the American 'Great White Fleet', Laurier's government requested a senior Royal Navy officer to lead Canada's sea service. Canadian-born Rear Admiral Charles Kingsmill, a 1904 War Course student, improved the status and efficiency of the service, and promoted the idea of a naval militia. In May 1908 the imperially minded anglophone *Toronto Globe* expected a naval militia would develop gradually, to 'keep pace with the advance of public opinion in assuming a large share in imperial defence'.[6] Sensing a shift in public opinion Grey transformed the planned national tercentenary into 'a really impressive Imperial splash', hoping to make Canadians proud to belong to the empire, to sell the seapower model, integrate the Dominion into a wider defence system, and encourage it to take some of the imperial naval burden. The cost of the Anglo-German arms race, which threatened British domestic reform programmes, had been emphasised at the 1907 Colonial Conference. The government supported Grey's agenda by sending a powerful imperial delegation, eight large warships, the Prince of Wales, Field Marshal Lord Roberts and the Roman Catholic Duke of Norfolk, to flatter French Canadian sensitivities, along with representatives from other parts of the empire. There were no British, imperial or foreign troops: the grand review of 12,000 militiamen showed that Canada's military concerns remained local and terrestrial. The nation-building military jamboree was combined with an international naval review that demonstrated who was really in charge, and why Canada survived America's era of 'Manifest Destiny'. Five thousand sailors marched with the Canadians; the great majority of them British.[7] The inference was obvious. British sea power made Canada possible. Canada's willingness to defend itself was appreciated, but London would expect more.

The Quebec event attempted to forge a 'white' Canadian nation from divergent European elements, sidelining Native peoples. It reflected contemporary views of what constituted a 'nation' and a desire to raise 'European' soldiers for Canada or the empire. The history on display carefully avoided anglophone triumphalism: the 'white' nations received equal billing and equal glory. Francophone sensitivities were appeased by linking two battles at Quebec, the British success in 1759 balanced by a French triumph in 1760, which upheld French honour, even as their Canada fell.[8] Native Americans, fortunate recipients of European civilisation, were window dressing; Inuit were ignored.

The official account of the festivities, *The King's Book of Quebec*, written by Dominion Archivist and historian Arthur Doughty, reflected an agenda chosen by Grey and Canada's anglophone elite: it ended with the War of 1812, when Canadians united to repel American invaders, standing shoulder to shoulder with British regulars, the Royal Navy having secured the Atlantic and the Lakes. Canada found security within the empire, by making a suitable contribution to its own security, and that of the wider empire. The synergy of this message with Corbett's 'Sea Commonwealth' was obvious, and he spent enough time with the directing minds of the pageant, Grey, Doughty and Colonel Wood, to recognise the fact. The task going forward would be to ensure Canada would be a contributing partner to the 'Sea Commonwealth'. French Canadians would be 'at home under the British Flag', if only because the stridently anti-clerical French Republic no longer offered an alternative.[9]

To become a nation Canada needed a suitable past. In an age dominated by nationalist approaches to history this attempt to shape an agreed narrative exploited all the contemporary tools: pageantry, text, mass-produced images and international endorsement.[10] The tercentenary attempted to forge a Canadian identity by fusing British and French perspectives at the place where Canada began, and saw its destiny change. Honouring French heritage at the centre of French Canadian culture with an international gathering would enable Canadians to take pride in a shared heritage and face the future together.

For Britain this was part of the long process of transferring power back to the colonies as they reached political maturity, in exchange for enhanced cooperation. Initially the attraction of self-government had been economic: imperial garrisons accounted for 90 per cent of the cost of British rule. By

1902 Britain recognised the Dominions and wider empire as a reservoir of military manpower, and potential naval support.[11] Canada had been gifted the imperial dockyards at Halifax and Esquimault, but demonstrated little interest in maintaining them, let alone developing a naval capability. Fisher doubted Canada would contribute at sea, recognising the profoundly continental focus of a Dominion dominated by inland provinces. It was time to show the Canadians the instruments of their security.

After the Diamond Jubilee Fleet Review of 1897, George Sydenham Clarke stressed the importance of public display:

> The fact that navies are powerful agents for the inter-change of national sentiment is little recognised, although the influence of the presence of British squadrons in the ports of our great colonies is one of the principal factors in promoting and maintaining the unity of the Empire.

During the Boer War, the Admiralty helped maintain British prestige through ceremonial ship launches, giving capital ships imperial names to forge the disparate elements of a maritime empire into something as coherent as a battlefleet.[12] All eight *King Edward VII*-class battleships along with the armoured cruisers *Good Hope* and *Natal* celebrated the empire, while Canadian Charles Kingsmill was chosen to command the Canadian battleship, HMS *Dominion*, which had visited Quebec in 1906.[13]

The Coronation Reviews of 1902 and 1911 and public warship launch ceremonies at Portsmouth were 'invented traditions' for an age of mass politics, popular media and early cinema. The identities being constructed could be national or supra-national. Across the quarter-century before 1914 the British Empire organised ever grander displays of naval and military power, highlighting imperial cohesion and effortless dominance. Diamond Jubilee events for Queen Victoria at Spithead and in London were linked to the Quebec ceremonials; the June 1909 fleet review, which Corbett attended, was staged to coincide with the Imperial Conference, targeting the imperial press corps; the Dehli Durbar of 1911, and in 1913 the inaugural display of a new Royal Australian Navy at Sydney, brought the project to a fitting climax. This imperial pageantry was funded by the imperial government.[14]

In 1902 Corbett wrote in lyrical terms about the Coronation Review, a 'breathing image of the mystery of [naval] power ... the silent pressure of sea power'.[15] By 1908 he may have realised there was little 'mystery' in overwhelming displays, crafted to impress tax-payers and deter foreign powers. No-one understood this better than Fisher, who emphasised the visual impact of his new ships, and took every opportunity to put them on display. He recognised that a major war would not serve Britain's interests, and demonstrations of overwhelming power were the key to deterrence. A peace-preserving victory in the naval arms race with Germany would be his greatest triumph. As Jan Rüger observed, the 'naval theatre' of reviews and pageants 'played a key role: it provided the stage on which the command of the sea could be claimed in front of domestic and foreign audiences'.[16] The presence of foreign warships, especially from potentially hostile nations, emphasised the need for security.

The Admiralty exploited the tercentenary to display imperial power, assess interest in a local navy, and test an evolving strategy for oceanic defence. Slade and Corbett discussed the defence of Canada against the United States in May 1908, aware that Haldane was seeking a significant Canadian military resource. Slade thought that raising a naval militia for the Great Lakes and securing the land frontier would provide useful support for the Royal Navy and imperial defence.[17] His belief that an American invasion would be limited to 100,000 men prompted Corbett to suggest the threat posed by amphibious divisions based at Newfoundland and Jamaica would enable the Canadians to hold the frontier. Fisher knew better: an American invasion was highly unlikely, but Canada could not be defended; the border was best left unprotected. In June Corbett proofread Slade's 'Canada Pamphlet', to familiarise himself with his friend's thinking.[18] He also commented on the new W series War Plans, drawn up at the War College, which Slade delivered to his apartment.[19] On 19 June he attended Fisher's 'dreadnought show' at Sheerness, travelling by train with Haldane, Ottley and Thursfield. Having discussed the possibility of improved Army–Navy relations when Fisher and General Sir William Nicholson retired, Corbett seized the opportunity to remind Haldane that 'conscription would wreck any government. Haldane agreed, while Balfour [leader of the Conservative Opposition] was of the same opinion'.[20] That conversation settled the parameters of Corbett's 'British way': Britain's great power status would continue to rest on the Navy.

Impressed by the display of dreadnought gunnery, torpedoes, submarines and destroyers, Corbett may have missed Fisher's deeper purpose. The display was one of many events, including the annual manoeuvres, that emphasised the North Sea as the Navy's future battlefield. Fisher had shifted the strategic centre of gravity in home waters to the Nore Command and the new Home Fleet. Nine months later,Lord Charles Beresford's disputatious Channel Fleet command ended.[21]

On 1 July Corbett attended the Chelsea Pageant: although he enjoyed pageants he found this one 'very poor, far too much dialogue and a bad stage'.[22] The next day he set off for the fleet anchorage at Berehaven, in south-west Ireland, joining the squadron on 3 July, he travelled with Lord Howick, the eldest son of Earl Grey, and fellow Coefficient Halford Mackinder.

The squadron detached to Quebec comprised four Duncan-class pre-dreadnought battleships, *Albemarle*, *Russell*, *Exmouth* and *Duncan*, built for imperial duties, initially in East Asia, with the cruisers *Arrogant* and *Venus*. They were commanded by Admiral Sir Assheton Curzon-Howe in HMS *Russell*. Corbett and Mackinder travelled in the flagship, as guests of Captain Ricardo and the Ward Room officers.[23] After dinner on the 4th, Corbett had a rewarding discussion with Rear Admiral John Jellicoe, whose flag flew in HMS *Albemarle*, 'perhaps the cleverest young flag officer in the service'.[24] Once at sea he observed wireless-directed manoeuvres in intermittent fog, fire control practice, and icebergs in the Straits of Belle Isle on the 11th. That night, 'Mackinder gave us a very good lecture on Canada as to historical geography in the Ward Room'. The following night Corbett spoke on the taking of Quebec, before discussing imperial tariff reform with Mackinder.[25]

On the 14th, the squadron anchored off the citadel at Quebec. Thereafter Corbett spent much of his time ashore, often in company with Mackinder, visiting the old city and key sites from 1759, discussing the Canadian naval situation with Curzon-Howe, Earl Grey, Lord Roberts, Rear Admiral Kingsmill and others. He cross-examined Roberts on the nature of command in amphibious operations, challenging the field marshal's preference for German methods, which gave the general control over all aspects of the campaign, including politics. Kingsmill and Grey reported that Canada had no interest in a navy, while he debated the events of 1759 with Dominion Archivist Arthur Doughty and fellow historian Colonel William Wood, and took Jellicoe to Wolfe's battlefield.

The battlecruiser HMS *Indomitable*, with the Prince of Wales on board, arrived on 22 July, accompanied by armoured cruiser HMS *Minotaur*. This grand entrance brought proceedings to a climax:

The ships created a sensation as they assembled in the harbour ... they stretched for several miles in their anchorages in mid-stream. The

British ships were anchored in pairs, the mighty *Indomitable*, flanked by the *Minotaur*, had pride of place opposite the Citadel. This unprecedented show of modern naval power drew vast crowds. The thunder of the guns as the ships saluted arrivals and departures startled residents and provided a constant reminder of the presence of the Navy, even to those far from the scene ... the effect was overwhelming.[26]

Three foreign warships, one American, two French, were grouped together at a distance, distinctive colour schemes and silhouettes emphasising both their alien identity and supporting role. This mighty naval demonstration may have been counter-productive, implying Britain needed no naval assistance.

Corbett had a front-row seat at all the events, and access to the key players. If the military review was 'very hot & badly managed', the grand pageant was 'beautiful against the St. Lawrence, background beyond description'. The imperial services dinner at the Citadel that evening had been 'A great function – a sort of Imperial debauch, but a real historic occasion'. The prince reviewed the fleet on Saturday, 25 July, his standard flying on HMS *Arrogant*, with a Canadian icebreaker and a fishery protection vessel as escorts. Corbett enjoyed the fleet light show and fireworks from the governor general's terrace. Six British capital ships on the majestic St Lawrence were a metaphor for the integration of the Dominion within a global empire, represented by imperial dignitaries, who had travelled on imperial ships across oceans secured by the Royal Navy. British warships commanded the river, dominating the view from the city.

The key business meeting was a working lunch with General Sir Percy Lake, Inspector General of Canadian Forces on 28 July. Lake saw no possibility of a local navy, from lack of interest and ingrained corruption. He advised preparing a torpedo boat flotilla to move to the Great Lakes by rail. Custance had reconnoitred the American side of the Lakes in 1898, but his confidential reports had not been retained in Canada. Sir Percy agreed to pass information to Slade discreetly, via the government bag.[27] The 'best authority by far on Canadian defence that I have met', knew his strategic history, suggesting the report that Wellington commissioned from General Carmichael Smythe on the defence of Canada shortly after the War of 1812 would repay study. Lake's local expertise reflected four years' service, and a Canadian mother; his discretion and diplomacy facilitated the military integration of the Dominion into imperial policy.[28]

On 29 July *Indomitable* and the rest of the fleet unmoored, making an impressive departure, racing downstream at 19 knots on the falling tide. As *Indomitable* worked up to full power Jellicoe's *Albemarle* was detached to maintain wireless connections with the prince's ship, until it was within range of home stations. *Indomitable*'s return passage tested key elements of Fisher's strategy: between Belle Isle and the Fastnet Light, the battlecruiser maintained an average speed of just over 25 knots – the designed top speed. Not only was this the fastest naval crossing to date, but *Indomitable* remained in wireless contact with the Admiralty throughout the passage.[29] These new technologies reinforced Britain's ability to dominate the ocean.

On the passage home Corbett read a paper on flotillas by Captain Huddleston, a recent War Course student commanding *Arrogant*, and wrote a report for Slade. On 5 and 6 August, the squadron exercised a key aspect of the contemporary fire control problem, while the cruisers conducted a night torpedo attack. Arriving in Berehaven on 7 August, Corbett had a final discussion with the admiral before boarding *Arrogant*, debating Huddleston's paper over lunch and landing at Bantry. 'So ended one of the best months I ever had.' The following morning he reached Paddington, joining his family at Stopham by mid-afternoon. Discussions on 22 August revealed that Fisher and Ottley had approved Slade's plan for an independent Australian Navy without serious consideration. Corbett sent copies of *England in the Seven Years' War* to Captain Ricardo, Earl Grey and Arthur Doughty; he anticipated Canadian sales.[30]

The naval message of the Quebec Tercentenary was clear: Britain ruled the waves, securing Canada against America, and Japan, while the Entente with France provided European security. Safe behind the imperial aegis, Canada could develop into a nation, taking a full part in the evolution of a Sea Commonwealth, helping to uphold existing collective security arrangements.

Warships, floating symbols of national power, emphasised modernity and imperial connections, messages reinforced by gun salutes, illuminations and fireworks. The naval presence divided the Canadian press: most franco-phone journals ignored the ships.[31] For all the fanfare and fireworks the pageantry of 1908 had little impact on the profoundly continental Canadian identity. The ocean was a long way from Quebec, Montreal or Toronto and, as the tercentenary had demonstrated, it belonged to Britain. That naval dominance made 1759 possible did nothing to endear the Navy to French Canada: there would be no Canadian consensus on naval issues before 1914.

Britain did all it could to make Canadians proud of their role in the world-girdling British Empire. The Royal Navy's presence overwhelmed French and American representatives. The French badly miscalculated, sending the *Admiral Aube* and *Leon Gambetta*, named for left-wing Republicans, icons of an alien state that had no attraction for francophone Canada.[32] Aube had created the *Jeune École* strategy of the 1880s. Detaching the new battlecruiser *Indomitable* combined public display and imperial bonding with a full-power trial for Fisher's new global strategy, which relied on turbine-powered, wireless-connected capital ships to sustain imperial communications in the age of self-governing Dominions and defence cooperation. Six years later, *Indomitable*'s sister ships would exploit that system to crush the last remnant of Germany's oceanic naval challenge off the Falkland Islands.

Indomitable's Atlantic crossings demonstrated how the steam turbine had changed maritime strategy. Corbett, a proponent of strategic speed, understood the message, and the connection with his mission. As Fisher focused his efforts on containing the High Seas Fleet in the North Sea, he needed an economical means to secure the world ocean and represent British power. His globally deployable capital rank battlecruisers were calculated to overwhelm hostile cruisers, and were equally impressive visual symbols of power. *Indomitable*'s modern profile, dominated by two tall tripod masts, three big funnels, four heavy gun turrets and a wireless array, reduced the French and American armoured cruisers to irrelevance. The presence of the Prince of Wales, himself a naval officer, reinforced the message. Fleet reviews were a unique opportunity to project power. *Indomitable* had commanded the river by day and night, the impressive profile picked out in lights as night fell. The ship represented a step change in strategic capability, but it is not clear whether it was sent to draw Canada into an imperial naval project, or to demonstrate that the Royal Navy would defend Canadian interests, not least the Atlantic shipping lanes that dominated the Dominion's economic activity. Such ships would be central to the 'Fleet Units' that Fisher decided were appropriate for the empire; the Royal Australian Navy of 1913 was a battlecruiser-led fleet unit, while New Zealand bought a battlecruiser for the Royal Navy.

Unlike the historical pageantry of the old world, the Quebec tercentenary did not project a single nation, or a specific nationalism;[33] the coming together of distinct peoples and traditions held out hope for other divided components of empire – South Africa, Ireland, perhaps even India. As Stefan

Berger observed: 'For many in England, control of the imperial past meant control of the imperial present, which is why the idea of a single Imperial Archive was at the heart of notions of how to improve communication and control in the empire.' This approach challenged the domestic/progressive fixation of Whig historiography. Seeley understood that empire had changed Britain, and so did Corbett.[34] Empire and seapower were indissolubly linked; without a large maritime empire Britain could neither justify nor afford the Navy that made it a great power. The 'Little Englanders' in his own party treated empire as barrier to domestic reform, an excuse for excessive defence spending. The sea, navies and oceanic commerce were the central pillars of English/British national and imperial history and identity after 1700. Empire and seapower made Britain different from other Europeans states, politically, economically and strategically. The key message of the Quebec Tercentenary, perfectly conveyed by eight grey hulls on the St Lawrence, was clear: the Senior Service secured the empire.

Corbett recognised the potential for a stronger empire emerging from an era of change. The Navy, and only the Navy, had the strategic and cultural power to sustain this unique system. Fisher's new Navy was configured for the task. Defeating the German naval challenge, without a war, was only a short-term problem.

Yet Canada offered a worrying portent. Quebecois opinion was deeply hostile to imperial commitments, other than the empire's commitment to defend Quebec. Quebec saw no need for naval power, and had no intention of providing men or money. Although Corbett found signs of interest, imperial Toronto was too far inland, while the coastal provinces were marginal political factors. It is unlikely his acute mind missed the deeply continental roots of Canadian identity. The strategist who identified Quebec as a pivot point of British grand strategy faced a deeper truth. Continental settler nations soon abandon any residual maritime identity; the anglophone majority, safely located in Ontario, took a terrestrial view – sea was distant and alien, while Quebec, the terminal point of oceanic navigation, had been celebrated as a fortress, fought over by soldiers. The naval heroes of 1759, Charles Saunders and James Cook, were nowhere to be seen. The oversight may have been deliberate, or merely a reflection of landlocked mentalities.

While Corbett attended as an agent of the DNI, Mackinder did so to promote the cause of imperial unity at the forthcoming Imperial Conference, working for Lord Milner. Milner favoured an imperial tariff. Mackinder remained in Canada for several months after the tercentenary, assessing the best way to enhance imperial ties. He advised tariffs that would enable imperial grain to undercut Argentine produce, a Canadian government ambition.[35] He missed the critical reality that much of Argentina was worked by British capital. Mid-Atlantic discussions with Corbett may have prompted Mackinder's observation that if all of North American were united it would, 'of necessity, take from us the command of the ocean'.[36] After entering Parliament in 1910, Mackinder used the German naval challenge to support the case for imperial unity: 'only by gathering together the several nations of the Empire can we cope in the international balance of power with the newly organised continental powers'.[37] If his future empire shared elements of Corbett's – a 'free partnership of democracies united by common interest' – his centralising, coercive tariff core was neither progressive nor Liberal.[38] Corbett knew the unified imperial navy and army that Mackinder favoured were politically impossible. Elsewhere the peculiar issues facing the South African Defence Force led the imperial officers in the Dominion to focus on defensive tasks, not least the security of vital ports and naval facilities, releasing imperial troops in wartime.[39] Among the imperial officers involved, George Aston was half Boer, a Royal Marine and a strategist. Aston took a distinctly different view of imperial needs to those of his army contemporaries, and was familiar with Corbett's work.[40]

Quebec challenged Corbett's approach to empire. It dissolved any hope Canada might look to the sea, and he was not surprised when Canada went to war in 1914 with soldiers. A Canadian Navy took shape only after the naval war came to Canada. Corbett accepted the Canadian choice, making the first Canadian troop convoy a highlight of 'the great imperial concentration'. Thirty-two thousand soldiers in thirty big ships were escorted to Britain by the battlecruiser HMS *Princess Royal*, an improved *Indomitable*.[41] The ship dominates Norman Wilkinson's picture *Canada's Answer*, much as *Indomitable* had commanded the St Lawrence six years before.[42] The empire answered the call to arms in different ways, as befitted the loose structures of a Sea Commonwealth. Most chose the land.

CHAPTER 12

Tactics, Signals and Trafalgar

Alongside his work on strategy and doctrine, Corbett studied naval tactical development in the age of sail, revisiting an old debate to inform the thinking of contemporary officers. Existing assessments of this work fundamentally misrepresent its origins and objects. Don Schurman attributed the initial impulse to the Trafalgar Centenary, and followed his mentor Brian Tunstall, a lifelong student of sailing tactics, in treating Corbett's purpose as essentially antiquarian.[1] This assessment ignores Corbett's own words, and the educational/doctrinal focus of his entire output after 1893. His two NRS texts were created to stimulate the study of tactics and tactical doctrine among serving officers, not to satisfy antiquarian curiosity. In 1905 he acknowledged the support of four senior officers: Admiral Sir Cyprian Bridge, Rear Admiral Sir Reginald Custance, Captain Prince Louis of Battenberg and Captain Edmond Slade. All four were NRS councillors and, of greater moment, had been or would become Director of Naval Intelligence. The Naval Intelligence Division shaped the NRS's publishing programme from its foundation by Laughton and DNI Bridge in 1893.[2] Corbett understood this, and concurred when Captain Reginald Bacon, a leading technologist, declared the NRS published 'too many books of no practical use to Naval Officers'.[3] Corbett also discussed tactics with Newbolt, who examined Nelson's methods in *The Year of Trafalgar*. Both men favoured the classic account, an attack in two columns, over fanciful theories advanced by those who tried to make Nelson appear consistent, and his ideas unnecessarily complex. They distinguished between the moral and tactical aspects of Nelson's attack. The merits of the former outweighed the 'vicious' defects of the latter, which made them irrelevant to the post-1815 codification of the Signal Book.[4]

This project began when the Earl of Dartmouth loaned his collection of tactical manuscripts to the NRS.[5] The Council decided they should become the basis of a collection of tactical material, to assist 'a fresh study of the principles which underlie the development of naval tactics' because, 'in the opinion of those best able to judge' (the naval officers on the council), they possessed 'practical value', for the contemporary Navy. The council also selected Corbett to edit them. Corbett thought the old texts remained useful because the primary weapon was still the heavy gun, hoping they would promote 'vitality of mind' in tactical thought.[6]

Fighting Instructions, 1530–1816 marked a step change for the NRS; it was the first artificial collection, defined by subject, not source, stretching across three centuries and several countries. Furthermore, the dry, technical documents required additional context and elucidation, prompting Corbett to distribute his editorial input across the volume to support his naval students.[7] The result was a draft history of naval tactics, aimed at contemporary tacticians. The model was widely used by historians teaching document-based courses.[8]

Corbett had already mastered the subject, in his *Drake* texts, adding Spanish, Dutch and French material, as well as evidence from other record societies. He had already written on Tudor and Stuart tactics.[9] He opened a new line of research on the eighteenth century just as he started working on the *Seven Years' War*, another project propelled by the intellectual needs of the contemporary Navy. Both projects benefited from the synergy.

Corbett argued that existing accounts of the battles in 1666 underplayed the contribution of his old hero George Monk and the impact of the victory he and Prince Rupert secured on St James's Day, overturning negative assessments of contemporary tactics by Samuel Pepys and William Penn.[10] Historians had been misled by Granville Penn's *Memorials of Penn*, which included a set of instructions and implied they were used in 1666. Dartmouth's collection demonstrated they were written no earlier than August 1672, and in all probability never issued.[11] Corbett printed Penn's text, with additions found in a later copy in the Admiralty Library, to emphasise the rapid development of tactics in wartime; the inserted material increased the admiral's ability to control attacks.[12] This was typical of Corbett's methodology, using new material to discredit old assumptions and slack scholarship, before constructing a fresh synthesis. The English had developed the line of battle to exploit superior firepower against the dynamic *mêlée* tactics of the Dutch, subtly encouraging readers to recognise the tactical advantages of superior range and volume of fire provided by Fisher's *Dreadnought*. With the design of future battleships in flux, the synthesis of tactics and technology was at the forefront of naval debate and many commentators, notably Mahan, had been misled by inadequate or inaccurate history.

Finally, Corbett demonstrated that such discussions were both normal and productive. Instructions issued during the Third Anglo-Dutch War came from two very different schools of thought. He dismissed those associated with James, Duke of York and William Penn, formal tactical systems, as 'pedantic', 'tending to confuse the means with the ends'. By contrast Monk and Rupert looked to 'unfetter individual initiative to almost any extent rather than miss a chance of overpowering the enemy by a sudden well-timed blow'. His preference was obvious, but he recognised that neither side had the complete answer. Progress reflected wartime experience and the constant interaction of the two schools, much as the Constitution had been shaped by a two-party political system. The Navy, then and now, needed 'the best adjusted compromise between free initiative and concentrated order'.[13]

Moving on to the French wars, Corbett countered Mahan's criticism of English tactics after 1688. Not only were the Instructions developed and improved from those of James II, but they worked. To assert his authority he noted that Mahan, a Francophile, consistently privileged French texts.[14] Corbett demonstrated that the 1691 Instructions issued by Admiral Sir Edward Russell were created by Arthur Herbert, Lord Torrington, who had already used them at Beachy Head.[15] Noting they were more defensively minded than previous editions, Corbett missed an obvious point: the French fleet was larger and more heavily gunned than the English, a complete reversal of the situation in the Dutch wars, one that demanded tactical change. The famous French tactical treatise of Père Hoste, L'Art des armées navales, ou traité des évolutions navales, of 1697 reflected and endorsed English practice, especially the single line ahead as the standard formation, and did so on the authority of the Comte de Tourville. Tourville thought attempting to break the enemy's line radically unsound.[16] Proof of the soundness of English practice came at the Battle of Malaga in 1704, when Rooke and Shovell, low on ammunition and men, defeated the Comte de Toulouse's attempt to recover Gibraltar with a superior force. This was precisely the scenario Torrington had envisaged in 1690. Having command of the sea, the English fleet used defensive strategies and tactics to preserve their advantage. Rooke and Shovell's priority was to secure Gibraltar, not destroy Toulouse's fleet. They used the 1703 edition of Herbert's Instructions

to control a defensive battle.[17] Once again Corbett left the critical importance of cohesion in a defensive battle to one side, perhaps because his
students did not anticipate having to employ such restraint. Modern analysts
of tactical ideas would identify the distinction drawn between *Auftragstakitik*,
or mission analysis, which in the naval context reached its zenith in Nelson's
1805 memorandum, and the altogether more precise directive control
systems embodied in the Fighting Instructions, which Nelson used, and
used brilliantly, to fight a very different battle at Copenhagen in 1801.

Corbett's analysis of tactical thinking stressed the constant interplay
between the dynamic offensive power of well-briefed initiative, devolved to
squadron or unit commanders, and the security of a well-ordered line
of battle, maintained by ferocious discipline. He recognised that the 1703
Fighting Instructions, only lightly modified across the next eighty years,
ensured a well-ordered line of battle but made little provision for flexibility
and initiative.[18] He did not mention that the problem had arisen because the
French Navy after 1714 was significantly weaker than the British, and
unwilling to engage in fleet battle. Those circumstances made the line of
battle a hindrance, not a help. Experienced commanders addressed the
problem by issuing Additional Fighting Instructions, enhancing the core text.
During the American War Rodney and Hood planned to concentrate the
fleet against portions of the enemy as the era of written instructions ended.[19]

By 1793 Lord Howe had replaced written Instructions with an illustrated Signal Book; each flag denoting a specific movement. The new
system enabled the Royal Navy to be more aggressive in the wars of the
French Revolution and empire, wars in which the marked moral and professional superiority of British fleets allowed them to operate with unprecedented flexibility.[20] Much of this section would be overtaken by a second
tactical publication three years later.

Corbett's mastery of the broader context included a brilliant evocation
of the British approach to battle. Don Domingo Perez de Grandallana, a
Spanish veteran of the Battle of Cape St Vincent, recognised that British
captains went into battle to win, attacking the enemy and assisting their
comrades, without requiring directions, while French and Spanish officers
lacked any feeling for mutual support, looking to the admiral for orders.[21]
Corbett stressed: 'in the British service formal tactics had come to be
regarded as a means of getting at your enemy, and not as a substitute for
initiative in fighting him'.[22]

When he reached Trafalgar, Corbett deliberately set out to shock. His discussion of the fabled Trafalgar memorandum, 'regarded by universal agreement as the high-water mark of sailing tactics', was intended to startle the unwary. There was, in reality, widespread disagreement about what Nelson meant, and whether he had fought the battle according to the text. The best captains, a term Corbett used to encourage those of 1905 to pay attention, 'those who had a real feeling for tactics saw that Nelson was making his attack on what were the essential principles of the memorandum'. Those 'possessed of less tactical insight' mistook the shadow for the substance, believing he had abandoned his design. They were excused, to a degree, because they had not been given access to a coherent account of the evolution of British naval tactics.[23] Even Collingwood had not fully grasped the intention of the memorandum, leading Corbett to question Nelson's expository powers. However, the 'most sagacious' officers, including Edward Codrington of HMS *Orion*, had understood.

Corbett contended the memorandum replaced the line of battle with mutually supporting squadrons in line ahead. This formation enabled Nelson to concentrate attacks on part of the enemy fleet, conceal the point of attack until late in the approach to combat, and block any counter-attack by the rest of the enemy force.[24] On the day of battle Nelson adopted a column attack 'for a suddenly conceived strategical object'. The perpendicular approach exposed the heads of his columns to serious damage, a tactical risk willingly taken in order to achieve his ulterior purpose.[25] To achieve significant strategic impact on the wider conflict, Nelson had to annihilate the enemy, as he had at the Nile. With wind and swell rising, indicating an imminent westerly gale, he had to hasten the approach to battle.[26]

The contemporary implication of these words are obvious; the increasingly large battlefleets of the era were too long and unwieldy for linear combat to produce decisive results. Something altogether more dynamic was required, potentially a fast wing or advanced squadron of faster capital ships, like the one Nelson had created in 1805. In 1905 these would have been the last generation of armoured cruisers, by 1907 they were dreadnoughts and battlecruisers.

Villeneuve had anticipated Nelson would not use linear tactics, placing one third of his fleet in a separate formation behind his battle line, commanded by Admiral Gravina, to counter the threat of a breakthrough. On the day of battle Villeneuve abandoned this approach when he saw

Nelson had more ships than he had anticipated. The Franco-Spanish fleet fought in a regular close-hauled line. Nelson had adopted divisional tactics in 1798, to maximise the fighting power of his fleet in an encounter battle with an amphibious task force, briefing his captains, and adjusting his Signal Book accordingly. These ideas were refined in 1803, for a bow-to-bow encounter battle with a similar enemy squadron. In all cases his purpose was to break the enemy's command, control and cohesion, setting up 'a pell-mell battle' in which superior British seamanship and firepower would triumph. On the day of battle he destroyed the enemy's command and control, disguising his point of the attack until he saw Villeneuve's flag.[27] While Nelson smashed the enemy's command, control, communications and intelligence (C3I) and cut off their van squadron, Collingwood would crush the centre and rear. Collingwood attacked in a line of bearing, intending his ships to cut through the enemy line at all points to prevent their opponents escaping. Nelson hoped to take twenty enemy ships. In the event he took nineteen. A British admiral using conventional tactics would have done well to match Sir Robert Calder's performance a few months earlier, taking four or five at best.

Corbett wanted his students to think about tactics in the strategic context in an era when the battlefleet remained the ultimate arbiter of sea control, not to master the antiquarian detail of a long-dead art. His friends in the Naval Intelligence community needed a fresh discussion based on the principles so clearly enunciated in the text. The unique status of Nelson's 1805 memorandum, sanctified as holy writ by the triumph and tragedy of Trafalgar, enabled Corbett to provide his readers with an object lesson in the tactical power of mission analysis. He invited readers to see Edward Codrington's brilliant tactical decisions in the battle as a model for future practice. Nelson had demonstrated that tactics must be adjusted to serve strategy.

To ensure readers recognised a radical revision of received wisdom he resorted to startling, emotive language. Nelson had used:

> a mad, perpendicular attack in which every recognised tactical card was in the enemy's hand. But Nelson's judgement was right. He knew his opponent's lack of decision, he knew the individual shortcomings of the allied ships, and he knew he had only to throw dust, as he did, in their eyes for the wild scheme to succeed.

While the moral advantage of pushing home an attack on an unformed enemy was great, this enemy showed no sign of seeking to avoid combat, so Nelson might have taken more time, and reduced the cost of victory. Corbett did not endorse unnecessary risk.[28] He contrasted the 'rare simplicity and abstraction' of Nelson's memorandum with what he saw as the glaring inadequacy of the 1816 Signal Book, and the widespread notion that Nelson's tactics were characterised by unthinking aggression, superior men and ships. Contemporary rivals were capable professionals, consequently it was necessary to recognise the 'nice combination' by which the master secured his victories.[29] In striving for effect, Corbett's criticism of the 1816 Signal Book missed the central point. The men of 1816 understood that neither Nelson's genius, nor the enemy's inadequacy were useful models for future development. They must prepare their successors to fight fleets of equal skill and determination. He changed his opinion of this document in 1910. The page proofs of *Fighting Instructions* were completed in early April 1905 after a bout of erysipelas,[30] which he had suffered before in periods of great stress. A letter to *The Times* in early July brought the book to public attention.[31]

Corbett's message was obvious, and consistent: master the principles, think logically, and only then use the past as precedent. His provocative treatment of Trafalgar sparked a major debate about Nelson's intentions, and his conduct of the battle. While it has been suggested Corbett found the debate unwelcome,[32] a closer examination of the origins of the NRS project, and the opinions of Newbolt and Bridge, suggest all three were playing to the gallery. Bridge's NRS Trafalgar Centenary Lecture praised Corbett's work as:

> the most useful to naval officers that has yet appeared among the Society's publications. It will provide them with an admirable historical introduction to the study of tactics, and greatly help them in ascertaining the importance of Nelson's achievements as a tactician.[33]

Their public disagreement had been contrived, to promote discussion in the service and among the public, as Corbett made clear two months before Bridge endorsed the volume.

> I am really proud of my book. It will give people a clearer view of what happened than before I wrote, though Custance tells me our views are not going to be swallowed quietly. I feel the stir of bellowing admirals

and cutlasses grinding to do us battle. Such at least is the impression he gives me. Bridge he says will follow Colomb. But we can remain all jolly and hearty ... thank God – and the more they argue over it the better for their brains. If together we succeed in starting again a real interest in the history of tactics our work is well done right or wrong.[34]

The phrase 'our views' is profoundly significant. Corbett sent copies to his friends. George Clarke declared 'your views on Trafalgar are impregnable'.[35] Charles Firth was equally impressed.[36] The Trafalgar debate delighted Fisher: 'I did read your reply to Bridge, and "chortled" with joy! I do so love to see a fellow properly kicked!'[37]

The other welcome result of publication was the discovery of more Fighting Instructions and Signal Books. Corbett had recognised significant gaps, which both he and the NRS Council hoped to address in the future. In the spring of 1908, Laughton's work on Lord Barham's papers provided vital insight into Richard Kempenfelt's tactical work, while the British Library's Bridport Collection, the papers of Admiral Sir Alexander Hood, Lord Bridport, and the Rodney papers lately donated to the Public Record Office addressed the critical period between the American War and the Glorious First of June 1794, when written instructions were replaced by Howe's signal-driven system.

These archival discoveries prompted the NRS Council to request another volume in March 1908. Corbett was far from pleased: 'Settled I was to begin New Vol of Fighting Instructions at which I refused as not likely to exceed 150pp.'[38] His response reflected a state of complete exhaustion after the hectic schedule of the past eighteen months. The demanding NRS Council included Bridge and fellow admirals Sir Arthur Fanshawe, Sir Albert Hastings Markham, who knew something about the importance of signals, Sir William May and Sir Edward Seymour, along with Trafalgar devotees Newbolt and Thursfield. Corbett began work the following day, work that would occupy many evenings; his days were occupied with more pressing tasks, including revising Frederick Dreyer's memorandum on the all-big-gun battleship. He met Laughton at the RUSI on 23 March, and hired a copyist to transcribe the Kempenfelt material in the Barham collection. Four days later he attended the Public Record Office and the British Library, examining Bridport's collection.[39]

Corbett immediately made a major discovery: Kempenfelt had reintroduced the signal for breaking the line in 1779, long before Rodney's battle on 12 April 1782. Soon afterwards he met the new Admiralty Librarian, William George Perrin, an expert on naval flag signalling.[40] Perrin would be a key ally, locating important material on James, Duke of York's Instructions.[41] Corbett also undertook the closely related NRS project of introducing contemporary sketches of the battles of Solebay and Texel, also loaned by the Earl of Dartmouth.[42] The drawings and text were issued in May 1908.[43] On the same day Corbett had a belated epiphany, going to bed he 'found the long lost Kempenfelt Signal Book, sent me on approval by Edwardes price 20/- (£1.00). Immediately sent him a cheque and had to read it in bed. One of the best bits of Godly luck I have had.' He acquired a set of Rodney's Fighting Instructions a week later.[44]

Progress on the new volume was interrupted when Slade asked him for a draft explaining 'how war plans should be constructed', to assist him in compiling suitable remarks: 'So I must lay aside Fighting Instructions'. The invitation to attend the Quebec Tercentenary provided additional distractions.[45] Even so, the new volume, *Signals and Instructions, 1776–1794*, went to the printers at the end the month, following a dinner with Custance and Slade.[46]

Returning from Canada in early August, Corbett spent ten days on the proofs before revising the 'Green Pamphlet'.[47] With the task effectively complete, the tactics project was thrown into confusion. On 5 September Captain Hubert Garbett RN, librarian at the RUSI, reported the belated rediscovery of Admiral Sir Thomas Graves' comprehensive collection of signals and instructions.[48] A brief description was enough to persuade Corbett that the current volume must be stopped. He wrote to halt printing, before consulting Perrin, William Graham Greene and Laughton, as Treasurer and Secretary, both to keep the discovery secret, and consider the impact it would have on his work.[49] Slade was certain the discoveries were important.[50]

Laughton provided a report on the box on 11 September. The following day Corbett went to the Admiralty Library, where it now resided, and worked all day with Perrin.[51] This was a serious problem, he was about to set off on a holiday to Ireland, needed to compile War Course lectures on combined operations and the Crimean War, and assess a draft naval history for cadets at Dartmouth.

Corbett finally had a chance to inspect the new discoveries a month later, at the end of a long day. His response was suitably laconic: 'Found many unknown things, which will mean a lot of work recasting my book.'

The following day, 13 October, he chaired the NRS Council, explaining why it was essential to revise the text, despite the additional cost and delay.[52] The council concurred.[53] He completed the modifications by the end of the month, just in time to switch to new War Course lectures, which became a book on Trafalgar.[54] The second half of November was taken up with checking and further revisions. The proofs ran into the New Year, followed by indexing and appendices, despite receiving serious attention during a Christmas break at Woodgate. The volume, Corbett's 'ninth historical work', appeared in March 1909.[55]

Signals and Instructions focused on the critical period, identified in 1905, when written Fighting Instructions were replaced by Signal Books, enhancing an admiral's tactical control over his fleet. The evidence that explained the process came from Barham's papers, and the Graves collection. Corbett thanked Perrin for finding references in Navy Board correspondence, helping to recast the text, reading the proofs, making the appendices, and providing lists of manuscripts and printed works on tactics and signalling. The 1909 text was integrated with the original volume, highlighting the importance of new developments.[56]

The purpose was to 'render possible a real study of the development of sailing tactics'. This was 'Admiralty work' and the students would be naval officers.[57] There remained a major gap in the sequence: he had not found the 1760 Printed Additional Instructions.[58] The 80-page introduction emphasised his mastery of the subject, rejecting the old idea that Rodney chose to break the line at the Battle of the Saintes after reading the pamphlet of John Clerk of Eldin. Such false deductions reflected inadequate evidence and a limited grasp of logic. The Navy had ignored Clerk's book, already familiar with the ideas he advanced, and unimpressed by the tactical credentials of a mere civilian. Corbett offered an alternative source of innovation, Richard Kempenfelt, who had studied in France, where the tactical lessons of the Seven Years' War had been taken to heart. Important post-1763 French tactical texts by Morogues and Villhuet were dedicated to the Duc de Choiseul, who was preparing the navy for a war of revenge.[59] Morogues combined a history of naval tactics since ancient galleys with detailed methods. His tactical preference was for a close-hauled line of large ships, because battles were won by firepower and mobility. The British printed partial translations of these texts in the late 1760s, while a new French edition of Morogues was produced in Amsterdam in 1779, in all probability to satisfy English demand during the American War. Corbett established Morogues' influence on Kempenfelt, while the evidence suggested the French text was widely consumed in the Royal Navy, not least by Rodney, where 'it found a more fertile soil than in his own service, and was more quickly and more thoroughly transformed into practical results'.[60]

Corbett exploited Robert Beatson's contemporary *Naval and Military Memoirs*, the best naval history of the American War, the author being connected to the Barham, Kempenfelt and Howe tactical school.[61] While the heavily footnoted narrative may have been unnecessary for naval students, it remained critical to establishing academic credibility.[62] He also followed Beatson's hint that Kempenfelt had been a model officer who reasoned in a 'scientific spirit', and 'the pith of his work ... was in freeing tactics from its fetters'. The *Barham Papers* would establish his 'genius' and explain the praise of his contemporaries.[63] Corbett used Kempenfelt as a model for contemporary students of tactics.[64]

He stressed the revolutionary nature Lord Howe's concept of breaking through the enemy line at all points, to hold their ships in position and secure a 'decisive' outcome, tracing the development of Nelson's thinking from Howe. That said, Corbett, a master of logical, precise prose, was horrified by Howe's 'tangled style'.[65] In 1790 Howe produced a new Signal Book, and new manoeuvre to pin the enemy in battle, a risky tactic used on 1 June 1794, because 'the times and peculiar circumstances of the country at that period ... called loudly in my opinion for some conclusive issue of the contest'.[66] This, Corbett noted, was 'exactly Nelson's frame of mind when he made his risky attack at Trafalgar'.[67] The subsequent discussion of Howe's thinking on the organisation of the battlefleet addressed an obvious contemporary problem: how to command an ever larger Home Fleet in a war that would be fought in an often murky North Sea.

Turning to Rodney, Corbett celebrated the recovery of six distinct sets of his 1778 instructions, linking them to the flagship's logbooks to show how Signal Books were distributed, and intermittently recalled, along with the signal lieutenants, for updates and amendments.[68] Rodney's instructions were the final word of Lord Hawke's highly aggressive school from the Seven Years' War, and a marked improvement over the 1759 instructions Corbett had cited in 1905, notably in their language and organisation.[69] This was critical for any tactical system. Then he rehearsed the vital role of doctrine in establishing understanding between admirals and captains.

Rodney had secured an ideal position to launch a concentrated attack on a portion of de Guichen's force, but Captain Carkett, who led the fleet, did not understand the purpose of his signal.[70] Corbett blamed Rodney's opaque orders, and failure to brief his captains in person, not the signal.

> A leader in real touch with his captains would have understood that tactical pre-occupations – traditional in the service – cannot be eradicated simply by new signals.[71]

There may have been a contemporary inference here, a criticism of Fisher's autocratic methods, by a man struggling to tone down the First Sea Lord's uncompromising intervention in the Invasion Inquiry.[72] Carkett's dilemma reappeared in *Some Principles*, to exemplify the importance of sound doctrine and effective communication.[73]

Hitherto unsuspected tactical developments on the North American Station, drawn from the Graves collection, included signals for combined and amphibious operations.[74] Corbett traced the evolution of the system through to 1794, emphasising the importance of Howe's cruise with the fleet assembled for the Nootka Sound Crisis of 1790. Exercising thirty-five sail of the line enabled Howe to test the tactical developments of the last war. He established that large fleets should be broken down into squadrons, and produced a new concept, cutting the enemy line at every interval.

> From this point it was but a step to the direct and drastic methods of Nelson, and it is easy to understand how the young admiral, when he came to appreciate what Howe's work really meant, was moved in his enthusiastic way to call him 'the first and greatest sea-officer the world has ever produced'.[75]

By contrast the French, as late as 1797, had made no progress beyond Morogues' text. The British, led by Kempenfelt and Howe, moved ahead, combining French theory and signalling concepts with British practice to shape a system that suited a well-organised, highly professional force with the skill and initiative to exploit fleeting opportunities. This was the secret of Nelson's success.

In March 1909 Captain Montagu Browning, lately Chief of Staff in the Channel Fleet, told Corbett that *Signals and Instructions* 'had been of great use in working out the tactical problems', especially in forming orders of battle from cruising stations.[76] Such responses encouraged Corbett to wrap up this work in *The Campaign of Trafalgar*, which he began immediately after *Signals and Instructions*. His forensic examination of the original Trafalgar memorandum argued that Nelson had abandoned his original intention of deploying from columns into line abreast for the final attack. The claim was based on copious contemporary evidence, emphasising the inclusion of this method in the 1816 Signal Book, suitably modified to reduce the obvious defects, as something altogether new. Corbett's view of the 1816 Signal Book had changed significantly since 1905.[77] He distinguished between the major and minor tactical ideas in the Trafalgar memorandum, emphasising that Nelson had retained the former but altered the latter to suit conditions on the day. Having established a coherent tactical doctrine in verbal and written briefings, Nelson did not need to explain these minor changes; his captains had no trouble following his lead and his example. Critically, Nelson took the lead, avoiding a repetition of Carkett's failure of understanding, while Collingwood led the lee line.[78]

British and French logbooks helped Corbett dismiss Thursfield's 'very ingenious attempt . . . to show that Nelson's attack was not perpendicular'.[79] The wind had veered during the approach, rather than remaining northerly as Thursfield contended, basing himself solely on *Victory*'s log. Corbett also rejected Philip Colomb's contention that the attack had been made in line abreast, pointing out how quickly even well-handled fleets lost cohesion when attempting to hold that formation, or even a line of bearing, something both Howe and Kempenfelt had recognised. A line or lines ahead was the most flexible tactical organisation for an attacking fleet. On the day of battle Nelson signalled the fleet to set all sail, including stunsails, and form in the wake of the flagships; Corbett traced the effect of the signal through the Master's Log of Thomas Fremantle's HMS *Neptune*, second behind the flagship. This had not been published in Admiral Thomas Sturges Jackson's NRS volume *Logs of the Great Sea Fights* or by Harris Nicolas in the *Nelson Letters*.[80] 'Otherwise', Corbett stressed, 'so careful an historian as Admiral Colomb would never have hazarded his unlucky conjecture that the fleet bore up together.' Colomb's essay, first published in the *United Services Magazine* and reprinted in 1905, had influenced Bridge and Custance. They, and not the long-dead Colomb, were Corbett's targets. Not only had Nelson attacked in columns, but the logbooks indicated some ships had anticipated this formation, evidence that Nelson's doctrine had been understood.[81] Colomb and Thursfield received their dismissal in a footnote. Corbett discussed his new findings, both signal logs and his new reading of the 1816 Signal Book, in a Trafalgar Day letter to *The Times*.[82] Nelson deliberately pressed the attack at maximum speed, signalling his followers to form as they could. The pace of Nelson's attack denied Collingwood the opportunity to form the line of bearing to attack at all points, following Lord Howe's model: his ships could only form a bow and quarter line, in echelon, one point of sailing off line head. The section closed with a magisterial denunciation of fancy theories, forced conclusions and idle speculation:

> It is, of course possible, by selecting fragmentary passages from the ill-kept Logs and Journals, and by calculations based on the various times at which ships alleged they engaged, to infer that possibly a real line of bearing was formed; but the rigour of historical science absolutely forbids such fragile web-spinning to obscure a question which is illuminated by direct and unimpeachable evidence to the contrary.

This was a less than subtle assertion of intellectual superiority in a debate sustained by the contemporary significance of the issue for the Navy. Corbett built his case around the operative word 'science', a word deliberately chosen to satisfy the naval mind that his conclusions were soundly based and final.[83] He hoped students would adopt his analytical method, even if they did not attempt to master this subject.[84]

Having settled that Nelson deliberately attacked in columns, Corbett examined his selection of the point at which to attack. He wanted to take out the enemy's command and control, reducing the Combined Fleet to a leaderless aggregation of units, individually inferior to his own ships in real combat power. When Villeneuve's flag broke, Nelson steered for him, and accepted the inevitable *mêlée*.[85] Once battle had been joined, Corbett passed swiftly through the action, his ten-page treatment focused on tactical choices, not fighting, death or heroics. He emphasised the repulse of Admiral Dumanoir's five ships by two British units as further proof that Nelson's intentions had been understood. His fleet had contained and then driven off the enemy's van, while crushing both the centre and rear. The result amply justified Nelson's tactical choices, whatever view was taken of the connection between the memorandum and the actual battle. In essence Nelson had used the major concepts of the memorandum but not the precise form, sacrificing scientific method and unity of impact for speed of execution, because the enemy was inferior in quality, and the weather was breaking.[86] Any other judgement 'depends upon the niceties of a dead art', a damning verdict on the so-called 'experts' who had tried to second guess events, and one that should be pondered by all those who study the past. Nelson's decisions on 21 October 1805 demonstrated the unique nature of genius:

> that final resolution remains as the stroke that above all others touches his leadership with divinity. Such flashes of genius will not submit to reasoned criticism, they are beyond rule and principle, and every effort to measure them by scientific standards can only be lost in the final comment – 'It was a glorious victory.'[87]

The synergy with Clausewitz's description of genius is striking. The Graham translation, which Corbett owned, read: 'this glance of genius ... sets aside a thousand dim notions which an ordinary understanding could only bring to light with great effort, and over which it would exhaust itself'.[88]

Corbett left the ultimate conclusion unspoken: it was one that he had been drumming home throughout the book. Nelson viewed battle as an opportunity to advance strategy and policy, rather than a tactical problem. Consequently he took risks to ensure the Combined Fleet would not be able to interfere with British strategy, in the Mediterranean or the Atlantic. That he also crushed the last attempt to challenge Britain's command of the sea was a predictable long-term benefit.

The tactical discussion of Trafalgar was widely welcomed. Édouard Desbrière agreed with Corbett, adding: 'As regards the tactics of Trafalgar ... the real peculiarity of the attack was his disorder. But such a disorder is simply apparent, and being caused by natural, human and generous reasons, deserves victory better than any complicated and theoretical scheme.'[89] Newbolt, delighted by two characteristic footnotes, 'admired the masterly way in which you have put aside old Colomb without appearing to make a point of it, and brushed away Bridge in the process without even naming him. The whole thing is seen in its true proportions.'[90] Charles Firth agreed, as far as his knowledge of the sea allowed, that Corbett had proved 'conclusively that the memorandum was one thing & the actual battle another'.[91]

However, there were worrying signs that the argument might not be settled after all: 'old Bridge has republished his Trafalgar nightmare in a new vol. of essays'.[92] Bridge had launched a substantial, if uninspired counter-attack by Thursfield and Captain Mark Kerr RN, who may have been working together. Kerr's views mattered, if only because he was a confidant of Prince Louis of Battenberg. Despite a long discussion with Corbett at the RUSI on 25 January 1911,[93] Thursfield repeated much of his old argument in the 1911 edition of *Brassey's Naval Annual*, while Kerr managed to invent something new in *The Nineteenth Century*. When these attacks failed, Thursfield used pages of *The Times* to demand an official enquiry to condemn Corbett's heresy. Bemused and not a little annoyed, Corbett told Newbolt:

> faintly in my ears are echoes of the Jabber of these clever gentlemen who think they know other than Nelson how Trafalgar should have been fought. It seems so far away and it matters so little. From a leader of Thursfield's in the *Times* he seems to want the Admiralty to put you and me in the Tower, or to burn us at the stake.[94]

In early April 1912 an official enquiry was ordered, by First Sea Lord Battenberg. Corbett expected Bridge and Custance, the naval members of the committee, would 'sit on my book'.

> who do you think is Chairman! None other than Bridge – a trial for heresy with the heresiarch for judge. Dear old sailormen they are very funny sometimes. They really think their committee will settle the controversy. Custance is the other naval member, Perrin, the Librarian and Secretary. They were going to appoint another sailor, but Perrin made them add Firth. I have seen him and explained. There may be fun. . . . P.S. I should have said that the real point at issue in the Trafalgar Committee – as it was appointed – is whether historians are to take their history from sailors or sailors from historians. It is a revolt of Bridge, Custance and Co. against people like you and me actively behind our backs – but especially me of course.[95]

Bringing Firth onto the committee was a masterstroke by Corbett and Perrin. Corbett may have recruited Firth, while Perrin, as Secretary to the committee, would control the evidence. Bridge decided not to call expert witnesses, denying Corbett a day in court he might have relished: 'the procedure is for Cyppy[96] to get up the evidence and then try I suppose to get Firth to agree with his view of it. At least that is what was going on when I heard, but I daresay Firth has had something to say.'[97] Indeed he did. Both Perrin and Firth understood and accepted Corbett's views. Perrin knew more about signals and Signal Books than anyone, including Corbett, and he would write the report. When selecting the evidence, Perrin excluded controversial material published since 1905, while employing Desbrière's majestic book as an authority, well aware that the Frenchman agreed with Corbett. On every point of consequence the committee found for Corbett, although he was not named, and against the equally anonymous Thursfield and Kerr. The report recognised the superiority of Corbett's academic methodology, the rigour of his analysis, and the coherence of his position. This was the point at issue.[98] Corbett was pleased: 'the Committee decided against Mark Kerr, Colomb and Bridge on all the main points'. However, Thursfield tried to have the last word on Trafalgar Day 1913, misrepresenting the outcome in *The Times*.[99] Corbett hoped Newbolt might provide a counter as 'I have no time for it.'[100] Nor, to his regret, did Newbolt, who feared a short letter would 'only rouse Thursfield to spin webs & webs of egotistic sophistry? My present idea is to go & see the Editor of the *Times* privately & expose to him the inwardness of the article.'[101] Corbett agreed they should boycott Thursfield, who was not playing by the rules, and advise the editor that his naval correspondent was falsifying history. Kerr, who had relied on Bridge and Custance to endorse his views, was annoyed.[102] Having committed the cardinal methodological sin of 'starting an historical investigation with a thesis', his case had been undone by the evidence.[103] Firth predicted Thursfield's nonsense would not endure.[104] He was right.

The Admiralty report provided a fitting conclusion to Corbett's tactical studies; work intended to stimulate contemporary thinking had generated private thanks, and public abuse. To mark the occasion he pasted letters from Newbolt, Firth and Perrin into the report. His work met the needs of the contemporary Navy so well that *Signals and Instructions* became the first NRS volume to sell out. That said, sailing-era battle tactics fascinated Corbett. He created an impressive collection of these texts, largely from specialist dealers.[105] After completing *Fighting Instructions* in 1908, he suggested a third, dealing with the 1760s, using the newly discovered Duff manuscripts.[106] Brian Tunstall argued Corbett had enough evidence to produce a history of tactics, but it is unlikely he would have done so. By 1918 there was ample modern tactical material for the Navy to process. Tunstall, whose approach was fundamentally antiquarian, considered the passage of time had 'triumphantly vindicated' some of Corbett's brilliant arguments,[107] among them Corbett's incisive deduction that Howe's 1790 Signal Book had inspired Nelson's approach at Trafalgar.[108] He also high-lighted occasions when Corbett went beyond the evidence, notably when he extended Morogues' point about the tactical value of big ships. Morogues' text did not refer to three-deckers, nor did it explain what Nelson did at Trafalgar, the points Corbett sustained from the French text.[109] Here Tunstall ignored the context: Corbett was addressing the *Dreadnought* controversy. Tunstall's antiquarian history of tactics lingered in manuscript for three decades. Written at a time when academic naval history remained the preserve of present-minded service colleges focused on nuclear exchange, it required a remarkable shift in intellectual habits, a bold and sympathetic publisher, and major editorial interventions to bring it to print in 1990.[110]

By contrast Corbett had taught the Edwardian Navy to think logically as it prepared for the future, using the history of naval tactics to stimulate fresh thinking in the Edwardian battlefleet. Past practice highlighted the issues that needed attention, and appropriate methods of study. These texts were suggestive, provocative and forward-looking. They provided evidence, methods of study and an invitation to join the debate. He demanded critical engagement, not rote learning.

CHAPTER 13

Maritime Strategy in a Total War

Corbett used *England in the Seven Years' War* to examine the efficacy of a 'British way' in a limited conflict, his next book would assess its relevance in the total war with the Napoleonic empire. *The Campaign of Trafalgar* focused on the opening phase of the Anglo-French War, linking the contest for command of the sea with Britain's attempt to create a pan-European coalition to resist Bonaparte's hegemonic ambitions. While that policy collapsed at Austerlitz, leaving France in control of Western and Central Europe, mainland Italy and Spain, Corbett demonstrated that maritime strategy remained critical to insular security, global power, economic warfare and the construction of future European coalitions.[1] Critically, this was a national approach that used an amphibious army to destroy hostile fleets and bases, and capture overseas possessions, keeping the enemy off balance and unable to focus on invasion. In 1805, Napoleon's response to a pair of small military expeditions sent his fleet to destruction.

Corbett had intended following the *Seven Years' War* with a similar text on the American War of Independence, a contrasting study of flawed strategy and defeat in another limited war. Instead he set the American War aside, bypassed the French Revolutionary conflict, and moved directly to Trafalgar, the 'Holy Grail' of naval history. In part he was responding to emerging opportunities and challenges. The War Course had requested Trafalgar lectures, while Nelson's tactics had become the battleground that would determine who had the authority to produce sea power doctrine. When Custance and Bridge asserted their superior authority, Corbett had to defeat them to preserve the credibility of methods and arguments that had been the basis of service education for much of the past decade.

Furthermore, the project offered a priceless opportunity to demonstrate the strikingly limited strategic consequences of the most 'decisive' naval battle. Trafalgar had not settled the Napoleonic wars.[2] Maritime strategy alone would not win a total war in Europe: Pitt the Younger recognised that was not a task for Britain alone, and did not require a mass conscript army. Pitt understood that only a pan-European coalition, one that included the other military great powers, could restore the Continent to balance. This argument would drive home Corbett's central themes that strategy, which had a base in theory, was ultimately a practical, specific national choice. In Britain that meant combining naval and military power under civilian direction, to meet the changing nature of conflicts. His new book focused on diplomacy and strategy between 1803 and 1805, reducing the battle to an afterthought, a mere 40 pages among 400, while the critical tactical debate that would establish his authority was relegated to the appendices. This structure encouraged readers to see the battle as a consequence of sound maritime strategy, a point emphasised in the title. Once again his primary targets were statesmen, soldiers and sailors, not academic historians.[3]

Trafalgar evolved at the intellectual juncture between suitably strategic War Course lectures, an ongoing public debate about contemporary tactics, and the need to establish the credibility of academic naval history. Corbett wrapped up *Signals and Instructions* in January 1909 and immediately started sketching War Course lectures on Trafalgar.[4] As usual he checked and reinforced the published scholarship with targeted access to primary sources, focusing on major controversies. On 21 January he read the dispatches of admirals Sir John Orde and Sir Robert Calder at the Public Record Office. Accepted wisdom held that both men had failed in 1805; the archives proved their actions were sound, consistent with national strategy.[5] He lectured at Devonport in the same week. Further research, which required a Foreign Office permit to consult dispatches from Lisbon, preceded the second delivery of the Trafalgar lectures at Sheerness. Here he was hosted by Admiral Sir Francis Bridgeman, commander-in-chief of the Home Fleet and soon to be Second Sea Lord, responsible for naval education. His audience included senior officers from the Home Fleet, Royal Engineers from Chatham and Gillingham, and Rear Admiral Alexander Bethell, the new DNI.[6]

In mid-February course director Lewis Bayly told Corbett his combined operations lectures at Portsmouth were the best he had heard for years.[7] Suitably encouraged, Corbett resumed work on Trafalgar: in late February he dropped the word 'lectures':

Began writing Trafalgar campaign, with many doubts as to wisdom thereof – in spite of being urged to by Slade, Bridgeman and many other naval officers. But I have found so much that is unknown about it that all recent criticisms go on a misconception of what its object was, thus I think I will go on with it, tho' against my feeling to crib history in scraps.[8]

Naval demand, new material and the weakness of existing scholarship made the subject irresistible. Before taking his words literally it should be remembered that his exposition of the strategic, political and tactical issues of the campaign had already persuaded three separate naval audiences, including the incoming Second Sea Lord and DNI, that a book was required. He needed little persuasion: both subject and material were attractive, while moving ahead to Trafalgar would bring the age of sail to a conclusion, releasing him to address more contemporary examples. It may not be a coincidence that he considered translating Colonel Édouard Desbrière's French Staff History of the campaign on the previous day.

With lecture notes and printed sources to hand, Corbett began work the following day, engrossed in the diplomatic preliminaries set out in John Holland Rose's *Select Dispatches relating to the Third Coalition against France, 1804–5*.[9] Outside it was snowing hard, and the 'We Want Eight' crisis threatened to split the Cabinet. Foreign Secretary Sir Edward Grey secured the eight ships by threatening to resign.[10]

Among the first issues to be addressed was the relative value of the large battleships. Mahan, Custance and Sir William White had cited the ubiquitous 74-gun third rate ship of the line of 1805 when criticising *Dreadnought's* 'excessive' size. Having established that Nelson, and most other naval men, reckoned three-decked first rates, like the 100-gun HMS *Victory*, equal to two two-decked 74-gun third rates in close combat, Corbett used that measure to calculate the relative power of the fleets and squadrons that surged across his pages. When he used the argument at Portsmouth in March, admirals Sir Edward Bradford and Doveton Sturdee were shocked, declaring their preference for Custance's judgement. Bayly provided support, but Corbett dropped the *Dreadnought* reference from later lectures.[11] It seems the excitement stressed a fragile author: another outbreak of erysipelas confined him to bed, delaying the Trafalgar lectures at Chatham.[12] Heavily bandaged, Corbett continued writing, reaching the end of chapter 4 inside a month. Devouring Napoleon's correspondence in the intervals between lecturing at Portsmouth, he discovered the emperor agreed with Nelson that three-decked ships were superior to 74s.

By 4 April Corbett, taking the usual family 'holiday' at Stopham, was engaged on chapter 8, Nelson's decision to go to the West Indies. Three weeks later, having wrapped up chapter 9, he returned to town, where DNI Bethell invited him to join the War Staff – just as the Beresford Inquiry was in full spate. Despite being on stand-by to attend the enquiry, Corbett delivered the postponed Trafalgar lectures at Chatham and conducted further research at the Public Record Office and British Library, adding new material to the drafts as he went. Reviewing Thursfield's Nelson essays for *The Times* provided some light relief. His criticism of Thursfield's imaginative tactical ideas reappeared in the appendices of *Trafalgar*, the book was 'bad in places, but [I] don't like to say how bad'.[13] Thursfield disputed Corbett's account of Nelson's tactics in his copy of *Trafalgar*, having ignored the first 340 pages.[14]

By contrast, a charming letter from Édouard Desbrière settled the target of Villeneuve's West Indian campaign, which had been troubling Corbett. The mystery turned on the difference between the direction north (Barbude in French) and the island of Barbade (Barbados), the British naval base. Desbrière sent a copy of his book, apologising that a colonel of the 27th Dragoons was no naval expert.[15]

Corbett made a critical breakthrough on the afternoon of 11 May, persuading Laughton to let him read Lord Barham's correspondence as First Lord of the Admiralty, which Sir John was editing for the NRS.[16] A week later he opened Calder's action, only to be overwhelmed by the birth of his son Richard on the 27 May. The doctor sent him to Woodgate, suffering from 'nervous breakdown and lumbago'. After a week's rest he returned home to find the family were doing well, resuming Calder's action the next day.[17] Visiting Laughton he uncovered a wealth of strategic material the professor had overlooked. The implications of these discoveries may have been emphasised by attending the Imperial Press Conference Review of the Home and Atlantic fleets at Spithead on 12 June. One hundred and forty-four warships moored in seven columns provided a potent demonstration of naval primacy, reinforced by dramatic torpedo boat exercises, emphasising the unity and resolve of Britain's global maritime empire. The message was understood in Germany.[18] Nor was Corbett short of professional input. Captain Huddleston, a former student and friend from the Quebec voyage, provided notes on Lord Keith's operations in the North Sea, and later 'some good cruiser stuff'.[19] This helped Corbett grasp the critical role of cruiser operations throughout the campaign. Frigate logbooks and reports revealed a striking consistency in decision-making, which looked like a common doctrine. Frigate captains with important intelligence to deliver consistently focused on the priorities that drove national strategy. Throughout the book, Corbett employed a variety of phrases to encapsulate the modern concept of doctrine, a word he began to use sparingly in *Some Principles* the following year, and fully adopted in the 1913 'Staff Histories' essay.[20]

By early July the manuscript was progressing to a conclusion: 'Having got Villeneuve to Cadiz feel the back of the book is broken'.[21] Exhausted by the concentrated intellectual effort of lecturing, researching and writing, public debate, domestic drama and ill-health, he took Edith for a week's holiday at Rye, where he sketched Camber Castle and dined with Henry James, Francis and other locally based Darwins. Chapter 19 was wrapped up soon after they returned to London.[22] The book would be dedicated to Edith, whose birthday fell on 21 October. A summer break at Woodgate was spoiled by heat and lumbago, but he made some revisions. Lieutenant Keate's discovery of the long-overlooked logbooks of *Temeraire* and *Defence* at the Public Record Office prompted a revision of the battle narrative. The draft was completed at Stopham on 9 October, an event recorded with pardonable pride after a mere seven months' work. A timely article on the *Temeraire* logbook appeared in *The Times* on 22 October. A week later he lectured on Trafalgar at the War College.

In November the chapters were typed while Corbett rewrote his Russo-Japanese War lectures.[23] When Corbett delivered the revised typescript on 4 February Charles Longman 'seemed glad to have it & inclined to be generous about maps etc'. The illustrations would include contemporary drawings and several large folding sheets in three colours, drawn by Lieutenant Keate. Corbett had long since evolved from a literary man using pictures to illustrate his text, into a strategist working with maps and charts, the method of his naval audience. His last two books would extend that approach, integrating words and images, the twin pillars of strategic comprehension. Everything had been settled before a contract was signed in mid-February – the relationship with Longman was personal, between gentlemen. A bad cold followed the proof corrections; he recuperated at Bournemouth. Proofs and index went to Longman on All Fool's Day, the maps required more work, and arrived on 13 April: 'so completed my Trafalgar campaign. Good luck go with it. I fear it is full of imperfections.'[24] Corbett and Edith set off for Florence the next day. The death of King Edward VII prompted Longman to delay publication until after the state funeral. By August, over a third of the 1,500 copies had been sold.

Alongside printed editions of contemporary documents illuminating the diplomatic and political background, including French and Spanish perspectives, Corbett used material created for the 1907 Invasion Inquiry to demonstrate how control of the Western Approaches, the Channel Isles and the North Sea rendered Napoleon's projects futile. Corbett reminded readers that *Trafalgar*, the naval highlight of Britain's greatest conflict, a total war lasting twelve years that had threatened the existence of the state, could only be fully understood by starting with the Cabinet, and 'the inward springs at work by which the fleets at sea were really controlled and mark the flow of intelligence ... that set them in motion, or stayed their action.'[25] He condemned the complacent attitudes of nation and Navy to the development and application of doctrine, a word nowhere written, but everywhere inferred, using *Trafalgar*, a striking reassessment of the opening two years of the Napoleonic conflict, to project his understanding of maritime strategy and national policy. The battle secured command of the sea but left Napoleon dominant in Europe, exposing the limits of Britain's power, and the limited/maritime strategic method. The future depended on coalitions, as Pitt understood. Corbett demolished the charming myth that Trafalgar prevented an invasion, and with it half a decade of misguided tactical speculation, his devastating footnotes eviscerating inadequate and incompetent work.

Alongside the focus on grand strategy, Corbett highlighted doctrinal lessons by reconnecting cruiser work with fleet operations:

> naval officers ... require ... a co-ordinated account of the movements of all classes of ships engaged in each operation, and a clear knowledge of the instructions and intelligence under which it was carried out. In short, if Naval History is to establish itself as a matter of real instructional interest, students must be able to find in accounts of the old campaigns at least an indication of what they would look for in a report on manoeuvres today.

Dismissing his book as 'tentative and imperfect', he called for an Admiralty Historical Section to rewrite virtually the whole of British naval history 'on Staff lines'. It would be 'a laboratory where civilian and naval experts can work side by side to supply each other's defects and ripen each other's ideas'.[26] A university professorship would not meet the practical needs of the service; it required a naval establishment, on a scale commensurate with Fisher's dreadnought fleet, to recover 'the soul of the matter', doctrine. A decade later he evinced less faith in the Admiralty's support for history, but the need to recover doctrine through the professional study of past practice persisted.

Trafalgar's opening chapter situated Britain's limited maritime strategy in a geo-strategic context. British policy focused on keeping hegemonic powers, like Napoleonic France, out of the Low Countries, Portugal and Sicily, and the strategy to achieve that end was necessarily linked to the balance of power and diplomacy. The prominence he accorded the Baltic said as much about the strategic situation in 1907–9 as that of 1803–5. Connecting Pitt the Younger, Pitt the Elder, Marlborough and William III stressed the continuity of a 'British way' and the critical role of educated statesmen. Pitt attempted to recover the initiative, building a coalition to restore Europe to balance.[27] That balance would secure Britain, its trade and empire, and remove the financial burden of war. The narrative opened with the recapture of Saint Lucia, using a small, distant action to critique the continental views of Army historian John Fortescue. Clearing the West Indies of Dutch and French privateer bases reduced 'the chief danger to our sea-borne commerce'. This mattered because: 'the retention of our financial position eventually enabled us to beat Napoleon down'. The exposition of maritime strategy ended with G.F.R. Henderson's line that the proper role of the British Army was to support the maintenance of sea power, condemning the unthinking application of concentration of force to global maritime strategy. He analysed Pitt's use of maritime strategy to counter-attack France, rather than waiting on the defensive in Clausewitzian terms.[28] Beyond strategy, Britain's role in helping to restore the balance of power was a 'fundamental law' of international politics, one that coincided with the continental interests of Russia, Prussia and Austria. Such insights reflected his attempt to master the strategic history of the state since the sixteenth century: they were among the 'principles of maritime strategy'.

Corbett traced the campaign that ended at Trafalgar back to Pitt's decision to open his counter-offensive by sending troops to support a Russian campaign in southern Italy. Here Russia's continental concerns coincided with Pitt's anxiety to secure Sicily, which fed and watered Malta, which in turn enabled the Royal Navy to command the Mediterranean. Despite the existential threat posed by Napoleon's invasion plans, Pitt refused to sacrifice Britain's strategic interests: he would not hand Malta back to the Knights of St John, or the Tsar, let alone sacrifice British maritime belligerent rights, because Russia was no more to be trusted than France. If Russia would not cooperate, Britain, Pitt informed their ambassador, would 'continue the war alone: it will be maritime'.[29] This was a threat: Russian trade would be crippled by an Anglo-French economic conflict. Russian procrastination delayed the application of British strategy; Pitt could not deploy his limited amphibious strike force until St Petersburg was committed. Thereafter naval dominance would give the Third Coalition against France the luxury of strategic choice.

Military manpower for British offensives was recruited, not conscripted, while reinforcing the south coast meant a Napoleonic invasion would have to bring more men and guns. The naval response to this threat was understood by senior officers: Lord Barham's instructions to Admiral Sir William Cornwallis in 1805 encapsulated everything that had been learnt in the eighteenth century and provided ample space for initiative.[30] Corbett did not believe the invasion threat was real: the troops never embarked. Napoleon maintained the illusion because *Delenda est Carthago!* had become the unifying war cry of France.[31] Pitt bluntly rejected Napoleon's peace terms, pointedly ignoring his imperial pretensions. He trusted the 'rising spirit of the nation', a link to Clausewitz's discussion of unlimited war.

Corbett's critique of Mahan, and others who accepted Napoleon's version of events was less than subtle. The demolition of old verities was critical to his argument that Britain would contribute effectively to a major European war without a mass conscript army. Nor was Mahan the only naval 'expert' criticised: Corbett ridiculed Custance's obsession with battle. Of Nelson he observed: 'No great Captain ever grasped more fully the strategical importance of dealing with the enemy's main force; yet no-one ever less suffered it to become an obsession, no one saw more clearly when it ceased to be the key of a situation, and fell to a position of secondary moment.' For good measure he shattered Custance's small battleship thesis:

Nelson and Napoleon reckoned a three-decked ship equal to two 74-gun two-deckers.[32]

Once the action moved from the Cabinet Council to the open ocean, Corbett emphasised the fluid, uncertain nature of command of the sea, when communications were slow and uncertain. This placed a premium on strategic insight, and explained how Nelson missed Villeneuve off Sardinia. He commended the decision-making of Sir John Orde and Sir Robert Calder, long dismissed as inadequate and short-sighted by those who did not recognise the limits of the art. Nelson's negative judgements were made in haste and, in Orde's case, coloured by personal factors. Ultimately the Royal Navy's doctrinal cohesion, built on long experience, defeated Napoleon's complex schemes. Cohesion was more important than 'genius' in the wider picture, because it could be relied upon. At the Admiralty, Barham, grappling with a rapidly changing situation and uncertain intelligence, assumed senior officers afloat shared his strategic vision, and expected them to use their initiative. Corbett used Barham to reinforce arguments made three years earlier, through Pitt the Elder and Anson.[33] Napoleon's 'interminable modification' ignored the reality of war at sea and the experience of his admirals. This masterly turn of phrase elevated British decision-making to a higher plane, demolishing myths of Napoleonic omnipotence. His self-serving claims to have outwitted the dull British, trumpeted in Adolphe Thiers' multi-volume history of the consulate and empire in the 1840s, evaporated under serious scrutiny.[34] Napoleon 'entirely failed to fathom either the subtlety or the strength of British strategy'.[35] The irony that the critical evidence came from France was not over-played.

Napoleon's condemnation of the opening moves of Pitt's counter-attack as 'the movement of pygmies' reflected his fury when the invasion threat failed to fix the British on the defensive. By mid-June 1805, British blockades had been re-established, Nelson was in hot pursuit of Villeneuve, and Britain remained secure against invasion. Furthermore, the willingness of General Craig, en route to secure Sicily with a small army, to detach his escort to ensure British naval superiority off Ushant demonstrated the synergy of the two services, 'and how complete was their mutual understanding of the principles of combined warfare'. Corbett's use of the past tense inferred that synergy no longer existed, while its restoration was both long overdue and essential to the development of national strategy. Craig, like G.F.R. Henderson, understood command of the sea was the primary concern of British strategy: when it became necessary to act on that principle he 'did not flinch'.[36] With the Straits of Gibraltar secure, British strategy could unfold, unhindered by France and Spain.

Ultimately, British doctrine triumphed over Napoleon's complex plans because 'a living instinct for naval war' was shared by every officer, not just men of Nelson and Barham's stamp: even 'the least of Drake's heirs' knew what to do in an emergency.[37] Collingwood easily penetrated Napoleon's schemes, as did Barham. A shared doctrine enabled admirals at sea to anticipate Barham's orders and use their initiative.[38] Unsettled by the emperor, and unsure of their strength, French admirals had no such confidence.

The dissection of Napoleon's strategy provided a striking contemporary lesson. Assessing British responses to Napoleon's assembly of an army in the Texel to divert attention from his real intentions, he observed:

> The disturbing power of an army by the sea with transports and escort alongside – a specially English device – is often questioned. Here at least is evidence of Napoleon's faith in it.[39]

This present-minded remark addressed continental strategists at the War Office who ignored the effect of British power in the Baltic on the outcome of the Crimean War. Napoleon's use of this device demonstrated how amphibious operations worked as strategy or deterrent. Having deliberately left the issue unresolved for fifty pages, Corbett revealed how easily Lord Keith had penetrated the sham. Half a dozen third rates contained a French demonstration designed to unlock the entire British defensive system.[40]

Ultimately, Napoleon's complex schemes collapsed in the face of a well-established British principle: 'When in doubt make sure of the mouth of the Channel.' Barham considered the Western Squadron 'the mainspring from which all offensive operations must proceed'. With the Channel secure, he detached Calder from Ushant to intercept Villeneuve, an order Cornwallis had anticipated.[41] French admirals knew that any battlefleet entering the Channel would be destroyed, leaving the Boulogne Flotilla to attempt an invasion without support. Napoleon's invasion force, both land and sea, was never ready: Corbett dismissed it as hoax, relying on Desbrière's detailed French Staff History.[42] The French soldier, the ultimate authority, exposed Napoleon's posturing, and ridiculed those who took it seriously, from Thiers and Mahan to a rising generation of British soldiers. Having admonished the soldiers, Corbett shifted focus, using Calder's engagement with Villeneuve on 22 July to demonstrate the limits of simple tactics, the impact of chance, and the importance of big ships. Calder's three-deckers shattered French and Spanish two-deckers, Fisher's *Dreadnought* would do the same.[43]

Having established that Napoleon was never going to launch an invasion, Corbett returned to the British counter-attack. Anticipating Napoleon would renew his attack on India the government sent an expedition to seize the Cape of Good Hope from the Dutch. This operation emphasised the irrelevance of 'crude' ideas of concentration, 'a warning that the broad combined problems of Imperial defence are not to be solved off-hand by the facile application of maxims which are the outcome of narrower and less complex continental conditions'.[44] Using challenging, provocative language and dismissing arguments based on Mahan and Jomini as facile and crude emphasised the profundity of Corbett's point.

When Villeneuve departed from Coruna in mid-August, Cornwallis's fleet off Ushant remained stronger than that of Ganteaume in Brest, because it had many more three-deckers, enabling him to detach Calder to secure the Mediterranean. With the fate of the nation in his hands, Cornwallis once again took a major decision that anticipated Barham's orders, confident in the soundness of his analysis.[45] The powerful synergy between Whitehall and the flagship explains Corbett's concern to develop and promulgate sound strategic and operational doctrine.

Napoleon called the division of Cornwallis's fleet stupid, a judgement Mahan echoed, but, as Corbett observed in a telling footnote, he was the only naval officer ever to do so. The put-down was necessary to prove that Mahan's continental approach to sea power did not work in the British maritime/imperial context. He softened the blow by observing that Mahan wrote before gaining experience of the higher direction of war in 1898: his discussion of the subject in *The War of 1812* of 1905 was 'incompatible with his censure of Cornwallis'. Mahan's claim also failed the most basic test: the Admiralty approved Cornwallis's decision. Nor were these moves defensive, they extended British power to support counter-attacks at the Cape and Sicily. Naval strategy should never be judged by 'the elementary maxims derived from warfare on land'. The discussion of concentration challenged Mahan's credibility, and destroyed the extreme positions taken by unsubtle followers and 'purists trained in the continental schools'.[46]

Concentration off Ushant would not secure the Mediterranean, where a fleet and an army were essential to sustain the emerging alliance with Russia and Austria.[47] This example of the deflection of strategy by politics on the largest scale explains why Cornwallis acted. Furthermore he had to consider the defence of floating trade, which occupied a prominent place in British decision-making, especially in the season when great oceanic convoys entered the Western Approaches, a risk that had no parallel on land. Losing an inbound East India convoy would be 'a disastrous blow to the national finance, and commercial . . . influence demanded that it must be saved at any cost'.[48]

Cornwallis knew that even if the fleets of Villeneuve, Allemand and Ganteaume combined, bringing fifty sail into the Channel, they would be annihilated before reaching Boulogne. However, the risk should not be run. On 25 August, the critical day of the entire campaign, Cornwallis drove Ganteaume's emerging fleet back into Brest.[49] Two days before, Villeneuve had limped into Cadiz, meekly submitting to be blockaded by Collingwood with three ships: the Royal Navy's moral ascendancy was absolute. Ten days later Calder arrived off Cadiz with eighteen sail. With the Combined Fleet locked up, only Allemand's five battleships remained unaccounted for.[50] The invasion threat, if it had ever been serious, had passed. Napoleon gave up before he knew where Villeneuve was heading, and did so in response to the threat posed by the tiny expeditions of Craig and Baird. He thought Baird would follow Craig into the Mediterranean.[51] On 31 August 1805, the emperor demobilised the invasion flotilla and split the battlefleet into raiding squadrons.

Corbett used examples of consistent work by detached cruiser commanders: men who understood their mission, and used their initiative, to link the fleets and the Admiralty. This stressed the continuing importance of sound doctrine for the development of maritime strategy.[52] These men had learnt their business on the quarter deck, from experienced officers, not French or German textbooks.[53] Barham and Nelson reorganised the patrol lines, using additional cruisers released by Keith to improve their ability to intercept the enemy, maintain communications between the main fleets, and protect trade, roles officers would recognise in 1910. This was 'a distinct advance towards more scientific systems of intelligence and commerce protection'.[54] Corbett included a classic example of a convoy escort sacrificing itself to enable the merchant ships to scatter, a model that students might have to emulate.[55] Concluding the discussion of trade defence, Corbett stressed the limits of cruiser warfare. The only area where French attacks might have a serious effect was the Western Approaches, where the near-permanent presence of the Grand Fleet made sustained operations impossible. Holding the terminal points was critical. Allemand's long and lucky cruise did not shake British strategy, or weaken its grip on the enemy: instead it demonstrated 'the futility of seeking to entice our fleets away, so long as a sound strategical tradition remains green in the service'.[56] This summed up his core message: the need to recover and teach doctrine.

Startled by Craig's expedition, Napoleon ordered Villeneuve to take his troops to Naples, before undertaking raiding operations. Pitt's approach had worked, 'by sheer force of strategical law'.[57] Nelson, a minor presence in the text until the very end, was determined to destroy the Combined Fleet, because he knew, from hard experience, how difficult it was to blockade Cadiz in winter, advising the Admiralty accordingly. Bomb vessels and Congreve rockets were prepared, in case the enemy remained in harbour, while Nelson hoped a blockade would drive them out.[58]

Corbett rewarded diligent readers with an assessment of the operational and tactical handling of the battle, before moving to the larger issue of what had been achieved.[59] His conclusion, a masterpiece of advocacy, set up the straw man of the battle's irrelevance: 'so barren of immediate result' that it inspired the legend that it prevented an invasion of England. This allowed him to develop a very different argument, and a far grander view of the war. Sicily, the central point of the campaign, was secured by 8,000 British troops, even though the Russians withdrew after Austerlitz. Austrian power in Italy disappeared, 'like the baseless fabric of a dream', while Prussia cringed before Napoleon. The continental coalition had failed, but Britain would fight alone, Trafalgar ensuring it did so with unchallenged command of the sea. Holding Sicily and Malta secured command of the Mediterranean, while control of the Cape went a long way to securing India. Trafalgar placed Britain, the empire and the wider world beyond Napoleon's grasp, but this was not victory: 'the sea had done all that the sea could do, and for Europe the end was failure'.[60] While his closing lines stressed the inability of naval power alone to settle the destiny of Europe, Corbett stressed the Army's vital, if limited, role in British strategy. The future for maritime strategy lay in Iberia, where sea communications would sustain a land campaign.

Copies were sent to friends and colleagues. Desbrière was delighted by high praise, subtle correction, and the synergy of their thinking.[61] Newbolt admired the facility with which Corbett had subtly yet unmistakably surmounted the account of Colomb, and silently dismissed that of Bridge. He concluded with a line that must have touched Corbett to the very core, 'My dear Julian, you know how proud I am of you and your work. I hope this will put the coping stone on your reputation and be recognised as a national service.'[62] This was precisely what Corbett had intended. Admitting he liked 'pleasant things from those who know', he also acknowledged an error Newbolt had spotted, placing Israel Pellew in command of *Colossus* rather than *Conqueror*.[63] Charles Firth was persuaded by Corbett's treatment of the Nelson memorandum, a point that would become significant two years later, and his handling of grand strategy.

> The explanation of the reasons for the different orders issued by the Admiralty & the process of reasoning which led Nelson or Cornwallis or Barham to come to the conclusions they did is extremely interesting, and excessively instructive. I felt that I understood not only that bit of the naval war but the whole war much better than I did before. No other book I know of throws the same sort of light on the principles of naval defence as they were worked out during that period. In particular I feel that the whole working of the blockade and the system of concentrating the fleet wherever it was necessary explains a great deal.

Firth sought Corbett's advice on naval aspects of King William's war and Macaulay's hostility to Lord Torrington before lecturing on the subject.[64] Admiral Sir Wilmot Fawkes reported reading the book twice, picked up three small errors, and demonstrated why he was held in high regard by Lord Selborne, Fisher and the naval intellectuals:

> I think you have made the whole campaign for the first time clear, given us the meaning of it all and told its story so clearly, by giving in detail what the Admiralty & the Admirals knew, the facts on which their decisions were based. How splendidly they worked together, anticipating orders & taking responsibility whenever necessary. I also like your battles so much. You have made Trafalgar, Calder's action and Strachan's

very clear & I congratulate you most heartily & hope the book will be well studied by the rising generation of naval officers.[65]

Fawkes hosted Corbett when he lectured at Devonport and joined the NRS Council in 1914.[66]

Jacky Fisher was so impressed that he sent the book, complete with reading directions, to former prime minister and CID founder Arthur Balfour. Balfour responded: 'I will certainly read the passage in Corbett's book to which you call my attention, indeed, I have already ordered the book; and propose reading the whole of it. Corbett is an admirable writer.' This letter disposes of the fallacy that no-one who mattered read Corbett. Fisher sent Corbett a brilliant epitome of the book from the *Times Literary Supplement*: 'about as admirable a bit of war Bovril that was ever boiled down from a great book such as yours. <u>Do read it!</u>'[67] Herbert Richmond, Staff Captain on HMS *Dreadnought*, recognised Corbett's overriding concerns:

It is a great work, and really will do something, I feel sure, to open people's eyes to the fact that the old wars were not a mere heedless jumble of ships running about like mad dogs looking for some one to bite, but were organised concerns, planned on definite lines, & governed always by some particular objects. If it should do something towards the formation of an Historical Section it will have done a great deal: but I hope it will do that & more besides.[68]

Marine George Aston thanked Corbett for his copy from Pretoria: 'I can only hope that every officer in the Fleet and Army, and every Statesman, will read the book and keep a copy by him. Your power of work must be wonderful.' He asked for Corbett's views on his *Letters on Amphibious Wars*.[69]

Among the leading reviews, the *Athenaeum* was quick off the mark, finding much to praise, enjoying the debate, and anticipating further discussion, even if it did not entirely agree. The reviewer even criticised Corbett's prose as, 'often unpleasant, savouring of "graphic" descriptions in the popular press', objecting to 'the author's fancy for rendering old-established names of things into twentieth-century jargon'.[70] It recognised the higher educational function of the book, elucidating principles for statesmen soldiers and sailors, and felt it was 'a very considerable success'. Predictably, the Conservative *Spectator* rejected to Corbett's challenging ideas and source criticism.[71] The Liberal *Westminster Gazette* disagreed:

> Mr Corbett excels as an historian because his strategical understanding it as great as the profundity of his knowledge of the facts, and he never fails to write in such a manner as to command the interest of the general as well as the professional reader.[72]

For the *Saturday Review*, it was 'a book that would rank among our naval classics', 'Mr Corbett understands how to make the most of any subject he takes in hand', defeating both 'Barfleur' and Thursfield.[73]

The longest, and most scholarly review, complete with footnotes, appeared in the *English Historical Review*. Charles Atkinson accepted the argument that Craig's expedition had brought on the battle, but questioned how far that justified describing the campaign as 'essentially offensive'. He found Corbett's arguments more ingenious than compelling, preferring Mahan's assertion that Trafalgar drove Napoleon to adopt the Continental System. However, Corbett's unusual approach was 'the price one must pay for those very qualities of insight and ingenuity which make his volumes so vivid and suggestive'. Atkinson then reversed course, acknowledging the centrality of Sicily to Pitt's planning, the brilliance of the division of the Western Squadron, and the striking endorsement of British cruiser work. He concluded with a delightful, barbed assessment of the 'tactics at Trafalgar' debate, implying Corbett was as guilty of 'fragile web spinning' as those he criticised, making such methods 'a rather double edged sword'.[74] Corbett may have enjoyed being taken seriously in the leading academic history journal, aware that few sailors read the *English Historical Review*.

Finally, Corbett received the endorsement he really wanted: Edmond Slade declared: 'I think it is just what we want and if men will only study it we shall not have so much loose talk going on.'[75] *Trafalgar* had passed the ultimate test, satisfying statesmen, the Regius Professor at Oxford, strategic sailors, a clever Royal Marine, and a master of English prose who happened to be an expert on the battle. As Don Schurman observed, the book demonstrated 'his unrivalled knowledge of the strengths and weaknesses of sea power'.[76] Good sales ensured the message was widely consumed.

Trafalgar restated the intellectual case for a 'British way' as set out in the *Seven Years' War*. Britain's distinctive character as a maritime-imperial power meant its strategy should not follow the tune of continental theorists, even in a total war. Instead it should develop Clausewitz's system to address a very different situation. By January 1911, with half the copies sold, Longman wanted to publish a reduced-type edition: Corbett demanded corrections.[77] He revised proofs for this edition immediately after completing the typescript of *Some Principles*.

Fisher was quick to make use of the new book: in July 1910 he advised the Australian High Commissioner in London: 'Next Time you write to Senator Pearce [the Australian Defence Minister] send him the last paragraph of *Pitt's Campaign* in Literary Supplement of *Times* July 7th.'[78] The strategic/cultural message registered.[79] It was no accident that Naval War Course graduates oversaw the creation of the Royal Canadian and Royal Australian navies. The establishment of consistent imperial doctrine governing the application of sea power was far more important than standardisation of technology. Only navies that thought like the Royal Navy would be able to fight alongside it in war.

Trafalgar would have been the first instalment of a larger project. In October 1910, course director Lewis Bayly requested lectures on the Great War after 1805.[80] Corbett delivered them in June 1911. Like the initial sketches of *Trafalgar*, they were written in a week, following a few days' research at the Public Record Office, and only 'finished' the day before they were given.[81] Corbett may have planned to develop them into a book, but the opportunity never arose. Instead they provided a text for his last public lecture. Work on the American Revolution, the Napoleonic conflict after Trafalgar, and the Crimean War would be restricted to lectures and aspirations as his writing became ever more closely aligned with the intellectual needs of the modern Navy. Yet it would be a mistake to regret the end of the historical phase: Corbett had little more to say in that format. Moving seamlessly from *Trafalgar* to *Some Principles* emphasised his maturity as a strategist, ready to develop his ideas within a conceptual framework, free from the constraints of narrative. Ultimately, historical narrative restricted his ability to deliver comprehensive arguments about maritime strategy and doctrine. His next book reversed the model, giving ideas and argument centre stage, supported by selected historical evidence.

Trafalgar demonstrated how Britain's limited maritime strategy had thwarted the military efforts of the greatest captain of war in modern history's first total war, laying the foundations for a successful counter-stroke, through economic warfare, limited military intervention in Europe, and the support of continental coalitions, without raising a mass conscript army. This strategic model remained the basis of British policy down to August 1914. The difference between 1814 and 1918 was not the result – Britain ensured the independence of the Low Countries and restored the European balance on both occasions – but the cost. The war of 1914–18 cost a million lives, shattered the British economy, polarised British politics, wrecking a Liberal party that stumbled into a continental war without a settled strategy, and saw the nation lose faith in the Senior Service and maritime strategy. Corbett had been acutely aware of those realities.

CHAPTER 14

Teaching National Strategy

Some Principles of Maritime Strategy was an Edwardian doctrine primer, created to explain the strategic context of Fisher's policy, in the civil/ military context provided by the CID.[1] Never intended to have universal applicability, it was written, as Herbert Richmond reported, 'with some diffidence' at Fisher's behest.[2] While Corbett used core strategic texts, especially *On War*, he carefully developed them to meet British needs, using the medium of historical experience. Both intellectual content and historical examples were drawn from his work across the preceding decade. Furthermore it was, like any good doctrine primer, merely a way-point in an intellectual continuum, not the terminus. This chapter will focus on the creation and immediate impact of the book.

Some Principles developed Corbett's strategy texts of the preceding decade, notably the 'Green Pamphlet', the introduction to the Ballard Committee War Plans and the memorandum for the 1907 Invasion Inquiry.[3] It took definite shape as Fisher's time in office came to an end. Anxious to secure his legacy, Fisher needed a compelling exposition of his strategic concepts, one that superseded Mahan's 'naval' approach and rebutted the 'continental' ambitions of the Army General Staff by highlighting the central role of economic warfare in maritime strategy. That Corbett was trusted to compile that text reflected a profound synergy of ideas, beliefs and values between the two men, a synergy that endured to the end. Corbett met Fisher's need by using Clausewitz's logic to argue for a unique 'British way'.

In mid-April 1909 Fisher invited Corbett to the Admiralty to assess the work of the War Plans Committee. Within days DNI Captain Alexander Bethell had offered him a position on the committee: his unique insight into 'the ideas and operations of the old Admirals' would assist the planning process. While this would have fulfilled a long-held ambition, Corbett doubted his suitability: Bethell pressed him to select a title and suggest a salary.[4] Nothing came of the initiative because Fisher's object in employing Corbett, to rebut Beresford's allegation that there were no war plans, had been overtaken by events. When the Beresford Inquiry opened, Lord Charles changed tack, accusing Fisher of leaking plans, by implication to Corbett, already a focus for social conservative criticism. Fisher needed to keep Corbett outside the Admiralty in case Beresford summoned him as a witness.[5] This sudden change, and Corbett's mental collapse after the birth of his son on 27 May, settled the matter. His ambition to support the planning process endured.

Retaining the Clausewitzian argument of the 'Green Pamphlet', Corbett insisted strategic theory was an educational tool that enabled commanders to make informed decisions, providing a common language to converse with soldiers and statesmen. By developing Clausewitz he could shape British experience into strategic doctrine.[6] For Corbett, the basic principles of strategy were consistent and could be drawn from Clausewitz and Jomini, but their practical application at the national level was necessarily a unique cultural construct, and subject to political control. This context distinguished British strategy from that of continental military powers. The General Staff's Germanic agenda was a profound threat to the future of the empire, wrecking Britain's established strategy so that the Army could replace the Navy as the 'Senior Service'.[7] Continental strategies, little more than large-scale operational military plans, were irrelevant to Britain, which depended on maintaining peace in Europe, and commanding the oceans. The direct link between continental planning, conscription and social conservative politics made it an anathema to any Liberal.

The critical impulse for *Some Principles* came in January 1910, when the CID sought a doctrine primer for an enhanced War Course. CID Secretary, ex-DNI Charles Ottley, observed the new programme would require a revision of the syllabus to improve staff training. It should impart 'sound strategical principles', 'strategy should therefore occupy a prominent place': 'naval history is valuable for the purpose of illustrating each of the subjects ... and the study of some particular campaign should be included in every course'. The curriculum would be approved by the Admiralty. 'It is submitted that the sole object of the instruction in strategy should be to throw into high relief the fundamental principles on which all sound strategy must be based.' While these were known, they were spread across many works, none 'sufficiently concise to serve as handbooks'. He was content with the existing history provision. The course would not discuss current diplomatic issues, focusing on principles 'illustrated by history'.[8] The course 'should not be encouraged to "Mind high things" such as secret plans of campaign for possible wars with other powers with who ... it is our desire and interest to live in amity'.[9] This stipulation would reduce the topicality of Corbett's text. Ottley's wish list, which he had discussed with Fisher, added a textbook to Corbett's existing contribution to the War Course.[10]

A few months earlier Fisher decreed that in future officers employed in Admiralty staff roles must qualify on the War Course, a concession he hoped would stave off the introduction of a formal Admiralty Staff. On 27 October 1909 Corbett received a finely bound volume of blank leaves from Fisher, who had been on holiday in Italy, inscribed 'In remembrance of much kindness'.[11] The inference was obvious.

Fisher had decided to retire early: Arthur Wilson would be his successor, preventing the post falling to one of Beresford's 'Syndicate' allies, who would wreck the project. Fisher had intended standing down in April 1910, Wilson holding office until he retired at the age of 70 in March 1912.[12] Having agreed this plan with First Lord Reginald McKenna, everything changed in late November 1909, when Prime Minister Asquith called a general election. Fisher decided to bring Wilson into office before either a pro-Syndicate Conservative ministry, or a Liberal Cabinet reshuffle, could alter the current favourable political climate. Wilson took office on 25 January 1910.[13]

After completing the *Trafalgar* page proofs on 13 April 1910, Corbett set off for Italy. In late May he spent two days with Fisher at Kilverstone; he did not record their discussions, but it is likely they involved the Admiralty/CID textbook.[14] Three weeks later, having cleared his in-tray, he began:

> an experiment to see if it is possible to produce a useful book on the subject. It seems possible to develop Clausewitz theory from the point where he left off – so as to make it apply to our case & explain or coordinate many things. Such a book ... seems badly wanted if I can only produce it.[15]

For Corbett the temporary, contingent nature of the book, and the hostile response he expected from old friends like Custance, made it, however necessary, a 'difficult tasteless' process.[16] He began work while teaching the sixteenth Naval War College Course. Within days he was re-reading Clausewitz, followed by Jomini, and French Mahanian strategists Gabriel

Darrieus and René Daveluy.[17] He wrote quickly, working from start to finish, and without significant modifications. Other commitments were stacking up. In late August he signed a commercial agreement to write the Admiralty Russo-Japanese War text, using early drafts of *Some Principles* to explain the proposed treatment.

On 10 October War Course director Lewis Bayly told Corbett he was keen to see the strategy book; not only had the Admiralty expressed a desire for such a work, but it had already been offered one.[18] The following day Corbett showed him the contents, but Bayly 'shied at the theory of war part saying naval officers would not read it'.[19] In reality the only 'offer' on the Admiralty table was a discussion between Corbett and DNI Bethell. By late October he had a typescript of the first two thirds of the book, and shared passages on limited and unlimited war (part 1, chs 3–6) with War Course alumnus Sidney Drury-Lowe, who was lecturing on the Russo-Japanese War at Camberley.[20] Bethell promised to read the completed draft of the theoretical section. Despite his initial objections Bayly read this section within a week, suggesting important modifications. He wanted fewer technical terms, fewer German authorities and more exposition of the argument about the defensive.[21] This was sage advice. Corbett understood that practical men like Bayly had no interest in arcane academic diversions on historical methods or strategic theory. They needed an official text that explained doctrine and informed future discussion. On 23 November 1910 he 'finished revising Maritime Strategy to work in Bayly's suggestions'.[22]

This was timely. Weakened by the recent election, the Liberal government was struggling to keep control of an Army General Staff pushing for a mass army, primacy in national strategy and increased funding, supported by a resurgent Conservative party in the House of Commons, happy to use defence as a political weapon. Haldane, the Secretary of State for War, responded by commissioning a report on conscription from General Sir Ian Hamilton, lately Adjutant-General.[23] Hamilton rejected conscription, and Haldane secured public support for the status quo by publishing the report as *Compulsory Service* in November 1910, just as Corbett began revising his draft text. Haldane's lengthy introduction made a strikingly Corbettian case for maritime strategy, and a long-service expeditionary army:

> The little islands on which we live are the centre of an enormous and scattered Empire, the parts of which are separated by great stretches of

ocean from the parent islands and from each other. No other nation possesses this peculiar feature to anything approaching the same extent. It is therefore no accident or result of haphazard conjecture, but rather a deep-seated instinct, that has, for generations past, led our rulers and our sailors and soldiers to base their strategy on a principle to which they have held tenaciously. It is that, first in the order of importance comes sea-power, backed up not only by adequate over-sea garrisons, but by an expeditionary army, kept at home in time of peace, but so organised that it is ready for immediate transport by the fleet to distant scenes of action, and is capable of there maintaining long campaigns with the least possible dislocation of the social life of the nation. Such an expeditionary army is essentially a long-range weapon and can be raised only on a long-service basis.[24]

Clearly he had not forgotten *England in the Seven Years' War*, continuing:

to make the Navy an effective weapon we require a military instrument capable of being used in conjunction with it. ... The true strategical [a favourite Corbett word] foundations of all adequate defensive preparations is the power of rapidly assuming the offensive, by striking wherever a blow will be most effective, it may be at some distant point in the enemy's organisation.[25]

An army relying on short-service reservists would not be ready to embark when needed. Haldane would support the 'British way' in the crisis of July–August 1914.[26] He continued:

if the Navy could not command the seas, then we should sooner or later starve and have to submit, not the less certainly for having the million men with us. Command of the sea lies at the root of the whole matter.[27]

In conclusion Haldane cited the Admiralty position, explained by First Sea Lord Arthur Wilson in the second and subsequent editions: 'The really serious danger' was the 'interruption of our trade and destruction of our Merchant Shipping'. The defence of shipping determined the size of the fleet, which would 'almost necessarily' prevent an invasion by 70,000 troops.[28] Wilson's text, Appendix VIII, provided a powerful closing argument, an important element of courtroom advocacy, as Haldane and Corbett knew. Without command of the sea a million men removed from useful labour would only hasten Britain's defeat. Corbett would have concurred. In conclusion Haldane referenced Pitt the Elder and Nelson as 'great British strategists': they were key figures in Corbett's latest books.[29] Haldane's text provided a powerful statement of national strategy, one that influenced *Some Principles*.

Haldane published the Hamilton report to satisfy mainstream Liberal opinion and counter the alternative views of the Army General Staff and the post-Balfour Conservative party. Within weeks the first edition had sold out, 'causing grief' to the conscriptionist cause. Haldane defended Hamilton's work in the House of Commons three months later.[30] Yet logic, history and advocacy could not stop a flood of conscriptionist continentalism, the press and the opposition working the issue for political gain. By the time *Some Principles* appeared, *Compulsory Service* had been reprinted four times, reflecting the importance of the debate.

With the conscription debate still raging, Corbett met Ottley in St James's Park on 9 December 1910: they discussed Thomas Gibson Bowles' attack on the as yet unratified Declaration of London in *Sea Law and Sea Power*. Ottley feared it would alarm the public. Corbett suggested it would be better to persuade the country than force it to accept, and an eminent lawyer, Prime Minister Asquith or Haldane, should respond. He offered to write for *The Nineteenth Century*, if invited. While the invitation never came, the conversation impacted *Some Principles*. By the end of 1910, Corbett had completed seventeen of a planned twenty chapters, and revised or rewritten nine. The section on trade defence was recast after reading Daveluy, who reinforced Corbett's assessment that commerce warfare was now a minor threat.[31] A final section on expeditions exploited George Aston's *Letters on Amphibious Wars*, which Corbett considered 'very good'.[32] The only primary research for the book was a single day at the Public Record Office, analysing Lord Howe's 1782 campaign in home waters and the relief of Gibraltar, which helped end the American War of Independence.[33] Corbett had abandoned a projected book about the American War when the War Course urged him to address Trafalgar.

Having established the theoretical argument in parts 1 and 2, Corbett examined methods of application through examples in part 3. Many of those examples reflect the fact that he began the book immediately after *The*

Campaign of Trafalgar, and completed it after starting the Confidential History *Maritime Operations in the Russo-Japanese War*, and lecturing to the War Course on the Crimean War – tasks that often overlapped on the same day. Corbett stressed the importance of doctrinal cohesion, examined in detail in *Trafalgar*, as the key to the most effective use of naval power, enabling a judicious combination of dispersed action and rapid concentration for battle. This was an enduring strength of the Royal Navy's approach to war. His target was Mahan's obsession with concentration, which he considered ill-suited to the British context. The Royal Navy needed seamless, fluid, movement between attack and defence, concentration and dispersal to meet the changing circumstances, something that required powerful, coherent, commonly understood doctrine like that which had informed cruiser operations in 1805.[34] Frigate captains had learnt by example to connect the main fleets, convoys and landfalls of the Atlantic theatre. He contrasted doctrine, a living body of experience with:

> the disease of formalism, that kind of superstitious reverence for the means, which tends to bring the end into oblivion. In the naval art it leads directly to strategical blindness, to tactical rigidity, and to the habit of relying on rules, till all power of initiative is atrophied and is replaced in action by a dread of responsibility that is barely to be distinguished from cowardice.[35]

Corbett understood the need to obtain the insight and understanding that connected the campaign of 1805 without the hard knocks of war, or the inspirational presence of Nelson.

Some Principles retained the 'Green Pamphlet's' emphasis on definitions and terminology. There were no conclusions – none were required. Corbett had no business telling naval officers how to wage war, instead he provided them with the intellectual equipment they needed to make plans and debate strategy with soldiers and statesmen. Significantly he altered the combative style of the 'Green Pamphlet', where he used irrefutable logic and withering scorn to demolish the fallacies of the unreflective, to less confrontational language and arguments based on historical evidence.[36]

Corbett completed the text in late February 1911, a mere eight months' work amidst a heavy literary and lecturing schedule.[37] However, he had no intention of publishing without Admiralty approval.[38] Official sanction would make it a national strategic doctrine primer and establish the credibility of the author. In March his friend Gwyneth Keate produced a full typescript, which he revised and circulated. On 3 April 1911 Corbett, working on the Russo-Japanese War project in Admiralty Room 43, discussed the draft with Bethell, Deputy DNI Captain Thomas Jackson and Captain Ernest Troubridge, Naval Secretary to the First Lord of the Admiralty, who promised to read the draft. The following day Corbett discussed it with Bethell, new War Course director Rear Admiral Henry Jackson, and Admiralty Librarian W.G. Perrin. He asked Bayly to read the typescript, but he declined. No longer director of the War Course, he thought it should be sent to Henry Jackson. Troubridge did not anticipate any problems getting clearance, but thought he 'should get Sir Arthur Wilson's opinion before finally writing to you'.[39]

Corbett used the delay to read the latest edition of the Army's ancient strategy primer, Sir Edward Hamley's *Operations of War*, newly updated by Brigadier General Launcelot Kiggell psc, director of Staff Duties at the War Office.[40] Attempting to bring this forty-year-old Jominian text into the modern era by introducing Clausewitz, Kiggell had sought advice from George Clarke, then Secretary of the CID. Kiggell refused to add a section on imperial defence, as Clarke suggested, claiming the book was not about the 'particular case' of Britain.[41] In reality the Army was anxious not to be constrained by the imperial and maritime needs of a 'British way'. Obsessed with the 'complete defeat of the enemy's forces in the field', Kiggell appeared genuinely surprised by the mutual support of armies and navies in the Russo-Japanese War, a commonplace of British experience.[42] Such parochial thinking left the field clear for Corbett, who had responded to Clarke with more discernment.

Wilson read the manuscript of Corbett's book over the first weekend in July, delayed by the demands of the Coronation Fleet Review. He raised no objections. This was hardly a surprise: he had already approved Corbett's Clausewitzian preface to the 1907 War Plans and other texts.[43] Wilson read the text because he believed the First Sea Lord should know what was being taught at the War College.[44] His promotion to Admiral of the Fleet had been prompted by a plan to appoint him President of the War College. Famously unwilling to delegate, and perfectly familiar with the War College's strategic and planning functions, Wilson's imprimatur was a genuine accolade. He had no hesitation in rejecting anything he considered unsound, impractical or speculative.[45] Wilson's silence should not be misunderstood. In office he fought for a maritime strategy, and used Corbett's text.

Seven weeks after approving Corbett's manuscript Wilson presented his strategic ideas to the CID on 23 August 1911, when the committee met to address the Agadir Crisis. His submission included an epitome of Corbett's maritime strategy, along with G.F.R. Henderson's argument, although Sir Arthur discussed the enemy's civil and military fleets, which politicians might understand, rather than the nebulous notion of command of the sea. 'Naval opinion on any proposed action by the Army must be mainly determined by the extent to which it helps or hinders that object'. Committing the Army to France rendered: 'joint action of any kind against the enemy ... impossible'. With elegant irony, Wilson declared himself ready to accept the Army plan if it would ensure Britain's allies could march to Berlin; 'but even the advocates of the scheme do not pretend that this is the case. The alternative to this scheme is joint action by the Army and Navy with the one main object in view, the destruction of the enemy's fleet, both Naval and Mercantile'. Destroying the enemy merchant fleet was the basis of economic blockade, while combined operations against the German coast would draw off considerable forces from the French frontier. The passage 'If the Army decides to act with the Navy, one division embarked in the transports, and acting with the Navy, keeps the whole Coast Army whatever its strength, on the move' reflects Corbett's view of the strategic value of amphibious threats, and Napoleon's panic-stricken response to the Walcheren Campaign of 1809.[46] While Fisher might have invited Corbett to produce a skilful brief for the meeting, highlighting the strategic irrelevance of an Army plan based on five or six divisions, Wilson's vision of British strategy was well-informed, consistent and effective.

For all the *ex post facto* criticism heaped on Wilson's performance and his proposals, the meeting did not endorse the Army's plans, or uphold those of the Navy. The primary reason for this abject dereliction of duty was Prime Minister Asquith's anxiety to avoid war. He willingly exposed the Home Fleet to the risk of a German surprise attack, preventing any precautions. Wilson obeyed the political decision, but recognised the risks.[47] Instead, Asquith's hand-picked section of the Cabinet agreed to support France, by raising the possibility that Britain might send a token military force to their aid, rather than deploy the fleet to deter Germany as Fisher had in 1905.

Wilson's room for manoeuvre at the CID had been restricted by the looming ratification of the Declaration of London, which called into question the efficacy of a blockade.[48] His response was shaped by the reality that if Britain wanted to prevent a war in Europe, it needed a powerful deterrent.

There were two choices: Britain could support France by moving the world's most powerful Navy, or hint that it might send a non-existent continental army to France. Wilson had known the Cabinet opposed the military option before he signed the memorandum in *Compulsory Service* in November 1910. Nothing had changed by August 1911: the Navy remained Britain's only strategic asset, the only force capable of influencing Germany. To render the fleet effective, Wilson, Fisher and Corbett agreed it would require an offensive posture, complete with an amphibious component. Fisher looked to economic pressure and the threat of a Baltic incursion, Corbett agreed because 'decisive' naval battles would only occur if the enemy could be forced to fight, by threatening or attacking vital trade routes. He shared Fisher's belief that, as Germany depended on iron ore imports from Sweden, the threat to enter the Baltic would secure such a battle. He had commented on the relevant war plans in 1908. Wilson preferred more direct methods on the strikingly short German North Sea coast. These would be conducted by older and specialist warships, including new minesweepers of his own design. The Home Fleet would support the attack, engaging the High Seas Fleet if it appeared. While the benefit of hindsight has encouraged many to criticise Wilson's plan to seize Heligoland as out of date and unrealistic, successful operations of this type were a commonplace in the Second World War.[49] Furthermore, the assumption that the five-division BEF of 1911 was always going to become the BEF of 1918 is unfounded. For all the *ex post facto* focus on operational specifics, Wilson had presented a national maritime strategy, using combined operations to enhance British sea control, conduct economic warfare and support a continental ally. As Britain did not have a mass army in 1911, or a binding continental alliance that required one, Corbett's strategic argument, titled *The Principles of Maritime Strategy* when Wilson approved it, was the only credible basis for strategic planning – both before and after the CID meeting of 23 August 1911. In a war with Germany Britain would have to secure command of the sea for self-defence, and the defence of floating trade; that command would enable effective economic warfare, even if the mechanism of blockade was uncertain in 1911, it could also apply direct pressure to the German coast, distracting troops from the French border. Wilson's offensive, like Fisher's Baltic concept, might bring the enemy to battle. A successful action would reinforce command of the sea, potentially enabling an effective blockade. Furthermore, an army afloat, as Corbett stressed, had the power to distract, one on the Franco-German frontier could only fight. Wilson recognised the central issue was control of national strategy: if the Army was committed to France, it would be impossible to withdraw it, even to meet British needs, a continental commitment would ensure the Army, however small, dominated strategy.

Not only were Wilson's strategic instincts correct, but he had examined the practical problems of coastal warfare: long-range fire control, mine-sweeping and offensive mine-laying. Churchill's oft-cited criticism of Wilson reflected a power struggle within the Admiralty, not a strategic divergence. In August 1914 he recalled Wilson to the Admiralty, specifically to develop the 1911 plans that he mocked in his memoirs.[50] Churchill ignored the fact that without British troops, which he helped send to France, any plans would be incomplete.

British strategy did not change in August 1911. Asquith merely demanded greater cooperation between the services, something the General Staff inter-preted as ordering the Admiralty to support their continental plan and allowing them to ignore amphibious options. This was not the intention. When Wilson demolished the minister's case for a Naval Staff, Asquith sent Churchill to the Admiralty to impose the concept. The obvious alternative, Lord Haldane, would have been more effective, taking professional advice, and more attuned to maritime strategy. Undeterred, Wilson restated his opposition to a staff in a devastating critique of the structural chaos that would result from applying German military methods to the wholly different conditions of naval warfare. Being convinced the new system would render the Navy inefficient, he refused to compromise. As Wilson had expected, Churchill used the memo to persuade Asquith to remove him. In line with Wilson's prediction, the new organisation dislocated the Admiralty system, enabling Churchill to usurp executive functions hitherto the preserve of Sea Lords. Churchill used Troubridge, a tame Chief of Staff, to circumvent the strategic role of the First Sea Lord.[51] The political imperative to create a Staff was so compelling that Churchill removed Wilson from office a mere three months before he had to retire on reaching the age of 70. Wilson obtained King George's permission to refuse the proffered peerage, to demonstrate that he had not been bought off with a trinket.

Having secured Wilson's approval, Corbett delivered the typescript to Longman on 21 July, but only signed a contract on 3 August 1911.[52] The initial print run would be 1,250 copies. A few days later Corbett changed the title from *The Principles* to *Some Principles*, finally resolving a dilemma that can be traced through the gestation of the book, reflecting Corbett's anxiety that some would question his standing to publish on national strategy. He had hoped to secure Slade's endorsement or co-authorship, but the publishers would not countenance waiting for a reply from the Commander-in-Chief East Indies.[53] Corbett also changed his identity. In the *Seven Years' War* and *Trafalgar* he was 'Lecturer in Naval History to the Royal Naval War College'; but *Some Principles* only credited him with a Law degree, distancing the book from the place where it had evolved and for which it had been written.

When the page proofs arrived Corbett lamented to Newbolt that he was condemned to re-read 'a difficult tasteless book on "Maritime Strategy"'.[54] Behind an obvious joke to a close friend and fellow author lay a doctrine primer written to satisfy a national need, one addressed to his naval audience rather than the public.

Some Principles, the first public statement of British strategic doctrine, was designed to inform high-level decision-making, integrating naval, military and civil action to deter or, *in extremis*, wage war. It appeared just as Churchill sought a textbook to educate future Staff Officers, emphasising 'the principles to be deduced from the events of war'. While Churchill recognised the need for a strategy text, he was at heart a continentalist.[55] His failure to apply the principles that Corbett advocated in 1914 did not reflect a failure of comprehension but a fundamental divergence on policy. Churchill's terrestrial strategic focus explains his obsession with naval offensive operations.[56]

Some Principles explained the intellectual basis of current naval thinking, making a powerful case that national strategy was limited and maritime, built on sea control and economic warfare. Although the word 'doctrine' appears four times in *Some Principles*, on the first three occasions referencing Clausewitz's doctrine of limited war, only the last, dealing with fleet operations, approaches the modern usage.[57] Corbett's terminology was evolving as he wrote. A year later 'doctrine' would dominate his mission statement.

Retaining the Clausewitzian form and structure of the 'Green Pamphlet', Corbett repeated the argument that strategic theory was not 'a substitute for judgment and experience'. It was an educational tool to help commanders reach their own decisions, providing them with a common set of terms and concepts to convey their meaning to colleagues and subordinates.[58] His sophisticated, nuanced use of Clausewitz's theoretical framework created a

'British way' from Britain's strategic experience, making limited maritime war the master principle.[59] Britain's command of the sea could isolate the enemy's overseas possessions, limiting the amount of military force required, making it the ideal strategy for a war waged for limited political aims. By contrast, the contemporary Great German General Staff had perverted Clausewitz's emphasis on the political nature of war to seek military solutions to complex political problems. Corbett also demonstrated that decisive battle could only be secured in favourable conditions by forcing the enemy to fight: the obvious occasion would be cutting vital trade routes. He shared Fisher's belief that a threat to the Baltic was the best way to bring the High Seas Fleet to battle.

Some Principles also enabled Corbett to address public criticism of his work, criticism primarily intended to discredit Fisher by association. In 1908 Spenser Wilkinson attacked Corbett in the pages of the Conservative *Morning Post*, part of the paper's support for the Army case at the recent Invasion Inquiry. Corbett was not impressed: 'Strong attack on Fisher & Admiralty employing me, sign of parlous condition of Navy etc, Confused reiteration of old fallacies of Mahan which he himself has abandoned plus his own way of trying to substitute continental theorists in place of our own experience.' Both Wilkinson and Custance confused 'Clausewitz's unlimited war with his absolute war'.[60] Edmond Slade agreed, linking Wilkinson's antediluvian views to Custance.[61] Neither had grasped the inner core of Clausewitz's thinking.[62] Wilkinson made 'a sort of apology' to Corbett for the article at a Navy League dinner a few months later, 'but was quite senile'.[63] He would challenge Corbett's interpretation of Clausewitz again in 1909, 1912 and 1916, attacks driven by divergent political and strategic views. A lifelong advocate of a larger British Army, based on German theory and practice, Wilkinson was predisposed to deny the validity of maritime strategy and limited war. Wilkinson promoted the dangerous delusion that strategy was universal and would work for any nation with the wit to copy the Germans, an obsession that predisposed him to favour Mahan's focus on 'decisive battle'. Corbett's radically different 'British way' challenged Wilkinson's standing as a strategic commentator, and his utility to Charlie Beresford and the General Staff. In August 1909, a mere four days before the report of the Beresford Inquiry was made public, he attacked Corbett's development of Clausewitz as 'erroneous'. A recently published essay by Lieutenant Thomas Fisher provided a stalking horse. Writing while attending the Naval War Course, Fisher had used Corbett's argument about the control of communications. Wilkinson had no argument, blustering, 'command of the sea is simply the advantage given by a crushing naval victory over an enemy who by that victory has been so weakened as to be obliged to abandon the conflict on the open sea'.[64] While this futile polemic was unworthy of attention, Lieutenant Fisher, who took Corbett's ideas with him onto the War Course staff in February 1913, was promoted to commander before the year was out, and served in the Admiralty Trade Division throughout the war, helping develop the convoy system.[65]

Corbett treated such nonsense with disdain; having taken the subject far beyond the 'naval' thought of Mahan, Bridge and Custance, he had nothing to learn from Wilkinson.[66] In selling 'Sea Power' as national strategy to his fellow Americans, Mahan had elevated it into a strategic alternative to land power, largely because American land power had no traction outside the New World. Only a big navy could make America a great power.[67] Corbett recognised that Britain, which had the necessary strategic reach, relied on the joint action of sea and land forces, in that order, to retain great power status. *Some Principles* would be the strategic doctrine for a hegemonic global maritime empire – one that stressed deterrence above war.

When the book appeared in early December, Troubridge congratulated him, and extracted some useful arguments for Churchill, who was already familiar with Corbett's work.[68] Within a month Troubridge would be the first Chief of the Admiralty War Staff.[69] Unfortunately he was Churchill's 'man', circumventing the naval chain of command and reinforcing the First Lord's control, rather than supporting the development of naval strategy.[70] Fortunately there were other intelligent readers, as Corbett observed:

> There was an excellent send off for my book in the *Times* yesterday. I saw it just as I was turning in. It was in an article on the late changes & the writer quoted my book at length to show that the Admiralty policy had been quite right. That is better than the best review for everyone interested in the Navy reads such articles.[71]

The Times recognised that *Some Principles* reflected current Admiralty thinking, and Corbett's influence on policy, approving both. Reflective men understood that Corbett had gone far beyond mere naval strategists, and dismissed his critics.[72] Sidney Drury-Lowe wrote:

a line to congratulate you, if you will allow me, on your last book 'Principles of Maritime Strategy'. It's a long time since I've gained such pleasure and instruction from reading a book, as I have from this one, & I'm sure there were very many in the Navy of the same opinion. You have done us a very great service, & we owe you a deep debt of gratitude. I have long looked for a book that would contain the various theories & principles of *maritime* strategy which you discuss, & have thought the want of it has been the cause of a great deal of loose talk amongst Naval officers, & of extraordinary actions too! Some of us have waded through Clausewitz, Jomini, von Cammerer etc, but there was so much that wanted re-adjustment, & so much that had nothing of interest to us (so far as I could see!), & in my own case you have just supplied the want. Your chapter on 'Constitution of Fleets' is splendid.[73]

The reference to Caemmerer suggests that Corbett cited him in War Course lectures. Corbett's maritime development of standard strategy texts enabled sailors to challenge the flimsy intellectual foundations of British continentalism.[74] War Course alumnus George Cayley stressed: 'it is a natural sequel to your *Seven Years' War* and *Trafalgar*'.[75] Navalist author and war-gaming pioneer Fred T. Jane thought the book would ensure officers used theory in war games, rather than relying on 'classical maxims'.[76]

Critically, Corbett's book emerged just as the work of the War Course was reconnected with war planning. In November 1912 Henry Jackson informed Corbett that the War Course, of which he had lately been director, would come under his control when he became Chief of the Admiralty War Staff, 'an arrangement which I have always wanted to see'.[77]

There were predictable objections from the continentalists. In February the *Morning Post* published Spenser Wilkinson's review. Confronted with an original, coherent national strategic doctrine, he fell back on German ideas and old excuses. His simplistic reading of Clausewitz sustained the fatuous contention that there was no rational basis for the idea that war could be limited.[78] Evidently he disliked the argument in *On War*, and objected to Corbett using it to address the practical and political needs of the British Empire. Citing Admiral Maltzahn among other contemporary continental theorists, he claimed limited war was no longer relevant.[79] While principles were essential to the conduct of war, Corbett's were wrong because they disagreed with those advanced by the uniformed authorities who wrote for navies: including Colomb, Bridge, Custance, Daveluy, Batsch, Stenzel, Maltzahn and above all Mahan. Despite his own forays into the field he did not believe civilians had any business writing on strategy, and avoided advancing any new ideas, 'not having the experience of a naval officer'. The obvious implication was that Corbett was equally incompetent. He suggested Corbett's ideas would have a 'disastrous' effect on the naval mind, casting doubt on the 'fundamental' principles advocated by uniformed experts. Finally, he insisted on reading the text as a guide to naval warfare, rather than a national 'maritime strategy'. Wilkinson ignored the strategic context in which navies operated, treating Britain as a misguided continental power.

The absurdity of Wilkinson's position became obvious when Admiral von Maltzahn reviewed *Some Principles* alongside Mahan's *Naval Strategy*, also published in 1911. Having compared both texts with Clausewitz's masterwork, he awarded the prize to Corbett. While Mahan effectively ignored Clausewitz, piling up history in a basic Jominian fashion, Corbett had developed *On War* to analyse naval warfare. Hitherto, Maltzahn had favoured Mahan, but *Some Principles* changed everything:

> Corbett's establishment of strategic doctrine is much clearer and tighter. His method proceeds from a logical development and, in contrast, falls back on examples which appear more judicious to me. Moreover, the historical basis – the history of naval warfare – is nowhere lost.[80]

This essay appeared in the French *Revue Maritime* the following year, accompanied by a review of *Some Principles* by an unnamed reviewer who preferred Mahan's principles, but stressed Corbett's purpose was to ensure his students thought about any principles before applying them, recognising the complexity of his historical examples.[81] By 1919 the French Navy recognised *Some Principles* was the epitome of British thinking, and Capitaine de Vaisseau Raoul Castex secured the rights to translate the book. Castex found familiar, Mahanian, reasons to dispute Corbett's text, because he wrote from a continental perspective. Nor was he prepared to accept the opinions of a civilian, however talented. Yet he admitted Corbett had made him re-think every aspect of his own theoretical work, to his considerable profit. He thought this 'subversive text' should be read by French officers, and found himself conforming to Corbett's ideas as he developed his own strategic project.[82]

Continental readers and serving officers invariably questioned the validity of Corbett's work. He did not expect them to follow him blindly: 'the British way' was not a religion, unlike Mahanian 'Sea Power', and he was not an evangelist. He taught his students to think, and to think logically, using the correct language, working within the national context. *Some Principles* demonstrated that Britain had never waged unlimited war, because it was not contending for continental dominion, even when it took part in unlimited wars. Liberal Britain was not prepared to create mass conscript armies because it had no political aims that could justify them, or the concomitant seismic social change they would entail. While Clausewitz advised against assuming wars would remain limited – in Europe there was no rational reason why they should – this was not the case once the sea became a critical factor, as it necessarily was for Britain. Wilkinson's ignorance of naval warfare, and geography, led him to claim that in the absence of strong defensive positions at sea: 'Naval warfare ... tends to be more decisive than land warfare, and approximates more to that absolute form towards which all warfare is driven as soon as it becomes national.' He wrote to discredit maritime strategy, and the primacy of the Royal Navy in British policy, to promote a continental military agenda. He feared Corbett's elegant advocacy would preserve the strategy that enabled a maritime state 'to realise her special strength'.[83] Corbett did not bother to record this perfunctory, partisan notice in his diary.[84]

Far from being a radical challenge to current orthodoxy, *Some Principles* codified the strategic thinking of the Fisher years, while successive Admiralty Boards approved its use on the War Course. Corbett's model of British strategy reflected a sustained historical analysis of hard-won experience dating back to the Tudor era, while working closely with successive DNIs and directors of the War Course for nine years, years in which those posts were at the centre of Admiralty war planning, using the War Course to test and refine evolving strategic concepts.[85] Not only did these men attend and approve his lectures, but several read drafts of *Some Principles*.

Corbett rejected the simplistic notion that strategic theory was universally applicable, and could be read across from nation to nation and age to age. He stressed the unique, contingent and specific needs of individual nations. It did not matter what strategy Clausewitz had recommended, because Britain in 1911 was not Prussia in the late 1820s. What mattered was that Clausewitz's philosophy of war enabled those in different ages and locations to shape their own doctrine, and address their own security needs. Corbett treated the Prussian theorist with profound respect, and remained deeply indebted to G.F.R. Henderson.

Shortly after the publication of *Some Principles*, Corbett was elected to the Athenaeum Club, 'a meeting place for the leading intellectuals and men of influence' of the era, a cultured institution located midway between his flat and Whitehall, well placed for working lunches and serious dinners, while possessing a fine library. Here he was among friends, discussing art, music, politics and policy with imperial pro-consuls, soldiers and sailors, artists and authors.[86]

Within months, Corbett wanted to revise his doctrine primer, updating content and adding Slade's name to the title page. However, despite some good reviews, few felt the need to buy a copy. Charles Longman was not enthusiastic; he had 700 copies in hand, sales were 'not very brisk just now' and he thought everyone knew that Slade was involved.[87] Slade disagreed, 'the fact that we are more or less of one mind on this subject is not known beyond a small circle'.[88] The opportunity passed. By mid-August 1912 Corbett was working on the Confidential History *Maritime Operations in the Russo-Japanese War*, a project that continued the development of national doctrine for his core audience of naval officers and statesmen.[89] He explained the initial Russian decision to send the Baltic Fleet to the Pacific had been taken to secure command of the sea, facilitating the invasion and overthrow of Japan. An additional force of coast defence ships was sent to provide inshore fire support for an advancing Russian army, much as Peter the Great had used his galley fleet in the 1710s. Assembling these ships delayed the departure of the battlefleet, with serious consequences.[90] The larger point, that coast attack assets were essential to project amphibious power, reflected the ideas of Fisher and Wilson: a fleet of monitors was ordered in 1914.[91]

Corbett also examined contemporary commerce raiding by two Russian Volunteer Fleet ships in the Red Sea and Indian Ocean in 1904. Leaving aside the dubious legal status of the ships, which were not commissioned warships, detaching prize crews soon left them incapable of high-speed steaming, emphasising 'the limitations of commerce destroying under modern conditions'. Neutral protests, from Britain and Germany, forced Russia to recall the ships, and release the prizes.[92]

The material points to note are that, unless such vessels are prepared to incur the moral responsibilities of sinking all their prizes, their steaming power will very quickly be reduced below operating efficiency by the drain of prize crews. In the next place it will be seen that they were powerless to act as a serious check on the flow of commerce except in narrow and fertile waters where weather conditions were exceptionally favourable [in this case the Red Sea].

The appearance of British cruisers obliged the Russians to move to less productive areas.

This is precisely what was always found to happen in the old wars. It was in fact being demonstrated that the changed conditions of naval warfare had not affected the fundamental principle on which our traditional system of commerce defence was based.

Russian action only served to 'annoy a powerful neutral and force her to interfere'.[93] This assessment demonstrates that although Corbett failed to anticipate unrestricted submarine warfare, his mastery of strategic principles had provided the basis for a structural response. Japanese success blockading Port Arthur led Corbett to suggest the threat surface torpedo craft posed to the blockading fleet had been overrated in Europe: 'in practice the torpedo danger proved to be no greater under steam than the weather obstacle under sail'.[94] This may have been valid for a secondary Russian port protected by surface torpedo craft, but both conclusions would be overturned in 1914 by submarines, greatly improved torpedoes and the unexpected willingness of belligerents to violate international law. The *Russo-Japanese* text continued developing national doctrine, indeed all Corbett's work after 1911 was linked to a projected revision of *Some Principles*.[95] The Royal Navy's War College would need a strategy textbook based on the latest experience.

After *Some Principles* ceased to be an up-to-date doctrine primer, it was reimagined as a contribution to strategic thought, but that was never Corbett's intention. He had used strategic theory to shape a coherent expression of British strategic doctrine for serving officers, one that captured the unique and contingent in national strategy. He had not developed a 'new' argument, and did not claim any novelty for his text beyond the contemporary British context. He used the work of leading strategists, especially

Clausewitz, to create a coherent rendition of the 'British way'. In 1972, Bryan Ranft, the last Professor of Naval History at the Royal Naval College Greenwich, introduced the first reprint of *Some Principles* in forty years with the observation that it read like a well-designed lecture course, 'measured exposition by a confident expert' adding gravitas to the argument.[96] That was Corbett's intention: he would have been surprised to learn that his insight, advocacy, rhetoric and restraint continue to influence those who think about a 'British way' and maritime strategy more widely.

The possibility of a revised edition was crushed by slow sales, despite the book being part of Admiralty ship's libraries, and a core teaching text at the Naval War Course and United States Naval War College by 1914.[97] In early 1913, 548 copies remained unsold, over 40 per cent of the print run, so the type was broken up.[98]

The original 1,250 copies finally sold out in 1918. Unable to get paper, or press time, in England, Longman had 1,000 printed in America, to satisfy the dramatic rise in American demand, notably at the United States Naval War College; only 150 copies were for the British market. The text was unchanged.[99] Corbett's friend Admiral William S. Sims, commander-in-chief of US Naval Forces in Europe, provided practical support:

> I was only too glad to have the opportunity of expediting the sending the [sic] England of the 150 copies of MARITIME STRATEGY. ... I thank you also for your offer to give us any further help in our naval historical work. We have already benefited greatly by your advice and assistance in bringing to the attention of our Navy Department what ought to be done in this line.[100]

This edition was used by students on the post-war War and Staff Courses.[101]

Corbett, like Clausewitz, was an inductive thinker: his strategic ideas evolving alongside, and through, historical writing.[102] Having imposed a strategic pattern on Britain's naval history, he rendered the issues clear for his students, and emphasised the fact that without professional historical research the work of strategists would remain flawed.[103]

While *Some Principles* annoyed Fisher's critics, notably Reginald Custance and George Clarke, too much has been made of their futile fulminations.[104] It remains the only intellectually coherent analysis of the grand strategy of a unique global maritime empire, a commanding synthesis informed by hard-won experience, addressed through the prism of Clausewitzian theory, and reduced to doctrinal clarity in order to support professional military education. Written amidst fierce political battles over the future of Britain, the empire and the precarious balance in Europe, *Some Principles* promoted a distinctive maritime strategy. Haldane had used Corbett's arguments in 1910, while the manuscript shaped Arthur Wilson's attack on the creeping continentalism of the Army General Staff at the CID in August 1911. The government did not endorse Henry Wilson's continental alternative. Corbett's text explained the government's strategic posture down to a fateful day in August 1914.[105] Britain had no binding commitment to France, the only reason for sending an army to the Continent was the defence of Belgian neutrality.[106]

Prime Minister Asquith's equivocation in August 1911 left the CID, run by Maurice Hankey, a junior officer with a strong sense of bureaucratic and personal survival, without a strategic role.[107] Hankey used the office to create the basis for global collaboration, the framework for a major war of imperial scale. His strategic thinking was informed by close contact with Corbett.[108] It was no accident that the CID would be Corbett's base of operations for the rest of his life.

That *Some Principles* remains relevant to British strategy more than a century later, surviving war, decline and alien strategic concepts, reflects the power and sophistication of Corbett's elegant text.

CHAPTER 15

'Doctrine – The Soul of Warfare'

Having completed *Some Principles*, Corbett continued teaching on the War Course, wrote a Confidential Strategic History for the Admiralty, led two publishing ventures that supported naval education, and enhanced the academic standing of naval history as the key to the long-term future of national strategy. His book had melded British practice and strategic theory to create a national doctrine to replace service-focused 'continental' and 'blue-water' arguments, while establishing the language and terminology for future debates. Despite the British focus, the book quickly became a core teaching text at the United States Naval War College in Newport. The contrast with Mahan's tired old strategy course, also published in 1911, demonstrated why the strategic baton had been passed.

Corbett understood strategic doctrine as a process, not a record. To secure his intellectual legacy, the unique maritime character of British strategy, he needed to mobilise the men and mechanisms to continue and develop his work. One promising sign was the emergence of the *Naval Review*, a restricted, private circulation journal created in 1911 to encourage naval officers to debate the policy, strategy and education behind the anonymity of a pseudonym. Founded in Captain Herbert Richmond's front room by a group of younger officers connected with the War Course, the *Review* stimulated intellectual debate within the service. Corbett influenced the journal through Richmond and the editor, Admiral Sir William Henderson. An old friend, Henderson discussed papers submitted to the journal on frequent visits to Hans Crescent.[1] Corbett saw the *Review* as an opportunity to equip the service to debate with soldiers and statesmen as equals, rather than relying on an eccentric civilian.[2] Ultimately he wanted the Navy to develop and sustain the intellectual capacity to fight its own battles, rising above the petty factionalism and lazy assumptions of enduring relevance that too often passed for thought when discussing strategy.

While he believed national strategy should remain maritime, Corbett recognised the continentalist challenge of the Army General Staff, laid bare at the inconclusive CID meeting in August 1911. The soldiers must be led back to the maritime vision of Wolseley, Maurice and Henderson. While his long-term agenda was to equip the Navy to meet that challenge, in the short term he took on the task of defending maritime strategy while the Navy acquired the necessary skills. After *Some Principles*, he focused on developing the resources needed to sustain strategic doctrine. It was as a contribution to this process that he judged Richmond's lectures on the War of the Austrian Succession 'very promising' and commissioned a book version. For every step forward, and there were many, occasional setbacks reminded him that the task remained unfinished. It was typical that just as Corbett established the intellectual credibility of naval history among university academics, the Admiralty set up a committee to investigate the tactics of Trafalgar. The object appears to have been the desire of well-meaning but ill-informed sea officers to overturn *The Campaign of Trafalgar*. The news came as a profound shock at a time when he had more pressing tasks to occupy his attention.[3]

The first of these tasks pre-dated *Some Principles*. In September 1904 Charles Repington called for a CID Historical Section in *The Times*:

> not confined to a single branch of the profession or arms, or under a deputy sub-assistant of the Secretary for War, but composed of soldiers, sailors, marines, and civilians of high standing, responsible to the Committee of Imperial Defence, which should properly decide the relative importance of the labours of an Historical Section of Imperial mould.[4]

The ideas belonged to George Clarke, who had briefed Repington.[5] Corbett may have read the essay; he was also using briefs from Clarke at this time. The history unit was created, only to fail its first test. Disillusioned by an Army-focused account of the Russo-Japanese War, which ignored the critical role of navies and lessons for imperial defence, DNI Ottley employed linguists Major Edmond Daniel RMLI (Royal Marine Light Infantry) and Naval Instructor Oswald Tuck to work on Russian and Japanese material for an Admiralty text, but needed someone to analyse the evidence. Corbett had assisted Captain Thomas Jackson RN on the naval section of the CID history, and in March 1907 Ottley recommended the CID should assign 'the literary completion of the history' to 'Mr Corbett's very capable hands'.[6] As the CID did not have the necessary funds, Ottley recommended waiting to 'engage Mr Corbett or some other literary expert to write a short history in two or three volumes'. In November 1907 Slade, the new DNI, declared:

> I am convinced that he is by far the best man to undertake this work as, from his position as lecturer in Naval History at the War College, he is in intimate touch with the service, and his published works on naval history show a grasp of strategtical and tactical questions which is greatly superior to that of any other writer with whom I am acquainted.[7]

Slade had hoped Corbett could improve drafts written by Thomas Jackson and Captain John Luce. Corbett refused:

> I could have nothing to do with such amateurish stuff & thought the Admiralty ought not either. It is going back to where we began – trivial stuff without a spark of understanding of what strategy means – done by a Commander – who could not possibly know enough to do it. I told Slade it was trifling with the whole thing & he should protest at all the NID work being wasted for lack of proper treatment.

Evidently annoyed, Corbett revised his letter the following day.[8] He had lectured the War Course on this conflict for three years, criticising the CID account for focusing on technical detail at the expense of strategic analysis. The next DNI, Alexander Bethell, agreed the CID history was useless for the War Course and the Navy. Although the suggestion that naval history should be written at the CID, by a civilian, hired by the Admiralty, prompted widespread criticism, Fisher's Admiralty persisted.

An official invitation to produce *Maritime Operations in the Russo-Japanese War 1904–1905* for the CID reached Corbett in 1910. He proposed a two-volume study modelled on *England in the Seven Years' War*, and a fee of £1,000. While he began work officially in October, before *Some Principles* reached a critical stage, Corbett knew that project had priority over the new book. When Bethell advised waiting for further information from Tokyo before commencing, Corbett told his wife: 'This will suit me exactly, for I can now go on with my strategy book & perhaps get it done before I have to begin the other.'[9] He began work a year later, having completed *Some Principles*, relaxing into a familiar task: 'it went all right. I know it so well now that it comes very easy.'[10] Critically, he kept draft chapters away from the First Lord's Naval Secretary and later Chief of the War Staff Captain Ernest Troubridge, who wanted to change his conclusions. The Admiralty wisely appointed Slade the official naval reader.

Corbett explained his aims and methods:

> In a war which from the nature of its object and the geographical conditions of its theatre was so essentially maritime the naval and military operations during this period are for the most part inseparable. While, therefore, the history of the struggle is viewed from the naval point of view and naval operations alone are dealt with in detail, it has been found necessary to follow the military developments closely enough to bring out the mutual reactions of the two spheres.[11]

Having clarified his object, Corbett discussed his sources: the Japanese Confidential Naval History 'a bare but minute record of the proceedings', provided the factual base for strategic analysis, free from intervening Japanese judgements. Additional unpublished Japanese reports, translated by Tuck, proved 'invaluable'. A French translation of the Japanese published official history was useful, not least because Corbett could take it home. In the absence of an official Russian naval history, he praised the General Staff History, which stressed the dependence of land operations on naval activity, effectively 'a combined history'.[12] The prominent role he gave the broad-minded Russian General Staff was a rebuke to the British General Staff, which would not have dreamt of doing the same. Here again he used a French translation, as far as it had been completed. Major Daniel translated Russian accounts of the naval war, including semi-official articles in the journals *Morskoi Sbornik* and *Ruskaya Starina*. Other texts had appeared in French or English translation. Attaché reports, Admiralty and Foreign Office correspondence were useful for the pre-war period, as were discussions with officers who had been present in the war zone. Having made maps and diagrams an integral element of his work a decade earlier, Corbett insisted on high-grade cartography of this distant, unfamiliar theatre, using place names from Admiralty charts, not the CID history. Each chapter opened with a reference to the relevant maps and tactical diagrams.

He followed the method of his last two histories, analytical narratives dealing with each theatre in chronological succession. This conscious rejection of the standard model for Staff Histories created some difficulties of execution, but it was 'the only way in which a clear impression can be given and retained of the inter-relation of the various parts of the struggle', while doing justice to commanding officers by enabling readers to 'appreciate the subsidiary and external deflections by which their decisions and conduct were necessarily influenced'. Analytical insight was woven into the narrative, contextualising decisions while the facts were still clear in the reader's mind. This commentary tended to be direct, avoiding the tendency towards 'facile generalisations' when judgement was reserved for a separate conclusion. He made an exception for Staff work, especially important in amphibious operations. As Japan had withheld the relevant volume of the Confidential History he reserved judgement for an overview.[13]

Corbett noted the parallel between Japan and Korea and Britain and Europe, and the critical importance of controlling the waters that linked islands and continent:

> From the middle ages onward the bulk of our diplomatic and military activities have been more or less concerned with securing the control of those intervening waters and particularly with efforts to prevent any great continental power from obtaining a footing on the Dutch or Flemish coasts.[14]

Those forty-seven words reminded readers of the underlying strategic realities that explained why Holland and Belgium were independent states. Yet he was quick to stress that maritime wars, 'such as ours have been either wholly or in part', cannot be traced to singular causes. To strategic position he added commercial and colonial ambition, the divergent interests of great capitalists, and the intangibles of the national spirit.

Then he subverted the lazy assumption that Japan was an Asian Britain. Korea was an appendage of Asia, not an integral part, as the Low Countries were of Europe. Therefore Japan could expand into Korea, while Britain could not absorb the Low Countries 'without becoming a continental power and losing the advantages of our insular position'.[15] Britain had consistently rejected the continental option that Japan sought. Although he never stated that Japan was a continental military power, as it would have weakened his strategic argument,

Corbett recognised the fact. Analogies were restricted to British and Japanese strategic geography, comparing the new Japanese naval base at Maizuru to Rosyth, then in progress to meet the German naval challenge.[16]

Ultimately Corbett stressed the outcome of the conflict could not be explained by principles derived from other wars, it was abnormal: 'a war in a maritime theatre, where, as with our last two European wars, the Peninsula and Crimea, naval and military operations were so intimately connected as to be inseparable'. The outcome turned on the balanced use of both forces, the one context where Japan had shown 'marked superiority' over Russia. This superiority compensated for inferior forces on land and sea, enabling Japan to achieve 'practically complete' victory. The moral for British strategy was obvious.

Corbett considered 'command of the sea' too facile an explanation, openly disagreeing with Mahan.[17] The dissenting voice continued. Togo's final report revealed that he had not sought 'decisive' battle with Russia's First Pacific Fleet: his aim had been to keep it in Port Arthur while he landed the Army. The Navy secured the strategic movement of the Army by holding a strategic location between Port Arthur and Vladivostok, using local offensives to drive the enemy back into their bases. Togo wanted the Russians in port, repairing damage, not forced out to sea, where a battle might undermine Japan's strategic position. Victory in the Yellow Sea had been 'unexpected' and, he inferred, lucky: it proved vital to counter Russian strategy. Togo's fleet had never been strong enough to seek out the enemy; the Japanese plan was to capture Port Arthur by land, destroying the fleet to prevent an overwhelming concentration of Russian naval power in Asia. After Port Arthur fell, Japan prepared for a defensive battle in home waters, while cutting Russia's regional sea communications. Japan fully exploited command of the sea after Tsushima, seizing Sakhalin Island and pressing Russian mainland positions.

Corbett attributed much of Togo's thinking to classic Chinese strategy, and the experience of the Sino-Japanese conflict a decade earlier, when the three elements of the Chinese fleet had been dealt with in detail. From these ancient texts, and Captain Ogasawara's *History of Japanese Sea Power*, he divined a 'Japanese Way', strategic ideas that differed from those in the Western canon. The connection with his distinctive 'British way' is compelling. Japan's wars with Russia and China were limited maritime wars waged for territory, the fleet protecting the home islands against an overwhelming counter-stroke.[18] The synergy with his analysis of Britain's Seven Years' War was clear. General Kuropatkin, like the French in 1759, believed it would be necessary to invade the enemy's home islands to secure victory. Korea, like Canada, was a relatively easy target for limited maritime methods, because Russia could not counter-attack without securing command of the sea. Japan succeeded in the first two phases of the war, down to the end of the Battle of Tsushima, by preventing Russia from obtaining command of the sea, *not* by seeking or exercising command itself.[19] Even if Russia had won the great battles in Manchuria, it would have faced an uphill task attempting to drive Japan out of Korea without command of the sea.

Corbett's central criticism of Russian strategy was that, Makarov apart, its leaders did not use the fleet to threaten Japan's sea communications. The critical landing of the Japanese 2nd Army at Liao-Tung had been exposed to attack at sea, but the Russians did nothing. Consequently, Togo's calculated risk secured the fall of Port Arthur, obliging Russia to send a larger Second Pacific Squadron, which seriously delayed its departure.[20]

Critically, Japanese public opinion supported the war, while that of Russia did not, as the Japanese knew. Being constantly on the defensive sapped Russian morale; the Japanese preserved their warlike spirit without resorting to mindless offensives. Corbett concluded with a powerful statement of the vital human component in war:

> It is here, then, if anywhere, in this enduring capacity to withstand the demoralising influences of a prolonged defensive that the Japanese showed upon the seas, at any rate, a distinctly higher genius for war than their enemy.[21]

He judged the Royal Navy had the same genius. In November 1913 Hankey approved volume I, and adopted Corbett's argument for employing civilians in the CID Historical Section.[22]

This magnificent book had a curious fate. Criticism of Japanese decision-making in volume I led the CID, unwilling to upset a close ally, to mark the text Confidential and print very few copies. They appeared in January 1914, for discreet use by the NID. Both volumes were marked: 'The lessons to be learnt from this History should not be divulged to anyone not on the active list.' The first volume had been read and appreciated by some senior officers, including First Sea Lord Prince Louis of Battenberg, before

August 1914. On 31 July 1914 Corbett completed the appendices and maps for volume II, liaising with Slade, and found an indexer.[23] More than 400 copies of volume II were produced in October 1915, but by then the Royal Navy was at war, and had more recent lessons to learn.

In 1994 the United States Naval War College and the Naval Institute Press published a new edition, but without the charts and diagrams that dominate Corbett's treatment of a conflict fought far, far away, in an area with unusual, inconsistently employed proper names. It is scarcely necessary to observe that the book is masterpiece, or that it conforms to the rest of Corbett's canon. It was curiously apposite that the page proofs of volume II passed through Corbett's hands in January 1915, just as the Dardanelles moved to the top of the strategic list. Having been written to inform the Royal Navy and those statesmen who thought about grand strategy, any criticism of the book's essentially parochial nature misses the point. It was carefully targeted, not blindly chauvinistic.

No sooner had Corbett begun work on the Russo-Japanese War than his leadership was required on another front. On 4 March 1912 Sir John Laughton resigned the secretaryship of the NRS. Failing eyesight had finally caught up with the grand old man of naval history. A week later the council hastily commissioned Corbett to represent the NRS at a meeting to discuss the forthcoming International Historical Congress in London, before turning to the critical issue of replacing Laughton at the interface between the Navy, naval education and academic history. Corbett had served on the NRS Council since 1897, and in the spring of 1912 was completing a four-year term as vice president. After toying with the option of taking on Laughton's role he stood back, refusing to join the editorial committee that replaced the great man. After the brief, unsatisfactory secretaryship of Laughton's son, Corbett deftly manoeuvred the NRS inside the Admiralty, to ensure it remained a naval educational asset, supported by powerful patrons.

In March 1912 Corbett represented the NRS at a meeting to discuss the forthcoming International Congress of Historical Sciences in London at the British Academy. He wanted to reinforce the connection between naval history and a rising academic tradition.[24] At the meeting he objected 'to their being no Naval and Military section', with the support of important allies, including George Prothero, a leading advocate of modern history.[25] Professor Adolphus William Ward, chairman of the organising committee, adopted Corbett's proposal, and requested his help in editing a new series for Cambridge University Press (CUP), where he chaired the Syndicate.[26] Ward had no doubt as to Corbett's suitability.[27]

Corbett accepted Ward's invitation because he could enhance the academic standing of naval history through the prestigious International Congress, while the new series would produce textbooks for the War Course, and encourage academics to support the course, thereby raising its profile.[28] Working closely with his friend Charles Firth, Regius Professor of History at Oxford, NRS councillor and one of the organising committee, Corbett ensured the naval and military sections were integrated . Their proceedings would be published in a volume to launch the Cambridge series, treating naval and military history as integral elements of a single subject. Firth and Corbett had been corresponding on the Trafalgar report, which Firth had helped to compile, while Firth sought Corbett's advice on naval issues for an illustrated edition of Thomas Babington Macaulay's *History of England*, published in 1913.[29] Firth envied Corbett his role at the centre of events, joining committees in London to escape a straitjacketed Oxford curriculum that he could not change.

With the International Congress agenda settled, Corbett discussed Admiralty support for the Cambridge series with Slade.[30] The proposal was shaped in his own image, intellectually sophisticated, broad-based and present-minded. He imposed the same agenda on the naval sub-section of the congress, creating an expert symposium on the present state and future prospects of naval history in both academic and service contexts. The published version can be read as a 'state of the discipline' manifesto for naval history, backed by the imprimatur of an International Congress, and a leading academic press.

By late October Corbett had settled terms with Cambridge University Press, inviting Douglas Owen and Alexander Pearce Higgins, the shipping and international law lecturers on the War Course, along with Captain Herbert Richmond, to contribute.[31] Owen's and Higgins' contributions were essential to develop practical aspects of doctrine. When all three authors agreed to contribute he demanded better terms from CUP: he could not ask the top men in their fields to work for an academic pittance. The Cambridge texts would join NRS volumes in the ward rooms of the fleet to improve the standard of debate. Discussions with War Course director Henry Jackson in mid-November confirmed Corbett's belief that there was an opportunity to shape the academic content of the programme, ensure expert contributions were available to a global Navy, and enhance the status of the course across the service.[32] When the series was announced, Rear Admiral David Beatty, Naval Secretary to the First Lord of the Admiralty and 1910 Naval War College alumnus, wrote for more details.[33] Delighted Corbett had taken the vital, if 'herculean task' of general editor, Beatty believed the series would 'fill a long felt want': works from Owen and Pearce Higgins would be a fine beginning.[34] Beatty ensured Churchill was familiar with the project.

The Navy's response disposes of two myths: first that it was in any way anti-intellectual and, second, that it did not appreciate Corbett. The Cambridge series, like *Some Principles*, was approved at the Admiralty, which consistently backed his efforts to improve professional education. Corbett also secured the endorsement of First Sea Lord Prince Louis of Battenberg, to whom the Secretary of the Press promised early results in return for naval support. In 1913 Corbett used that promise to browbeat the Press into action: 'I cannot afford to be associated with an undertaking that lets me down in this way, nor can you afford to trifle with the navy if you want its support.'[35] Corbett also explained his plans to Hankey at the CID. 'Such work, he thought, ought to secure scholarly as well as military recognition. Hankey understood and agreed.'[36]

Before the war Cambridge produced two texts. One was *Naval and Military Essays*, from the International Congress, the only coherent group of papers from the congress to be published, in which academic history and the study of war met in a joint enterprise that combined distinctive forms of professional expertise. The second, Douglas Owen's *Ocean Trade and Shipping*, emphasised the range and sophistication of the pre-war course. A user's guide to global commerce *'primarily'* for 'naval and military officers', the final section explained the paperwork a boarding officer would find when they stopped neutral ships. Furthermore, Owen replaced old precedents with current practice, since the 'laws of maritime warfare themselves have been modified to the advantage of the neutral flag.'[37] Although the outbreak of war may have limited the book's impact, Owen's lectures were familiar to War Course graduates. The series was always intended to be topical, so in May 1914 Corbett considered pre-empting a major event. 'I have been thinking of a volume on the "Capture of Private Property at Sea", but am not yet certain who to invite to do it. It would be timely if we could get it out before the next Hague Conference.'[38]

The 1913 London International Congress of Historical Studies ran from 3 to 9 April. Firth, as President of the Royal Historical Society, welcomed the 'innovation' of a 'special sub-section devoted to military and naval history'.[39]

Corbett bent the high-profile meeting to his agenda, positioning the history of war between an academic tradition uncomfortable with modern subjects, especially those studied for practical 'lessons', and professional military education, which had no interest in the status anxieties of a relatively new academic discipline. Corbett organised the programme's only coherent sub-section[40] and delivered the stand-out paper, a powerful critique of the prevailing German trend in historical scholarship, meeting A.W. Ward's call for a 'history of historians'.[41]

The naval and military sub-section met in the well-appointed Whitehall lecture theatre of the Royal United Services Institute,[42] only minutes from the Admiralty and the War Office. This enabled serving officers to attend. The meetings were chaired by General William Robertson, Commandant at Camberley, Charles Firth and the First Sea Lord, Prince Louis, all three contributing to proceedings. This combination of service and academic leadership gave the lectures a strikingly present-minded tone. Corbett opened the sub-section on 3 April with Robertson in the chair; the remaining papers that day were military. On 4 April Firth chaired a mixed naval and military panel. Prince Louis chaired a naval panel on 6 April, demonstrating the Admiralty's high-level support for 'the intellectual equipment of the sea service'.

The Times repeated Corbett's agenda:

We are only just beginning to understand what naval history really is, what its relations are to political history on the one hand, and on the other, to the military history which is its contemporary counterpart. The incidents of naval history are seldom, perhaps never, isolated and purely naval incidents. We shall never understand them unless we can penetrate the minds of those engaged in conducting the operations recorded, unless we can study the instructions given to them, unless we can see how they interpreted those instructions themselves, unless we can reproduce the perplexing atmosphere of conflicting information and befogging ignorance in which they had to move and act as best they could.[43]

Despite the international agenda Corbett focused the naval sub-section on a domestic audience, primarily in uniform, advancing clear, present-minded and above all practical agendas.[44] His philosophical enquiry into the type of naval history needed for strategic education was paired with Laughton's critique of naval historical writing, by generalists and specialists alike.

Corbett reflected on his recent experience, teaching strategy and doctrine to senior naval officers, writing strategic histories, including an official text, editing documentary collections, and producing a national strategic doctrine that linked academic work to defence planning. To connect his varied audiences he focused on the recent upsurge of Staff, or Official Histories of war. His masterly overview emphasised service/academic connections, stressing the positives, eliding the reality that history still had many battles to fight before it became a core discipline for the development of strategic doctrine. Accustomed to ransacking the past for evidence to support pre-determined conclusions, an obvious criticism of Mahan, naval officers soon discovered others could use the same method to sustain counter-arguments, persuading 'practical men' that history, like statistics, could prove anything. The service only became receptive when historians adopted a 'sound and philosophical method', which valued history as 'a treasure house of rich experience' in which they could search for principles. These methods transformed the past from a heap of jumbled facts into 'a mine of experience . . . from which right doctrine – the soul of warfare – can be built up'.[45] The critical role of strategic theory in the process was inferred, a task that required educated, rather than experienced, intellects.

Having established the doctrinal utility of history, Corbett considered the construction of Official Histories, intended to inform and instruct rising generations. He divided them into two categories, those dealing with older wars, which could only inform 'broader doctrines', and recent conflicts, 'in which, in spite of the rapid development of material, we seek for closer and more direct light on the wars of to-morrow'.[46] Analysts of older conflicts should sweep away 'unimportant detail' and bring out 'general principles . . . inseparable from the conduct of all wars', including 'the deflections of purely military operations which were caused by political exigencies and influences . . . to which modern military theory attaches so much importance'. The uniquely maritime nature of British strategy led him to dismiss the widely lauded German Staff History of the Seven Years' War because 'it was confined to the continental and European theatre of the war and the influence of the maritime theatre is ignored'. His target lay just across Whitehall, where the Army General Staff dreamt German dreams of mass conscript armies and 'decisive' theatres.

Rather than examining older conflicts in detail Corbett believed Staff Histories should address 'special problems'.[47] Some in the audience might have recognised this as the NRS model, a point Laughton would develop. General histories of older wars were best left to civilian historians, although he modestly avoided referencing *England in the Seven Years' War*. The solution to Britain's methodological dilemma lay in Colonel Desbrière's *Projets et tentatives de dèbarquement aux Iles Brittaniques, 1798–1805*, produced by a French General Staff searching for the 'solution to a particular war problem'. A 'complete collection of documents, orders and statistics' would enable students to extract their own conclusions, guided by 'lucid comment'. He did not need to explain why his ideal strategic study was one that dismissed the danger of invasion.

Studies written in the immediate aftermath of modern conflicts needed to be comprehensive, as 'their object is avowedly to study the mistakes that were made with ... an illuminating frankness which is the marrow of real history'. However, it was impossible to be wholly honest about political and other external deflections in the lifetime of those involved, rendering such works, like collections of documents, more 'materials for history' than history itself. Professional historians might render such books 'more digestible to a hard-worked officer seeking to improve his knowledge of his profession'.[48] Corbett's model Staff History, Frederick Maurice's account of Wolseley's 1882 Tel-el-Kebir campaign, had been written by an accomplished soldier-historian, avoiding the 'inordinate length and heaviness of recent Staff Histories'. He valued 'the art of narrative and the art of selection' provided by experienced historians.[49]

Britain needed a Historical Section where officers and academics would cooperate. Here naval history was at a disadvantage, most evidence dated back to the age of sailing ships, while Army officers were significantly better educated for historical work than their seagoing colleagues, and possessed a more impressive literature. The training and occupation of a sea officer were uncongenial to historical work. Attempting to grasp the wisdom of 'long dead masters' was a complex problem, one in which 'scholarship', the ability to keep conclusions 'as free as fallible human minds can make them, from preconceived ideas' had, like seamanship, to be learnt by experience. To secure the respect it deserved from naval officers, Corbett emphasised the 'long and devoted service' required to become a historian, while admitting that he needed the help of naval officers to round out his comprehension of the naval past.[50]

Historical conclusions, based on the balance of evidence and 'disciplined judgement', were not intended to resolve 'modern technical problems', those belonged to service experts – but those experts must employ historical methods. His case study was the use of history in the *Dreadnought* controversy, specifically the tactical importance of three-decked ships. Historical conclusions should not be used 'to prove that a particular modern type is either right or wrong'.[51] In criticising Fisher's *Dreadnought*, Custance, Bridge, White and Mahan had all failed as historians. To avoid such dangers he favoured 'free collaboration' between the two forms of expertise, linked by historically trained naval officers, like congress speaker Herbert Richmond.

Britain posed a unique problem for Staff Histories, a point Corbett had made in *Some Principles*, because maritime war, the combined action of Army and Navy, received 'little attention from any staff'. Historical Sections concentrated on great continental wars, 'into which the sea factor hardly entered'. These histories, however good, ignored 'the most pronounced deflections in war – those which naval operations exercise upon land operations and *vice versa*'. This made it essential to treat the two services as 'units of one combined force'. The British attempt to study the Russo-Japanese War in service Historical Sections had failed, leaving the CID 'to emphasise the essential unity of the land and sea forces of an island country'.[52] Corbett was confident the best model for such work was an analytical narrative, the province of the historian. He was quietly confident his own as yet unpublished Official History would transcend service agendas.

Corbett's lecture fused two streams of authority, urging the Navy and the academy to take each other seriously, to study national or grand strategy. In the event, few historians took up the challenge. Corbett's vision remained effectively unique, his close working relationship with senior officers like Slade, Battenberg and Jackson helped him understand the needs of a service struggling for doctrinal comprehension in an age of rapid technological progress. The collaborative CID Historical Section he discussed was no paper exercise: it already existed. In 1914 it became the Official Historical Section, and Corbett led it for the rest of his life.

The London congress located naval history, and its service education role, on the intellectual map of world history. The sub-section was an organisational and public relations triumph, the quality and coherence of the naval papers demonstrating the maturity of the discipline, and the intimate connection between subject and audience – a connection made explicit by locating the lectures in the forum of British strategic debate, instead of the university. The papers addressed military audiences, and it is likely more officers than academics attended. Corbett's message about creating strategic doctrine, carefully wrapped in the newly won professionalism of history, exploited the congress's international seal of approval to establish the 'scientific' standing of his work. Publishing the papers in the 'Naval and Military' series provided academic endorsement for his doctrinal message. Corbett had exploited an unforeseen opportunity to promote naval history in the academic world and regularise civilian input to doctrine development and the War Course, the focus of his historical output.

In December 1913 the NRS Council, prompted by Corbett, increased the print run of volumes deemed of 'interest' to the Navy, and began to sell them to officers who were not members.[53] This decision was linked to his latest publication, volume I of *The Private Papers of George, Second Earl Spencer, First Lord of the Admiralty, 1794–1801*, issued two months before. A second volume appeared in the autumn of 1914. These texts reflect the view of naval history as an educational tool for the War Course expressed in Corbett's 'Staff Histories' essay.

The papers of the 2nd Earl Spencer (1758–1834) had been deposited in the Admiralty Library by the 5th Earl, founding President of the NRS and former First Lord, to be considered for publication.[54] After his death in October 1910 the 6th Earl agreed to their publication.[55] In January 1911 William Graham Greene put them in Admiralty Room 43; Corbett reported their significance to Council on 14 March 1911 and agreed to edit them.[56] He selected the documents that summer, and probably completed the editorial content a year later, during a summer break at Stopham.[57] References were added after returning to London.[58]

Corbett had discovered a rich vein of strategic insight, 'material which, above all, the Society exists to deal with.'[59] Correspondence between flag officers, the First Lord and his Cabinet colleagues illuminated the main lines of strategy and policy, free from the restraint of official communications. Such material had been central to the *Seven Years' War* and *Trafalgar*, distinguishing his work from that of historians who overestimate official records. His strategic selection addressed 'the main flow of naval affairs', discounting politics, promotion, patronage, the persiflage of Sir Sidney Smith and the dockyard reforms of Sir Samuel Bentham.

In a concession to the NRS's educational role, Corbett arranged the letters by subject, following each issue to a conclusion, rather than using a simple chronology, to better illustrate 'the principles of naval and maritime warfare'.[60] While he used little material on domestic politics, Corbett ensured his readers understood the divergent strategic ideas within Pitt's post-1794 coalition ministry, and explained how the Cabinet worked. Spencer was appointed to the Admiralty in December 1794, following the failure of Admiralty planning for operations in support of the royalist rising in the Vendée, which had forced Pitt to recognise the limitations of his elder brother Lord Chatham. Corbett disputed the argument that Henry Dundas's colonial and imperial expeditions had been wasteful diversions, developed in John Fortescue's *History of the British Army* and *British Statesmen of the Great War*. That argument reflected contemporary continental obsessions, not the realities of 1794. Corbett subtly promoted Dundas's merits, including his protest against the excessive concentration of naval power in home waters.[61] The real problem was that both Pitt and Dundas were trying to repeat the limited maritime strategy of the Seven Years' War, despite facing an 'unlimited' war. The object they had in view, the overthrow of the Revolutionary regime, could not be secured by limited methods, an argument sustained by quoting 'the great German strategist'.[62]

Fortescue's criticism of the West Indies campaigns reflected flawed assumptions. Many of the troops used in 1793 were already in theatre, defending British planters from the danger of a slave revolt inspired by events on St Domingue (Haiti). French planters had invited the British to occupy an island that commanded the approaches to Jamaica. While the French counter-attack obliged the government to act, the expedition was shaped by the Army. Appointing a junior flag officer to command the fleet handed overall direction to a senior general: 'insufficient thought was given to the naval difficulties it would cause'. The First Sea Lord Admiral Sir Charles Middleton resigned because the decision was 'in conflict with ... the best traditions of maritime warfare', leaving office 'as a protest against War Office domination'.[63] The contemporary relevance of Corbett's argument was entirely intentional.

The Navy registered a collective protest at an extraordinary court martial. Sir William Cornwallis, Vice Admiral of Great Britain, refused to obey an order issued by the Duke of York, commander-in-chief of the Army, excusing Army officers from naval discipline while travelling on warships as being degrading to a naval officer. Spencer, pressurised by Dundas, the Duke of York and General Sir Ralph Abercromby, demanded a trial. The largest number of admirals ever assembled for a court unanimously acquitted Cornwallis.[64] The situation in the West Indies was largely restored in 1796 by the intelligent application of adequate resources.[65]

While narrative historians focused on battles, Corbett emphasised strategy, examining intentions and plans, an approach that made the Channel the central focus. The danger of a French invasion loomed large in 1794, with the Channel Isles an obvious target. Securing the islands with effective cruiser patrols turned them into 'a base from which the British would operate offensively against the French coast. This forced the French onto the defence'. To reinforce control of French coastal waters the Navy seized the Saint-Marcouf islands east of Cherbourg, 'an anchorage from which Havre could be watched', which interrupted coastwise shipping, much as Alderney and Jersey controlled that on the north coast of Brittany and the west coast of Normandy. With Desbrière's majestic text to hand, Corbett revealed 'the other side of the hill' and the constant interaction of British and French strategies.[66] He encouraged students to consult the French text while sustaining larger points about invasions, the seizure of offshore islands and the relative importance of Navy and Army in the defence of the United Kingdom for the Admiralty and CID. Unlike the tit-for-tat seizures in limited wars – Belle Isle for Minorca in the Seven Years' War was well known to Corbett's readers – Saint-Marcouf conferred significant strategic advantage in a total war, contributing to insular defence and economic blockade.

Throughout Corbett's years teaching on the Naval War Course, the Army had sought to replace the Navy as the prime instrument of British strategy, urging the need for a large land force to provide security against invasion, before switching tack to urge the need to fight in France, while deprecating offensive naval strategies, especially the seizure of offshore islands. *The Spencer Papers* equipped naval officers to make better arguments in future, especially if they took the trouble to consult Desbrière.

Corbett's handling of the ill-fated Quiberon expedition was more detailed than other sections; the subject appealed, having formed the basis of *A Business in Great Waters*. While the new text offered a warning against relying on rebels, enthusiasts and discredited royalists, it also highlighted serious operational and strategic concerns. Amphibious operations were high risk, but also very powerful: 'how precarious is the movement of troops over sea when there is an active fleet, however despicable, within striking distance'. Despite serious errors, the expedition demonstrated that combined operations could achieve strategic surprise, 'the most difficult, and valuable advantage that war can show'. However, concentrating the fleet to cover the expedition 'tended to throw open the sea to the enemy's counter-attacks on trade'. While it was possible to uphold a general control of the sea for defensive purposes, the offensive required a higher concentration of force, a point illustrated by a powerful letter from Middleton.[67]

Corbett's discussion of the strategic situation in 1796 and early 1797 focused on the balance of effort between colonial expeditions, home defence and the protection of trade. He echoed Dundas's view that too many ships had been held back in home waters. Desbrière had demonstrated how British sea control had wrecked French invasion plans: nervous troops refused to embark at Dunkirk. Corbett inferred the problems of this period were at least in part a consequence of the lack of status and strategic insight among the junior flag officers at the Admiralty.[68]

The final section focused on the decision to evacuate the Mediterranean. France, Holland and Spain outnumbered Britain in capital ships, invasion projects were increasing, and extending in geographical reach. This forced the Admiralty to make hard decisions. Once again, Dundas remained positive, confident the Navy would win any battle. Spencer and his flag officers refused to take the risk, but Dundas would be proved correct.

Despite the press of other business, Corbett used the Spencer material to revise orthodox assessments of British strategy in the French Revolutionary War, undermine Fortescue's red-coated continental assumptions, and rehabilitate the energetic, imperial and above all maritime ideas of Henry Dundas. His text would educate contemporary naval officers about the development and application of strategy, within the wider context of his examination of the evolution of British strategic practice. Despite the different format there were important similarities with *England in the Seven Years' War*, while it followed *Some Principles* in using the American War to highlight continuities and discontinuities. That he was writing the CID text on the Russo-Japanese War, a modern version of the *Seven Years' War*, at the same time was reflected in an underlying synergy of audience and analysis.

In volume II, Corbett pressed on with the broadly chronological sequence. He noted how admirals broke down under pressure, 'nervous collapses were not unknown in the old navy, even amongst younger and less severely tried officers'.[69] His discussion of the Great Mutiny profited from Conrad Gill's *The Naval Mutinies of 1797*, which he had read as a Cambridge

Fellowship thesis in 1911.[70] He resolved the debate about Admiral Duncan's tactics at Camperdown, assisted by the Earl of Camperdown, biographer of his illustrious ancestor and fellow Liberal navalist. Duncan attacked the Dutch in general chase, to bring on the battle before they could escape into shoal water, 'not the expression of any subtle tactical idea like that which inspired the similar attack designed by Nelson in his Trafalgar memorandum'.[71] Corbett's stress lay on the word 'designed'. This was no criticism of Duncan, a smart, strategically minded officer, combining rare determination with an iron will and a delight in battle.

Returning to the theme of invasion, Corbett highlighted the distinction to be drawn between the various schools of thought inside the service. Few senior officers were worried; some hoped the French would make the attempt – they would be annihilated at sea. Yet Naval Lord Rear Admiral William Young 'was obviously frightened by the idea of attempting to re-occupy the Mediterranean at a time when invasion was threatened'. His real target was not Young, but those who advanced such views in the modern context, when infinitely superior communication technologies had reduced the risk. This group included the Army General Staff, playing politics with national strategy for service advantage. Henry Dundas provided the answer, shaping a dynamic strategy to re-enter the inner sea: Britain needed to re-establish and maintain moral superiority over the enemy, ready to risk much to put heart into the country by offensive action.[72] For Corbett the relevant 'Inner Sea' was the Baltic – and the strategic message was clear.

The discussion of attacks on privateer bases, 'from which the main damage to our trade was done', culminated in the destruction of the canal locks at Ostend, a 'thoroughly well-designed and brilliantly-executed enterprise . . . its strategic purpose . . . preventing the Dutch section of the invasion Flotilla from using the Bruges-Ostend canal to concentrate on those in the French channel ports'. The contemporary relevance of these comments is reflected in the wartime work of the Dover Patrol, attacking lock gates at Ostend and Zeebrugge. He may have developed these points after the outbreak of war.[73] This operation prevented a dangerous concentration of invasion shipping, and could have been repeated with effect if petty inter-service jealousies had not hampered preparations. The next target was Flushing, the jumping-off point for any serious invasion of England. Dundas's attacks split and weakened the French 'Army of England' and, as Desbrière demonstrated, obliged it to expend resources and manpower on defences that quickly absorbed its limited capabilities.[74]

Turning to the Mediterranean in 1797, Corbett emphasised how the Battle of Cape St Vincent altered the naval balance but had little strategic impact on the wider war, because the Royal Navy remained too weak to re-enter the Mediterranean and link up with potential allies. The Spanish fleets at Cadiz and Cartagena were too powerful to leave between a British fleet and the Atlantic, while France had a strong Mediterranean fleet. This restricted Jervis's fleet to blockading Cadiz, rather than cooperating with Austria and Russia in Italy. When France and Spain tried to break the blockade by pressuring Portugal to close its ports to the British, Jervis, prompted by Spencer, left the blockade of Cadiz to Commodore Collingwood and headed north to Lisbon, where he stiffened Portuguese resolve. Corbett used this incident to shift attention away from battles and 'action' to the reality of seapower:

> the struggle for the Tagus scarcely finds a place in our histories, but [it] was considered vital to our ability to continue the war . . . . the results of our long war experience had been rather to enhance than diminish the strategic importance of such naval positions. The men who knew what naval war was were dominated by the idea that though battles might place in our hands the command of the sea, the exercise of that command was impossible without advanced bases rightly distributed.

The Portuguese alliance had been critical to English/British control of the great sea routes for two centuries, and he implied that it became more important in a total war. Another powerful, present-minded passage linked this naval defensive to the subsequent development of a strategic offensive in Iberia.[75]

The 1798 Mediterranean papers addressed a more agreeable theme, the Battle of the Nile and dramatic reoccupation of the inner sea. Corbett stressed the strategic impulse followed Pitt's diplomatic offensive to create a new coalition, 'which would force France to turn her eyes away from the ocean', opening new fronts on land, with Austrian and Russian armies. The coalition would only come to pass if the Royal Navy could command the Mediterranean. Jervis, now Earl St Vincent, acknowledged the diplomatic imperative, and the naval risks it entailed, because he took a statesmanlike view of the situation. Praising St Vincent's 'courageous assumption of responsibility' encouraged contemporary senior officers to prioritise national strategy over operational concerns.[76] The Mediterranean was critical to a Second Coalition against France. Spencer turned policy into strategy by shifting ten battleships from home waters, appointing Nelson, and giving St Vincent the resources to conduct the operation. The volume ended at a point when the war was going well: Britain had recovered the Mediterranean and the base at Minorca, while Austria was about to join the coalition.[77] In December 1914, the NRS promised more from the Spencer papers, but by then Corbett had another war to study.[78]

The *Spencer Papers* were handled in the manner Corbett had developed in 'Staff Histories', the material arranged and explained to enable students to address modern problems by analogy. It highlighted 'how the old men thought' at the level he believed his audience, mid-career and senior officers, needed, the civil/military interface and the making of national strategy, integrating naval, diplomatic and military activity. Arranging the documents by theatre and theme turned each section into a case study, a digestible fraction, which he expected students to master. There were also parallels with *The Russo-Japanese War*, his primary literary task in this period. He picked out the major themes, selected the evidence and equipped readers with the context to profit from the documents, without dictating a Staff solution.

The *Spencer Papers* also demonstrate that Corbett was running the NRS. He had avoided any of the offices of business, after briefly considering becoming Hon. Secretary, if he could delegate the routine administration.[79] Instead he established a leadership cadre based in the Admiralty: the new Hon. Secretary was Admiralty Librarian William Perrin; Admiralty Secretary Oswyn Murray continued as Treasurer, with Admiral Reginald Custance providing the essential naval voice. This team refreshed the original intellectual purpose of the NRS, serving the Navy's educational needs. Corbett's NRS was an Admiralty doctrine cell, linked to war planning and higher education. The new leadership cleared a publications backlog that had built up during Laughton's closing years: Herbert Richmond's strategic *Papers Relating to the Loss of Minorca* appeared in 1913–14.[80] NRS publication in 1913 and 1914 paired Corbett's *Spencer* volumes with the fourth and fifth volumes of the decidedly antiquarian *Naval Tracts of Sir William Monson*, which, for all their scholarly merit, had limited value for naval education.[81] To link the society with the Cambridge Series, Corbett secured volumes focused on Naval and Maritime Law, linked to Pearce Higgins' projected Cambridge textbook.[82] Yet the *Spencer Papers* also highlighted an old problem. Corbett had grasped their significance and edited them because no-one else had the expertise to do so. His input had transformed historical records into a teaching text for the War Course. There was no-one else working at this level.

Corbett's work on *Spencer* and the *Russo-Japanese War* was driven by a sense of danger. In late 1912 he confessed to his wife:

> I have just done my lecture, the first in the Jap war which they always like & I have had a long talk with some of the soldiers about it. They are always interesting & seem to know so much more of their subject & to have clearer ideas than the sailors. The Army has certainly been going ahead of the Navy of late.[83]

Although he had worked hard to counter that trend, delivering intellectual resources, the acid test would arrive before his work was complete.

Corbett believed that doctrine emerged from a synthesis of experience, engagement and education. While he addressed many aspects of the process, his core contribution lay at the higher levels, where policy, strategy, law, economics, shipping and communications became a seamless grand strategic whole. *Some Principles* was but one element of a multi-faceted complex of educational resources that he created to ensure the continuing vitality and national character of national doctrine. His object was nothing less than the consolidation of a 'British way'. Between 1902 and 1914 he had challenged the Army's adherence to continental methods. When he struck a controversial note, for example downplaying the significance of fleet battle, he did so deliberately, to prompt debates he was confident of winning. He stressed the importance of economic warfare through shipping control, international law, cable and wireless communications, while referencing future developments in submarine and air technology, because it was imperative that Britain responded to change in a timely and intelligent fashion, guided by past experience, but always looking forward. His doctrine was progressive; it would inform the men of the moment without becoming hidebound or restrictive. His attempt to update *Some Principles* before 1914 reflected an anxiety to retain relevance. Ultimately, Corbett recognised that British strategy was limited and weak; it was only effective when all national resources – naval, military, financial, industrial, commercial and human – were directed by the guiding maritime principle. He did not create specific strategies, that was not his role; he provided the conceptual tools to shape national strategy, a maritime compound that drew its strength from the integration of the two services under civilian direction towards a common purpose. That purpose was the security of Britain, the empire and the essential sea communications as the empire morphed from central direction towards a 'Sea Commonwealth' of self-governing nations. By 1914 Corbett's strategic ideas, and methods of study, filtering out from naval education into wider consciousness, were raising the quality of the debate.

Corbett's ideas were familiar to the wartime naval leadership, statesmen who thought about war, the Secretary of the CID and a wider group of opinion-formers in Britain and beyond. His arguments were central to national strategy. In February 1914 his work was recognised by the Council of the Royal United Services Institute, which awarded him the Chesney Gold Medal, despite the opposition of an Army faction.[84] His friends Herbert Richmond and Arthur Leveson, leading the Admiralty's Operations Division, countered the continentalist views of General Sir Henry Wilson. As Colonel George Aston RMA noted, Corbett's work had 'an authority which it would be impossible to question'.[85] He had been in line for a knighthood, but the political priorities of the Irish Home Rule crisis saw him bumped from the list.

While such esteem indicators were welcome, Corbett was still refining and deploying a national doctrine based on limited maritime strategy when war broke out. War marked the failure of British policy: having no positive interest in a European conflict, Britain would have been far better served by the preservation of peace, by diplomacy or deterrence. Deterrence, not warfighting, had been the core of Jacky Fisher's Admiralty programme: big ships, public displays and timely deployments to the Baltic, backed by 'loose talk' about 'Copenhagening' the German fleet had been effective. After 1912 the global situation changed. The Anglo-German naval arms race had been won, and it seemed a rapprochement might follow. Mainstream Liberal opinion remained pro-German, and anti-Russian. As Russia regained the strength to balance Germany, it was unlikely the Anglo-Russian Entente would be renewed, reflecting irreconcilable differences across Eurasia.[86] Soon Britain might be released from a 'balancing' role in great power politics, to refocus on the wider world, global trade, the evolving Commonwealth and empire, resolving the Irish crisis, and shaping a new era of 'Splendid Isolation'. The British economy continued to grow, if not as fast as those of other major powers, which had far larger industrial bases. The key indicator of strategic success was that Britain continued paying down the National Debt between 1902 and 1914.[87] Britain dominated global shipping, shipbuilding, and related services; it was the major exporter of capital, and controlled global communications. Corbett, who understood all of this as well as anyone in London, created a strategic concept that could secure Britain's global power as the empire transitioned into a 'Sea Commonwealth'. He does not seem to have been surprised by the German leadership choosing '*Weltpolitik*' and war over domestic reform.[88] By contrast, Sir Edward Grey's assumption that keeping the fleet mobilised in late July would be 'a clear enough signal' of intent proved unfounded.[89] It would have been difficult to deter the irrational leadership of Imperial Germany; the best option would have been Fisherite grandstanding in or about the Baltic ... but Fisher was neither in office nor available, and no-one else understood the art of deterrence.

The one thing that no-one expected, not even Henry Wilson and the continentalists at the War Office, was that five years of mass European warfare would eviscerate the British seapower state. Wilson dreamt of a short war, British troops arriving just in time to play a significant role, not half a decade of grinding attrition. Corbett had not crafted doctrine for such an outlandish, unprecedented contingency. His strategy for a progressive liberal future held the field down to August 1914, when strategically illiterate statesmen allowed ambitious soldiers to join a continental war, without imposing political control. There had been another way, a 'British way', and Corbett would be condemned to repeat himself.

CHAPTER 16

The 'British Way' at War

When war broke out in August 1914 Corbett's reputation as a strategist and educator had never stood higher: he had recovered and explained national strategy as a doctrine that stressed the primacy of political direction, limited war, sea control, economic warfare and inter-service cooperation.[1] These arguments were familiar to statesmen and admirals: he had an audience at the heart of government at the CID, and the Admiralty. In July 1914 British strategy was, essentially, the limited/maritime construct Corbett had developed across the previous decade. The government had rejected the continental option in 1911, leaving the army with a small expeditionary force, and a Territorial reserve made up of men who had only signed on for a home defence role. The contrast between these limited preparations and the widespread assumption that a European war would be waged on the largest scale, and settled in a single season, is compelling. Successive governments had allowed the Army General Staff to reject joint service planning for maritime warfare, despite the best efforts of Clarke, Esher and the CID, forcing the Admiralty to plan for a naval war.

Corbett would be drawn into the war effort because the nation and the Navy needed his intellect, his legal and literary skills, and his unique ability to impose order and coherence on the chaos of war. He would help shape wartime policy, and dominate the manner in which it would be recorded, trying to write the new conflict with the same detachment he had used when discussing the Seven Years' War, linking the current conflict with past practice as he refined his thinking.

A limited maritime strategy threatened the social, political and professional agendas of a military caste, agendas lately on display in the Curragh Mutiny.[2] The influence of the Army was redoubled when Prime Minister Asquith appointed Field Marshal Lord Kitchener Secretary of State for War, a distorting combination of military rank and political office in an otherwise civilian Cabinet. In the past, senior admirals had held the political post of First Sea Lord, Anson, St Vincent and Barham being highly effective in shaping and directing national strategy. Fisher was well aware of these examples, which Corbett had addressed, and Kitchener's appointment only reinforced his concern to secure a seat in the War Cabinet. As First Sea Lord he attended Cabinet meetings as the professional advisor to the First Lord, only contributing when consulted.

Despite past experience, and current doctrine, the government committed most of the small BEF to France, a decision heavily influenced by the Army General Staff, notably Director of Military Operations General Sir Henry Wilson. The decision was taken late in the afternoon of 5 August by an extemporised 'War Council' consisting of Asquith, Grey, Haldane, Churchill and Kitchener. The four politicians were outnumbered by nine senior soldiers, who presented them with a movement and logistics schedule to move a few divisions to France, a plan entirely bereft of strategic consequence, merely adding a few British divisions to the ninety-division army of France. The ministers, who were using the possibility of such support to stiffen the diplomacy of the Entente, may not have thought through the implications. Critically Grey, the Foreign Secretary, went along with a decision entirely out of step with his long-held Liberal preference for sea power and economic warfare because he was reluctant to challenge the authority of military 'experts'.[3] Only one minister positively backed the military option, Churchill, an avowed continentalist. As First Lord of the Admiralty he deprived the Navy of the 'Expeditionary Force' that British experience indicated would be essential to secure and exploit command of the sea. In consequence Britain waged war with two separate service-led strategies, dominated by an open-ended commitment to defend France, a risk Fisher and Arthur Wilson had highlighted across the previous decade. This undermined the strategic model of global maritime power based on the combined action of the two services. The soldiers had assumed a war between European great powers could only be won on the Continent, and that they should be involved. The obsession with short wars and decisive battles, perfectly rational in France and Germany, distorted British policy because British statesmen, who had no understanding of war, assumed it should be left to soldiers. The last point was obvious on 5 August. The only admiral in the room, Prince Louis of Battenberg, the First Sea Lord, outnumbered by no fewer than nine generals, remained silent while his political master overturned national strategy. Asquith's Cabinet, which had wavered before declaring war, proved incapable of settling on or implementing a coherent strategy, allowing itself to be swayed by the deep sense of personal grievance engendered by German duplicity, newspaper headlines, military advice and political pressure from the Conservative opposition.

Churchill was one of many who expected this would be a short war, settled by a single climactic battle, consistent with German theory and practice. While this was the view of the dominant 'General Staff' clique, there were other voices in the Army, echoing Henderson, Maurice and Wolseley. Sir John French, the designated commander-in-chief, argued that the BEF should be deployed to Belgium. That option disappeared when the Admiralty refused to take responsibility for delivering the BEF to Antwerp, and with that the last fleeting chance to keep the services linked and focused on British interests was lost.

Committing the BEF to France separated the Expeditionary Force from the fleet it was intended to support, sacrificing the overriding national strategic imperative – securing and enhancing sea control – to provide a tiny continental force, which became the guarantee of British commitment to France, a guarantee France was quick to exploit.

The War Council decision marked a clear break with pre-war policy; there had been no binding commitment to assist France, and all previous British experience, experience Corbett had reduced to doctrinal consistency in *England in the Seven Years' War* and *Some Principles of Maritime Strategy*, stressed that British aims in Europe were limited to keeping Germany out of the Low Countries and maintaining a balance of power. Churchill's military focus and Battenberg's passivity left the Navy in the background as all eyes focused on the anticipated clash of great armies. Transfixed by events on land, no-one in the Cabinet, or the Naval High Command, had the insight or aptitude to produce a clear statement of national strategy. Those in power took far longer to recognise the disaster they had set in train, and later tried to evade responsibility. Corbett dedicated the rest of his life to ensuring their mistakes were not repeated.

Later in the year Maurice Hankey, Secretary to the CID and then the War Cabinet, took a similar view, but in August 1914 he had been among the majority, rushing enthusiastically into battle. He came to rely on Corbett's insight, judgement and priceless ability to draft a compelling memorandum to counter the drift into total war.[4] Many more took something of Corbett to the war, from Lord Esher to a generation of dynamic captains and commanders.

Vice Admiral Sir Edmond Slade, an old friend and intellectual companion, returned to the Admiralty Staff in August, ensuring Corbett would continue to work in the building, as he had throughout the Russo-Japanese project. Captain Herbert Richmond, Assistant Director of the Operations Division, used both men as sounding boards for his own thinking. All three realised that the positive opportunities of the war lay in the colonial and imperial spheres as they discussed the situation on 5 August, their discussions shaped by *England in the Seven Years' War*.[5]

At the CID Corbett moved seamlessly from the Russo-Japanese book, at the press when war broke out, to leading the Official History project and the civilian staff of the Historical Sub-Committee – critical tasks that have been ignored.[6] Corbett's roles were settled, albeit unofficially, before the war was a week old. Slade wanted him to join the Admiralty War Staff, while Major Daniel approached him unofficially to write the CID war history. Leaving the latter offer to one side until it had official sanction, Corbett worked at the Admiralty, although without an official title. He drafted memoranda that were beyond the competence of the Chief of Staff, Vice Admiral Doveton Sturdee. These included the covering instructions sent to Jellicoe as commander-in-chief of the Grand Fleet![7] On 11 September Corbett had a 'Long talk with Sturdee over strategy & possibility of getting German fleet to come out. Told him I thought they would husband it for coast defence later on – this had not occurred to him.'[8] Corbett's point was critical. He had demonstrated that the sublime moments of naval history had to be worked for: the enemy would not offer battle unless compelled by a strategic threat. The only way to force the High Seas Fleet to fight would essentially be to threaten Germany's vital interests; Corbett's reference to the 'coast' referred to Germany's long Baltic coast, the focus of Fisher's thinking since the 1890s. The synergy of Corbett's theory and Fisher's practice shaped a suitable 'British way' of waging the war. Sadly, Henry Jackson advised Corbett that Churchill had consistently ignored his senior professional advisors since the outbreak of war.[9] While Sturdee's obvious failings saw him replaced in late October, the new man, Henry Oliver, an old friend of Richmond, was an unimaginative micro-manager with a deep animus against civilian historians.[10] Oliver consistently obstructed Corbett's work.

In late August 1914 Corbett discussed North Sea strategy with former War Course director and DNI Sir Alexander Bethell, commanding the Channel Fleet. His work, compiling a running record of events, a basic war diary, was going 'laboriously but pleasantly enough. My only trouble is that I find a difficulty in getting at secret matter (instructions, war orders and the like) without which it is impossible to tell the whole story properly.'[11] Filling in the gaps, elevating narrative into strategic analysis, occupied the rest of his life.

Corbett recorded the war as it happened from his office at the CID, No. 2 Whitehall Gardens, five minutes' walk from the Admiralty. These locations gave him access to confidential material, key decision-makers and any fleet commanders who passed through.[12] His friendship with Vice Admiral Sir Henry Jackson, who directed Overseas Operations in the first six months of the war, proved significant. Having worked together on the War Course and after, Jackson looked to Corbett for the guiding concept of the oceanic campaign: the detailed execution was, properly, in other hands. Reviewing War Office papers on Home Defence in early October only confirmed his worst fears. They were 'useless, being confusing and narrow minded criticism of ministers for not doing all WO required. WO really makes me sick with their hide-bound ideas & ignorance of political friction.'[13]

Already unwell, Corbett underwent major surgery on 18 October, only returning home, and to Whitehall, on 30 November. By then Fisher had replaced the compliant Battenberg.[14] Fisher, the one admiral who understood deterrence and grand strategy, had been out of office, and out of town, unable to influence the July crisis or the opening moves of the conflict. His strategic thinking had been shaped by Corbett's work, work that he consistently referenced in his strategy and policy papers. He had sought Corbett's help in drafting and explaining his memoranda for a decade. War revived their partnership. Corbett's strategic concept provided the context for Fisher as he focused on the strategic and technological means of enhancing the Navy's ability to deliver strategic effect.[15]

Recalled to office in late October, despite the protests of the king, and several old Tory admirals, Fisher brought 'elan, dash initiative, a new spirit' to the naval war effort. He quickly set about acquiring the specialist hardware required to conduct major offensive operations, the spearhead of a projected maritime strategy.[16] His return was timely: new battleships had shifted the naval balance decisively in Britain's favour, while the anticipated return of three battlecruisers, detached to annihilate Admiral Graf von Spee's squadron, would reinforce the Grand Fleet. Germany, with fewer capital ships, and fewer under construction, could not contest British superiority.[17] At this juncture the strategy of sea control and economic warfare was evolving rapidly: the global war would be over within weeks.

Fisher was not prepared to cede the strategic direction of the war to the soldiers, let alone the French, or allow their continental methods to persist. He faced several problems, beginning with the taciturn Kitchener, who combined ministerial responsibility as Secretary of State for War with a field marshal's baton, and a formidable popular reputation.

Having supported the deployment of the BEF to France, Churchill had to develop naval offensives that did not require troops. These were necessarily limited to small offshore targets of little strategic consequence. By contrast, Fisher wanted to recover control of national strategy, and the BEF, to conduct a grand strategy that reflected British strengths, and British interests. These included the destruction of the German Navy, and naval bases, which would ease the post-war economic burden. In late 1914 Fisher developed a suitable grand strategy from the pre-war Admiralty Plan G.U., created during his initial term as First Sea Lord.[18] He had adopted Corbett's concept of maritime strategy in a continental conflict from *England in the Seven Years' War*, a war won without a mass army. The lesson of Fisher's favourite book was clear:

> In the long series of wars between France and England ... [t]he most telling move of France had always been to concentrate her operations against the Netherlands in order to get possession of them and so increase at one her own industrial wealth and destroy the security of the English naval position.[19]

In 1914 Germany replaced France, but the security of the Low Countries remained critical, something Corbett had stressed on the first page of his Russo-Japanese War text.[20] Fisher also shared Corbett's conviction that Britain went to war to secure imperial advantage, not continental success. In 1907, after the completion of the Entente system, Corbett had informed the Naval War Course that the purpose of British diplomacy, insofar as Europe was concerned, was:

to confine the threatening war to the theatres beyond the sea where lay our special objects and our peculiar strength. Our controlling aim was to ensure that we should not be drawn into a European struggle and forced to fight for our ends where our power was weakest. To purchase the ___ alliance at the price of sending a serious military force into the very cockpit of Europe was to ensure the consequences which it was the sole object of the alliance to prevent. Moreover it was to offer a price which the instinct of the country had determined not to pay. The spirit with which the people of a country go into a war is as much an element of strategical calculation as its army or its navy. For a maritime and Colonial war with ___ the people of this country were eager and resolute, but of Continental wars they had had enough.[21]

Fisher recognised the German occupation of the Belgian coast was a strategic disaster, one that must be rectified, and quickly.

Since 1898 Fisher had shaped his strategy for dealing with Germany, in peace or war, on the Baltic, recognising German dependence on regional trade, especially in iron, and the difficulty of securing two coasts separated by the Jutland Peninsula. This concern had prompted the creation of the Kiel Canal in the early 1890s, and the costly widening he had obliged Germany to make by building HMS *Dreadnought*. When he learnt the canal would be ready for dreadnoughts in August 1914, Fisher declared this would be Germany's signal for war. The ability to unsettle and deter the German High Command dominated his initial term at First Sea Lord. His 'Copenhagen Complex' combined the threat to attack the High Seas Fleet in harbour with a potent reminder that the Royal Navy had, on several occasions, smashed its way into the Baltic. Had he been in a position of influence in August 1914 he would have urged moving the already mobilised Grand Fleet towards the Baltic, reprising the successful move from the autumn of 1905. He had a better understanding of grand strategy, deterrence and the national interest than any other senior officer, of either service.

Standard accounts of the war have tended to accept Churchill's dismissive aside that Fisher's Baltic plan was an unrealistic fantasy, which the senile admiral had no intention of attempting. While this line dovetails neatly with the familiar argument that the British role on the Western Front was 'inevitable', for the want of realistic alternatives, it is dishonest, and inaccurate. It also begs some very big questions: why did Churchill use up so much of his political capital to recall this senile old man? Why did he try to revive this strategy in 1939–40? The answer is obvious. With Fisher and Corbett dead, he deliberately misrepresented their views, and traduced their reputations to save his own.

The Baltic had long been the focal point of Fisher and Corbett's thinking. It offered a serious challenge to the emerging orthodoxy of the Western Front and purely naval operations at the Dardanelles, and Churchill persuaded Asquith to prevent the Baltic being raised at the War Council. The Baltic would be the occasion for Fisher's resignation, and the focal point of Corbett's Official History, central to his explanation of what had gone wrong, and the lessons to be learnt.

The primary problem for any Baltic strategy remained the diplomatic status of Denmark, which controlled the entrance to the enclosed sea.[22] These straits had been a critical focus of British diplomacy since the 1830s. In August 1914 Denmark, although a neutral, had mined the Great Belt, the only route for dreadnought battleships, under German diplomatic pressure and the unspoken menace of yet another invasion of Jutland. As these were international waters this gave Britain *casus belli*. However, Fisher had no interest in lazy ideas that relied on fighting: he wanted the Danes to be allies. His target was the Baltic anxieties of the German High Command.

He ordered a new fleet of specialist naval assets to threaten the Danish Narrows, while fast merchant ships laid minefields in the North Sea. While there were few mines in store, and those not of the best quality, he had twelve to eighteen months to acquire more and better, while their role was not so simple as has been assumed. As Corbett demonstrated in *Some Principles* and *The Russo-Japanese War*, minefields were more important as intelligence assets than tactical weapons: their presence would compel the Germans to conduct extensive minesweeping before any fleet sortie, something that could be observed by British submarines. This role has been forgotten, because within months signals intelligence had become the most useful indicator of German activity.[23]

Corbett had highlighted the importance of specialist coastal forces, both purpose-built and modified older units designed for coastal work in the Russo-Japanese War, a 'siege fleet'.[24] This force would be essential to the effective exploitation of naval power in coastal waters, especially when conducting amphibious operations.[25] They would supplement the sea control fleet of modern battleships, cruisers and destroyers. Such a force had been provided in the Ballard Committee and later war plans.[26] In 1914–15 Fisher ordered shallow-draught, torpedo-proof heavy gun monitors and light-draught battlecruisers, fitted obsolete cruisers with torpedo-proof bulges and advanced fire control, while a host of submarines, destroyers and mine-sweeping sloops, along with 260 motorised armoured landing craft, for 'Home Operations', a useful phrase covering the North Sea and Baltic.[27] These assets ensured a 'Baltic' strategy would not risk command of the sea: Fisher had no intention of deploying the Grand Fleet in the Baltic. He would deploy the 'siege fleet' towards, but not into the Danish Narrows, with the Grand Fleet in support in case the High Seas Fleet appeared. He expected a German reaction to this threat, on land and sea. That reaction would set up his counter-stroke.

It appears Fisher discussed this concept with Churchill in early December, probably after victory at the Falklands on 8 December had ended the oceanic campaign. The First Lord was not persuaded. Although he shared Fisher's enthusiasm for monitors, and the Baltic, Churchill thought Baltic operations would follow a direct assault on the High Seas Fleet, inside heavily defended harbours: 'going in to fetch them', because, unlike Fisher, he had no idea how to force the enemy to come out and fight.[28] Where Churchill looked for a costly 'decisive' battle, Fisher relied on deception and economic warfare.

Fisher saw command of the Baltic as the culmination of a war-winning maritime strategy that avoided the need for a continental army. His plan had two stages. In the summer of 1915 he envisaged using monitors, mine-sweepers and obsolescent warships to support a British Army operation to recover the Belgian coast. This was the essential preliminary for the Baltic project, and a key element in the defence of merchant shipping. He demanded the War Council sanction this operation on 13 January 1915, rejecting purely naval attacks on Belgian ports as wasteful and inconclusive. His ultimate object was to secure control of the BEF, returning it to the expeditionary role of a maritime strike force. Having secured control of national strategy he would wage a 'British' war from the sea.

That war would be won in 1916. Fisher believed a threat to enter the Baltic with a significant naval force, but not the Grand Fleet, would touch a raw strategic nerve in Berlin, prompting an invasion of Jutland, bring the High Seas Fleet to battle and prompt Danish accession to the war as an ally of Britain. He would act when the second instalment of his new fleet, including light battlecruisers and submarines, was ready, the British Army standing ready to secure the Danish Islands of Funen and Zealand, which would keep open the two main routes into the Baltic, the Great Belt and the Sound. A German invasion of Denmark would also change the diplomatic landscape – potentially ending Swedish trade before the Royal Navy could impose a blockade. The synergy between the British occupation of Zealand in 1807, which Fisher had used to spark the 'Copenhagen Complex' in 1907, and his plan to hold the island against Germany in 1915, was neither accidental, nor novel. If Anglo-Danish land forces held the Danish islands, Fisher could dominate the Baltic, with or without a fleet action in the North Sea.

If Germany did not react as he expected, Fisher's light battlecruisers and submarines would enter the Baltic, using Russian bases to blockade Germany's Baltic coast, and cut the supply of iron ore, steel products and copper that sustained German war industries, along with other vital commodities, including food and fuel. The ultimate threat of British sea power remained economic.

On 17 December Fisher phoned to summon Corbett to his residence in Mall House for lunch 'to talk over his project for hastening end of war by getting command of Baltic – combined with his method of making sure of the North Sea. Wanted me to write memo thereon.' *England in the Seven Years' War* was the model, and Fisher needed a powerful memorandum to win over a reluctant War Council. Fisher did not mention Churchill's role. Corbett wrote the paper over the weekend of 19–20 December, delivering it directly to Fisher on Monday morning.[29]

'On the Possibility of using our Command of the Sea to Influence More Drastically the Military Situation on the Continent' developed Fisher's case for the Belgian coast and the Baltic. As Corbett explained: 'I have endeavoured to state your case for the Baltic as well as I can – setting out such objections as occurred to me and meeting them to show the difficulties had been considered.'[30] Fisher's appreciation was obvious: apologising for Asquith's failure to recognise his services in the latest Honours List. 'I do really hope that the plighted word will be kept next time! Anyhow I mean to keep pegging away.'[31]

Corbett did far more than compile a memorandum; his text synergised the admiral's thinking with the strategic doctrine encapsulated in *Some Principles*. It resolved the troubling question of how Britain could make its maritime strength felt by Germany, and best support its continental allies.

In 1919 Corbett allowed Fisher to publish the memorandum in his memoir *Records*, to give the Baltic a prominent place in post-war strategic debates.[32] He placed control of the Baltic at the heart of the Official History, as the logical culmination of British strategy. Having cleared the outer oceans of German ships in volume I of *Naval Operations*, Corbett opened volume II with a Fisherite statement of national strategy:

> Now that the outer seas had been cleared the paramount need was to obtain a closer hold on the North Sea, with a view to the possibility of ultimately pressing our offensive into the enemy's waters. Such operations would involve coastal attack and inshore work, and required a special class of vessel.[33]

A 'closer hold' would involve occupying the Belgian coast, and pushing the Germans back into their own coastal waters, including the Baltic, Germany's longest sea coast. This would involve opening the Baltic. The two-stage plan depended on a British military force.[34] This was Fisher's concept of national strategy. At the War Council of 1 December, Fisher 'pointed out the importance of adopting the offensive'.[35] He agreed with Corbett that such plans required careful development, and could not be rushed. He wanted to be ready if the current maritime strategy, based on sea control and economic warfare, failed to break the German economy. Minefields would keep the High Seas Fleet out of the North Sea, while the 'siege fleet' approached the Baltic.[36] If the High Seas Fleet attempted to interfere it would be engaged by the Grand Fleet. The ultimate aim was to complete the blockade of Germany, not the amphibious smokescreen Fisher deployed to obscure his intentions from talkative politicians. Russian bases would be very useful, but Russian troops were not required. Fisher only mentioned them to connect his paper to Churchill's 'Baltic' letter to Grand Duke Nicholas on 19 August 1914.[37] As Corbett observed:

> The risks, of course, must be serious; but unless we are fairly sure that the passive pressure of our Fleet is really bringing Germany to a state of exhaustion, *risks must be taken to use our Command of the Sea with greater energy*; or, so far as the actual situation promises, we can expect no better issue for the present war than that which the continental coalition was forced to accept in the Seven Years' War.[38]

In essence, defeat. Corbett was referencing the Prussian crisis of 1761, when the Russian fleet opened Prussia's vulnerable Baltic coast, leaving Berlin defenceless, only for a miraculous political change to avert the fatal stroke. This was Fisher's favourite passage, from his favourite book, which invests the passage with considerable weight.[39] Corbett had written those lines after the First Moroccan Crisis, when Fisher's coercive Baltic strategy had settled great power diplomacy.

Corbett acknowledged doubts about the efficacy of economic warfare. Foreign Office directives were restricting its impact, to avoid problems with neutral powers, especially the United States. A blockade under the current modified Declaration of London rules would only be fully effective if the Entente controlled the Baltic. These historical and legal flourishes demonstrate that this was Corbett's paper, and not, as Marder argued, 'in substance, Fisher's work'.[40] While Fisher used the memorandum to secure War Council support, he had no intention of revealing the details. Even Corbett was deliberately left guessing, which explains his erroneous assumption that the Grand Fleet would enter the Baltic.[41] Fisher had no such intention. Furthermore, Corbett was not clear how Fisher would stop German minefields closing the Danish Narrows.[42] Even so, Fisher was delighted.[43] He had twenty-four minesweeping sloops under construction, and they would be ready when the rest of his 'Baltic Fleet' entered service.[44] He had no intention of discussing strategy, for the Baltic or anywhere else, with garrulous, gossiping politicians. Both he and Corbett always believed control of the Baltic was the key to an Entente victory, with or without the destruction of the German fleet.

Unable or unwilling to recover the Expeditionary Force, created to support maritime strategy and conduct joint operations, Churchill had no better option than purely naval, or, in Corbett's terms, 'minor' strategies. Without the designated amphibious strike force, such naval offensives involved excessive risk for limited reward. That Churchill pressed for purely naval attacks on the German North Sea island of Borkum and the Dardanelles, despite receiving eloquent maritime strategy papers signed by Fisher and Hankey, but written by Corbett, was a testament to his anxiety to do something, and his rejection of maritime strategy. Churchill blocked Fisher's minefield strategy in the North Sea, preferring an amphibious attack on the island of Borkum, which the soldiers had already rejected.[45] The division at the head of the Admiralty was obvious, and ruinous. Where great statesmen of the past, like Pitt the Elder, adopted the strategic advice of senior admirals, Churchill thought he knew better.

Fisher's timetable was too slow for Churchill, who remained optimistic the war would be over in 1915. Annoyed by the Fisher/Corbett memorandum, he refused to sanction Fisher's 'Baltic' battlecruisers, arguing: 'Long before they can be finished we shall have smashed up the German Navy <u>in harbour</u> with our monitors, or they will have fought their battle in blue water, or peace will have been signed.'[46] The difference between the two men was one of time, not target, Churchill observing, 'the Baltic is the only theatre in which naval action can appreciably shorten the war'.[47] Hearing an echo of his own ideas, Fisher left the energetic young minister to take the lead in Cabinet while he concentrated on strategy and shipbuilding. This was a serious mistake.

Churchill was not prepared to wait on economic and strategic pressure to win the war, nor the completion of Fisher's coastal fleet, designed to force the Germans to risk the High Seas Fleet in battle, or lose command of the Baltic. Nor was he prepared to fight the taciturn Kitchener and the Army General Staff for control of the BEF, lacking support from a passive War Cabinet paralysed by the enormity of its responsibilities. Without an amphibious Army, British strategy would remain limited, weak, and essentially operational. This suited the soldiers. Instead, Churchill anxiously sought an early naval offensive to bolster his leadership credentials.[48] He was angry, as Hankey told Corbett, that the Baltic paper had been produced. Fisher's concept would take too long for an ambitious young minister anxiously awaiting the siren call of battle and convinced the war would be won in a year. He pressed on with an improvised scheme for the Dardanelles, developed from a suggestion by Hankey.[49]

Hankey recognised that Fisher was using Corbett's mastery of strategy and history to deflect and disarm the ill-considered sketches that emerged from Churchill's fertile mind in the hours of darkness, the hours when Fisher slept. Churchill's December 2nd proposal for Borkum, the westernmost of the German Frisian Islands, was wildly optimistic and based on unwarranted assumptions.[50] While Fisher was able to block these naval attacks,[51] the task wasted time and energy better used waging war on Germany.

Fisher avoided an open break with Churchill, hoping to secure his escalating resource demands, backed by not infrequent threats of resignation. In exchange for withdrawing his resignation in late January, the War

Council authorised the three *Courageous*-class light battlecruisers, the largest units of the projected 'Baltic Fleet'. Only then would he agree to support Churchill's Dardanelles plan, although only to distract Winston from the even more dangerous Borkum concept.[52] It should be stressed that Fisher did not believe in the Dardanelles, confident it would be cancelled when the impossibility of the task became obvious. He had navigated those waters and knew the defences. Disappointed by Churchill's failure to grasp the Baltic concept, Fisher turned to Lloyd George, the Chancellor of the Exchequer, and the only other man of action in the Cabinet. Hoping he had found a contemporary Pitt the Elder, Fisher directed the Chancellor to read the Baltic passages of Corbett's *Seven Years' War* in mid-January.[53] In March Churchill belatedly backed Fisher's demands, reminding the War Council 'that the ultimate object of the Navy was to obtain access to the Baltic ... this operation was of great importance as Germany was, AND ALWAYS HAD BEEN, very nervous of an attack from the Baltic. For this purpose special vessels were required.' Corbett's words and Churchill's declaration of faith prompted Lloyd George to sanction the expenditure.[54]

Fisher's *Courageous* was 'imperatively demanded for the Baltic, where she can go through the international highway of the Sound owing to her shallow draught'. The Swedish side of the Sound was not mined, but it was shallow[55] and 'quite impossible for any of our present larger ships or indeed the larger vessels of the enemy'.[56] Combining the firepower to deal with older German battleships, the speed to outrun anything more powerful, and very long endurance, these ships could dominate the Baltic. Their primary design stipulation was a draught of water not greater than 22 feet, to pass the Swedish Sound.

Ultimately Fisher's new fleet of approximately six hundred ships and vessels included five battlecruisers, a larger pair codenamed 'Rhadamanthus' in case anyone doubted the judgement he wished to render on Germany,[57] thirty-seven monitors, two light cruisers, fifty submarines, minesweeping sloops, anti-submarine escorts and motorised landing craft. Eight fast merchant ships were purchased to mine Germany's North Sea approaches.[58] This 'Baltic Fleet' would be ready by early 1916.

In the interval, Fisher wanted to regain control of national strategy through a combined operation to recover the Belgian coast. Obsolete warships, the first new monitors and the BEF would secure the Channel, close German submarine and destroyer bases at Ostend and Zeebrugge, push the Germans back onto their own coast, and remove the BEF from the French line, reconnecting the elements of maritime strategy. The next step, from Flanders to Copenhagen, would follow logically, once Fisher's second fleet was complete. Corbett stressed combined operations as the proper use of British troops in the *Seven Years' War*, an argument reduced to doctrinal orthodoxy in *Some Principles*, backed by a highly relevant quote from Napoleon. After the destruction of the French invasion base at Flushing in 1809, not many miles from Ostend, Zeebrugge, or Antwerp, the emperor declared that 30,000 English troops embarked in transports would tie down 300,000 French troops, reducing France to a second-class power, emphasising the strategic power of an uncommitted amphibious force.[59] Corbett also cited G.F.R. Henderson's argument that Antwerp remained the focus for any future British military intervention on the Continent, especially if Germany violated Belgian neutrality. Henderson's 'great maxim [was] that the naval strength of the enemy should be the first objective of the forces of a maritime power, both by land and sea'.[60] The primary role of an expeditionary army should be to secure and enhance command of the sea.

Not that Fisher was looking for anything as banal as an operation of war. He expected to unsettle and confuse the German High Command, expecting them to make mistakes, as Corbett understood:

> it is for consideration whether, even if the suggested operation is not feasible, a menace of carrying it out – concerted with Russia – might not avail seriously to disturb German equilibrium and force her to desperate expedients, even hazarding a fleet action or to alienating entirely the Scandinavian Powers by drastic measures of precaution.[61]

Fisher anticipated that threatening the Danish Narrows would trigger a 'drastic' German response, the invasion of Denmark. This would enable a British army to 'aid' Denmark, securing the islands that held open the Baltic, while Sweden and Norway moved closer to the Entente, cutting trade with Germany. This was classic Fisher, manipulating the German High Command into acting as he desired, something he had achieved on several occasions.[62] The Russian army was merely a useful element in his deception plan, and he had no intention of using the Grand Fleet in the Baltic. Holding the Danish Narrows and deploying submarines and high-speed, long-endurance battlecruisers would suffice. The threat to the iron ore trade should bring the High Seas Fleet to battle. If the German fleet was sunk, the blockade could be extended into the Baltic, crippling the German war economy.[63] If not, battlecruisers and submarines would act as commerce destroyers. The ultimate object was a complete economic blockade of Germany.

Yet defeating Germany was not the sole object. Securing the empire was a global concern. On 10 February 1915, after a morning of meetings at the CID and the Admiralty, Corbett noted: 'Then to War Room with Richmond helping him with memo; on proposed combined operation in Medn'.[64] While Slade also provided useful input, Richmond noted that Corbett's wording 'got into some of the paragraphs'. Richmond's 'Remarks on Present Strategy' combined a powerful argument to rebalance strategy away from the Western Front, using a dynamic offensive campaign in the Mediterranean to defeat Turkey, linked to a wider concept of the war.[65] The basic concept was to exploit command of the sea, deploy 20,000 troops from Egypt with powerful naval support on the Ottoman coast between Palestine and Alexandretta, cutting the strategic rail link and pre-empting an attack on the Suez Canal. This would seriously damage the Turkish regime, and potentially raise Balkan allies. Comparing command of the sea to strategic railway links, Richmond argued that fighting on the Continent was playing the enemy at their own game, 'conforming like sheep to their strategic plan'. Ultimately the Mediterranean theatre could be used to knock Turkey out of the war and enhance Russian military might with British fleets and fortunes. This was a conscious reprise of the Napoleonic era. He thought the Baltic unsuited to this method. Richmond gave the paper to Fisher on 14 February when they met in an Admiralty corridor. Fisher and Hankey approved.[66] But with the Dardanelles plans already settled, such inspired ideas had little impact: Fisher and Hankey may have seen them as useful counters to Churchill's schemes.

From his position inside the planning process, Corbett recognised that, Fisher aside, the Navy's leadership, both civilian and professional, seriously overestimated Germany's willingness to use the High Seas Fleet for offensive operations, and thereby risk command of the Baltic.[67] Control of the Baltic, and the ability to pass dreadnoughts through the Kiel Canal, had been critical prerequisites for Germany going to war, as Fisher had anticipated in 1911.[68]

Having begun life as a joint Royal Navy/Greek Army plan, enthusiastically backed by Churchill and Lloyd George, the Dardanelles morphed into purely naval operation, in violation of everything Fisher and Corbett had written, and the objections of other experts. It gained traction because there was nothing else the Navy, acting alone, could do, and there were no troops for a combined operation. The battlecruiser action on the Dogger Bank on 23 January 1915 underlined Britain's mastery of the North Sea, and the value of signals intelligence, encouraging Churchill to believe that he could commit considerable resources to an offensive. He envisaged the Channel Fleet – pre-dreadnought battleships – forcing the Dardanelles, defeating Turkey and linking up with Russia. Fisher tolerated this folly to distract Churchill from his absurd plan to attack Borkum, and because it would not interfere with the Baltic. While Fisher did not disapprove of a combined operation using Greek or British troops, he condemned any thought of a 'futile bombardment'. Vice Admiral Sir Henry Jackson's astute memorandum of 15 January 1915 dissected Churchill's folly.[69] Having examined the possibility while steaming up the Dardanelles in 1900, Fisher did not believe a fleet could pass the Narrows without an army in support. If the Turkish batteries were competently manned, and the minefields remained intact, the fleet would be defeated.[70] As Corbett observed:

> when the enterprise began to take on the aspect of a serious attempt to force the Straits, and reduce Constantinople, without military co-operation, he [Fisher] began to contemplate it each day with graver apprehension. . . . So much, indeed, would have to be staked for success, that it would gravely prejudice, and even render impossible, the plans he was elaborating to secure a perfect control of Home Waters and the Baltic.[71]

Fisher made his views clear on 25 January 1915, sending Churchill another powerful memorandum crafted by Corbett, with input from Hankey. Risking heavy ships in purely naval bombardments was playing into the hands of the Germans:

> The pressure of sea power to-day is probably not less but greater and more rapid in action than in the past; but it is still a slow process and requires great patience. In time it will almost certainly compel the enemy to seek a decision at sea, particularly when he begins to realise that his offensive on land is broken.

[W]e ought to aim at a complete closure of the North Sea, and the declaration of a blockade....

The sole justification for coastal bombardments and attacks by the fleet on fortified places, such as the contemplated prolonged bombardment of the Dardanelles forts by our Fleet, is to force the decision at sea, and so far and no further can they be justified....

It has been said that the first function of the British Army [a paraphrase of G.F.R. Henderson] is to assist the fleet in obtaining command of the sea. This might be accomplished by military co-operation with the navy in such operations as the attack of Zeebrugge, or the forcing of the Dardanelles, which might bring out the German and Turkish fleets respectively. Apparently, however, this is not to be. The English Army is apparently to continue to provide a small sector of the allied front in France, where it is no more help to the navy than if it were at Timbuctoo....

Being already in possession of all that a powerful fleet can give a country, we should continue quietly to enjoy the advantages without dissipating our strength in operations that cannot improve the position.[72]

This was not a negative or passive document, as Churchill later claimed. It established a dynamic, positive maritime strategic concept, and demanded the government back it by reconnecting the Navy and Army. Fisher and Corbett made the Baltic operation the central pillar of a strategy to secure sea control, defeat Germany by economic pressure, without the human cost of a mass army, while securing the empire beyond Europe. Little wonder they derided Churchill's grandiose vision of an obsolescent fleet single-handedly defeating Turkey, creating a Balkan alliance and driving on to Vienna. This option was unnecessarily risky because it ignored the critical need to reconnect the increasingly alienated elements of national power into a coherent national strategy.

There are few more important statements of Fisher's strategic concept, or of Corbett's direct influence on him than the phrase 'our position at sea gives us all we want', which first appeared in Corbett's diary on 13 August 1914.[73] Only Fisher's strategic concept, threatening the entrance to the Baltic, could provoke a German invasion of Jutland and draw out the High Seas Fleet, enabling Britain to complete the economic blockade. It depended on redeploying the British Army in an amphibious role, something Corbett and

Fisher considered axiomatic. Corbett's mature teaching stressed the synergy of naval and military resources as the core of a maritime strategy, and that this was Britain's only option. Fisher was not interested in action for its own sake and saw no reason to rush. His critique of Churchill's relentless search for a purely naval offensive used Corbett's arguments to shape a policy recommendation from the Crown's senior naval advisor. Although the paper was drafted by Corbett, the line about Timbuctoo was pure Fisher.

On 28 January Fisher walked out of the War Council intending to resign. His Baltic plans had been kept off the agenda. He was persuaded to return by Kitchener. Characteristically, Asquith hushed up the incident, and did not mention the Baltic – lest the demand for an expeditionary army split the Cabinet and alienate Kitchener. Asquith and Churchill had prevented the circulation of Fisher's paper to the other members of the War Council.[74] That self-serving sleight of hand overturned three centuries of British experience to sustain the cohesion of a failing Cabinet. It placed Britain on the slippery slope that led to conscription, the Somme, Passchendaele and economic catastrophe.

Asquith's fudge made the Dardanelles, by default, Britain's only offensive option. In the short term Fisher could do little, his new ships were not ready, while the weather in the English Channel, the North Sea and the Kattegat was adverse. As the global war was effectively over, Fisher needed an amphibious army for an offensive maritime strategy in Europe, but the BEF was committed to France, tied to a continental campaign by War Office ambition and alliance politics. It seemed impossible to extract the Army without rupturing the French alliance. Rather than trying to rein in Kitchener and the continentally minded General Staff by adopting the Baltic plan, which he admitted was 'the operation', Churchill deluded his ministerial colleagues with the promise of major diplomatic, strategic and economic gains when Turkey collapsed. This cornucopia was to be secured by a purely naval assault that his professional advisors did not support. He eased concerns by claiming the fleet could withdraw if the initial attack did not succeed. Churchill displayed no interest in preparing for the failure that his advisors anticipated, let alone providing the fleet with adequate supplies of the high-explosive shells needed to demolish forts. Elsewhere the 'steady pressure' of sea power brought Italy into the Entente. With a long, exposed coastline, and reliant on imported coal and oil, Italy could not fight Britain. Balkan neutrals were less impressed.[75]

Nor was Fisher the only strategist to consult Corbett. As the naval attack began, Hankey belatedly requested a paper on Admiral Sir John Duckworth's passage of the Dardanelles in 1807, the obvious analogue for Churchill's offensive. Duckworth's fleet had passed the Dardanelles, but failed to impress the Turkish government.[76] Corbett and Hankey agreed that a hasty, half-baked naval attack would fail, for the same reasons. Corbett's logical analysis ensured readers grasped the key issues. In both cases, aiding Russia had been the political object, and wise men had objected to leaving British troops in Egypt when the fleet went to the Dardanelles. Duckworth managed to pass the batteries, but could not hold his station without troops. His retreat dealt 'a severe blow to our prestige in the Near East', and 'our relations with Russia were poisoned', leading the Tsar to sign a separate peace with Napoleon. By contrast, a combined operation at Copenhagen a few months later had 'entirely defeated and outwitted Napoleon'. Not only was the message clear, but references to the Baltic and the danger of Russia making a separate peace were deliberate.[77]

This paper persuaded Henry Jackson, leading the CID sub-committee on overseas attacks, that a naval attack was not feasible. Hankey and Jackson then used it to press a reluctant Kitchener to release two divisions, the 29th and the Anzacs.[78] By contrast, a delusional Churchill persisted in viewing the Dardanelles as a short-term naval commitment. On 3 March he told the War Council that the Baltic was still 'our proper line of strategy', to be attempted 'later on when our new monitors were completed'.[79] A month later Fisher, equally anxious to secure military cooperation at the Dardanelles, to reduce the risk to the fleet, requested Corbett write on the analogous operation at Nanshan during the Russo-Japanese War, to inform Kitchener, whom he described as 'the best of the bunch [on the War Council] but not brilliant and rather slow on the uptake'.[80] Although Corbett considered the Dardanelles/Gallipoli a distraction from the primary theatre, Flanders and the Baltic, he supported the method, and the strategic ambition, primarily for doctrinal purposes. As a result, his account of the fiasco would be more positive than most modern assessments.

The working relationship between Churchill and Fisher collapsed because Churchill's naval offensive at the Dardanelles violated the principles of maritime strategy which, as Corbett had demonstrated, depended on effective combined operations. This, rather than mania, hysteria, senility or even a personality clash, caused the breakdown. The wisdom of Fisher and Corbett's position was confirmed on 18 March, when the naval attack stalled. Subsequent amphibious operations, too late and inadequate in scale, were no more successful, and far more costly. Corbett and Fisher had urged using a large military force alongside the initial naval attack, the 'combined strategy' both men consistently advocated. Ultimately the entire enterprise failed because it had been woefully under-resourced from the start, in men and munitions.

Having failed to secure control of national strategy, Fisher was left with no option other than resigning. Not only had Churchill failed to fight for maritime strategy in the War Council, but he persuaded his colleagues to approve a deeply flawed naval operation that Fisher, the senior naval advisor, opposed. By April 1915 Churchill was systematically wrecking Fisher's Baltic strategy to reinforce failure at Gallipoli, stripping away key assets. The final straw came when two E-class submarines, which Fisher intended to use against German iron ore shipping in the Baltic, were deployed to the Dardanelles. He resigned and refused to return to office unless Churchill was removed from the higher direction of the war and the War Council restored maritime strategy. Alongside this fight for the Corbettian principles of British strategy, Fisher, and other senior officers, were profoundly alarmed by the First Lord's unconstitutional assumption of executive authority. Fisher blew up the system to get rid of Churchill, but overplayed a strong hand in a desperate attempt to secure control of the Admiralty and shift national strategy back to a maritime focus.[81] He wanted to join the Cabinet and direct national strategy. Old enemies like Beresford and Custance helped secure his defeat. He remained close to: 'my beloved Corbett ... the most beautiful writer I know'.[82]

It should not be thought that May 1915 ended Fisher's potential to shift the balance of British strategy. Lloyd George had not forgotten the lure of the Baltic, and Balfour, who replaced Churchill at the Admiralty, was a maritime strategist, having read and understood Corbett's work. Balfour and Hankey decided against the Baltic because they were unable to see beyond the simple, kinetic version that overlay the real purpose. As late as 8 March 1916 Fisher had a chance to win the argument at a special session of the War Committee, courtesy of Lloyd George, who was hoping to rein in the Army, and a resurgent Churchill. Balfour's interrogation undermined Fisher's case, largely it appears to discredit Churchill, and Lloyd George gave way.[83]

The following year, the *First Report of the Dardanelles Commission* provided a ringing endorsement of Corbett's 'fundamental principle of naval strategy that the attack of ships on forts, without military aid, was rarely productive of satisfactory results'.[84] Clearly the authority of *Some Principles* was recognised beyond the naval classroom, even if the report mistakenly referred to maritime strategy as naval strategy. Papers Corbett wrote for Fisher and Hankey were cited throughout the report, the intellectual core of a stinging indictment of the failings of war government and Admiralty direction. However, all mention of Fisher's Baltic plans was excised from the report, for reasons of wartime security as it remained a serious option, leaving his strategic thinking, and his objection to the extension of naval commitment at the Dardanelles, looking inconsistent and incoherent. While this omission was rectified in Corbett's Official History, Churchill's panegyrists and army historians have consistently failed to acknowledge the critical battle in 1915 concerned the higher direction of the war, not personalities. The Baltic concept was a serious alternative to the continental commitment, based on long experience and sound analysis. The enduring anxiety of continental apologists, then and now, to dismiss a strategy based on completing the economic encirclement of Germany, is illogical, but predictable. Fisher's strategy exploited British strength: Henry Wilson's alternative destroyed lives and livelihoods for no appreciable benefit.

While Corbett recognised the Dardanelles was a poor example of strategic thinking and operational execution, the basic concept was sound, and above all consistent with British strategic practice, unlike the concurrent, costly mass army operations in France. Britain did not go to war to save France in 1914: it went to war to prevent a potential continental hegemon from securing control of the Low Countries, from which it could threaten Britain's vital maritime communications. This time-honoured task should have been the strategic priority in August 1914: it became Fisher's first concern on returning to office in October. His demand for a British combined operation was blocked by British generals and French statesmen who preferred simple battles to the more elegant, incisive ideas of Britain's leading strategist, and the dynamic First Sea Lord who relied on his work.

The Dardanelles cost Churchill his post, destroyed Fisher's decision to blow up the Admiralty and fight for a maritime strategy. The departure of Fisher and Churchill left no alternative to the misery of the Western Front.

Working in tandem to implement a maritime strategy, Fisher and Churchill might have changed the course of war. When they left the stage the politicians accepted the General Staff assertion that theirs was the 'decisive theatre' and served up the necessary mass conscript army.

When assessing Corbett's role in the most dynamic phase of British wartime strategy, it is important to acknowledge that both Churchill and Fisher used his doctrine to describe their strategy and defend themselves against critics. So did their replacements, Arthur Balfour and Admiral Sir Henry Jackson, and so did the Dardanelles Commission. Everyone who mattered knew that Corbett had developed a coherent British strategic doctrine from historical evidence, processed through the medium of Clausewitzian theory. There was no alternative, as Corbett's critics soon discovered when they tried to denigrate his work. He maintained his opposition to the 'decisive' theatre obsessions of the General Staff, writing his advocacy of British limited maritime strategy, focused on completing the economic blockade in the Baltic, into the DNA of the Official History. He would spend the rest of war looking for a way out of the 'German way', along with a few like-minded men.

In May 1916 Hankey consulted him:

> to see if nothing could be done to break down rigid General Staff ideas of concentration in Main Theatre – he agreed concentration no good unless chances of getting sufficing preponderance for a decision – but he said they would not listen & even resented ministers asking how they were going to get on in France.[85]

This terrifying conversation reflected Hankey's experience as Secretary to a War Council whose civilian leadership had long since capitulated to the soldiers.[86] The primacy of civilian direction of war, a core theme in Corbett's work, not to mention that of Clausewitz, had been forgotten. In Britain the damage was far greater than in Imperial Germany, because the tradition had been far more important. Politicians who had not considered their responsibilities in the event of war, tamely passed that role to soldiers who only thought about one kind of war, one that would fulfil their long-held ambition to create a mass conscript army. Only Fisher had the strategic understanding to challenge the soldiers, who consistently outnumbered the sailors at the War Council. Corbett made it his mission to ensure strategy returned to pre-war maritime norms, contesting the dominant position of bloody sacrifice on the Western Front in the national memory. In the process he coined a famous phrase. Ever on the lookout for signs of hope, he found some encouragement in the minutes of an Anglo-French confer-ence in Paris in the summer of 1917, observing; 'our old British way of waging war seemed to be coming up again and clashing with continental ideas'.[87] The soldiers refused to reconsider, and the politicians lacked the courage to restrain them. The belated post-war revolt against the carnage of the Western Front was no more than a return to deep-rooted British cultural norms. On this, and so much else, Corbett and T.E. Lawrence were in complete accord. There was a 'British way', the one that Corbett was working into his book.

The central issue was the reassertion of civilian direction. When the Dardanelles Commission created an opportunity to make that case in public, Hankey made an urgent appeal to Corbett. With Asquith about to give evidence before the commission, Hankey needed to 'coach' him on the higher conduct of the war, dealing with the responsibilities of the War Council, the Cabinet, and the departments of state. That Asquith, of all people, still needed help explaining wartime leadership in late 1916 is compelling evidence of the absence of authority at the head of government. While Hankey had explained the constitutional position of the War Council, he had not dealt with the Cabinet, or the departments of state. He needed a 'short discourse' on the subject to append to Asquith's statement, from 'the greatest living authority on this question. ... I know of no-one who has given as much consideration to what is, after all, a very vital matter in the direction of a war. I quite well remember references to the matter in some of your works.' While Hankey said there was no hurry, Corbett understood that to mean he had two or three weeks.[88]

The two men had no chance to meet before Corbett began work on 30 September, alongside a memorial lecture for John Laughton.[89] Research at the Public Record Office and the Athenaeum drew blanks, but he finished the paper on 8 October, before turning to his annual accounts. Matter-of-fact diary entries reflected the pedestrian nature of the work for an expert with a legal background. He exploited the 1904 essay 'Queen Anne's War Council' and sections of the *Seven Years' War*, which Hankey had referenced.

On 11 October Hankey described the memo as 'quite priceless & just what was wanted by the PM', a fine compliment that was followed by another request, for a paper on 'practice as to Armistice preceding peace'. The second paper was finished the following day.[90] It came to hand in late 1918.

Corbett's confidential memo was printed for the Cabinet, and widely circulated. There is a copy among Churchill's papers.[91] The five-page document, a model of clarity, traced the evolution of British practice on key issues: how far Cabinets had directed past wars; how far they had delegated that responsibility, and how far ministers were responsible for decisions taken by departments, or higher councils, when the Cabinet had not been formally consulted. This was especially important in the case of the decision to send troops to Gallipoli, which had been taken without a War Council. Even Hankey remained uncertain who had been involved. Opening with an account of practice in the reign of Queen Anne, Corbett demonstrated how a Secret Committee, including the secretaries of state, the commander-in-chief of the Army and the lords of the Admiralty, had been assembled to prevent leaks. In Walpole's era the Cabinet had taken responsibility, although Pitt the Elder directed the Seven Years' War with the service chiefs, Lord Anson and Lord Ligonier. However, the Cabinet had blocked his plan for a pre-emptive attack on Spain. The badly conducted American War provided no precedent, or any evidence of Cabinet-level decision-making. The modern Cabinet had emerged with Pitt the Younger, establishing joint responsibility. In practice, Pitt, Dundas, Grenville and Lord Spencer had run the Revolutionary War – a conclusion derived from the *Spencer Papers*. The four men met before full Cabinets, settled operational matters, and then reported to their colleagues. He demonstrated that 'diplomacy or diplomatic deflection of war plans', a classic Corbett phrase, had been settled in Cabinet.

Recognising the limits of the evidentiary base, Corbett left room for future enquiries, but settled the principles:

1. In periods of tension before war, control tended to rest with the Cabinet.
2. Important wartime operations were usually submitted to the Cabinet for approval after they had been agreed by key ministers. Those ministers had a wide discretion, and the operation was rarely discussed again at Cabinet, unless the expertise of other ministers was required.
3. While the key issues were naval or military such meetings were not necessary – but major changes of plan, or of relations with allies, did require a Cabinet.

4. Individual ministers could not disclaim responsibility because the issue had not been presented to Cabinet, as they had a theoretical right to call for a meeting.

5. In each war the government invariably ended up placing the direction of the war in the hands of as few men as possible. After 1790 the prime minister represented the sovereign as the chief executive at such meetings.

6. The connection between the current War Council and the Cabinet was as hard to define as any previous secret committee, but it was only the latest example of a recurrent practice. The prime minister decided if he needed to call a Cabinet, or some form of secret committee, and precedent suggests that the other ministers were responsible for the outcome. Corbett closed with a discussion of practice in the Crimean War, the last major conflict, drawn from a parliamentary enquiry. Prime Minister Lord Aberdeen, following the practice of Pitt and Liverpool, had not thought it necessary to summon a Cabinet through the critical period after they had agreed to invade the Crimea, despite several changes of plan.

In the event Asquith was not questioned on the issue. However, in June he had used notes produced by Corbett to meet the demand for a public enquiry into the Dardanelles campaign, securing a major victory in the House of Commons on 20 July 1916, an occasion Corbett watched from the Strangers' Gallery.[92] This success prompted Asquith to honour an old promise: the New Year Honours List of 1917 contained a long overdue knighthood.

Corbett had also produced critical papers for the Admiralty in 1916, notably the appreciation published with the heavily censored edition of Jellicoe's Jutland dispatches on 6 July. Admiral Brownrigg, the Admiralty Censor, requested he undertake the task on 27 June, working at the Admiralty from the official dispatches, and in close consultation with Jellicoe and Henry Jackson. He returned home late, 'very tired after an interesting and strenuous day'. The following day Beatty arrived to join the discussion at the Admiralty, which settled on the name of the battle. Corbett rejected a request from the *New York Times* for an analysis of the action.[93]

While Corbett's Jutland paper was published anonymously, the underlying strategic analysis, which linked the action with other battles, notably Trafalgar, indicated the authorship to more discerning readers.[94] On

9 October Reginald Custance used the Jutland paper to re-launch his old attack on Corbett's tendency to minimise the importance of battle in a letter to *The Times*. If this was annoying then the rehearsal of the issue by George Clarke, now Lord Sydenham, in the House of Lords at the end of November made it a matter of public interest. It was all the more annoying as Corbett had lunched with Sydenham six weeks before. Hankey advised him to reply, pointing out that in 1906, as Secretary of the CID, Sydenham had signed off on the 'Green Pamphlet' he now chose to criticise. The real significance of these random attacks, including one from Churchill, was that they acknowledged the strategy of the war at sea followed Corbett's ideas, a reality emphasised by First Lord Arthur Balfour.[95]

Fisher never lost his belief that a Baltic operation, feint or stroke, was the only way that British sea power could defeat Germany, to avoid military mobilisation for total war, a concept closely linked to Corbett's *Seven Years' War*, which in turn had been inspired by Admiralty planning in 1905–7.[96] Britain's primary weapon was economic, with a Baltic blockade completing the process. Fisher's thinking continued to develop after he left office for the second time in May 1915, adding a note on the 'New Danish Defence from Roeskilde to Kiöge, like the lines of Torres Vedras' to his chart.[97] The Baltic remained unfinished business: it was the reason why he wanted to return to office, and why he printed Corbett's Baltic memorandum in his memoirs. Nor was it forgotten within the Admiralty, prompting Jellicoe's plan of May 1916, or a more direct intervention in 1917, to support the faltering Russian government. One problem remained: there was no Army to support the operation; the soldiers were unwilling and, while the government had the authority to compel them, it lacked the courage to act.

Corbett shared Fisher's Baltic vision and wove it into the fabric of *Naval Operations* at every opportunity. He used the August 1915 incident near Copenhagen, when German destroyers entered Danish territorial waters and opened fire on the stranded British submarine E13 and Danish warships, killing sailors from both nations, to highlight German anxieties about the command of the Baltic, and willingness to violate international law.[98] Corbett held up the Baltic as a warning, so future generations might recognise how the best-laid plans could be deflected into futile sideshows by political interference, how service rivalries could wreck national strategy, and how men of genius, acting in tandem, could cancel one another out. The failure to threaten Germany's grip on the Baltic was, in Corbett's judgement, the central tragedy of the war; and Fisher the ultimate British strategist.

Fisher published Corbett's 'weighty memorandum' in 1919, as a criticism of Churchill's strategic judgement, a critique Corbett emphasised in volume II of the Official History. Churchill hit back in 1923, when both Fisher and Corbett were dead. His claims were unconvincing; a later attempt to deflect criticism onto the dead admiral in *Great Contemporaries* grossly misrepresented Fisher's thinking and ignored Corbett's rationale. Ironically, Churchill took the lesson to heart. In 1939 he dreamt of reprising a bastardised, purely naval version of Fisher's elegant scheme as 'Operation Catherine'. This time wiser men prevailed.[99]

Ultimately the Fisher/Corbett concept was never attempted. The War Office would not consider it, and the Cabinet would not challenge Kitchener or the General Staff. Instead, the politicians had compromised on Churchill's Dardanelles delusion, wasting the amphibious weapon in a secondary theatre. In late 1916 Jellicoe, now First Sea Lord, solicited a memo on naval attacks on fleets in defended harbours without military support.[100] The qualification only emphasised the incoherence of national strategy.

The 'Cabinet Council' paper survived the change of leadership. In mid-November 1917, Philip Kerr, Lloyd George's Private Secretary, 'phoned Corbett to tell him the prime minister wanted the memo compiled for Asquith on the Cabinet and conduct of war, for a speech on the following Monday'.[101] How far this paper empowered Lloyd George to challenge military control of the war is unknown, but it is unlikely so canny a lawyer would have missed the message. While little changed on the Western Front, Lloyd George had developed some strategic insight. When Jerusalem was taken he linked the success to the Battle of Plassey and the fall of Quebec, the central events of Corbett's *Seven Years' War*, the book Fisher had urged him to read in 1915. In a carefully contrived assault on the continental view of the war, the prime minister expressed the hope that this event would 'hold a more conspicuous place in the minds and in the memories of our people than many events which loom much larger for the moment'.[102]

As the war ground on into a fifth year Corbett – exhausted and alarmed by a combination of over-work, aerial bombardment, the German 'Michael' Offensive and domestic stresses – sensed his career had been in vain. The War Council, prompted by the Army, had ignored his argument that the most effective way of waging war involved the combined efforts of both services to secure the strategic and policy goals established by political direction. The past four years had demonstrated the consequences of leaving war to generals who rejected any alternative to forms of power Britain did not possess in 1914, a 'German' army, and a 'German' strategy, tools created to conquer Europe, not protect a global maritime empire. Such choices carry heavy penalties. By 1918 he could only hope his message might make a difference the next time. By June he was close to despair, sharing his innermost thoughts with Fisher. His letter should be read by every student of war, and every author who ever thought their work might make a difference. It seemed the war would go on for ever:

> I wept when I knew our whole Expeditionary Force was going to France, and felt what it would mean, and how Pitt would turn in his grave. Perhaps as Germany had got the initiative so completely, it could not be helped; but there is the cause of tears all the same. When the time came to strike amphibiously for a decision, we had nothing to strike with. The first chance, as you saw, was at the Dardanelles, and once the decision was obtained there we could have passed to the final one in the Baltic. Oh these blessed Germanised soldiers with their 'decisive theatre'. . . .
>
> It is the most bigoted 'soldier's war we have ever fought, and this at the end of all our experience. Why didn't I devote my life to writing comic opera, or collecting beetles? I might just as well. But now my fate is to tell the stupid story of the war as it is; not, alas, as it might have been. I had hoped when you came back, but already the soldiers had entangled us too far even for you to drag us out. We deserve each other's pity.[103]

Corbett and Fisher believed their country had been shattered by a war that might have been prevented, or waged with more intelligence, an intelligence informed by the past practice Corbett had used to shape current doctrine. It seemed their work had been in vain – it had not been possible to turn experience and insight into policy and action. Britain, it seemed, had thrown away a million lives, blasted many more and wrecked the most successful economy in history, opening a veritable Pandora's box of misery stretching from the influenza pandemic to chaos and genocide. Yet attempts to rationalise the disaster persist, desperate attempts to equate cost with consequence.

There was a golden opportunity to make the case outside the Official History project. Fisher died on 10 July 1920, and Corbett attended the state funeral. Having settled the treatment of Fisher's resignation in discussions with George Lambert MP, one-time Admiralty Civil Lord and Fisher's literary executor, Corbett was invited to write the official life. He was obliged to decline, in view of the ongoing Official History.[104] A study of Fisher written by the man who helped shape his strategic thinking, and his wartime policy, would have transformed our understanding of the man and his age, shattering the reputations of weak-willed statesmen and narrow-minded generals, while emphasising Fisher's grasp of the higher direction of war and peace, rather than the prosaic focus on naval service and technology that Admiral Bacon eventually provided. Given Fisher's admiration of Corbett's *Seven Years' War* book, it is likely the link with Lord Anson might have featured, but the Baltic would have provided the major theme.

CHAPTER 17

Propaganda, Peace and the Liberal Empire

Alongside his role in war planning, shaping Fisher's alternative grand strategy and directing the Official History project, Corbett's mastery of language, law and logic became part of the national response to more profound challenges, German 'Navalism' propaganda and the looming menace of an American peace. His approach to these tasks was consistent with his core concerns, the evolution of the empire into a liberal seapower commonwealth, the maintenance of the legal bases of naval power, and the recovery of national strategy from continental delusions. His work in this field should be read as part of a synthesis that linked the Official History to a revised edition of *Some Principles* and the strategy for an evolving empire.

At the core of Corbett's agenda lay maritime economic warfare, Britain's right arm and the core of imperial strategy. In 1911 his argument for maritime economic warfare appeared as national doctrine, reworking the combative 'Capture of Private Property' into a more benign form. This strategy depended on the: 'right to forbid, if we can, the passage of both public and private property upon the sea'. It would be enforced by a distant or 'strategical blockade of the great trade routes' since the close blockade, the only system considered in the 1856 Declaration of Paris, had been rendered obsolete by modern technology. Any attempt to impose a close blockade would exhaust the fleet. To be useful at the strategic level, command of the sea must translate into the ability to 'exert pressure on the citizens and their collective life' because: 'it is commerce and finance which now more than ever control or check the foreign policy of nations'. The possibility of their destruction would tend to reduce the risk of war. This, Corbett argued, was the sea power deterrent.[1] Without the legal right and naval strength to conduct effective maritime economic warfare against a state like Imperial Germany, under modern conditions, Britain would cease to be a great power. When these critical constituents of national strategy were threatened by

German propaganda and American armed diplomacy, Corbett provided the response. His powerful, persuasive papers were critical to the preservation of British global power for another quarter-century.

Corbett knew that Britain had no interest in waging war in 1914, and no need for more empire, recognising that however the war ended the imperial edifice, from Ireland to India, must continue to evolve, the more so to reflect the strains and stresses of war. That process would require the security of a maritime strategy. Yet a post-war British Empire that dominated the world ocean, as it must, having demonstrated the unprecedented capacity to raise mass armies, would inevitably provoke fear and hostility, much like the greatly expanded British Empire after the Seven Years' War, which had provoked a revolution, and foreign intervention.[2]

In 1914 Germany willingly sacrificed the moral high ground, violating the 1839 Treaty of London, the foundation stone of modern European diplomacy, in a vain attempt to win the war quickly. Leading German historians rallied to the cause, the more liberal among them hoping Britain would stand aside, the rest happily anticipating the destruction of 'Perfidious Albion'. As the short-war delusion faded, these men became propagandists, penning futile, violent outpourings of Anglophobic rage. Much of the argument could be traced back to Treitschke and his fellow ideologues, melded with older French critiques of the new Carthage, using seapower and foolish continental allies to deny Germany its rightful claim to a place in the sun.[3] German propaganda also reflected deep-rooted anxieties about the rising domestic threat of socialism, reform and the prospect of German 'decline'. German academics had long prostituted their profession to the state, Friedrich Meinecke, Eduard Meyer and others updating 'delenda est Carthago'.[4] The war unleashed decades-old cultural anxieties among those who saw Britain as the only obstacle to world power, inculcating a visceral hatred into the national consciousness.[5] By 1914 the message was so engrained that no-one in Berlin thought it might be wise to exercise restraint. Whatever they might have thought about British sea power, most neutrals understood that Germany was seeking a Universal Monarchy, a new Roman Empire, under a northern Eagle. If the new Carthage went under, who could stop Germany?

Shortly after the war began, Lloyd George, learning that Germany had a state propaganda bureau, persuaded Asquith that Britain had to counter German attacks and influence neutral opinion. The Cabinet agreed on 31 August, creating a new bureau under Charles Masterman, a junior Cabinet minister and former Coefficient who had had recently lost his seat at a by-election.[6] While Asquith's selection was predictably expedient it proved fortunate. As literary editor of the Liberal *Daily News*, Masterman knew the London cultural scene, assembling the leading professional authors at his headquarters, Wellington House, 8 Buckingham Gate, on 2 September. His twenty-five-strong list represented the past and present of English talent, men of middling or advanced years, too old to serve and, perhaps, too comfortable to challenge the establishment. Popular literature would wage war, with Arthur Conan Doyle, Arnold Bennett, John Masefield, Ford Maddox Ford, G.K. Chesterton, Owen Seaman, Henry Newbolt, John Galsworthy, Thomas Hardy, Rudyard Kipling, Gilbert Parker, G.M. Trevelyan and H.G. Wells in the vanguard. Others wrote to pledge their support. Masterman had mobilised the liberal intelligentsia to combat German militarism; there were no pacifists and, Wells aside, no socialists.[7] He also secured the support of leading newspapers.[8] Corbett, who had known Masterman for many years and had many friends at the meeting, was already busy writing the war.

Closely linked to the Foreign Office and conveniently located for Whitehall and Parliament, Wellington House had previously housed the National Insurance Commission, where Masterman had worked. It was absorbed into the Ministry of Information in February 1918.[9] The staff included intellectual heavyweight Arnold Toynbee, who referred to it as 'the Mendacity Bureau'. After five months working on American material, Toynbee moved to the Armenian question and German atrocities, before joining the Political Intelligence Department in 1917.[10]

Wellington House published more than a thousand pamphlets, subsidised and distributed suitably patriotic publications, and produced John Buchan's monthly *Nelson's History of the War*, providing a British view for audiences domestic and foreign. The long arm of the British state reached out through many interconnected organisations: millions of propaganda prints were exported on the state-subsidised steamship lines.[11]

While much British output provided simple messages about German atrocities and inequities, or vindicated Allied actions, some achieved lasting significance. These included Lord Bryce's *Report on Alleged German Outrages* published in early 1915, documenting war crimes against Belgian civilians, the text enhanced by Dutch artist Louis Raemaekers' powerful, emotive images. Like many prominent Liberals, Bryce's pre-war German sympathies had turned to dust as he read the evidence. If recent scholarship has questioned both the assumptions of the report and some of the evidence, the raw, emotive power of disenchanted liberalism was all too obvious.[12]

Corbett did not share Bryce's distress, having long viewed Imperial Germany as a menace. Dismissing criticism of the Royal Navy in 1901 as 'a mere rant for their inexpressible jealousy', he characterised an entire nation as savage, suspicious and envious.[13] The German naval challenge had shaped his 1907 essay on maritime belligerent rights.[14] The subject resurfaced early in 1915, in a new, more pressing form.

As the British blockade took effect, Germany attacked the legal basis of sea power, targeting influential American business groups with links to the president, notably the Chicago meat packers and Southern cotton growers, excluded from German markets by British economic warfare.[15] Anxious to create a counter-narrative to Entente accounts of rampant militarism, Belgian atrocities and indiscriminate mine-laying, the Germans argued that 'Navalism' was the moral equivalent of 'Militarism', and a greater threat to world peace. The message primarily targeted German and Irish Americans, through their political representatives and newspapers. Grey recognised the hand of the German Foreign Office in the new offensive.[16]

German propagandists argued they were fighting a thalassocratic tyrant to obtain 'freedom of the seas' for the benefit of all mankind. Neither the rhetoric nor the ideas were new, or German. Representing Britain as a sea tyrant, a new Carthage, had bolstered the fragile self-regard of the French *ancien régime*, republic and empire – militarised states that aspired to be the new Rome. France, Russia and the United States had each espoused 'freedom of the seas' as they felt the hard hand of blockade. Germany's only original contribution to an old argument was the label. Ironically, 'Navalism' had been coined by radical left-wing activist Karl Liebknecht in a 1907 attack on the Tirpitz Plan that saw him jailed for eighteen months.[17] When it reached audiences across the Atlantic 'Navalism' would empower an Anglophobe American president and his naval leadership.

The only neutral great power would be the critical market for wartime propaganda, and the focus of Wellington House's most important section. Sir Gilbert Parker MP, Canadian-born novelist, politician and imperialist with a wealthy American wife, used American connections to recruit 13,000 influential individuals to help distribute British material.[18] Parker moved to New York when the United States entered the war.[19]

British counter-propaganda for America audiences was dominated by policy summaries provided by leading statesmen, Balfour, Grey, Sir Edward Carson, fellow Coefficient Lord Robert Cecil and others, with lively naval texts from Sir William Dixon, Parker, Robert Donald and Archibald Hurd; War Course lecturer Alexander Pearce Higgins addressed the legal issues of the U-boat war.[20] Summoned to counter the impact of 'Navalism' propaganda in America, Corbett realised his task had been eased by the incoherence and violence of the argument. He responded by combining the philosophy of seapower, international law, and the evolution of the British Empire into a self-governing free trade commonwealth, linked by mutual dependence on legally restrained sea control, into a compelling alternative to German continental hegemony. He contrasted liberal, progressive Britain with an aggressive militaristic Germany that posed a fundamental threat to the international order. The target shifted to Woodrow Wilson's 'freedom of the seas' mantra, which became the primary threat to Britain's long-term interests in 1916. Within those texts he wove another message with another audience. The wartime revival of Conservative interest in imperial federation and tariff barriers – policies that would alienate America and prompt fresh challenges to British sea control – along with the possibility that the war might add more territory to the empire, made it a pressing issue. Corbett's last two essays specifically targeted America, where the 'violent anti-British propaganda' of William Randolph Hearst's press empire threatened Britain's war effort and long-term interests. None of Corbett's propaganda essays were translated for audiences beyond the Anglosphere.[21]

The obvious indication of propaganda impact was provided by extensive re-publication and citation in America. In March 1915 Masterman reported that Bryce's pamphlet *Britain's Attitude to the United States* was 'doing an enormous lot of good', having appeared in the *New York Times*. Masterman wanted more texts that appealed to influential American newspapers.[22] In April 1915 Parker approached Corbett, 'a writer of eminence',[23] to counter 'Navalism'.

> They say that the war is a war for the open seas and against the tyranny of Great Britain's naval power and the evils of Navalism. . . . We were anxious that some distinguished naval authority should show that the history of the British navy had been one of the protection of small

nations, had never been one of offence or aggression, that we had policed the seas for the world, that the United States had profited by the honest policing of Great Britain, and that there was no need to fear British Navalism in the light of its past record, while there is every reason to fear German Militarism with its past record. . . . It is essential that the thing should be done at once, and the need is great.[24]

Parker invited Corbett to reinvent the Royal Navy as a morally acceptable global police force, upholding a benign *Pax Britannica*. Corbett hurried back to town from a brief holiday at Stopham, met Masterman and Parker, and promised to write, if the CID 'made no objection'. Stopping briefly at his apartment to collect materials, he headed back to the country and worked for three days.[25] Parker was delighted to have copy in hand within a week.[26] Corbett corrected the proofs on 15 May, two days after learning that his beloved nephew Denis Corbett-Wilson had been killed in action over the Western Front. He suffered a nervous breakdown, his highly strung nature pushed beyond endurance by the stress of trying to comfort his sister, find out what had happened to Denis and carry on working.[27] Corbett's text was complete in late April, before the sinking of the *Lusitania* on 7 May: 3,500 copies of *The Spectre of Navalism* appeared after that watershed moment.[28]

Although the *New York Times* referenced Corbett's essay on 24 May, achieving Masterman's primary object, not all of its American readers were impressed. While few would disagree with Corbett's 'skilful defence', the critic thought 'Navalism' focused on the past, while current policy was different, an implication of hypocrisy sustained by referencing Archibald Hurd's latest article in the *Fortnightly Review*, which espoused the doctrine that might makes right.[29]

It is not known if either essay reached Woodrow Wilson's desk, but Wilson, an avowed Anglophobe, like many Democrats, adopted elements of German propaganda, notably that 'Navalism' was a moral equivalent to U-boat warfare.[30] Along with Lenin, he believed the war had been caused by competing imperial economic systems, seeking exclusive control of large swathes of territory. This harmed American interests. Destroying the empires of Britain and Germany would facilitate the advance of American capitalism. He had no interest in the rights of subject peoples, happily replacing political subjugation to old world empires with economic subjugation to a new master.[31]

Propaganda work brought Corbett into contact with Lord Robert Cecil, younger son of Lord Salisbury, Conservative prime minister on several occasions between 1885 and 1902. After a successful career at the bar Cecil turned to politics, but his politics were driven by ideas and connections, rather than party ties. In 1914 Asquith, aware that Cecil was an old Oxford friend of Sir Edward Grey, eased Cecil into a junior ministerial post at the Foreign Office to direct economic warfare. This suited Grey, who wanted the Foreign Office to control a complex interaction involving the Admiralty, War Office, Board of Trade and Treasury.[32] Cecil's passion for order made him an effective minister, not least because he rarely compromised on issues of principle. In February 1916 Grey secured Cecil a seat in the Cabinet, as Minister for Blockade, an unprecedented, but effective method of reinforcing Foreign Office control. Grey's support ensured Lloyd George retained Cecil in post in the December 1916 reconstruction of government. Cecil worked closely with Grey and his successor, Cecil's cousin Arthur Balfour, leaving the daily business of blockade to civil servant Eyre Crowe, while improving vital intelligence-gathering and data-processing capabilities. His legal expertise was a key asset: economic warfare was imposed by courts, not cruisers. Close blockades had been replaced by a War Trade Intelligence Department, which exploited Britain's dominance of global information flows, especially in the maritime sector, to identity cargoes and companies that attempted to supply Germany, directly or indirectly. The new department enabled Britain to wage economic warfare, and avoid the complications with neutrals, which Corbett had anticipated.

Cecil and Grey also shaped British thinking about a post-war international order. Cecil's positive assessment of economic warfare informed his thinking about how a League of Nations could coerce recalcitrant powers.[33] This combination of idealism and legality became a contentious issue in January 1916, when President Wilson's close confidant 'Colonel' Edward House arrived in London. Grey had encouraged the visit, hoping to secure American support for the Entente. House carried a document that emphasised the need for a post-war 'league of peace' to secure all nations against aggression, promote international disarmament, and ensure freedom of the seas. If either side was willing to adopt those terms the Americans would act. Both Wilson and House knew 'freedom of the seas' would be a red line for Britain. Nor was it clear what America would do if either alliance accepted their terms: it had no army, and only a top-heavy peacetime navy.

Grey carefully avoided an overt negative. He was not convinced by Cecil's contention that the first role of a league should be to promote disarmament, while both he and Crowe doubted the efficacy of blockade as a coercive strategy. They expected a league would need military force to be effective. Furthermore, Wilson was resolved to remove blockade from the international arsenal, to advance American commercial interests. He even had the audacity to claim that the Allies were using blockade to prolong the war.[34] Nothing could have been further from the truth. Well aware that sea power was critical to Britain's great power status, Wilson wanted to disarm the Navy that secured Britain's global economic hegemony.

When Wilson addressed the League to Enforce Peace on 2 May 1916, he secured a reputation as a liberal statesman committed to the league concept.[35] His speech obliged the British government to respond. Cecil was not impressed, on 1 August telling the War Cabinet that the United States would only act 'if it was in her economic interests to do so', countering Wilson's demand for 'freedom of the seas' by stressing that the right to blockade would be the ideal coercive power for a post-war 'league of peace'. Although Eyre Crowe concurred, he believed a league would be impractical and risk British strategic interests, 'especially in the deployment of sea power'.[36] Crowe's response reflected a long engagement with the reality of British strategy, famously expressed in his 1907 memorandum.[37] As a realist, Crowe expected American mediation would lead to Irish independence, freedom of the seas, disarmament and compulsory international arbitration.[38]

Masterman read Wilson's speech as 'dangerously flirting with Germany' on the issue of 'freedom of the seas': Wellington House published an interview with Arthur Balfour, First Lord of the Admiralty, while the Admiralty and the Foreign Office responded to requests for relevant information.[39] In November Bryce suggested combining pamphlets by Balfour, Haldane and Lloyd George with speeches by Asquith and Grey that stressed the benign character of British aims in a book that he would introduce for the American market.[40]

In December Corbett advised Hankey that the Fourteen Points could be a lure to draw out Germany's war aims.[41] That Corbett felt the need to raise these issues as Lloyd George reconstructed the government suggests his views were taken seriously at the highest level. His analysis of Wilson's thinking was shrewd. For British liberals the optimism of May 1916 had been tempered by Wilson's procrastination and blatant self-interest.

A month later Admiral Brownrigg, the Admiralty Chief Censor, asked Corbett to write another essay for 'the "Foreign Office Propaganda people"'; they needed a 'weighty article' to counter German arguments about British Navalism then gaining traction in the USA. There was 'nobody better': Brownrigg had already cleared the request with the Admiralty leadership, Sir Edward Carson and Jellicoe.[42] Brownrigg and St John Hutchinson of the Foreign Office Propaganda Committee told Corbett their primary concern was to 'meet President Wilson's manoeuvres ... on Freedom of Seas for FO for foreign press'.[43] He began work on 30 January 1917, completing a longhand draft the following day. The typescript arrived on 2 February; suitably corrected, it was in Brownrigg's hands that afternoon.[44] A week later Corbett was offered a knighthood, although there was no direct connection between the paper and an honour that had been mooted before the war. A month later he was coaching the naval writer 'Bartimaeus', pseudonym of Paymaster Ritchie, who was writing a reply to Hans Delbrück's threadbare justification of unrestricted submarine warfare.[45] *The League of Peace and a Free Sea* was printed as a pamphlet in New York to explain the benign nature of British aims and policies to an audience hesitating on the brink of conflict.[46] War Course lecturer Alexander Pearce Higgins provided powerful support for Corbett's arguments, demonstrating the incoherence of German attempts to undermine British economic warfare, noting how German lawyers had read across from land to sea, treating defensively armed merchant ships as guerrilla forces to justify sinking them without making provision for passengers and crew.[47]

Corbett's response to the diplomatic context of the conflict intersected with his concern for an evolving British Empire. He lectured to an Imperial Studies course at King's College London in the autumn of 1917; the subject had been developed by Laughton to contextualise naval history. Just as the Passchendaele offensive opened, Professor Arthur Newton shifted attention:

> from an excessive preoccupation with the momentous events taking place on the continent of Europe to a remembrance that Britain's true concern is rather with the affairs of the world as a whole than with the narrower details of purely territorial questions with which the land powers of Europe are so intimately concerned.[48]

This invitation reconnected Corbett with the ultimate purpose of his work. His 'Sea Commonwealth' opened the lecture series, providing both the core argument and the title of the book version.[49] He re-examined the bases of British power as it faced the president's demand for 'freedom of the seas', backed by a major naval programme. War may have obscured the future, but Corbett retained his faith in historically informed analysis. An empire that absolutely depended on command of the sea must make that command appear suitably benign, lest the appearance of great strength aroused the opposition of an irresistible coalition. A modern 'Armed Neutrality' of 1801, backed by the impending American Armada, would cripple Britain's ability to secure the empire. Furthermore, British sea power would only be palatable if it resisted the siren call of 'Tariff Reform' protectionism. War would change the empire; the best model would be his 'Sea Commonwealth', a looser federation of self-governing nations. There was nothing especially radical in this: he had advanced the concept of 'a democratic, autonomous commonwealth' back in 1900.[50] He expected the Dominions and India would take more prominent roles in external policy, but mutual dependence on sea power would ensure cohesion. If the sea remained just as much 'all one' as it had been before the war, the sea power needed to secure the empire would require 'a united effort of the whole organism'.[51] The empire/commonwealth must share the culture and identity of a seapower state, sacrificing individual interests to build mutual support. The sympathy, restraint and concessions required to manage the commonwealth would be equally important for Britain's post-war relations with the wider world.[52]

This looser federation of nations, with the connecting sea as the main check on calls for independence, would avoid a critical risk ignored by those fixated on the Western Front, then as now. The British might believe their empire stood for peace and trade, but others saw 'an overpowering combination which is solely moved by lust of dominion and greedy self-interest'. Reusing the concept of the Royal Navy as a benign global police from 'Navalism', Corbett contended the world had accepted British dominion in the nineteenth century, 'because it was felt on the whole to be a convenience to the world. Certainly it was not employed, as it might have been, to thwart the spirit of the age.'[53] Widening the focus, he observed that Britain had profited from the example of other empires which, in attempting to secure complete control, brought on their end. Aware that closed markets prompted opposition, Britain had opened the imperial trade to all, making sea power a 'convenience to the world'. To remain so in future, the empire must resist the siren lure of protectionism. Rather than attack the protectionists, Corbett called for reflection. Protectionism and sea power were antithetical concepts, pulling the empire in different directions, weakening the whole. Seapowers depended on expansive oceanic free trade systems to fund the costly fleets that protected their empires, and the trade that justified them. Tariff barriers would sustain German and American claims that British sea power was 'tyranny'.[54] Hitherto this danger had hardly featured in British imperial discussions, which took the sea and sea power for granted. This was a dangerous delusion in a changing world. New naval powers, continental military states with big navies, had emerged, while 'vague aspirations for disarmament and what is called "Freedom of the Seas"' challenged simple notions of security. Policymakers must recognise that absolute security for the British Empire equalled insecurity for everyone else, leading the insecure to coalesce to restore the equilibrium. America's 1916 Navy Programme suggested the attack on British 'Navalism' would continue after the war. It would be wise to disarm critics by retaining free trade. Acutely aware of the problems Britain faced in conducting economic warfare against Germany while avoiding disputes with powerful maritime neutrals, Corbett stressed the need to recognise Britain's strengths and weaknesses, and act accordingly. Only a relatively loose free trade sea commonwealth would be allowed to possess the necessary naval power to secure Britain's interests. Corbett wrote the published version of 'The Sea Commonwealth' a year later, alongside his final propaganda piece, with which it shared key themes.[55]

While America entered the war in April 1917, President Wilson offered no concrete plans for a League of Peace. Cecil proposed the government should review the history of the idea, to inform their approach to peacemaking: 'its [the committee's] remit should also include possible terms of peace when hostilities ceased'.[56] While Cecil hoped a British report might encourage Wilson to act, he had little faith in Wilson's integrity, or his international credentials.[57]

Eminent jurist Sir Walter Phillimore would chair the committee, having recently published *Three Centuries of Treaties of Peace and Their Teaching*.[58] In late November 1917, Hankey, sensing a new threat to national security, sought Corbett's assistance.[59] Hankey relied on his legal and strategic expertise to prevent the discussions being hijacked by idealists like Phillimore, or Foreign Office bureaucrats, much as Fisher had used it to block Churchill's wilder schemes. Fearing the Foreign Office might weaken Britain's maritime belligerent rights, Hankey shared Corbett's anxiety to restrict the negative impact of a post-war league on imperial security. He suggested that any league should be a continuation of the newly established Allied Supreme War Council, a proto-world government that would need a powerful secretariat, which he could lead. Such empire building was typical, and unlikely to garner support at the Foreign Office. It is unlikely Hankey shared his own enthusiasm for a world government that dealt with 'blockade, munitions, shipping, finance, terms of peace etc and all other matters' with Corbett.[60] A fortnight later Cecil formally invited Corbett to join the committee.[61] Disingenuously claiming he had 'no fixed ideas on the subject', Corbett agreed to serve.[62]

Although invariably described as one of three historians on the committee, Corbett had been selected for his strategic, legal and literary abilities, along with his ability to debate and draft a state paper, skills that Hankey was already exploiting. When the committee assembled on 30 January 1918 Corbett was writing the Official History account of the Dardanelles and the amphibious landings at Gallipoli. He found Phillimore a dreadful bore, while Foreign Office heavyweights Eyre Crowe, William Tyrell and legal expert Cecil Hurst opposed Cecil's agenda. They were balanced by Corbett and fellow historians Arthur Pollard and John Holland Rose, both admirers of Corbett's work. While Hankey looked to combine wartime cooperation and sea power to impose peace, the committee adopted a narrow diplomatic focus on rights and sanctions.[63] The Foreign Office men were 'obviously bored with the whole thing'.[64] Hankey gave evidence to the committee on 20 February, but relied on Corbett to shape the outcome.[65] Finally Corbett, Pollard and Holland Rose took control of proceedings, to the consternation of Phillimore, 'who seems a bigger ass the more you know him'.[66]

On 13 February Pollard launched the historians' counter-attack, insisting on a discussion of 'fundamental factors', rather than Phillimore's 'pet scheme', a neo-Kantian project for perpetual peace.[67] In the end the committee members out-voted Phillimore, adopting Corbett's draft report on 20 March. The historians agreed to produce a memorandum by late April.[68] Corbett's report forcefully expressed his concern that a 'League of Nations' would undermine Britain's age-old reliance on naval power for national and imperial security. Presented to Foreign Secretary Balfour, it reinforced the government's suspicions of Wilson, representing 'freedom of the seas', as a deliberate, direct threat to the strategic significance of sea power, and with that the global status of the British Empire. Wilson expected the 'league' to achieve an old American aim, the disarmament of the British Empire, to make the world safe for American capital and commerce. The report neatly countered that threat without overtly criticising the American president, while providing the basis for the eventual Charter of the League of Nations.[69]

In May the Cabinet sent the report to Wilson, Edward House providing a confidential channel. Diplomatic discussions revealed French opposition, Lloyd George was unenthusiastic, while Leo Amery, Lord Curzon and Hankey were sceptical. In August Wilson requested Britain delay publication of the text, fearing a hostile response in a Republican-dominated Senate. Claiming it 'had no teeth' was a fig leaf to cover his political weakness.[70] Corbett and his allies had replaced Phillimore's well-intentioned platitudes with a crisp text that drew attention to the nationalist agenda behind Wilson's 'Points' and ensured the government recognised the threat to national strategy.

This agenda dominated Corbett's final wartime essay.[71] By January 1918 British propaganda was focused on Anglo-American relations, with Corbett enlisted among those explaining British responses to Wilson's proposed league – alongside Sir Edward Grey, Gilbert Murray, Sir Frederick Pollock, Arthur Pollard and Arthur Henderson.[72] The approach came in mid-April, as he worked on the historical memorandum for the Phillimore report. His task was to address 'freedom of the seas' and a League of Nations. He did so against a dismal background.

> Cold & Dull all day writing chapter on League of Nations Freedom of Seas for Ministry of Information book. Boiling down previous pamphlet, but hard work with head full of dark situation in France. I begin to fear the worst.[73]

Wilson's decision to make the league public had forced the government to act. Corbett's pamphlet *The League of Nations and a Free Sea*, a key part of that response, targeted American audiences. The draft reached the Ministry of Information on 20 April.[74]

In Wilson's original concept, 'freedom of the seas', the abolition of maritime belligerent rights was 'an essential condition of such a League'. He offered no justification for his position, beyond pre-war ideals.[75] Corbett recognised the oversight, his withering logic easily exploded the president's ambiguous concept. In peace all seas are free, and if the league achieved its ultimate aim, preventing war, the question of belligerent rights would never arise. In reality the advocates of 'freedom' wanted to abolish the right of belligerents to stop commercial shipping on the high seas, and seize that belonging to enemy states, or that of neutrals found to contain contraband. However, the right to interfere with non-combatants and private property was as much the key to naval strategy as the occupation of territory was to war on land. Naval warfare was not a matter of navies fighting navies, the Custance fallacy:

> It is only by the prevention of enemy's commerce that fleets can exercise the pressure which armies seek, in theory or practice, to exercise through victories ashore; and it is only by the capture and the ability to capture private property at sea that prevention of commerce can be brought about. Without the right to capture private property naval battles become meaningless as a method of forcing the enemy to submit. ...
>
> It comes then to this – that if Freedom of the Seas is pushed to its logical conclusion of forbidding altogether the capture and destruction of private property at sea, it will in practice go far to rob fleets of all power of exerting pressure on an enemy, while armies would be left in full enjoyment of that power. The balance of Naval and Military power, which has meant so much for the liberties of the world, would be upset, and the voice of the Naval Powers would sink to a whisper beside that of the Military Powers.[76]

Maritime strategy converted sea control into strategic effect on land through economic warfare. Without that right, sea power would be toothless and Britain disarmed, an intolerable development.

These arguments reappeared in the report of the British government's International Law Committee, which had met intermittently through 1918, chaired by Viscount Cave, the Home Secretary, with representatives from the Admiralty, the Foreign Office, the War Office and the Air Ministry, Pearce Higgins providing legal expertise and a conduit for Corbett's strategic vision of seapower, economic warfare and British interests. By the time of the second meeting, in May, both the Phillimore Report and Corbett's *The League of Nations and a Free Sea* were in print, while the Admiralty was arguing that Britain should withdraw from the 1856 Declaration of Paris.

The committee report to the Attorney General melded legal argument with Corbett's concept of sea power strategy dominated by economic warfare. If the wording was subtly different, the message was identical. The report criticised pre-war agreements, including the Declaration of London: 'hypotheses which were not realised not only hampered the striking power of the British Navy, but broke down in practice when vital issues were at stake'. Pre-war anxieties about economic ruin and food shortages had proved unfounded, while international agreements could not secure the food supply. Unrestricted submarine warfare demonstrated how easily the international consensus could be shattered by self-interest and opportunism, without powerful international sanctions.[77] The committee viewed 'freedom of the seas' with concern and adopted Corbett's arguments.

Corbett left unspoken the reality that the United States, like previous continental military powers, wanted to disarm sea power strategy, the easier to dominate the world. He saw no reason why Britain should unilaterally abandon its primary strategic instrument. Furthermore, the exercise of belligerent rights at sea would be the key to enabling a league to act as 'an effective instrument for peace'.[78] Blockade, or in modern parlance 'embargo', would be the 'most readily applied', providing 'the most immediate and humane' sanction against recalcitrant powers.[79]

Corbett skilfully contrasted Wilson's original pronouncement on a league, which called for the sea to be open for 'the common unhindered use of all the nations of the world', with his more realistic message to congress of 9 January 1918, to suggest the realities of war, including the strategic value of economic blockade, had caused him to qualify a simplistic position. Corbett claimed Wilson had recognised belligerent rights were essential to enforce league authority.

While the extension of belligerent rights at sea had been a feature of the current war, the solution to this age-old problem did not require 'freedom of the seas'. In a total war, old-fashioned neutrality simply did not exist. The only remedy was a league with the power to coerce recalcitrant states, using naval power to uphold the rights of small states against military aggression. The case of Belgium and Germany in 1914 may have shaped that argument.

While Corbett made a strong case, he had a deeper purpose. A league with the power to blockade would be a powerful force for stability, binding members to protect the interests of all states, large and small. Such support for the status quo would benefit a satiated imperial power like

Britain, which could build coalitions to maintain peace within a functioning League of Nations, as the backbone of another century of peace – a peace that would suit British interests – as the empire evolved into a 'Sea Commonwealth'. At a time when the majority were focused on current disasters, Corbett looked ahead, charting a course that would sustain British imperial seapower into the future: reworking past experience, filtered through the experience of total war, to address new challenges. The failure of naval power to secure obvious strategic success in the war made his case all the more important.

When Germany accepted Wilson's 'Fourteen Points' as the basis for peace negotiations on 12 October 1918 it unwittingly transformed Corbett's *The League of Nations and a Free Sea* from high-grade propaganda into a policy primer. On the same day Lloyd George made it quite clear that Britain 'could not accept his [Wilson's] views about the Freedom of the Seas'. When the First Lord of the Admiralty, Sir Eric Geddes, met Wilson on 13 October, the president would not admit his desire to end British maritime dominance, but the inference of 'freedom', extended territorial waters and redefining blockades was obvious.[80] They were central to an American programme that would disarm the last great seapower.

On 17 October First Sea Lord Rosslyn Wemyss emphasised Corbett's link between sea power strategy and the security of the British Empire when advising the War Cabinet.

> Acceptance of the proposal would result in making sea-power of little value to a nation *dependent upon it* for existence whilst providing a military power with free lines of overseas communication.[81] ...
>
> It would prevent us from using our strongest weapon and place in the hands of our enemy a power he does not [currently] possess. The value of military power, both for attack and defence, would be enhanced, and its radius of action increased, while the value of naval power for attack and defence and its radius of action would be correspondingly reduced.[82]

It appears Foreign Secretary Arthur Balfour had also read Corbett, echoing his argument that 'only militarism would be the gainer'.[83] Both men knew and valued Corbett's work. While Arthur Marder claimed 'The Freedom of the Seas controversy revealed to the British in a flash the apparent American ambition to achieve naval supremacy',[84] there was nothing 'apparent' about

Wilson's plan. He wanted to disarm Britain with a combination of internationalist rhetoric and a multi-year battleship-building programme, strikingly similar in form and function to the Tirpitz Plan.

'Freedom of the seas' returned to prominence when Germany accepted
the Fourteen Points as a basis for peace on 12 October. On 25 October the
War Cabinet informed the US government that Britain would not agree to
'freedom of the seas', recommending the fact be communicated to the inter-
allied conference, and the Germans, before an armistice was signed.
Furthermore, the First Lord of the Admiralty would attend the meeting in
Paris to reflect the importance of naval issues.[85] Anxious to secure his
point by international covenant before a triumphal arrival in Europe,
Wilson directed House to redouble the pressure on Britain. House threatened that America would out-build the Royal Navy if Britain did not
accede. Revealing the mailed fist that lay behind American diplomacy was
a serious mistake. Britain, an imperial seapower, had no choice but to strive
for naval superiority, a core element of national identity, and as a democracy it had the political strength to sustain costly long-term policies.
Although weakened by war, Britain had a far stronger connection with the
sea than America, a reality demonstrated by post-war events. The War
Cabinet rejected Wilson's posturing on 'freedom' and his attempt to preserve
Germany's battlefleet, to tie the Royal Navy to European waters. In Paris
Geddes quickly secured the internment of the modern German fleet, which
he linked to the need to sustain the prestige of the Navy, following Corbett's
Cabinet memorandum in making the surrender of the fleet a precondition
for the armistice.[86]

When Lloyd George rejected 'freedom' at the Supreme War Council,
House threatened that America would withdraw from the conflict, directing
two tame journalists to produce a more benign explanation of Point 2. The
resulting gloss did not make the text any more acceptable. Wilson, still in
Washington, remained determined to secure his prize, anticipating the
other Entente powers would rally to his cause if he threatened to walk away
from the peace process. House quickly discovered that the British delegates
would not to allow 'freedom' to be discussed at the Peace Conference.[87] Had
he known a little more history he might have been less surprised. Britain
had resisted attempts to discuss such fundamental issues in the context of
general peace in 1814 and 1815, keeping the subject off the agenda at Paris,
Ghent and Vienna by threatening to end financial support for their allies.[88]

On 3 November Lloyd George made Britain's position clear, telling House: 'Great Britain would spend her last guinea to keep a navy superior to that of the United States or any other power. . . . No Cabinet official could continue in the Government in England who took a different position.' He refused to join a League of Nations which included Point 2.[89] Corbett's work on the Phillimore Committee ensured British policymakers recognised the threat, and informed the positions adopted by the government and the Admiralty in the decisive engagement at Versailles.

The Paris Conference agreed that 'freedom' was open to 'various interpretations', the Allies reserving complete freedom on the subject.[90] After these exchanges, Corbett's views were canvassed: on 24 October he lunched with Foreign Office heavyweight Sir Charles Nicholson to discuss the issue, and on 4 November Wemyss called him to the Admiralty: 'to draw Admiralty case against Freedom of Seas for Peace Conference'. The following day Wemyss provided the Admiralty position papers, which Corbett dismissed. Having read the minutes of the Paris Conference 'to see where we are with regard to Freedom of Seas – seems to me no one believes in it – not even Wilson, but feels he has to make good his uninstructed pronouncements', he devoted almost a week to a draft, completed on Saturday, 9 November – two days before the Armistice took effect. On 14 November he wrote to Wemyss, 'showing lines on which Freedom of the Seas must be discussed since what was said at Versailles & suggesting he should set up a committee'.[91] Wemyss presented Corbett's arguments to the Imperial War Cabinet on 20 November, under his own signature.[92] The Cabinet adopted them, setting up a major diplomatic battle with the American president. A full-length memo on freedom of the seas was sent to Wemyss on 29 November.[93] When Wemyss spoke on the League of Nations in Paris on 18 December, he echoed Corbett's views.[94]

American naval planners feared that a post-war world where only a League of Nations could use seapower to enforce international covenants would jeopardise American interests.[95] Wilson and his administration were well aware that Britain's red lines were all at sea. On 19 December the American Ambassador in London, John W. Davis, stressed 'Freedom of the Seas' was 'the sole source of real anxiety in London', while House advised Wilson the British were 'crazy' on this issue and Foreign Secretary Balfour insisted on the right to blockade.[96]

Having met the president on 19 January 1919, Cecil judged him to be a vain, pompous bully, dominated by American opinion polls, advising Lloyd

George accordingly.[97] The prime minister believed Anglo-American cooperation was critical to securing British aims, including a durable peace in Europe,
basing his approach on the wise statesmanship of Castlereagh and Wellington
at the Congress of Vienna, where Britain balanced the military powers and a
defeated France in the interests of long-term stability while avoiding costly
defence commitments. While he was prepared to adopt Wilson's League of
Nations to tie the Americans into a new European system, in effect reinforcing the long-standing British policy of maintaining peace and a 'balance
of power', and compromise on other points, he would not purchase that result
by neutering British sea power. An Anglo-American entente would be useful,
but he had no intention of allowing the American president to pose as the
conquering hero. The Cabinet agreed to join the league, but only after Wilson
had recognised Britain's red lines, and dropped 'freedom of the seas'.[98]

Wilson agreed to cut the 1918 Naval Program, which had the added
benefit of curbing a worrying 'Big Navy' party in Washington and reducing
costs. Having agreed to postpone naval negotiations for future discussion,
America and Britain combined to block the French attempt to raise their
own naval issues at Versailles. Lloyd George's key asset in curbing Wilson's
ambitions was the growing reluctance of congress to sanction the league.[99]
The prime minister made British support for a clause in the League Treaty
to exclude the Monroe Doctrine from the general terms of the League, to
avoid domestic opposition, conditional on removing 'freedom of the seas'.
Wilson bought that concession by avoiding any challenge to 'British coloni-
alism through his self-determination agenda' and 'quietly dropped the
demand for Freedom of the Seas'. Britain had retained the empire, and the
legal right to impose naval blockade.[100]

Wilson adopted Corbett's argument that a league would need the right
to impose economic sanctions by blockade. At the same time his threat to
launch a naval arms race collapsed. Not only was congress unwilling to
fund the project, but it would have made a mockery of the league's disarmament agenda. Extracting the Monroe Doctrine concession, which violated
several of the 'Fourteen Points', from the other powers at Versailles was a
vain attempt to persuade the Republican-dominated Senate to support the
league. The 'Monroe' clause was drafted by Robert Cecil, who provided a
suitable legal formula. It was admitted in a separate article, highlighting
American double standards. The process left the president dependent on
British support, an opportunity Lloyd George exploited.[101]

Naval issues came to a head during a heated confrontation between the senior British and American naval advisors on 29 March. On 1 April Lloyd George breakfasted with Josephus Daniels, the American Navy Secretary, refusing to consider joining a League of Nations while Point 2 remained on the list.[102] He was strongly backed by the French, the Entente powers jointly hinting that they would continue the war alone.

Britain finally accepted the league on 10 April, after the outstanding naval issues had been resolved, with Lloyd George supporting Wilson's Monroe Doctrine clause. As congress had already cut the 1918 Naval Program, Wilson did not have very far to climb down.[103] Britain abandoned plans to neutralise or destroy the Kiel Canal – it was a valuable economic asset – but insisted on destroying the fortress of Heligoland.

Meanwhile Robert Cecil worked the Peace Conference to promote his own league agenda, joining with House to promote Corbett's Phillimore Report. He realised Lloyd George had lost interest. Negotiations with the Americans produced a workable draft by late January, replacing an 'inelegantly written' American version. Cecil's room for manoeuvre was limited: the Cabinet treated the draft covenant as 'one of a growing number of bargaining tools, still subject to possible revision, that could be used to broker concessions on other issues at the peace conference'.[104]

Cecil understood Lloyd George's use of the league to end the American naval challenge as classic old-fashioned diplomacy, while James Goldrick stressed that Wemyss secured 'practically all that Britain wanted in the naval terms for the final peace treaty with Germany'.[105] Corbett provided the intellectual core of those victories: his mastery of past practice, legal and strategic, equipped the government and Admiralty to defeat Woodrow Wilson's hostile measures. His arguments had been shaped by two decades of study.

Ultimately, Wilson knew he would not have America behind him if he started a naval arms race with Britain, or forced the country into a League of Nations it did not support. His bluff had been called. Speaking to a domestic audience on 19 September 1919, he glossed over his defeat in Paris, reusing the core argument of Corbett's 1918 *League of Peace and a Free Sea*.[106] He may have read the paper. Ultimately the Senate refused to ratify both the Versailles settlement and the League in November 1919.[107] Wilson's dreams had come to nothing, out-manoeuvred by the agile intellects of two British lawyers. Corbett may have been amused to find Reginald

Custance in complete accord on 'freedom of the seas': the latter's lecture of 15 July 1919 was reprinted in the *Proceedings of the United States Naval Institute* just as the Senate rejected Wilson's projects.[108]

By 1920 Britain had defeated the existential challenges of Imperial Germany and the United States, challenges that shared an obvious continental agenda. Both wished to disarm the British Empire by restricting the application of economic warfare at sea, expressed in the propaganda of 'Navalism' and 'freedom of the seas'; both backed that policy by building Mahanian battlefleets to challenge the naval hegemony that secured Britain, the empire, and global trade. Corbett responded by focusing on the unique character of British strategy, the overriding importance of economic warfare, and the distortion of the international system that would follow if continental arguments triumphed. This may have been his most important national service, and it is typical that it garnered neither praise nor publicity. Self-effacing to the end, Corbett would have appreciated the irony. His elegant, strategic contributions built on a sustained effort to analyse the strategy of global empire as a living problem, not an academic exercise, across two decades. But this work continued. He had the expanding Official History project to complete; and he wanted to enhance the alliance between professional military education and academic history, and reduce the experience of global war to coherent doctrine. The 'British way' was about so much more than war, or battle; it was a complex system designed to minimise the need for violence and reduce the cost of security.

Consequently, while the Versailles Conference ended the war, it did not end Corbett's connection with war planning. In January 1921 he compiled a memorandum on the role of the Panama Canal in a war with the United States for Hankey, while assisting Herbert Richmond with a paper on trade defence in such a conflict.[109] These were among the pressing tasks that engaged his attention alongside the writing of volume III of the Official History. He remained a strategist for the present, not a historian of the past.

It has been customary to see *Some Principles* as the culmination of Corbett's career, and his wartime role as a sad, declining coda, his ideas vitiated by the hard realities of total conflict in the industrial age. In reality, Corbett rose to the challenge, informing national strategy, contesting the drift into a 'German way' and the invidious threat of German and American propaganda. He remained committed to the ultimate task, the security, stability and cohesion of an economically vibrant, politically progressive

British Sea Commonwealth, one where self-determination was tempered by mutual dependence on the ocean, and the Navy. In 1918 he helped shape a post-war world in which such ideas were possible, despite a League of Nations and the dynamic spread of nationalism, new strategic rivalries and the end of old certainties. His thought continued to evolve as he worked through the grand strategy of a global total war, while his contribution to British policy was widely acknowledged. He had become one of the nation's indispensable eminences. It may be a surprise to learn that he was closely involved in the project that led to the tank.[110]

CHAPTER 18

Naval Operations
A STUDY IN DISARTICULATED STRATEGY

While Corbett's work stretched across many aspects of the conflict, his primary roles were writing the official account of British grand strategy and naval operations, and the direction of the British Official History project. Those linked tasks commenced with the outbreak of war and remained unfinished at his death. His experience of the higher direction of the conflict informed the history, enabling him to master the blizzard of official paper, while the survival of an evolving seapower empire as a great power informed every page of the history project. The need to profit from the educational opportunities provided by the war was recognised by many, not least his friend Herbert Richmond, the historically minded Assistant Director of the Operations Division. On 2 August Richmond directed Staff Commander Oswald Tuck, Head of the Admiralty Historical Section, 'to collect and arrange the documents of the war'.[1] Both men were closely connected to Corbett's work. The project would expand to encompass the entire war effort, and Corbett would be responsible for all of it.

On 5 August 1914 Corbett offered his services to Admiralty Secretary William Graham Greene, noting 'there is little chance of being accepted'. Within days Edmond Slade had placed him at the heart of a system that evolved from the ongoing Admiralty–CID history of the Russo-Japanese War. Slade summoned Corbett to town on 10 August, asking him to compile the War Diary, 'but mainly as he said to have me at hand to discuss strategy & draft memoranda embodying ideas of staff as Sturdee could not do it'.[2] He quickly acquired a large-format page-a-day desk diary and began recording all aspects of the war.[3] In constant contact with Slade, Leveson and Richmond, Corbett watched and advised through the dynamic phase on the Franco-Belgian frontier, with a special focus on the Belgian coast, emphasising the value of keeping the Army in hand as an amphibious strike force. He would work between the two organisations for the rest of his life.

Corbett's central contribution, *Naval Operations*, the Official History of British grand strategy and the naval war, would be dominated by the need to understand and promulgate national strategic doctrine.[4] It would be the culmination of a career stretching back to the late 1890s, analysing the evolution of English/British strategy, and recovering the guiding principles for naval officers, statesmen and even soldiers. The text would be the basis of post-war service education and updated doctrine, agendas that obliged him to reconcile the ghastly reality of total war on the European continent with pre-war expectations of a limited maritime conflict, consistent with previous British experience.

When Arthur Marder wrote the next multi-volume study of Britain's naval war, he ignored the strategic dimension of Corbett's work, and his didactic agenda, and grossly underrated Corbett's influence on the Navy and national strategy, dismissing his 'detailed, authoritative; restrained judgements' as a semi-popular treatment aimed at the public. Yet Marder, beguiled by Corbett's superior prose and incisive analysis, imported substantial passages without attribution.[5] Marder's assumption that the 'real' official account was contained in the Staff Histories, 'written by the Historical Section of the Naval Staff', was incorrect.[6] These detailed operational and tactical studies served a very different purpose from Corbett's strategic assessment, providing detailed analysis to inform operational and tactical doctrine. Corbett never claimed to possess the necessary expertise for such work; it was properly conducted by naval officers. His book, primarily intended for the War Course, was a teaching text modelled on *England in the Seven Years' War* that explained British strategy to post-war audiences. He revealed how the 'British way', the time-honoured methods of limited maritime strategy, with the two services acting in concert, under intelligent political direction, to secure control of sea communications and break the enemy's economy, had been distorted and disarticulated by politics, alliances and alien strategic concepts. By 1918 he recognised it would provide a striking contrast to the strategic successes of the Seven Years' War and the Napoleonic conflict.

Corbett focused on high-level decision-making, where civilian government, diplomacy and enemy policy interacted to shape strategy. Alongside the archives he had access to strikingly rich human sources, reflecting close professional and personal relationships with Cabinet ministers, the head of the War Cabinet Secretariat, all five wartime First Sea Lords, and other senior officers, many of them former students. He would discuss the Grand Fleet, Jutland and the crisis of 1917 with Jellicoe, who commented on relevant drafts of the Official History.[7] He had access to the records of the Dardanelles Commission, Ian Hamilton's diaries, and the personal correspondence of Henry Jackson, Rosslyn Wemyss and Roger Keyes, and worked closely with Reginald Tyrwhitt. Maurice Hankey provided insights from within the High Command in exchange for a succession of brilliant memoranda.

After the war Corbett's work would be contested by Winston Churchill and then David Beatty, who tried to block or deflect critical analysis of their failings. Both men recognised Corbett's official opinions could damage their careers.[8] While they caused many problems, Corbett's commitment and the support of many prominent figures saved the project. By 1918 Corbett's public reputation was so high that Admiral Sir Berkeley Milne's public challenge to his account of the escape of the *Goeben* was roundly condemned by the mainstream press, which upheld the Official History and Corbett's magisterial judgements.[9]

After an intellectual career spent tracing the upward curve of British strategic insight, success and power, Corbett had to explain a war in which the 'British way' made only fleeting appearances, one that seemed to have been settled by 'German' methods. In the *Seven Years' War* he had explained how the decisive fleet battle at Quiberon was brought on by a successful amphibious strike at Quebec:

> it must not be forgotten that convenient opportunities of winning a battle do not always occur when they are wanted. The dramatic moments of naval strategy have to be worked for, and the first preoccupation of the fleet will almost always be to bring them about by interference with the enemy's military and diplomatic arrangements.[10]

By contrast volume III of *Naval Operations* had to explain Jutland and Gallipoli, altogether less compelling examples that seemed to call into question his pre-war arguments. The educational importance of his texts, as the 'Bible' of the post-war Naval War Course, made it essential to situate the Dardanelles, Gallipoli and Jutland in the grand strategy of a great power alliance, while emphasising the maritime focus of the 'British way' and challenging the continental narrative of the British Army, and the 'decisive battle' school of blue-water navalists.

While Corbett did not live to complete the project, his voice effectively stilled on the morrow of Jutland, he left ample evidence of his intentions in other formats.[11] Ultimately he would demonstrate how the war should have been waged, and why it had followed very different lines.

By 1914 Britain had extended the concept of official history, which had its roots in German and French practice, beyond the individual armed services to the CID, where Corbett was completing an Official History, funded by the Admiralty. Working at the CID, a civil–military coordinating body, gave him licence to study the new conflict at the same level he had chosen in his major histories, the interface where war, politics and diplomacy shaped national strategy. Strategy flowed from Cabinet decisions and alliance politics, setting the context before the conduct of operations was assessed.

On 21 February 1907 the CID had accepted the principle that it should direct 'histories of naval and military operations', creating a Historical Section in April. The staff consisted of a Secretary, Major Edmond Daniel RMLI, a Russian linguist, and a confidential clerk. Daniel adopted Lord Esher's critique of existing histories produced by service ministries as amateurish, unduly delayed, wasteful, present-minded and unconnected with service education. The *Official History of the Russo-Japanese War* kept the CID Historical Section busy until July 1914, the final volume being delayed by the outbreak of war. The military bias of the project saw Corbett commissioned to write a Confidential Staff History 'for the use of the Admiralty'. He relied heavily on the language skills of Daniel and Oswald Tuck. Although Admiralty funded, the project was housed at the CID. Corbett had explained his approach to official history to an audience of international academic historians and British naval officers in April 1913. He emphasised strategic analysis and political context over tactical/operational detail, the grand sweep of the past, not the piling up of facts, a characteristic of the massive compilations produced by the Historical Section of the Great German General Staff.[12]

In December 1913 Esher's Historical Section sub-committee reported that, in future, foreign wars would not be studied; the Russo-Japanese conflict had been an exception, with 'special and unique sources of information'. Future British wars would be dealt with as necessary.[13] It appears the sub-committee were content to leave the task to Corbett, who already had an office in the building, as a sponsored guest. He was the only historian working at the CID, while his first Official History had been approved by key figures, including Prince Louis and Maurice Hankey

At the outbreak of war the CID Historical Section began collecting and arranging naval and military material, a lesson learnt from the South African

War project. The decision to create histories was taken three weeks later, on 27 August, Asquith setting up an advisory sub-committee under Edmond Slade. The original members were Slade, Hankey, Corbett – the Admiralty representative and the only civilian – Major General Frederick Maurice, Rear Admiral J.F. Parry, Hydrographer of the Navy, Lieutenant Colonel A. Leetham and Major F.S. Brereton of the Royal Army Medical Corps.[14] Slade secured Corbett's appointment and confirmed Daniel as Secretary. Hankey, the increasingly powerful Secretary of the War Council, pushed the Official History project and secured the necessary funding against stiff opposition from the Treasury, using Corbett's memoranda to challenge the department's penny-pinching predilections. He provided Corbett with strong, if not always consistent, support.[15] Corbett's transition from the Russo-Japanese history to the new conflict proved seamless – he used the same office and worked with the same people. Daniel would administer the project while Tuck remained Head of the Admiralty Historical Section.

With Slade and Hankey holding the ring, Corbett's position was secure. Both men were advocates of maritime strategy. He was acutely conscious of the educational opportunities that could be developed in a skilfully handled history project.[16] As the scale of the task became apparent, he recruited additional staff: authors, sailors and administrators, largely through personal contacts. He worked in the section without pay until 27 January 1915, when he and fellow NRS councillor Captain C.T. Atkinson were formally appointed to supervise the collection of naval and military material 'for the ultimate compilation of an Official History'. Corbett continued working at No. 2 Whitehall Gardens, but Atkinson, for reasons of space, dealt with military material at the Public Records Office in Chancery Lane. The separation was unfortunate, given the ultimate object was to understand how Britain waged war, rather than compiling operational-level single-service texts, especially as the two men were well acquainted. Although the CID was effectively suspended in 1915 the Historical Section continued, with Corbett as the civilian head, combining work on the Official History with active roles in the development of strategy, policy and propaganda.[17]

Work began with the creation of a running record, containing such operational detail and strategic analysis as his inconsistent access to the higher direction of the war would allow. Used to the intellectual freedom of old wars and the papers of long-forgotten men, he found security and bureaucratic restrictions deeply frustrating, prompting frequent complaints in his diary and correspondence. 'I find a difficulty in getting at secret matter (instructions, war orders and the like) without which it is impossible to tell the whole story properly.'[18] Despite the obstructionism of the Admiralty Chief of Staff, Admiral Sir Henry Oliver, Corbett's team began producing narrative drafts.[19] Most began with Oswald Tuck digesting the evidence into factually accurate 'readable' narrative.[20] These were developed by Daniel and Corbett, whose marginalia can be found on surviving copies. Once Tuck had incorporated their suggestions Corbett integrated the draft into the broad structure of the work, emphasising the overarching strategic concept, and crafted a final text: he owned every line.[21] After the war, official material was supplemented by private papers, interviews and a growing stream of British, German and French publications.

The Official History project became public knowledge in April 1915, when 'historians of the Defence Committee' appeared in the 1915–16 Civil Service Estimates, prompting Carlyon Bellairs MP, former Coefficient and Tory naval spokesman, to request their names, and if the work would be public or confidential. While Asquith said as little as possible, leaving the character of the work for future decision, he named Daniel, Atkinson and Corbett.[22] This prompted unwelcome questions. To square public demand for information with the need to preserve 'Official Secrets', a relatively new concept, ministers agreed 'a popular Official History' would appear at the end of the war. Confidential Staff Histories would be produced later, exploiting the archival organisation established for the popular study.

With Hankey absent at the Dardanelles in August 1915, the Historical Sub-Committee proposed two histories, each in two volumes, dealing with naval/colonial and military operations. Corbett would produce the former, Sir John Fortescue, 'the historian approved by Lord Kitchener', the latter. In December the Treasury refused to fund the project, prompting an eloquent response from Corbett, which Hankey presented to Asquith:

> Owing to the development of modern rapid communications, censorship and secrecy have been carried to a pitch unknown in previous wars. The result is that the general public and even the professional sailor and soldier know very little of the history of the war. To this day, for example, very little is known of the movements of the Allied Fleets, nor of the great concerted naval and military operations which brought about the extinction of the German commerce destroyers. Such vitally important matters

as the escape of the *Goeben* are a closed book to all but a very few. The despatches of the British Generals only illuminate one narrow portion of the land operations and give little idea of the huge combinations of which they formed but a minor part. The objectives and intentions of the Dardanelles and Salonica operations are quite imperfectly understood.[23]

Treasury parsimony was subjected to withering scorn: at a trifling annual cost, equal to three 15-inch shells, the nation would ensure 'the useful services of the Section as an educational centre must be added to the actual history'.

> Hundreds of millions are spent on the war and yet a few thousands are grudged to enable the State and the Services to benefit by its experiences. . . . For history is the 'Memory' of the services, and without it the lessons will be forgotten, alike by statesmen, sailors and soldiers.[24]

Corbett believed the primary role of Official History was to develop doctrine, the 'Soul of Warfare'.[25] This intervention saved the project. After prolonged negotiations between the Admiralty, the War Office and the Treasury, Corbett was commissioned to write the official 'interim' public history for the CID in March 1916. It would be published commercially, by Longman, his publisher since 1898.[26] Corbett had bound the government into a contractual relationship, a critical asset if the project ran into difficulty.[27]

Corbett's volumes would cover:

Preparation for War
The General Policy of the War (Grand Strategy in modern terms)
The Naval Operations
All Overseas Operations (the maritime campaigns)
Foreign Policy in Relation to the War (the critical context of strategic decision-making).[28]

Linking grand strategy, global war and naval operations, while restricting Fortescue's Army volumes to operational and tactical matters reflected Corbett's concept of national strategy, one he shared with Slade, Hankey and Daniel, who dominated the sub-committee. It also made sense in terms of the growing scale and narrowing focus of the military effort. Above all, Corbett wanted to keep strategic analysis out of the hands of Fortescue, a

365

'continental' enthusiast whose misguided criticism of 'Overseas' operations in the French Revolutionary War was already in print.[29]

Corbett adopted the three-stage concept of the war that Churchill had submitted to the War Council of 28 January 1915, based on Fisher's views, as elaborated by Corbett:

1st Phase: The clearing of the outer seas.
2nd Phase: The clearing of the North Sea.
3rd Phase: The clearing of the Baltic.[30]

This structure did not change: commanding the Baltic remained critical to an effective maritime strategy. Corbett's elegant exposition of the 'British way' had all the deft touches to be expected of an experienced lawyer. He emphasised 'the deflection of strategy by politics', situating the British experience in a theoretical structure developed from Clausewitz. The conceptual/doctrinal framework was drawn from his officially sanctioned text *Some Principles of Maritime Strategy*. He approached the new project with two overriding aims: to emphasise the unique, specific nature of British strategy, based on sea control, economic warfare and combined operations, and to contribute to the intellectual development of the War Course. His anxiety to ensure the experience of mobilising mass conscript armies to fight in the 'decisive' theatre was recognised as aberrational, was widely shared among the naval and political leadership. It was no accident that *Naval Operations*, the strategic capstone of the entire Official History project, would be the first text to appear in print.

Corbett wanted to demonstrate the 'influence of fleet on war and prevent Army from getting out of focus to keep the Navy paramount'.[31] Locating the strategic narrative in the naval volumes would counter the 'continental' impression created by the unprecedented scale of the military effort, and prevent it from distorting post-war strategy.[32] It was also essential to the development of naval education. When he resumed lecturing at Greenwich in 1920, he used drafts from *Naval Operations*.[33] The new text would refresh and reinforce lessons from the age of sail and inform the revision of *Some Principles*.

Corbett's agenda was reinforced when a third text was added to the project through the good offices of the Garton Foundation.[34] The foundation funded Charles Ernest Fayle to compile an account of 'the Economic Effect of the Attack and Defence of Trade' in concert with the Historical

Section. *Seaborne Trade* had been prompted by Corbett's observation that War Course students frequently asked how they could study the actual effects of operations against seaborne trade in past wars when 'nothing trustworthy existed on the subject'.[35] Archibald Hurd's *Merchant Navy* project, which examined on the impact of the war on merchant shipping, was also taken into the CID. Placing all three 'maritime' works under Corbett's direction ensured intellectual synergy, as Asquith announced in the House of Commons on 28 June 1916.[36] Critically, they emphasised the crucial role of the sea in winning the war: the strategic analysis in Fayle's first volume closely followed Corbett.[37] The fourth element of Corbett's project, a study of the economic blockade of the central powers, was entrusted to Lieutenant Archibald C. Bell RN, largely based on Foreign Office material. Security concerns hampered Bell's work. Although completed in the 1930s it only appeared in print in 1961.[38] Unaware of the synergy between the four texts students of the war and of the Official History project have ignored Corbett's attempt to produce a coherent treatment of maritime strategy. The oversight is strange; it was recognised by contemporary American reviewers.[39]

The decision to proceed with the histories was made public on 28 June 1916, when Corbett was explaining Jutland to the public.[40] Thereafter most of his time was dedicated to the project. Not only were the early drafts written during the war, while the outcome remained unknown, but they were shaped by Corbett's conviction that national strategy had been distorted by weak-willed politicians, self-interested soldiers and narrow-minded admirals. He denigrated those who refused to contemplate alternatives to the unprecedented, costly commitment of a mass army to Europe. By the time he began drafting in 1916, the 'German way' shaped British strategy. Corbett's frustration with the conduct of the war and lack of naval leadership can be traced in his diary. He criticised Jellicoe, now First Sea Lord, whose pessimism and narrow-mindedness hampered both the waging of war and the writing of history. Disappointed by an officer he knew and respected, he helped to remove Jellicoe from the Admiralty, bringing Herbert Richmond into contact with Lloyd George.[41] No sooner had Jellicoe left office than the two men resumed their friendship, Jellicoe providing acute, effective commentary on relevant portions of the history.

Jellicoe's successor, Rosslyn Wemyss, understood the importance of Corbett's work, helping ensure it was published before the Army texts.[42] A star War Course student in 1911, and a friend, Wemyss often summoned

Corbett to tea at Admiralty House, although he upheld the ban on wartime publication.[43] Corbett had drafted the first two volumes by July 1918.[44]

In June 1917 Daniel explained Corbett's concept to the Cabinet: the military volumes, based on operational and tactical records, War Diaries, Intelligence Summaries and the like, would leave the strategic level to the naval volumes, which examined the civil/military interface. Work progressed in step with the sorting of such material as the Admiralty released. With everything prior to 15 December 1914 in hand, volume I was largely complete by mid-1917. From 1915 onwards, vital records, of 'a more secret character', remained closed. Many concerned the Grand Fleet and Room 40 intelligence work. Without them it was futile to essay a coherent narrative. At the same time the section compiled a 'comprehensive Diary of the War', divided into military, naval and political material, while 'continuously engaged in supplying information to other Departments and individual officers'.[45] Mr Layard, a volunteer in the section, was assisting Oxford historian H.W. Carless Davis of the Trade Clearing House, part of the War Trade Intelligence Department, with a history of blockade policy for the Foreign Office.[46] Layard would add a blockade section to the War Diary in 1918.

Daniel's report reflected Corbett's frustration at the lack of access to Admiralty records. When he asked for support, Hankey tasked Daniel to compile a Cabinet memorandum. Discussions with Jellicoe led Hankey to accept the need to withhold key material, advising the Cabinet 'a delay must occur in carrying out the promise made to Parliament, that publication would take place at or soon after the conclusion of peace'.[47]

In June 1917 the naval section was staffed by three senior assistants, two female assistants and five female clerks, among them family friend Gwyneth Keate, a talented writer who worked on Tuck and Bell's drafts, and helped plan volume I.[48] Two of the senior assistants and all the female clerks were funded by the Admiralty. They sorted and arranged material for binding and produced draft narratives. They also liaised with the other Official History sections and government departments on the War Diary.

When the sub-committee met in July 1918, General Maurice had been replaced by a new War Office representative, Major General P.P. de B. Radcliffe, while Leetham and Brereton were absent. Atkinson, new Official Historian Sir Walter Raleigh (no relation to the Elizabethan adventurer) and two representatives of the Air Ministry attended, but were not members of the sub-committee. Corbett reported access to Admiralty documentation had improved, and his first volume would, 'most probably, be ready for publication directly the war came to an end'. Having read the draft, Slade considered 'it would require no material alteration'.[49] Publication of the Army volumes, constantly revised to include new evidence, was less certain. Hankey's suggestion that volumes should appear regularly once the war had ended, to keep the public 'interested', prevailed.

Slade found early chapters of Fayle's book 'quite good, but rather heavy'; Corbett advised that some material would be better placed in Hurd's *Merchant Navy*. He anticipated Fayle's account of the submarine war would be 'much better, and lighter' and 'a very valuable book'. The committee reviewed the scope of Hurd's work, which covered pre-war preparations for trade defence, and the mercantile marine in the war, in relation to the Admiralty, Board of Trade, Ministry of Shipping and other departments. The sub-committee inspected a bound copy of the October 1914 War Diary, and Slade proposed it be printed as a Confidential book after the war, Corbett and Hankey having found it very useful in their respective roles. Daniel reported the arrangement and binding of Admiralty papers in the naval section had kept ahead of Corbett's work, with preliminary operational narratives prepared down to the middle of 1915. The Admiralty rejected the option of publishing before the end of the war; the necessary 'rigorous censorship' would remove so much material that the book would not satisfy the public or the committee.[50] Corbett had accepted the inevitable after discussions with Wemyss in February 1918.[51]

The main item of business was a new history, *War in the Air*, which would need additional funds to catch up with the other volumes. The Air History had been prompted by the creation of the Royal Air Force (RAF) in April 1918. Placing air history in a single volume proved to be a major error.[52] The RAF had, as the Section Report noted, been formed 'by the amalgamation for administrative purposes of the RNAS [Royal Naval Air Service] and the RFC [Royal Flying Corps]': it was not a separate armed service, nor a strategic asset. Allowing the Air Ministry to shape a history of air operations imposed an 'RAF' version on events that long pre-dated its foundation, to reinforce the consequence of a stand-alone service. In addition, the work would be profoundly imbalanced, dominated by the RFC/Army agendas in the post-war air service, minimising treatment of the RNAS. It became the RAF's foundation myth. Appointing an Oxford professor of English Literature ensured the book would be readable: Raleigh had been recommended by Corbett's friend, historian H.A.L. Fisher, President of the Board of Education.[53] The sub-committee, focused on the procedural issue of disentangling the relevant records from Navy and Army archives for the new author, did not anticipate the propaganda value the Air Ministry would extract from the project.

Finally, Daniel reported a visit from the French Naval Historical Section, approved at the last meeting in February. On 21 February Rear Admiral Mercier de Lostende and Captain Comte de Douville Maillefeu were shown how the British processed documents and discussed related issues with the naval section. They left, 'apparently pleased with their reception and impressed with the organisation'.[54] The French had yet to start work and doubted anything would be done before the war ended. In 1918 the French naval history centre had the same staff as the CID in July 1914 – a secretary and a clerk. It was unable to exchange information, having nothing to share. The French officers were 'astonished at the magnitude of the work', reporting the need for a similar organisation in France. They hoped to return and study the British system. The section had also been assisting the Americans.[55] Admiral William S. Sims was effusive:

> I thank you also for your offer to give us any further help in our naval historical work. We have already benefited greatly by your advice and assistance in bringing to the attention of our Navy Department what ought to be done in this line.[56]

The value of *Naval Operations* became apparent long before publication, in a way that echoed Corbett's original argument. In early February 1919 Jellicoe refused to sail on his mission to consider imperial naval policy without advance copies of volume I, because he 'knew nothing that had occurred in the outer seas' while commanding the Grand Fleet. This was precisely the role Corbett had outlined in his December 1915 Cabinet paper. Proof copies and charts were supplied for Jellicoe and Chief of Staff Frederic Dreyer 'just in time' to sail on HMS *New Zealand*.[57] The impact of what Corbett described as 'ammunition' can be traced in Jellicoe's report on the 1919 mission. At the same time Corbett reported the reorganisation of the Historical Section, to satisfy pressure for cuts, and new policies for military archives.[58] Typically he wrote on a Sunday, never a day of rest, despite the end of the war. 'Freedom of the seas' and American battleships had replaced 'Navalism' and the High Seas Fleet.

The plan to publish immediately after the war proved unduly optimistic. Corbett fought many battles before volume I appeared. In the spring of 1919 the Admiralty had more important issues at hand than approving the book that would explain the Navy's critical role in winning the war, and contain critical arguments to support post-war programmes. Corbett carried on correcting and updating the text, but mounting anxiety triggered a sequence of health problems, ranging from Spanish flu and rotten teeth to high blood pressure and bladder stones.[59] In May he heard the Admiralty 'did not want it to come out yet', with Wemyss anxious to avoid any 'rows'.[60] Within a week Winston had started a row.

Restored to power as Secretary of the State for War and the Air, Churchill was profoundly anxious about how his less than stellar war would be remembered. He had been quick to read the draft volume: praising Corbett's 'great care and literary skill', but objected to publication 'in its present isolated form', demanding the addition of 'a full and fair selection of authentic documents . . . very little of historic value needed to be concealed on public grounds and nothing on private grounds'. The next paragraph garbled his message: the documents would have to be edited and provided with 'such comments as are required to make the account fully intelligible', processes that would qualify the 'authentic' facts he wished to place before the public. Corbett received the paper the following day: he called on Wemyss, who drafted a minute for the First Lord, 'advising determined opposition'. Wemyss, now keen to get the book published, agreed Corbett should follow the report on the book produced by the Director of Plans, 'saying I should be frank', and they settled how to handle the *Goeben* incident.[61] By late May the final revision was complete.

After a considerable delay, Sir Arthur Leetham responded to Churchill on behalf of the sub-committee with some classic Whitehall hair-splitting. The book was not an Official History, merely a Popular History written from official documents. An Official History was many years away. Churchill's Private Secretary, Sir Herbert Creedy, came back with a missive evidently dictated by his master.[62] A book written by an Official Historian, from Official Documents, would be considered Official whatever it was called. The fact that it had been deliberately written for a wide public audience made it all the more important to ensure that it conveyed as true a perspective on events 'as history affords'. Churchill feared Corbett's text would be 'the verdict of history', which 'in nearly every case is based upon the history book that is most widely read'. He cited the enduring power of Tacitus' judgement of Nero, and Macaulay's of the later Stuarts as proof of his contention – and evidence of his vanity. It was also a high, if unintended, compliment for Corbett.

Rather than wait years for an Official History, a document collection could be produced in six months, with merely 'a thread of narrative'. Analysis of the evidence would go on far longer: 'It is probable that events such as the Battle of Jutland will be hotly debated so long as naval history is written and read'. In this, at least, Churchill proved prescient. Leetham admitted defeat, Churchill's memo was submitted to the Cabinet.[63]

Corbett secured powerful support for early publication from Longman, based on contractual priority. Longman feared any delay would hurt sales. Corbett urged Barstow at the Treasury to press for a resolution while he worked through the page proofs.[64] Hankey read the draft preface and asked for a copy to show the Cabinet. He did not think they would listen to Winston, and asked Corbett to credit the late Major Grant Duff for the general design of the War Book.[65]

Hankey's optimism proved unwarranted. Corbett broke off a much-needed summer break at Stopham to attend a Cabinet meeting, but the subject was not settled. Then he met Wemyss, who was annoyed that Longman had announced the volume without his sanction. When Corbett explained that the Treasury had sanctioned publication, the First Sea Lord calmed down and promised to pass the book if the DNI was content with the latest version. Nothing happened. Corbett returned to London, writing another Cabinet memo four days later. The following week he returned to meet Churchill, who cancelled.[66]

The Admiralty Board considered the issue on 19 August. First Lord Walter Long noted 'certain passages had been pointed out as open to objection, especially some which reflected on the action taken by previous Boards'. Such points would not be covered by a disclaimer, because the Admiralty had permitted publication. Therefore he requested the War Cabinet suspend publication until the text had been 'fully examined and approved by the Board'.[67] This was craven nonsense, Long knew it had already been approved by two senior officers, including the First Sea Lord.

Hankey's reaction was uncommonly frank: reflecting his engagement with the project, a close working relationship with Corbett that stretched back before the war and his view that publication was a matter of urgency.

We were instructed to produce a history; we engaged the best historian we could; he produced the best history he could.

The decision is now with the War Cabinet.

I see no harm in the simultaneous production of documents, provided the Admiralty agree.

In the mean time publication must be suspended both here and in America.

PS I feel great sympathy with Corbett.[68]

Two days later Hankey advised Daniel to produce a 'full & unvarnished account of all the proceedings of the Historical Section with a view to the discussion of Churchill's paper'. Before sending the letter he replaced the last two words with 'the naval history'. He also sent Daniel a sketch of the memorandum he needed to take to France for Lloyd George. Only the prime minister could bring Winston to heel in this 'most troublesome matter ... if the Departmental Ministers can't play up we had much better scrap the whole thing'.[69] Daniel signed the memo, but it was drafted by Corbett.[70]

Alongside the memo, Daniel reported dining with Captain Rushton, who had reported on the book as Deputy Director of Training and Staff Duties:

His view is that it is priceless for our navy, but will also be invaluable to any potential enemy, and for that reason doubts whether it ought to be published. He is also absolutely opposed to Mr Churchill's proposals. I told him my view was that Corbett's history ought to be spread broadcast all over the Empire, so that all our partners shall know what the navy has done and what sea-power means. ... In my opinion it is the very best form of propaganda and I would go so far as to subsidise it so that a cheap edition could be issued.

Corbett's views and legal insight burst through the usual departmental discretion. He dismissed the idea that the book libelled Sturdee over the *Cressys* and Coronel as irrelevant: official statements were covered by Crown privilege. Sturdee's name was removed from contentious passages before publication. Insiders knew who had been Chief of Staff at the time, the public only needed to know that mistakes had been made. While he saw little need for the Army histories, as the subject was 'pretty well-known', the three maritime works were so closely linked that they must stand or fall together. He remained anxious to publish because his book had great professional and educational value.[71] It would inform a public that knew little about the work of the Grand Fleet, or 'the widespread operations against the German commerce destroyers', while 'the object and intention of the Dardanelles, Salonica and Mesopotamia operations are still quite imperfectly understood'.[72] These were Corbett's views, and can be traced back to his 1915 memorandum for Hankey.[73]

The histories would 'provide an antidote to the usual unofficial history which, besides being generally inaccurate, habitually attributes all naval and military failures to the ineptitude of the Government'.[74] The naval and military works were to be distinct, but coordinated, a vital point for a CID document. The memo emphasised Corbett's roles as War Course lecturer, author of the Confidential Admiralty History and director of the document collection process. Then he detailed ministerial commitments to publish, including Bonar Law's comments the previous November. This proved critical.

Corbett's first volume was ready to print, it would be the first Official History to appear, giving maritime strategy due prominence. The print run was 9,500 copies at 17s 6d (75 pence) for a volume and a map case. The text had been sent to the Admiralty for approval on 19 March, and reached the War Cabinet on 13 September, dates highlighted as an admonition.

Corbett had an additional line of defence, the bottom line. Not only was the Historical Section budget remarkably small, but he estimated no more than three years' work were required. He expected the final volume, at that stage the fourth, in the summer of 1922. Adding the memorandum of agreement between the Stationery Office, acting for the government, and commercial publishers, reminded the Cabinet that cancellation risked financial penalties and political embarrassment.[75] Hankey praised Corbett's draft, telling Lloyd George there was nothing in the book to cause offence.[76]

With the sorry saga dragging on into the winter Corbett reported feeling 'seedy'. An interview with James Masterton-Smith, Winston's right-hand man, in late September seemed to clear the air; the necessary alterations only took a few days.[77] But Winston returned to the charge, and the Admiralty procrastinated. Hankey proposed a stiff letter, but Corbett preferred a less drastic course, asking Walter Long 'to support me for the sake of naval officers who are keen to get my book and learn what the Navy had done'. When the Cabinet met on 23 October Hankey feared they meant to quash the whole project. Corbett's spirits sank: it seemed that five years' hard work had been for nought. 'They said it could be made up to me some way, but it can't.'[78] That night he met fellow historians Charles Oman MP and Firth: Firth was incensed, and Oman promised to raise the matter. Five days later, on 28 October, Corbett had to amend the Cabinet minute, to explain Sir John Fortescue's dismissal: his article 'Lord French 1914' in the *Quarterly Review* had violated the Official Secrets Act.[79] This pleased Brigadier James Edmonds, who had replaced Atkinson at the Military History Section in April 1919. Fortescue had refused to alter old-fashioned drafts, remained ignorant of wartime realities, and strayed into contentious areas of high policy. Edmonds would produce suitably soporific alternatives.[80]

On 3 November Oman spoke in the House of Commons, but the business was badly bungled by the Clerk: the Admiralty reply was evasive, and Churchill emerged unscathed. Yet the warning shot worked: Winston 'threw up the sponge' on 5 December. Within a fortnight an appendix had been inserted, and approved by the Admiralty, addressing Churchill's main anxiety, avoiding blame for the loss of the three *Cressys* and Coronel. The Admiralty Board, now led by David Beatty, dismissed much of Churchill's argument as 'silly' and passed the book. Beatty, who knew Winston better than most naval officers, recognised his objections had been prompted by: 'the attacks made on him personally as the responsible Minister'. A few days later, the Board discussed publishing Churchill's minute, which they described as 'vindicating his own actions'. This would require some rewriting, 'and the addition of notes in each case, referring the reader to the Appendix'. They also invited Sturdee to comment.[81] The Cabinet passed the book for publication on 26 November, eight months after it had been submitted: Hankey apologised to Corbett 'for all the inconvenience I had suffered through no fault of my own'. Three days earlier his blood pressure had been so high that the doctor demanded he give up tobacco, alcohol, coffee, tea and meat.[82] The impact of delay, uncertainty and procrastination on the fragile health of a man already stressed by five years of war work was incalculable. It may well have shortened his life; it definitely shook his faith in the Navy, and the nation.

On 5 December the Cabinet agreed to publish the first volumes by Corbett, Fayle and Hurd, reserving a final judgement on the entire project until they could gauge the public response. The casting vote came from Bonar Law, who refused to go back on his word, having previously committed the Cabinet to publication in the House of Commons.[83] Corbett's use of precedent secured publication, the success of his first volume secured the entire project.[84]

Churchill's attempt to bury the bad news in a massive documentary collection ended as a two-page appendix, four documents dealing with two issues, 'in view of the criticism passed on the then First Lord'. As he had wished, there was no analysis.[85] When his fears about the judgement of history were borne out, Winston's view of Corbett became increasingly sour. Recognising a continuing threat to the project, Hankey shaped Cabinet presentations accordingly. In April 1920 Daniel advised James Edmonds that 'Winston will like anything German that tends to prove the Antwerp Expedition did some real good'.[86] Churchill criticised Corbett's Official History because the disasters of 1914–15, the *Cressys* debacle, Antwerp, Coronel and the Dardanelles cast doubt on his judgement, and highlighted his unconstitutional assumption of executive authority, threatening his political future. His attempt to block the publication of Corbett's book, exploiting his privileged position as a Secretary of State, risked wrecking the entire Official History project.

Defeat in Cabinet prompted Churchill to begin his own book, initially restricted to his period at the Admiralty. While Martin Gilbert attributed that decision to the relatively benign Second Report of the Dardanelles Commission, it was the prolonged, unsuccessful battle over volume I of *Naval Operations* that focused Churchill's attention. Winston began work in November 1919, using Admiralty and Cabinet documents in his possession, along with Lord Fisher's papers, those of Sir Edward Grey and even the Admiralty. The opportunity to restore his finances helped to concentrate his mind and expand the project. Having become his own Macaulay, Churchill's *World Crisis*, initially a two-volume treatment of his Admiralty service, appeared in late 1922. By then both Corbett and Fisher were dead.[87] Yet his discussion of Coronel hid behind Corbett's account.[88]

Having been involved in the development of strategy, Corbett understood that his problems with volume I would be as nothing to those sparked by volume II, which had to grapple with the Dardanelles, while volume III would address Gallipoli and Jutland.

The Dardanelles posed a serious intellectual problem for Corbett. He had never approved of the naval attack, writing memoranda to help Fisher, Hankey and Jackson block Churchill's scheme, yet he recognised that the attempt to open the straits had been the only attempt to exploit maritime strategy, in the manner highlighted in his pre-war historical and doctrinal studies. Ultimately he would endorse the strategic ambition and the amphibious phase of the campaign, as consistent with British doctrine, explaining that failure flowed from the 'deflection' caused by alliance politics, the continental focus of the Army General Staff, and the failure of civilian direction.

Having assembled an operational narrative by the spring of 1918, Corbett began analysing the larger issues, using War Council papers and other high-level sources, along with personal correspondence from leading actors, including his friend Sir Rosslyn Wemyss, the First Sea Lord. On 3 March Lady Wemyss handed Corbett her husband's letters home during tea in Admiralty House.[89] Wemyss's insight and candour, in person and on paper, were critical to the development of the Dardanelles/Gallipoli chapters.

Just as he began writing the initial landings at Gallipoli, General Sir Ian Hamilton, the commander-in-chief, asked Captain Atkinson for copies of signals he had exchanged with Admiral de Robeck about reinforcing Y beach and the French evacuation of Kum Kale on the day of the initial landings, along with telegrams requesting the East Lancashire Division should be sent up from Egypt on the following day. Having passed between warships they were recorded in signal logs. Corbett replied, personally transcribing much of the material.[90] Delighted to find his views vindicated, Hamilton offered to lend Corbett the first volume of the war diary he was preparing for publication. Corbett grabbed the opportunity: it was 'just the material I value most. It enables one, without giving away anything, to clothe with flesh the skeleton we construct from the official papers'. He reminded Hamilton of mutual friends and distant days riding to hounds.[91] Hamilton brought his diary to the CID on 26 March; old acquaintances, which included Lady Hamilton, were renewed over dinner two days later.[92]

The diary enabled Corbett to make rapid progress. He secured the rest with overt flattery: 'I find as you anticipated that it will not do to break off there and the Diary is so indispensable for getting a land view of affairs. . . . Without it I could not have written an account which would have been at all satisfactory.'[93] He also corrected the manuscript, 'pointing out slight inaccuracies of detail which I hope you might like to put right, only one of any importance: concerning reinforcement for Y beach'.[94]

Hamilton thanked Corbett and sent the next volume.[95] He may have recognised the subtle insertion of an amphibious case. A fortnight later Hamilton explained that the diary had been compiled from three sources: 'a bald, official diary dictated every night to the Sergeant-Major', 'my own personal scripts, very shorthand and elusive – so much so that in several instances in coming to work them out there were passages I could not elucidate at all', and 'carbon copies of cables and letters which were marked to be woven in at leisure'.[96]

Hamilton's diary established the precise timings of the critical opening phase, naval logbooks correcting his assumption about the location of HMS *Queen Elizabeth* on the night after the landing. The ship had been midway between Helles and Anzac, ideally placed if either beach needed support.[97] Eight months later Hamilton invited Corbett to dinner. Although the last section of the diary was returned the next day, Corbett begged he might have it back later, having only completed his text down to 4 June 1915: 'Your record is so valuable that I do not feel that I can deal with the operations adequately without the help of it.'[98]

In June 1918 Fisher warned Corbett 'not to commit yourself over much as to the Dardanelles! There has been champion lying over it! Even you don't know the truth or anything like it. I think I do.'[99] In late 1919, with volume I of *Naval Operations* at the press, Corbett's treatment would be dominated by the need to save national strategy from the consequences of a debacle, and the 'decisive theatre' obsessions of the Army. Hamilton, an important ally, called at the CID on 9 October 1919 to ask Corbett for help locating signals he had exchanged with Admiral Sir John de Robeck on the day of the initial landings, signals that Commodore Roger Keyes had referred to in evidence to the Dardanelles Commission. Corbett spent most of 24 October locating the signals, work that paid dividends. On 28 October he informed the general: 'there was no such signal as Roger Keyes alleged calling him to Suvla'.[100] When Corbett asked Keyes for confirmation of his claims, the hero of Zeebrugge breezily declared: 'There can be little doubt that my evidence is all there, but I will be delighted to visit you at 2 Whitehall Gardens when I can get away.'[101] Corbett let that one slip; he was making good use of Keyes' input elsewhere. Such subterfuge was necessary; he was playing for high stakes, the future of maritime strategy, and the necessary doctrine. To this end he had to impress his version of Gallipoli on the entire Official History project. Finding Captain Gordon, another of H.A.L. Fisher's academic nominations, was struggling with the land operations at Gallipoli, Corbett demanded he get on, or give up.[102] It would be another two years before Gordon resigned.[103]

Published in May 1920, Hamilton's *Gallipoli Diary* received excellent reviews which, Corbett noted, emphasised amphibious warfare. His position on the naval attack had not changed, dismissing claims in *The Times* that a renewed naval attack could have succeeded: 'the writer cannot have seen the latest information obtained from the Turks'. He was entertained by Sir John Fortescue's effusive notice: 'what a convert he has become to my much abused "heresy" that amphibious warfare is our peculiar strength. If some people would not see it he himself is much to blame, for in all his writings, till very lately, he has always derided it, chorusing Napoleon and the continentals'.[104] Ultimately Corbett used Hamilton's text to prove that British maritime strategic methods 'would have made hay of the continental, if only we had had sufficient faith in them to give them an adequate organisation'.[105]

Corbett continued to consult Hamilton, notably on the origins of the Suvla operation.[106] Later Hamilton requested signal transcripts from the landings of 8 August 1915. Having read them he pondered the consequences of the delay they revealed: 'Even at the time the mishap was recognised by GHQ as serious; but now, – from the historical standpoint – it looms very large indeed. From the whole course of the narrative it is perfectly clear that for good or evil things would have been drastically modified had I only reached Suvla with an hour or two more daylight before me': characteristically he blamed Admiral Nicholson for the lost opportunity.[107]

When Roger Keyes, Admiral de Robeck's Chief of Staff throughout the campaign, arrived at the Admiralty in May 1921, Corbett sent draft chapters dealing with the final phase. Keyes considered them 'quite excellent', advising him to stress the contrast between the views of Admiral Wemyss and those of de Robeck. 'The former and I were entirely in agreement as to the folly and impropriety of asking the Army to hold it for naval reasons unless we meant to get on and eventually force the Straits.' Keyes sent Corbett his diary and letters home, including notes written after interviews with Kitchener and Arthur Balfour in London in October and November 1915. 'I think they will help you to understand the extraordinary situation in Dec[r] 1915 and what led up to it more clearly.' He trusted Corbett would treat the loaned material in absolute confidence, not least because it included Keyes' view of General Charles Munro, Hamilton's replacement.

I could not hide my contempt for his narrow minded views or my disgust at his absurd behaviour after the first evacuation.... Monro and his Staff never were in sympathy with the Army in Gallipoli or the Navy or *tried* to understand the Campaign – or except for a few brief half-hours went nearer to it than Mudros. It was a soldier on [General Sir

William] Birdwood's Staff who remarked to me when Monro's dispatch arrived that Monro ought to have added at the end of his dispatch – 'and then the Army swam to Mudros'.[108]

Corbett discreetly used Keyes' evidence to ensure readers realised the campaign had been allowed to fail for want of understanding on the part of the Army, the vacillation of Kitchener, and the objections of de Robeck. He did not go on to determine whether it could have succeeded: that might have undermined his case for combined operations. Sir Roger was 'very glad to hear that you are on my side of the fence – I am so sure we are right!'[109]

Before he wrote up the end at Gallipoli, Corbett's account of the opening naval and amphibious operations appeared in volume II of *Naval Operations*, published in late October 1921. Hamilton's response was suitably fulsome, and packed with unique insights:

> I did very much enjoy your clear, logical and unbiased way of unrolling the facts. I think it is frightfully good and I don't see how the devil you could have carried along without, for instance, linking up the amphibious Dardanelles with the Turkish attack on the Canal. Anyone who probes deeply into the innards of the matter will find that the Turkish attack once and for all upset the nerve of McMahon and Sir John Maxwell so that from that time onwards they were seeing ghosts advancing on Egypt. Even K. was affected thereby although not so much as Maxwell to whom he sent a cable, which may or may not be on the official files but the existence of which I can prove, saying 'I want you to defend the canal, not to let the canal defend you.' The failure to use our amphibious power to catch the Turkish forces on that occasion profoundly affected the course of the war in the Near East. We never got so wonderful a chance again and it was missed not from stupidity but simply from lack of nerve in the higher command in Egypt.

He looked forward to Corbett's treatment of 'the agonies of indecision and back and forward policy' during Kitchener's visit to the Dardanelles and then at the Admiralty and War Office.[110] With his account approved by Hamilton and Admiral Carden, Corbett complained that newspaper critics had missed most of his big points:

because I suppose I had not put them into capitals. e.g. Beatty's false move that lost the German cruisers at the Dogger Bank, the cramping of our strategy by that abominable pre-war compulsory service invasion scare etc. Also as you say, Egypt, but I can put that line in my vol. III. I have a whole chapter (just completed) on the agonies of indecision. It was so mixed up with Salonica that it could not be included with vol. II.

Alongside Hamilton's and Keyes' material Corbett made excellent, if discreet use of Balfour's private telegrams to de Robeck, while Wemyss's official telegrams were 'priceless. ... I have also all Roger Keyes' papers, as he is a very good friend of mine & has just come to the Admiralty.' Keyes' support boosted his confidence: 'I don't think I will be asked to modify much.' He met Hamilton's complaint that de Robeck had not sustained the naval bombardment during the preparation for the initial landing by pointing out that the admiral had been obliged to husband his limited supply for the amphibious operation. 'I should not consider, if "ammunition" is found graven on his heart when he dies.' He ended by congratulating Hamilton on his new book, *The Soul and Body of an Army*.[111] They met for lunch and discussed the evacuation, which Corbett was then writing up. The first draft was completed on Sunday, 4 December 1921.[112] Sensing the strategic tide had turned, Hamilton was exultant: 'May your ink flow and flow with fertilising flood until we all begin to know something of sea power. No one will do it if you don't!'[113]

After drafting his account of Jutland, Corbett reviewed the Gallipoli evacuation in early April 1922. A month later he sent a copy to Keyes, and requested his confidential material. He already knew Keyes' views, and his agenda, but the chance to get first-hand testimony from inside the decision-making process added 'a certain liveliness which would otherwise be lacking & a greater certainty of judgement'. He had already worked Keyes' condemnation of Munro into the text.[114] Keyes brought the papers to Corbett's flat on the evening of 19 May, obliging Corbett to send Herbert Richmond away! Sir Roger proceeded to rehearse his version of the last stages of the campaign 'to explain relations with de Robeck, the Generals & K. also how keen Balfour was to go on'.[115] Balfour, the one wartime statesman to demonstrate 'a sound grasp of naval strategy and the art of naval warfare', was both a philosopher and a thoroughly practical strategist.[116]

Despite Keyes' anxiety to prove the viability of a purely naval assault, Corbett exploited his material.[117] He stressed that Munro had not bothered to discuss the situation with Wemyss at Gallipoli, violating a basic principle of combined operations. The next day Corbett began 'correcting my evacuation chapter on Keyes' information'.[118] To preserve confidentiality he worked on Keyes' material at home for three days, sustaining maritime amphibious strategy. It was priceless for a historian of the higher direction of war:

> I can't be too grateful to you for they lucidly explain all the points I had to leave hazy. They fit in exactly with all that was going on in the War Cabinet which I was at a loss to understand. It means a pretty extensive recasting of the first chapter you saw but that I have been very happy to do. I don't know whether you would care to see that chapter again when it has been retyped so that I may be sure that I have made no indiscreet use of your material. I should like to have put in a good deal more than I have, but I have tried to keep a brake on my pen down so tortuous a road.

He kept Keyes' material until the final revision was complete, and then carried it back across Whitehall. Keyes used the same documents for his 1934–5 text claiming a second naval attack would have succeeded.[119] In 1921 Keyes accepted Corbett's version, laughingly complaining 'of my having made so much of the part he played in the evacuation'. After returning the papers, Corbett settled down at the CID to correct the night action at Jutland.[120]

The synergy between Hamilton and Corbett reflected a shared strategic tradition and a profound aversion to mass conscript armies. They wrote up Gallipoli to raise its profile, to account for the ultimate failure and to rescue maritime/amphibious strategy. The partnership with Roger Keyes, if less cerebral, provided priceless insights into the last days of the debacle, supercharged with the relentless energy of a true believer. Although Corbett did not share Keyes' faith in a purely naval assault, his papers provided a glimpse of strategy in action, like those of Hamilton and Wemyss.[121] Corbett used them to situate the campaign in the British strategic tradition, to ensure it was not the last hurrah of amphibious warfare.

CHAPTER 19

Explaining the Unpalatable Truth

GALLIPOLI AND JUTLAND

As Corbett began work on volume III of *Naval Operations*, still focused on refining pre-1914 strategic doctrine in the light of hard-won experience and countering the Army's 'continental' obsessions, he had to address a new strategic situation. While German naval power had been destroyed, a new challenge to Britain's global position had emerged. Woodrow Wilson's attempt to crush British 'Navalism' at Versailles with a League of Nations and a massive battlefleet had been thwarted by British statesmen using Corbett's arguments, but both they and he recognised the threat would persist, even after the Washington Treaty of 1922. Had he lived, this issue would have occupied much of Corbett's attention as he moved towards a conclusion, linking his wartime role combating German 'Navalism' propaganda in the United States to his advocacy of more inclusive empire/commonwealth structures. His thinking remained subtle and elegant, stressing the need to avoid the appearance of seeking or acquiring overwhelming power at sea, which would only provoke others, while reducing internal frictions within the imperial system, the better to secure the reality of power.[1]

Corbett began sketching the strategic context of volume III after the war ended, and the Cabinet had come close to abandoning the Official History project.[2] He began on 31 May 1920, well aware that failure at Gallipoli and the seemingly 'indecisive' outcome of Jutland posed critical challenges to his concept of British strategy and the Royal Navy's primacy in national defence.[3] Returning to work after surgery, Corbett told Newbolt: 'I mean it to be my book, not the Admiralty's or anyone else's. I find it fairly easy to employ my opinion in telling the story without saying anything that is likely to cause obstruction.'[4] That last claim may have been overly optimistic.

He opened the discussion of the Suvla Bay landings with a lyrical exposition of British strategy:

In the long history of British warfare there is a special feature which distinguishes it from that of any other country. The precession of years is marked by a series of great combined expeditions which, over and above those which were planned as diversions or for seizing subsidiary strategical points, were aimed as definite thrusts at the decisive points of a world-wide war. Quebec, Havana, Walcheren and the Crimea to name only the more conspicuous, occupy a position in our annals which, at least in modern times, is not to be matched elsewhere till we come to the decisive use of the device by another Island Power in the Russo-Japanese War.

Suvla had surpassed the initial (Gallipoli) landings, demonstrating 'the vitality of the old spirit, emphasising the superiority of British combined operations doctrine, based on joint command, over continental practice which handed supreme command to generals.[5] Rather than focus on the reality of failure, Corbett emphasised how close the campaign had come to success, with war-changing consequences, an argument backed by passages from the memoirs of General Liman von Sanders. The amphibious strike had failed by 'a hair's breadth', it had needed reinforcements, which shifted the focus to the Allied war plan.[6] In his view, the Allies found themselves forced to choose between continental and maritime strategies at a point when, as Kitchener had advised Hamilton, Russia's collapse made an early success in France or Turkey vital to Allied cohesion. Hamilton could do no more without reinforcements. The strategic situation became more complex in early September 1915, when the French government created a new command for recently dismissed left-wing General Maurice Sarrail, to quell domestic political tensions. The original plan had Sarrail replacing the injured French general commanding at the Dardanelles, landing with six divisions on the Asiatic shore. When Sarrail refused to serve under Hamilton, his force was switched to a new front, Salonica in northern Greece. Hamilton had been willing to serve under Sarrail, who would have commanded the larger force, but that information was never shared with the French. Instead the switch to Salonica removed French troops from Gallipoli without engaging any enemy forces. Corbett used Sarrail's memoir to explain the grand strategic causes of failure at Gallipoli.[7] The British government accepted this absurdity, frightened that without a suitable gesture Russia would make a separate peace, as it had with Napoleon in 1807, a point taken from the Dardanelles memo of February 1915.[8] Some in

British councils, notably Balfour, had wanted to continue the 'well conceived but ill-provided' offensive at Gallipoli, and link up with Russia, thereby 'confining the war to Europe'. This was consistent with British practice, and served British regional and imperial interests. Yet the majority on the Allied War Council in Paris considered Gallipoli eccentric to the 'decisive' theatre.

To highlight their error, Corbett turned to Erich von Falkenhayn's *General Headquarters, 1914–1916*. The Chief of the German General Staff had halted a major offensive into Russia to secure the Dardanelles, as 'incomparably more important', shifting troops south. Having amplified the importance of Gallipoli, Corbett linked it to the failure of the British autumn offensive in France, implying such resources employed at Gallipoli might have secured victory before Falkenhayn's counter-move. Corbett's critique highlighted the strategic problems created by weak political leadership and the 'Western Front' obsession of the French and the British armies. Landing the French army at Salonica added a massive, open-ended drain on seriously over-stretched British shipping resources, resources the French were quick to call on, yet it achieved nothing. Once again, the troubled politics of Greece disappointed the easily raised hopes of wishful Western politicians who trusted Eleftherios Venizelos, the Cretan magician, to bring Greece into the war.[9]

Despite that failure, the French government insisted on continuing at Salonica, ignoring the advice of naval and military experts. This decision doomed Gallipoli. British politicians lamely complied, to avoid political tension with an embarrassed ally. This was 'the deflection of strategy by politics', a core element of Corbett's pre-war teaching, one he echoed when summing up the campaign. In a foolhardy attempt to compensate for the failure to reinforce Gallipoli, the War Council sanctioned a risky offensive in Mesopotamia, reversing the policy of maintaining a strong defensive position around vital oil terminals. Overstepping the limits of British capability, the river-based offensive was halted at Ctesiphon where, in an echo of Gallipoli, the troops were unable to advance because the gunboat flotilla could not pass the Turkish position. General Townsend's army fell back on Kut and capitulated after a long siege.[10] Gallipoli and Kut were flawed political decisions that ignored military advice, emphasised the problems of waging alliance warfare – and sustained the maritime method.

The last hope for a major combined operation having passed, Corbett examined Keyes' naval plan to pass the Dardanelles Narrows at night. This had the support of Wemyss, but not de Robeck, the commander-in-chief, or the khaki-clad 'adherents of the continental war doctrine'. When it became necessary to evacuate the beachheads, Wemyss, in temporary command, objected. He believed the British submarine offensive in the Sea of Marmara had crippled Turkish logistics, the failure of recent attacks had crushed Turkish morale, while improved naval bombardment capabilities would enable the army to advance onto the critical high ground overlooking the straits. Wemyss's striking paper employed Corbett's strategic logic. The evacuation condemned Britain to fight Germany with the Army alone, 'the Navy ... being practically left out', echoing Fisher's 'Timbuctoo' argument. Rather than risk the Anglo-French alliance, ministers had caved in, tying their forces for 'an indefinite time to [Salonica] an adventure of which we heartily disapproved and which made the defence of Egypt a task of increased difficulty'.[11] Wemyss's uninhibited criticism of the civilian leadership was inspired by Corbett's teaching on the War Course. His paper should remove any lingering doubts about Corbett's impact on the service, and the war. Wemyss had a profound grasp of maritime strategy: it was no accident he ended the war as First Sea Lord.

Failure at Gallipoli, the only major amphibious operation of the war, called into question the maritime strategy Corbett considered to be the highest form of British warfare, the single greatest challenge to his project. He had to rescue a vital strategic principle from near universal condemnation, after a single operational failure. Volume III made the best of a very bad job.[12] He demonstrated that Gallipoli failed for want of resources, and that the shortages were a direct result of political decisions, driven by the needs of allies, and the soldiers' continental obsession. Read in that context, Gallipoli was not a failure of the British method, but a warning about the 'deflection of strategy by politics'. Russian weakness and French domestic politics created a futile distraction at Salonica, which absorbed the manpower needed to win at Gallipoli. In Britain, the case had been undermined by the 'Kill more Germans' school of strategy, which dominated the War Office, echoing the understandable French perspective that the Western Front was the 'decisive' theatre of war. French and British soldiers knew Russia was in no position to support a major offensive from the east, and that without such support there was no chance of reaching a decision in the west. Finally, he echoed Wemyss's strikingly Corbettian condemnation of the abandonment of the campaign as a decisive break with the established strategy where sea power gave the British army the mobility and logistics it needed to achieve an effect out of all proportion to its size. He reinforced the point by demonstrating how the initial difficulties of land/sea cooperation at Gallipoli had been overcome. The account of the ease with which the army, brilliantly supported by elements of Fisher's inshore siege fleet, crushed successive Turkish offensives in the autumn of 1915 was designed to raise doubts about the need to evacuate, a point amply reinforced by the bloodless brilliance of the final operation. This section reflected the encouragement he had received from Wemyss, who appreciated how skilfully he had drawn the threads together in volume II.[13] Finally, Corbett masked the failure of the British method with a lyrical, uplifting account, with the evacuation providing the rhythm 'of that immortal symphony'.[14] Despite allies, soldiers and politicians, maritime strategy had produced a masterpiece, albeit belatedly, and in the minor key of defeat. His friend Elgar would have recognised the allusion.

Having rescued combined operations from obloquy, Corbett took care to lay the foundations to segue into the Arab Revolt, and the combined arms offensive that conquered Palestine. He noted that Wemyss moved from evacuating Gallipoli to commanding the Eastern Fleet, to secure the Suez Canal and Egypt, and sustain the Arab Revolt.[15] Wemyss had more wartime experience of combined operations than any other senior officer, and Corbett had seen his private letters to First Sea Lord Henry Jackson.[16]

Corbett's doctrinal overview of the lessons learnt stressed the superiority of naval officers and maritime strategy over soldiers and continental operations:

> With the broader outlook their world-wide activities gave them, they were in a better position to know all the order meant than men whose view of war had for long been almost entirely confined to the continental aspect of the great wars of the past, and who had been nurtured on doctrine bred in France and Germany. As naval thought read our long and rich experience, it was by close co-ordination of naval and military force that we had always held the balance and had built up the Empire. Now there was to be a complete divorce, and each service was to play a lone hand. Whether inevitable or not, at the moment it was a thousand pities; for not only did it mean that, so far as could be seen, all hope of free strategical design which sea power gives was abandoned, but never

did the true method and spirit of combined action attain a higher mani-
festation than was exhibited in the last act of the great drama.[17]

Corbett extracted positive lessons from a major defeat, both for Britain and
amphibious warfare. As abandoning Gallipoli delivered only 'a slightly
increased power of "killing Germans" in France, while at the same time shut-
ting out our navy from the continental struggle, then, however desirable on
political grounds, it is far from clear that its strategical advantages balanced
its drawbacks'.[18] Britain and France conformed to the 'German way', fighting
the enemy where they were strongest, and best placed to resist, rather than
attempting to confound and confuse their thinking, as Fisher had planned a
few months before, and as T.E. Lawrence would demonstrate in 1917.

To reinforce his point, Corbett emphasised the positives: Gallipoli had
seriously weakened Turkey, demoralised its army, and facilitated the
Russian offensive into Armenia by sinking the Ottoman transport fleet.
Indeed, the evacuation hardly affected the British position in the region.

Corbett located failure at Gallipoli in the politics of grand strategy,
Russian weakness and the continental obsessions of the General Staff.
Closing the chapter with Russia advancing into Armenia was deeply ironic,
given that attempts to aid Russia had prompted the whole campaign.
Britain had not employed its 'normal' maritime strategy because it was tied
to France and Russia, who called for support on land, lending weight to the
'Western Front' focus of the General Staff. Corbett implied that under effective political direction Britain would have employed a maritime/expedi-
tionary strategy, supporting the national interest against the needs of
temporary allies. Referring back to the eighteenth century, Corbett admired
how the ruthless British statesmen abandoned allies to secure national
objects.

The amphibious operation at Gallipoli was a lost opportunity, although
the naval assault had been misguided. His account of the initial landings, and
those at Suvla, emphasised chance, contingency and the Clausewitzian friction of war. He worked to preserve the maritime/amphibious core of British
strategy, the strategy he had done so much to capture and explain, from the
unthinking continental obsessions and 'decisive theatre' of an Army pursuing
a 'German way' deep inside Europe. The consequences were clear; failing to
secure Antwerp in 1914, or recover the Flemish coast in mid-1915, as Fisher
proposed, gave Germany the ability to stage a submarine offensive from

Flanders that threatened Britain's vital interests. Britain went to war for British and imperial interests, not those of France, or the British Army. Fisher and Corbett saw this, working to secure a national strategy that served those interests, but the failure of political leadership compromised the entire imperial edifice to remove Germany from France. This was not Britain's business: it had often helped and supported continental powers to resist the hegemonic ambitions of over-mighty states but, as the events of 1793–1815 demonstrated, sea power enabled Britain to survive the defeat of continental allies, using a small professional army to reinforce command of the sea, the basis for economic war. Mass conscript armies should be raised by continental states with men to spare and no Navy to fund.

Corbett's strategic argument for Gallipoli shaped the key inter-war texts, beginning with Wemyss's *The Navy in the Dardanelles Campaign* of 1924, Cecil Aspinall-Oglander's Official History of the land campaign, *Military Operations: Gallipoli*, published between 1929 and 1932, and Roger Keyes' expansive *Memoirs*.[19] If Wemyss's account lacked the grandstanding self-satisfaction of Keyes' memoir, it demonstrated a superior grasp of grand strategy. He did not mention the Official History, or Corbett, but the influence of text and teacher were clear, especially in the concluding chapters, which argued that a great opportunity had been lost, while praising the fortitude of the fighting men. The final sentence made Corbett's subtle critique of war government explicit:

> the campaign of the Dardanelles will remain through all ages to come an imperishable monument to the heroism of our race, to the courage and endurance of our soldiers and sailors, to the lack of vision and incapacity of our politicians.[20]

Corbett's first two volumes had traced the strategic direction of the war as Britain systematically cleared the outer seas of German ships and colonies, crushed the cruiser threat to ocean shipping, and launched the naval attack on the Dardanelles and the follow-on amphibious strike at Gallipoli. His position on the Turkish adventure was clear: the war's solitary strategic-level combined operation deserved serious study. He remained convinced the strategy outlined in the 'steady pressure' paper was correct, and that driving the Germans off the Belgian coast and back into the Heligoland Bight, before threatening to enter the Baltic, was viable.[21]

He had closed volume II with the dramatic departure of Fisher and Churchill from the Admiralty, with an as yet small Army committed to the Western Front and the Navy entangled in the Gallipoli debacle. He traced these events back to a series of political blunders that severed the critical strategic synergy of Navy and Army. Without a military strike force, the Navy could not conduct the obvious strategic offensives, recovering the Flanders coast, threatening the Baltic and defeating the Ottoman Empire.

The challenge of 'Official History' did not end with rescuing maritime strategy and combined operations from the debacle at Gallipoli. Corbett's next task would be explaining that Jutland – the solitary main fleet action of the war – had been a victory, one he could link to past precedent, and a critical element in the ultimate Allied success. While death denied him the opportunity to develop the latter theme, he sketched the argument in October 1921, addressing an audience that included the First Lord and members of the Naval Staff.

As an Admiralty insider with a wide range of contacts, Corbett was well placed to analyse the battle. He had been able to discuss it with senior officers over the past four years, including Jellicoe, whose book *The Grand Fleet* would influence his treatment.[22] This publication sparked a controversy, prompting First Sea Lord Wemyss to commission a detailed narrative of events, without analysis, from navigational records. Wemyss may have hoped to end an unseemly row then brewing between the officers of the Battle Cruiser Fleet and the Grand Fleet, and it would be of great value to the official historian. Navigator Captain John E.T. Harper completed a masterly text just before Beatty replaced Wemyss at the Admiralty. Publication was delayed while Beatty, and the former Battle Cruiser Fleet officers who dominated his team, attempted to remove facts that showed them and their leader in a bad light, including *Lion*'s 360-degree turn, poor signalling and gunnery, and the failure to report the enemy's position to Jellicoe. When Harper requested a formal written order to make these revisions, none was forthcoming. Jellicoe believed the report should be published without interference from Beatty or himself. The affair showed Beatty and his team in a very bad light.[23] As Herbert Richmond observed, 'it will open the way to controversy afterwards'.[24] Corbett would have been aware of the situation, but he had more pressing matters in hand at the time.

Corbett's 'battle' of Jutland began on 9 August 1920, while holidaying with his family in North Wales. Receiving a telegram from Beatty, requesting an urgent meeting, he returned to London where he was asked to contextualise Harper's report.[25] Corbett recorded: 'they wanted me to write a foreword to Jutland report to explain how good our gunnery was & only failed thro' bad shells against good armour – mean to get out of doing it if I can'. Without missing a beat he reverted to the law, his original profession, telling Beatty that Longman's contract with the Admiralty gave them the exclusive right to publish an account of the battle based on official records. Admiralty Secretary Oswyn Murray, the long-serving Treasurer of the NRS, 'jumped at the idea that Longman's position might provide an occasion for dropping the whole thing & handing it all over to me'. Despite the legal position, Beatty remained hopeful.[26] In the end he would block publication, because he could neither alter Harper's report, nor explain away the tactical and gunnery failings it revealed. Soon afterwards Jellicoe reported that he had previously rejected a draft Admiralty foreword, and the Board's proposed alterations to the text, which 'are not justi-fied by the records taken at the time, particularly the gunnery records and ranges'. While the foreword was withdrawn, battle still raged over Beatty's textual alterations. Jellicoe insisted on seeing any changes to Harper's original report and was anxious to have Corbett's account. Corbett promised to keep him informed.[27] A second meeting at the Admiralty revealed the secretariat's anxiety to suppress Beatty's 'Admiralty' foreword. Corbett persuaded Longman to send a written protest, which he had 'redrafted in official style'.[28]

In June 1921 Corbett informed Jellicoe his as yet unwritten account of Jutland would appear at the end of volume III. His staff were creating preliminary drafts. He was content with Harper's charts, as was Jellicoe, who offered to help. He would share any new material before publication.

I may add that I have reason to believe there is no intention of interfering with my discretion in the matter. My only desire is the same as I know yours to be – to give to the best of my ability a plain unvarnished tale, and I shall always look to you to help me to do it with perfect confidence.[29]

Frustrated by his inability to change the Harper report, and Corbett's skilful use of contract law, Beatty commissioned an alternative text.[30] In November 1920, Captain Walter Ellerton, Director of Training and Staff Duties, directed brothers Captain Kenneth and Lieutenant Alfred Dewar to prepare a secret appreciation based on Admiralty records, including the Harper report. They were assisted by navigator Lieutenant John Pollen, attached to Corbett's section at the CID to work on charts, and part of Harper's team. Dewar met Corbett at the CID on several occasions.

While Dewar echoed Corbett's pre-war War Course agenda, 'if the history of this war is studied critically and fearlessly it will form the foundation stone of a new navy', his conclusions were distorted by a predetermined agenda.[31] Dewar's text was complete by September 1921, but Captain Alfred Chatfield, Assistant Chief of the Naval Staff, demanded revisions to tone down criticism of Jellicoe. Dewar discussed the battle with Corbett four days before Corbett lectured on the naval war after Trafalgar, a lecture in which he criticised the concept of 'decisive battle'.[32] His closing remarks directly countered Dewar's argument: 'what material advantage did Trafalgar give that Jutland did not give? It is one that, in the present state of our knowledge, I will not venture to answer.'[33] This provocative passage may reflect the confidence he drew from early reviews of volume I. He did not live to answer that riddle.

While he did not make the point explicit – it may have been too radical for any audience in 1921 – Corbett inferred that British strategy against Napoleon had not only been very different to that adopted in 1914–18 but also far wiser. Several times in the paper he emphasised that a limited maritime strategy, shaped by the fundamental importance of trade and merchant shipping, deploying a small, volunteer army to enhance sea power, and waiting for the other great powers to share the burden of resisting pan-European hegemonic ambitions, would have been both wiser and more realistic. This approach was consistent with *Some Principles*, which stressed the need for a national strategy that did not unthinkingly ape the continental ideas of Napoleon's successors, modern German militarists. The distinction between Corbett's subtle, sophisticated elucidation of his theme and the blustering journalese of Basil Liddell Hart's 'British Way in Warfare' was at heart a question of method. Corbett had the intellectual power and literary skill to construct an argument that could not be ignored by those who disagreed at a purely visceral level.

Dewar responded to the Jutland jibe in the last paragraph of the *Staff Appreciation*, printed as Confidential Book 0938 in late December. The date is important. Dewar's final paragraph opened with a direct rebuttal:

It has been said that a great victory would have given us no more than we had. This is a lame commentary on the battle. It is not only a repudiation of the teachings of Nelson and Mahan, but it involves an entire misconception of the subsequent workings of the submarine campaign, and reduces contemporary British strategy to the level of a farce. It is better to look facts in the face. The Battle of Jutland can only be regarded as the beginning of a great battle which was never driven home. By studying its history we may redeem our shortcoming and discover another and sounder conception of tactics and command.[34]

At this stage Beatty's Admiralty wanted an expurgated 'Fleet edition' of Dewar's text for wider naval circulation and, after removing any criticism of Jellicoe, for public consumption. John Pollen was directed to produce a version 'free from criticism and comment'.[35] Corbett reminded Pollen of Longman's legal claim.[36]

Dewar visited the CID in late December, informing Corbett that he had finished his work, handing over all the evidence, and the 'super secret appreciation unexpurgated'.[37] Corbett received copy number 9 of the *Staff Appreciation* in early 1922, just as he began writing up Jutland. By the second week in February he was engaged on the 'Run to the South', advising Captain Vernon Haggard, the new Director of Training and Staff Duties, that the Dewar version was divisive and misleading. A week later Haggard reported that the volume would not be published, requesting Corbett return his copy.[38] He resisted the request, and informed Jellicoe.

I have now got well into the battle [of Jutland] and find, so far as I have got ... that my reading of the whole affair differs materially from the 'Staff Appreciation'. After I had read it – for they were good enough to let me have a copy – it appears to me that merely as a piece of history it ought not to go out with the Admiralty imprimatur. The presentation of the facts seemed to me so faulty that I felt it my duty to intimate that my narrative would have to be entirely different. Whether similar opinions were expressed in other quarters I do not know. But in a few days I was informed that its issue was to be stopped.[39]

When Dewar lectured at Greenwich in 1922, his arguments were rejected by an audience that included John Harper and several Jutland veterans.[40]

While he disagreed with Dewar's handling of the battle, Corbett would have concurred with his argument for the role of the Baltic in British strategy:

Germany's practically undisputed control of the Baltic was a grave obstacle to the blockade, and acted as a powerful impetus to neutral trade. In addition to supplies from the West, it covered the important Swedish iron ore traffic, which, in the opinion of the French General Staff, was as vital to Germany as the supplies from the Lorraine and Luxembourg districts.

If the High Seas Fleet 'had been decisively defeated, a British squadron could have entered the Baltic. Operating from Russian bases such a squadron would have tightened the commercial blockade, and opened the road for moral and material support to the Russian armies.' Dewar also stressed the High Seas Fleet kept the Heligoland Bight open for the passage of submarines.[41] Corbett might have taken a similar approach in volume IV, making the Baltic the focal point of British grand strategy.

Corbett's account of the battlecruiser action, the 'First Phase' was ready to be typed up on 16 February 1922. Two days later he discussed the next section with Richmond, enlightening him on 'strategical aspects of the battle which he had never understood'. He discussed the 'First Phase' with John Pollen and Commander Archibald Bell, the naval members of his team, at the Naval Club on 10 March. Recognising he would need a more detailed treatment, Corbett advised Longman that he would cut volume III in half, adding a fifth volume to the project.[42] In what may have been his last public speech, Corbett amused diners at the Naval Club with some reflections on his task and his relationship with the Admiralty.[43] By 27 March he was working on the 'Second Phase', the Grand Fleet approach to action. He spent 31 March at the Admiralty with Captain William 'Bubbles' James, Assistant Director of the Intelligence Division, checking 'on various points on Jutland, especially on my differences with Dewar, whose facts were I fancied very loose'.[44] The revised typescript of the 'Second Phase' was discussed with Daniel and Bell on 6 April, the 'Third Phase', the main fleet actions, on 8 April. Corbett sent the draft to Jellicoe, before taking his customary Easter holiday.[45]

At this point Corbett broke off from Jutland to review the Gallipoli evacuations, completed in late 1921, before the chapters were typeset. Once settled at Stopham, he began work on the night actions of the 'Fourth Phase', which was complete by early May, when he began the 'Last Phase', the morning after.[46] Back in London he spent May correcting Jutland and the end at Gallipoli, before clearing contentious passages with the Naval Staff.

Determined to complete the task, he ignored obvious signs of failing health working six or seven days a week, often long into the evening. The last section of Jutland went to the typists in mid-June. At the end of the month he worked in further corrections from John Pollen, which he shared with Jellicoe.[47] While Jutland was being revised, Corbett began the two 'Home Waters' chapters (chapters 13 and 14), linking the evacuation of Gallipoli to Jutland. Jellicoe approved his Jutland chapters, and sent new text prepared for a second edition of his book, *The Grand Fleet*.

> My general impression of the whole affair now is that nothing you could have done could have forced Scheer to decisive action except meeting him in the morning between him and his base and this he prevented simply because the necessary information which the Admiralty had intercepted was not passed on to you.

At the same time he pressed Jellicoe for details of the routes he had believed open to Scheer, perhaps the most acute question that anyone asked.[48] Having worked through the evidence, and formed his own conclusions, Corbett sent the first half of the book to the Admiralty, Foreign Office and War Office. On 18 July he heard that Dewar's account would not be published, taking full credit for the decision.[49] Captain Vernon Haggard's decisive report reflected Corbett's argument and legal focus:

> The mental attitude of the writer was rather that of a counsel for the prosecution than of an impartial appraiser of facts, and an obvious bias animates his statements throughout the book, leading to satirical observations and certain amount of misrepresentation.

Chatfield and Keyes recommended the text be suppressed, and all copies pulped. Despite their 'Battlecruiser sympathies' they recognised publication would 'rend the Service to its foundation.'[50]

At a meeting on 27 June Hankey praised Corbett's industry, and noted his impact on the Cabinet Committee. Having blocked Dewar's account, Corbett explained that his version 'would show how Beatty spoiled the battle. If he objected I could not alter. Hankey said then it would have to go to Cabinet.'[51] He would not back down. He had defeated Churchill and would defy the First Sea Lord.

On 1 August Corbett took the family to Stopham for the summer, where he reviewed the Jutland material, a task that occupied the entire month. There were major issues to address, as he told Jellicoe:

> Since writing the battle-cruiser action I have seen the secret report and am altering or rather reinforcing their gunnery failure as contrasted with that of 5th BS.
>
> The way the Operations Division dealt with the intercepts seems to have left much to be desired and I have already noted specially the omission to send you the one about the air reconnaissance off Horns Reef. From the nature of the case I cannot say as much as I would like on this point. The summaries that were sent you were obviously misleading. I have *all* the intercepts now ...

Corbett's text evolved through constant interaction with evidence and actors, even as the final draft was being compiled. Jellicoe's input would: 'enable me to improve and strengthen the narrative in many places. But it is a great satisfaction to me to have your approval of it as a whole.'[52] Dewar's text was finally suppressed in August, not only was it full of 'satirical observations', 'bias' and 'misrepresentation', but it deprecated the line of battle, and could hardly be sent out while this tactic remained central to naval doctrine. Haggard and Pollen settled the abridged edition for public issue.[53]

Three chapters were deleted, along with all references to Room 40. The deleted chapters 1, 2 and 8 contained Dewar's argument that a 'decisive victory' would have prevented the submarine campaign and opened the Baltic, his critique of Jellicoe's Grand Fleet Battle Orders, and the deployment of the fleet at 6.15 p.m. There was little chance of the revised work appearing before the *Naval Operations* volume, not least because Longman insisted on their contractual right.[54] Their letter had been drafted by Corbett. The bland *Admiralty Narrative* appeared in 1924.[55]

Corbett began sending completed chapters to London in early September. On 13 September first page proofs of the volume arrived. Bell came down on 19 September to work on charts and papers. Corbett observed that 20 September had been 'A Lovely Day'. He died suddenly on the 22nd.

Colonel Edmond Daniel RM, a friend and colleague for twenty years, undertook to ensure his text was not 'interfered with in any way after it has left this office. But I anticipate considerable trouble with the present Board of Admiralty over certain passages.'[56] Beatty tried to alter the text, retained the relevant Admiralty file among his private papers, and used his copy of the *Staff Appreciation* to influence others. Corbett's text survived.[57]

To ensure his readers would connect the failure to put pressure on the enemy outside the North Sea with the limited success of naval action within it, Corbett crafted a strategic overview of the campaign in home waters after the evacuation of Gallipoli that stressed how that campaign had crippled the development of maritime strategy. It had, as Fisher feared, put 'it out of the power of the fleet to influence the general course of the war by high offensive action in Home waters'. Carefully avoiding overt judgement on the relative strategic merits of Gallipoli and the Baltic, he observed how failure at the Dardanelles had dragged critical human and materiel resources to the Mediterranean, weakening the combat power of the Grand Fleet.[58] He echoed Fisher and Jellicoe's protests against Army recruiting that took skilled manpower from the shipyards, delaying the completion of new ships and exacerbating the difficulty of fitting them out. This faulty use of national resources flowed from the adoption of a continental strategy.

Corbett set up Jutland by demonstrating that the Royal Navy had crushed Germany's ability to use the North Sea for trade and fishing, and reduced the threat of surface mine-laying by active patrolling into the Skagerrack. More ambitious operations, on the German coast, or in the Baltic, were impossible without deployable troops, and so many heavy ships, destroyer and submarine flotillas, and most of Fisher's 'siege fleet' were committed to the Aegean.[59] Ever on the lookout for corroborating evidence, Corbett noted Reinhard Scheer's judgement that the British understood the wisdom of holding 'immovably on the ocean communications' too well 'ever to throw it away by clamouring for a hazardous advance into German waters'.[60] Recognising the Corbettian nature of British strategy and the crushing impact of the blockade on Germany's war effort, Scheer had no option but to challenge the Grand Fleet's grip. This subtle message, reworking the events of 1759, undermined the 'decisive battle' school.

The strategic emphasis stretched beyond British decision-making: 'The sanguine illusions with which the Great General Staff has plunged into the war had faded away. Their cherished doctrine was failing them. The cardinal article of their creed was to crush the armed forces of the enemy by a swift and unrelenting offensive.'[61] While he stressed the failure of German thinking, Corbett's real target was closer to home, leaving out the signifier that the Staff in question was German encouraged readers to treat the passage as a criticism of British continentalism, a point emphasised in the next section, where he assessed the impact of British and Allied operations outside Europe. Here he exploited memoirs by Falkenhayn and Kurt Helfferich, the Secretary of State, explaining the change in German strategy and the shift towards unrestricted U-boat warfare.[62] Corbett worked German sources into his text as they became available. Tirpitz's *Memoirs* arrived in December 1919, and were retrospectively worked into volumes I and II, those of Reinhard Scheer appeared four months later.[63]

Corbett's build-up to Jutland began with the British realisation that the failure at Gallipoli meant something must be done to force the Germans to shift their focus to the north, 'reviving Fisher's "still-born plan"' for the Baltic, and seizing any opportunity 'to upset the German war plans by forcing them to dissipate forces for the defence of their northern front', ideally leading to a German violation of Danish neutrality.[64] The Baltic would be the culmination of British strategy, using maritime/economic power to defeat larger, more populous continental states. He criticised the misuse of Fisher's 'special fleet', drip-fed to the Dardanelles, while keeping troops evacuated from Gallipoli festering uselessly at Salonica meant there were no reserves to support operations in the North Sea region, not even enough to hold Copenhagen.

In the summer of 1916 the absence of deployable armies in the northern theatre effectively confined both sides to naval or, in Corbett's terms minor, strategies, any prospect of a major offensive further constrained by the critical defensive roles both main fleets occupied in increasingly continental strategies. Despite this, the movements that culminated at Jutland were the most ambitious yet undertaken by either fleet. After a succession of sorties which tried to bring on a major battle through air raids and mine-laying, Jellicoe accepted Fisher's strategic logic. Only by threatening Germany's control of the Baltic could he challenge German strategy. Consequently:

he had prepared a plan that went beyond anything he had yet hazarded. Two squadrons of light cruisers were to proceed to the Skaw, which they were to reach by dawn on June 2. Thence they would sweep right down the Kattegat as far as the Great Belt and the Sound, while a battle squadron would push into the Skagerrak in support. Such a bait, it was hoped, could scarcely fail to draw a strong enemy force from the Bight. Possibly, as had happened before, they would not come far enough north to ensure an action, but at least they might be lured into a trap.[65]

The trap included a new minefield and submarines at the Horn's Reef, the northernmost exit from the German minefields.

In the event signals intelligence revealed Scheer's planned sortie, also based on a submarine ambush, before Jellicoe executed the plan. How Germany would have responded to Jellicoe's original plan is unknown, but the overriding importance of the Baltic in British war planning explained why the fleets met in the Skagerrak, the Baltic approaches, on 31 May. Both sides needed a victory. In 1916, as David French observed, the British government 'badly needed some spectacular victories to increase its waning authority'.[66] Little wonder there was widespread disappointment that the great naval battle was not a new Trafalgar.

While Jellicoe's defensive role, covering the British coast and the 10th Cruiser Squadron, and the limited steaming range of his destroyers, left little to find and fight the enemy fleet in the German Bight, Corbett concluded Jellicoe's plan was working, and the chances of battle were high when the Clausewitzian friction of war intervened. He drew a pointed analogy between Jellicoe's position and that of Nelson in March 1805, when Villeneuve evaded a brilliantly placed ambush by pure luck. Referring to *The Campaign of Trafalgar* stressed his contention that Jutland and Trafalgar had secured the same result.[67] Finally there was the all-important issue of friction. The chance sighting of a Danish steamer brought the fleets into contact before Scheer had come far enough north to suit Jellicoe, a stroke of luck Scheer readily admitted.[68]

To smooth the passage of the book across an Admiralty Board packed with Battle Cruiser Fleet officers, Corbett accepted some of their excuses for their strikingly poor gunnery during the 'Run to the South', including destroyers obscuring the range, and cited Jellicoe's contention that poor-quality shells had saved the Germans.[69] He made his real point in a positive stress on the 'magnificent' gunnery of the 5th Battle Squadron. There was no need to contrast it with the battlecruiser's lamentable efforts. Further evidence of Corbett relying on 'irrefutable' facts, many drawn from Harper's work, to establish critical points can be found in passages dealing with Beatty's turn to the east, his failure to maintain contact with the enemy, or his own light cruisers, during the Run to the North, and his failure to provide Jellicoe with accurate information about enemy course and speed. He was also criticised for passing across the front of the Grand Fleet, obscuring Jellicoe's range at a critical moment. The infamous 360-degree turn by HMS *Lion* was mentioned, as a 'complete circle', along with the seven minutes that it took to complete.[70] Recognising the limits of his position, Corbett selected dry facts that would encourage his key audience, mid-ranking and senior ranking naval officers, to read between the lines.

Jellicoe emerged as a paragon of command. Corbett explained his doctrine of fighting a main fleet battle at 15,000 yards, to reduce the torpedo threat.[71] He reckoned Jellicoe's deployment from the steaming formation into a line of battle the 'supreme moment of the naval war', a tactical move that placed him among the great admirals, the heir of Wilson, Bridgeman, May and Callaghan. The decision to avoid night action was explained by referring to 'The Glorious 1st of June' 1794, assuming readers would know the details of the older battle. Lord Howe's decision to wait for another day to ensure he had enough time to complete his battle was a powerful precedent – not least because the dates so nearly matched. Both Jellicoe and Howe had outmanoeuvred the enemy, placing their fleets between the enemy and their base, forcing them to give battle if they wished to regain the safety of harbour.[72]

To explain how the enemy had escaped, despite Jellicoe's strategic success, Corbett emphasised the role of contingency, including 'the good fortune which the Germans had earned by their bold movement stood by them' in the night action. Furthermore, there had been serious failures by British divisional commanders. The most glaring, that of Commodore Farie leading the 13th Destroyer Flotilla, opened a path for Scheer through the British destroyers. Farie had changed course to the east under the mistaken impression that he could not reach the enemy. As a result 'the impossible had happened. In spite of the massed flotilla rear guard Admiral Scheer had succeeded in passing across his adversary's wake during the hours of darkness, and without injury to a single capital ship.' Not only was Jellicoe excused, but Staff College students would understand that destroyer flotillas could not be relied on to stop battlefleets at night.[73]

Critically Corbett gave the Germans agency. Unlike the brave amateurs Nelson had annihilated at Trafalgar, they were the equal of the British, unit for unit, man for man, and Jellicoe had been wise to treat them with respect.

Corbett emphasised Scheer's 'bold and skilful' performance, as he had the 'skill and boldness' of Lieutenant Commander Hersing of U21's 'brilliant' attack on HMS *Majestic* at Gallipoli. Retreating in the face of 'a greatly superior force' because he could not risk a fleet action, Scheer had done 'enough for honour'. Evading Jellicoe's trap was 'enough to enrol his name high upon the list of fleet leaders'. Just how high became clear in a long footnote connecting Scheer's battle plan and Nelson's Trafalgar memorandum. Scheer had a final stroke of luck: he avoided the ambush Jellicoe had positioned at the Horn's Reef for his Baltic sortie, because the submarines had been told to expect the enemy on 2 June.[74] Emphasising the skill and determination of the enemy made them worthy opponents, distancing Jutland from Trafalgar, reinforcing his stress on the contingent nature of battle, where chance, friction and the unforeseen compromised every plan. Raising Scheer to the pantheon of great admirals and stressing the quality of the High Seas Fleet reduced the disappointment of an incomplete victory. Finally, a 'decisive' victory had not been a necessary or even a wise object. The Official History was, as Gibson and Harper observed in 1934, the 'true turning point in the Jutland controversy'.[75]

Volume III ended without a conclusion on Jutland. Whether Corbett elected not to essay one in what was already a profoundly controversial volume or thought it better to link that assessment to the shift of strategic focus that would follow in volume IV is unknown. It was not a question of space. Corbett had developed his book along the same lines as the *Seven Years' War* and *Trafalgar*, using long, detailed narratives to emphasise that 'decisive' battles had to be worked for, employing large-scale combined operations against strategically critical enemy targets, followed by relatively compact battle narratives. *Naval Operations* should be read as an extended analysis of how British strategy was intended to work, and why it had failed on this occasion. The argument was carefully constructed to explain failure without challenging the underlying pattern. Gallipoli or Fisher's Baltic plan could have been the contemporary Quebec, combined operations that obliged the enemy to risk his fleet in offensive operations, leading to its destruction in a dreadnought version of Quiberon. The causes of failure were primarily the disarticulation of combined strategy, which saw the BEF, intended to support a maritime strategy, committed to open-ended continental operations, leading to a purely naval attack on the Dardanelles, followed by an under-resourced amphibious effort. Fisher's Baltic vision had the power to unsettle the Germans; all the evidence from Germany indicated that entering, or even threatening to enter the Baltic would have prompted a German invasion of Denmark.[76] Corbett never lost sight of Fisher's vision, or the resources he created to conduct it. An opportunity to test the idea in early June 1916 had been pre-empted by Scheer's sortie.

For Corbett the critical point in 1916 was the absence of a modern version of General Craig's Expeditionary Force. The dispatch of Craig's small force to Sicily prompted Napoleon to order Villeneuve to sea in October 1805, just as the loss of Canada dragged France into the attempted invasion of 1759. That Craig's destination had been a strategically vital island which, like Zealand, commanded a key maritime artery was no accident. Corbett had noted the contemporary resonance of the analogy back in 1910 – stressing 'the old law which gives to such expeditions as Craig's a disturbing power out of all proportion to their intrinsic force'.[77] In 1916 the strategic significance of Jellicoe's projected advance into the Kattegat was compromised by the lack of military force to exploit any success. A British advance on the Baltic that included troop transports offered the best chance of bringing the High Seas Fleet to battle.

Corbett's treatment of the contested issues of 1915 and 1916 massaged events to ensure the book worked effectively as doctrine primer, a feature of all his work since 1907. This was the book the Navy and the nation needed. Furthermore, the experience of the First World War had changed his assessment of the Napoleonic conflict, now he understood the true significance of Trafalgar had been obscured by morale-boosting triumphalism. Had he lived to complete the Official History, Corbett would have developed his 'unimportance of battle' thesis. Comparing German attacks on seaborne commerce with Napoleon's desperate search for a strategy after 1805 would have been consistent with his wider thinking, and given shape to what became, in lesser hands, a rambling narrative of losses and counter-attacks. Corbett, and Corbett alone, could have rendered the latter stages of the naval war coherent and compelling at the strategic level. That this would have been consistent with *Some Principles*, and advanced the writing of a new edition, should be obvious. *Naval Operations* was always intended to advance the understanding of national strategy, a priority that shaped the text, and the treatment.

Corbett's work was taken very seriously by all concerned – Beatty had been desperate to secure his endorsement, but he awarded it to Jellicoe.

Despite Beatty's anxiety to avoid the appearance of yet another critical account of the battle, especially one labelled 'Official', he was powerless. Instead he took a coward's revenge, back-stabbing a dead man. The Admiralty famously burdened the book with a disclaimer:

> Their Lordships find that some of the principles advocated in this book, especially the tendency to minimize the importance of seeking battle and of forcing it to a conclusion, are directly in conflict with their views.[78]

The minute was written by Keyes, with Churchill's help.[79] In publicly dis-associating the Navy from a book consciously crafted to enhance public appreciation of its role in the war the Admiralty shot themselves in the collective foot. In his defence Beatty, a First Sea Lord at war with the Treasury, could not allow his public standing to be lowered. The aura of glory was vital to his political position. Set against the medium-term future of the Navy, factual truth and strategic insight were not such great prizes as historians might imagine.[80] The astonishing response to volume III from Chatfield, Walter Cowan and Kenneth Dewar, compounding gross distortions of fact with personal abuse, are ample testimony to Corbett's success.[81] Dewar's observations are typical:

> It will be very regrettable if certain false doctrines are perpetuated there. For example the idea that the destruction of the High Sea Fleet could give us no more than we already had, or the argument that Jellicoe's retirement was justified by the threat of torpedo attack. Not only is such teaching thoroughly demoralizing but it is a short step to the abolition of the capital ship and the belief that the fruits of seapower can be gathered by aircraft, submarines and such like auxiliary craft. Personally I attach no importance to Corbett's opinion on the battle.[82]

Jellicoe urged the text be left unaltered, despite noting one or two errors: 'I find it difficult to express my admiration for the style of the narrative, the language in which it is expressed, and its accuracy.'[83] Longman neatly hid the offensive disclaimer behind a diagram of Jellicoe's masterly deployment on the port column, the critical moment of the entire war.

Yet the disclaimer did not end the Admiralty's attempt to undermine Corbett's account of Jutland. It continued to withhold the Harper report.

Elsewhere, Alfred Dewar's response in the *Naval Review* repeated passages from the *Staff Appreciation*, generating further dispute in the leading naval forum. He had been appointed to lead the tiny Admiralty Historical Section, possibly Beatty's reward for his efforts.

When Churchill sought advice on Jutland for his overblown memoir, both Beatty and Keyes recommended consulting Kenneth Dewar, Beatty loaning his copy of the *Staff Appreciation*. Winston enjoyed the book, telling Keyes that it was 'admirable', and made considerable use of it, for fact and faction. Dewar drew the charts for Churchill's book. When the relevant volume of *The World Crisis*, volume III, part 2, appeared it prompted a sharp retort from Admiral Sir Reginald Bacon, Jellicoe's literary champion and later biographer.[84] Beatty also showed the *Staff Appreciation* to American journalist Langhorne Gibson, but Gibson and John Harper's *The Riddle of Jutland* of 1934 came down firmly on Jellicoe's side, Archibald Hurd, formerly of the Official History Section, echoing Corbett's judgement in the introduction. Harper had revised Dewar's text for publication.[85] Arthur Marder consulted Beatty's copy of the *Staff Appreciation*, and adopted Dewar's indictment of the pre-1914 Navy, but he was not swayed in his assessment of Jutland.

Corbett's death left the Official History unfinished. While his friend Henry Newbolt produced the last two volumes, they were a sad shadow of Corbett's work. Newbolt was unable to sustain Corbett's strategic and doctrinal treatment, let alone upset anyone in authority. The decision to entrust the project to him was taken by H.A.L. Fisher, Minister of State for Education. He considered the poet 'the best man' for the task.[86] While the Official History Unit continued to produce accurate narratives, Oswald Tuck and his team had never attempted to provide Corbett's incisive analysis of the strategic, diplomatic and political contexts, the large sweep of the conflict, or any consistent standard of judgement. Newbolt incorporated some of Tuck's chapters 'with little beyond a few verbal alterations', although others underwent significant cuts.[87] Without Corbett, the strategic concept and educational thrust of the text faltered amidst the tactical drama. Corbett had done little work on volumes IV and V, which would have been drafted by his team from the autumn of 1922. His assessment of the war after Jutland, unrestricted U-boat warfare, the intervention of the United States, and the final destruction of the High Seas Fleet was never written. The harassing delays imposed on the first two volumes consumed

precious time and energy. In 1922, the only author with the insight, aptitude and confidence to complete the task was Herbert Richmond, but it is
highly unlikely the Admiralty would have favoured the appointment, let
alone paid a flag officer to think and write. That said, Richmond thought
deeply about the issues, advising the next official naval historian, Captain
Stephen Roskill RN of the appalling treatment accorded to Corbett.[88]

By the time Newbolt published volume IV of *Naval Operations* in 1928,
Beatty had left the Admiralty, and the Jutland debate had cooled. Reflecting
on the 'irreparable' loss the project had suffered through Corbett's death, he
noted the 'coincidence' that:

> the first stage of the war had been brought to a definite conclusion at
> Jutland. The period of great naval operations in the old sense was over:
> the remaining volumes would deal with a new kind of war, a naval war
> on a vast scale, conducted mainly by blockade and counter-blockade,
> both unexampled in kind: and with a moral struggle in which the vital
> conflict at sea was inseparably interwoven with a conflict of imponder-
> able forces.[89]

This strikingly Mahanian passage echoed the division of *The Influence of
Sea Power upon the French Revolution and Empire*, where Trafalgar ended
the first phase of the war, and the 'Continental System' began the next. This
may have been Corbett's scheme, perhaps sketches of this structure had
been left in the office, or discussed with Daniel. The appearance of a
favourite Corbett word 'strategical' on the first page of Newbolt's book may
reflect that legacy. Newbolt stressed that command of the North Sea had
not been challenged, the blockade remained unbroken, and the superiority
of the Grand Fleet had been enhanced.

Ultimately, *Naval Operations* had been designed to support the work of
a revived Senior Officers War Course. In 1919 the Board offered Corbett
£1,000 a year to become Professor of Naval History at Greenwich, his book
becoming the basis of post-war naval education and doctrine development,
connecting the latest war with past practice, and, above all, to rescue national
strategy from the dangerous assumption that the only way to defeat
Germany was the 'German way'– mass armies and 'decisive battle'. It was
well that Corbett did so; the next time Britain went to war it ended up
waging a Corbettian war against a major European coalition for more than

a year, much as it had between 1807 and 1812. In both cases the enemy over-reached themselves: invading Russia provided allies who took the burden of mass warfare on land.

Naval Operations laid out the underlying strategic concepts with compelling clarity, alongside Corbett's judgement that Fisher, and Fisher alone, had the vision to shape an effective British grand strategy, consistent with experience, and exploit the strategic opportunities that emerged, a point emphasised by the plan of the book. His treatment of Jutland emphasised how the effective development of British strategy depended on the combined action of Navy and Army, that 'decisive' naval battles were set up by effective combined operations and/or economic warfare, and, unless the enemy was compelled to fight to secure critical strategic interests, naval combat was unlikely to produce significant strategic impact. Victory in naval battle was remarkably unimportant, as long as Britain retained sea control and conducted economic warfare. Judged on those criteria, Jutland had served Britain as well as Trafalgar. While he did not live to complete the 'official' version of that argument, or bring his deep engagement with the importance of commanding the Baltic to a resolution, *Naval Operations* signposted conclusions that can be supplemented from other texts, his correspondence and diaries.

Contemporary judgements of Corbett's work and the wider maritime dimension of the Official History project were positive and strikingly consistent. More sophisticated reviewers recognised the wider ambition to connect the war with the development of doctrine from the long run of strategic experience. They acknowledged the primacy of seapower and limited war, and even those who, like Beatty and his followers, attacked Corbett's treatment, did so because it was powerful and persuasive. Corbett's eloquent case for Gallipoli being a strategically sound near-run thing has ensured it remains one of the great 'what ifs' of the First World War.

Naval Operations was a typical Corbett text, an elegant, easily understood exposition of the maritime core of British strategy, the deft touches of an experienced analyst and master of literary composition illuminating every page. In October 1921 Archibald Colbeck, who may have been connected to the Historical Section, or perhaps a pseudonym for someone in the section, used an *Edinburgh Review* notice of the first volumes by Fayle and Hurd to examine the nature of wartime trade defence.[90] It could also be read as a sketch for the post-war revision of the penultimate section of *Some Principles*, with which it shares both concepts and language. If the essay was not written by Corbett, the author was very familiar with his work, and that of many other authors he used. Colbeck separated Corbett's work from the 'old' naval history of William James and Mahan, 'who dismissed with contemptuous indifference . . . how our seaborne trade had been attacked and defended for more than two centuries'. In the past, Corbett had emphasised the impact of trade defence on naval thought, but lacked the data to measure the effect of such operations on British commerce. This need was addressed by Fayle. Colbeck emphasised the two methods of trade defence, convoy or patrolled sea lanes and focal points, while assessing the impact of steam and wireless on the problem. In the French wars, trade defence had combined both systems. Where the focal points were widely separated the routes could be left to patrols, where they were close, convoy was required between them. German cruiser warfare on the open oceans had not required convoy, because the focal points were so far apart and the threat so small. The U-boat war in home waters posed a different threat. Colbeck recognised the cruiser period had been one of dislocation, with shipping movements interrupted by the presence of raiders while actual losses were relatively small. Such interruptions were averted when ship-owners had confidence in local naval defence, Colbeck cited examples from 1914 when the mere presence of British warships maintained or restored confidence. Successful raiders operated at focal points, those that did not took few ships, and had little impact on confidence. He condemned the pursuit of raiders using stale intelligence, preferring the educated assessment made by officers on the spot – the reason why Corbett crafted strategic doctrine. He challenged the idea that the next war would be waged in the same way as the last, 1917 and 1918 did not constitute an 'everlasting pattern'. The U-boat campaign had been conducted in a 'foolish, unmilitary way ... for the device of indiscriminate sinkings was the outcome of a narrow bigoted method of thought, which regarded strategy as a science capable of being studied apart from policy'. The Armed Neutralities and the War of 1812 reminded Britain 'that command of the sea must be exercised with judgement; and the lesson was not forgotten when we extinguished German trade with neutral States by a steady, gradual process'.[91] Colbeck thought German methods 'ignorant' of naval history, referencing Tirpitz's *Memoirs* just as Corbett was reading them.[92]

Colbeck dismissed U-boat successes as merely a reflection of the old truth that raiders able to operate for long periods in focal areas close to the home ports would be successful. He compared them to French privateers: both had been able to reach their hunting ground within three days of their bases. Consequently, the close proximity of Germany was critical, not the nature of the threat, a point emphasised by the poor returns made by surface raiders and cruiser submarines on the open oceans. He used data from Raoul Castex's essay, 'Synthèse de la guerre sousmarine'.[93] 'A submarine is dangerous to commerce in direct proportion to her ability to act against her opponent's home terminals', which was largely a factor of the proximity of bases; the data suggested that, once driven to a distance, submarines were less dangerous than surface raiders. In the next war, the defence of trade would be settled by geographical proximity, not submersibility. Any navy devoting effort to commerce raiding was admitting inferiority, citing Napoleon's orders to raiding squadrons after Trafalgar, from another of Castex's essays.[94] Ultimately, Colbeck stressed, 'politics and strategy are inseparable', and illustrated his point with a Clausewitzian flourish, reminiscent of the famous passage on the war plans of 1830.

In early 1922, Colbeck reviewed Corbett's first volume in the *Journal of the Royal United Services Institute*. He compared it to a judicial summing up, noting its impartiality, clarity, restraint and dignity, which, 'without taking sides does persuade a jury to draw the proper deductions from the case before them'. He highlighted how Corbett worked in his strategic ideas, notably that maritime/amphibious strategy was the British way, and that such operations in secondary theatres 'may be decisive'. Colbeck's discussion of the Dardanelles/Gallipoli combined Corbett and Ian Hamilton's texts, seeing victory as always close, apparently unaware how the texts had been coordinated. Colbeck recognised that the war aims set by the Cabinet in 1914 demanded an unlimited effort, open ended and total in nature, in sharp contrast to the measured, restrained, diplomatically contingent aims of previous conflicts. These aims gave the soldiers an opportunity to press for mass armies and decisive theatres. In reality, the practical war aims, removing the Germans from Belgium and France by the most economical and efficacious means, did not require total war, or mass mobilisation. Furthermore the Entente failed to achieve those aims, without American support. Britain and France would have been forced to negotiate after Russia collapsed. Consequently Gallipoli had been a sensible option, consistent with past practice, an opportunity to secure a major prize for the diplomatic endgame. It was consistent with the great strikes on Havana and Manila in the Seven Years' War; it had been 'rightly conceived and wrongly executed.'[95] The suspicion that 'Colbeck' was a pen-name for Corbett is hard to avoid.

The Official History had a major impact on international audiences, none more so than in the United States Navy. The *American Historical Review* sent Corbett's work to naval reviewers. In October 1920 Admiral Bradley Fiske USN, a radical reformer and a long-term admirer of Corbett's work, reflected on volume I. He thought Corbett's 'ability and knowledge' beyond question, while 'the field covers almost the whole surface of the earth', amply illustrated by maps. Fiske realised Corbett had not stressed the failure of pre-war planning and preparations, to avoid problems with politicians, a key constraint in any official text. He also picked up the doctrinal core:

> Sir Julian does a great service to naval strategy by giving the weight of his authority to the doctrine that the primary function of the British fleet is to secure the command of home waters for the safety of British coasts and trade, and not merely to 'seek out and destroy the enemy's main fleet'. His narrative develops this doctrine quite naturally, and shows that fighting is objectless and resultless, unless it is done for a definite cause.

Corbett's method transformed apparently random events at sea into 'the harmonious and correlated movements of the parts of a gigantic organism', making the book a work of unparalleled scope and significance.[96] The following year, athlete, consular official, spy and now curator of the US Navy's archives, Edward Breck, began a review of Fayle's first volume with a *résumé* of Corbett's work and the wider Official History project, in the vain hope of persuading the US government to follow 'this generous and far-sighted policy'. The British histories 'did not shrink from drawing historical conclusions', on their own authority, the Admiralty having disclaimed any responsibility for the analysis of the evidence.[97] In 1924, Breck lamented the death of 'the foremost naval historian since Mahan', before addressing his final book. Corbett's comprehensive view of the conflict, taking in grand strategic, military and political developments, contextualised the use of naval power. Breck found the account of the decision to evacuate Gallipoli 'heartbreaking', precisely the effect the former novelist had intended, picking out some beautifully written passages and Corbett's link between Gallipoli and Russian advances. Breck agreed with Fiske that Corbett's 'amiable habit of dealing gently with reputations' exposed the absurdity of the infamous

Admiralty minute applied to volume III. Corbett's account was the best guide to Jutland, and explained what had been achieved.[98]

In 1924 Royal Marine General Sir George Aston delivered the verdict of British history, reviewing the volumes II and III of *Naval Operations* in the *English Historical Review*. Aston stressed the 'official' status of the work reflected Corbett's access to the evidence, rather than his judgements. Beatty's infamous minute prompted him to analyse the place of battle in strategy. He clarified Corbett's objection to seeking out the enemy, referring to *Some Principles*, which had explained that it was not possible to force battle on an unwilling foe in a secure base or, if encountered at sea, they elected to turn away. Aston adopted Corbett's subtle distinction, that the Navy should develop its strategy to secure a decision, as soon as the wider war effort permitted. Corbett demonstrated how successive wartime Boards of Admiralty and fleet commanders had done this. Having found no strategic reason for the Admiralty disclaimer, he turned to the tactical discussion of Jutland, observing that no specific statements had been criticised. He argued that it was essential to have access to the Harper report, to see how far Corbett had followed the official narrative. Corbett's untimely death had deprived him of the opportunity to deliver a strategic judgement on the action, as he had for the Dogger Bank. Ultimately Corbett's book demonstrated that the Navy's successes were:

> due to adherence to principles based upon the lessons of history. His references to the war as a whole show that conflicts between allied interests, and between personalities, political and military, in different countries, prevented any such consistency in its general conduct. There was neither 'simplicity of design, unity of purpose, nor concentration of resources', and we are reminded forcibly of Napoleon's dictum about the simplicity of the strategy whereby he defeated so many good generals who saw too many things at a time, while he concentrated upon essentials, thus causing all accessories to fall by themselves.[99]

With that, one suspects, Corbett would have been content.

CHAPTER 20

Carrying On

During the war Corbett built or reinforced connections across the dramatically expanded defence sector, and used them to advance his long-term project to establish naval history as an academic discipline, based in a major university. This would ensure the subject sustained its hard-won position as the key to advanced naval education and doctrine development. Although the demanding schedule of the Official History project and his own writing left little time, he consistently made space for this project.

Although he enjoyed a brief respite at the end of the war, as the office and the rest of London enjoyed a 'Maffic', echoing the euphoria prompted by the relief of Mafeking two decades earlier, Corbett's job was far from finished. The return of peace hardly affected his working week, normally six days, and often seven, punctuated by high-level meetings and endless delays as ministers, mariners and bureaucrats cramped his freedom of action, and challenged his judgement. Meanwhile, the pressure to complete his book grew as the country, and the Navy, sought a coherent exposition of what had happened, and why so many pre-war expectations had proved false. More time was lost to the Spanish flu pandemic, which left the entire family bedridden for weeks. Producing a masterpiece of strategic analysis despite these pressures reflected absolute dedication. That the work killed him should be no surprise: a catalogue of health issues, many of them stress-related, had undermined his fragile constitution before the war.

Fortunately there were compensations: the knighthood and the Official History raised his social profile, extending his intellectual networks. Profoundly social, engaged with the broad sweep of contemporary culture, and close to the heart of the literary world, Corbett's friends ranged from the editor of *Punch* to civil servants, sea captains and composers. His lifelong interest in music culminated in friendship with that most English of composers, Sir Edward Elgar. They met through art expert and literary critic Sir Sidney Colvin, a mutual friend.[1] Corbett had known Colvin, another Trinity man, since his Cambridge days, when Colvin had been Slade Professor of Fine Art. As Keeper of Prints and Drawings at the British Museum, Colvin helped Corbett find illustrations and consulted him on new discoveries.[2] Yet Colvin's first love was literature, sharing Corbett's enthusiasm for Robert Louis Stevenson. Elected to the Literary Society in 1884, Colvin had dined with Matthew Arnold, Robert Browning and Algernon Swinburne, while Henry James and Joseph Conrad were close friends.

Having written nothing since the war broke out, Elgar underwent a tonsil-lectomy in March 1918. As the anaesthetic wore off he began sketching the immortal cello concerto, one of four instrumental pieces completed within a year, and dedicated it to Colvin. In April Colvin conveyed Elgar's invitation for Corbett to visit his holiday cottage, Brinkwells, near Pulborough.[3] It proved to be a meeting of minds. On 11 September, Corbett, Edith and their daughter Elizabeth walked over, the Elgars returned the visit a week later.[4] Lady Elgar was delighted. 'To tea at Stopham Manor Farm – very pleasant tea in old panelled room – house really beautiful. . . . Most amusing & friendly.'[5]

Both men were in the last stages of important projects, and both enjoyed a long country walk.[6] With volume II of *Naval Operations* complete, Corbett and Elgar walked through Flexham wood. A week later the Corbetts went up to Brinkwells, took tea and heard 'samples of his new violin sonata.'[7] Elgar was 'delighted to see Sir Julian Corbett & we have had one good walk. It is painful for us that their stay here is so short. We had a happy tea at Stopham & regret hugely that they are going.'[8]

Family visits resumed in the following summer, as Elgar developed the cello concerto and, like Corbett, found relief from composition. One evening in August Elgar, out fishing, stepped on a wasp's nest and was stung, just as Corbett rowed his family past the stricken composer. 'Sir Julian said he only heard words that sounded like "Dear Me!!!"' Taking pity on the wounded knight, the Corbetts took him to Stopham and dressed his wounds. A week later the Corbetts returned the call, when Elgar played for them. There were further visits, long walks, tea and conversation.[9]

Corbett did not attend the unsatisfactory premiere of the cello concerto. Cellist Felix Salmond and the London Symphony Orchestra's under-rehearsed performance failed to engage an audience that may have expected a little more Edwardian swagger. In February 1920 Corbett and Edith heard Elgar and Salmond play the concerto at Elgar's house, a pleasure they shared with Elgar's muse 'Windflower', Lady Alice Stuart-Wortley.[10] 'Very fine,' Corbett observed, 'but too modern for my understanding except the last pages, which they played twice.'[11] The concerto expressed a profound sense of loss, the human tragedy of war, and the passing of the Edwardian world that had shaped both men. Elementally raw and profoundly moving, Elgar's music shared sentiments expressed in Corbett's elegant lament for the lost genius of British strategy.

Three weeks later Colvin invited Elgar to join the Literary Society, Samuel Johnson's famed dining group: Corbett was already among the more assiduous diners at the monthly gathering.[12] Elgar was pleased to escape a lonely house after Lady Elgar died in April 1920.[13] Later that year Elgar empathised as Corbett recovered from surgery, offering to collect him for the dinner, 'if you feel that you could stand it'.[14] This time the doctors had the last word: Corbett had to decline.[15] Elgar spent a last summer at Brinkwells in 1921, depressed and often lonely, finding solace in Corbett's company.[16]

If Elgar's friendship lifted Corbett's spirits, other aspects of his private life only added to the public pressures. Deeply sensitive and easily depressed, he had struggled to deal with the loss of his beloved nephew and his sister's grief. He found many of the more mundane aspects of domestic life profoundly distressing, especially those related to his children. In 1920 Corbett's health would be affected by an unfortunate choice of school for Richard. While Elizabeth went to school with pleasure, Richard made himself ill at the very thought of returning, leaving Corbett equally unwell. 'A melancholy day as usual' is the lugubrious note for January; five months later 'Richard made himself ill because he did not want to go', and in September he was 'much wearied by the effort' of getting the children back to school.[17] The problem was Durnford, a notoriously spartan and uncomfortable boy's preparatory school linked to Eton. Located at Langton Maltravers, Dorset, it was run by former Eton master Thomas Pellatt. Pellatt, a violent bully and a naturist who delighted in watching his pupils swim naked in the sea, had no time for sensitive, homesick boys who lacked an interest in sport. It seems Richard, like his father, met all of these criteria. Corbett eventually accepted that Richard was deeply unhappy, had learnt nothing, and was not up the demands of a top-tier public school.[18] This sorry saga impacted Corbett's fragile health. Diary entries record moments of crisis: rushing down to Dorset, usually alone, to spend weekends with a desperately sad boy, on whom he doted. It was hardly the ideal relaxation for the occasional breaks he took from the Official History. Edith's frequent absence suggests she was no better equipped to deal with the problem. Travelling to Dorset in November 1920 left Corbett disabled by constipation, the very last thing a man with high blood pressure needed.[19] It must have been a relief to get back to the office, where the stresses of his official life were tempered by the confidence and compliments of prominent figures. The pressure of work was the more destructive for being entirely self-inflicted. In 1922 Corbett and his brother Charles rejected an offer of £250,000 for a London street owned by the family.[20] He had no need to work, let alone to carry on the punishing schedule recorded in his diaries, yet he pushed on with the Official History and found time to promote naval history in academic and service contexts.

Corbett was convinced the development of British strategy and doctrine depended on creating close connections between academic history and naval education, to train the next generation of naval educators. His commitment never wavered. Even at the height of the war he made time to support the development of academic history, the basis of his work, work he hoped would be developed by succeeding generations. Despite the overriding urgency of his primary task, recording a global conflict and developing strategic doctrine, Corbett supported historical scholarship and hoped to resume his pre-war projects. He provided the first Lees Knowles lectures on military history at Cambridge in 1915, 'The Great War After Trafalgar', and a second series in 1917, dealing with 'Imperial Concentration' from early drafts of the Official History.[21] It was appropriate that Corbett should inaugurate a lecture series founded in 1912 by a fellow Trinity man, barrister, politician and public servant. Elsewhere he lectured to the Historical Association, commemorated the tercentenary of Richard Hakluyt, led the NRS, sustained the naval element of the Cambridge University Press Naval and Military series, and supported plans to create a naval history chair in London.[22] Nor was he alone in his concern for the future. In March 1918 George Aston urged the need for a naval professorship at Cambridge, 'to combat the heresies Spenser Wilkinson was spouting from Oxford'.[23] Corbett, who ensured the subject remained connected to the historical mainstream, thought a Professor of War would be more useful.[24]

Corbett's academic leadership was built on the intellectual and bureaucratic alliances that sustained naval scholarship. The oldest, the NRS, was also the most demanding. Not only was Corbett a founder member, but he had remained on the NRS Council ever since 1897, a unique record of unbroken service. War led to a dramatic reduction of naval support and academic input, with the NRS's distinctly limited pool of talent drawn into war work. His colleague Charles Atkinson, running the Army Official History Section, was one of many NRS men caught up in the conflict. Corbett and the 'Admiralty' management team he had created in 1912 – Oswyn Murray, W.G. Perrin and Custance – shepherded the NRS through the war, with many naval friends on the council.[25] It was never far from his thoughts. In a rare moment of leisure in late 1919, created by delays to the publication of the first volume of *Naval Operations*, he dreamt of resuming work on the *Spencer Papers*. Such thoughts proved fleeting, but he remained busy, approving Geoffrey Callender's manuscript *Life of Sir John Leake*.[26]

In 1920 the council delegated Corbett to represent the NRS at a British Academy meeting addressing the social and economic consequences of the war. He also served on the council and the editorial committee of the Society for Nautical Research, attending the meeting, chaired by old antagonist Admiral Sir Doveton Sturdee, to raise funds to restore HMS *Victory*.[27] While these organisations were useful, naval history needed a powerful presence in British academe if it was to meet Laughton's ambition.

In November 1918 newspaper proprietor Harold Harmsworth, Viscount Rothermere, younger brother of Lord Northcliffe, offered to endow the first and only permanent naval history chair ever established at a British university. He did so in memory of his son, Vere Sidney Tudor Harmsworth, killed on 13 November 1916 while serving in the Royal Naval Division at the Battle of the Ancre.[28] Those heroic Elizabethan names reflected Rothermere's ideology, while his philanthropic projects invariably had an element of self-interest.[29] Rothermere offered £20,000 to endow a chair in naval history at Cambridge, described 'for all time' as the Vere Harmsworth Chair of Naval History, in honour of his son. He would appoint John Holland Rose. If Rose refused, the university could fill the vacancy.[30]

The Council of the University Senate recommended acceptance on 27 January 1919; Congregation adopted the recommendation on 16 May. The professor was expected to 'deliver courses of lectures on naval History, to apply himself to the advancement of knowledge in this subject, and to promote the study of naval History in the University'. Income from the endowment would provide a stipend, less the income from any college positions held by the incumbent.

At the same time, the Admiralty launched a scheme to send young officers to the university for a few terms, that they might learn something of life beyond the service, to save them from 'the besetting sin of all professions viz narrowness'. The initiative came from Herbert Richmond, Director of Training during last eight months of 1918, who believed officers should not be restricted to a mathematical curriculum. Initially he envisaged sending 400 officers, later reduced to 140. In 1923 the scheme was terminated by the Treasury, which pleased both the university and undergraduates, who feared being 'swamped'. John Holland Rose had been providing naval history lectures within a broad liberal curriculum.[31]

The offer to found a chair and appoint a professor prompted a debate about the nature and purpose of naval history at the university and in British academe. Noted for work on Pitt the Younger, Napoleon and other aspects of the Revolutionary and Napoleonic era, Rose was not a naval specialist, and it is not clear why Rothermere selected him. Rose declined because:

> the new Professorship would exercise the most beneficial influence, both on the University and on the nation at large, if it became not merely a historical Professorship, but also one which would contribute to the development of the study of naval strategy and tactics in the present age. While realising to the full the value of the study of the campaigns of previous centuries, I hold that the investigation of modern developments (even of recent developments) of naval warfare is equally important. Only that investigator who has been in close touch with the present problems of naval administration and marine warfare can, in my judgement, impart to his teaching that vitality, that authority, which will enable him to build up in this University a strong School of Naval History. . . . It is my earnest desire to see such a School founded and developed here. The present opportunity may never occur again.[32]

He did not need to name Corbett, with whom he had worked closely on the Phillimore Committee. This was not what the university wanted to hear. Within days James Smith Reid (1846–1926), Professor of Ancient History and a member of the Council of Senate,[33] had 'a long talk' with Rose, stressing his decision would be 'unfortunate, both for the university and for himself', dismissing the idea of founding a 'School of Naval Strategy and Tactics', ridiculing naval history since the introduction of steam as 'almost farcical', and sweeping aside Rose's preferred candidate 'as quite without the gift of exposition for which Rose is conspicuous'.[34] Opinions on such matters vary: when Rose lectured at King's College London in January 1920, Corbett thought him 'very bad indeed and most disappointing'.[35]

Alongside an understandable anxiety to avoid upsetting a wealthy donor, Reid wanted to maintain a strict separation between academic and professional interest in history. In his view, history was not a useful subject: if it was it had no place at Cambridge. His comical characterisation of modern naval warfare reflected concerns about the validity of 'modern' history typical of cloistered communities. Dismissing Corbett revealed something worse than ignorance: not only did the 'man' have excellent expository powers, but he was a university alumnus, a knight and the recognised master of the subject. Fundamentally Reid objected to the presence of a relevant subject in the university, or was Corbett's law degree a permanent bar to historical eminence?

Rose recognised the development of the subject from the 1880s had been driven by the expanding educational needs of the Navy, pioneered by Laughton and extended by Corbett.[36] He thought the chair should establish an academic/service partnership at Cambridge. Shortly after the discussion with Reid, Rose informed Corbett he had stood down, lacking 'a sufficient grip of the most modern developments of the British Navy and of its actual working, and that therefore my teaching would lack vitality and freshness'. He had mentioned Corbett to 'three or four persons of influence up here & . . . all who are acquainted with naval history recognise the strength of your claims'. Above all, 'you have that touch with the Navy of the present which will make your teaching fresh & powerful, & will contribute towards the building up of a School of Naval Study of truly national importance'.[37] Ill and overworked, Corbett declined, but Rose persisted, hoping he could rest and be ready by late spring.[38]

Reid's letter was passed to Sir Arthur Shipley (1861–1927), the vice chancellor.[39] A week later Corbett wrote to Shipley – they had worked together on British propaganda for the United States – recommending Richmond, 'who I am sure is far the best you could find. . . . He is a disciple of mine.' He invited Shipley to discuss the subject in London.[40] Shipley pressed him to accept, but Corbett declared: 'so long as I have to run the Historical Section I see no prospect of being able to take on anything else. It is a back-breaking load.'[41]

Rose, prompted by Rothermere, had second thoughts. If Corbett declined he would be willing. 'All that I want is that the best man possible shall gain the Professorship and shall build up in Cambridge a strong school of Naval Studies.'[42] Rose wanted a chair in 'Naval Studies', rather than naval history narrowly conceived, which would need someone 'in close touch with the Admiralty'. He recognised that unless the chair was founded on Corebettian lines it would wither, from inattention or malice, demonstrating a sound grasp of university politics. He lived to see those fears borne out.

Corbett discussed the opportunity with Richmond, who enthused: 'My strongest inclination is to go to Cambridge where I should like to build up a really big thing out of that lectureship.'[43] Richmond's case was supported by Arthur Hungerford Pollen, naval journalist, barrister and fire control pioneer, who wrote at Rothermere's invitation. His effusive letter was perfectly calculated to defeat Richmond's candidacy: not only did this arcane branch of knowledge 'need a seaman to really understand what seamen wrote to each other', but the chair would enable Richmond to become 'an English Mahan', 'a really great authority'. The suggestion that Shipley might dig out the manuscript of Richmond's three-volume book from the University Press hardly compensated for his ignorance of academic concerns.[44] The idea that the university should house a school of war and strategy would have appalled all right-thinking academics. A reference from Admiral 'Blinker' Hall, lately Director of Naval Intelligence, emphasised Richmond's historical expertise had 'carried him into the realms of both major and minor strategy on both of which he is competent to speak from his intimate knowledge.... If a naval officer be selected for the Chair ... Richmond is admirably suited for it.'[45] Two more names were recommended, South African statesman Jan Christian Smuts backed George Aston. Although not a naval historian, he was an experienced and popular Staff College teacher who had 'written a number of interesting books on war'.[46] *Daily Mail* journalist and popular naval writer H.W. Wilson provided his own reference, after meeting Rothermere at the Paris Peace Conference. He sent both an official application and a personal letter, with Northcliffe, Rothermere, defence correspondent and Chichele Professor of the History of War Spenser Wilkinson, George Prothero of the *Quarterly Review* and Admiral William Henderson, 'the British Mahan', as referees.[47] Despite his Oxford credentials it is unlikely Wilson excited any interest; he was deeply tainted by a long and active role in compiling, editing and managing the vulgar rags that had provided the money for the chair.

On 2 February Corbett discussed the chair with Lady Richmond; Herbert was interested, and with his great book at the press the opening was timely. Two days later Corbett discussed the possibility of a naval history chair at King's College London with Professor Arthur Newton. Then he was 'offered Chair of Naval History' at the revived Naval War Course, based at Greenwich.[48] This suited his interests and his location. Any lingering interest in Cambridge was crushed by flu, surgery for bladder stones and the opening rounds of his battle with Churchill over *Naval Operations*. When old friend George Prothero urged him to stand, he wrote to Shipley for details of the post, residence qualifications and other requirements. A month later the Treasury raised the salary of the Greenwich chair to £1,000.[49] A welcome by-product of his renewed links with Cambridge was his election as an honorary Fellow of Trinity; attending the ceremony revived cherished college memories.[50]

On 18 May 1919 Richmond noted: 'Saw Corbett & discussed Cambridge with him. He has decided that he can't do the work, and said the field was open for me, if I cared for it. But as I find that it meant living in Cambridge & becoming a tutor, I don't want it. I think I can do more than that with my life.'[51] Richmond's decision prompted Corbett, despite poor health and the Official History, to reconsider. The opportunity to establish the subject in such an august setting might not recur, but tutorial work and residence stipulations made it impossible.[52] This cleared the way for the university to oblige Rothermere, appointing his candidate as their choice.

On 14 June 1919 Rose became the Vere Harmsworth Professor, while the Council of the Senate set up a board of electors for future appointment comprising Corbett, Arthur Quiller Couch, Admiral of the Fleet the Marquis of Milford Haven, H.H. Brindley, the two Regius Professors of History Charles Harding Firth and John Bury, and R.V. Lawrence of Trinity College.[53] Corbett maintained his Cambridge connections, visiting Trinity in late May 1920 as the guest of the Master, distinguished physicist Sir Joseph Thomson (1856–1940), President of the Royal Society 1915–20 and a significant contributor to wartime Admiralty research.[54] Unfortunately Rose's tenure neither added lustre to the university nor advanced the subject, facilitating a brutal annexation of the chair by other historical interests in 1936.

That a man past retiring age, in poor health and desperately busy, should even consider the option was striking. The Cambridge initiative reinforced Corbett's anxiety to secure a permanent home for naval history within British academe. Appointing Rose would not be enough. He lunched with the Navy League in May 1919 to 'encourage national study of naval history': the delegates agreed to 'raise funds to found a chair at London University'. Attending another Navy League event a fortnight later, Corbett revealed his true priorities, leaving early to attend the Society for Nautical Research. While prepared to work a crowd to raise funds, he found some uncongenial. Well aware that the Navy was uninterested, he was hardly surprised when Slade reported that attempts to create an Admiralty Historical Section were not going well.[55] A tiny office would endure, under Lieutenant Alfred Dewar, joint author of the infamous *Staff Appreciation* of Jutland. Beatty's Admiralty had no interest in objective scholarship.

With the Navy League faltering, the Admiralty beyond hope and King's College London dithering, Corbett joined the University of London Historical Studies Appeal Committee, chaired by his friend Professor Albert Pollard.[56] Long an advocate of naval history and of Laughton's work, Pollard wanted a department to study naval and military history, 'two aspects of the same subject, particularly so far as the British Empire is concerned, and nothing has hampered its understanding more than the habit of treating each in isolation'.[57] These were Corbett's words. The department would be based in a postgraduate School (now Institute) of Historical Research. Having initially opposed teaching naval history at a university, Corbett's view had been changed by close contact with the Navy.[58] In 1916 he publicly endorsed Laughton's contention that the long-term future of naval history depended on combining the academic standards of the university with the contemporary relevance of the Staff College.[59]

Historian-minister H.A.L. Fisher provided Cabinet-level support for Pollard's vision. In February 1920 University College, King's College and the London School of Economics' committee on postgraduate historical studies recommended the Senate sanction an appeal to raise £20,000. The list of influential persons appealed to included statesmen, financiers, public figures and Corbett. Enthused by an echo of his own opinions, Corbett contributed £20. In July 1920 Fisher demanded a school to prepare students for work in the national archives, bringing 'the experience of the past to bear on the problems of the present'. The absence of such teaching was 'a reproach not merely to the capital of the Empire, but the nation at large'.[60] Pollard envisaged a national intellectual resource, like the American 'Board of National Historical Services for the purpose of bringing to bear upon present problems the light of historical knowledge'.[61] The links he drew between the new Institute of

Historical Research (IHR) and Staff College at Greenwich reflected their prominence as the twin poles of Corbett's intellectual world. When he needed to prove that history was a significant national resource, Pollard cited Corbett's CID Historical Section, inferring that something better might be done in future, if historians had benefited from a central school of advanced studies, detached from the day-to-day business of undergraduate education. The prominence of naval history, and contemporary relevance, reflected Pollard's belief that Corbett was an exemplar, linking Laughton's NRS, the Phillimore Committee and Richmond's revived Staff College. Echoing Corbett, Pollard envisaged the IHR becoming a shared resource to broaden the horizons of naval officers by teaching historical method and political history.[62] That synergy would feature in Corbett's last lecture.

In June 1920, Corbett joined other eminent historians at a university dinner for City men, hoping to raise £20,000 for the IHR. Only Thomas Selfridge obliged, providing £1,000.[63] Corbett continued to press the case with cabinet ministers and joined the IHR Committee, the lone voice of Official History among leading academics.[64]

Corbett's support also took a more obvious form. In January 1921 he prompted the NRS Council to donate a set of volumes to the new institute.[65] The vice chancellor conveyed the thanks of the university to the NRS and thanked Corbett for providing the one missing volume.[66] That *Signals and Instructions* had been the first NRS text to sell out emphasised how skilfully it had been tailored to the naval audience of the dreadnought generation. Corbett also offered some of his own 'textbooks'. IHR secretary Miss Davies' reply persuaded him that she shared his doubts about their value.[67] Corbett's description said more about his innate modesty than the merits of the texts: Miss Davies did not consult Pollard, who knew better. When the building opened it included a dedicated 'Naval and Military' room with relevant books and materials. The introductory pamphlet of 1921 explained:

> On the other side of the English History room we connect England with the European Continent by the three inevitable means of contact, Diplomatic, Naval and Military . . . diplomacy precedes naval action and, for an insular State, the navy comes before the army.[68]

The Naval and Military room survived into the 1990s, when it was consigned to the basement, with the order of the names reversed, spoiling a critical element of Pollard's scheme. Today the collection includes a full run of NRS volumes and half of Corbett's library.

If the Naval and Military room suggested that war had changed the academic landscape, the presence of an explicitly present-minded British Institute of International Affairs across the corridor, enabling students to share resources, completed Pollard's vision.[69] At the inauguration H.A.L. Fisher echoed Pollard's agenda, commending the co-location of the two institutes.[70] Corbett and Edith attended, lunching with leading university figures and the fund-raising committee. Corbett returned a few days later on committee business, opening a discussion of naval history as chairman of the Colonial Section of the History Conference.[71] The IHR project allowed Corbett to command the attention of academics, warriors and statesmen to his vision for the future of naval history. Based at the heart of the federal university, an expanding intellectual resource at the centre of the empire Corbett lived to serve, it was far removed from the dusty disdain of Oxford and Cambridge. Naval history needed to be in central London, close to the Greenwich Staff College, Westminster and the City, not in an academic enclave. He spent a final afternoon at the IHR on 28 June 1922, still working for the long-term interests of his subject.[72]

In a mark of his consequence, and that of his subject, Pollard invited Corbett to give the Annual Creighton Memorial Lecture for 1921 in the margins of an IHR Committee meeting on 8 April 1921.[73] Despite being desperately busy, Corbett accepted. The Creighton was a major event in the university calendar, an ideal opportunity to promote their shared vision. With his experience of the Vere Harmsworth Chair in mind, and the 1916 Laughton Memorial Lecture in hand, he restated the academic case for naval history. It was significant that he spoke in the Great Hall at King's College on the evening of 11 October 1921.

Corbett accepted the invitation despite the obvious problem that he had no time to write a new lecture. Instead he reused material originally produced for the War Course, at Lewis Bayly's request, dealing with the naval war after Trafalgar. When Corbett delivered the 'Walcheren' lecture on 28 November 1911, he overran the hour: 'really much too big a subject to deal with in one lecture'. By then Bayly had been relieved by Sir Henry Jackson, 'who said I ought to make two of it & write a book about it. But I think everyone was very much interested.'[74] Six months later the revised lectures generated great interest: 'the war after Trafalgar is such a perfect blank to them'.[75]

The lecture was chaired by Lord Lee of Fareham, First Lord of the Admiralty.[76] Lee complained of university 'indifference' to sea power; only Cambridge made any provision, and even there, as Corbett would have advised him, naval history was a recent, unwelcome addition to the curriculum. Lee linked the lecture to pre-war plans for a chair in the University of London. Many mistakes made during the war might have been avoided 'if those charged with the direction of affairs had studied and applied the lessons learned by our ancestors in the naval wars of the past'. The greatest of these lessons concerned 'the diplomatic use of sea power, which often attained greater ends than fighting did'.[77] *The Times*' brief account of Lee's introduction served Corbett's agenda of creating a School of Naval History. The lecture stressed how much work remained to be done, with the period between Trafalgar and Waterloo a 'trackless desert'. While this gap was not unique, the period surpassed all others 'in importance and instruction', being relatively recent, and a 'striking analogy' for the Great War. Focusing on the defence of trade enabled him to stress how 'naval' history should address 'the whole activities of our life at sea'.[78] The separation of maritime history into naval and commercial aspects encouraged general historians to ignore the subject.

Corbett quickly moved to the strategic argument. Continental strategists, obsessed with the principle of concentration, judged the British war effort between 1805 and 1812 'amateurish child's play, yet it was this child's play that won'. It was not a violation of sound strategic principles, and he stressed that Britain had survived, prospered, and funded the coalition that finally destroyed Napoleon. The repetition of his argument from *Some Principles* addressed continentally minded soldiers, and the dominance of the 'Western Front' as the focal point of the conflict. The war had seen these approaches, already a problem in 1911, harden into unthinking dogma, invulnerable to reason. Corbett advised the application of 'historical massage' to relax ossified, khaki-clad minds, and recover the reality of Britain's limited maritime strategy. Citing the poem *Libylle of Englysshe Policie* of 1436 and G.F.R. Henderson's maxim that 'the first objective of the forces of a maritime power, both by land and sea' was the naval strength of the enemy, produced a new strategic model, 'which binds the sporadic incidents [of the period 1806–12] into a consistent whole'. This 'British way' required a concentration of effort in a decisive theatre, namely command of the sea.[79]

Although he did not mention strategic doctrine, it is evident Corbett was thinking about the revision of *Some Principles*, a task that might be possible after completing the Official History. Many had questioned the need to keep attacking Napoleon's fleet after Trafalgar. Even Mahan, 'for all his philosophic outlook', had fallen into this trap, treating Nelson's victory as the end of Napoleon's sea power. Having neatly set up a paradox, Corbett resolved it to make his point, while emphasising his superior insight. Napoleon had not accepted the judgement of one battle: his massive energies were devoted to resuscitating French naval power, through allies, satellites and national effort. Down to 1812 the British were responding to a real, growing threat, one that Corbett traced through the emperor's correspondence.[80] In response, the British attacked French naval bases, fleets and resources in a series of combined operations, which tended to be ignored by both services. While they might be condemned as weak by German theorists, they were in reality a powerful concentration of effort on the most important object for British security. Colonial privateer bases were taken to reduce shipping losses and consequent economic damage, while captured islands became outlets for trade. So, while Napoleon tried to destroy Britain by economic exhaustion, Britain defeated his offensives, and struck back, destroying his navy, opening new markets and attacking his economy. This was the best use of a limited military capability unable to face the French in a 'decisive' theatre.

Napoleon's greatest effort was made on the North Sea. New dockyards were created at Antwerp and Hamburg to harness Scandinavian resources, Antwerp and Flushing replacing Brest as the 'cradle for his new fleet'.[81]

Referring to Sir James Craig's Sicilian expedition of 1805 revealed how early the counter-attack had begun. The need to act, to encourage allies, was tempered by the limited number of troops, and the major economic interests to be secured by keeping Napoleon out of the Levant. Sicily acted as a bastion against French expansion.

Attempts to achieve more, with an army based on Rügen in the Baltic, collapsed when Prussia and Russia made peace. After Tilsit, the naval arm of the Continental System included over eighty Baltic capital ships. Napoleon, Corbett stressed, was already counting on this new fleet when the British struck. The seizure of the Danish Navy at Copenhagen in 1807, using amphibious power, removed sixteen of them from the list and alarmed Russia. Far from apologising for Copenhagen as an unwarranted strike against little, neutral, Denmark, Corbett rightly celebrated it as a 'victory over the great, unsuspecting Napoleon'.[82] While Copenhagen denied Napoleon a useful fleet, the wider strategic impact was far greater: it denied him the ability to close the Baltic. He did not stress the contemporary resonance. The seizure of Heligoland opened new avenues for smuggling, both goods and people, obliging the emperor to fortify German ports and estuaries, and contemplate an amphibious operation to remove the 'ulcer'. Corbett noted how Saumarez's armed diplomacy kept the Baltic open, despite Napoleon's best efforts, undermining the Continental System.

The attack on Walcheren and the destruction of Flushing were the intended follow-on operation in 1807, using Sir Arthur Wellesley's force. After that, the remaining allied ships at Cadiz would be torched. However, Napoleon's reaction to Copenhagen, seizing Lisbon, obliged the British to respond: 'as a naval base the Tagus was far too valuable to be allowed to fall into the enemy's hands'.[83] The Scheldt and Cadiz were postponed while a fleet secured the Portuguese fleet, royal family, gold and trade, but left the French in Lisbon, with nine Russian battleships. A difficult blockade was avoided by amphibious power: the oft-derided Convention of Cintra gave Britain control of Lisbon, the Tagus and the Russian fleet, a major strategic success.

Then Napoleon tried to create an overwhelming naval concentration in the Mediterranean, to seize Sicily, only to be distracted by the threat to Corfu, and the Balkan ambitions of his Russian ally. Two French squadrons were redirected to relieve the Ionian Islands, passing up a chance to win the Mediterranean. Not that it was much of a chance; Collingwood knew where the danger lay and deployed accordingly. Napoleon's delusional plans assumed the Royal Navy could be decoyed away, leaving Britain, Sicily or other key strategic positions unguarded. The last French attempt to combine forces for a strategic move ended in disaster at the Aix Roads in 1809, prompting a redeployment of naval resources to defensive roles. When the Spanish Revolt handed Britain control of Minorca, Toulon was completely neutralised, leaving the fleet in the Scheldt as the only strategic threat. Corbett questioned the assumption that the Walcheren operation had been a failure. He stressed the shock it had given Napoleon. Far from laughing at British amphibious operations as 'the combinations of pygmies',

Napoleon redoubled his efforts to fortify the North Sea coast. However, he had been dealt a major blow, for 'without Flushing, where before leaving, we had completely destroyed the port and arsenal, Antwerp, for technical reasons, was of little value, either as a base or a dockyard'.[84] Napoleon poured money into the reconstruction of Flushing, and a new basin at Antwerp, but his resources were never equal to the task of outbuilding Britain at sea, let alone acquiring an effective battlefleet. The scale of victory was obvious in Whitehall: 'after Walcheren, our fleet was able to devote its main energy for the rest of the war to supporting the army in the Peninsula'.[85]

He had a larger point to make, about the utility of history for current thinking; and of recent experience for grasping the realities of past events. Not only had the First World War changed his assessment of the Napoleonic conflict, leading him to reconsider the impact of Trafalgar, but, he concluded:

> Going even lightly over the ground, its striking analogy to our latest struggle brings forth a whole harvest of unsettled queries: and the one which for me at least is the most insistent is this: What material advantage did Trafalgar give that Jutland did not give? It is one that, in the present state of our knowledge, I will not venture to answer.[86]

He was ready to take on his critics, hinting at a startling development of the 'unimportance of battle' heresy, which would confound Lord Sydenham, Spenser Wilkinson, Custance and other narrow-minded Mahanian thinkers, and advance the revision of Some Principles.

Unspoken, perhaps because it was too radical for any public audience in 1921, was the fundamental point that British strategy against Napoleon had been very different to that adopted in 1914–18, and far wiser. Corbett's text subtly implied that a limited maritime strategy, one which recognised the fundamental importance of trade and merchant shipping, which he emphasised several times in the paper, while deploying a small, volunteer army to secure British sea power, and waiting for other powers to carry their share of the burden of resisting a pan-European hegemonic drive was both wiser, and more appropriate. British strategy should not be driven by the continental obsessions of modern soldiers.

The audience included several officers from the Admiralty: Captain John Kelly of the Operations Division begged for a copy: 'It delighted the ear; and it interested and instructed the mind; it inspired the soul; it set the imagination working. Thank you a thousand times.'[87] The rising stars of the post-war Navy wanted to hear what Corbett had to say, and he reminded his diverse audiences that only university-level teaching would ensure the Navy had 'useful' historians.[88] His old friend George Prothero published the lecture in the prestigious *Quarterly Review*, a brilliant introduction to his work and ideas.[89]

Two months later Professor Israel Gollancz invited Corbett to deliver the 1922 Raleigh Lecture on behalf of the Council of the British Academy; the lecture would be required in October 1922. The lectureship had been founded on the tercentenary of the Elizabethan hero's execution.[90] In view of his eminence it is likely membership of the Academy would have followed: a great man of British scholarship recognised by his peers. Corbett accepted the invitation and began drafting a lecture on 9 September 1922, having completed the proofs of volume III. He found another two days for the project, and some gardening, before the Official History returned to his desk.[91] Time ran out. Herbert Richmond took up the task, delivering 'National Policy and Naval Strength, XVIth to XX Century'. While he may have developed Corbett's initial sketches, the lecture marked Richmond's emergence as a strategist.[92]

Although Corbett may be considered the godfather of the *Naval Review*, he scrupulously avoided taking a public role in a journal by and for naval officers. His only published contributions were an unsigned three-page essay 'Methods of Discussion'[93] of 1920, and an old essay, 'United Services', that Richmond printed posthumously in 1923.[94] He produced the first, a brief tutorial, at a time when he was heavily committed to the Official History, and in poor health, prompted by Richmond, then Director of the Senior Officers War Course at Greenwich. When the course re-opened in March 1920, Richmond's strategy lectures were followed by Corbett's series on 'Imperial Concentration'.[95] The Official History was already in use as the basis for post-war education.[96]

Corbett's old concern about the limited debating skill of naval officers, when dealing with soldiers and politicians, was revived by a paper published in May 1920. 'War from the Aspect of the Weaker Power' argued that battle could suit the interests of the aforesaid power, as opposed to commerce destroying. A paper that concluded: 'there is no support in the theory of war or in history, as far as can be seen, for a policy of avoiding battle and aiming at some lesser form of destruction' required a response.[97]

Rather than simply rebutting the contention, Corbett provided an essay on logic. To excuse the intervention of a civilian, albeit unsigned, in a restricted naval journal, Corbett stressed that the *Naval Review* existed to 'promote discussion', therefore discussants must accept 'elementary principles' if they hoped to achieve any useful results. Legal experience had taught him that without a logical and consistent methodology the fruits of debate would be diffuse and incompatible, effectively useless. His experience of the wartime Admiralty had provided ample evidence of muddled thinking, ill-considered argument and unfortunate outcomes. He explained the difference between inductive and deductive reasoning, the first working from the particular to the general, through the assembly of evidence to develop an argument of general application, while the latter began with general principles and then applied them to specific cases. The deductive method, he warned, was more difficult, and likely to lead the unwary to 'fallacious conclusions'. This argument applied to Mahan, a classic deductive thinker.

Taking his usual delight in the counter-attack, he noted the author began with Spenser Wilkinson's erroneous argument about the functions of government. Wilkinson, the primary target of the paper, was a long-term advocate of German military methods and closely associated with the Army General Staff 'continental' school that had done so much, as Corbett saw it, to distort British strategy in the Great War. Nor had his ill-informed, unintelligent *Morning Post* review of *Some Principles* been forgotten.[98] Corbett did not need to name Wilkinson, carefully noting the failure to understand Clausewitz, and some striking examples of twisting words beyond their meaning. Confusing means and ends was a classic problem among contemporary naval officers, predictable enough in a service that trained men to do before it encouraged them to think. Limited objects did not mean limited means; limited war was a political choice, not an operational decision. In 1904–5 Japan had used its entire strength to seize a limited belt of territory from Russia. Anyone who dismissed Clausewitz's analysis that it was not always necessary to destroy an enemy's armed forces as a 'fallacy' was hardly going to impress Corbett, who had developed *On War* for the British context. Nor was he impressed by the old chestnut that battle was a means to an end, another Wilkinson error. Once again his purpose was not to lambast the lieutenant, but to administer a lesson at a higher level, to critics of his pre-war writing and his influence on the conduct of the First

World War. What really annoyed Corbett was that a false premise and lax methodology led to the bizarre conclusion that the object of war was always the destruction of the enemy's armed forces, and that this was a prerequisite for peace. Two recent examples sufficed to annihilate such nonsense, the Russo-Japanese War and the First World War.

The original essay had then reversed course, abandoning the initial dogmatic position, grasping at the alternative, the Corbettian way, of attacking the economic vitals as an alternative to the defeat of the enemy's armed force. As Corbett stressed, states must accept defeat if they found their 'sources of strength for carrying on the war are getting exhausted, and this is the cause, so long experience tells us, why most wars come to an end. Hence it is unnecessary to destroy armed force if you can more easily, more quickly, or with greater certainty destroy the power of sustaining it.' He accepted there were good reasons to prefer a direct attack on the enemy's armed forces, and regretted these had not been developed. Failing to develop the logic of these alternatives risked practitioners missing opportunities to secure a decision by indirect means that were equally rapid, and less costly. This methodological critique emphasised the difference between British maritime and continental military strategies: he implied that a British officer could only arrive at the conclusion that the German total war doctrine of mass mobilisation and decisive battle was appropriate to British strategic interests by starting from unsound propositions, and using 'un-consequential inference' to build a doctrine 'which breaks down the moment it is tested by past experiences'. German strategic writing provided a model for German strategy and doctrine, but it did not translate into English, and should not be held up as the solution to the security needs of a very different state.[99] It is likely that a revision of *Some Principles* was at the forefront of Corbett's mind as he lectured to the revived War Course, the locus of his life's work.

The evolution of Corbett's strategic thinking over the last eleven years of his life, years filled with striking new examples, the hard lessons of war, and the discipline of official writing, had been profound. The *Naval Review* note suggests he was preparing to demolish Wilkinson, Custance and Sydenham, who had publicly blamed him for the 'failure' at Jutland.[100] While Corbett protested in private, his full response would have appeared in the closing sections of the Official History and a revision of *Some Principles*. Instead of completing that task, he wasted time battling an ambitious politician who feared for his reputation, and an Admiralty Board packed with War Course graduates who chose to forget his key points: the educational role of the past; the need for a national, not a service-based approach to strategy; and the importance of a widely disseminated, intelligent understanding of how history supported the evolution of doctrine. History provided the ultimate test of any theory, but only if it was accurate, carefully considered and consistent. The unfortunate lieutenant had bundled up a lot of Elizabethan history in a profoundly unhistorical package to support false deductions. Corbett concluded by advising naval officers to avoid the deductive method:

> Far better to stick to the inductive method. Collect and study the ascertained facts of war history, and patiently build up your doctrine on the solid foundations they afford. It is a practical method far better suited than the other to a naval officer's training and habit of thought.[101]

He might have added, had he not made the point so well elsewhere, that this was his method, and Clausewitz's. These giants stand apart from the system-building political science methodologies espoused by lesser strategists. This was the advice of a gifted teacher and a sophisticated strategist who had given his life to the service of an organisation he loved. Corbett's death left the Official History, the education of the Navy and the academic standing of naval history incomplete. This was widely recognised, and deeply regretted. His death left a void that no-one else could fill: the search for an endowed chair in naval history at a British university continues.

Jellicoe lamented a friend and observed: 'who will carry on his work . . . no-one living can really do it satisfactorily'.[102] A decade later Edmond Daniel revised the Official History, declaring: 'He has no successor. There is no-one living who can set out the lessons to be learned from the study of naval history as he did.'[103] Albert Pollard placed on record the IHR's 'high appreciation of the services which he rendered', words that were greatly appreciated by Edith.[104] Pollard's continuing concern for the subject led the IHR to appoint George Aston to fill Corbett's place.[105] Corbett made the IHR the academic centre for naval history, a legacy reinforced by half of his library, while a Naval History Prize, funded by brother Herbert in 1926, ensured it retains a prominence unusual among schools of advanced historical study. The Society for Nautical Research called a special meeting to mark their sense of his importance, recognising 'his magnificent literary achievement' and regretting an 'irreparable' 'national loss'.[106] The NRS was quick to join the list. Both societies would need new leadership, and new means of communicating with the academic mainstream. Neither would be entirely successful: naval history slowly drifted to the academic margins, a process that culminated a decade later in the destruction of the Vere Harmsworth Chair. Perhaps it had all been in vain.

Conclusion

Corbett's work suffered the cruellest of fates, derided by those it had been designed to help, disparaged by those who would exploit it in the next great conflict, and popularised by a journalist to such effect that few realise who created the 'British way of waging war'. Admiral Sir Herbert Richmond, his friend and intellectual heir, helped journalist Basil Liddell Hart shape a 'British Way in Warfare' in 1931, enabling an infantry tactician to discuss higher policy, but Liddell Hart's failure to engage with naval history or seapower theory left his essay a pale shadow of the original.[1]

Death denied Corbett the chance to render the First World War as a strategic morality tale, unfolding the tragedy of poor decisions and missed opportunities. Fortunately the main lines of his argument are clear, and can be fleshed out. A deeper engagement with his wartime work demonstrates how the synthesis of history, strategy and national policy that informed his work before 1914 informed critical arguments that won the peace. Those arguments secured the seapower state against the malice of an American president bent on disarming seapower through the legal notion of 'freedom of the seas', while ensuring a 'League of Nations' would serve British interests, by preserving the post-war status quo. Woodrow Wilson had abandoned 'freedom of the seas' in a speech that paraphrased Corbett's argument. The Official History shaped post-war strategic planning, starting with Jellicoe's Empire Mission, and post-war naval education. During the same hectic post-war years, Corbett secured a place for naval history at the heart of British academic life, in the University of London's School of Advanced Study. This gave naval history, the core of any advanced naval education system, intellectual respectability. He hoped university-trained lecturers would be ready to support an expanding defence education sector, relieving him from duty. Whether his subject was Francis Drake or the First World War, he lived in the present and he wrote for the future.

At the heart of Corbett's intellectual endeavour lay a progressive, liberal British state, one that needed a national strategy that could secure the empire as it transitioned into a post-imperial collective, a 'Sea Commonwealth'. He analysed the history of British strategic policy to guide future thinking, harmonising it with contemporary realities, diplomatic, legal, economic, political and technological, an evolving strategic concept that shaped national doctrine. He emphasised the need to harmonise all aspects of national power, not the narrow interests of an individual service, the fiscal horizons of the Treasury, or the constant pressure of short-term agendas that shaped the period 1904–14, when Britain temporarily took a more active role in balancing Europe. The aim was always the preservation of peace, and the onward march of progress, social, political and economic. Deterrence, not war, was the aim.

By 1914 there were grounds for optimism: the dramatic revival and growing hostility of Russia was challenging the relevance of the Entente system, while the Anglo-German naval race that had dragged Britain into Europe, by necessitating the Anglo-French Entente, had ended in 1912. In a world without war, Britain could address the future of the empire, change the relationship with Ireland, and sustain the liberal progress of the past century. Britain's primary concern was to prevent a major European war, which might create a hegemonic super-state, a concern that prioritised effective deterrence. While Fisher had a visceral understanding of deterrence, which he demonstrated in 1905, sending a powerful British fleet into the Baltic to influence German decision-making, Corbett developed a sophisticated strategic rationale for this strategy. The development of this strategy was compromised by the absolute refusal of the Army General Staff to join the necessary joint service planning, in defiance of the CID, and successive governments. The fleet needed an amphibious army to secure choke points and offshore bases, and attack maritime targets. The civilian leadership did not challenge the soldiers, in part because the Anglo-French Staff Talks linked to the soldiers' preferred strategy of dispatching a small army to support France, helping to sustain the Anglo-French Entente of 1904, which in turn promised to preserve peace. It was not, it must be stressed, a strategy for war, merely a mobilisation and movement plan to send a token force of between four and six divisions to Europe, where France and Germany would each put between ninety and a hundred divisions in the field. The French valued the gesture above any fighting power. British strategy in August 1914 remained maritime, but the commitment to

Europe, and the failure of ministers to limit the scale of the military commit-ment, a commonplace of all previous major alliance wars, in part shaped by the prevailing expectation of a short war, separated the two armed services, and left Britain waging two separate wars.[2]

In the July crisis the government did not attempt to deter Germany, and ignored the Baltic. After declaring war in 1914 four civilian ministers, not the full Cabinet, committed the BEF to France. Despite having the ultimate responsibility, the civilians were unwilling to challenge the 'experts', nine generals and a field marshal, with only one admiral. All four knew Corbett and his work, work that the government planned to recognise with a knighthood in December.

Corbett would explain the consequences of that decision: directing the entire Official History of the war project, and writing the grand strategic overview at its centre. He ensured lessons were learnt, but died before he could complete the task, leaving much of his argument to be recovered from other sources. Having developed a distinctive national approach to strategic doctrine for sailors, soldiers and, above all, statesmen, he was obliged to begin afresh, as the short war scenario faded, casualties mounted, and civilians abdicated their duty to direct the conflict.

His 'British way' of war concept, which explained how Britain, his Britain, a global empire of titanic scale, could be defended in a new century, was the culmination of a sustained intellectual effort dating back thirty years. It was no easy task, hampered by those who feared his ideas would damage their interests – small-minded servicemen, ignorant politicians and lightweight defence commentators. There was something heroic, and also tragic, in the arc of Corbett's life – not the heroism of physical danger and personal risk, but the heroism of an ageing man in poor health taking on a task that required more time, effort and resource than he could hope to apply. His synthesis of history, strategic theory, international law, education and politics was all-encompassing and rich. It provided the intellectual rationale for Jacky Fisher's dynamic policy and strategy, influenced leading statesmen from Arthur Balfour and Richard Haldane to Lloyd George, and informed the develop-ment of defence policy, not least through Maurice Hankey, the maritime-minded bureaucrat who led the CID and the War Council Secretariat.

Corbett was unique. He did not need money; he worked because he had a powerful public service ethic, loved the Navy and relished the intellectual challenge. He integrated history and strategy as the twin pillars of advanced defence education, providing the framework that embraced legal, technical and financial insights, the first coherent exposition of national strategy.

Corbett's strategic thought was original because it focused on the unique and specific concerns of Britain. The limited maritime methods he set out were only applicable to an insular seapower great power, one that depended on oceanic communications and that could afford to create and sustain a dominant navy for prolonged periods. While all strategic theory is contingent, Corbett's had especially restricted relevance. His model depended on limiting commitment on land to secure dominance at sea, meeting the heavy costs of naval power through economic success and an inclusive political system. In a total war, this strategy prevented invasion, the obvious mechanism for defeating an insular seapower, and supported continental allies. Britain was not capable to imposing order on Europe, but it could support allies in opposing hegemonic powers. Today, Corbett's ideas are especially relevant to the liberal, or 'Western', economic and security collective, whose members include key elements of Corbett's 'Sea Commonwealth'. It favours deterrence over war, dominates the maritime domain, and shows little interest in mobilising large conscript armies. The synergy of this model with the geopolitical thinking of his contemporaries Mahan and Mackinder is not accidental. They were responding to the same concerns. His place in the canon of strategic theory is secure.[3]

Corbett's ideas endured because they were securely founded in a sophisticated understanding of past experience. Strategic theory imposes system and order on experience, supporting the development of doctrine, the critical output that educates the minds of decision-makers. His key text of 1911, *Some Principles of Maritime Strategy*, was an officially sanctioned doctrine primer. It flowed from the dialectical relationship of history and strategy: history informs strategic questions, which direct further historical research, refining strategic arguments until they can be deployed as doctrine. The constant dialogue between history and strategy that Corbett employed to build the 'British way' was difficult to sustain, but vital. Making strategy without history may be easier, but historians have long understood the danger of applying simple solutions to complex political problems. In 1914 the Great German General Staff tried to resolve the existential problems of Imperial Germany with a masterpiece of military operational art. The plan failed, and the empire collapsed, because force of arms was no substitute for domestic reform. The 'German way' did not work, even for Germany, while Corbett's limited maritime strategy met the needs of a unique maritime great power, despite the abberration of a mass conscript army. Strategy is a national construct, a practical response to specific problems, not a universal panacea. Consequently Corbett developed Clausewitz's theory, replacing the focus on Central Europe with the world ocean and the empire. He used Clausewitz's concept of friction to explain why in war nothing works as it was intended, but reinforced the point with a peculiarly British variant, 'the deflection of strategy by politics'. Above all it is essential that we understand that Corbett used history and strategy to educate his contemporaries. He did not expect his methods and his message would still command the attention of those who think about strategy, war and history a century later. Corbett would have agreed with Friedrich Nietzsche, 'You can explain the past only by what is most powerful in the present.'[4]

Some Principles, the first national strategic doctrine primer, informed Britain's highly effective global war between 1914 and 1918. It also persuaded the Admiralty, the CID and ultimately the government that Corbett should record and analyse the conflict from the grand strategic perspective, restricting Army histories to operational and tactical matters. This role sustained his central task, the strategic education of navy and nation, while producing teaching texts for post-war naval education.[5] His ideas survived the catastrophe of war becoming, by default, the strategic system that enabled Britain to survive a war with Germany and Italy, the collapse of France, the occupation of Denmark, Norway, Holland, Belgium and Greece, along with the hostility of Imperial Japan. The Second World War was truly global: the Grand Alliance linked by maritime communication – the Axis fractured by the same oceans, crippled by inadequate resources and terrestrial communications. After the Second World War, Corbett's ideas inspired the development of post-atomic limited war theory, keeping alive the idea that war should remain a political act, not the ultimate expression of nihilism.[6] They survived the ill-informed attacks of Cold War historians, unable to recognise that a strategic and political landscape shaped by the commitment of major British Army and Air Force assets to the defence of West Germany was both temporary and anomalous. When the Cold War ended, Corbett's work returned to prominence, the only intellectually coherent explanation of a national, as opposed to an alliance strategy. His arguments resumed their rightful place in the 1990s, prompting renewed interest in the man and his agenda. Meanwhile, Britain slowly shifted towards a global maritime posture.

Corbett's ideas endured because they were securely based in past experience, accurately appraised, and cogently explained. Corbett was an outstanding educator, as many of his successors have recognised. He would be central to the development and delivery of national strategy before, during and after the First World War; he was studied and used by the Royal, United States, German, Italian and French navies. In France, Raoul Castex recognised that his doctrine primer deliberately challenged received wisdom, forcing students to think with system and logic. He remains a major influence on naval thought today because the same problems persist: busy careers, hierarchical command structures and rapid technological progress allow little time to reflect on the cerebral aspects of professional development.

Corbett's life matters because strategic ideas must be understood in context before they can assume any wider utility. Understanding their aims and audiences is critical to developing their insights.[7] *Some Principles* was written for 'Jacky' Fisher, the Edwardian empire and the CID, the strategic doctrine of a global seapower. It developed Clausewitz's theoretical structure to frame the argument, and ensure it would be understood by all those involved in the higher direction of war. It was the culmination of a long engagement with the strategic history of a unique seapower great power, the last to depend on the ocean for security, prosperity and deterrence. Approved for publication by the CID and the Admiralty, it was rejected by soldiers and social conservatives in favour of a 'German way'.

It might be assumed that Winston Churchill, historian and strategist, recalled Corbett's arguments when Britain entered another major war in 1939. However, Churchill was a continental military thinker, and his view of Corbett remained profoundly negative. Corbett's exposure of his failings as First Lord of the Admiralty in the Official History prompted Churchill to create his own version of the war, *The World Crisis*, and inspired a stream of hostile comments. His dismissive treatment of the Fisher/Corbett Baltic concept in *The World Crisis* has misled many. The Baltic was the only British strategic option that had the potential to win the war: something the 'continental' alternative signally failed to achieve. Not only had defeating Germany on the battlefield proved beyond the strength of Britain, France and Russia, but American support, as Corbett recognised, posed a fundamental threat to the survival of the empire. The critical role of the Baltic had been clear from the beginning of the Anglo-German naval arms race, shaping naval planning throughout the Fisher era, a reality that shaped Corbett's integration of history, law and strategy.

When Churchill began a biography of Marlborough, he consulted *England in the Mediterranean*, which provided the strategic template. Hiring Commander John Owen to draft the naval side of Marlborough's war, Churchill advised him to consult the work of 'that poor little man who wrote the official naval history'.[8] Despite the sneering slight Churchill found himself waging a Corbettian total war six years later, forced to abandon Europe and avoid another 'stupid soldiers' war'. Like many another twentieth-century continentalist, Churchill assumed the continental role had been inevitable, and should become Britain's primary focus.[9] From the longer perspective of the third decade of the twenty-first century, it is clear that this was an aberration. Small, weak, insular states, fundamentally reliant upon global commerce and resource flows, must prioritise sea control or perish. In two world wars, no amount of military force, or land-based aviation, could secure the oceanic communications on which Britain depended. Although Corbett's maritime strategy might appear better suited to the political context of limited conflict, he demonstrated that it had functioned effectively in the strikingly 'total' wars of the French Revolution and Napoleonic empire, as the central block for grand coalitions that restrained the hegemonic ambitions of France, and in the First World War. His work remains the basis of a distinctive 'British' strategic culture and has never been more widely appreciated.

Strategic innovation begins by mastering the past: a sophisticated understanding of how we arrived at the present is the essential baseline for thinking about the future. Strategy serves the wider national interest and it is ultimately the responsibility of statesmen, advised by experts. It is not the business of generals, or admirals, to set national strategy, because the armed forces are only one element of a national effort. Corbett used Pitt the Elder as a model of wartime leadership, but Jacky Fisher could not find a contemporary equivalent.[10] In August 1914 the statesmen Corbett had tried to educate abdicated their responsibility; he spent the rest of his life explaining what had gone wrong. His record of sustained strategic innovation reflected legal, literary, historical and strategic expertise, developed across a twenty-year career at the civil–military interface, as journalist, educator, historian and theorist. Such work cannot be produced to meet short-term agendas, three-year cycles or individual deployments. If there are no easy answers, Corbett set himself, and his students, some profound questions. Who is responsible for setting national strategy, how can we promote effective choices, and how should we profit from the rich veins of experience to be recovered from the past? Corbett's peers did understand, if only belatedly. Ironically, he would be knighted in February 1917, for drafting the memorandum explaining how Cabinet government functioned in war, the very thing that had failed in 1914.

Aware that his career would have been in vain if he allowed the First World War to shatter the 'British way', replacing it with a false idol of German manufacture, Corbett had pressed on with the demanding schedule set by a constellation of interlinked projects after the war, well aware that his health was failing and the nation was no longer dancing to the siren song 'We Want Eight'. He could only hope his ideas would make a difference the next time. Perhaps they did.

NOTES

Abbreviations

ADM	Admiralty Papers
Beatty Papers	B.M. Ranft (ed.), *The Beatty Papers*, 2 vols, London, NRS, 1989–93
CAB	Committee of Imperial Defence and Cabinet Papers
CBT	Sir Julian Stafford Corbett Papers, Royal Museums Greenwich
CCC	Churchill College, Cambridge
Churchill Companion	M. Gilbert (ed.), *Winston S. Churchill: Companion*, vols III–V, London, Heinemann, 1972
Diary	Diary of Sir Julian Stafford Corbett, Royal Museums Greenwich
Fisher Papers	P. Kemp (ed.), *The Papers of Admiral Sir John Fisher*, 2 vols, London, NRS, 1964
FISR	Admiral Lord Fisher Papers, Churchill College, Cambridge
FO	Foreign Office Papers
EHR	*English Historical Review*
FGDN	Arthur Marder (ed.), *Fear God and Dread Nought*, 3 vols, London, Cape, 1956
FDSF	Arthur Marder, *From the Dreadnought to Scapa Flow*, 5 vols, Oxford, Oxford UP, 1960–70
Jellicoe Papers	A. Temple Patterson (ed.), *The Jellicoe Papers: Selections from the Private and Official Correspondence of Admiral of the Fleet Earl Jellicoe of Scapa*, 2 vols, London, NRS, 1966–8
JRUSI	*Journal of the Royal United Services Institute*
Keyes Papers	Paul Halpern (ed.), *The Keyes Papers*, 3 vols, London, NRS, 1980
Laughton	A.D. Lambert, *The Foundations of Naval History: John Knox Laughton, the Royal Navy and the Historical Profession*, London, Chatham Press, 1998
LHCMA	Liddell Hart Centre for Military Archives, King's College London
LSE BLPES	London School of Economics, The British Library of Political and Economic Science
NMM	National Maritime Museum (Royal Museums Greenwich)
NRA	*Naval Review* Archive
NRS	Navy Records Society
ODNB	Oxford Dictionary of National Biography
RNWC	Royal Naval War College
THU	James Thursfield Papers, National Maritime Museum
USNIP	United States Naval Institute Press
USNWC	United States Naval War College Archives
WO	War Office Papers

Abbreviated titles of books by Corbett

Drake	*Sir Francis Drake*, London, Macmillan, 1890
Fighting Instructions	(ed.) *Fighting Instructions, 1530–1816*, London, NRS, 1905
Mediterranean	*England in the Mediterranean: A Study of the Rise and Influence of British Power within the Straits, 1603–1713*, 2 vols, London, Longman, 1904
Monk	*Monk*, London, Macmillan, 1889
NO	*Naval Operations: History of the Great War based on Official Documents, by Direction of the Historical Section of the Committee of Imperial Defence*, 3 vols, London, Longman, 1920–3
Russo-Japanese War	*Maritime Operations in the Russo-Japanese War 1904–1905* (printed 1914–15), ed. J. Hattendorf and D.M. Schurman, Annapolis, MD, USNIP, 1994
Seven Years' War	*England in the Seven Years' War: A Study in Combined Strategy*, 2 vols, London, Longman, 1907
Signals	(ed.) *Signals and Instructions 1776–1794*, London, NRS, 1909
Some Principles	*Some Principles of Maritime Strategy*, London, Longman, 1911
Spanish War	*Papers Relating to the Navy during the Spanish War 1585–1587*, London, NRS, 1898
Spencer	(ed.) *The Private Papers of George, Second Earl Spencer, First Lord of the Admiralty, 1794–1801*, London, NRS, I (1913), II (1914)
Successors	*The Successors of Drake*, London, Longman, 1900
Trafalgar	*The Campaign of Trafalgar*, London, Longman, 1910
Tudor	*Drake and the Tudor Navy, with a History of the Rise of England as a Maritime Power*, 2 vols, London, Longman, 1898

Introduction

1. Corbett had spent the day dealing with the details of a botched operation in the North Sea (the Scarborough Raid of 1914), rather less satisfying work, but an equally important element of his great project to ensure Britain learnt from the hard-won experience of a global conflict.
2. Ernest Tatham Richmond (1874–1955), architect and administrator, worked in Egypt 1895–1911, and then as an administrator for the British Palestinian Mandate, 1918–37.
3. Diary 31 March 1920: CBT 43/19.
4. Barry D. Hunt, *Sailor-scholar: Admiral Sir Herbert Richmond 1871–1946*, Waterloo, Wilfrid Laurier UP, 1982, pp. 43–54.
5. T.E. Lawrence, 'Three Unsigned Articles in *The Times* of 26–28 November 1918', in M. Brown (ed.), *T.E. Lawrence in War and Peace: An Anthology of the Military Writings of Lawrence of Arabia*, London, Greenhill Books, 2005, pp. 221–31; see pp. 221, 225 for Wemyss and command of the sea.
6. Diary 1 August 1917: CBT 43/16: Corbett found traces of a return to this method in the minutes of the latest Anglo-French Conference in Paris.
7. D.M. Schurman, *Julian S. Corbett, 1854–1922: Historian of British Maritime Policy from Drake to Jellicoe*, London, Royal Historical Society, 1981; see pp. 17, 152–4.
8. Arthur Marder, *From the Dreadnought to Scapa Flow* (henceforth *FDSF*), 5 vols, Oxford, Oxford UP, 1960–70, vol. I, p. 380 citing ADM 116/1043B.
9. J.S. Corbett (unsigned), 'Some Principles of Naval Warfare', in P. Kemp (ed.), *The Papers of Admiral Sir John Fisher* (hereafter *Fisher Papers*), London, NRS, 1964, vol. II, pp. 318–45. Kemp's introduction to the Ballard Committee plans at pp. 316–17 is inaccurate, promoting Edmond Slade to Director of Naval Intelligence (DNI) when he remained Director of the War Course, conflating events in 1906 and 1907 with those of 1909, long after the document was completed.
10. Battenberg to Fisher, 11 February 1902: M. Kerr, *Prince Louis of Battenberg: Admiral of the Fleet*, London, Longman, 1934, pp. 161–4. Slade to Corbett, 20 May 1906: CBT 13/2/1.

11. R. Gardiner (ed.), *Conway's All the World's Fighting Ships, 1906–1921*, London, Conway, 1985, p. 175. In 1907 the Royal Navy had 40 submarines; see pp. 86–7.
12. Richard Dunley, *Britain and the Mine, 1900–1915: Culture, Strategy and International Law*, London, Palgrave, 2018, pp. 135–6, 149.
13. Ibid., pp. 338, 433.
14. *Fisher Papers*, II, pp. 432, 436.
15. *FDSF*, V, p. 306. See also p. 373.
16. D. M. Schurman, *The Education of a Navy: The Development of British Naval Strategic Thought 1867–1914*, London, Cassell, 1965, pp. 152–4. This assessment reflected the views of his tutor, Brian Tunstall.
17. Nicholas Lambert, Review Essay, 'False Prophet? The Maritime Theory of Julian Corbett and Professional Military Education', *Journal of Military History* 77, 2013, pp. 1055–78, at p. 1076. The 'review' was actually a paper on economic warfare delivered at HMS *President* on 23 November 2012, largely ignoring the book under review.
18. Captain Charles Ottley (DNI) to Corbett, Dictated 'Secret', Naval Intelligence Division (NID), 1 July 1905: Richmond Papers, NMM RIC/9, cited at p. 1068. The letter is positive and encouraging: Ottley effectively commissioned *Some Principles of Maritime Strategy*.
19. Corbett to Fisher, 4 April 1909: Arthur Marder (ed.), *Fear God and Dread Nought* (henceforth *FGDN*), 3 vols, London, Cape, 1956, vol. II, p. 243 fn.
20. Corbett's diaries contain dividend certificates, along with a record of monthly bank payments.
21. Douglas Owen, *Ocean Trade and Shipping*, Cambridge, Cambridge UP, 'Naval and Military Series', 1914. Alexander Pearce-Higgins' book appeared in a different format.
22. Julian Corbett, *Some Principles of Maritime Strategy* (henceforth *Some Principles*), London, Longman, 1911, pp. 92–3, 95, 97, 101. Unless otherwise stated, all references in this book are to this 1911 edition, which has become universally accessible online.
23. A position he shared with Fisher: Andrew Lambert, *Admirals*, London, Faber, 2007, pp. 292–8.
24. Julian Corbett, *Naval Operations* (henceforth *NO*), 3 vols, London, Longman, 1920–3.
25. James Goldrick and John Hattendorf (eds), *Mahan Is Not Enough: The Proceedings of a Conference on the Works of Sir Julian Corbett and Admiral Sir Herbert Richmond*, Newport, RI, Naval War College Press, 1993, reflected the US Navy's long relationship with an author it had greatly admired before and after the First World War. See Julian Corbett, *Some Principles of Maritime Strategy*, ed. Eric Grove, Annapolis, MD, USNIP, 1988. Jerker J. Widen, *Theorist of Maritime Strategy: Sir Julian Corbett and his Contribution to Military and Naval Thought*, Farnham, Ashgate, 2012, analyses *Some Principles* and Corbett's methods.
26. Beatrice Heuser, *The Evolution of Strategy: Thinking War from Antiquity to the Present*, Cambridge, Cambridge UP, 2010, emphasises Corbett's critical place in maritime theory.
27. Corbett, diary 13 February 1913: Liddle Collection. Brigadier General Hubert John Foster (1855–1919) British and later Australian Army officer, was appointed Director of Military Science at the University of Sydney in 1906, becoming a major contributor to the debate on Australian defence. He advocated an expeditionary strategy, with a major role for the Australian Army, rather than a policy of continental defence. He served as Chief of the Australian General Staff from 1916 to 1917.
28. Julian Corbett, *England in the Seven Years' War: A Study in Combined Strategy* (henceforth *Seven Years' War*), 2 vols, London, Longman, 1907; Julian Corbett, 'The Capture of Private Property at Sea', *The Nineteenth Century*, June 1907; Earl Loreburn, *Capture at Sea*, London, Methuen, 1905, 1913.
29. Richmond's letters are in Liddell Hart's archive at King's College London.
30. Michael Howard, *The Continental Commitment: The Dilemma of British Defence Policy in the Era of the Two World Wars*, London, Temple Smith, 1972; 'The British Way in Warfare: A Reappraisal', in Howard, *The Causes of War and Other Essays*, London, Temple Smith, 1980.

31. *Some Principles*, p. 38, cited in David French, *The British Way in Warfare, 1688–2000*, London, Unwin Hyman, 1990, p. xiv.

32. Basil H. Liddell Hart, 'Economic Pressure or Continental Victories', *Journal of the Royal United Services Institute (JRUSI)* 76, 1931, 486–503.

33. Hew Strachan, *The Direction of War: Contemporary Strategy in Historical Perspective*, Cambridge, Cambridge UP, 2013, p. 141.

34. Ibid., pp. 6, 15, 31–3, 78, 127, 141–8, 150, 154–5, 157, 172–3, 176–7. Quote at p. 141.

35. Heuser, 2010, p. 3 A work of critical importance for all who study the subject. The integration of maritime and naval thought into the wider process is exemplary.

36. Strachan, 2013, pp. 155–6.

37. Ibid., pp. 153–4.

38. English writers were well aware of Thucydides in the sixteenth century; Heuser, 2010, citing Matthew Sutcliffe's 1593 text *The Practice, Proceedings and Lawes of Armies*, at p. 201. John Dee and Walter Raleigh also referenced the Peloponnesian War.

39. Andrew Lambert, *Seapower States*, New Haven, CT, and London, Yale UP, 2018; see ch. 2 for democratic methods as a weapon.

40. This is stressed in Julian Corbett, *Maritime Operations in the Russo-Japanese War 1904–1905* (henceforth *Russo-Japanese War*), ed. Hattendorf and Schurman, Annapolis, MD, USNIP, 1994, vol. I, p. 1.

41. Strachan, 2013, p. 127.

42. Heuser, 2010, p. 170. For a contextualised analysis of naval and maritime strategy see chs 8 and 9.

43. Sir John Fortescue, the king's Librarian, told Corbett that Fisher sent many of his memoranda to the king; Schurman, 1981, pp. 6–7.

44. Jon Sumida, 'The Historian as Contemporary Analyst: Sir Julian Corbett and Admiral Sir John Fisher', in Goldrick and Hattendorf, 1993, pp. 125–40.

1 Victorian Empire

1. Diary 25 March 1921: CBT 43/20.

2. The event delighted Corbett. Diary 22 April 1912: CBT 43/11.

3. D. MacCarron, *Letters from an Early Bird: The Life and Letters of Denys Corbett Wilson 1882–1915*, Barnsley, Pen & Sword, 2006. The family history is inaccurate.

4. Hallam Tennyson to Corbett, 25 July 1891: CBT 14/6/23. F. MacCarthy, *William Morris: A Life for our Times*, London, Faber, 1994, pp. 29–48. K. Jeffery, *Field Marshal Sir Henry Wilson: A Political Soldier*, Oxford, Oxford UP, 2006, pp. 4–5. Wilson (1877–80) returned to the college for an old boys' event on 5 March 1921. There is no record of Corbett doing so.

5. S.L.G. Rickard, 'Hallam, Second Baron Tennyson (1852–1928)', *ODNB* 57219 (http://www.oxforddnb).

6. Corbett to Newbolt, 16 December 1904: CBT 3/7/31.

7. C. Repington, *Vestigia*, London, Constable, 1919, p. 21.

8. For Headmaster Bradley see M. Girouard, *The Return to Camelot: Chivalry and the English Gentleman*, New Haven, CT, and London, Yale UP, 1981, pp. 126, 165–9, 171–9, 245, 250. C. Poulson, *Morris, Burne-Jones and the Quest of the Holy Grail*, the 1998 Kelmscott Lecture, London, William Morris Society, 2001.

9. Girouard, 1981, p. 176.

10. N. Vance, 'Farrar, Frederic William (1831–1903)', *ODNB* 33088.

11. Information from the archivist at Trinity College. His contemporaries included barrister Sir Charles Nicholson (1857–1918, MP 1915–18), CBT 43/17, 24 October 1918: 'Dined with Sir Chas Nicholson at 35 Harrington Gardens to talk over my "Freedom of Seas" pamphlet.'

12. H. Lloyd-Jones, 'Jebb, Sir Richard Claverhouse (1841–1905)', *ODNB* 34166. Caroline Jebb, *Life and Letters of Richard Claverhouse Jebb*, Cambridge, Cambridge UP, 1907.

13. Sir John Fortescue was struck by this mastery of the architectural and historical details. Schurman, 1981, pp. 6–7.

14. Simon Reynolds, *Sir William Blake Richmond*, Norwich, Michael Russell, 1995. See C. Wood, *Olympian Dreamers: Victorian Classical Painters, 1860–1914*, London, Constable, 1983, p. 191 for Burne-Jones' *Cophetua* – a work that inspired Corbett, itself inspired by Tennyson's poem. R.J. Barrow, *The Use of Classical Art and Literature by Victorian Painters, 1860–1912: Creating Continuity with the Traditions of High Art*, London, Edwin Mellen, 2007, p. 220 reports Richmond's 1910 attack on the Post-Impressionist Exhibition in London in the *Morning Post*.

15. F. MacCarthy, *The Last Pre-Raphaelite: Edward Burne-Jones and the Victorian Imagination*, London, Faber, 2011.

16. Hunt, 1982, p. 5.

17. Reynolds, 1995, pp. 298–9. Diary: CBT 43/11.

18. The bookplate was used on books loaned to the Institute of Historical Research (IHR), London, and the Naval Staff College, Greenwich. M. Hopkinson, *Ex Libris: The Art of the Bookplate*, London, British Library, 2012.

19. H.F. McGeach and H.A.C. Sturgess, *Register of Admissions to the Honourable Society of the Middle Temple, from the Fifteenth Century to the Year 1944*, London, Butterworth, 1959, vol. II, p. 591.

20. J.A. Venn, *Alumni Cantabrigiensis, 1752–1900*, Cambridge, Cambridge UP, 1944, vol. II, p. 135

21. Diary 29 January 1921: CBT 43/20. This reflection was important: it was written more than a week later. The connection between the two forms of enquiry is close; notably on standards of evidence.

22. G.R. Rubin, 'Finlay, Robert Bannatyne', *ODNB* 33132.

23. Corbett to Miss Davies, 26 January 1921: Institute of Historical Research, XII correspondence 1921–6 C.

24. Freda Harcourt, *Flagships of Imperialism: The P&O Company and the Politics of Empire from its Origins to 1867*, Manchester, Manchester UP, 2006, links the shipping line with imperial strategy and identity.

25. Built 1870, 3,664 tons. Sold 1889. Thanks to Dr Richard Osborne of the World Ship Society for information on P&O ships.

26. Corbett to his mother, 23 October 1877: CBT 8/3/1. Charles wrote to their father, usually by the same post.

27. Corbett to his mother, 28 October 1877: CBT 8/3/1.

28. This unconscious bias endured, although only expressed in private. He described the wife of the Mayor of Toronto as 'a homely little charwoman' in 1908: Schurman, 1981, p. 107.

29. Corbett to his mother, 4 January 1878: CBT 8/3/1.

30. Corbett to his mother, 17 January 1878: CBT 8/3/1. Campbell and the 93rd were Scottish Highlanders.

31. Corbett to his mother, 6 February 1878: CBT 8/3/1. The Imber, a tributary of the Thames, ran past the family home.

32. Built 1871, 3,742 tons.

33. Built 1858, 2,021 tons.

34. Corbett to his mother, 14 April 1878: CBT 8/3/1. K. Dharmasena, *The Port of Colombo, 1860–1939*, Colombo, Ministry of Higher Education, 1980, pp. 1–26.

35. *Poona*, built 1863, 2,152 tons. Julia Margaret Cameron (1815–79), Indian-born photographer. J. Cox and C. Ford, *Julia Margaret Cameron: The Complete Photographs*, Los Angeles, CA, J. Paul Getty Museum, n.d.

36. The 4,000-ton wooden steam frigate HMS *Undaunted* was commanded by Captain Nathaniel Bowden-Smith. Rear Admiral John Corbett, possibly a distant relative, was not on board at this time. Rif Winfield, *British Warships in the Age of Sail, 1817–1863: Design, Construction, Careers and Fates*, Barnsley, Seaforth, 2014, p. 122.

37. Andrew Lambert, 'Wirtschaftliche Macht, technologischer Vorsprung und Imperiale Stärke: GrossBritannien als einzigartige globale Macht: 1860 bis 1890', in M. Epkenhans and G.P. Gross, *Das Militär und der Aufbruch die Moderne 1860 bis 1890*, Munich, De Gruyter Oldenbourg, 2003, pp. 243–68.

38. Bernard Porter, *Absent-minded Imperialists: What the British Really Thought about Empire*, Oxford, Oxford UP, 2004, p. 18. The expression was coined by Seeley.

39. John Robert Seeley, *The Expansion of England*, London, Macmillan, 1883, p. 288. Deborah Wormell, *Sir John Seeley and the Uses of History*, Cambridge, Cambridge UP, 1980, pp. 41–2.

40. Seeley, 1883, wrote: 'sooner or later we must lose India because sooner or later some war in Europe will force us to withdraw our English troops', pp. 291–2, 300–1.

41. Wormell, 1980, p. 129.

42. R.N. Soffer, *Discipline and Power: The University, History and the Making of an English Elite, 1870–1930*, Stanford, CA, Stanford UP, 1994, pp. 90–1.

43. John Seeley, 'War and the British Empire', *Journal of the Military Service of the United States* 10, September 1889, pp. 488–500. The paper had been read at Aldershot on 24 April 1889 as 'The Empire' and published locally. Mahan to Stephen Luce, 7 October 1889 in Robert Seager II and Doris Maguire (eds), *Letters and Papers of Alfred Thayer Mahan*, 3 vols, Annapolis, MD, USNIP, 1975, vol. I, pp. 711–13.

44. Thomas George Otte, *Statesmen of Europe: A Life of Sir Edward Grey*, London, Allen Lane, 2020, pp. 31, 65 and 70. Grey's politics and strategic instincts were closely aligned with Corbett's.

45. R.T. Van Arsdel, 'Macmillan family (c.1840–1986), publishers', *ODNB* 63220/34798. Maurice and elder brother Frederick (1851–1936) were Corbett's friends as well as his publishers. C. Morgan, *The House of Macmillan (1843–1943)*, London, Macmillan, 1944. Corbett does not appear in this charming catalogue of famous authors.

46. Edmund Burke's *Reflections on the French Revolution* was a universal tract of the age, along with Thomas Carlyle's massive, alarming account and Alexis de Toqueville's *Democracy in America*.

47. Corbett versus Beyer: *Fishing Gazette* 26 and 21, 15 April and 20 May 1893, pp. 272 and 352.

48. William Morris's visits to Iceland in 1871 and James Anthony Froude's excursion to Norway were far from unique. MacCarthy, 2011, pp. 278–310, 662–4. Ciaran Brady, *James Anthony Froude: An Intellectual Biography of a Victorian Prophet*, Oxford, Oxford UP, 2013, p. 391. Edward Augustus Freeman lamented not going: W.R.W. Stephens, *Life and Letters of Edward A. Freeman*, 2 vols, London, Macmillan, 1895. Andrew Wawn, *The Vikings and the Victorians: Inventing the Old North in 19th-century Britain*, Woodbridge, Brewer, 2000, p. 312.

49. For rambles around Rome with Twain, see Diary April 1892: CBT43/3.

50. Stefan Collini, *Matthew Arnold*, Oxford, Oxford UP, 1988. Matthew Arnold, *Culture and Anarchy: An Essay in Political and Social Criticism*, London, Smith Elder, 1869 and later editions. First published in the *Cornhill Magazine* 1867–9. Richard Jebb advocated Arnold's work.

51. F.M. Turner, *The Greek Heritage in Victorian Britain*, New Haven, CT, and London, Yale UP, 1981, p. 30.

52. Ibid., pp. 32–3. Jebb was also influenced by George Grote, liberal historian of ancient Greece, ibid., p. 234.

53. B.J. Day, 'The Moral Intuition of Ruskin's "Storm Cloud"', *Studies in English Literature 1500–1900* 45(4), 2005, pp. 917–33.

54. Turner, 1981, p. 231, citing Grote's *History of Greece*, vol. XI, p. 82.

55. Matthew Arnold to sister Frances, 11 November 1865: C. Lang (ed.), *The Letters of Matthew Arnold*, Charlottesville, VA, University of Virginia Press, 1997, vol. II, pp. 471–2.

56. Brady, 2013, pp. 440, 457–62. Brady's incisive assessment is vital to understand Froude's impact on Corbett. Froude's work, only tangentially about the past, addressed current concerns.

57. Schurman, 1981, p. 17.

58. The list of Corbett's publications by John Hattendorf, 'A Bibliography of the Works of Sir Julian Corbett', in Goldrick and Hattendorf, 1993, pp. 295–309, has minor errors.

59. K. Flint, 'The Victorian Novel and its Readers', in D. David (ed.), *The Cambridge Companion to the Victorian Novel*, Cambridge, Cambridge UP, 2001, pp. 17–36.

60. S. Eliot, 'The Business of Victorian Publishing', in David, 2001, pp. 37–60.
61. J.N. Figgis and R.V. Laurence (eds), *Historical Essays and Studies by Lord Acton*, London, Macmillan, 1907, pp. 273–304.
62. J. Kucich, 'Intellectual Debate in the Victorian Novel: Religion, Science and the Professional', in David, 2001, pp. 212–33.
63. Fred Macmillan to Corbett, 19 January 1886: CBT 1/2/3.
64. Fred Macmillan to Corbett, 30 December 1885: CBT 1/2/2.
65. Morgan, 1944, pp. 104, 122, 147.
66. B. Willey, 'Arnold and Faith', in M. Allott (ed.) *Matthew Arnold: Writers and their Background*, London, Bell, 1975, p. 257.
67. Diary 23 November 1890: CBT 43/1.
68. *Punch* 90, 1 May 1886, p. 214.
69. A weekly review of literature and general topics published in London between 1869 and 1902. Signed reviews were unusual. *The Academy* 729, 24 April 1886, pp. 285–6.
70. *Contemporary Review*, August 1886, p. 298.
71. Strachey (1860–1927), cousin of Lytton Strachey. See *ODNB* 36340. His reviews were unsigned, but obvious.
72. *Spectator*, 11 September 1886, p. 19.
73. Hans Ross to Corbett, 27 June 1886: CBT 1/2/4.
74. 'Contemporary Literature', *Scottish Review*, January 1888, p. 199.
75. Morgan, 1944, p. 136.
76. 'Novels of the Week', *Athenaeum* 3139, 24 December 1887, p. 859.
77. 'Belles Lettres', *Westminster Review*, January 1888, p. 266.
78. Maurice Macmillan to Corbett, 26 February 1888: CBT 1/1/8.
79. 'Smiling Ford', *Time*, December 1888, pp. 727–36. He received £1 a page for the essay from editor E.M. Abdy-Williams: CBT 1/1/7. The 'Smiling Ford' is a river crossing.
80. L.T. Meade to Corbett, 15 February and 9 March 1888: CBT 1/1/10-11. Meade was the pen-name of Alicia A. Leith. Mary Louisa Molesworth had encouraged him to try the juvenile market.
81. 'Jezebel', *Universal Review*, 15 August 1889, pp. 555–64.
82. Ibid., p. 564.
83. 'Current Literature', *Spectator*, 24 August 1889, p. 25.
84. The monthly literary journal *Time* was edited by Walter Sichel. Vol. 7, 1888, carried three instalments. Sichel to Corbett, 31 January 1888 and 28 February1889. The Sichels and Corbetts took each other's children on holiday.
85. Julia Molesworth to Corbett, 16 February 1888: CBT 14/4/38. Mrs Molesworth to Corbett, 8 April n.d. and 10 February n.d.: CBT 14/4/39-40.
86. MacCarthy, 2011, pp. 341–4.
87. J.S. Corbett, *Kophetua XIII*, single vol. edn, London, Macmillan & Co., 1889, p. 1–2. All references are to the online Gutenberg edition: http://www.gutenberg.org/files/47030/47030-h/47030-h.htm
88. F.G. Rohlfs, *Adventures in Morocco: Journeys through the Oases of Draa and Tafilet*, London, Sampson Low, 1874. Rohlfs was a gold medallist of the Royal Geographical Society, the strategic intelligence organisation of the British state. His pioneering expeditions opened up a region of Morocco hitherto unknown to Western travellers. See pp. 68–74 for the Draa oasis.
89. *Kophetua XIII*, p. 263.
90. 'Current Literature', *Spectator*, 25 May 1889, p. 19.
91. George Locke, *A Spectrum of Fantasy: The Bibliography and Biography of a Collection of Fantastic Literature*, London, Ferret Press, 1980, p. 58. Darko Suvin, 'Ruritania rather than SF', *Victorian Science Fiction in the UK: The Discourses of Knowledge and Power*, Boston, MA, G.K. Hall, 1983, p. 104. L.T. Sargent, *British and American Utopian Literature, 1516-1985*, New York, Garland, 1988, p. 49. Andrew Lambert, *Crusoe's Island*, London, Faber, 2016, pp. 9–13.

92. The Methuen edition of *For God and Gold* is not mentioned in Hattendorf's bibliography of Corbett's works. Fred Macmillan to Corbett, 15 May 1889: CBT 1/2/14.
93. 'Current Literature', *Spectator*, 11 September 1886, p. 19. Corbett addressed this issue openly in 1893, in his essay on Thomas Doughty – see ch. 3.
94. William Doyle, *The Oxford History of the French Revolution*, Oxford, Oxford UP, 1898, pp. 289–340.
95. A.P. Watt Literary Agency to Corbett, 16 June 1894: CBT 1/2/16.
96. After Cambridge, Colles (1865–1926) was called to the bar at the Inner Temple in 1880, and practised on the Midlands circuit, also working as a leader writer for the *Standard*. In 1889 he published *Literature and the Pension List: An Investigation*, and two books on copyright and literature. Colles' papers are divided between UCLA and Columbia University, New York. Columbia holds letters from Corbett, and Fred Jane. http://www.columbia.edu/cu/lweb/archival/collections/ldpd_4078626
97. Colles to Corbett, 14 November 1895: CBT 1/3/33.
98. 'Recent Novels', *Spectator*, 21 August 1895, p. 18.
99. Rendell to Corbett, 4 August 1891: CBT 1/3/34. *The Deserters* MS is CBT 1/6.
100. Imber Court was sold in 1900. The building is now the Metropolitan Police Training Academy.

2 Making Waves

1. Andrew Lambert, *The Foundations of Naval History: John Knox Laughton, the Royal Navy and the Historical Profession* (henceforth *Laughton*), London, Chatham Press, 1998, p. 100.
2. Mowbray Morris to Corbett, 4 and 6 March 1888: CBT 1/2/6-8.
3. Corbett and Firth, later Regius Professor of History at Oxford, remained friends. Firth's edition of Macaulay's *History of England*, London, Macmillan, 1913–16, referenced Corbett in vols III and IV, at pp. 1860–2 and pp. 1955–57. Firth's *Commentary on Macaulay's History of England*, London, Macmillan, 1938, referenced Corbett's *England in the Mediterranean*, 1904, at pp. 166, 179–82.
4. Gardiner to Corbett, 26 March 1889: CBT 14/3/10.
5. Fred Macmillan to Corbett, 14 and 15 April 1889, and Morris to Corbett, 27 April, 3 and 12 May 1889: CBT 1/2/10-13.
6. This was a literature Corbett greatly enjoyed: 'The Colonel and his Command' was his most 'antiquarian' essay.
7. Julian Corbett, *Monk*, London, Macmillan, 1889, pp. 96, 43–4.
8. Ibid., pp. 45, 68, 93.
9. See fn at pp. 25, 68, 74, 89, 93.
10. General Wolseley to Corbett, n.d.: CBT 14/5/36: Halick Kochanski, *Sir Garnet Wolseley: Victorian Hero*, London, Hambleden Press, 1999. Wolseley was then commander-in-chief in Ireland.
11. Gardiner to Corbett, 26 March to 15 September 1889: CBT 14/3/10-15. See *Laughton* for the new journal.
12. 'Books', *Spectator*, 12 October 1889, p. 15.
13. Diary 17 January 1890: CBT 43/1 – the first diary.
14. These insights were used: Julian Corbett, *Drake*, London, Macmillan, 1890, pp. 87–8 (henceforth *Drake*).
15. Diary 23 April 1893: CBT 43/3
16. Diary 16 February–10 April 1890: CBT 43/1.
17. Diary 21 and 17 April 1890: CBT 43/1. James A. Froude, *History of England from the Fall of Wolsey to the Death of Elizabeth*, 10 vols, London, Longman, 1856–66. Brady, 2013, p. 227.
18. Fernandez Duro, *La Armada Invencible*, Madrid, de Rivadeneyra, 1884–5. Corbett's set is in the library of the Institute of Historical Research, University of London.
19. E. Jones, *John Lingard and the Pursuit of Historical Truth*, Brighton, Sussex Academic Press, 2001, pp. 82, 151, 225 for Drake and the Armada.

20. Charity established 1790. J. Adam Smith, 'A Short History', http://www.rlf.org.uk/wp-content/uploads/2013/10/10/RLFShortHistory.pdf
21. Sir Clinton Dawkins (1859–1905), Under Secretary in Egypt, financial advisor to the Viceroy of India 1899, partner in J.P. Morgan's London branch 1899, chaired the War Office Administration Committee of 1901, for which he was knighted, member of the Coefficients. Purchased the Tudor mansion Polesdon Lacey in 1902. Corbett remained in contact with his wife, taking tea in March 1920.
22. Diary 5 July 1890: CBT 43/1. Patrick Jackson, *Lulu: Selected Extracts from the Journals of Lewis Harcourt, 1880–1895*, Madison, NJ, Fairleigh Dickinson UP, 2006 and Patrick Jackson, *Harcourt and Son: A Political Biography of Sir William Harcourt, 1827–1904*, Madison, NJ, Fairleigh Dickinson UP, 2004. Liberal election funds were exhausted, so Harcourt needed wealthy volunteers. Otte, 2020, p. 116.
23. *Drake*, pp. 205, 7, 129.
24. Ibid., p. 114.
25. Ibid., p. 164. Corbett did not name 'the great German historian' but the inference was obvious. For Ranke's *History of England Principally in the Seventeenth Century* see George Gooch, *History and Historians of the Nineteenth Century*, London, Longman, 1913, pp. 93–4. The history of states in the history of mankind was his central concern.
26. *Drake*, p. 112. Corbett inserted the ultimate chivalric connection into an otherwise functional sentence on Drake's career in Parliament, where he represented Tintagel, 'King Arthur's Castle', p. 195.
27. Bruce Wathen, *Sir Francis Drake: The Construction of a Hero*, Brewer, Woodbridge, 2009, pp. 143–62, a fine analysis of Corbett's work and the wider context. *Drake*, pp. 159 and 172.
28. Colomb quoted Laughton extensively. *Laughton*, p. 99. Diary 23 June 1890: CBT 43/1. The article appeared in the *Naval and Military Magazine* published by W.H. Allen, who produced the book: see Schurman, 1965, pp. 36–59 for Philip Colomb.
29. *Drake* quotes at pp. 92, 114, 117.
30. Schurman, 1981, p. 21.
31. *Drake*, p. 117. Philip Colomb, *Naval Warfare: Its Ruling Principles and Practice Historically Treated*, London, W.H. Allen, 2nd edn, 1895, p. 24. He was 'Lecturer on Naval Strategy and Tactics and the Royal Naval College Greenwich'.
32. *Drake*, pp. 124, 151.
33. Ibid., p. 59.
34. Ibid., pp. 154–5, 158.
35. Ibid., pp. 159, 169.
36. Ibid., pp. 167–8, 171.
37. Ibid., p. 168 The words 'chivalry' and 'chivalric' recur with striking frequency, e.g. pp. 176 and 186, passages that align perfectly with Corbett's bookplate.
38. Ibid., pp. 180, 184–6.
39. Ibid., pp. 175, 189–90.
40. Ibid., pp. 208–10.
41. Brady, 2013, p. 191. Kingsley and Froude were close friends and their wives were sisters.
42. Ibsen (1838–1906). Translator William Taylor reported the 'unanimously favourable reception'. Ibsen to Taylor, 29 April 1891: J.N. Laurvik and M. Morison (eds), *Letters of Henrik Ibsen*, New York, Fox, Duffield & Co, p. 440.
43. Martin Andrew Sharp Hume (1843–1910), independent scholar. Unsuccessful Liberal parliamentary candidate, and from 1892 editor of *The State Papers relating to Spain*, published several works on Spanish and Tudor history. Gooch, 1913, p. 401. Hume's *Sir Walter Raleigh: The British Dominion of the West* appeared in 1897. Hume criticised Laughton's *Spanish Armada* volumes in the *English Historical Review (EHR)*.
44. *Athenaeum* 3305, 28 February 1891, pp. 277–8.
45. *Speaker*, 7 March 1891, pp. 290–1.
46. *London Quarterly and Holborn Review* 16(151), April 1891, pp. 177–8.
47. *Westminster Review* 135(1), January 1891, pp. 462–3.

48. Hallam Tennyson to Corbett, 25 July 1891: CBT 14/6/23.
49. Diary 29 January 1891: CBT 43/2.
50. Diary 9 and 10 February 1891: CBT 43/2.
51. Diary 23–4 November 1891: CBT 43/2.
52. *Laughton*, pp. 114–42 for the Royal Naval Exhibition and late nineteenth-century navalism.
53. Unless otherwise indicated the routine of Corbett's life has been drawn from his epigrammatic diary.
54. Diary 22 July 1891: CBT 43/2.
55. The rakish Clyde-built 233-ton steamer belonged to London paint and varnish manufacturer James Rolls Hoare (1849–1922).
56. Diary 21 October 1891: CBT 43/2.
57. Diary 27 October 1891: CBT 43/2.
58. Diary 7 December 1891: CBT 43/2.
59. Diary 30–31 December 1891: CBT 43/2.
60. Wathen, 2009, pp. 170–2, stresses the work of Garrett Mattingly, Harry Kelsey and Kenneth Andrews.
61. Elizabeth Elliot-Drake to Corbett, 5 May 1895: CBT 26/1/8. Lady Elliot-Drake, *The Family and Heirs of Sir Francis Drake*, 2 vols, London, Smith Elder, 1911. Corbett's copy is at the IHR. He was discussing a monument in London in 1914: Corbett, diary 17 July 1914: Liddle Collection.
62. Wathen, 2009, pp. 148–53.
63. Morgan, 1944, p. 189.
64. Diary 28 February 1912: CBT 43/12. George Macmillan raised the issue again on 11 March.
65. Morris, to Corbett, 1 March 1901 and JSC marginalia on the letter: CBT 1/3/31.
66. Morris to Corbett 28 April 1901: CBT 1/3/32.

3 Finding an Audience

1. His friend William Richmond may have made the connection. William Richmond, 'Lord Leighton and his Art', *The Nineteenth Century* 39, March 1896, pp. 465–76.
2. Diary 27 April 1892: CBT 43/3.
3. Julian Corbett, 'Tragedy of Mr Thomas Doughty: His Relations with Sir Francis Drake', *Macmillan's Magazine* 68, August 1893, pp. 258–68 and *The Living Age* 199, 21 October 1893, pp. 146–56 (henceforth 'Doughty'). *Macmillan's* (1859–1907), the publisher's house journal, shared the conservative taste of their books. *The Living Age*, an American weekly, reprinted work from British and American journals and newspapers.
4. 'Doughty', p. 258
5. Julian Corbett, 'Our First Ambassadors to Russia', *Macmillan's Magazine* 68, May 1893, pp. 58–69, repeated in *The Living Age* 198, 15 July 1893, pp. 67–77 (henceforth 'Russia'). John Hattendorf's claims that the essay was illustrated by Shannon and Ricketts confuses it with 'Jezebel'. 'Russia' was not illustrated. See Hattendorf's 'Bibliography' in Goldrick and Hattendorf, 1993, p. 304.
6. Richard Hakluyt, *The Principal Navigations, Voyages and Discoveries of the English Nation, made by Sea or over Land to the most remote and farthest distant Quarters of the earth at any time within the compass of these 1500 years,* London, Bishop and Neewberie, 1589.
7. 'Russia', p. 69. This was a Liberal commonplace, based on John Morley's *The Life of Richard Cobden*, London, Fisher Unwin, 1883.
8. Diary December 1891, 25 January 1892: CBT 43/2 and 3.
9. The double portrait of Arundel and his wife is normally dated to 1639, but 1637 would be more likely.
10. Julian Corbett, 'Sancho Panza of Madagascar', *Macmillan's Magazine* 71, March 1895, pp. 358–64, at p. 364.

11. Diary 22 September 1890: CBT 43/1: 'went to Record Office re forts for Col. Richardson'. Richardson was then on the Artillery Staff in London. He became Commandant of the Gunnery School in March 1892, a post he held for two years. By 1916 he was a Major General and Colonel Commandant of the Royal Artillery.

12. Diary 23–4 November 1891: CBT 43/2. George Sydenham Clarke, *Fortification: Its Past Achievements, Recent Developments, and Future Progress*, London, Murray, 1890, Preface to the 1st edn.

13. Diary 28 June 1892: CBT 43/3.

14. Diary 2 June 1891: CBT 43/2 Julian Corbett, 'The Colonel and his Command', *American Historical Review* 2, October 1896, pp. 1–11. Peter Novick, *That Noble Dream: The 'Objectivity Question' and the American Historical Profession*, Cambridge, Cambridge UP, 1998, p. 15.

15. Julian Corbett, 'Introduction' to Thomas Taylor, *Running the Blockade*, London, John Murray, 1896. Diary 10 March–11 September 1896: CBT 43/3.

16. Diary 1–17 May 1893: CBT 43/4.

17. Laughton to Corbett, 8 August 1893: CBT/14 approving his application.

18. See *Laughton*, pp. 142–73 for this argument.

19. Laughton to Corbett, 28 September 1893: CBT/14.

20. Laughton to Corbett, 8 August 1893 and 24 September 1893: CBT/14. *Laughton*, pp. 142–72.

21. Laughton to Corbett, 3 and 5 January 1895, 1 February 1895, 8 and 11 May 1895: CBT/14.

22. Laughton to Corbett, 1 and 8 May 1895: CBT/14.

23. Diary 30 December 1894: CBT 43/5.

24. Corbett to Laughton, 4 October 1895: Laughton MS NMM LGH 43/14-15.

25. *Laughton*, pp. 156–7.

26. Diary 25 February and 11 March 1896: CBT 42/6. Rodd (1858–1941) won the Newdigate Prize at Oxford for a poem on Raleigh, wrote a life Sir Walter for the *English Men of Action* series ', and published *Ballads of the Fleet* in 1897.

27. Reports in the *Pall Mall Gazette* on 13, 14 and 16 April 1896, 'Dongolay' on 15 May 1896: CBT 31/3. Sir Reginald Wingate to Corbett dated Firket, 1 July 1896: CBT 14/5/35.

28. Diary 12 February 1896: CBT 43/6

29. Julian Corbett, 'Ubaldino and the Armada', *Athenaeum* 109, 17 April 1897, p. 508. Julian Corbett, *Drake and the Tudor Navy, with a History of the Rise of England as a Maritime Power* (henceforth *Tudor*), 2 vols, London, Longman, 1898, vol. II, pp. 412–20.

30. The subject is discussed in *Tudor*, Appendix B.

31. *Laughton*, pp. 158–60. Diary 21 August and 10 December 1896: CBT43/6.

32. Diary 15–24 November 1896: CBT 43/6.

33. *Tudor*, II, pp. 368–9. D.M. Schurman, 'Civilian Historian: Sir Julian Corbett', in Schurman, 1965, pp. 154–5.

34. Lambert, 2007, ch. 1.

35. Julian Corbett, *The Successors of Drake* (henceforth *Successors*), London, Longman, 1900, pp. 235, 291–2.

36. Correspondence between C.J. Longman, Corbett and his agent leading to the contract for the second edition of *Tudor* is fraught, Colles implying that Longman deliberately withheld sales to avoid triggering the step in royalties due after 1,000 copies had been sold: CBT 1/2/24-25, CBT 2/1/1.

37. James A. Froude, *English Seamen in the Sixteenth Century*, London, Longman, 1896. Froude revived interest in the Tudor era, but his work was too deeply engaged with contemporary political issues for his academic peers.

38. H.W. Wilson, 'Drake of Devon', *Graphic*, 5 March 1898.

39. Sir James Richard Thursfield (1840–1923), *The Times'* naval correspondent since 1887, and a significant contributor to the naval debate in other formats.

40. *The Times*, 4 May 1898, p. 3, col. A.

41. *The Times*, 15 March 1898, p. 12, col. D.

42. 'Books of the Week', *The Times*, 4 April 1898, p. 9, col. A. W.L. Clowes (ed.), *The Royal Navy: A History from the Earliest Times to 1900*, 7 vols, London, Sampson Low, 1897–1903.
43. Laughton review of *Tudor*, *EHR*, July 1898, pp. 581–4.
44. *Morning Post*, 3 October 1899, p. 7.
45. N.A.M. Rodger, *The Safeguard of the Sea: A Naval History of Britain*, vol. I: *660–1649*, London, Harper Collins, 1997. Kenneth Andrews, *Drake's Voyages: A Reassessment of their Place in Elizabethan Maritime Expansion*, London, Weidenfeld & Nicolson, 1967, challenges the Victorian version of Drake. Wathen, 2009, continues the process. For Tudor strategy and diplomacy: R.B. Wernham, *Before the Armada: The Growth of English Foreign Policy 1485–1588*, London, Cape, 1966; *After the Armada: Elizabethan England and the Struggle for Western Europe, 1588–1595*, Oxford, Oxford UP, 1984; and *The Return of the Armadas: The Last Years of the Elizabethan War against Spain, 1595–1603*, Oxford, Oxford UP, 1994. John Sugden, *Sir Francis Drake*, London, Barrie & Jenkins, 1990 remains the standard life. See Paul Hammer, *The Polarisation of Elizabethan Politics: The Political Career of Robert Devereux, 2nd Earl of Essex, 1585–1597*, Cambridge, Cambridge UP, 1999 for the politics of Elizabethan strategy.
46. Julian Corbett (ed.), *Spanish War 1585–87* (henceforth *Spanish War*), London, NRS, 1898, p. xxxi.
47. Duro, 1884–II. Michael Oppenheim, *A History of the Administration of the Royal Navy, 1509–1660*, London, Bodley Head, 1896.
48. *Spanish War*, p. xiv.
49. Ibid., p. xxii.
50. Ibid., pp. xxv and 110.
51. Ibid., pp. xxix–xxxiii.
52. Ibid., p. xli.
53. Ibid., p. xliii. He may have known that in a war the Navy planned to seize French overseas cruiser bases, and bombard metropolitan naval bases. The Fashoda crisis brought that prospect closer.
54. Ibid., p. xliiv.
55. F. York Powell, Review, *EHR*, April 1899, pp. 366–8.
56. *The Times*, 18 May 1898, p. 9, col. E; 3 May 1900, p. 6, col. G; 22 July 1898, p. 11, col. E.
57. 'Election Intelligence', *The Times*, 17 January 1899, p. 10, col. D. His decision was widely reported, e.g. in *Daily News*, 17 January 1899.
58. *Morning Post*, 8 February 1899, p. 1.
59. Julian Corbett, 'The Plan of Campaign', 'Letters to the Editor', *Daily News*, 14 February 1900. In 1901 the editorial policy of the *Daily News* shifted to oppose the war, following its purchase by Quaker chocolate-maker George Cadbury.
60. Colles to Corbett, 4 December 1899, and related correspondence: CBT 2/1/6.
61. Diary 13 and 26 February, 18 April, 2 May, 7 and 31 July 1900: CBT 43/8.
62. Diary 5 and 11 October 1900: CBT 43/8.
63. John Robert Seeley, *The Growth of English Policy: An Historical Essay*, Cambridge, Cambridge UP, 1895. Corbett cited vol. I, p. 216 on pp. v–vi of *Successors*.
64. *Successors*, p. vii.
65. Ibid., p. 410.
66. John Guilmartin, *Gunpowder and Galleys: Changing Technology and Mediterranean Warfare at Sea in the 16th Century*, London, Conway, 2003, pp. 111–18.
67. *Successors*, p. 353.
68. Hammer, 1999, p. 82.
69. *Successors*, Preface, pp. vi and vii.
70. Ibid., pp. 407–9.
71. Hammer, 1999, p. 402.
72. Critically George Sydenham Clarke and James Thursfield, *The Navy and the Nation*, London, Murray, 1897.
73. *Successors*, p. 410.

74. L.W. Henry, 'The Earl of Essex as a Strategist and Military Organiser (1596–7)', *EHR* 68(268), 1953, pp. 363–93, at pp. 368–9, 390; see also p. 373 fn 3. *Successors*, p. 163 credits Essex 'with being one of the first men who tried to give England an army in the modern sense'.
75. Henry discussed this material with Charles T. Atkinson, an NRS councillor and editor before 1914. Paul Hammer has demonstrated the paper was intended for Sir Francis Vere, the pre-eminent English soldier of the day, who served at Cadiz, in Essex's retinue. Hammer, 1999, p. 255.
76. Paul Hammer, 'Myth-making, Politics, Propaganda and the Capture of Cadiz in 1596', *Historical Journal* 40(3), 1997, pp. 621–42.
77. Hammer, 1999, pp. 74–5, 260. K.R. Andrews (ed.), *The Last Voyage of Drake and Hawkins*, Cambridge, Hakluyt Society, 1972, pp. 15–17.
78. Henry, 1953, pp. 366–7. Hammer, 1999, pp. 187–9, for Essex's excellent intelligence-gathering system.
79. *Successors*, Conclusion, pp. 415–38 is a discussion of warship design.
80. Ibid., p. 350.
81. Hammer, 1999, pp. 234–5, 307 for Thucydides. Lambert, *Seapower States*, chs 1 and 2 for these wars.
82. Hammer, 1999, p. 232. The link with Castiglione's influential guide *The Courtier* is instructive. Essex was a good student. Raleigh, an exemplary poseur, acknowledged Essex to be the master of this art in 1596.
83. Hammer, 1999, pp. 243–9, 261.
84. *Successors*, pp. 440–2. See also Hammer, 1999, pp. 250–2.
85. 'Literature', *Leeds Mercury*, 31 October 1900.
86. Longman used the notice in an advert in the *Pall Mall Gazette*, 5 November 1900.
87. 'Books of the Day', *Standard*, 23 November 1900, p. 4.
88. 'Recent Naval Literature', *The Times*, 12 May 1901, p. 13, col. C.
89. 'Reviews', *Pall Mall Gazette*, 13 December 1900.
90. A.F. Pollard, review in *EHR*, July 1901, pp. 577–8.
91. Julian Corbett, 'War Correspondence and the Censorship under Elizabeth': *Anglo-Saxon Review: A Quarterly Miscellany* 10, September 1901, pp. 54–62. Hammer, 1999, offers a modern approach.
92. J.K. Laughton (unsigned), Review, *Edinburgh Review* 397, July 1901, pp. 1–27.
93. G. Mattingly, *The Defeat of the Spanish Armada*, London, Cape, 1959.
94. For the intellectual consequences of salaried historians serving the state see: Lionel Gossman, *Basel in the Age of Burckhardt: A Study in Unseasonal Ideas*, Chicago, IL, University of Chicago Press, 2000, pp. 160–70. Burckhardt and Nietzsche shared a profound antipathy for Prussian/German statist scholarship.

4 Politics and Policy

1. For a discussion of this concept see: Lambert, *Seapower States*.
2. Corbett to Newbolt, 16 December 1904: CBT 3/7/31, envying Newbolt his chance to talk with the explorer and imperial expansionist Sir Francis Younghusband, leader of the recent expedition to Tibet.
3. Notably in the pages of the *Naval Annual*. The 1908 edition argued for imperial contributions to the Royal Navy. *Athenaeum*, 6 June 1908, p. 694. 'Election Intelligence', *The Times*, 17 January 1899, p. 10.
4. Richard J. Evans, *Cosmopolitan Islanders: British Historians and the European Continent*, Cambridge, Cambridge UP, 2009, p. 111, referring to Harold Temperley, a colleague at the 1913 International Congress and a fellow recruit to the war effort. Thomas Otte (ed.), *An Historian in Peace and War: The Diaries of Harold Temperley*, Abingdon, Routledge, 2016 (first published Farnham, Ashgate, 2014).
5. Ian F.W. Beckett and Keith Jeffery, 'The Royal Navy and the Curragh Incident', *Historical Research* 62, 1989, pp. 54–69.

6. H.C.G. Matthew, *The Liberal Imperialists: The Ideas and Politics of a Post-Gladstonian Elite*, Oxford, Oxford UP, 1973. Otte, 2020, pp. 160–1 for Rosebery's diplomacy, of which Grey and Corbett approved.
7. Charles Corbett was proposed for a peerage in the political crisis of 1909.
8. For service politics: Peter M. Keeling, 'The Armed Forces and Parliamentary Elections in the United Kingdom, 1885–1914', *EHR* 134(569), August 2019, pp. 881–913.
9. Morley's *Life of Cobden* became an ideological pillar of the Gladstonian party, an influence that endured down to 1914.
10. Matthew, 1973, p. 216. Clarke and Thursfield, 1897. Corbett owned a copy.
11. *Laughton*, p. 192. A.W. Ewing, *The Man of Room 40: The Life of Sir Alfred Ewing*. London, Hutchinson, 1939, p. 134.
12. *Laughton*, pp. 235–7.
13. Rosebery to Gladstone, 16 July 1891: cited in Matthew, 1973, p. 200.
14. J.E. Tyler, *The British Army and the Continent, 1904–1914*, London, Arnold, 1914, pp. 63–4.
15. Matthew, 1973, p. 219. Nicholas d'Ombrain, *War Machinery and High Policy: Defence Administration in Peacetime Britain, 1902–1914*, Oxford, Oxford UP, 1973, p. 15.
16. Fisher to Thursfield, 29 November 1901 and enclosed cutting, source not given: THU 1/3/59.
17. Fisher to Thursfield, 17 January 1903: THU 1/3/17.
18. Fisher to Thursfield, 6 March 1903: THU 1/3/43.
19. Fisher to Thursfield, 24 December 1903: THU 1/3/37.
20. Fisher correspondence with Joseph and Austen Chamberlain: AC10/1B et seq. Chamberlain MS, University of Birmingham Cadbury Archives Centre.
21. *Scotsman*, 17 February 1903: Matthew, 1973, p. 216. Ruddock Mackay, *Fisher of Kilverstone*, Oxford, Oxford UP, 1973, pp. 309–10 for this relationship. Later Haldane called for a single Ministry of Defence, which enraged Fisher.
22. Haldane, speech of 6 January 1904: Matthew, 1973, p. 216. Thursfield's input is obvious.
23. Haldane speech, *Scotsman*, 17 February 1903. Matthew, 1973, pp. 217–18.
24. Corbett to Newbolt, 31 August 1901: CBT 3/7/5. Paul M. Kennedy, *The Rise and Fall of the Anglo-German Antagonism, 1860–1914*, London, Allen Lane, 1980. Otte, 2020, p. 209.
25. Otte, 2020, pp. 170, 209. Edward Grey, 'Mr Chamberlain's Fiscal Policy', *Monthly Review*, October 1903, pp. 11–25.
26. Newbolt's private life was complex. His wife brought her cousin, and lover, into the marriage. Newbolt lived at 14 Victorian Road, Kensington, a short walk from Corbett in Knightsbridge.
27. Haldane, 'Great Britain and Germany: A Study in Education', *Monthly Review*, November 1901: Matthew, 1973, p. 228.
28. Corbett to Newbolt, 19 July 1900: CBT 3/7/3.
29. Matthew, 1973, pp. 151–94
30. Corbett to Newbolt, 19 July 1900: CBT 3/7/3. The essay was unsigned, but Edith wrote in his diary: 'Henry's new magazine *The Monthly Review* published Julian's contribution "The Paradox of Empire", gave it 1st place!': Diary 19 and 22 September 1900: CBT 43/08.
31. T.A. Brassey to Corbett, 27 February 1901: CBT 14/1/24. Brassey served in the Second Boer War.
32. Thomas A. Brassey, *Problems of Empire*, London, Arthur H. Humphreys, 1904.
33. James Bryce, *The Holy Roman Empire*, London, Macmillan, 1866. This book was almost a commonplace of Victorian reading. Corbett's copy of the 8th edition of 1889 is in the IHR collection, see p. 378 for the quote.
34. Julian Corbett (unsigned), 'The Paradox of Empire', *Monthly Review*, October 1900, pp. 1–14.
35. Ibid., p. 14
36. Julian Corbett (unsigned), 'The Little Englander', *Monthly Review*, January 1901, pp. 10–19, at p. 11.

37. Ibid., p. 12.
38. Hunt, 1982, pp. 9–10.
39. Mackay, 1973, pp. 274–5. Hunt, 1982, pp. 5–19
40. Corbett to Newbolt, 3 February 1902: CBT 3/10.
41. Corbett to Newbolt, 1 February 1902: CBT 3/7/8.
42. Julian Corbett, 'Education in the Navy I', *Monthly Review*, March 1902, pp. 34–40, at pp. 37–8, 40.
43. Ibid., p. 45. Hunt, 1982, p. 27.
44. Mackay, 1973, p. 275.
45. Julian Corbett, 'Education in the Navy II', *Monthly Review*, April 1902, pp. 43–57, at pp. 44, 45 and 46.
46. Ibid., p. 56.
47. Ibid., pp. 56–7.
48. Julian Corbett, 'Lord Selborne's Critics', *Monthly Review*, July 1902, pp. 64–75, at p. 65.
49. Ibid., p. 67.
50. Corbett to Newbolt, 29 July 1903: CBT 3/11.
51. Julian Corbett, 'Education in the Navy III', *Monthly Review*, September 1902, pp. 42–54, at pp. 42, 44, 54.
52. Ewing, 1939, pp. 133–7, 153–4.
53. Corbett to Newbolt, 3 May 1902: CBT 3/7/9.
54. Julian Corbett, 'Lord Selborne's Memorandum I & II', *Monthly Review*, February 1903, pp. 28–41, at pp. 28–9.
55. Ibid., pp. 34–6, 41. See 'The February Reviews', *Saturday Review*, 14 February 1903, p. 205, for press reactions.
56. Julian Corbett, 'Lord Selborne's Memorandum III', *Monthly Review*, March 1903, pp. 40–52, at pp. 49 and 52, for Corbett's effective use of a Parliamentary Return, a financial statement from the Treasury.
57. Ibid., p. 53.
58. Corbett to Newbolt, 3 March 1903: CBT 3/17.
59. Corbett to Newbolt, 9 July 1903: CBT 3/18.
60. Dinner at the Athenaeum, 7 November 1903, signed menu: CBT 13/3-4.
61. Corbett to Newbolt, 19 September 1903: CBT 3/21.
62. Corbett to Newbolt, 10 October 1903: CBT 3/25.
63. Julian Corbett, 'Found Wanting', *Monthly Review*, October 1903, pp. 82–90, at p. 84.
64. Ibid., p. 86.
65. Clarke to Corbett, 16 February 1904: CBT 14/5/18.
66. Henry Spenser Wilkinson (1853–1937), Germanist tactical writer, founder of the Navy League, advocate of a Naval Staff in the early 1890s. An ally of Lord Charles Beresford, later Chichele Professor of the History of War at Oxford. Jay Luvaas, *The Education of an Army: British Military Thought 1815-1940*, London, Cassell, 1964, pp. 253–90, at pp. 277–8.
67. Julian Corbett, 'The Reorganisation of the War Office', *Monthly Review*, March 1904, pp. 26–36, at p. 28.
68. Ibid., pp. 31–3.
69. Ibid., pp. 34–5.
70. Corbett to Newbolt, 17 May 1904: CBT 3/25.
71. Julian Corbett, 'Queen Anne's Defence Committee', *Monthly Review*, May 1904, pp. 55–65 (henceforth 'Queen Anne's Defence Committee').
72. Ibid., pp. 63 and 59.
73. Ibid., pp. 61–5.
74. Julian Corbett, 'Home Rule for the Volunteer', *Monthly Review*, June 1904, pp. 29–39, at p. 38.
75. Ibid., p. 38.
76. Julian Corbett, 'The One-eyed Commission', *Monthly Review*, July 1905, pp. 38–49, at p. 39.

77. Ibid., p. 40.
78. Ibid., p. 49. For the invasion debate see: David G. Morgan-Owen, *The Fear of Invasion: Strategy, Politics and British War Planning, 1880–1914*, Oxford, Oxford UP, 2017.
79. Corbett to Newbolt, 15 June 1904: CBT 3/27.
80. Corbett to Newbolt, 5 July 1904: CBT 3/29.
81. Julian Corbett, 'A Russian Privateer in the Mediterranean', *Monthly Review*, February 1904, pp. 140–52, at p. 152.
82. Corbett to Newbolt, 20 August 1903: CBT 3/19.
83. *The Times*, 20 November 1903, p. 15; see also 20 August 1903, pp. 5–7 and 21 August 1903, p. 10. Goldrick and Hattendorf, 1993, p. 307.
84. Corbett to Newbolt, 20 August 1903: CBT 3/19.
85. Julian Corbett, 'The Report on the Fleet Manoeuvres', *Monthly Review*, December 1903, pp. 85–94.
86. Ibid., pp. 92–3.
87. Susan Chitty, *Playing the Game: A Biography of Sir Henry Newbolt*, London, Quartet, 1997, pp. 149–55.
88. Webb to Wells, 12 September 1902: N. Mackenzie (ed.), *The Letters of Sidney and Beatrice Webb*, vol. II: *Partnership, 1892–1912*, Cambridge, Cambridge UP, 1978, p. 170.
89. See his 'The Navy and the Empire', in *The Empire and the Century*, London, John Murray, 1905, pp. 197–212. Other Coefficients also contributed: Reeves, Haldane, Garvin and Amery.
90. Beatrice Webb to Russell, n.d. May 1903: Mackenzie, 1978, p. 185.
91. Ibid., pp. 186–7.
92. Coefficients printed minutes: XXIII and XXIV, 19 February and 19 March 1906: ASSOC 17 BLPES. Amery and Mackinder took the minutes.
93. Corbett to Newbolt, 1 November 1907: CBT 3/54.
94. Mackenzie, 1978, pp. 265–6.
95. Corbett's Diary records meeting on 18 May 1908 with Lord Robert Cecil speaking, 18 January 1909 when Newbolt spoke, and 24 May 1909 with Webb on Poor Laws, when they decided to keep the Coefficients going.

5 *England in the Mediterranean*

1. Clarke had been Secretary to both the Interdepartmental Colonial Defence Committee (1885–92) and the Hartington Commission on Army and Navy Administration (1888–90). His public critique of War Office obstructionism was deeply resented, and wholly justified.
2. Clarke and Thursfield, 1897. Corbett's copy is on the Staff College Loan list. T.A. Brassey, 'Great Britain as a Sea Power', *The Nineteenth Century*, July 1898, reprinted in Brassey, 1904.
3. Clarke to Corbett, 30 June 1900: CBT 14/2/21.
4. Clarke to Corbett, 28 November 1900: CBT 14/2/14.
5. *Laughton*, pp. 137–9. Clarke's devastating 'England and the Mediterranean', *The Nineteenth Century*, April 1895, reprinted in *The Navy and the Nation*, pp. 228–42, was a key text for Corbett's project. Matthew, 1973, p. 219.
6. Laughton to Corbett, 11 November 1900: CBT 14.
7. May to Corbett, 19, 25 and 27 August 1902: CBT 13/1/50-52. May was well read, and a key figure in the development of naval war-gaming.
8. There is nothing on the subject among Corbett's papers. *Laughton*, pp. 235–7, for membership of the NRS's Council between 1897 and 1922.
9. *The Times*, 21 May 1903, p. 6, col. E.
10. Corbett to C.J. Longman, 15 March 1903, draft: CBT 2/2/3.
11. C.J. Longman to Corbett, 17 March 1903: CBT 2/2/4.
12. C.J. Longman to Corbett 20 March 1903: CBT 2/2/8: *England in the Mediterranean* agreement signed 1 May 1903: CBT 2/2/14.
13. Corbett to Newbolt, 31 August 1901: CBT 3/7/4.

14. Julian Corbett, *England in the Mediterranean: A Study of the Rise and Influence of British Power within the Straits, 1603–1713* (henceforth *Mediterranean*), 2 vols, London, Longman, 1904, vol. I, pp. 23, 142–54. John Jordan and Philippe Caresse, *French Armoured Cruisers, 1887–1932*, Barnsley, Seaforth, 2019.

15. *Mediterranean*, I, p. 80.

16. 'Books of the Week', *The Times*, 4 April 1898, p. 9, and Chapter 3 of this book.

17. Within two years the Dutch Wars became topical, as the main theatre shifted to the North Sea.

18. *Mediterranean*, I, p. 96.

19. Ibid., Preface dated November 1903, pp. v–viii.

20. For use of footnotes see ibid., p. 212 fn 2, and pp. 363–4.

21. Ibid., pp. 36–8, 46, 72. This point has not received the attention it deserves from Raleigh scholars. Mark Nicholls and Penry Williams, *Sir Walter Raleigh in Life and Legend*, London, Continuum, 2011, do not address the wider context in which the voyage was permitted.

22. *Mediterranean*, I, p. 201.

23. Ibid., pp. 197–8.

24. Ibid., pp. 196–7.

25. Ibid., p. 308, referencing John Colomb, *The Protection of our Commerce and Distribution of our Naval Forces Considered*, London, Harrison, 1867. For Colomb, see Schurman, 1965, pp. 16–35. In *Seven Years' War*, I, p. 308, Corbett defined command of the sea as 'nothing but the control of sea communications'.

26. *Seven Years' War*, II, p. 207.

27. Ibid., pp. 240, 244, 252–3, 278.

28. Nelson relied on Tetuan to revictual his fleet holding station off Cadiz in October 1805.

29. *Mediterranean*, II, p. 354.

30. Ibid., p. 420, for the critical passage.

31. Ibid., p. 470. The singular 'military state' may imply Germany.

32. F.A. Johnson, *Defence by Committee: The British Committee of Imperial Defence*, Oxford, Oxford UP, 1960, p. 54.

33. *Mediterranean*, II, pp. 493–5.

34. Ibid., p. 506.

35. John Hattendorf, *England in the War of the Spanish Succession: A Study of the English View and Conduct of Grand Strategy, 1702–1713*, New York, Garland, 1987, Preface, pp. 53–75, 138–48.

36. *Mediterranean*, II, pp. 519–20.

37. Ibid., p. 555. The historians included a descendant of Stanhope.

38. Ibid., pp. 557–8.

39. Student lecture notes survive: 'Naval History – as it affects the rise of Great Britain as a maritime power and the Strategical situation in the Mediterranean'. Notes from lectures by Mr Julian Corbett: Royal Museums Greenwich Archive, GET/13, 18 pages, 36 openings.

40. *Athenaeum* 3391, 23 April 1904, pp. 524–5.

41. *Speaker*, 21 May 1904, p. 189.

42. J.K. Laughton (unsigned), 'England in the Mediterranean', *Edinburgh Review*, July 1905, pp. 100–30, esp. pp. 129–30.

43. Corbett, 'Queen Anne's Defence Committee', pp. 55–65, at pp. 64–5.

44. The second edition of 1917 reused moulds taken from original typesetting with the spacers knocked out.

45. Hunt, 1982. The relationship with Corbett is a major theme of the book. Herbert Richmond, *The Navy in the War of 1739–48*, 3 vols, Cambridge, Cambridge UP, 1920.

46. George M. Trevelyan, *England under Queen Anne*, 3 vols, London, Longman, 1930, vol. I, pp. vi, 129, 259. Basil Williams, *Stanhope: A Study in Eighteenth-century War and Diplomacy*, Oxford, Oxford UP, 1932, p. 28 fn, and Stetson Conn, *Gibraltar in British Diplomacy in the Eighteenth Century*, New Haven, CT, and London, Yale UP, 1942, p. 295, all cite Corbett as an academic standard

47. It is a curiosity of the profession that Liddell Hart's concept has generated far more literature than Corbett's more powerful and original output. Catchphrases matter more than ideas.
48. John Ehrman, *The Navy in the War of William III*, Cambridge, Cambridge UP, 1953, p. 517.
49. See Ehrman's footnotes, pp. 519, 521–2.
50. Linda Colley, *Captives: Britain, Empire and the World 1600–1850*, London, Cape, 2002, p. 389.
51. Julian Corbett, *A Note on the Drawing in the possession of the Earl of Dartmouth illustrating the Battle of Sole Bay May 28th 1672 and the Battle of the Texel, August 11, 1673*, London, NRS, 1908, 45 pp.
52. Diary April–May 1907. CBT/43/8.
53. Remmet Daalder, *Van de Velde & Son: Marine Painters*, Leiden, Primavera, 2016, pp. 150–5.
54. Corbett, *A Note on the Drawing*, p. 29.
55. Ibid., p. 45.

6 The Naval War Course

1. Admiralty to President Royal Naval College [RNC] Greenwich, 2 June 1900: ADM 203/64.
2. Arthur J. Marder, *The Anatomy of British Sea Power*, London, Putnam, 1940, p. 389.
3. Mackay, 1973, p. 237.
4. Mackay, 1973, pp. 238, 259. Fisher to Lord Selborne, 29 July 1901: *FGDN*, I, pp. 202–4. Custance to Bridge, 17 October 1901; NMM BRI 1/15.
5. Battenberg to Fisher, 11 February 1902: Kerr, 1934, pp. 161–6.
6. Slade to Corbett RNC Greenwich, 20 May 1906: CBT 13/2/1. Slade's Notes in the origins of the Course. May was working with Fred T. Jane on naval war-gaming.
7. Admiralty to Admiral President RNC Greenwich, 20 and 22 September 1900: ADM 203/64.
8. Schurman, 1981, pp. 32–4.
9. 'The War Training of the Navy, VII: The Naval War Course', *The Times*, 25 January 1902, p. 6, col. A.
10. Reginald Tupper to Corbett, 26 October 1906: CBT 13/3/69. R. Tupper, *Reminiscences*, London, Jarrolds, n.d., pp. 112–15. Tupper served in the NID in 1896.
11. Brian Bond, *The Victorian Army and the Staff College, 1854–1914*, London, Eyre Methuen, 1972, pp. 197–8.
12. Henry May to Corbett, 19 September 1902, RNC: CBT 13/3/50.
13. *Laughton*, pp. 200–1, 235–7. K.G.B. Dewar, *The Navy from Within*, London, Gollancz, 1939, pp. 134 and 137. Dewar used these books to study tactics, but ignored Corbett, following their feud over Jutland.
14. David Hannay, journalist and naval writer; his cursory approach to evidence was anathema to professionals, who took their lead from Laughton. *Laughton*, pp. 152, 161, 164.
15. H.J. May to Corbett, 27 August 1902, RNC: CBT 13/3/51.
16. Julian Corbett, 'The Teaching of Naval and Military History', *History*, April 1916, pp. 12–24.
17. Julian Corbett, 'War Course lecture notes October 1903': LHCMA.
18. Reginald Bacon, *From 1900 Onward*, London, Hutchinson, 1940, pp. 30–5.
19. H.J. May to Corbett, 30 October and 2 November 1902, RNC: CBT 13/3/54-5.
20. Dinner at the Athenaeum, 7 November 1903, signed menu: CBT 13/3-4.
21. Schurman, 1981, pp. 21, 26 and 34.
22. Corbett to Newbolt, 15 and 17 June 1904: CBT 13/2/25 and 27.
23. *Successors*, p. vii.
24. Tupper, n.d., pp. 143–4 at RNC and Camperdown Committee.
25. Admiralty to Pres. RNC, 16 July 1903: ADM 203/9.

26. Report on the 2nd War Course 1902–1903, Submitted by Rear-Admiral H.J. May, 23 June 1903, with minutes. H.J. May to Admiral President RNC, 25 July 1903. Admiralty to Treasury, 19 August and reply, 21 August 1903: ADM 1/7713.
27. R.H. Harris, *From Naval Cadet to Admiral*, London, Cassell, 1913, pp. 408–9. Admiralty to Admiral President, 21 August 1903: ADM 1/7713.
28. May to Corbett, 20 January 1904: CBT 13/3/56-57: Admiralty to Pres. RNC, 4 May 1903: ADM 203/9.
29. **Presidents of the Naval War College**

Name	Destination
Rear Admiral Henry May, Sept. 1900–Apr. 1904	Died
Captain Edmond Slade, 13 May 1904–Oct. 1907	DNI
Rear Admiral R.S. Lowry, n.d.–Nov. 1908	2nd Cruiser Squadron
Rear Admiral Lewis Bayly, 22 Nov. 1908–23 Feb. 1911	1st Cruiser Squadron
Rear Admiral Sir Henry B. Jackson FRS, 24 Feb. 1911–27 Jan. 1913	War Staff
Vice Admiral Alexander Bethell, 28 Jan. 1913–1915 (ex-DNI)	Channel Fleet

30. For NRS councillors 1893–1915 see *Laughton*, pp. 235–7.
31. Admiralty to Pres. RNC, 1 March 1905: ADM 302/9.
32. Capt. of War College to Pres. RNC, 13 March 1905: ADM 203/9.
33. Fisher to Corbett, 6 July 1903: FISR 3/26/3722: FG I, pp. 274–5.
34. Corbett minute in Fisher to Corbett, 24 May 1905, and Fisher to Corbett, 22 May 1905: FISR 1/4/166–8.
35. Schurman, 1965, p. 164.
36. Schurman, 1981, pp. 61, 167.
37. Ibid., pp. 44–5. D. Baugh, *The Global Seven Years' War*, London, Longman, 2011, p. 667.
38. Schurman, 1981, p. 47.
39. Corbett to Newbolt, 30 January 1906: CBT 3/44.
40. Fisher to Corbett, 12 May 1906: FISR 1/4/201: FG & DN, pp. 81–2.
41. Corbett to Fisher, 13 May 1906: FISR 1/5/202: FG & DN II, pp. 81–2.
42. Slade to Corbett, 20 May 1906: CBT 13/2/1.
43. Julian Corbett, 'The Naval War Course I', *The Times*, 5 June 1906, p. 6.
44. The relevance of this remark became clear in August 1911, when Sir Arthur Wilson's plans were subjected to CID scrutiny.
45. Fisher to Corbett, 11 June 1906: FGDN, II 1956, p. 82. CBT 12/108.
46. *Manchester Guardian*, 7 June 1906 and *Western Mercury*, 3 July 1906: CBT 13/2/3-4.
47. Terpsichore was the muse of dance. Admiralty to the President of the RNC, 9 November 1906: ADM 203/10. For experiments to spot periscopes in 1909: FISR 1/9.
48. Admiralty Order, 1 July 1907: ADM 203/100.
49. Tenth War Course: ADM 203/69, pp. 25–9. The dedicated planning team Corbett mentioned in *The Times*.
50. Watson to Admiralty, 9 January 1912: M. Seligmann (ed.), *Naval Intelligence from Germany*, Aldershot, NRS, 2007, p. 367.
51. A project that ultimately involved Corbett. *Fisher Papers*, II, pp. xii and 316–468. Corbett's essay is at pp. 318–45.
52. Fisher to Corbett, 9 March 1907: FGDN, II, p. 120 and Schurman, 1981, p. 67.
53. Fisher to Corbett, 17 March 1907: FISR 1/5/2322.
54. Published in *The Nineteenth Century*, February 1907.
55. Julian Corbett, 'The Strategical Value of Speed', *JRUSI*, July 1907. Delivered 6 March 1907.
56. Barfleur (pseud. Reginald Custance), *Naval Policy: A Plea for the Study of War*, London, 1907. Corbett's copy has significant marginalia. Chapter 9 was the target of his RUSI paper. Slade to Corbett, 16 April 1908: CBT 13/2/20.
57. *The Nineteenth Century*, June 1907 (journal title changed in 1901): also A.T. Mahan, *Some Neglected Aspects of War*, Boston, MA, 1907, pp. 115–54.
58. ADM 203/100, f. 19.

59. ADM 203/100, ff. 89–91.
60. ADM 203/100, f. 59
61. ADM 203/100, f. 96. Beatty to Corbett, 25 November 1912: CBT 13/3/5. My copy of J. Corbett and H. Edwards (eds), *Naval and Military Essays*, Cambridge, Cambridge UP, 1914, bears the Naval War College stamp and that of the Imperial Defence College.
62. Richmond, 1920.
63. ADM 203/100, ff. 11–15.
64. ADM 203/100, f. 25.
65. Slade to Corbett, 17 August 1907, War College Portsmouth: CBT 13/2/11. Slade to Corbett, 19 February 1908, 16 April and 19 September 1908: CBT 13/2/16, 20 and 28.
66. Slade to Corbett, 11 September 1908: CBT 13/2/25. Slade to Corbett, 18 September 1908: CBT 13/2/27.
67. Slade to Corbett, 23 September and 19 October 1908: CBT 13/2/24, 29 and 30.
68. Slade to Corbett, 16 November 1908: CBT 13/2/35.
69. Lewis Bayly, *Pull Together*, London, Harrap, 1939, pp. 129–32.
70. Slade to Corbett, HMS *Hyacinth*, Colombo, 5 August 1909: CBT 13/2/42.
71. Slade to Corbett, HMS *Hyacinth*, at sea, 29 October 1909: CBT 13/2/45.
72. Bayly, 1939, p. 131.
73. Slade to Corbett, 4 May 1910: CBT 13/2/(50).
74. Corbett to Newbolt, 20 April 1909: CBT 3/7/65.
75. *FDSF*, I, p. 21.
76. Henry Jackson to Corbett, 4 December 1916: CBT 13/3/39.
77. The four lectures on 'The Great War after Trafalgar' formed the basis for Corbett's last published essay of 1922. They demonstrate that before he contracted for *Some Principles*, took on the *Russo-Japanese War* book and the Official History, he planned to carry his historical/strategic analysis to 1815 or 1856.
78. ADM 203/99, pp. 45–6.
79. ADM 203/100, p. 136.
80. Status of Antwerp and the Scheldt: ADM 116/1884.
81. I disagree with Professor Schurman's conclusions in Schurman, 1981, pp. 56–9.
82. Alfred Chatfield, *The Navy and Defence: The Autobiography of Admiral of the Fleet Lord Chatfield*, London, Heinemann, 1942, p. 91.
83. Bryan M. Ranft (ed.), *The Beatty Papers*, 2 vols, London, NRS, 1989–93, vol. I, pp. 33 and 60.
84. Ibid., p. 59.
85. *FDSF*, I, p. 39.
86. For Arbuthnot see John Brooks, *The Battle of Jutland*, Cambridge, Cambridge UP, 2016, which explains the fate of his squadron.
87. Battenberg, memo for Fisher, 25 February 1902: Kerr, 1934, pp. 144–9.
88. *FDSF*, I, p. 248.
89. Ottley memo submitted with Hankey to Fisher, 10 January 1910: FISR 1/9/455.
90. Churchill memo, 28 October 1911: R.S. Churchill (ed.), *Winston S. Churchill: Companion*, 3 vols, London, Heinemann, 1969, vol. II, part 2, pp. 1303–12, at p. 1307.
91. *Some Principles* had been published in November 1911.
92. Stephen W. Roskill, *Hankey: Man of Secrets*, vol. I: *1877–1918*, London, Collins, 1970, p. 100. Nicholas Black, *The British Admiralty War Staff in the First World War*, Woodbridge, Boydell, 2009. See ch. 7 for 1917–18.
93. K. Dewar, 'Naval War Staff Course': ADM 203/69, pp. 9–11. For a less than flattering appreciation of War and Staff Courses see Dewar's *The Navy from Within*, 1939, pp. 129–58. Even Marder considered it 'excessively critical of the Establishment', *FDSF*, V, p. 374.
94. Lady Wemyss, *The Life and Letters of Lord Wester Wemyss*, London, Eyre & Spottiswoode, 1935, pp. 100, 130.
95. ADM 203/69, pp. 19–23.
96. Fisher to Corbett, 22 June 1914: *FGDN*, II, pp. 507–8.

97. *FDSF*, I, pp. 32–3.
98. Ibid., pp. 400–1, citing Dewar, 1939, pp. 131–3.
99. Chatfield to Keyes, Private & Personal, January 1923: in Paul Halpern (ed.), *The Keyes Papers* (hereafter *Keyes Papers*), 3 vols, London, NRS, 1980, vol. II, pp. 85–7.

7 Strategy, Culture and History

1. For membership of the NRS Council see *Laughton*, pp. 235–7; see also Robert Vetch, *General Sir Andrew Clarke*, London, Murray, 1905, for an NRS councillor (1893–99) who made important contributions to the imperial, political and strategic debates of the era. Andrew Clarke was a Liberal, unusual among senior soldiers.
2. Robert Citino, *The German Way of War: From the Thirty Years' War to the Third Reich*, Lawrence, KS, Kansas UP, 2005. Gerhard Gross, *The Myth and Reality of German Warfare: Operational Thinking from Moltke the Elder to Heusinger*, Lexington, KY, Kentucky UP, 2016. This scholarship highlights the irrelevance of German strategic aims, and thus operational methods, to British conditions.
3. Citino, Foreword in Gross, 2016, pp. vii–x.
4. Gross, 2016, p. 1.
5. The contrast between the arguments of von der Goltz and Clausewitz is compelling.
6. Gross, 2016, p. 12. See also Robert Foley (ed. and trans.), *Alfred von Schlieffen's Military Writings*, London, Cass, 2003, pp. xv–xxviii.
7. Motto to G. Aston, *Sea, Land, and Air Strategy: A Comparison*, London, Murray, 1914. The quote came from the English edition of Colmar von der Goltz's *The Conduct of War*, London, W.H. Allen, 1896.
8. H. Delbrück, *The History of the Art of War*, vol. IV: *The Modern Era*, trans. W. Renfroe, Lincoln, NE, Nebraska UP, 1985, p. x, original edition Berlin, 1919. Delbrück (1848–1929) was a civilian contemporary of Corbett.
9. Colomb, 1891. Corbett owned the revised 2nd edition of 1895 (IHR). Colomb approved of Frederick Maurice's strategic views. Harry Dickinson, *Wisdom and War: The Royal Naval College Greenwich 1873–1998*, Farnham, Ashgate, 2012, pp. 68–95.
10. J.A. Rawley (ed.), *The American Civil War: An English View. The Writings of Field Marshal Viscount Wolseley*, Mechanicsburg, PA, Stackpole, 2002, for Wolseley's acute analysis of the American Civil War, which Corbett may have read. G.F.R. Henderson, *The Science of War: A Collection of Essays and Lectures 1891–1903*, ed. Col. Noel Malcolm, London, Longman, 1905. John F. Maurice, *The Balance of Military Power in Europe: An Examination of the War Resources of Great Britain and the Continental States*, London, Blackwood, 1888. Corbett owned and used Henderson's and Maurice's work.
11. Philip Colomb, *Essays on Naval Defence*, London, W.H. Allen, 2nd edn, 1896, records Colomb's exchanges with doubtful soldiers. He approved Maurice's strategic views. My copy has Ward Room stamps from two pre-dreadnought battleships.
12. Laughton had been appointed Professor of Modern History at King's College London in 1885, but continued to lecture at Greenwich for several years. Schurman, 1965, pp. 43–50.
13. *Why We Are at War with Germany: Great Britain's Case*, Oxford, Clarendon Press, 1914. The many authors involved, including H.W. Carless Davis, would have important wartime careers.
14. Corbett owned the key texts of Seeley, Philip Colomb and Mahan, and may have heard Seeley lecture on empire at Cambridge.
15. Gordon Martel, *Imperial Diplomacy: Rosebery and the Failure of Foreign Policy*, Kingston, ON, Ontario, McGill-Queen's, 1986, pp. 151–7.
16. Brady, 2013, p. 406.
17. Mahan, who was no Liberal, recognised the issue in *The Influence of Sea Power upon History, 1660–1783*, Boston, MA, Little, Brown, 1890.
18. Viscount Wolseley, *The Story of a Soldier's Life*, London, Constable, 1905, vol. II, pp. 226–56.
19. Adam Dighton, 'Jomini versus Clausewitz: Hamley's *Operations of War* and Military Thought', *War in History* 27(2), 2020, pp. 179–201, provides a detailed analysis.

20. 'The Strategic Pedagogue: General Sir Edward Bruce Hamley', in Luvaas, 1964, pp. 130–68.
21. Ibid., p. 187.
22. E.B. Hamley, *The Operations of War: Explained and Illustrated*, Edinburgh, Blackwood, 1866, 1st edn, p. 2. William Blackwood & Sons of Edinburgh was a leading outlet for defence writing across the next fifty years. The final 1909 edition was updated by Brigadier Launcelot Kiggell psc.
23. Hamley, 6th edn, 1909, pp. 44, 58–9, 227, 235.
24. Luvaas, 1964, p. 141. Clarke's essay was published in the *Edinburgh Review*, 1896, pp. 1–38, and Clarke and Thursfield, 1897.
25. D.P. O'Connor, *Between Peace and War: British Defence and the Royal United Services Institute, 1831–2010*, London, RUSI, 2011, p. 115. Kochanski, 1999.
26. Wolseley to Corbett, n.d.: CBT 14/5/36: Wolseley was then commander-in-chief in Ireland.
27. All four were in Corbett's library.
28. Luvaas, 1964, 'The Second Pen of Sir Garnet: Major General Sir John Frederick Maurice', pp. 173–215. Lt Col. E. Maurice, *Sir Frederick Maurice: A Record of his Work and Opinions, with Eight Essays of Discipline and National Efficiency*, London, Edward Arnold, 1913. My copy was presented by Major General Sir Charles Callwell to the Library of the United Service Club after 1918. Callwell studied at Camberley in 1884–5, when Maurice was professor, which explains his maritime approach to national strategy. Bond, 1972, p. 141.
29. Maurice, 1913, pp. 25–6, 40–3, 54.
30. Ibid., pp. 55–7.
31. Schurman, 1965, traces British naval thought back to John Colomb's 1867 essay 'The Protection of Commerce in War'. An engineer and imperial administrator, Clarke built docks and harbours, advised on major infrastructure projects and imposed order and logic on coast defence at home and abroad: Vetch, 1905.
32. Maurice, 1913, p. 59. Repington, 1919, pp. 76–7.
33. Maurice, 1913, p. 61.
34. Ibid., p. 65. Rodney Atwood, *Life of Field Marshal Lord Roberts*, London, Bloomsbury, 2015, chs 7 and 8.
35. Henderson, 1905, p. 202.
36. Maurice, 1913, pp. 68–9.
37. John Maurice, 'Mahan's Testimony to England's Power', *United Services Magazine*, 1893, pp. 792–98. Luvaas, 1964, pp. 209–11. Corbett owned Maurice's *War* of 1891, developed from his *Encyclopaedia Britannica* contributions, *National Defence* of 1897, and *Sir John Moore's Diary*.
38. Maurice, 1913.
39. Luvaas, 1964, 'The Unfinished Synthesis', at pp. 216–47, remains the best study of Henderson's thinking. Luvaas's Civil War perspective stressed the role of anglophone lessons in Henderson's work, rather than the influence of Clausewitz.
40. Bond, 1972, p. 157. Corbett would have positive encounters with both soldiers.
41. Diary 4–9 June 1894: CBT 43/5.
42. Henderson, 1905, pp. 394–5, from 'The British Army' of 1903, pp. xxxiii, 10, 16, 26, 88, 186, 396, 429.
43. Ibid., ch. 7 (first published 1894) and ch. 5 (first published 1897) contain the earliest references to Mahan.
44. Ibid., pp. 129–30.
45. These comments date to 1898: Luvaas, 1964, p. 227.
46. J. Stone, 'The Influence of Clausewitz on G.F.R. Henderson's Military Histories', in S. Berger, P. Lambert and P. Schumann (eds), *Historikerdialoge: Geschichte, Mythos und Gedächtnis im deutsch-britischen kulturellen Austausch 1750–2000*, Göttingen, Vandenhoeck & Ruprecht, 2003, pp. 197–218, at p. 215, fn 69.
47. Christopher Bassford, *Clausewitz in English: The Reception of Clausewitz in Britain and America 1815–1945*, Oxford, Oxford UP, 1994, pp. 64–74. *The Times*, 23 March 1905, article by Colonel Repington, the military correspondent.

48. Henderson, 1905, pp. 12 and 173.

49. Ibid., p. 2 stresses British exceptionalism in the European context.

50. Ibid., pp. 16 and 20.

51. Maurice, 1913, p. 124.

52. Henderson, 1905, pp. 25–6.

53. *Some Principles*, p. 14.

54. Henderson, 1905, p. 37.

55. Ibid., pp. 25–6, 35–6, 92.

56. Ibid., p. 33.

57. Ibid., p. 28.

58. Julian Corbett, *The Campaign of Trafalgar* (henceforth *Trafalgar*), London, Longman, 1910, p. 4 fn 1.

59. Henderson, 1905, pp. 31, 33. Julian Corbett, 'Napoleon after Trafalgar', *Quarterly Review*, April 1922, pp. 239–40.

60. Henderson, 1905, pp. 33–4. Mahan, 1890, pp. 25–6.

61. Henderson, 1905, pp. 34–5 and 39 citing George McClellan's campaign in the Yorktown Peninsula of 1862, unaware it had been based on the 1854 Crimean campaign.

62. Henderson, 1905, p. 36.

63. Ibid., pp. 25–8, 256. Corbett referred to this in the 'Green Pamphlet'.

64. Henderson, 1905, p. 434.

65. *Successors*, p. 410.

66. Henderson, 1905, pp. 100 and xxxi.

67. Bond, 1972, p. 159. Wolseley, 1905, II, p. 142. Lord Esher to his son, 17 September 1905 in M.V. Brett (ed.), *Journals and Letters of Reginald Viscount Esher, 1903–1910*, London, Nicholson & Watson, 3 vols, 1934–6, vol. II, p. 112.

68. Charles Callwell recognised the irony, highlighting those words in *Field Marshal Sir Henry Wilson: His Life and Diaries*, 2 vols, London, Cassell, 1927, vol. I, p.13. Jeffery, 2006, echoed those sentiments, pp. 17 and 19.

69. My copy of Henderson bears the stamp of the Officers' Mess at the Depot of the Worcestershire Regiment. Although somewhat shaken and marked by use, many pages remained uncut, including 'The British Army' of 1903, the most important essay.

70. See endmatter in Corbett's *Trafalgar* and *Some Principles*.

71. Rudolf von Caemmerer, *The Development of Strategical Sciences*, London, Rees, 1905, cited in *Some Principles* at p. 72. German edition 1904.

72. T. Moreman, 'Callwell, Charles', *ODNB* 32251. Charles Callwell, *The Effect of Maritime Command on Land Campaigns since Waterloo*, Edinburgh, Blackwood, 1897.

73. Charles Callwell, *Military Operations and Maritime Preponderance: Their Relations and Interdependence*, Edinburgh, Blackwood, 1905, p. 179. Quoting *Mediterranean*, II, p. 242.

74. Callwell, 1905, pp. 179, 183.

75. George Aston, *Letters on Amphibious Wars*, London, Murray, 1911. Aston acknowledged Corbett's influence: *Sea, Land and Air Strategy*, London, Murray, 1914, pp. vii, 92, 93, 132. Bond, 1972, pp. 194, 198, 252. J. Beach, 'The British Army, the Royal Navy, and the "Big Work" of Sir George Aston, 1904–1914', *Journal of Strategic Studies* 29(1), 2006, pp. 145–6.

76. Ludmilla Jordanova, *History in Practice*, London, Arnold, 2000: for links between history and theory see ch. 3. Azar Gat, *The Development of Military Thought: The Nineteenth Century*, Oxford, Oxford UP, 1992, p. 49.

77. Kennedy, 1980, p. 36 for Treitschke.

78. W.H. Allen of 13 Waterloo Place, close by the Naval and Military Club, the Royal Geographical Society, the Athenaeum, and not a hundred yards from Corbett's club, the Reform, published Colmar von der Goltz's *Nation in Arms* in 1887 and Philip Colomb's *Naval Warfare* in 1891. It faded away in the early 1900s, leaving the market to Hugh Rees on Pall Mall, who produced a new edition of von der Goltz in 1907, by the same translator.

79. Gat, 1992, pp. 100–2, and Foley, 2003, pp. xv–xxviii

80. Ideas encapsulated in Bernhardi's *On War of Today*, 2 vols, London, Rees, 1912. See John G.C. Rohl, *The Kaiser and his Court: Wilhelm II and the Government of Germany*, Cambridge, Cambridge UP, 1995, pp. 162–89 on Wilhelm II's desire for European hegemony and the defeat of Britain.
81. Andreas Dorpalen, *Heinrich von Treitschke*, New Haven, CT, and London, Yale UP, 1957, pp. 148–51 for Treitschke's views on war, views echoed by Goltz, Bernhardi and Moltke the Elder, p. 124. See also Alfred Tirpitz, *My Memoirs*, London, Hurst & Blackett, 1919, vol. I, pp. 254, 295–6.
82. Lord Bryce, *Neutral Nations and the War*, London, Macmillan, 1914.
83. Colmar von der Goltz, *The Nation in Arms*, trans. Philip Ashworth, London, W.H. Allen, 1887, pp. 1–2.
84. Ibid., pp. 123, 350–3. Schurman, 1981, pp. 42–3. Shawn Grimes, *Strategy and War Planning in the British Navy, 1887–1918*, Woodbridge, Boydell & Brewer, 2012, pp. 62–74.
85. Goltz, 1896. Corbett signed and dated his copy 1904. IHR collection. This edition was critical to Goltz's impact in the anglophone world: see p. 211.
86. Ibid., pp. 388–91.
87. Kennedy, 1980, p. 371. The National Service League journal was titled *The Nation in Arms*.
88. The book opened with a passage from Clausewitz which compared war with commerce, rather than art or science (book II, ch. 3), which Michael Howard and Peter Paret translated as 'War is an act of human intercourse.' M. Howard and P. Paret (eds), *Clausewitz: On War*, Princeton, NJ: Princeton UP, 1976, p. 149.
89. Goltz, 1896, p. 212; passage marked by Corbett.
90. Ibid., p. 215.
91. The margin of Liddell Hart's 1913 edition is heavily marked. Liddell Hart Library, King's College London.
92. Caemmerer, 1905, esp. pp. 72–130. Unfortunately Corbett's copy, loaned to the IHR, was removed by Brian Tunstall in 1937, along with his marginalia.
93. Ibid., p. 54. emphasis in the original. Corbett's 1894 French edition of Jomini's *Précis de l'art de la guerre* is at the IHR.
94. For Slade's signed copy see Bookseller Inventory # 15302, http://www.abebooks.com/servlet/BookDetailsPL?bi=3162884458&searchurl=sortby%3D1%26an%3Dcaemmerer
95. Caemmerer, 1905, pp. 72–3.
96. Ibid., p. 75.
97. Ibid, pp. 111–12.
98. *Some Principles*, p. 47. Diary 6 January and 9 October 1915: CBT 43/14.
99. Caemmerer, 1905, pp. 116–17, 123.
100. Ibid., p. 124. Rear Admiral Kurt von Maltzahn, 'What Lessons has General von Clausewitz's work "On War" for the Naval Officer?', from *Marine Rundschau*, 1905, citing the English translation produced for the Naval War Course, p. 16.
101. Bassford, 1994, pp. 97–9.
102. *Seven Years' War*, II, p. 130.
103. Caemmerer, 1905, pp. 95–7 and 108. This linked to alternative German thinking, explored in Arthur Kuhle, 'Putting Theory into Practice: Ludwig von Wolzogen and the Russian Campaign of 1812', *War in History* 27, 2020, pp. 156–78. See *Some Principles*, part 1, ch. 2 for Corbett's development of this critical argument.

8 Shaping the 'British Way'

1. Rhodri Williams, *Defending the Empire: The Conservative Party and British Defence Policy, 1899–1915*, New Haven, CT, and London, Yale UP, 1991, pp. 68, 123 for Corbett. Ruddock Mackay, *Arthur Balfour: Intellectual Statesman*, Oxford, Oxford UP, 1985, pp. 116, 133. Johnson, 1960, p. 53.
2. Otte, 2020, pp. 222–3, 272.

3. Matthew Seligmann, '"Failing to Prepare for the Great War": The Absence of Grand Strategy in British War Planning before 1914', *War in History* 20(4), 2017, pp. 414–37 demonstrates how the failure to harmonise service strategies before 1914 compromised the conduct of the war. Corbett had addressed the issue in *Some Principles*, a national doctrine primer, not a naval document. His maritime strategy included military and combined operations, it was not 'naval'.

4. D'Ombrain, 1973, p. 1.

5. Ibid., pp. 4–5.

6. Ibid., p. 2.

7. Jeffery, 2006, pp. 75–6. Wilson was close to Roberts.

8. Tyler, 1914, pp. 19–20.

9. Ibid., pp. 15–16, 21–3. Most commentators are unaware that Fisher's 'loose talk' was backed up by deploying the Channel Fleet to the Baltic.

10. Ibid., pp. 37–8.

11. Grimes, 2012, p. 70.

12. Tyler, 1914, p. 43. These views were in stark contrast to his *Times* contributions two years earlier.

13. D'Ombrain, 1973, p. 10.

14. Tyler, 2014, pp. 40, 51.

15. Ibid., pp. 61–2.

16. The conscriptionists included Field Marshal Sir William Nicholson, Chief of the Imperial General Staff (CIGS), and Henry Wilson, both linked to Roberts, along with Conservative politicians including Leo Maxse and Lord Milner. Jeffery, 2006, pp. 75–6. Fisher, it should be noted, hated Nicholson as a matter of policy.

17. Tyler, 2014, pp. 63–70.

18. Ibid., pp. 71–3.

19. Ibid., pp. 77–88, 91–2. R. Bacon, *Lord Fisher of Kilverstone*, London, 1929, vol. II, pp. 182–3. Fisher to Mrs McKenna, 14 November 1909: *FGDN*, II, pp. 278–9.

20. D'Ombrain, 1973, p. 15.

21. Ibid., p. 150. Jeffery, 2006, p. 85. In August 1914 the only functional plan envisaged sending the BEF to France, because the responsible ministers had failed in their duty to establish a national strategy.

22. Callwell, 1927, I, pp. 122–3 for seapower. This revelation must have been deliberate.

23. David Morgan-Owen, 'Cooked Up in the Dinner Hour? Sir Arthur Wilson's War Plan Reconsidered', *EHR* 130, 2015, pp. 865–906. An important revision of old assumptions.

24. Troubridge to Corbett, 11 July 1911, Admiralty: CBT 13/3/66 and Diary: CBT43/13.

25. Tyler, 2014, pp. 112–16, 141.

26. Ibid., pp. 174–5.

27. The Kaiser dismissed the British Army as contemptible on account of its size. This rendered it equally contemptible as the strategic element of British diplomacy. Fisher understood that command of the Baltic, backed by an amphibious force ready to secure the Danish archipelago, would be the most effective deterrent.

28. Esher to Asquith, 14 February 1913: Asquith MS Bodleian MS 24: cited in d'Ombrain, 1973, pp. 209 and 272.

29. There is no evidence of a direct connection between Corbett and Esher, although they had many mutual friends and Esher read Corbett. Esher was a Conservative and continued working with Repington, despite opposing his continental views and his prominent anti-Fisherite role in the invasion and Beresford inquiries.

30. D'Ombrain, 1973, p. 267. Hankey admitted seeing the light in late August: Corbett, diary 25 August 1914: Liddle Collection.

31. D'Ombrain, 1973, p. 23.

32. Andrew Lambert, '"The Army is a Projectile to be Fired by the Navy": Securing the Empire 1815–1914', in Peter Dennis (ed.), *Armies and Maritime Strategy: 2013 Chief of Army History Conference*, Canberra, Big Sky Publishing, 2014, pp. 29–47, shows how Corbett's ideas were used to shape Dominion navies.

33. *Some Principles*, p. 55.
34. Corbett to Fisher, 6 March 1914: *FGDN*, II, p. 500. The letter referenced Maurice's edition of Sir John Moore's *Diary*, which Corbett owned.
35. Ottley to Corbett. Dictated. Secret NID, 1 July 1905. RIC/9.
36. 'Lectures on Naval Strategy by Sir Julian Corbett', bound volume cited in *Some Principles*, ed. Grove, 1988, p. xvi.
37. 1905–7 lectures. Slade to Corbett, 22 August 1905: LHCMA.
38. 1905–7 lectures. Rawlinson to Corbett, 25 August 1905: LHCMA.
39. 1905–7 lectures. Corbett draft reply of 2 October 1905 on Rawlinson to Corbett, 25 August 1905: LHCMA.
40. 1905–7 lectures. Rawlinson to Corbett, 2 October 1905: LHCMA.
41. Corbett to Edith, 7 January 1907, Aldershot: CBT 10/4/1.
42. Caemmerer, 1905, p. 54.
43. Translated by W.H. Hancock, 30 March 1906. 'For the Use of Officers Studying at the Naval War Course', print no. 4. There is a copy in Corbett's papers. I own a photocopy of the paper, made by Professor Bryan Ranft, editor of the 1972 edition of *Some Principles*. Bassford, 1994, pp. 94–5. Corbett's copy has significant marginalia. Matthew Seligmann, *Spies in Uniform*, Oxford, Oxford UP, 2006, p. 63.
44. The point is made by Maltzahn, 1905, on p. 4. Corbett added: 'He thought it would end the war but it didn't.'
45. Ibid., p. 9. *Some Principles*, p. 14.
46. Maltzahn, 1905, p. 8.
47. *Some Principles*, p. 157.
48. Maltzahn, 1905, p. 13. Corbett marked this passage. See *Some Principles*, book 1, ch. 2 for his development of an argument he had first encountered in Caemmerer.
49. Maltzahn, 1905, p. 16.
50. Ibid., p. 17 and Corbett marginalia.
51. Baron Kurt von Maltzahn, *Naval Warfare: Its Historical Development from the Age of the Great Geographical Discoveries to the Present Time*, trans. John Combe Miller, London, Longman, 1908, p. 81.
52. The most accessible texts are an appendix to Eric Grove's 1988 edition of *Some Principles*, pp. 307–25. There are original copies in Corbett's papers. Schurman, 1981, pp. 50–5.
53. Corbett to Miss Davies (Secretary, Institute of Historical Research), 23 June 1921: IHR XII 1921–26 C.
54. Maltzahn, 1905, pp. 3, 5.
55. *Some Principles*, ed. Grove, pp. 307–9. The argument was Maltzahn's.
56. Ibid., p. 309.
57. Ibid., pp. 312 and 332. The repetition suggests no-one noticed.
58. Ibid., p. 313.
59. Ibid., p. 315.
60. Ibid., pp. 316–21.
61. Ibid., p. 322.
62. Ibid., pp. 322–5.
63. Ibid., p. 324. The Navy's use of the Dutch Wars as an analogue for a German conflict prompted the NRS to begin work on the subject in 1900. *Laughton*, pp. 147–9.
64. Andrew Lambert (ed.), *Twenty-first-century Corbett*, Annapolis, MD, USNIP, 2017, chs 1–3.
65. Slade to Corbett, 2 December 1906: CBT 13/2/6.
66. Mahan letters of 20 December 1908 and 4 March 1911: Seager and Maguire, 1975, III, pp. 273 and 389–94.
67. Alfred Thayer Mahan, *Naval Strategy*, Boston, MA, Little, Brown, 1911, pp. 26–7.
68. Suzanne Geissler, *God and Sea Power: The Influence of Religion on Alfred Thayer Mahan*, Annapolis, MD, USNIP, 2015, pp. 99–104.
69. Schurman, 1981, pp. 58–9, citing correspondence of November–December 1916.

70. *Some Principles*, ed. Grove, pp. 326–45, new example at p. 337. This would appear as *The Campaign of Trafalgar* in 1910.
71. *Some Principles*, ed. Grove, p. 331.
72. Ibid., p. 341.
73. Ibid., p. 345.
74. *Some Principles*, 1911, pp. 69–71.
75. Ibid., p. 94.
76. Spenser Wilkinson, *Morning Post*, 3 August 1909, and review of *Some Principles*, 19 February 1912: CBT/13/54.
77. Heuser, 2010, p. 169, citing Henry Spenser Wilkinson, *War and Politics*, London, Constable, 1910, p. 181.
78. *Some Principles*, ed. Grove, p. xliii. Bassford, 1994, pp. 98–9. Wilkinson was dismissed by the *Morning Post* for opposing the 'We Want Eight' dreadnought campaign, Keith Wilson, 'Spenser Wilkinson at Bay: Calling the Tune at the *Morning Post* 1908–1909', *Publishing History* 19, 1986, pp. 33–52.
79. James Thursfield, *Naval Warfare*, Cambridge, Cambridge UP, 1913, pp. 4, 89, 105, 118. Bassford, 1994, p. 103.

9 'Radiant with the Genius of a Maritime State'

1. *Seven Years' War*, I, p. 9. Fisher's memorandum 'The Strangest Thing in the War' refers to 'the unrivalled History of the Seven Years' War': FISR 3/19/3208-9 early June 1918.
2. Corbett loose memo on 1907 in the 1908 Diary: CBT 43/7.
3. Fisher to Corbett, 22 and 24 May 1905: FISR 1/4/163, 166, 168. Corbett to Fisher, 3 June 1905: FISR 1/4/171.
4. Ottley to Corbett: Admiralty, Secret, 1 July 1905: RIC/9.
5. Ottley to Corbett: Admiralty, Secret, 3 July 1905: RIC/9.
6. A point Corbett developed in his *Russo-Japanese War* book.
7. Clarke to Corbett, 21 July 1905: CBT 14/5/20. Corbett sent Clarke a copy of his new NRS volume *Fighting Instructions*.
8. Tyler, 1914, pp. 38–88, for the Belgian focus of Grierson's period as DMO.
9. D. McCartney, *W.E.H. Lecky: Historian and Politician*, Dublin, Lilliput Press, 1994, p. 150.
10. Richard Middleton, *The Bells of Victory: The Pitt–Newcastle Ministry and the Conduct of the Seven Years' War, 1757–1762*, Cambridge, Cambridge UP, 1983, p. 225. W.E.H. Lecky, *A History of England in the Eighteenth Century*, 8 vols, London, Longman, 1878–90. This book went to the Staff College in 1923: ADM 1/8650/244. His friend Frederic Harrison's 1905 Pitt biography may have added another influence.
11. Slade to Corbett, 22 August 1905: LHCMA 1905–07 lectures.
12. Fisher to Corbett, 28 July 1905, Admiralty: FISR 1/4/182a; and *FGDN*, II, at p. 63. See also FISR 1/182 and 183.
13. Corbett to Newbolt, 22 October 1905: CBT 3/42. Schurman, 1981, p. 44, takes the comment seriously.
14. Corbett to Edith, 14, 16 and 17 January 1906: CBT 10/2/1, 4 and 7.
15. Corbett to Edith, 14 March 1906: CBT 10/2/21.
16. Slade to Corbett, 16 December 1905: Confidential RIC/9.
17. Andrew Lambert, *The Crimean War: British Grand Strategy against Russia 1853–1856*, 2nd edn, Farnham, Ashgate, 2011. A narrowly 'Crimean' version of the war was almost universal at this time.
18. Slade to Corbett, 26 December 1905: RIC/9. *Some Principles*, ed. Grove, pp. 307–25.
19. Corbett to Newbolt, 12 September 1906: CBT 3/48. The seafaring metaphor was significant.
20. *Seven Years' War*, I, p. 2.
21. Corbett to Newbolt, 22 September 1906: CBT 3/50.
22. Corbett to J. Franklin Jameson (editor, *American Historical Review*), 4 November 1906: CBT 2/5/3. Novick, 1998, p. 30 etc.

23. Corbett to Newbolt, 5 December 1906: CBT 3/52.
24. Slade to Corbett, 29 July 1907: CBT 13/2/8.
25. Detached memo in the 1908 Diary: CBT 43/7 The first reference to the house was in July 1907.
26. Lady Wolseley, *Some of the Smaller Manor Houses of Sussex*, London, Medici Society, 1925, pp. 116–29.
27. Corbett loose memo on 1907 in the 1908 Diary: CBT 43/7.
28. Corbett to Newbolt, 1 November 1907: CBT 3/54.
29. Schurman, 1965, p. 164.
30. *Seven Years' War*, II, pp. 373–5.
31. Corbett to Newbolt, 31 January 1906: Schurman, 1981, p. 47 and CBT 3/44.
32. *Seven Years' War*, I, p. v.
33. Ibid., pp. vi–vii.
34. *Seven Years' War*, pref. dated November 1907.
35. *Some Principles*, ed. Grove, pp. xviii–xxi and 307–25.
36. Brendan Simms, *Three Victories and a Defeat: The Rise and Fall of the First British Empire, 1714–1783*, London, Allen Lane, 2007, reflects the European emphasis of many Cambridge scholars. *Seven Years' War*, I, p. 9.
37. Seeley, 1883, pp. 291–2, 300–1.
38. *Seven Years' War*, I, pp. 74–5.
39. Mahan, 1890, pp. 50–9.
40. *Seven Years' War*, I, p. 1.
41. Ibid., p. 7.
42. Ibid., p. 4.
43. Ibid., p. 5.
44. Ibid., pp. 8–9.
45. Ibid., pp. 19–20.
46. Ibid., p. 84; see ch. 8 of this book for invasion.
47. Ibid.; for Minorca and Byng, see pp. 97–135, 143.
48. Ibid., p. 166.
49. Ibid., pp. 188, 192. The point comes from Caemmerer.
50. Ibid., p. 260.
51. Ibid., p. 277.
52. Ibid., p. 336.
53. Bedford to Newcastle, 9 May 1761: cited in ibid., II, p. 171.
54. Ibid., pp. 466–71. Julian Corbett, 'The Strategical Value of Speed', *JRUSI*, July 1907, pp. 824–39. Delivered 6 March 1907.
55. *Seven Years' War*, II, p. 325.
56. Ibid., pp. 375–6.
57. H. Doughty, *Francis Parkman*, Cambridge, MA, Harvard UP, 1983, ch. 15 on Parkman's *Montcalm and Wolfe* of 1884. See Gooch, 1913, pp. 419–21 for a contemporary judgement that Corbett would have echoed. He owned Parkman's book.
58. Richard Haldane to Corbett, 6 December 1907, War Office. Endorsed by Corbett, 'Haldane on "Seven Years War"': CBT 14/3/27.
59. Firth to Corbett, 26 December 1907: CBT 14/3/2.
60. Diary 10 and 15 March 1908: CBT 43/10.
61. Diary 31 March 1908: CBT 43/10. This entry was prompted by Wilkinson's article attacking Fisher and the Admiralty for employing Corbett. See Bassford, 1994, for Wilkinson.
62. Slade to Corbett, 31 March 1908: CBT 13/2/18.
63. Diary 19 May 1908: CBT 43/10.
64. Corbett to Newbolt, 25 May 1908: CBT 3/57.
65. See Novick, 1998, pp. 50, 69, 82–3.
66. George Louis Beer, 'Seven Years' War Newly Studied', *New York Times*, 16 August 1908.
67. Beer to Corbett, 14 June 1908: CBT 14/1/17.

68. 'Our Greatest War Minister', *Spectator*, 16 May 1908, p. 19.
69. *Laughton*, p. 234. Councillor 1903–6, 1909–14. Atkinson completed Samuel Rawson Gardiner's editorial work on the papers of the First Anglo-Dutch War.
70. Charles T. Atkinson, Review, *EHR*, July 1908, pp. 585–8.
71. Doughty to Corbett, 23 January 1909: CBT 14/2/28.
72. Fisher to Corbett, 20 December 1907: FISR 1/5/271. The reward came in February 1918.
73. Fisher memo: 'Plain Speaking', February 1915: FISR 5/4348.
74. John Hattendorf, 'Conference Issues and Themes', in Goldrick and Hattendorf, 1993, pp. 7–9.
75. John Hattendorf, 'Technology and Strategy: A Study of the Professional Thought of the US Navy, 1900–1916', *Naval War College Review* 24, 1971, pp. 25–48, at p. 31.
76. Sturdee circular: ADM 1/8326/X2229/12 covering cruiser operations 1756–1815. I am indebted to my friend Dr Tim Dougall for this and an important discussion of American responses to Corbett.
77. Middleton, 1983, pp. 225–6, citing *Seven Years' War*, I, pp. 8–9.
78. Middleton, 1983, p. 226.
79. Baugh, 2011, at p. 685 Baugh criticises Corbett's *Seven Years' War*, I, pp. 68–72, which 'lacks crucial dates and is marred by factual errors as well as unwarranted speculations'. In this case Corbett focused on Admiral Hawke, as a study in command. At pp. 687 and 716 Baugh criticises Corbett for taking the French invasion threats of 1756 and 1762 seriously, without mentioning the contemporary 1907 Invasion Inquiry or his Admiralty memoranda. Corbett wanted his students to take the contemporary subject seriously and therefore had to do so himself, even though, as Baugh implies, the evidence suggested it was not serious. At both pp. 689 and 702 he criticises Corbett for 'speculations', which clearly addressed the educational needs of his audience.
80. Richard Pares, *War and Trade in the West Indies, 1739–1763*, Oxford, Oxford UP, 1936. Pares wrote for a small academic community; his claim that Corbett's book was 'somewhat less valuable' than Herbert Richmond's *Navy in the War of 1739–48* is one few would now accept. Pares challenged one of Corbett's judgements, relying on French archival material, while Corbett's assessment of British intentions for Manila used more consequential evidence. Pares, 1936, pp. viii, 184 fn 3, p. 594. *Seven Years' War*, I, pp. 237–8, 255–60, and II, pp. 248, 254.

10 Policy, Strategy and International Law

1. Julian Corbett, 'Recent Attacks on the Admiralty', *The Nineteenth Century*, February 1907, pp. 195–208.
2. 'Barfleur', 1907. Corbett's copy was loaned to the Staff College in 1923, and his marginalia appear alongside passages that were criticised in 'Recent Attacks' and 'Strategical Value'. The 'Syndicate' label was acknowledged by White, see 'Civis' (pseud. Sir William White), *The State of the Navy in 1907: A Plea for Inquiry*, London, Smith, Elder, 1907, p. 25.
3. Sir William White as 'Civis', 1907. Corbett's copy is at the IHR Library.
4. Esher to Fisher, 21 October 1906: Brett, 1934–6, II, pp. 198–9.
5. 'Civis', 1907, pp. 12–15. The Conservatives had appointed Fisher.
6. Ibid., pp. 39–41, 45, 58, 111.
7. 'Barfleur', 1907'. Corbett's copy at Joint Services Command and Staff College (JSCSC) Library at Shrivenham.
8. Slade to Corbett, 5 August 1909: CBT 13/2/42.
9. Cyprian A.G. Bridge, 'Amateur Estimates of Naval Policy', *The Nineteenth Century*, December 1906, pp. 883–8.
10. Ibid., p. 897.
11. Fisher to Corbett, 12 May 1906: FISR 1/4/201: Corbett to Fisher, 13 May 1906: FISR 1/5/202. Fisher to Corbett, 5 June 1906: CBT 12/107.
12. Fisher to Corbett, 10 January 1907: FISR 1/5/214 and 215.

13. Fisher to Corbett, 15 January 1907, Admiralty: FISR 1/5/217: FG & DN II, p. 113. Nicholas Lambert, *Sir John Fisher's Naval Revolution*, Columbia, SC, University of South Carolina Press, 1999, pp. 137, 345 fn 69.
14. 'Recent Attacks', p. 208.
15. Fisher to Corbett, 16 January 1907: FISR 1/5/218.
16. Fisher to Corbett, 17 January 1907: FISR 1/5/219. Fisher to Corbett, 11 February 1907: FISR 1/5/227. *FGDN*, II, p. 109 fn.
17. Fisher to Corbett, 11 February 1907: FISR 1/5/227: FG II, p. 109 fn.
18. Fisher to Cawdor, 25 November 1907: *FGDN*, II, p. 151 fn. For the quote, 'Recent Attacks', p. 196.
19. Julian Corbett, 'The Strategical Value of Speed', *JRUSI*, July 1907. Delivered 6 March 1907, pp. 824–39.
20. Barfleur, 1907, ch. 9, pp. 230–64; several of Corbett's marginalia were deployed in the lecture.
21. Fisher to Corbett, 2 and 4 January 1907: FISR 1/5/212-13.
22. 'Strategical Value', pp. 825–8. In the fn on p. 832 Corbett thanked Laughton for Kempenfelt letters, which would be published in a forthcoming volume of Lord Barham's correspondence.
23. Ibid., pp. 829–30.
24. Alfred T. Mahan, 'Reflections Historic and Others, suggested by the Battle of the Japan Sea', *United States Naval Institute Proceedings*, June 1906, pp. 447–71, reprinted *JRUSI*, November 1906, pp. 1327–46.
25. 'Strategical Value', p. 831.
26. Ibid., p. 833.
27. Ibid., p. 839.
28. Fisher to Corbett, 17 March 1907: FISR 1/5/2322.
29. Schurman, 1981, pp. 67–8 and ADM 116/1043B.
30. Slade to Corbett, 2 December 1906: CBT 13/2/6 discussing the final edits of the pamphlet.
31. Corbett, 'Some Principles of Naval Warfare', in *Fisher Papers*, II, pp. 318–45.
32. Battenberg to Fisher, 11 February 1902: Kerr, 1934, pp. 161–4. Slade to Corbett, 20 May 1906: CBT 13/2/1.
33. Gardiner, 1985, pp. 175. The Royal Navy had 40 submarines in 1907; see pp. 86–7.
34. Dunley, 2018, pp. 135–6, 149.
35. *FDSF*, I, p. 380, quoting ADM 116/1043B.
36. *Fisher Papers*, II, p. 432, 436.
37. Ibid., pp. 338 and 433.
38. The 1770 edition of Montecuccoli's *Memoirs*, in three volumes, now at the IHR.
39. *Fisher Papers*, II, p. 321.
40. Ibid., p. 322.
41. Goltz cited in Aston, 1914.
42. *Fisher Papers*, II, p. 327.
43. Slade to Corbett, n.d. 1907: CBT 12/72, and 30 March 1907: CBT 13/2/5.
44. *Fisher Papers*, II, pp. 327, 335.
45. Ibid., p. 336.
46. Andrew Lambert, '"This is All We Want": Great Britain and the Baltic Approaches 1815–1914', in J. Sevaldsen (ed.), *Britain and Denmark: Political, Economic and Cultural Relations in the 19th and 20th Centuries*, Copenhagen, Museum Tusculanum Press, 2003, pp. 147–69. *Fisher Papers*, II, p. 338. Mackay, 1974, pp. 367–9.
47. *Fisher Papers*, II, p. 338. Corbett underlined the quote for emphasis. It was printed in italic.
48. Michael Clemmesen, 'The Royal Navy North Sea War Plan 1907–1914', *Fra Krig og Fred: Journal of the Danish Commission for Military History* 2, 2014, pp. 58–112 for the North Sea ambush concept. I am indebted to Brigadier Clemmesen for his generous support of this and other projects across many decades. His paper is a critical contribution to the discussion of British war planning before 1914.

49. *Fisher Papers*, II, p. 340. Mahan based this on Jomini, naval concentration served continental needs, not those of a seapower empire.
50. Ibid., p. 341.
51. Fisher to Corbett, 28 July 1905: FISR 1/4/182a. *FGDN*, II, p. 63.
52. *Fisher Papers*, II, p. 341.
53. He chose to lecture on this aspect of the opening phase of the war at Greenwich in 1919.
54. *Fisher Papers*, II, pp. 344–5.
55. Slade to Corbett, n.d. 1907: CBT 12/72, and 30 March 1907: CBT 13/2/5.
56. *Fisher Papers*, II, p. 454. Schurman, 1981, p. 69.
57. Ibid., p. 459.
58. Mackay, 1974, p. 370.
59. Corbett to Edith, 11 and 14 March 1907: CBT 10/4/7-8.
60. Diary 4–5 April 1908: CBT 43/9.
61. Fisher to Corbett, 9 March 1907, Secret: *FGDN*, II, p. 120 and fn.
62. Corbett Introduction, in Thomas Taylor, *Running the Blockade*, London, John Murray, 1896, p. vii.
63. Julian Corbett, 'The Capture of Private Property at Sea', *The Nineteenth Century*, June 1907. Schurman, 1981, p. 71.
64. H. Harris Brown, 'Reid, Robert Threshie', *ODNB* 35719.
65. A revised version was published 1913 (London, Methuen).
66. Julian Corbett, 'The Capture of Private Property at Sea', reprinted in Alfred T. Mahan, *Some Neglected Aspects of War*, London, Sampson Low, 1907, at p. 118, Corbett's italics.
67. Fisher to Corbett, 8 June 1907: FISR 1/5/246.
68. Alan Anderson, 'The Laws of War and Naval Strategy in Great Britain and the United States, 1899–1909', unpublished PhD thesis, King's College London, 2016.
69. Fisher to Corbett, 10 October 1907: FISR 1/5/260 also CBT 12/67.
70. Mahan, 1907, pp. xxi–ii and 115–54.
71. *Some Principles*, p. 93.
72. Ibid., pp. 93–4.
73. Mackay, 1974, p. 223.
74. *Some Principles*, pp. 97–100. Loreburn was the target.
75. Morgan-Owen, 2017, is the standard account.
76. Initially opposed to conscription, Repington changed his mind to support France. A.J. Morris, *The Scaremongers: The Advocacy of War and Rearmament, 1896–1914*, London, Routledge, 1984, p. 117.
77. Schurman, 1981, pp. 79–80. Clarke's letter was signed 'Navalis'. Clarke's usefulness was compromised by his simple Mahanian views; he did not approve of *Dreadnought*, or the Home Fleet. His main concern was to impose his own control over a maritime strategy. Esher to his son, 1 September 1906: Brett, 1934–6, II, p. 179. Fisher was bound to fall out with Clarke, who 'is all agog against the "Dreadnoughts". He has there a supporter in Mahan, who criticizes the strategic value of those vessels. Still it is no affair of Clarke's. That question must be left to the Admiralty.'
78. Fisher to Corbett, 28 September 1907: FISR 1/5/257. *FGDN*, II, pp. 137–8.
79. Slade to Corbett, 18 July 1907: CBT 13/2/2. Morgan-Owen, 2017, pp. 163–4.
80. Repington was corresponding with Beresford, his chief of staff, Doveton Sturdee and retired admirals Bridge and Gerard Noel. Morgan-Owen, 2017, pp. 166, 170.
81. The paper is RIC 9/1, having been handed to Richmond by Corbett for use in *The Navy in the War of 1739-1748*, 1920.
82. Schurman, 1981, pp. 81–9.
83. Slade to Corbett, 12 December 1907: Schurman, 1981, p. 87.
84. Slade to Corbett, 19 February 1908: Schurman, 1981, pp. 95–6.
85. Diary 10 March 1908: CBT 43/10. May met Corbett at the NRS Council, and discussed *England in the Seven Years' War*. See Morgan-Owen, 2017, pp. 163–76 for Corbett's role.
86. Schurman, 1981, pp. 90–5.
87. Diary 22 August 1908: CBT 43/10.

88. Nicholas Lambert, 1999, p. 138.
89. Schurman, 1981, p. 97. Diary 19 June 1908: CBT 43/9.
90. Fisher to Esher, 15 March 1909: *FGDN*, II, p. 232.
91. Memorandum Diary 1908: CBT 43/9.
92. Charles Callwell, *The Life of Sir Stanley Maude*, London, Constable, 1920, pp. 93–4. Diary 31 January 1908: CBT 43/9.
93. *Some Principles*, pp. 235–63. In both texts invasion has a separate index entry.
94. Memorandum Diary 1908: CBT 43/9.

11 Imperial Pageantry

1. For an imperial perspective on the post-Boer War shake-up of imperial military assets, the emergence of the CID and the origins of the Army's continental focus, see Douglas E. Delaney, *The Imperial Army Project: Britain and the Land Forces of the Dominions and India, 1902–1945*, Oxford, Oxford UP, 2018, pp. 6–43.
2. Colonial Conference 1907, CAB 17/77: cited in ibid., pp. 37–8.
3. Grimes, 2012, ch. 4. Morgan-Owen, 2017, pp. 166–78. *Fisher Papers*, II, pp. 316–468 for 1907 War Plans. Diary 12 June 1908: CBT 43/9.
4. Schurman, 1981, pp. 87–97.
5. Keeling, 'Armed Forces', *EHR*, 2019.
6. *Toronto Globe*, 18 May 1908. William Johnston, William Rawlings, Richard Gimblett and John MacFarlane, *The Seabound Coast: The Official History of the Royal Canadian Navy, 1867–1939*, Toronto, Dundurn Press, 2010, pp. 108–30, at p. 124.
7. H.V. Nelles, *The Art of Nation-building: Pageantry and Spectacle at Quebec's Tercentenary*, Toronto, University of Toronto Press, 1999, pp. 198–9, 211.
8. Inuit peoples were not mentioned. For 1759 and 1760, see ibid., pp. 74, 266.
9. Ibid., pp. 299–301.
10. For an incisive introduction to the global context see: Thomas Otte (ed.), *The Age of Anniversaries: The Cult of Commemoration, 1895–1925*, Abingdon, Routledge, 2018. British views are examined in Andrew Lambert, 'An Entente Centenary: Commemorating Trafalgar without Wounding "the Susceptibilities of France"', in Otte, 2018, at pp. 61–81. For pageantry, see Angela Bartie, Linda Fleming, Mark Freeman, Tom Hulme and Paul Readman, 'Commemorating through Dramatic Performance: Historical Pageants and the Age of Anniversaries, 1905–1920', in Otte, 2018, at pp. 195–218
11. Delaney, 2018, pp. 6–10.
12. Jan Rüger, *The Great Naval Game: Britain and Germany in the Age of Empire*, Cambridge, Cambridge UP, 2007, pp. 175–7. George Clarke, *Russia's Sea Power*, London, Murray, 1898, pp. 132–3. In 1898 Russia was considered a serious threat.
13. Robert Davison, 'A Most Fortunate Court Martial: The Trial of Captain Charles Kingsmill, 1907', *Northern Mariner* 19(1), 2009, pp. 57–86.
14. Rüger, 2007, pp. 178–82. Eric Hobsbawm and Terence Ranger, *The Invention of Tradition*, Cambridge, Cambridge UP, 1983.
15. Corbett in H.W. Wilson (ed.), *The Navy League Guide to the Coronation Review June 28, 1902*. London, 1902, p. 7, cited in Rüger, pp. 203, 206.
16. Lambert, 2007; Rüger, 2007, pp. 204–6.
17. Schurman, 1981, p. 101.
18. Diary 15 and 22 May 1908: CBT43/9.
19. Diary 12–15 June 1908: CBT 43/9. Grimes, 2012, pp. 115–24.
20. Diary 19 June 1908: CBT 43/9.
21. Mackay, 1974, pp. 361–2, 401–3.
22. Schurman, 1981, p. 97. Diary 1 July 1908: CBT 43/9.
23. Diary 12 and 13 June 1908: CBT 43/9.
24. Schurman, 1981, p. 101.
25. Diary 9–13 July 1908: CBT 43/9. W.H. Parker, *Mackinder: Geography as an Aid to Statecraft*, Oxford, Oxford UP, 1982.

26. Nelles, 1999, pp. 213–16.
27. Slade to Corbett, 11 August 1908: CBT 13/2/23.
28. Delaney, 2018, pp. 69–73. Lake remained in Canada until 1911.
29. Nelles, 1999, p. 314.
30. Diary 10 and 22 August 1908: CBT 43/9.
31. Nelles, 1999, pp. 217–18.
32. Ibid., at p. 216 the French ship is named *Admiral Aude*, garbling the political message.
33. Nelles, 1999, p. 317. Otte, 2018.
34. Stefan Berger with Christoph Conrad, *The Past as History: National Identity and Historical Consciousness in Modern Europe*, London, Palgrave, 2015, pp. 215–16 for the British imperial vision. Also Thomas Richards, *The Imperial Archive: Knowledge and the Fantasy of Empire*, London, Verso, 1993. Duncan Bell, *The Idea of Greater Britain: Empire and the Future of World Order, 1860–1900*, Princeton, NJ, Princeton UP, 2007, p. 108 for Seeley and 'Greater Britain'.
35. Johnston et al, 2010, p. 108.
36. Parker, 1982, p. 40, quoting Mackinder in *The Times*, 15 December 1908, and p. 71 for Argentina.
37. Parker, 1982, p. 41
38. Ibid., pp. 68–9, quoting *The Times*, 19 October 1910.
39. Delaney, 2018, pp. 93–4.
40. George Aston, *Memoirs of a Marine*, London, Murray, 1919, p. 269. Both lectured at Camberley 1905–7.
41. Julian Corbett, *Naval Operations: History of the Great War based on Official Documents, by Direction of the Historical Section of the Committee of Imperial Defence* (henceforth *NO*), 3 vols, London, Longman, 1920–2, vol. I, pp. 203–6. Delaney, 2018, pp. 106–9.
42. Norman Wilkinson, *Canada's Answer*, Canadian War Memorial, Ottawa.

12 Tactics, Signals and Trafalgar

1. Schurman, 1981, pp. 113–30. Brian Tunstall, *Naval Warfare in the Age of Sail: The Evolution of Fighting Tactics 1860–1815*, ed. Nicholas Tracey, London, Conway, 1991. Tunstall died in 1970.
2. *Laughton*, pp. 150, 189–90.
3. Diary 20 February 1909: CBT 43/10: Bacon, Custance and Corbett were discussing the subject.
4. Corbett to Newbolt, 17 February 1905: CBT 3/32. Newbolt thanked Prince Louis and Rear Admiral Sir Wilmot Fawkes in his book.
5. Dartmouth became a councillor of the NRS in 1906. His ancestor served in the Restoration Navy, and commanded James II's fleet in 1688.
6. Julian Corbett (ed.), *Fighting Instructions, 1530–1816* (henceforth *Fighting Instructions*), London, NRS, 1905, pp. vii–xi. He also thanked the librarians at the RUSI and the Admiralty for their help in finding source material.
7. Ibid., p. viii.
8. Ibid., p. ix
9. Ibid., pp. 164–5, citing *Mediterranean*, II, pp. 97–105 on Sir John Narborough's fleet.
10. Ibid., pp. 110–30, esp. pp. 120–2: 'Pepys's acrid and irresponsible pen can have no weight at all.'
11. Ibid., pp. 137–40.
12. Ibid., pp. 153–63.
13. Ibid., pp. 134–5.
14. A point Laughton had emphasised: *Laughton*, p. 125.
15. *Fighting Instructions*, pp. 175–8. Mahan's critique can be found in *Types of Naval Officer*, London, Sampson Low, 1902, at p. 15.
16. *Fighting Instructions*, pp. 179–83.
17. Ibid., pp. 195–6.
18. Ibid., p. 196.

19. Ibid., pp. 205–14.
20. Ibid., pp. 233–8.
21. Ibid., p. 267. Corbett translated the passage from Fernandez Duro's *Armada Española*, vol. VIII, p. 111.
22. *Fighting Instructions*, p. 268.
23. Ibid., p. 282.
24. Ibid., pp. 282–3.
25. Ibid., p. 284.
26. Andrew Lambert, *Nelson: Britannia's God of War*, London, Faber, 2004, pp. 285–308.
27. *Fighting Instructions*, pp. 286–310.
28. Ibid., pp. 311–13.
29. Ibid., pp. 335–42.
30. Corbett to Newbolt, 6 April 1905: CBT 3/7/34.
31. Julian Corbett, 'The Tactics of Trafalgar', *The Times*, 27 July 1905, p. 11a.
32. Schurman, 1981, pp. 120–30.
33. Cyprian A.G. Bridge, 'Nelson: The Centenary of Trafalgar', in *Sea-Power and Other Studies*, London, Smith, Elder, 1910, pp. 206–26, at p. 211. Corbett's copy is in the author's collection. Bridge's lecture was delivered in July 1905, and subsequently published in the *Cornhill Magazine*, 'the most useful' was very high praise indeed, given the NRS's intent that all volumes should be useful.
34. Corbett to Newbolt, 27 May 1905: CBT 3/36.
35. Clarke to Corbett, 21 July 1905: CBT 14/5/20.
36. Firth to Corbett, 24 May (1905): CBT 14/3/4. Firth used Corbett's work in *Commentary on Macaulay's History of England*, London, Macmillan, 1938, at pp. 166, 179–82.
37. Fisher to Corbett, 28 July 1905, Admiralty: FISR 1/4/182a. *FGDN*, II, p. 63. He was referring to Corbett's letter to *The Times* of 27 July 1905 on 'The Tactics of Trafalgar', a critique of Bridge's Centenary Lecture.
38. Diary 10 March 1908: CBT 43/9.
39. Diary 11, 14, 23 and 27 March 1908: CBT 43/9.
40. W.G. Perrin, *British Flags*, Cambridge, Cambridge UP, 1922. Corbett was series editor for this book.
41. Diary 1–3 April 1908: CBT 43/9.
42. See ch. 5 of this book. Diary 28 May 1908: CBT 43/9.
43. Julian Corbett (ed.), *Views of the Battles of the Third Dutch War: The Battle of Sole Bay and the Texel with a Note on the Drawings in the Possession of the Earl of Dartmouth illustrating the battle of Sole Bay, May 28, 1672 and the Battle of the Texel, August 11, 1673*. London, NRS, 1908, volume xxxiv.
44. Diary 28 May and 7 June 1908: CBT 43/9. Edwardes was a prominent London dealer in books and manuscripts: Corbett must have requested such material be sent to him.
45. Diary 12 June 1908: CBT 43/9.
46. Diary 30 June and 1 July 1908: CBT 43/9.
47. Diary 10–18 August 1908: CBT 43/9.
48. Hubert James Garbett, promoted captain on the retired list 1894, produced a *Catalogue of Naval Manuscripts in the Library of the Royal United Service Institution* in 1914. He also wrote *Naval Gunnery*, London, George Bell, 1897, part of a series on naval subjects.
49. Diary 5–6 September 1908: CBT 43/9.
50. Slade to Corbett, 8 September 1908, Admiralty: CBT 13/2/24.
51. Diary 11 September 1908: CBT 43/9.
52. Diary 12 and 13 October 1908: CBT 43/9.
53. Julian Corbett (ed.), *Signals and Instructions 1776–1794* (henceforth *Signals*), London, NRS, 1909, pp. viii–ix.
54. The last Diary reference to this work is 26 October 1908: CBT 43/9.
55. Diary 1 March 1909: CBT 43/9.
56. *Signals*, pp. 41, 74 and 135.
57. Opening matter, 1908 Diary: CBT 43/9.

58. *Signals*, pp. x–xi.
59. Sébastian François de Bigot, Vicomte de Morogues, *Tactique navale ou traité des évolutions et des signaux*, 1763. Bourdé de Villhuet, *Le Manoeuvrier ou Essai sur la théorie et la pratique de movements du navire et des évolutions navales*, 1765. *Signals*, pp. 3–8.
60. *Signals*, p. 8.
61. Ibid., p. 40. Robert Beatson, *Naval and Military Memoirs of Great Britain, from the year 1727 to the present time*, London, Strahan, 3 vols, 1790; 6 vols, 1804. Corbett owned the 1804 edition.
62. *Signals*, pp. 23 fn 3, 29 and 32.
63. Ibid., pp. 34–5. J.K. Laughton (ed.), *The Barham Papers*, vol. I, London, NRS, 1907, pp. 288–364. Laughton expressed his 'gratitude to Mr Julian S Corbett, who has read the proof slips and offered many valuable suggestions', p. lxii. This labour secured Corbett access to the Barham manuscripts.
64. Tunstall missed the pedagogical point, wondering why Corbett made so much of 'old Kempy . . .'
65. *Signals*, p. 139.
66. Ibid., p. 71, citing Howe to Rear Admiral Sir Roger Curtis: John Barrow, *The Life of Richard, Earl Howe*, London, Murray, 1838, p. 379.
67. *Signals*, p. 71.
68. Ibid., pp. 180–1.
69. Ibid., pp. 180–1, 219–25.
70. Laughton, *Barham*, I, pp. xliv–xlvii. Corbett reused the example in *Some Principles*, p. 2, to emphasise the role of doctrine.
71. *Signals*, p. 187.
72. Diary 19 December 1908: CBT 43/9.
73. *Some Principles*, pp. 2–3.
74. *Signals*, p. 235.
75. Ibid., p. 318. The reference is to the letter, Nelson to Howe, 8 January 1799: Sir Harris Nicolas, *Letters and Dispatches of Lord Nelson*, vol. III, London, Bentley, 1845, p. 230.
76. Diary 25 March 1909: CBT 43/10.
77. *Trafalgar*, Appendix D and E, pp. 445–6, 447–9.
78. Ibid., pp. 345–58.
79. Ibid., p. 361 fn 1, referring to James Thursfield, *Nelson and other Naval Studies*, London, Murray, 1909.
80. T.S. Jackson (ed.), *Logs of the Great Sea Fights*, London, NRS, 1899–1900. Nicolas, *Nelson*, vol. VII: *1846*, pp. 142–211.
81. *Trafalgar*, p. 363 fn 1.
82. Julian Corbett, 'New Lights on Trafalgar', *The Times*, 22 October 1909, p. 8a.
83. *Laughton*, pp. 47–9 for Laughton's important paper 'The Scientific Study of Naval History' of 1874.
84. For Corbett's emphasis on the importance of logical argument see: Julian Corbett, 'Methods of Discussion', *Naval Review*, 1920, pp. 322–4.
85. *Trafalgar*, p. 385.
86. Ibid., pp. 391–5.
87. Ibid, p. 396.
88. C. von Clausewitz, *On War*, trans. Col. J.J. Graham, 4th edn, London, Kegan Paul, 1940, vol. I, p. 69.
89. Desbrière to Corbett, Versailles, 8 June 1910: CBT 14/2/24.
90. Newbolt to Corbett, 12 June 1910: CBT 3/6/4.
91. Firth to Corbett, 28 June 1910: CBT 14/3/3.
92. Corbett to Newbolt, 16 July 1910: CBT 3/72.
93. Diary 25 January 1911: CBT 43/12, and Bridge, 'Centenary of Trafalgar', in Bridge, 1910, pp. 206–26.
94. Corbett to Newbolt, 12 October 1911: CBT 3/75.
95. Corbett to Newbolt, 21 April 1912: CBT 3/87.

96. A reference to Cyprian Bridge.
97. Corbett to Newbolt, 6 May 1912: CBT 3/79.
98. Schurman, 1981, pp. 128–30.
99. A cutting of Thursfield's *Times* letter of 21 October 1913 is in Corbett's copy of the report (IHR). He did not mark the report.
100. Corbett to Newbolt, 22 October 1913: CBT 3/84.
101. Newbolt to Corbett, 23 October 1913: IHR pasted into the report.
102. Corbett to Newbolt, 24 October 1913: CBT 3/82. Kerr pointedly ignored Corbett in his life of Prince Louis.
103. Corbett to Newbolt, 27 October 1913: CBT 3/86.
104. Firth to Corbett, 28 October 1913: IHR Report.
105. Diary 18 December 1908. He recorded buying a Signal Book for £4 from a private individual.
106. Diary 22 December 1908: CBT 43/9.
107. Tunstall, 1991, p. viii.
108. Ibid., p. 196. *Signals*, pp. 331–3.
109. Ibid., p. 160, relying on Rodney to Sandwich, 25 April 1782: John Owen (ed.), *The Sandwich Papers*, vol. IV, London, NRS, pp. 264–5. *Signals*, p. 229.
110. Donald Schurman provided an appreciation of his teacher, Nichols Tracey rendered the text accessible, and Robert Gardiner, at Conway Press, produced and published a fine illustrated edition.

13 Maritime Strategy in a Total War

1. *Trafalgar*.
2. Bridge, 1908. In Corbett's copy the chapter 'Strategy at Trafalgar' was marked up twice, pp. 276–7.
3. Jon Robb-Webb, 'Corbett and *The Campaign of Trafalgar*: Naval Operations in their Strategic Context', *Defence Studies* 8(22), 2008, pp. 157–89, addresses the relevance of the text in 1910 and 2008.
4. Diary 20 January 1909: CBT 43/10.
5. Diary 27 January 1909: CBT 43/10. Both had been approved by the Admiralty.
6. Diary 8–12 February 1909: CBT 43/10.
7. Diary 15–19 February 1909: CBT 43/10.
8. Diary 23 February 1909: CBT 43/10.
9. John Holland Rose (ed.), *Select Dispatches relating to the Third Coalition against France, 1804–5*, London, Camden Society, 1904.
10. Otte, 2020, pp. 350–5.
11. *Trafalgar*, pp. 44–9.
12. Diary 17 March 1909: CBT 43/10.
13. Diary 6–7 May 1909: CBT 43/10.
14. I am indebted to my friend Stephen Mclaughlin for access to the relevant pages of Thursfield's copy of *Trafalgar*. The marginalia run from pp. 342 to 396, restricted to battle plans, tactics and the battle.
15. Desbrière to Corbett, Versailles, 17 May 1909: CBT 14/2/23.
16. *Barham* was published after Corbett's book.
17. Diary 25 May–8 June 1909: CBT 43/10.
18. Diary 12 June 1909: CBT 43/10. Rüger, 2007, pp. 79, 179, 214 and 222 stresses the scale and novelty of a review laid on for the Imperial Press, and the impact it had in Germany.
19. Diary 30 June and 13 July 1909: CBT 43/10.
20. *Some Principles*, pp. 44, 56, 68, 179–80. 'Staff Histories', in Corbett and Edwards, 1914.
21. Diary 6 July 1909: CBT 43/10.
22. Diary 21–8 July 1909: CBT 43/10.
23. Diary 5 and 17 November 1909: CBT 43/10.
24. Diary 13 April 1910: CBT 43/11.
25. *Trafalgar*, p. viii.

26. Ibid., pp. xi–xii.
27. Ibid., p. 25 cited the sound advice of Charles Dumouriez from J.H. Rose and A.M. Broadley, *Dumouriez and the Defence of England against Napoleon*, London, Bodley Head, 1909, pp. 240–6, a text published too late to affect his general approach.
28. *Trafalgar*, pp. 1–4. A key argument. Although unmentioned, *On War* shaped his treatment.
29. *Trafalgar*, p. 21.
30. Corbett cited Desbrière in a brilliant footnote: ibid., p. 34.
31. Ibid, p. 19. The profound cultural meaning of that phrase, the anti-British war cry of the French for more than half a century, was not lost on British audiences.
32. Ibid., pp. 26, 32, 94 and 43–7.
33. Ibid., pp. 113–26.
34. The success of Thiers' massive history of France between 1790 and 1815, *Histoire du Consulate et de l'Empire*, Paris, Paulin, 1840–62, made it a standard reference. His claim that Nelson had been 'decoyed' to the West Indies, outwitted by Bonaparte, appeared in English in 1845, sparking an invasion scare. Robert Gildea, *The Past in French History*, New Haven, CT, and London, Yale UP, 1994, p. 98.
35. *Trafalgar*, pp. 127–9.
36. Ibid., p. 149.
37. Ibid., p. 171.
38. Ibid., p. 179.
39. Ibid., p. 174.
40. Ibid., pp. 227–9, 243.
41. Ibid., pp. 183, 231.
42. Ibid., p. 191, from Édouard Desbrière, *Projets et tentatives de dèbarquement aux Iles Brittaniques, 1798–1805*, Paris, Chapelot, 1900–4, vol. V, p. 406.
43. *Trafalgar*, pp. 201–6. Corbett criticised Calder for being too concerned to secure his prizes, sacrificing an opportunity to renew the action; a mistake he hoped his readers would not repeat.
44. Ibid., p. 237.
45. Ibid., p. 247.
46. Ibid., pp. 248–52. The final quote may have been aimed at Spenser Wilkinson and Repington. For another example of Corbett's incisive historiographical analysis, see p. 294 fn 1.
47. Ibid., p. 251.
48. Ibid., p. 279.
49. Andrew Lambert, 'Sir William Cornwallis: 1744–1809', in Peter le Fevre and Richard Harding (eds), *Precursors of Nelson: British Admirals of the Eighteenth Century*, London, Chatham, 2000, pp. 353–75.
50. *Trafalgar*, pp. 260–70.
51. Ibid., p. 278.
52. See, for example, ibid., pp. 74 and 111.
53. Ibid., pp. 265–6.
54. Ibid., pp. 297–301.
55. Ibid., p. 309. The *Jervis Bay* in 1940 is the best modern example.
56. Ibid., pp. 313–14.
57. Ibid., pp. 296 and 303.
58. Ibid., pp. 320–1.
59. For tactical issues see ch. 12 of this volume.
60. *Trafalgar*, pp. 416–24.
61. Desbrière to Corbett, 8 June 1910: CBT 14/2/24. Bridgeman to Corbett, Admiralty, 8 June 1910: CBT 13/3/15.
62. Corbett to Newbolt, 9 June 1910: CBT 3/7/70. Newbolt to Corbett, 12 June 1910: CBT 3/64.
63. Corbett to Newbolt, 16 June 1910: CBT 3/69.

64. Firth to Corbett, 28 June 1910, Oxford: CBT 14/3/3.
65. Wilmot Fawkes to Corbett, 29 June 1910: CBT 13/3/28.
66. Mackay, 1974, pp. 149, 245–6 and 275.
67. Balfour to Fisher, 9 July 1910, in Fisher to Corbett, 16 July 1910: CBT 12/54-56.
68. Richmond to Corbett, 30 June 1910: CBT 13/1/10.
69. Aston to Corbett, Pretoria, 9 September 1910: CBT 5/2/41. He obliged in *Some Principles*.
70. *Athenaeum*, 2 July 1910, pp. 5–6.
71. *Spectator*, 23 July 1910, p. 17.
72. *Westminster Gazette*, 28 July 1910.
73. *Saturday Review*, 6 August 1910, pp. 173–4.
74. C.T. Atkinson, Review, *EHR* 26, April 1911, pp. 398–402.
75. Slade to Corbett, Calcutta, 27 December 1910: CBT 13/2/51.
76. Schurman, 1981, pp. 62–3.
77. Diary 10 January 1911: CBT 43/13.
78. Fisher to Reid, 8 July 1910: George Pearce, *Carpenter to Cabinet: Thirty-seven Years of Parliament*, Melbourne, Hutchinson, 1951, pp. 100–1. Pearce's inclusion of Fisher's letter and a passage from the review in a short memoir cannot be accidental. Lambert, 2014, pp. 29–47.
79. John Connor, *Anzac and Empire: George Foster Pearce and the Foundations of Australian Defence*, Cambridge, Cambridge UP, 2011 demonstrates the long-term impact of Fisher's strategic tutorial.
80. Diary 10 October 1910: CBT 43/11.
81. Diary 21 May–4 June 1911: CBT 43/12.

14 Teaching National Strategy

1. Widen, 2012, recognises doctrine was more important than theory, p. 153.
2. Corbett obituary by Herbert Richmond, *Naval Review*, February 1923, p. 18.
3. Schurman, 1981, p. 67. For March 1907 correspondence between Fisher and Corbett, leading to the pamphlet 'Some Principles of Naval Warfare'. ADM 116/1043B. *Some Principles*, ed. Grove, p. xxiv, including the 'Green Pamphlet'. *Fisher Papers*, II, pp. 318–45.
4. Diary 12 February 1909: CBT 43/11. Fisher to Corbett 13 April 1909: *FGDN*, II, pp. 243–4: Corbett to Bethell, 21 April 1909 draft and Bethell to Corbett, 22 April 1909: CBT 12/43.
5. Diary 25 April 1909: CBT 43/11.
6. *Seven Years' War*, I, p. 207 fn 1. This is the first statement of what became the dominant theme of part 1 of *Some Principles*; similar insights can be found in other texts as far back as 1900.
7. See Henry Wilson's response to a potential Channel Tunnel. Keith Wilson, *Channel Tunnel Visions 1850-1945*, London, Hambleden, 1994, pp. 74–5, 88, 132, 137–8.
8. Ottley typescript, with Ottley to Fisher, 12 January 1910, in Hankey to Fisher, 10 January 1910: FISR 1/9 f. 455.
9. Ottley typescript memo of conversation with Fisher, December 1909: FISR 1/9 f. 456.
10. Ottley had been working with Corbett since 1905.
11. Diary 27 October 1909: CBT 43/11. Fisher to Corbett, 3 October 1909, sold in Sienna: it remains unused TUN/226.
12. Fisher explained the plan to Corbett on 6 February 1910: Diary CBT 43/11.
13. Nicholas Lambert, 'Admiral Sir Arthur Knyvet Wilson, V.C. (1910–1911)', in Malcolm Murfett (ed.), *The First Sea Lords: From Fisher to Mountbatten*, Westport, CT, Praeger, 1995, pp. 35–53, at pp. 35–7.
14. Diary Italy 15 April–13 May 1910; Kilverstone, 28–30 May 1910; 'strategy' 19 June 1910: CBT 43/11.
15. Diary 25 June 1910: CBT 43/11.
16. Corbett to Newbolt, 12 October 1911: CBT 3/75.

17. Captain Gabriel Darrieus, Professor of Strategy and Naval Tactics at the French Naval War College, *La Guerre sur mer: Stratègie et tactique. La Doctrine*, Paris, 1907, translated into English by Professor Philip Alger and published at the US Naval War College in 1908. Copies were acquired for the Royal Navy. It is not clear if Corbett consulted the French or English edition. Darrieus demanded the French Navy accept English ideas on sea power, from Mahan's work, for a future conflict with Britain, see, pp. 255–88. Arne Røksund, *The Jeune École: The Strategy of the Weak*, published PhD thesis, University of Oslo, 2005, pp. 216–17.
18. Diary 10 October 1910: CBT 43/11.
19. Diary 11 October 1910: CBT 43/11.
20. Diary 28 October 1910: CBT 43/11.
21. Diary 27 October and 9 November 1910: CBT 43/11.
22. Diary 23 November 1910: CBT 43/11.
23. Diary 19 June 1908: CBT 43/9.
24. Ian Hamilton, *Compulsory Service: A Study of the Question in the Light of Experience*, London, Murray, 1st edn November 1910, multiple editions thereafter. Haldane's 'Introduction' (pp. 9–42) retailed the government position, pp. 11–12.
25. Ibid., p. 20.
26. Stephen Koss, *Lord Haldane: Scapegoat for Liberalism*, New York, Columbia UP, 1969, pp. 117–18.
27. Hamilton, 1910, p. 33.
28. Arthur Wilson, in ibid., pp. 208–12. Morgan-Owen, 2017, pp. 198–9.
29. Hamilton, 1910, p. 41.
30. Koss, 1969, pp. 102–3.
31. Diary 13 November 1911: CBT 43/12. A French Mahanian author focused on decisive battle, Captain René Daveluy's *Études sur la Strategie naval*, Paris, Berger-Levrault, 1905, pp. 240–76, dismissed commerce destroying as a minor function that could be left to obsolescent vessel on colonial stations. Heuser, 2010, pp. 240–5.
32. Aston, 1911. Corbett's copy is in the IHR Library.
33. Public Record Office visit on 9 February 1911: CBT 43/12.
34. *Some Principles*, pp. 128–52.
35. Julian Corbett, review of A.T. Mahan, *Types of Naval Officer* (Boston, 1901), *American Historical Review* 7(3), 1902, pp. 556–9. If Corbett did not use the word 'doctrine' in 1902 he recognised the concept.
36. Grove, 'Introduction' to the 1988 edition of *Some Principles*, ed. Grove, pp. xxiv–xxv.
37. The manuscript survives, in a second-hand paper wrapper addressed to Mrs Corbett from the nearby department store Harvey Nichols, dated 12 March 1912. Corbett labelled it 'M.S. Maritime Strategy': CBT 41.
38. Diary 26 January 1911: CBT 43/12.
39. Keate to Corbett, n.d.: CBT 41, and Troubridge to Corbett, 10 July 1911, Admiralty: CBT 13/3/64. Diary 24 September 1908: CBT 43/9.
40. Hamley, 1909 edn.
41. Dighton, 2020, p. 191.
42. Ibid., p. 192
43. Troubridge to Corbett, 11 July 1911, Admiralty: CBT 13/3/66, and Diary: CBT 43/12.
44. Wilson to Churchill, n.d. 1911: Admiral Sir Edward Bradford, *Life of Admiral of the Fleet Sir Arthur Knyvet Wilson*, London, Murray, 1923, p. 230. Bradford recognised Wilson's intellectual penetration and practical expertise.
45. As he did when Arthur Pollen's fire control equipment failed on trial. John Brooks, *Dreadnought Gunnery and the Battle of Jutland*, London, Routledge, 2005.
46. Bradford, 1923, pp. 235, 237 and 238. *Some Principles*, pp. 64–6.
47. Nicholas Lambert, 'Wilson', in Murfett, 1995, p. 45. *FDSF*, I, pp. 248–51.
48. Nicholas Lambert, 'Wilson', in Murfett, 1995, p. 45.
49. *FDSF*, I, pp. 388–93 is the classic statement. The essential corrective is Morgan-Owen, 2015. See also Bradford, 1923, pp. 235–6, who cites Wilson's now lost handwritten MS.

50. On 9 August 1914, Wilson revived his plans for Heligoland and other coastal attacks because 'If the Germans succeed in entering France, the Navy will have to take a more active line.' He understood the risks, but realised political necessity might soon overrule tactical and operational caution. This is what happened at the Dardanelles, an operation he did not approve, probably because the secondary object did not warrant the risks: Bradford, 1923, pp. 240, 243.

51. Nicholas Lambert, 'Sir Francis Bridgeman', in Murfett, 1995, p. 57.

52. Longman to Corbett, agreement for *Some Principles*, 3 August 1911: CBT 2/3/12.

53. C.J. Longman to Corbett, 8 August 1911: CBT 2/3/11.

54. Corbett to Henry Newbolt, 12 November 1911: CBT 3/75.The reference is to the 1911 Admiralty Committee that considered the tactics at Trafalgar. It vindicated Corbett. Schurman, 1981, pp. 120–7.

55. Nicholas Lambert, 'Wilson', in Murfett, 1995, p. 48, suggests Churchill was not convinced by Henry Wilson on 23 August 1911.

56. Morgan-Owen, 2017, p. 208 for his links with Henry Wilson; also d'Ombrain, 1973, p. 265. Esher to Hankey, 15 March 1915: Brett, 1934–6, III, p. 221. Corbett owned Hamley's text, Dighton, 2020, p. 187.

57. *Some Principles*, pp. 44, 55, 68, 179–80 refer to Clausewitz's doctrine of limited war, and the overestimation of the importance of fleet battle in the seventeenth century.

58. Ibid., pp. 1–8.

59. Ibid., pp. 54–5.

60. The *Morning Post* article was published on 30 March 1908. Diary 31 March 1908: CBT 43/7.

61. Slade to Corbett, 31 March 1908, Admiralty: CBT 13/2/1.

62. Slade to Corbett, 16 April 1908, Admiralty: CBT 13/2/20.

63. Diary 19 May 1908: CBT 43/7.

64. S. Wilkinson, 'Strategy in the Navy', *Morning Post*, 3 August 1909. The *Morning Post*, a Unionist newspaper, opposed the Liberal government, and Fisher's policy.

65. ADM 203, pp. 5 and 167. Black, 2009, pp. 87, 108–9, 288.

66. *Some Principles* only mentioned Mahan twice, 1911, pp. 131 n, 171, illustrating strategic concentration and control of communications. Corbett did not engage with Mahan's overall thesis; it was common knowledge, and he rejected such unthinking maxims.

67. Alfred T. Mahan, *The Influence of Sea Power upon the French Revolution and Empire, 1793–1812*, 2 vols, London, Sampson Low, 1892, vol. II, pp. 353–96.

68. Troubridge to Corbett, 5 December 1911, Admiralty: CBT 13/3/67. Churchill memo on War Staff, 28 October 1911: R.S. Churchill, 1969, II, part 2, p. 1307.

69. Troubridge to Corbett, 9 January 1912, Admiralty: CBT 13/3/68.

70. Murfett, 1995, p. 57.

71. Corbett to Edith, 6 December 1911, RNWC Portsmouth: CBT 11/2/30.

72. Corbett to Edith, 28 May 1912, RNWC Portsmouth: CBT 11/3/35.

73. Sidney Drury-Lowe to Corbett, 27 December 1911, Compiègne, France: CBT 13/3/48.

74. Widen, 2012, pp. 155–6.

75. George Cuthbert Cayley to Corbett, 5 February 1912 – China Station: CBT 13/3/16.

76. Fred Jane to Corbett, 30 November 1911: CBT 14/4/1. Jane had worked with Henry May on war games.

77. Corbett to Edith, 26 November 1912, RNWC: CBT 11/3/27. *FDSF*, I, p. 77.

78. Wilkinson cited Colmar von der Goltz, 'the ablest of the recent German writers on war', and quoted French soldier Jean Colin's line that the limited–unlimited distinction 'can no longer be pressed, at any rate in regard to European wars', without recognising that Colin had restricted his remark to the operational level by including the word 'offensive'.

79. Wilkinson, *Morning Post*, 3 August 1909 and review of *Some Principles*, 19 February 1912.

80. Kurt von Maltzahn, 'Seestrategie in ihren Bezieungen zuir Landstrategie nach english-amerikananaschen Urteil', *Marine Rundschau*, 23 July 1912, pp. 869–86. See Hervé Coutau-Bégarie, 'Corbett and Richmond in France', in Goldrick and Hattendorf, 1993, pp. 277–85.

81. Maltzahn, *Revue Maritime* 196, January–March 1913, pp. 109–18, April–June 1913, pp. 94–101. Review, *Revue Maritime* 197, November–December 1913, pp. 272–7. Coutau-Bégarie, in Goldrick and Hattendorf, 1993, pp. 277–8.

82. Ibid., pp. 281–4.

83. *Some Principles*, p. 9.

84. *Some Principles*, ed. Grove, p. xliii. Bassford, 1994, pp. 98–9.

85. See ch. 6, this volume, on 'The Naval War Course'.

86. *Armchair Athenians: Essays from the Athenaeum*, London, The Athenaeum, 2001. See especially Felipe Fernandez-Armesto, 'Preface', p. vii, and Michael Howard, 'The Athenaeum and the Military', p. 278.

87. Longman to Corbett, 5 July 1912: CBT 2/3/16.

88. Slade to Corbett, 8 July 1912: CBT 2/3/15.

89. Longman to Corbett, 9 July and 14 August 1912: CBT 2/3/16 and 17.

90. *Russo-Japanese War*, II, pp. 7–15.

91. Ian Buxton, *Big Gun Monitors: Design, Construction and Operations, 1914–1945*, Barnsley, Seaforth, 2008, pp. 8–12.

92. *Russo-Japanese War*, II, p. 19

93. Ibid., pp. 25–6.

94. Ibid., p. 73

95. Andrew Lambert, 'Sir Julian Corbett and the *Naval Review*', in P. Hore (ed.), *Dreadnought to Daring: 100 Years of Comment, Controversy and Debate in the Naval Review*, London, Chatham, 2012, pp. 37–52.

96. Bryan Ranft, 'Foreword' to *Some Principles*, London, Conway, 1972, pp. vi –xvii, at p. x. This was the first print edition of the book since the 1930s. Ranft's copy of the 1911 edition, acquired new by Geoffrey Callendar in 1911, was gifted to Michael Lewis, his successor as Professor at Greenwich, and then to Ranft.

97. Testimony of the French officer with the Grand Fleet in 1918: Coutau-Bégarie, in Goldrick and Hattendorf, 1993, p. 279. Accession Book, Library USNWC, vol. I titles, lists copies of *Some Principles* acquired 1912–15: 4388, 4687, 5078–9, 5839–43, 6710– 15. J.B. Hattendorf, B.M. Simpson and J.R. Wadleigh, *Sailors and Scholars: The Centennial History of the U.S. Naval War College*, Newport, RI, War College Press, 1984, p. 79 for Corbett's presence on pre-1914 reading lists.

98. Charles Longman to Corbett, 12 February 1913: CBT 2/3/18.

99. Printed by F.H. Gilson Company, Boston, MA.

100. W.S. Sims to Corbett, 9 October 1918, 30 Grosvenor Square, London: CBT 1/2/36.

101. My copy of this edition belonged to Lt Cmdr Alec Fearn, who dated it 1922. It shows evidence of use on that year's Staff Course. Fearn also owned wartime editions of *Successors* and *Mediterranean*.

102. Mahan was a deductive thinker, a method Corbett considered dangerous.

103. While Schurman, 1981, only mentioned *Some Principles* twice, pp. 56 and 62, Widen, 2012, does not address the historical context.

104. Professor Schurman gave undue importance to the critics: Schurman, 1965, pp. 183–4, and 1981, pp. 168–9, 177, 194.

105. Otte 2020, pp. 416–18, for Grey's clear-sighted assessment.

106. William Philpott, 'The General Staff and the Paradoxes of Continental War', in David French and Brian Holden Reid (eds), *The British General Staff: Reform and Innovation, 1890–1939*, London, Cass, 2002, pp. 95–111, at p. 100.

107. D'Ombrain, 1973, p. 273.

108. Ibid., p. 111. Hunt, 1982, p. 42.

15 'Doctrine – The Soul of Warfare'

1. G. Grainge, 'A Family of Rare Naval Distinction: The Hannam Hendersons of Worth, East Kent', *Topmasts*, 15, 2015, pp. 11–15. Corbett knew both Sir William (1845–1931) and Sir Reginald (1846–1932).

2. Correspondence with Admiral William Henderson, especially 16 May 1914 and 17 June 1914: Naval Review Archive, courtesy of Admiral James Goldrick RAN.
3. Diary 2 April 1912: CBT 43/13. Corbett to Newbolt, 17 and 21 April 1912: CBT 3/87 and 79.
4. 'A Plea for History', *The Times*, 10 September 1904, in *Imperial Strategy by the Military Correspondent of 'The Times'*, London, John Murray, 1906, p. 213.
5. Ibid., p. 10.
6. Ottley to Admiralty, 8 March 1907: ADM 1/7878.
7. Ottley minute 11 June 1907, Slade minute 6 November 1907: ADM 1/7878
8. Diary 17–18 October 1908: CBT 43/9. Hattendorf and Schurman, 'Introduction' to *Russo-Japanese War*, I, pp. v–xvii, at p. xii.
9. Corbett to Edith, 9 November 1910, RNWC Portsmouth: CBT 10/10/5.
10. Corbett to Edith, 30 November 1911, RNWC Portsmouth: CBT 11/2/26.
11. *Russo-Japanese War*, I, p. xxv.
12. Ibid., p. xxvii.
13. Ibid., pp. xxviii.
14. Ibid., p. 1.
15. Ibid., p. 3.
16. Ibid., pp. 6–13 and p. 85 for a British naval analogy.
17. *Russo-Japanese War*, II, p. 382.
18. Ibid., pp. 383–92.
19. Ibid., p. 393.
20. Ibid., pp. 395–6.
21. Ibid., p. 398.
22. Schurman, 1981, dates the decision to 6 November 1913.
23. Diary 10 and 31 July 1914: WW1/RNMN/059, Leeds University Library, Liddle Collection: https://explore.library.leeds.ac.uk/special-collections-explore/26597
24. NRS Council Meeting, 12 March 1912: Diary (and NRS Minute Book 2).
25. George Prothero (1848–1922), a Cambridge historian, edited the *Quarterly Review* from 1899, NRS councillor 1901–9.
26. Adolphus William Ward (1837–1924), president of the British Academy 1911–13. The series had been proposed by Henry John Edwards (1869–1923), Fellow and lecturer at Peterhouse, Colonel Commanding the Cambridge Officer Training Corps, 1908–19, Secretary of the Board of Military Studies, 1904–20. David McKitterick, *A History of Cambridge University Press*, vol. III: *New Worlds for Learning, 1873–1972*, Cambridge, Cambridge UP, 2004, p. 167.
27. Diary 22 June 1912: CBT 43/13 and A.W. Ward to JSC, 24 June 1912, Peterhouse: CBT 14/5/31.
28. University Pr/V.74 minutes V.74, 11 June 1912: Cambridge University Archives.
29. Thomas Macaulay, *The History of England*, 6 vols, ed. Charles Firth, London, Macmillan, 1913. Firth to Corbett, 28 June 1910: CBT 14/3/3.
30. Diary 12 August 1912: CBT 43/13.
31. Corbett to Admiral William Henderson, 17 June 1914: Naval Review Archive Bundle ref. N. Review /1/38/16.
32. Corbett to Edith, 19 November 1912, RNWC Portsmouth: CBT 11/3/11.
33. Beatty to CUP, 16 November 1912, and CUP to Beatty, 18 November 1912: CBT 13/3/6-7.
34. ADM 203/100 f. 96. Beatty to Corbett, 25 November 1912: CBT 13/3/5. Corbett and Edwards, 1914.
35. Corbett to Waller, 1 and 3 June 1913: CUP Ua. Pr. A.C. 479 ff. 13, 14.
36. Schurman, 1981, p. 143.
37. Owen, 1914, Preface, pp. v–vi, italics added.
38. Corbett to Waller, 28 May 1914: CUP Ua. Pr. A.C. 479 f. 41.
39. *The Times*, 2 April 1913, p. 8. Lord Bryce, 'Presidential Address', and Charles Firth, 'The Study of Modern History in Great Britain', delivered 3 April 1913, in *Proceedings of the British Academy 1913-1914*, London, British Academy, 1914, pp. 139–50, p. 128 for war, p. 145 for the NRS.

40. The President of the British Academy lamented that could not fund a complete publication of the congress: *Proceedings*, p. 7.
41. A.W. Ward in *Proceedings*, at p. 116. K.D. Erdmann, *Toward a Global Community of Historians: The International Historical Congresses and the International Committee of Historical Sciences, 1898–2000*, New York, Berghahn, 2005, pp. 64–5. *Laughton*. 'Historians and Naval History', in Corbett and Edwards, 1914.
42. O'Connor, 2011, does not mention the International Congress.
43. *The Times*, 7 April 1913, p. 7.
44. Soffer, 1994, p. 233, fn 81.
45. 'Staff Histories', in Corbett and Edwards, 1914, p. 24.
46. Ibid., p. 25.
47. Ibid., pp. 26–7.
48. Ibid., pp. 27–8.
49. Ibid., p. 29. J. Luvaas, 'The First British Official Historians', *Military Affairs* 26(2), 1962, pp. 49–58.
50. 'Staff Histories', in Corbett and Edwards, 1914, pp. 30–1.
51. Ibid., pp. 32–3.
52. Ibid., pp. 34–5. The echo of G.F.R. Henderson's essay 'War' was obvious, and intentional.
53. NRS Council meeting, 9 December 1913: NRS Minute Book 3.
54. Archive now at the British Library. P. Gordon (ed.), *The Red Earl: The Papers of the Fifth Earl Spencer, 1835–1910*, Northampton, Northamptonshire Record Society, 1986.
55. NRS Council minutes: NRS Minute Book 2.
56. Diary 26 and 30–31 January 1911, and 14 March 1911: CBT 43/12.
57. Corbett worked at the Admiralty Library between 20 and 25 May, on 10, 24 and 26–7 June, and 1, 3–5 and 7–8 July. On 16 July, he had the material typed by Miss Keate, Diary 1912: CBT 43/13.
58. NRS insert in Julian Corbett (ed.), *The Private Papers of George, Second Earl Spencer, First Lord of the Admiralty, 1794–1801* (henceforth *Spencer*), 2 vols, London, NRS, I (1913), II (1914), vol. I, dated October 1913. *Spencer*, II was issued in the autumn of 1914.
59. *Spencer*, I, 'General Introduction', p. vii.
60. Ibid., p. x.
61. Ibid., p. xvi.
62. Ibid., p. xx. Clausewitz was not named, lest he alarm the unthinking.
63. Ibid., pp. 133–5.
64. Ibid., pp. 136–7. Lambert, 2004, pp. 362–3.
65. *Spencer*, I, p. 281. Michael Duffy, *Soldiers, Sugar and Seapower: The British Expeditions to the West Indies and the War against Revolutionary France*, Oxford, Oxford UP, 1987.
66. *Spencer*, I, 'General Introduction', p. 4.
67. Ibid., pp. 42, 65–70, quote from p. 70.
68. Ibid., pp. 233–4.
69. *Spencer*, II, p. 3.
70. Ibid., p. 103. Corbett records reading Gill's thesis six weeks after completing *Some Principles*. Diary 15 December 1911: CBT 43/10.
71. *Spencer*, II, p. 178.
72. Ibid., p. 224.
73. He worked on page proofs in July–August 1914. Diary 28 August 1914: Liddle Collection.
74. *Spencer*, II, p. 225.
75. Ibid., pp. 365–7, at p. 367.
76. Ibid., p. 425.
77. Ibid., pp. 425–7. The strategic role of Minorca had been a key theme in *Mediterranean*. Two more volumes would be edited by Herbert Richmond after Corbett's death.
78. List of titles and future publications: *Spencer*, II, Appendix following, p. 518.
79. P.R. Harris, *The Life of Edward Montague, First Earl of Sandwich*, 2 vols, London, Methuen, 1912. Corbett provided loans and editorial assistance. Diary 16 October 1908 and 30 April 1911: CBT 43/9 and 12.

80. Annual Report of the NRS 1913–14.
81. The Monson volumes, edited by pioneer naval historian Michael Oppenheim, were a legacy from the founding years of the NRS, the original volumes appearing in 1902.
82. R.G. Marsden (ed.), *Documents Relating to the Law and Custom of the Sea*, 2 vols, London, NRS, 1915.
83. Corbett to Edith, 26 November 1912, RNWC Portsmouth: CBT 11/3/27.
84. Schurman does not mention this prestigious accolade in his biography, perhaps because it contradicted his thesis that Corbett had been ignored and undervalued.
85. Aston, 1914, pp. 92–3, 132.
86. Jennifer Siegel, *Endgame: Britain, Russia and the Final Struggle for Central Asia*, London, I.B. Tauris, 2002, pp. 143–97, for the impending collapse of the Entente.
87. Martin Slater, *The National Debt: A Short History*, London, Hurst, 2018.
88. His diaries say nothing about German policy in July–August 1914: Liddle Collection.
89. Otte, 2020, p. 521.

16 The 'British Way' at War

1. Andrew Lambert, '"Doctrine – The Soul of Warfare": Teaching Strategy in the Royal Navy before 1914', in D. Delaney and R. Engen (eds), *Military Education and Empire*, Vancouver, University of British Columbia Press, 2018 (papers from the 2015 RMC Kingston conference).
2. Hew Strachan, *The First World War*, vol. I: *To Arms*, Oxford, Oxford UP, 2000, pp. 201–3. Jeffery, 2006, pp. 127–34.
3. Otte, 2020, pp. 543–5, 587.
4. These often appeared under Hankey's signature. In the index to Hankey's self-congratulatory memoir, *The Supreme Command*, Corbett, long dead, was dismissed as 'a Historian who worked for me'.
5. Arthur Marder, *Portrait of an Admiral: The Life and Papers of Sir Herbert Richmond*, London, Cape, 1952, p. 92.
6. Andrew Green, *Writing the Great War: Sir James Edmonds and the Official Histories, 1915–1948*, London, Routledge, 2003, mentions Corbett at pp. 7 and 9, but ignores his leading role, following Schurman.
7. Diary 15 August 1914: Liddle Collection. Schurman, 1981, p. 166.
8. Diary 8 September 1914: Liddle Collection, see Widen, 2012, pp. 120–5 and Corbett, 1911 pp. 167 and 182 for his stress on the strategic approach to securing a 'decisive battle'.
9. Diary 5 September 1914: Liddle Collection.
10. Marder, 1952, p. 156. 'The prejudice against laymen writing on naval subject dies very hard, if indeed it does at all. It is responsible for a great deal of the lamentable strategy of this war.'
11. Corbett to Bethell, 28 August 1914: Bethell MSS LHCMA ff. 4–5.
12. Schurman, 1981, pp. 152–7. *Survey of London*, vol. XIII: *St Margaret, Westminster*, part 2: *Whitehall*, London, Batsford, 1930, frontispiece. The Georgian town house stood in a cul de sac. The site is now occupied by the Ministry of Defence Main Building.
13. Diary 6 October 1914: Liddle Collection.
14. Fisher to Corbett, 12 December 1914: *FGDN*, III, p. 93.
15. Lambert, 2014, pp. 48–74.
16. Asquith to Venetia Stanley, 2 November 1914: M. Gilbert (ed.), *Winston S. Churchill: Companion* (henceforth *Churchill Companion*), London, Heinemann, 1972, vol. III, p. 247. Mackay, 1974, pp. 455–505 underplays the Baltic, accepting Churchill's self-interested post-1927 claim that Fisher never intended to carry out the plan, at pp. 463–4.
17. A fourth battlecruiser, HMAS *Australia*, would join the Grand Fleet, after clearing the Pacific.
18. Grimes, 2012.
19. *Seven Years' War*, I, p. 142.
20. *Russo-Japanese War*, I, pp. 1–2.

21. *Seven Years' War*, I, pp. 74–5. The missing words are Austrian and French, replacing them with French and German fits the situation in 1914. This had been the intention in 1907.
22. These waters witnessed major battles in 1801 and 1807, with the Royal Navy opening the Danish Narrows and securing major strategic advantages.
23. *Russo-Japanese War*, I, pp. 146–9; *Some Principles*, pp. 206–7, 298; Dunley, 2018, pp. 240–66.
24. *NO*, III, p. 149. Corbett took the term 'siege fleet' from French literature, where it described the armoured batteries of the Crimean War and later coast attack ships.
25. Black, 2009, pp. 116–19.
26. *Fisher Papers*, II, pp. 441–3, and later war plans.
27. Mackay, 1974, p. 490. These landing craft were used at Gallipoli. Norman Friedman, *Fighting the Great War at Sea*, Barnsley, Seaforth, 2014, p. 214.
28. Churchill to Fisher, 11 December 1914: FISR 866: see Buxton, 2008, pp. 8–12, for the British monitors, a unique warship type created for coast attack.
29. Diary 17–21 December 1914: Liddle Collection.
30. Corbett to Fisher, 19 December 1914: FISR 1/17/874. MS in Corbett's hand, with his corrections and changes: there is no indication of other input. Typescript copies: FISR 5/24/4337–8, 4344 as 'The Baltic Project'.
31. Corbett to Fisher, 19 December 1914; FISR 1/17/874: Fisher to Corbett, 2 January 1915: FISR 1/17 895.
32. Fisher to Corbett, 22 July 1918 and 3 December 1919: *FGDN*, III, pp. 546 and 602. Mackay, 1974, p. 472. Diary 3 December 1919: CBT 43/18.
33. *NO*, II, p. 3.
34. Ibid., p. 3. Fisher to Jellicoe, 9 and 16 December 1914, and Fisher to Beatty, 11 December 1913: *FGDN*, III, pp. 90–3.
35. War Council minutes, 1 December 1914: *Churchill Companion*, III, part 1, p. 290.
36. Lord Fisher, *Records*, London, Hutchinson, 1919, pp. 217–22; the missing paragraphs are in *FGDN*, III, p. 45.
37. W.S. Churchill, *The World Crisis 1915*, London, Thornton Butterworth, 1923, pp. 37–9.
38. Fisher, 1919, p. 222. The careful use of language and potent historical analogy leave no doubt this was Corbett's work. At *FGDN*, III, p. 602, Fisher refers to it as 'your Baltic paper'. W.S. Churchill, 1923, p. 39. Mackay, 1974, p. 472.
39. *Seven Years' War*, II, pp. 287–91. Fisher to Jellicoe, 25 May 1916: *FGDN*, III, p. 351. J. Dull, *The French Navy and the Seven Years' War*, Lincoln, NE, Nebraska UP, 2006, p. 190, provides a modern account.
40. *FGDN*, III, p. 45. Marder's judgement may explain why Gilbert's *Churchill Companion*, III, pp. 284–7 ignores Corbett.
41. Fisher, 1919, p. 220.
42. Schurman, 1981, pp. 159–60.
43. Fisher to Corbett, 3 December 1914: *FGDN*, III, p. 45.
44. The British had a wealth of information on Japanese minesweeping and the uses of advanced bases in 1904–5, see Dunley, 2018, and CAB 45/1. Corbett had used this material before the war. Gardiner, 1985, p. 94. Mackay, 1974, p. 494.
45. Diary 12 December 1915: CBT 43/14. Andrew Lambert, '"The Possibility of Ultimate Action in the Baltic": Die Royal Navy im Krieg, 1914–1916', in M. Epkenhans, J. Hillman and F. Nägler (eds), *Skagerrakschlact: Voorgeschichte - Ereignis - Verarbeitung*, Munich, R. Oldenbourg Verlag, 2009, pp. 73–112. Lambert, '"This Is All We Want"', 2003, pp. 147–69. Dunley, 2018, for British policy, pp. 12, 58, 62, 135, 206–7, 247–8.
46. Churchill to Fisher, 21 December 1914: *FGDN*, III, p. 105 and *Churchill Companion*, III, part 1, pp. 323–4.
47. Churchill to Fisher, 22 December 1914: *Churchill Companion*, III, pp. 325–6.
48. Asquith observed this in letters to Venetia Stanley, and in discussion with his wife.
49. Churchill had been thinking about the subject since 19 August 1914: *Churchill Companion*, III, pp. 44, 75, 83, 95.

50. Churchill memo, 2 December 1914: *Churchill Companion*, III, pp. 291–4. The use of historical examples in this paper reflects Corbett's influence on Bayly, who worked with him as War Course director, and read *Some Principles*.
51. Corbett captured this information, and recorded it for posterity in *NO*, II, p. 161.
52. *Churchill Companion*, III, pp. 272–3.
53. Fisher to Lloyd George, 11 January 1915: LG/C/4/11/2 History of Parliament Archives.
54. W.S. Churchill, 1923, pp. 42–6. Fisher's notes of the meeting in Fisher to Churchill, 13 March 1918: *FGDN*, III, pp. 521–2. Order approved by Treasury, 23 May 1915: Friedman, 2014, p. 179.
55. Fisher to Churchill, 25 January 1915: *FGDN*, III, p. 145. Lambert, '"This Is All We Want"', 2003, pp. 147–69.
56. Director of Naval Construction minute, 28 January 1915, cited in Norman Friedman, *The British Battleship*, Barnsley, Seaforth, 2015, pp. 178–9. E.H.T. D'Eyncourt, *A Shipbuilder's Yarn: The Records of Naval Construction*, London, Hutchinson, n.d., pp. 65–7, 86, 129. D'Eyncourt designed *Courageous* for Fisher.
57. Fisher to D'Eyncourt, 14 December 1914, facing p. 39 in D'Eyncourt, n.d. On completion they became *Renown* and *Repulse*. Rhadmanthus, brother of Minos, the first thalassocratic ruler, judged the dead in Hades, and was noted for his inflexible integrity. The Navy had used the name before, when Fisher began his career. The reference may also reflect recent excavations at Knossos on Crete.
58. Black, 2009, pp. 116–18 confirms that this was a 'Baltic Fleet' contra Mackay, 1974, pp. 459–76, using significant new evidence. The 'X' lighters, ordered in February 1915, were delivered between April and July – timing that connects them to the projected Flanders offensive.
59. *Some Principles*, p. 66, Corbett quoted Napoleon to ensure the point would not be contested.
60. Henderson, 1905, p. 28. Corbett used this quote in *Some Principles* and in War Course lectures.
61. Fisher, 1919, pp. 221–2.
62. Lambert, 2007, pp. 306–16.
63. Avner Offer, *The First World War: An Agrarian Interpretation*, Oxford, Oxford UP, 1989, on the development of blockade and Fisher's thinking, pp. 237–9, 252. Black, 2009, p. 119.
64. Diary 10 February 1915: CBT43/14.
65. Diary 10–12 February 1915: CBT 43/14, and Richmond memo, 14 February 1915: FISR 5/25/4349. Corbett's influence on Richmond is clear.
66. Marder, 1952, pp. 143–5. Hunt, 1982, pp. 40–50.
67. The obvious explanation is that they were mirror-imaging British thinking.
68. Hankey to Fisher, 28 May 1917: Fisher, 1919, pp. 214–15. Fisher to Hankey, 28 May 1917: *FGDN*, III, p. 429.
69. Grimes, 2012, pp. 203–11. Mackay, 1974, 478. Dardanelles Memoirs by Charles Callwell, 3 September 1914 and Rear Admiral Henry Jackson, 5 January 1915: FISR f. 4346.
70. Michael Forrest, *The Defence of the Dardanelles*, Barnsley, Pen & Sword, 2012, pp. 80–3.
71. *NO*, II, p. 105.
72. Fisher Cabinet memo, 25 January 1915: *Churchill Companion*, III, pp. 263–4. Diary 25 January 1915: CBT43/14 for authorship.
73. Diary 13 August 1914: Liddle Collection: Schurman, 1981, p. 158.
74. Mackay, 1974, pp. 482, 45–6.
75. David French, *British Strategic and Economic Planning 1905-1915*, London, Allen & Unwin, 1982, p. 74–8.
76. Schurman, 1981, p. 161; see also CAB 24/1 of 5 February 1915.
77. Diary 4 February 1915: CBT 43/14. CAB 42/1/32. Roskill, 1970, I, p. 162. Corbett to Hankey, 4 February 1915: The Dardanelles, Secret. Churchill's copy of the paper is: CHAR 2/89/3.

78. Roskill, 1970, I, pp. 163–8.
79. *Churchill Companion*, III, p. 324. See Buxton, 2008, for the completion dates of these ships.
80. Corbett to Fisher, 1 March 1915 and Fisher to Churchill, 15 March 1915: *Churchill Companion*, III, part one pp. 604–5 and 698. See also CBT 7/4 and Diary 1–3 March 1915: CBT 43/14. This suggests Fisher had read the *Russo-Japanese War* text.
81. There is no evidence to support the assertion that Fisher was either mad or senile.
82. Fisher to Corbett, 3 May 1918: *FGDN*, III, pp. 532–3.
83. Mackay, 1985, pp. 263, 270–3, 290.
84. *The First Report of the Dardanelles Commission*, part 1, Command 8490, London, HMSO, 1917, pp. 13–14. CAB 19/1.
85. Diary 19 May 1916: CBT 43/15.
86. Bassford, 1994, p. 80 demonstrates the insubordinate, unconstitutional contempt in which 'Wully' Robertson, CIGS, held his civilian 'masters'. He was not alone: the clash of culture between liberal progressive civilians and social conservatives with serious status anxieties was profound.
87. Diary 1 August 1917: CBT 43/16.
88. Hankey to Corbett, 28 September 1916: CBT 43/15. Original MS letter in the opening pages of the 1916 diary.
89. Delivered on 4 October, in a crammed room at King's College London, with Prince Louis in the chair, the lecture was 'quite a success'.
90. Diary 29 September–12 October 1916: CBT 43/15.
91. Churchill's copy, 'The Cabinet and the Conduct of War': Confidential: CHAR 2/73/5.
92. Diary 19–20 July 1916: CBT 43/15.
93. Diary 27 June–7 July 1916: CBT 43/15.
94. Langhorne Gibson and John E.T. Harper, *The Riddle of Jutland: An Authentic History*, London, Cassell, 1934, pp. 277–86.
95. Schurman, 1981, pp. 167–9. Diary 29–30 November 1916: CBT 43/15.
96. Fisher to Jellicoe, 25 May 1916: *FGDN*, III, pp. 350–1.
97. I am indebted to Michael Clemmesen for this reference. He has demonstrated that the new defences were planned in October 1915.
98. *NO*, III, p. 136 on the incident of 19 August 1915.
99. Christopher Bell, *Churchill and Sea Power*, Oxford, Oxford UP, 2013, pp. 169–82.
100. Diary 27 June–1 July 1916 and 14 July 1917: CBT 43/15 and 16.
101. Diary 16 November 1917: CBT 43/16. Kerr, later Lord Lothian.
102. News cutting of 20 December 1917 in Corbett's 1917 Diary: CBT 43/16, and Justin Fantuzzo, 'The Finest Feats of the War? The Captures of Baghdad and Jerusalem during the First World War and Public Opinion throughout the British Empire', *War in History* 24(1), 2017, pp. 64–86, at p. 65.
103. Corbett to Fisher, 12 June 1918: *FGDN*, III, pp. 538–9. Written in response to Fisher's paper 'The Strangest Thing in the War', passed to him by George Aston. Fisher warned him the Dardanelles issue was politically complicated, Fisher to Corbett, 15 June 1918: FISR 3/19/3212.
104. Diary 29 December 1920, 16 and 24 February 1921, 16 March 1921: CBT 43/19 and 20. Lambert spoke in the House of Commons on the subject. A year later he recruited Henry Sidebottom: Lambert to Austen Chamberlain, 2 December 1921: AC 7/1B/7, Chamberlain MS, Cadbury Library, University of Birmingham. Admiral Sir Reginald Bacon's book appeared in 1929.

17 Propaganda, Peace and the Liberal Empire

1. *Some Principles*, pp. 90–6, 190, 284. Bernard Semmel, *Liberalism and Naval Strategy: Ideology, Interest and Sea Power during the Pax Britannica*, London, Allen & Unwin, 1986, p. 98.
2. This conundrum explains Corbett's enduring interest in the American War.

3. H.W. Carless Davis, *The Political Thought of Heinrich von Treitschke*, Oxford, Oxford UP, 1914, dissected the deep roots of German Anglophobia. He was unaware of the links between Treitschke and Tirpitz.

4. See Hugh Trevor-Roper, 'Jacob Burckhardt', Master-mind lecture, *Proceedings of the British Academy* 70, 1984, pp. 359–78 for an elegant exposition of the defects of German scholarship.

5. M. Stibbe, *German Anglophobia and the Great War, 1914–1918*, Cambridge, Cambridge UP, 2008, pp. 70–1, 96–7, 177, 206. Oswald Spengler responded to Germany's defeat by arguing the West was declining. Kennedy, 1980, is the classic study; see, pp. 462–3 for 1914.

6. In July 1909 Corbett read Masterman's *Condition of England*; 'if not too deep it is a suggestive book – poetic or prophetic', 6 July 1909: CBT 43/9.

7. G.M. Messinger, *British Propaganda and the State in the First World War*, Manchester, Manchester UP, 1992, p. 25.

8. Report, 7 September 1914: CFGM 53/3/1, Charles Masterman MS, Cadbury Library, University of Birmingham.

9. J.D. Squiers, *British Propaganda at Home and in the United States from 1914 to 1917*, Cambridge, MA, Harvard UP, 1935, pp. 27–8.

10. Report, 7 June 1915: CFGM 53/3/2, Masterman MS. W.M. McNeil, *Arnold Toynbee: A Life*, Oxford, Oxford UP, 1989, pp. 72–81.

11. Royal Mail Steam Packet Company to Gossop, 30 February 1918: CFGM 32/2/4/4, Masterman MS.

12. C. Sylvest, *British Liberal Internationalism, 1880–1930: Making Progress?*, Manchester, Manchester UP, 2009, p. 161.

13. Corbett to Newbolt, 31 August 1901: CBT 3/7/5.

14. Julian Corbett, 'The Capture of Private Property at Sea', *The Nineteenth Century*, June 1907.

15. John Coogan, 'The Short-war Illusion Resurrected: The Myth of Economic War as the British Schlieffen Plan', *Journal of Strategic Studies* 38(7), December 2015, pp. 1045–64.

16. Otte, 2020, p. 578.

17. Karl Liebknecht, *Militarismus and Antimilitarismus*, 1907: cited in Dirk Bonker, *Militarism in Global Age*, Ithaca, NY, Cornell UP, 2012, p. 1. Liebknecht predicted that the Kaiser's navy would cause a war.

18. D. Atkinson, 'Parker, Sir Gilbert George, 1860–1932', *ODNB* 35384.

19. Squiers, 1935, p. 56. Corbett read Parker's *In Old Quebec* when he visited in 1908: Schurman, 1981, p. 102.

20. For a full list of Wellington House output see Squiers, Dixon, the Regius Professor of English Language and Literature at Glasgow 1904–35, was a keen yachtsman.

21. Masterman Report, 29 December 1917: CFGM 53/6: CFGM 53/3/5.

22. Masterman to Bryce, 31 March 1915: Bryce MS Bodleian Library 242 f. 29.

23. Bureau Report, 7 June 1915: CFGM 53/3/2.

24. Parker to Corbett, 27 April 1915: CBT 14/5/9.

25. Diary 28 April–2 May 1915: CBT 43/14.

26. Parker to Corbett, 4 May 1915: CBT 14/5/5.

27. Diary 12–15 May 1915: CBT 43/14.

28. Squiers, 1935, p. 51.

29. Allen F. Westcott, 'The Lion's Changing Voice', *New York Times*, 30 May 1915. Westcott taught naval history at the United States Naval Academy, Annapolis.

30. For Wilson's Anglophobia see: William Still Jr, *Victory without Peace: The United States Navy in European Waters, 1919–1924*, Annapolis, MD, USNIP, 2018, pp. 33–4 et seq.

31. Adam Tooze, *The Deluge: The Great War and the Remaking of Global Order, 1916–1931*, London, Allen Lane, 2014, pp. 45, 120.

32. John Robert Ferris, 'The War Trade Intelligence Department and British Economic Warfare during the First World War', in Thomas Otte (ed.), *British World Policy and the Projection of Global Power, c.1830–1960*, Cambridge, Cambridge UP, 2019, pp. 24–45.

Archibald Colquhoun Bell, *History of the Blockade of Germany*, London, HMSO, completed 1937, printed 1961.

33. Gaynor Johnson, *Lord Robert Cecil: Politician and Internationalist*, Farnham, Ashgate, 2013, pp. 65–7.
34. Ibid., pp. 86–7.
35. Ibid., pp. 80–1.
36. P.J. Yearwood, *Guarantee of Peace: The League of Nations in British Policy, 1914–1925*, Oxford, Oxford UP, 2009, p. 27; and Johnson, 2013, pp. 82–3.
37. Herbert Richmond, *Statesmen and Seapower*, Oxford, Oxford UP, 1946, pp. 355–6. It is significant that Corbett's friend and follower delivered his statement of British strategic exceptionalism in Ford lectures thirty-nine years after Corbett.
38. Johnson, 2013, p. 86.
39. Masterman to Bryce, 3 and 10 April 1916: Bryce MS 242 ff. 32, 51a.
40. Masterman to Bryce, 3 November 1916: Bryce MS 284 ff. 116–18.
41. Corbett to Hankey, 22 December 1916: Corbett Papers, Queen's University Kingston Ontario: Box 13.
42. Brownrigg to Corbett, 25 January 1917, letter enclosed in Diary 1917: CBT 43/16.
43. Diary 26 January 1917: CBT 43/16.
44. Diary 30 January to 2–3 February 1917: CBT 43/16.
45. Diary 23–8 February 1917: CBT 43/16.
46. Julian Corbett, *The League of Peace and a Free Sea*, New York, George Doran, and London, Hodder & Stoughton, 1917.
47. Alexander Pearce-Higgins, *Defensively Armed Merchant Ships and Submarine Warfare*, London, Stevens, 1917, pp. 9–12 a text aimed at American lawyers using American precedents: see, pp. 43–4.
48. Prefatory Note in A.P. Newton (ed.), *The Sea Commonwealth and Other Essays*, London, Dent, 1919. See Yearwood, 2009, for Newton.
49. Newton, 1919, pp. 1–10.
50. Julian Corbett, 'The Paradox of Imperialism', *Monthly Review*, October 1900, pp. 1–14.
51. Newton, 1919, p. 3.
52. Ibid., pp. 8–10.
53. Ibid., p. 4.
54. Ibid., p. 7.
55. Corbett lost the original lecture notes, writing a new text in June–September 1918: CBT 43/17.
56. Cecil to Balfour, 20 November 1917: FO 371/3439; also Yearwood, 2009, pp. 75–9 and Johnson, 2013, p. 89.
57. Johnson, 2013, p. 89.
58. London, John Murray, 1917.
59. Yearwood, 2009, pp. 49–78. G.R. Crosby, *Disarmament and Peace in British Politics, 1914–1919*, Cambridge, MA, Harvard UP,1957, pp. 68–75.
60. Hankey diary 7 November 1917: Yearwood, 2009, p. 48.
61. Diary 24 November and 5 December 1917: CBT 43/16.
62. Corbett to Cecil, 5 December 1917: FO 371/3429, p. 70.
63. Yearwood, 2009, p. 50.
64. Diary 30 January 1918: CBT 43/17.
65. Diary 6 and 9 February 1918: CBT 43/17. Roskill, 1970, I, pp. 471, 482 and 500.
66. Diary 13 March 1918: CBT 43/17.
67. This approach was rejected by Cecil Hurst: Yearwood, 2009, pp. 76–7.
68. Diary 13–14 March 1918 and 9 May 1918: CBT 43/17. Corbett to Pollard, 19 and 26 May 1918: Pollard MS University of London Library 860/16/1.
69. Johnson, 2013, p. 90.
70. Ibid., p. 91. Yearwood, 2009, pp. 55, 75, 82.
71. Julian Corbett, *The League of Nations and Freedom of the Seas*, Oxford UP, 1918.

72. J. Bryce (ed.), *The League of Nations*, Oxford, UP, 1919, reprinted the best of these papers, including Corbett's.
73. Diary 13 April 1918: CBT 43/17.
74. Diary 14–20 April 1918: CBT 43/17. The proofs arrived on 6 June 1918. Printed in New York.
75. Corbett, 1918, p. 1.
76. Ibid., pp. 8–9.
77. Bruce Russell, *Prize Courts and U-boats: International Law at Sea and Economic Warfare during the First World War*, Dordrecht, Republic of Letters, 2009, pp. 205–11. The report is FO 800/920/11472.
78. Corbett, 1918, p. 2.
79. Ibid., p. 9, a typical example of Corbett's foresight, combining logic, legal insight and hard-won understanding of past practice. As he anticipated, the use of such 'embargoes' has been the key instrument of United Nations coercion.
80. Lloyd George to Eric Geddes (First Lord of the Admiralty then in Washington), 12 October 1918: FO 371/3493 file 169051, cited in D.F. Trask, *Captains and Cabinets: Anglo-American Naval Relations, 1917–1918*, Columbus, MO, Missouri UP, 1972, pp. 308–10.
81. Wemyss memo: ADM 1126/1771 cited in *FDSF*, V, p. 239. The similarity of expression is obvious.
82. Wemyss memo: ADM 1126/1771, cited in Trask, 1972, p. 320.
83. *FDSF*, V, p. 239: ADM 116/1804-10. Stephen Roskill, *Naval Policy between the Wars*, vol. I: *The Period of Anglo-American Antagonism, 1919–1929*, London, Collins, 1968, p. 82.
84. *FDSF*, V, p. 242.
85. Trask, 1972, pp. 325–6.
86. Ibid., p. 319.
87. Ibid., pp. 337–41.
88. Andrew Lambert, *The Challenge: Britain versus America in the Naval War of 1812*, London, Faber, 2012, pp. 383–401.
89. Roskill, 1968, I, pp. 53–4. Roskill, *Hankey: Man of Secrets*, vol. II, London, Collins, 1972, pp. 75–6.
90. Lloyd George to House, 3 November 1918: House MS cited in Trask, 1972, p. 341.
91. Diary 24 October 1918 and 4–14 November 1918: CBT 43/17.
92. *FDSF*, V, p. 239. Marder was unaware of Corbett's authorship.
93. Diary 29 November 1918: CBT 43/17.
94. *FDSF*, V, p. 243.
95. Trask, 1972, p. 329.
96. A. Walworth, *Wilson and his Peacemakers: American Diplomacy at the Paris Peace Conference, 1919*, New York, Norton, 1986, pp. 303–6. FO 800/215.
97. Walworth, 1986, p. 113.
98. P.O. Cohrs, *The Unfinished Peace after World War I: America, Britain and the Stability of Europe, 1919–1932*, Cambridge, Cambridge UP, 2006, pp. 43–4.
99. M. Macmillan, *The Peacemakers: The Paris Peace Conference 1919*, London, Murray, 2018, p. 189.
100. Cohrs, 2006, p. 45. CAB 25/14 and 25/42.
101. Tooze, 2014, pp. 269–70.
102. Roskill, 1968, I, pp. 53–4. Roskill, 1972, II, pp. 75–6.
103. Macmillan, 2018, p. 105.
104. Johnson, 2013, p. 108.
105. James Goldrick, 'Wemyss, Rosslyn Erskine', *ODNB* 36832.
106. *FDSF*, V, p. 242. Within days he suffered a disabling stroke.
107. Johnson, 2013, pp. 111, 166.
108. Reginald Custance, 'The Freedom of the Seas', *Proceedings of the United States Naval Institute* 45(11), 1919, pp. 1851–5.

109. Diary 13 January 1921–19 January 1921: CBT 43/20.
110. Diary 24 September 1915 and 24 October 1916: CBT 43/14 and 15. Corbett knew Ernest Swinton before the war. Diary 6 June 1911: CBT 43/10.

18 Naval Operations

1. Tuck to Richmond, 12 January 1934: TUCK 2/5 TUCK MS CCC. By 1934 Tuck had produced 'nine large volumes of what is practically the staff history, written by my own hand & based on my own research'.
2. Diary 5 and 10 August 1914: Liddle Collection.
3. 'Charles Letts's Popular One Day Diary 1914': Liddle Collection.
4. Julian Corbett, 'Napoleon after Trafalgar', Creighton Memorial Lecture, delivered 11 October 1921. Published in *Quarterly Review*, April 1922.
5. Details courtesy of my student James Ulry.
6. *FDSF*, V, pp. 306, 362.
7. Diary 20 May 1920: CBT 43/19.
8. Schurman, 1981, pp. 163–95, rehearses the process from Corbett's perspective. For Jellicoe and Captain John Harper's assessments of the Jutland dispute see: A. Temple Patterson (ed.), *The Jellicoe Papers* (hereafter *Jellicoe Papers*), 2 vols, London, NRS, 1966–8, pp. 399–490.
9. Cuttings and notes in the 1920 Diary from *Punch*, *The Times* and the *Pall Mall Gazette*: CBT 43/20.
10. *Seven Years' War*, I, pp. 3–4.
11. Corbett, 'Napoleon after Trafalgar'. Julian Corbett (unsigned) 'Methods of Discussion', *Naval Review* 8, 1920, pp. 322–4.
12. Corbett, 'Staff Histories', in Corbett and Edwards, 1914, and *Russo-Japanese War*.
13. Colonel Edmond Y. Daniel, 'Official Histories', 3 September 1919, Cabinet memo: CAB 103/83, p. 3.
14. Ibid., p. 4.
15. Ibid., p. 3. Slade, Hankey, Daniel and Corbett were colleagues and friends.
16. Ibid., p. 3.
17. Diary 27 June–1 July 1916 and 14 July 1917: CBT 43/15 and 16.
18. Corbett to Admiral Sir Alexander Bethell, Commander-in-Chief Channel Fleet, 29 August 1914: Bethell MS LHCMA 4–5.
19. Marder, 1952, p. 156.
20. Daniel to Secretary of the University Extensions Delegation, Oxford, 5 November 1923: TUCK 2/5 CCC.
21. Corbett's Diary makes constant reference to Tuck and his work from 1912.
22. Bellairs and Asquith, 27 April 1915: House of Commons Debates, *Hansard* vol. 71, col. 560.
23. Hankey memo, 23 December 1915: CAB 103/68, p. 4.
24. Diary 20–22 December 1915: CBT 43/14. Hankey memo 23 December 1915: CAB 103/68, pp. 8 and 9.
25. Corbett, 'Staff Histories', in Corbett and Edwards, 1914, p. 24.
26. The official histories would be handled by several publishing houses, mainstream and academic.
27. Official Histories, Confidential 238-B. Edmond Y. Daniel, 3 September 1919: CAB 103/83, pp. 4, 6.
28. 'Historical Section of the Committee of Imperial Defence', Daniel memo, 8 June 1917: CAB 24/4.
29. John W. Fortescue, *British Statesmen in the Great War 1793–1814*, Oxford, Oxford UP, 1911: the 1911 Ford lectures. Corbett's copy IHR collection. For criticism of Henry Dundas's West Indies campaigns, pp. 95–117.
30. Churchill statement to the War Council of 28 January 1915: *Churchill Companion*, III, part 1, p. 463.

31. Diary 16 March 1916: CBT 43/15. Schurman, 1981, p. 165.
32. Ibid., p. 176.
33. 'Imperial Concentration 1914', four lectures, War College, Greenwich, 8–11 March 1920: CBT 23/3.
34. Established by wealthy brewer Sir Richard Charles Garton MP in 1912 to study international relations, with a focus on the relationship between military and political power and social conditions. The other trustees were Arthur Balfour and Lord Esher.
35. Daniel, 1919: CAB 103/83, p. 5. The maritime volumes were published by Longman; Blackwood and Murray handled the army and trade volumes.
36. House of Commons Debates, 28 June 1916: *Hansard* vol. 83, cols 838–9. Hurd, later Sir Archibald (1869–1959), was a noted pre-war writer on naval and maritime issues. He remained on the staff of the CID between 1918 and 1926.
37. Daniel, 1919: CAB 103/83, p. 9.
38. Bell, 1961.
39. Edward Breck, review of Fayle, *Seaborne Trade*, vol. I, *American Historical Review* 26(3), 1921, pp. 531–3. Breck lamented the lack of a similar Historical Section in America.
40. Daniel, 1919: CAB 103/83, pp. 4, 6.
41. Hunt, 1982, ch. 4. Marder, 1952, pp. 235–79; Diary 5–8 June 1917: CBT 43/17.
42. Wemyss to Corbett, 14 April 1917: CBT 13/3/74. A charming and personal letter from the Commander-in-Chief East Indies and Egypt, promising to help write up the naval role in the Arab Revolt.
43. Diary 26 February 1918: CBT 43/17.
44. Schurman, 1981, p. 179.
45. Daniel, 8 June 1917: CAB 24/4, p. 4.
46. Davis (1874–1928), later Regius Professor of History at Oxford, did not complete his 'History of the Blockade'.
47. Hankey, Confidential Note, 11 June 1917: CAB 24/4, p. 1.
48. Schurman, 1981, p. 178.
49. CID Official History of the War, Proceedings of the Sub-committee, 24 July 1918: CAB 24/60, p. 1.
50. Daniel report to sub-committee, 22 July 1918, Daniel, 1919: CAB 103/83, p. 4.
51. Diary 26 February 1918: CBT 43/17.
52. Corbett referred to 'our plan', which he cleared with Maurice, Diary 4 April 1918: CBT 43/17.
53. Daniel, 1919: CAB 103/83, p. 4, clause 19. Herbert A.L. Fisher, *An Unfinished Autobiography*, Oxford, UP, 1940, pp. 89–128.
54. Diary 21 February 1918: CBT 43/17.
55. The Americans visited on 15 May, Diary: CBT 43/17.
56. Sims to Corbett, 9 October 1918: CBT 1/2/36.
57. Jellicoe to Corbett, 1 February 1919 and Corbett's endorsement: CBT 7/15. *Jellicoe Papers*, II, p. 324. See pp. 283, 400–3, 412–19 for correspondence with Corbett. Diary 29 January 1919 and 1 February 1919: CBT 43/18.
58. Corbett memo, 3 February 1919: CAB 103/97. Diary 2 February 1919: CBT 43/18.
59. The diaries chronicle his ailments in unsparing detail.
60. Diary 29 March and 6 April 1919: CBT 43/18.
61. Diary 9–10 April 1919: CBT 43/18.
62. Creedy (1878–1973), a high-flying civil servant with a double first from Oxford, understood Churchill's concerns.
63. 'Official Histories' memo by Churchill, 8 April 1919; draft response by Leetham, n.d. and Sir Herbert Creedy, 10 June 1919; Leetham draft response, 21 June 1919: WO 32/4825.
64. Diary 9 July 1919: CBT 43/18.
65. Hankey to Corbett, 8 August 1919: Corbett MS LHCMA.
66. Diary 15–30 August 1919: CBT 43/17.
67. Admiralty Board minutes, 19 August 1919: ADM 167/56, minute 927.
68. Hankey to Daniel, 26 August 1919: CAB 103/82.

69. Hankey to Daniel, 27 August 1919: CAB 103/82. Roskill, 1972, II, chs 2 and 3.
70. Diary 19 August–10 September 1919: CBT 43/19.
71. Daniel to Hankey, 3 September 1919: CAB 103/82.
72. Daniel, 1919: CAB 103/83, p. 4.
73. Roskill, 1972, II, pp. 125–6. 'Official Histories', Confidential 238-B. Daniel, 3 September 1919: CAB 103/83.
74. Churchill paraphrased this passage in the Preface to *The World Crisis*. See *Churchill Companion*, III, part 3, 1975, p. 758.
75. Daniel, 1919: CAB 103/83, part 4, pp. 9–14.
76. Diary 4 September 1919: CBT 43/18.
77. Diary 23 September 1919: CBT 43/18.
78. Diary 23 October 1919: CBT 43/18.
79. Diary 28 October 1919: CBT 43/18. Roskill, 1972, II, p. 126.
80. Green, 2003, pp. 6–10.
81. Admiralty Board minutes, 6 and 10 November 1919: ADM 167/56, minute 1042.
82. Diary 23–6 November 1919: CBT 43/18.
83. Diary 5–8 December 1919: CBT 43/18.
84. Green, 2003, p. 9.
85. *NO*, I, Appendix D, pp. 441–2.
86. Daniel to Edmonds, 13 April 1920: CAB 103/97.
87. M. Gilbert, *Winston S. Churchill, 1917–1922*, London, Heinemann, 1975, ch. 41, pp. 750–9 ignores Churchill's 1919 attack on Corbett's text.
88. Churchill to Jackson, 22 July 1921: *Churchill Companion*, IV, pp. 1562–3.
89. Diary 5 March 1918: CBT 43/17.
90. Corbett to Hamilton, 18 March 1918: LHCMA Hamilton 13/28. See Ian Hamilton, *Gallipoli Diary*, 2 vols, London, Edward Arnold, 1920, vol. I, pp. 133, 146, 164–7 for these points.
91. Corbett to Hamilton, 20 March 1918: LHCMA Hamilton 13/28.
92. Diary 26 and 28 March 1918: CBT 43/17.
93. Corbett to Hamilton, 11 May 1918: LHCMA Hamilton 13/28.
94. Corbett to Hamilton, 7 May 1918: LHCMA Hamilton 13/28.
95. Hamilton to Corbett, 13 May 1918, typed flimsy: LHCMA Hamilton 13/28.
96. Corbett to Hamilton, 14 May 1918: LHCMA Hamilton 13/28. Hamilton to Corbett, 24 May 1918, 1 Hyde Park Gardens: CBT 14/3/31.
97. Corbett to Hamilton, 25 May 1918: LHCMA Hamilton 13/28. Hamilton, 1920, I, pp. 157–8.
98. Hamilton to Corbett, 19 and 21 March 1919, copy, and Corbett to Hamilton, 20 March 1919: LHCMA Hamilton 13/28.
99. Fisher to Corbett, 15 June 1918: FISR 3/19/3212.
100. Diary 28 October 1919: CBT 43/18; Corbett to Hamilton, 17 October 1919: LHCMA Hamilton 13/28.
101. Keyes to Corbett: HMS *Douglas*, Dover, 19 October 1919: CBT 13/3/43.
102. Diary 10 March 1921: CBT 43/20.
103. Green, 2003, pp. 90–3. Appointed in February 1919, and commissioned as captain, Gordon fell ill on a visit to Gallipoli and only produced three introductory chapters in four years. He resigned on becoming Professor of English Literature at Leeds University.
104. Fortescue's pre-war Army histories reflected the General Staff focus on continental war, dismissing maritime strategy and amphibious operations as distractions. Forrest, 2012, pp. 138–9.
105. Corbett to Hamilton, 29 May 1920: LHCMA Hamilton 18/5/32. Congratulations also came from John de Robeck, Roger Keyes and Spenser Wilkinson.
106. Corbett to Hamilton, 15, 17 and 20 July 1920. Hamilton to Corbett, 16 and 19 July 1920, copy: LHCMA Hamilton 13/28.
107. Corbett to Hamilton, 27 October 1920; Hamilton to Corbett, 30 October 1920: LHCMA Hamilton 13/28. Hamilton, 1920, II, p. 58. General C.F. Aspinall-Oglander, *Military*

Operations: Gallipoli, 2 vols, London, Heinemann, 1929–32 blamed General Sir Frederick Stopford and Hamilton for the delay in exploiting the landing at Suvla.

108. Keyes to Corbett, 8 May 1921: CBT 13/3/42-7; also *Keyes Papers*, II, pp. 53–4. See also 'Two pages from Private Journal of Keyes', in Brian Tunstall's hand, pp. 22 and 23: CBT 13/3/45.
109. Keyes to Corbett, 6 December 1921: CBT 13/3/44. *Keyes Papers*, II, pp. 66–75.
110. Hamilton to Corbett, 9 November 1921, flimsy: LHCMA Hamilton 13/28.
111. Corbett to Hamilton, 10 November 1921: LHCMA Hamilton 13/28.
112. Diary 16 November 1921: CBT 43/20. They discussed the evacuation which Corbett was then writing up. Corbett to Hamilton, 4 December 1921, LHCMA Hamilton 13/28.
113. Hamilton to Corbett, n.d. Friday (the close link to Corbett's of 4 December makes 9 December 1921 the most likely date): CBT 14/3/32.
114. Corbett to Keyes, 10 May 1922: *Keyes Papers*, II, p. 74.
115. This assessment is confirmed in Mackay, 1985; see pp. 278–88 for Balfour's struggle to sustain the Gallipoli campaign as First Lord of the Admiralty.
116. *FDSF*, V, p. 341 and Mackay, 1985, p. 306.
117. Corbett to Keyes, 10 February 1922: *Keyes Papers*, II, pp. 74–5.
118. Diary 19, 20, 25 and 27 May 1922: CBT 43/21.
119. Corbett to Keyes, 29 May 1922: *Keyes Papers*, II, pp. 74–5. He also pressed Keyes to ensure the papers were preserved. 'The letters &c. are such valuable historical material that I hope you have a copy of it all. They would leave a big hole in the story if they were lost.' Marder used them in *FDSF*, II, 1965: see fn 26, p. 326. Roger Keyes, *The Naval Memoirs of Admiral of the Fleet Sir Roger Keyes*, 2 vols, London, Thornton, 1934–5, vol. I, reflected Keyes' aggressive spirit, his absolute conviction that a second naval attack would succeed, and his contempt for cautious men and measures.
120. Diary 21 June 1922: CBT 43/21.
121. Diary 5 March 1918: CBT 43/17.

19 Explaining the Unpalatable Truth

1. Corbett to Sir George Aston, 23 May 1918: Aston MS LHCMA. Aston was not convinced, he preferred absolute dominion.
2. Corbett's Diary between January 1919 and April 1920 demonstrates that he was not working on Jutland, the second phase at Gallipoli, or anything else covered in volume III.
3. Diary 31 May 1920: CBT 43/19.
4. Corbett to Newbolt, 12 November 1920: CBT 3/7/92.
5. *NO*, III, pp. 84, 87, 92–3.
6. Ibid., pp. 106–7, citing Liman von Sanders, *Fünf Jähre Turkei*, p. 116.
7. Corbett began reading Sarrail's *Mon Commandement en Orient, 1916–1918*, Paris, E. Flammarion, 1920, on 29 January 1921: CBT 43/20. Keyes, 1936, I, adds telling detail here, pp. 426–7, 521–2.
8. *NO*, III, pp. 108–11.
9. Ibid., pp. 144, 154–5. Erich von Falkenhayn, *General Headquarters, 1914–1916 and Its Critical Decisions*, London, Hutchinson, 1919, p. 133. See also Robert Foley, *German Strategy and the Path to Verdun: Erich von Falkenhayn and the Development of Attrition, 1870–1916*, Cambridge, Cambridge UP, 2005.
10. *NO*, III, p. 165.
11. Ibid., pp. 219, 223 and 246.
12. Diary 31 May 1920: CBT 43/18.
13. Wemyss to Corbett, 15 February 1922: CBT 13/3/73.
14. *NO*, III, pp. 221, 240.
15. Corbett discussed this campaign with T.E. Lawrence on 31 March 1919; Lawrence 'Spoke highly of Wemyss': CBT 43/18.
16. Wemyss to Corbett, 14 April 1917: CBT 13/3/74 provides a useful *résumé* of the Red Sea Campaign.

17. *NO*, III, pp. 243–4.
18. Ibid., pp. 257–8.
19. Both Wemyss's and Keyes' memoirs were based on letters and papers that Corbett had used. Lord Wester Wemyss, *The Navy in the Dardanelles*, London, Hodder & Stoughton, 1924. Keyes, 1934–5, 'the underlying theme of vol. I (1910–1915) is "If only de Robeck had taken my advice"': *FDSF*, V, pp. 384–5. Aspinall-Oglander, 1929–32, and his authorised *Roger Keyes*, London, Hogarth Press, 1951, repeated positions both men had adopted in the 1930s.
20. Wemyss, 1924, pp. 247–84, quote at p. 284.
21. The 'steady pressure' paper refers to Fisher memorandum, 'On the possibility of using our Command of the Sea to influence more drastically the Military Situation on the Continent', n.d., sent to Churchill on 2 January 1915: *Churchill Companion*, III, part 1, pp. 284–7. Fisher Cabinet memorandum, 25 January 1915: *Churchill Companion*, III, part 1, pp. 263–4. Diary 25 January 1915: CBT 43/14.
22. Corbett to Jellicoe, 13 February 1919: Add. MS 49,037 f. 128.
23. Jellicoe's side of the story was published in *Jellicoe Papers*, I, pp. 458–90.
24. Marder, 1952, p. 361.
25. Beatty to Corbett, 12 August 1920: Corbett MS LHCMA.
26. Beatty to Corbett, 17 August 1920: Corbett MS LHCMA.
27. Diary 9–18 August 1920: CBT 43/19. Jellicoe to Corbett, 16 August 1920: Corbett MS LHCMA.
28. Diary 3–4 September 1920: CBT 43/19.
29. Corbett to Jellicoe 13 June 1921: Add. MS 49,037 ff. 162–3. Modern sensors proved Harper's charts were highly accurate. See Innes Macartney, *Jutland: The Archaeology of a Naval Battlefield*, London, Bloomsbury, 2016, for the latest survey of the battlefield, and Brooks, 2016, for the battle. Diary 19 August 1921: CBT 43/20.
30. W. Schleihauf and S. McLaughlin (eds), *Jutland: The Naval Staff Appreciation*, Barnsley, Seaforth, 2016.
31. Dewar to Corbett, 15 February 1917: CBT 13/3/24. He was effusive about Corbett's concept of control of communications. On 31 May 1916 Dewar commanded a monitor at Great Yarmouth. Buxton, 2008, pp. 31–2.
32. Diary 6 October 1921: CBT 43/20. Schleihauf and McLaughlin, 2016, p. 208. Stephen Roskill, *Admiral of the Fleet Earl Beatty: The Last Naval Hero: An Intimate Biography*, London, Collins, 1980, p. 333.
33. Corbett, 'Napoleon after Trafalgar'.
34. Schleihauf and McLaughlin, 2016, p. 208. Approximately 100 copies were produced,
35. Director of Training and Staff Duties (DTSD) to Pollen, 28 November 1921: NMM BTY /9/5.
36. Diary 17 October 1921: CBT 43/20.
37. Diary 23 December 1921: CBT 43/20.
38. Diary 15, 24 and 27 February 1922, and 10 March 1922: CBT 43/21. Captain Haggard DTSD to Corbett, 23 February 1922: BTY /9/5. Schleihauf and McLaughlin, 2016, p. xxiv.
39. Corbett to Jellicoe, 10 March 1922: Add. MS 49,037 ff. 172–3. For Harper's papers see *Jellicoe Papers*, II, pp. 458–90.
40. Harper to Admiralty, 3 June 1927: *Jellicoe Papers*, II, p. 482.
41. Schleihauf and McLaughlin, 2016, pp. 10–12.
42. Diary 15 March 1922: CBT 43/21.
43. Diary 21 March 1922: CBT43/21.
44. Diary 31 March 1922: CBT 43/21.
45. Diary 6–10 April 1922: CBT 43/21.
46. Diary 12 April–11 May 1922: CBT 43/21.
47. Diary 13–20 June 1922: CBT 43/21.
48. Corbett to Jellicoe, 19 June 1922: Add. MS 49,037 ff. 177–9. There is no evidence of a reply. Lord Jellicoe, *The Grand Fleet 1914–16*, London, Cassell, 1919. The second edition was never published.

49. Corbett to Jellicoe, 18 July 1922: Add. MS 49,037 f. 182. Diary 17–8 July 1922: CBT 43/21. Corbett's innate modesty makes the claim compelling.
50. Memo by Director of Training and Staff Duties [DTSD] to First Sea Lord (Beatty) and Deputy Chief of Naval Staff [DCNS] (Roger Keyes), 26 July 1922: *Beatty Papers*, II, pp. 454–5.
51. Diary 27 July 1922: CBT 43/21.
52. Corbett to Jellicoe, 3 August 1922: Add. MS 49,037 f. 183.
53. Haggard (DSTD) to 1SL and DCNS, 26 July 1922: *Beatty Papers*, II, pp. 454–5.
54. Corbett to Jellicoe, 20 August 1922: Add. MS 49,037 ff. 186–7.
55. Schleihauf and McLaughlin, 2016, p. xxv.
56. Diary August–September 1922: CBT 43/21. Daniel to Jellicoe, 2 October 1922: Add. MS 49,037 ff. 189–90.
57. Admiralty docket M70047/23 Hist Sect H.S. 4 February 19C 21 Dec. 1922: 'Naval History by Sir Julian Corbett Proofs of Volume III Chapters XVI to XXI' (the Battle of Jutland) was evidently not returned to the Registry. The battered file shows evidence of heavy use: BTY /9/40. At a later date Beatty added proofs and a copy of Alfred Dewar's *Naval Review* notice of vol. III: BTY/9/4/9, pp. 286–300. Beatty MS NMM.
58. *NO*, III, p. 259.
59. Ibid., p. 273.
60. Ibid., pp. 274–5, citing Reinhard Scheer, *Germany's High Seas Fleet in the World War*, London, Cassell, 1920, p. 96. Taking command in January 1916, Scheer expected British resolve to harden, along with the economic blockade, because of the high cost of the conflict, 'and to compensate for the blunders made, such as the surrender of Antwerp and the abandonment of the Dardanelles enterprise'. The link between Scheer's remarks on Antwerp and Corbett's view of the subject in 1907 is compelling. *Seven Years' War*, I, pp. 74–5, 142.
61. *NO*, III, p. 279.
62. Ibid., pp. 280–1, 287.
63. For Tirpitz: Diary 30 November 1919–2 December 1919: CBT 43/18. For Scheer, Diary 7–8 April 1920: CBT 43/19.
64. *NO*, III, p. 314.
65. Ibid., p. 320.
66. French, 1982, p. 181.
67. *NO*, III, pp. 328–9, and *Trafalgar*, pp. 55–6. Corbett might have made use of the synergy between the positions of Jellicoe and Cornwallis at the crisis of the earlier 'Great War' in August 1805, when the British admiral had to content himself with driving the enemy back into port, to ensure it could not escape and threaten British sea control. Instead he linked Jutland with two famous battles, Trafalgar and the 'Glorious First of June' 1794, so his points would be understood without instructing readers to consult *Trafalgar*.
68. Scheer, 1920, p. 141.
69. Diary 24 January 1919: CBT 43/18. 'Long talk in which he said failure at Jutland was mainly due to our bad armour piercing shells.' *NO*, III, pp. 333–7.
70. *NO*, III, pp. 355–6, 360, 365, 373.
71. Ibid., p. 347.
72. Ibid., pp. 361, 368, 388, 407. Barrow, 1838, p. 232. Corbett owned a copy of this book.
73. *NO*, III, pp. 404–5.
74. Ibid., pp. 418, 30–31, 374 fn.
75. Gibson and Harper, 1934, pp. 383–4. Corbett's text was reinforced by the German Official History in 1925.
76. G.P. Gross, 'German Plans to Occupy Denmark "Case J" 1916–1918', in M. Clemmesen and G.P. Gross (eds), *The Danish Straits and German Naval Power 1905–1918*, Potsdam, Militärgeschictliches Forschungsamt, 2010, pp. 155–66.
77. *Seven Years' War*, II, pp. 1–4. *Trafalgar*, p. 274. In both cases the purpose of the discussion was current doctrine, not historical reflection.
78. *NO*, III, Introduction.
79. Keyes to Churchill, 2 November 1940: CHAR 20/5/82. Churchill MS, CCC.

80. Lambert, 2007, ch. 9.
81. *Keyes Papers*, II, pp. 85–90.
82. Kenneth Dewar to Keyes, 24 May 1932: *Keyes Papers*, II, pp. 88–9. Dewar made an equally ill-informed attack on Fisher's Baltic strategy.
83. Jellicoe to Daniel, 16 February 1923: *Jellicoe Papers*, II, 1968, p. 438.
84. Churchill to Keyes, 25 August 1924: *Keyes Papers*, II, p. 104. His indebtedness included following Dewar's misspelling of Major Hervey's name. Schleihauf and McLaughlin, 2016, p. xxvii, also Robin Prior, *The World Crisis as History*, London, Croom Helm, 1983, p. 308 fn 58.
85. Schleihauf and McLaughlin, 2016, p. xxvii. *Jellicoe Papers*, II, 1968, p. 482 n. See Hurd's introduction to Gibson and Harper, 1934, pp. viii–xi and p. 384.
86. H.A.L. Fisher to Lt Cmdr E. Hilton, Treasury Chambers, 11 October 1922: CAB 103/73. Fisher consistently favoured literary types over historians for the Official History project.
87. For surviving drafts and notes see: Preliminary Studies TUCK 4/5 CCC. The printed copy of what would become ch. 9 of vol. III, dealing with Salonica and the evacuation of the Serbian Army has Corbett's characteristic marginalia. TUCK 4/4 has material used in vol. I and also includes Corbett marginalia: CBT 43/14-21. See, for example, 22–5 February 1915: CBT 43/14.
88. Hunt, 1982, p. 119.
89. Henry Newbolt, *Naval Operations*, London, Longman, IV, 1929.
90. A. Colbeck, 'The Strategical Aspect of War Against Commerce', *Edinburgh Review*, October 1921, pp. 358–74, reviewing C.E. Fayle, *Seaborne Trade*, vol. I: *The Cruiser Period*, London, Murray, 1920; A. Hurd, *The Merchant Navy*, vol. I, London, Murray, 1921; and J.A. Hall, *The Law of Naval Warfare*, London, Chapman Hall, 1921.
91. Colbeck, 1921, p. 370, referenced an article by Admiral von Muller in *Deutsche Politik* of November 1919, and the original German edition of Tirpitz's *Memoirs*.
92. Corbett noted reading Tirpitz's *Memoirs* in his Diary 30 November 1919-2 December 1919: CBT 43/18.
93. Colbeck, 1921, p. 372. Corbett noted reading Castex on submarines on 27 February and 7 March 1921: CBT 43/20.
94. Colbeck, 1921, p. 373, citing R. Castex, 'L'Envers de la Guerre de Course', described as 'a fine example of methodical scholarship applied to polemical writing'.
95. A. Colbeck, 'Reflections on Sir Julian Corbett's Official History', *JRUSI* 67, 1922, pp. 326–35.
96. Bradley Fiske, review of *Naval Operations*, vol. I, *American Historical Review* 26(1), 1920, pp. 94–6.
97. Edward Breck, review of *Seaborne Trade*, vol. I, *American Historical Review* 26(3), 1921, pp. 531–3.
98. Edward Breck, review of *Naval Operations*, vol. III, *American Historical Review* 29(3), 1924, pp. 556–8.
99. Aston review: *EHR*, 1924, pp. 301–4.

20 Carrying On

1. Sidney Colvin (1845–1927), Slade Professor of Art at Cambridge 1873–85. Colvin was a friend of Richard Claverhouse Jebb and director of the Fitzwilliam Museum until 1884, when he became Keeper of Prints and Drawings at the British Museum, remaining until his retirement in 1912. He was on familiar terms with the leading literary and artistic figures, from Matthew Arnold and John Ruskin to Edward Burne-Jones, Robert Louis Stevenson and Joseph Conrad. E.V. Lucas, *The Colvins and Their Friends*, London, Methuen, 1928. From 1912 Colvin lived in Kensington, close to Corbett.
2. Diary 28 May 1908 and 18 January 1909: CBT 43/7 and 8.
3. Diary 27 April 1918 and 1 May 1918: CBT 43/17. The cottage was rented from artist Rex Vicat Cole.

4. Diary 11 and 17 September 1918: CBT 43/17.
5. This was on 16 September 1918: Alice Elgar Diary 1918: Martin Bird Transcript, Elgar Birthplace Museum.
6. Diary 11–29 September 1918: CBT 43/17.
7. Diary 22 and 26 September 1918: CBT 43/17. Alice Elgar Diary.
8. Elgar to Colvin 26 September 1918: Elgar Birthplace Museum EB 3476. See also L. Foreman (ed.), *The Music of Elgar*, vol. II: *'Oh My Horses!' Elgar and the Great War*, Rickmansworth, Elgar Editions, 2001, pp. 225, 450.
9. On 16, 21 and 25 September 1919: Alice Elgar Diary 1918: Elgar Birthplace Museum.
10. Diary 8 February 1920: Edward Elgar Diary 1920: Elgar Birthplace Museum.
11. Diary 8 February 1920: CBT 43/19.
12. Elgar to Colvin, 5 February 1920: Jerrold Northrop Moore (ed.), *Edward Elgar: Letters of a Lifetime*, Oxford, Clarendon Press, 1990, p. 374.
13. Corbett's letter of condolence is both heartfelt and reflective of a deep friendship: Corbett to Elgar, 9 April 1920. Elgar MS Letter 592 Condolence Box.
14. Elgar to Corbett, 28 October 1920: CBT 14/4/35.
15. Corbett to Elgar, 29 and 31 October 1920: Letter 6001, 6005, Elgar Birthplace Museum.
16. Carice Elgar Diary August–September 1921: Martin Bird Transcript, Elgar Birthplace Museum. Elgar to Edith, 1921 n.d.: CBT 14/4/34.
17. Diary 24 January 1920, 6 May 1920: CBT 43/19.
18. Diary 23 January 1920: CBT 43/19; 12 November 1921: CBT 43/20. The school in question was Winchester.
19. Diary 2–5 November 1920: CBT 43/19. On 21 January 1921 he noted: 'Richard in bed with school sickness': CBT 43/20.
20. Diary 4–6 June 1922: CBT 43/21.
21. Brian Bond, *The Unquiet Western Front: Britain's Role in Literature and a History*, Cambridge, Cambridge UP, 2002, pp. 102–8 for Sir Lees Knowles (1857–1928) and the lectures he founded at Trinity College on the last day of 1912.
22. On 16 February 1917 Corbett attended the University of London Board of Historical Studies with many of his academic friends: Diary: CBT 43/16.
23. Diary 20 March 1918: CBT43/17.
24. Diary 15 February 1918: CBT 43/17.
25. NRS Annual General Meeting, 30 June 1913: NRS/3, p. 1. Although he was never Hon. Secretary, the minutes are in Corbett's hand. He had been editing the minutes since Laughton held the office.
26. Herbert Richmond edited two more *Spencer* volumes, part of his work to secure Corbett's legacy.
27. Diary 8, 10 and 25 July 1920; 28 February 1921; 17 February 1922 and 14 June 1922: CBT 43/19-21.
28. V.S.T. Harmsworth, Rothermere's second son, had retired from the Navy as a midshipman due to gun deafness, and had been due to go to Trinity College in Michaelmas term 1914. Instead he joined the Royal Naval Division and went to Antwerp. Interned after the city fell, he escaped and rejoined the division. He served through Gallipoli and on the Western Front in Hawke Battalion: he was only 21.
29. D.G. Boyce, 'Harmsworth, Harold Sidney (1868–1940), *ODNB* 33718.
30. Rothermere to T.C. Fitzpatrick, Acting Vice Chancellor, 27 November 1918: CUR 39.52 f. 1.
31. Stephen W. Roskill, 'The Navy at Cambridge, 1919–23', *Mariner's Mirror* 49, 1963, pp. 178–91, at p. 188.
32. Rose to Fitzpatrick, 26 December 1918: CUR 39.52, Appendix, f. 1.
33. F.E. Adcock, revised by R. Small, 'Reid, James Smith', *ODNB* 35716.
34. Reid to President, 28 December 1918: CUR 39.52, Appendix 1, f. 2.
35. Diary 14 January 1920: CBT 43/19.
36. There are echoes of Corbett's 1916 Laughton Memorial Lecture.

37. John Holland Rose to Corbett, 1 January 1918 (clearly meant 1919): CBT 14/4/23.
38. John Holland Rose to Corbett, 6 January 1919: CBT 14/4/24.
39. Fitzpatrick to Shipley, 3 January 1919: CUR 32.50, Appendix 1, f. 2a. Sir Arthur Everett Shipley, Vice Chancellor of the University 1917–19, and Master of Christ's College 1910–27, was a prominent zoologist. *ODNB* 36069.
40. Corbett to Shipley, 12 January 1919: CUR 32.59, Appendix 1, f. 3.
41. Corbett to Shipley, 19 January 1919: CUR 32.59, Appendix 1, f. 5.
42. Rose to Shipley, 12 January 1919: CUR 32.59, Appendix 1, f. 4.
43. Richmond to Corbett, 24 January 1919: CBT 13/1/14.
44. Pollen to Shipley, 11 January 1919: CUR 32.59, Appendix 1, f. 6.
45. Hall reference, 13 January 1919, in Pollen to Shipley, 15 January 1919: CUR 32.59, Appendix 1, f. 8.
46. Smuts to Shipley, 19 January 1919: CUR 32.59, Appendix 1, f. 9.
47. Wilson to Shipley, 7 May 1919: CUR 32.59, Appendix 1, ff. 15 and 15b.
48. Diary 2–5 February 1919: CBT 43/18.
49. Diary 14 and 20 April 1919 and 21 May 1919: CBT 43/18.
50. Diary 6 March and 29–31 May 1920: CBT 43/19.
51. Herbert Richmond Diary 18 May 1919: Marder, 1952, p. 343.
52. Corbett to Shipley, 26 April 1919: CUR 32.59, Appendix 1, f. 14.
53. CUR 39.52, f. 3. Four were members of the NRS.
54. Corbett to Thomson, 3 May 1920: Thomson MS CUL Add. 7674 C26.
55. Diary 28 May and 1 June 1919: CBT 43/18.
56. *Laughton*, pp. 212–13, 225. Pollard, an NRS councillor was also involved in the Congress of Historical Sciences. In 1903 Pollard used naval history as the leading argument for the projected 'School of Advanced Historical Studies', which became the IHR. D.J. Birch and J.M. Horn (eds), *The History Laboratory: The Institute of Historical Research 1921–1996*, London, IHR, 1996, p. 3.
57. A.F. Pollard, *The Claims of Historical Research*, pamphlet, London, 1920.
58. *Trafalgar*, p. xii.
59. Lecture at King's, 1916, published as J.S. Corbett, 'The Revival of Naval History', *Contemporary Review* 110, December 1916, pp. 734–40.
60. J. Cecil Power to A.F. Pollard, 12 July 1920: cited in Birch and Horn, 1996, p. 8. Power provided £5,000.
61. Pollard memo: 'Joint Committee of University College, King's College and the School of Economics on Advanced Historical Studies', AC2 IHR MS para. 2 and 9. See Novick, 1998, pp. 120–1, 127: this link to propaganda work prompted some opposition to 'the pseudo-historian of the ultra-modern tendency'.
62. Pollard memo: para. 8.
63. Diary 30 June 1920: CBT 43/19. The dinner was held at the Athenaeum.
64. Diary 14 July 1920: CBT 43/19. Corbett to the Secretary of the University of London 17 February 1921: IHR XII correspondence 1921–26 C. Diary 2 March 1921: CBT 43/20.
65. Perrin to IHR, 5 February 1921: IHR I 10. Corbett to Miss Davies, 26 January 1921: IHR XII 1921–26 C.
66. Vice Chancellor to Corbett, 18 March 1921: IHR XII correspondence 1921–26 C.
67. Corbett to Miss Davies, 23 and 29 June 1921: IHR XII correspondence 1921–26 C.
68. Birch and Horn, 1996, p. 13.
69. Plan of buildings: ibid., p. 14.
70. *Morning Post*, 9 August 1921: Birch and Horn, 1996, p. 17.
71. Diary 11 July 1921: CBT 43/20.
72. In 1923 Lady Corbett, at Herbert Richmond's suggestion, agreed to loan half of Sir Julian's books to the IHR – a silent testament to his vision.
73. Diary 8 April 1921: CBT 43/20.
74. Corbett to Edith, 28 November 1911, dated RNWC Portsmouth: CBT 11/2/24.
75. Corbett to Edith, 12 June 1912, dated RNWC Portsmouth: CBT 11/3/20.

76. Reports do not specify where the lecture was held: the Great Hall was the only large lecture theatre in the college in 1921. *King's College Calendar, 1923–24*, p. 294, LHCMA, notes he was a Fellow of the Society of Arts (FSA), but not where he spoke.
77. 'Trafalgar and Jutland', *The Times*, 12 October 1921, p. 7. Quotes are from the report.
78. 'Napoleon after Trafalgar', p. 238.
79. Ibid., pp. 239–40.
80. Ibid., p. 241.
81. Ibid., p. 244.
82. Ibid., p. 247.
83. Ibid., p. 248.
84. Ibid., p. 253.
85. Ibid., p. 254.
86. Ibid., p. 255.
87. Captain John Kelly to Corbett, 12 November 1921: CBT 13/3/41.
88. Press cutting from the *Daily Telegraph* of 12 October 1921. A.P. Newton to Corbett, 13 October 1921: CBT 7/17. *Historical Records of the University of London 1856–1926*, London, 1926.
89. The *Quarterly* was no longer a Tory journal. Lambert, 2017, ch. 7: text, pp. 130–46.
90. Gollancz to Corbett, 14 December 1921: CBT 14/3/20.
91. Diary 9–11 September 1922: CBT 43/21.
92. Herbert Richmond, 'National Policy and Naval Strength, XVIth to XX Century', off-print from *Proceedings of the British Academy* 8, 1922.
93. 'Methods of Discussion', *Naval Review* 8, 1920, pp. 322–4.
94. 'United Services', *Naval Review* 11, 1923, pp. 210–14.
95. Course list reconstructed from ADM 203/100.
96. Hunt, 1982, pp. 107–20.
97. 'War from the Aspect of the Weaker Power', *Naval Review* 8, 1920, attributed to Lieutenant J.S. MacKenzie-Grieve RN, pp. 152–66, quote at p. 166.
98. Schurman, 1965, p. 183. *Morning Post*, 19 February 1912.
99. 'Methods of Discussion', p. 323.
100. Schurman, 1981, pp. 45, 57–8.
101. Corbett, 'Methods of Discussion', p. 324.
102. Jellicoe to Lady Corbett, 14 March 1923: CBT 7/15.
103. Daniel to Lady Corbett, 31 December 1934: CBT 7/13.
104. IHR Committee minutes, 27 September 1922, pp. 1–4. On 25 October 1922 the committee recorded receiving a letter of thanks from Lady Corbett.
105. IHR Committee minutes, 31 October 1923, p. 6.
106. Geoffrey Callender to Charles Corbett, 23 September 1922: CBT 14/2/1.

Conclusion

1. Diary 1 August 1917: CBT 43/16. Strachan, 2013, p. 141 restores the credit to Corbett.
2. In the wars between 1688 and 1815, British statesmen had always specified the level of military commitment to their continental allies.
3. Heuser, 2010; Strachan, 2013.
4. Friedrich Nietzsche, 'The Use and Abuse of History', trans. Adrian Collins, New York, Liberal Arts Press, 1957, p. 40 (originally publishined as *Vom Nutzen und Nachteil der Historie für das Leben*, 1874).
5. Corbett led the entire CID Historical Section, wrote *Naval Operations*, the critical strategic text, and used it to teach on the War Course in 1920.
6. Lawrence Freedman, *Strategy*, Oxford, Oxford UP, 2013, p. 135. Corbett inspired post-1945 limited war theory, which developed from Bernard Brodie's work on seapower. Heuser, 2010, is the best guide to Corbett's stature as a strategist.
7. Peter Paret, *Clausewitz and the State*, Oxford, Oxford UP, 1976, is the exemplary text. The notes on the original dust jacket are the best concise statement of this argument.

8. Churchill to John Owen, 6 January 1934: *Churchill Companion*, V, p. 700.
9. Sir Michael Howard's *The Continental Commitment*, London, Temple Smith, 1972, provided a basis for most of these arguments. His eminence and authority masking an almost complete lack of interest in maritime strategy, and a distinctly hostile view of its proponents. He barely mentioned Corbett, preferring to attack the far easier target provided by Basil Liddell Hart's hasty sketch.
10. Corbett had idealised Pitt, for emphasis.

BIBLIOGRAPHY

Manuscript sources

Official papers

Admiralty Papers (ADM)
Committee of Imperial Defence and Cabinet Papers (CAB)
Foreign Office Papers (FO)
The National Archives of the United Kingdom (TNA)
War Office (WO)

National Maritime Museums (Royal Museums Greenwich)

Admiral Lord Beatty
Admiral Sir Cyprian A.G. Bridge
Sir Julian Stafford Corbett
Admiral Sir Reginald Custance
Professor Sir John Knox Laughton
Admiral Sir Herbert Richmond
Admiral Sir Edmond Slade
James Thursfield
Papers of the Navy Records Society

Liddle Collection, Leeds University

Julian Stafford Corbett, Diaries 1913 and 1914: LIDDLE/WW1/RNMN/059, https://explore.
library.leeds.ac.uk/special-collections-explore/26597 (I am especially indebted to the Liddle
archivists who provided photographic copies of the 1913 and 1914 Diaries during the
COVID pandemic: these volumes and other material had become separated from the rest of
the collection after Schurman consulted them)

British Library

Admiral Lord Jellicoe
Admiral Lord Keyes

Liddell Hart Centre for Military Archives, King's College London

Admiral Sir Alexander Bethell
Sir Julian Stafford Corbett: Lectures
General Sir Ian Hamilton
Basil Liddell Hart

Institute of Historical Research, London

Correspondence 1921–6

London School of Economics, British Library of Political and Economic Science

Coefficients Papers

University of Birmingham, Cadbury Library

Charles Masterman
Austen Chamberlain

Bodleian Library Oxford

Lord Bryce

Cambridge University Library

University archives
UP archives
Owen Seaman MS

Churchill College Cambridge

Winston Spencer Churchill
Admiral Lord Fisher
Paymaster Oswald Tuck

Elgar Birthplace Museum

Elgar family MS

United States Naval War College Archives

Library accession records

Naval Review Archive

Courtesy of Admiral James Goldrick RAN

Works by Julian Corbett

These were published in London unless otherwise specified. The standard bibliography is by John Hattendorf in Goldrick and Hattendorf (eds), 1993, at pp. 295–309. I have noted a few minor additions in the text.

The Fall of Asgard, Macmillan, 1886.
For God and Gold, Macmillan, 1887.
Kophetua XIII, Macmillan & Co., 1889.
Monk, Macmillan, 1889.
Sir Francis Drake, Macmillan, 1890.
'Tragedy of Mr Thomas Doughty: His Relations with Sir Francis Drake', *Macmillan's Magazine* 68, August 1893, pp. 258–68.
'Our First Ambassadors to Russia', *Macmillan's Magazine* 68, May 1893, pp. 58–69.
'Sancho Panza of Madagascar', *Macmillan's Magazine* 71, March 1895, pp. 358–64.
A Business in Great Waters, Methuen, 1895.

'The Colonel and his Command', *American Historical Review* 2, October 1896, pp. 1–11.
Introduction to Thomas Taylor, *Running the Blockade*, John Murray, 1896.
'Ubaldino and the Armada', *Athenaeum* 109, 17 April 1897.
Drake and the Tudor Navy, with a History of the Rise of England as a Maritime Power, 2 vols, Longman, 1898.
The Spanish War 1585–87, NRS, 1898.
The Successors of Drake, Longman, 1900.
'The Plan of Campaign', *Daily News* 14 February 1900, 'Letters to the Editor'.
(unsigned) 'The Paradox of Empire', *Monthly Review*, October 1900, pp. 1–14.
(unsigned) 'The Little Englander', *Monthly Review*, January 1901, pp. 10–19.
Review of A.T. Mahan, *Types of Naval Officer* (Boston 1901), *American Historical Review* 7(3), 1902, pp. 556–59.
'War Correspondence and the Censorship under Elizabeth', *Anglo-Saxon Review: A Quarterly Miscellany* 10, September 1901, pp. 54–62.
(unsigned) 'The War Training of the Navy: The Naval War Course', *The Times*, 25 January 1902, p. 6, col. A.
'Education in the Navy I', *Monthly Review*, March 1902, pp. 34–40.
'Education in the Navy II', *Monthly Review*, April 1902, pp. 43–57.
'Lord Selborne's Critics', *Monthly Review*, July 1902, pp. 64–75.
'Education in the Navy III', *Monthly Review*, September 1902, pp. 42–54.
'Lord Selborne's Memorandum I & II', *Monthly Review*, February 1903, pp. 28–41.
'Found Wanting', *Monthly Review*, October 1903, pp. 82–90.
'A Russian Privateer in the Mediterranean', *Monthly Review*, February 1904, pp. 140–52.
'The Report on the Fleet Manoeuvres', *Monthly Review*, December 1903, pp. 85–94.
'The Reorganisation of the War Office', *Monthly Review*, March 1904, pp. 26–36.
'Queen Anne's Defence Committee', *Monthly Review*, May 1904, pp. 55–65.
'Home Rule for the Volunteer', *Monthly Review*, June 1904, pp. 29–39.
'The One-Eyed Commission', *Monthly Review*, July 1905, pp. 38–49.
'The Tactics of Trafalgar', *The Times*, 27 July 1905, p. 11a.
England in the Mediterranean: A Study of the Rise and Influence of British Power within the Straits, 1603–1713, 2 vols, Longman, 1904.
(ed.) *Fighting Instructions, 1530–1816*, NRS, 1905.
'The Naval War Course I', *The Times*, 5 June 1906, p. 6.
England in the Seven Years' War: A Study in Combined Strategy, 2 vols, Longman, 1907.
'The Capture of Private Property at Sea', *The Nineteenth Century*, June 1907. Reprinted in Alfred T. Mahan, *Some Neglected Aspects of War*, Sampson Low, 1907.
'The Strategical Value of Speed', *JRUSI*, July 1907.
'Recent Attacks on the Admiralty', *The Nineteenth Century*, February 1907, pp. 195–208.
(unsigned) 'Some Principles of Naval Warfare', in P. Kemp (ed.), *The Fisher Papers*, NRS, 1964, vol. II, pp. 318–45.
A Note on the Drawing in the possession of the Earl of Dartmouth illustrating the Battle of Sole Bay May 28, 1672 and the Battle of the Texel, August 11, 1673, NRS, 1908.
'New Lights on Trafalgar', *The Times*, 22 October 1909, p. 8a.
(ed.) *Signals and Instructions 1776–1794*, NRS, 1909.
The Campaign of Trafalgar, Longman, 1910.
Some Principles of Maritime Strategy, Longman, 1911.
Some Principles of Maritime Strategy, ed. E. Grove, USNIP, 1988.
(ed.) *The Spencer Papers*, I, NRS, 1913.
(ed.) *The Spencer Papers*, II, NRS, 1914.
Naval and Military Essays, ed. Julian Corbett and Henry Edwards, Cambridge UP, 1914.
Maritime Operations in the Russo-Japanese War 1904–1905 (printed 1914–15), ed. J. Hattendorf and D.M. Schurman, USNIP, 1994.
The Spectre of Navalism, Darling & Sons, 1915.
'The Teaching of Naval and Military History', *History*, April 1916, pp. 12–24.
'The Revival of Naval History', *Contemporary Review* 110, December 1916, pp. 734–40.

The League of Peace and a Free Sea, George Doran; Hodder & Stoughton, 1917.
The League of Nations and Freedom of the Seas, Oxford UP, 1918.
'Methods of Discussion', *Naval Review*, 1920, pp. 322–4.
'Napoleon after Trafalgar', *Quarterly Review*, April 1922, pp. 239–40.
(unsigned) 'United Service', *Naval Review*, 1923, pp. 210–14.
Naval Operations, 3 vols, Longman, 1920–3.

Published works

Allott, M. (ed.), *Matthew Arnold: Writers and their Background*, London, Bell, 1975.
Andrews, K., *Drake's Voyages: A Reassessment of their Place in Elizabethan Maritime Expansion*, London, Weidenfeld & Nicolson, 1967.
Andrews, K. (ed.), *The Last Voyage of Drake and Hawkins*, Cambridge, Hakluyt Society, 1972.
Armchair Athenians: Essays from the Athenaeum, London, The Athenaeum, 2001.
Arnold, M., *Culture and Anarchy: An Essay in Political and Social Criticism*, London, 1869, and later editions.
Aspinall-Oglander, General C.F., *Military Operations: Gallipoli*, 2 vols, London, Heinemann, 1929–32.
Aspinall-Oglander, C.F., *Roger Keyes*, London, Hogarth Press, 1951.
Aston, G., *Letters on Amphibious Wars*, London, Murray, 1911.
Aston, G., *Sea, Land, and Air Strategy: A Comparison*, London, Murray, 1914.
Aston, G., *Memoirs of a Marine*, London, Murray, 1919.
Atwood, R., *Life of Field Marshal Lord Roberts*, London, Bloomsbury, 2015.
Bacon, R., *Lord Fisher of Kilverstone*, London, Hodder & Stoughton, 1929.
Bacon, R., *From 1900 Onwards*, London, Hutchinson, 1940.
Barfleur, R. (pseud. Reginald Custance), *Naval Policy: A Plea for the Study of War*, London, Blackwood, 1907.
Barrow, J., *The Life of Richard, Earl Howe*, London, Murray, 1838.
Barrow, R.J., *The Use of Classical Art and Literature by Victorian Painters, 1860–1912: Creating Continuity with the Traditions of High Art*, London, Edwin Mellen, 2007.
Bassford, C., *Clausewitz in English: The Reception of Clausewitz in Britain and America 1815–1945*, Oxford, Oxford UP, 1994.
Baugh, D., *The Global Seven Years' War*, London, Longman, 2011.
Bayly, L., *Pull Together*, London, Harrap, 1939.
Beatson, R., *Naval and Military Memoirs of Great Britain, from the year 1727 to the present time*, London, Strahan, 3 vols, 1790; 6 vols, 1804.
Beckett, I.F.W. and Jeffrey, K., 'The Royal Navy and the Curragh Incident', *Historical Research* 62, 1989, pp. 54–69.
Bell, A.C., *History of the Blockade of Germany*, London, HMSO, 1961.
Bell, C., *Churchill and Sea Power*, Oxford, Oxford UP, 2013.
Bell, D., *The Idea of Greater Britain: Empire and the Future of World Order, 1860–1900*, Princeton, NJ, Princeton UP, 2007.
Bellairs, C., 'The Navy and the Empire', in *The Empire and the Century*, London, John Murray, 1905, pp. 197–212.
Berger, S. with Conrad, C., *The Past as History: National Identity and Historical Consciousness in Modern Europe*, London, Palgrave, 2015.
Bernhardi, F. von, *On War of Today*, 2 vols, London, Rees, 1912.
Birch, D.J. and Horn, J.M. (eds), *The History Laboratory: The Institute of Historical Research 1921–1996*, London, IHR, 1996.
Black, B., *The British Admiralty War Staff in the First World War*, Woodbridge, Boydell, 2009.
Bond, B., *The Victorian Army and the Staff College, 1854–1914*, London, Methuen, 1972.
Bond, B., *The Unquiet Western Front: Britain's Role in Literature and History*, Cambridge, Cambridge UP, 2002.

Bonker, D., *Militarism in Global Age*, Ithaca, NY, Cornell UP, 2012.

Bradford, E., *Life of Admiral of the Fleet Sir Arthur Knyvet Wilson*, London, Murray, 1923.

Brady, C., *James Anthony Froude: An Intellectual Biography of a Victorian Prophet*, Oxford, Oxford UP, 2013.

Brassey, T.A., 'Great Britain as a Sea Power', *The Nineteenth Century*, July 1898, reprinted in Brassey, 1904.

Brassey, T.A., *Problems of Empire*, London, Arthur H. Humphreys, 1904.

Breck, E., Review of *Naval Operations*, vol. III: *American Historical Review* 29(3), 1924, pp. 556–8.

Brett, M.V. (ed.), *Journals and Letters of Reginald Viscount Esher, 1903–1910*, 3 vols, London, Nicholson & Watson, 1934–6.

Bridge, C.A.G., 'Amateur Estimates of Naval Policy', *The Nineteenth Century*, December 1906, pp. 883–8.

Bridge, C.A.G., *Sea-Power and Other Studies*, London, Smith, Elder, 1910.

Brooks, J., *Dreadnought Gunnery and the Battle of Jutland*, London, Routledge, 2005.

Brooks, J., *The Battle of Jutland*, Cambridge, Cambridge UP, 2016.

Bryce, J., *The Holy Roman Empire*, London, Macmillan, 1866.

Bryce, J., *Neutral Nations and the War*, London, Macmillan, 1914.

Bryce, J. (ed.), *The League of Nations*, Oxford, Oxford UP, 1919.

Buxton, I., *Big Gun Monitors: Design, Construction and Operations, 1914–1945*, Barnsley, Seaforth, 2008.

Caemmerer, R. von, *The Development of Strategical Sciences*, London, Rees, 1905.

Callwell, C., *The Effect of Maritime Command on Land Campaigns since Waterloo*, Edinburgh, Blackwood, 1897.

Callwell, C., *Military Operations and Maritime Preponderance: Their Relations and Interdependence*, Edinburgh, Blackwood, 1905.

Callwell, C., *The Life of Sir Stanley Maude*, London, Constable, 1920.

Callwell, C., *Field Marshal Sir Henry Wilson: His Life and Diaries*, 2 vols, London, Cassell, 1927.

Chatfield, A., *The Navy and Defence: The Autobiography of Admiral of the Fleet Lord Chatfield*, London, Heinemann, 1942.

Chitty, S., *Playing the Game: A Biography of Sir Henry Newbolt*, London, Quartet, 1997.

Churchill, R.S. (ed.), *Winston S. Churchill: Companion*, London, Heinemann, vol. II, 1969.

Churchill, W.S., *The World Crisis 1915*, London, Thornton Butterworth, 1923.

Citino, R., *The German Way of War: From the Thirty Years' War to the Third Reich*, Lawrence, KS, UP of Kansas, 2005.

'Civis' (pseud. Sir William White), *The State of the Navy in 1907: A Plea for Inquiry*, London, Smith, Elder, January 1907.

Clarke, G.S., *Fortification: Its Past Achievements, Recent Developments, and Future Progress*, London, Murray, 1890.

Clarke, G.S., *Russia's Sea Power*, London, Murray, 1898.

Clarke, G.S. and Thursfield, J., *The Navy and the Nation*, London, Murray, 1897.

Clausewitz, C. von, *On War*, trans. Col. J.J. Graham, 4th edn, London, Kegan, Paul, 1940.

Clausewitz, C. von, *On War*, trans. M. Howard and P. Paret, Princeton, NJ, Princeton UP, 1976.

Clemmesen, M., 'The Royal Navy North Sea War Plan 1907–1914', *Fra Krig og Fred: Journal of the Danish Commission for Military History* 2, 2014, pp. 58–112.

Clowes, W.L. (ed.), *The Royal Navy: A History from the Earliest Times to 1900*, 7 vols, London, Sampson Low, 1897–1903.

Cohrs, P.O., *The Unfinished Peace after World War I: America, Britain and the Stability of Europe, 1919–1932*, Cambridge, Cambridge UP, 2006.

Colbeck, A., 'The Strategical Aspect of War Against Commerce', *Edinburgh Review*, October 1921, pp. 358–74.

Colbeck, A., 'Reflections on Sir Julian Corbett's Official History', *Journal of the Royal United Services Institute* 67, 1922, pp. 326–35.

Colley, L., *Captives: Britain, Empire and the World 1600–1850*, London, Cape, 2002.

Collini, S., *Matthew Arnold*, Oxford, Oxford UP, 1988.

Colomb, J., *The Protection of our Commerce and Distribution of our Naval Forces Considered*, London, Harrison, 1867.

Colomb, P., *Naval Warfare: Its Ruling Principles and Practice Historically Treated*, London, W.H. Allen, 1891; 2nd edn 1895.

Colomb, P., *Essays on Naval Defence*, London, W.H. Allen, 2nd edn 1896.

Conn, S., *Gibraltar in British Diplomacy in the Eighteenth Century*, New Haven, CT, and London, Yale UP, 1942.

Connor, J., *Anzac and Empire: George Foster Pearce and the Foundations of Australian Defence*, Cambridge, Cambridge UP, 2011.

Coogan, J., 'The Short-war Illusion Resurrected: The Myth of Economic War as the British Schlieffen Plan', *Journal of Strategic Studies* 38(7), December 2015, pp. 1045–64.

Cox, J. and Ford, C., *Julia Margaret Cameron: The Complete Photographs*, Los Angeles, CA, J. Paul Getty Museum, n.d.

Crosby, G.R., *Disarmament and Peace in British Politics, 1914–1919*, Cambridge, MA, Harvard UP, 1957.

Daalder, R., *Van de Velde & Son: Marine Painters*, Leiden, Primavera, 2016.

David, D. (ed.), *The Cambridge Companion to the Victorian Novel*, Cambridge, Cambridge UP, 2001.

Davis, H.W.C., *The Political Thought of Heinrich von Treitschke*, Oxford, Oxford UP, 1914.

Davison, R., 'A Most Fortunate Court Martial: The Trial of Captain Charles Kingsmill, 1907', *Northern Mariner* 19(1), 2009, pp. 57–86.

Day, B.J., 'The Moral Intuition of Ruskin's "Storm Cloud"', *Studies in English Literature 1500–1900* 45(4), 2005, pp. 917–33.

Delaney, D.E., *The Imperial Army Project: Britain and the Land Forces of the Dominions and India, 1902–1945*, Oxford, Oxford UP, 2018.

Delbrück, H., *The History of the Art of War*, vol. IV: *The Modern Era*, trans. W. Renfroe, Lincoln, NE, Nebraska UP, 1985.

Dewar, K.G.B., *The Navy from Within*, London, Gollancz, 1939.

D'Eyncourt, E.H.T., *A Shipbuilder's Yarn: The Records of Naval Construction*, London, Hutchinson, n.d.

Dharmasena, K., *The Port of Colombo, 1860–1939*, Colombo, Ministry of Higher Education, 1980.

Dickinson, H., *Wisdom and War: The Royal Naval College Greenwich 1873–1998*, Farnham, Ashgate, 2012.

Dighton, A., 'Jomini versus Clausewitz: Hamley's *Operations of War* and Military Thought', *War in History* 27(2), 2020, pp. 179–201

d'Ombrain, N., *War Machinery and High Policy: Defence Administration in Peacetime Britain, 1902–1914*, Oxford, Oxford UP, 1973.

Dorpalen, A., *Heinrich von Treitschke*, New Haven, CT, Yale UP, 1957.

Doughty, H., *Francis Parkman*, Cambridge, MA, Harvard UP, 1983.

Doyle, W., *The Oxford History of the French Revolution*, Oxford, Oxford UP, 1898.

Duffy, M., *Soldiers, Sugar and Seapower: The British Expeditions to the West Indies and the War against Revolutionary France*, Oxford, Oxford UP, 1987.

Dull, J., *The French Navy and the Seven Years' War*, Lincoln, NE, Nebraska UP, 2006.

Dunley, R., 'Sir John Fisher and the Policy of Strategic Deterrence', *War in History* 22(2), 2015, pp. 155–73.

Dunley, R., *Britain and the Mine, 1900–1915: Culture, Strategy and International Law*, London, Palgrave, 2018.

Duro, F., *La Armada Invencible*, Madrid, de Rivadeneyra, 1884–5.

Ehrman, J., *The Navy in the War of William III*, Cambridge, Cambridge UP, 1953.

Elliot-Drake, Lady, *The Family and Heirs of Sir Francis Drake*, 2 vols, London, Smith Elder, 1911.

Erdmann K.D., *Toward a Global Community of Historians: The International Historical Congresses and the International Committee of Historical Sciences, 1898–2000*, New York, Berghahn, 2005.

Evans, R.J., *Cosmopolitan Islanders: British Historians and the European Continent*, Cambridge, Cambridge UP, 2009.

Ewing, A.W., *The Man of Room 40: The Life of Sir Alfred Ewing*, London, Hutchinson, 1939.

Fantuzzo, J., 'The Finest Feats of the War? The Captures of Baghdad and Jerusalem during the First World War and Public Opinion throughout the British Empire', *War in History* 24(1), 2017, pp. 64–86.

Fayle, C.E., *Seaborne Trade*, vol. I: *The Cruiser Period*, London, Murray, 1920.

Ferris, J.O.R., 'The War Trade Intelligence Department and British Economic Warfare during the First World War', in T. Otte (ed.), *British World Policy and the Projection of Global Power, c.1830–1960*, Cambridge, Cambridge UP, 2019, pp. 24–45.

Figgis, J.N. and Laurence, R.V. (eds), *Historical Essays and Studies by Lord Acton*, London, Macmillan, 1907.

Firth, C., *Commentary on Macaulay's History of England*, London, Macmillan, 1938.

Fisher, Lord, *Records*, London, Hutchinson, 1919.

Fiske, B., Review of *Naval Operations* vol. I, *American Historical Review* 26(1), 1920 pp. 94–6.

Foley, R. (ed. and trans.), *Alfred von Schlieffen's Military Writings*, London, Cass, 2003.

Foley, R., *German Strategy and the Path to Verdun: Erich von Falkenhayn and the Development of Attrition, 1870–1916*, Cambridge, Cambridge UP, 2005.

Forrest, M., *The Defence of the Dardanelles*, Barnsley, Pen & Sword, 2012.

Fortescue, J.W., *British Statesmen in the Great War 1793–1814*, Oxford, Oxford UP, 1911.

Freedman, L., *Strategy*, Oxford, Oxford UP, 2013.

French, D., *British Strategic and Economic Planning 1905–1915*, London, Allen & Unwin, 1982.

French, D., *The British Way in Warfare, 1688–2000*, London, Unwin Hyman, 1990.

Friedman, N., *Fighting the Great War at Sea*, Barnsley, Seaforth, 2014.

Friedman, N., *The British Battleship*, Barnsley, Seaforth, 2015.

Froude, J.A., *History of England from the Fall of Wolsey to the Death of Elizabeth*, 10 vols, London, Longman, 1856–66.

Froude, J.A., *English Seamen in the Sixteenth Century*, London, Longman, 1896.

Gardiner, R. (ed.), *Conway's All the World's Fighting Ships, 1906–1921*, London, Conway, 1985.

Gat, A., *The Development of Military Thought: The Nineteenth Century*, Oxford, Oxford UP, 1992.

Geissler, S., *God and Sea Power: The Influence of Religion on Alfred Thayer Mahan*, Annapolis, MD, USNIP, 2015.

Gilbert, M. (ed.), *Winston S. Churchill: Companion*, London, Heinemann, vols III–V, 1972.

Gilbert, M., *Winston S. Churchill, 1917–1922*, London, Heinemann, 1975.

Gildea, R., *The Past in French History*, New Haven, CT, London, Yale UP, 1994.

Girouard, M., *The Return to Camelot: Chivalry and the English Gentleman*, New Haven, CT, and London, Yale UP, 1981.

Goldrick, J. and Hattendorf, J. (eds), *Mahan Is Not Enough: The Proceedings of a Conference on the Works of Sir Julian Corbett and Admiral Sir Herbert Richmond*, Newport, RI, Naval War College Press, 1993.

Goltz, C. von der, *The Nation in Arms*, trans. P. Ashworth, London, W.H. Allen, 1887.

Goltz, C. von der, *The Conduct of War*, London, W.H. Allen, 1896.

Gooch, G., *History and Historians of the Nineteenth Century*, London, Longman, 1913, pp. 93–4.

Gordon, P. (ed.), *The Red Earl: The Papers of the Fifth Earl Spencer, 1835–1910*, Northampton, Northamptonshire Record Society, 1986.

Gossman, L., *Basel in the Age of Burckhardt: A Study in Unseasonal Ideas*, Chicago, IL, University of Chicago Press, 2000.

Grainge, G., 'A Family of Rare Naval Distinction: The Hannam Hendersons of Worth, East Kent', *Topmasts*, 15, 2015, pp. 11–15.

Green, A., *Writing the Great War: Sir James Edmonds and the Official Histories, 1915–1948*, London, Routledge, 2003.

Grimes, S., *Strategy and War Planning in the British Navy, 1887–1918*, Woodbridge, Boydell & Brewer, 2012.

Gross, G.P., 'German Plans to Occupy Denmark, "Case J" 1916–1918', in M. Clemmesen and G.P. Gross (eds), *The Danish Straits and German Naval Power 1905–1918*, Potsdam, Militärgeschictliches Forschungsamt, 2010.

Gross, G.P., *The Myth and Reality of German Warfare: Operational Thinking from Moltke the Elder to Heusinger*, Lexington, KY, UP of Kentucky, 2016.

Guilmartin, J., *Gunpowder and Galleys: Changing Technology and Mediterranean Warfare at Sea in the 16th Century*, London, Conway, 2003.

Hakluyt, R., *The Principal Navigations, Voyages and Discoveries of the English Nation, made by Sea or over Land to the most remote and farthest distant Quarters of the earth at any time within the compass of these 1500 years*, London, Bishop & Newberie, 1589.

Halpern, P. (ed.), *The Keyes Papers*, 3 vols, London, NRS, 1980.

Hamilton, I., *Compulsory Service: A Study of the Question in the Light of Experience*, London, Murray, 1st edn November 1910.

Hamilton, I., *Gallipoli Diary*, 2 vols, London, Edward Arnold, 1920.

Hamley, E.B., *The Operations of War: Explained and Illustrated*, Edinburgh, Blackwood, 1st edn 1866. The final 1909 edition was updated by Brigadier Lancelot Kiggell psc.

Hammer, P., 'Myth-making, Politics, Propaganda and the Capture of Cadiz in 1596', *Historical Journal* 40(3), 1997, pp. 621–42.

Hammer, P., *The Polarisation of Elizabethan Politics: The Political Career of Robert Devereux, 2nd Earl of Essex, 1585–1597*, Cambridge, Cambridge UP, 1999.

Harcourt, F., *Flagships of Imperialism: The P&O Company and the Politics of Empire from its Origins to 1867*, Manchester, Manchester UP, 2006.

Harding, R. and Le Fevre, P. (eds), *Precursors of Nelson: British Admirals of the Eighteenth Century*, London, Chatham, 2000.

Harris, P.R., *The Life of Edward Montague, First Earl of Sandwich*, 2 vols, London, Methuen, 1912.

Harris, R.H., *From Naval Cadet to Admiral*, London, Cassell, 1913.

Hattendorf, J.B., 'Technology and Strategy: A Study of the Professional Thought of the US Navy, 1900–1916', *Naval War College Review* 24, 1971, pp. 25–48.

Hattendorf, J.B., *England in the War of the Spanish Succession: A Study of the English View and Conduct of Grand Strategy, 1702–1713*, New York, Garland, 1987.

Hattendorf, J.B., Simpson, B. and Wadleigh, J.W., *Sailors and Scholars: The Centennial History of the U.S. Naval War College*, Newport, RI: War College Press, 1984.

Henderson, G.F.R., *The Science of War: A Collection of Essays and Lectures 1891–1903*, ed. Colonel N. Malcolm, London, Longman, 1905.

Henry, L.W., 'The Earl of Essex as a Strategist and Military Organiser (1596–7)', *EHR* 68(268), 1953, pp. 363–93.

Heuser, B., *The Evolution of Strategy: Thinking War from Antiquity to the Present*, Cambridge, Cambridge UP, 2010.

Hobsbawm, E. and Ranger, T., *The Invention of Tradition*, Cambridge, Cambridge UP, 1983.

Hopkinson, M., *Ex Libris: The Art of the Bookplate*, London, British Library, 2012.

Howard, M., *The Continental Commitment: The Dilemma of British Defence Policy in the Era of the Two World Wars*, London, Temple Smith, 1972.

Howard, M., *The Causes of War and other Essays*, London, Temple Smith, 1980.

Hunt, B.D., *Sailor-scholar: Admiral Sir Herbert Richmond 1871–1946*, Waterloo, Wilfrid Laurier UP, 1982.

Hurd, A., *The Merchant Navy*, London, Murray, vol. I, 1921.

Jackson, P., *Harcourt and Son: A Political Biography of Sir William Harcourt, 1827–1904*, Madison, NJ, Fairleigh Dickinson UP, 2004.

Jackson, P., *Lulu: Selected Extracts from the Journals of Lewis Harcourt, 1880–1895*, Madison, NJ, Fairleigh Dickinson UP, 2006.

Jebb, C., *Life and Letters of Richard Claverhouse Jebb*, Cambridge, Cambridge UP, 1907.

Jeffery, K., *Field Marshal Sir Henry Wilson: A Political Soldier*, Oxford, Oxford UP, 2006.

Jellicoe, J., *The Grand Fleet 1914–16*, London, Cassell, 1919.

Johnson, F.A., *Defence by Committee: The British Committee of Imperial Defence*, Oxford, Oxford UP, 1960.

Johnson, G., *Lord Robert Cecil: Politician and Internationalist*, Farnham, Ashgate, 2013.

Johnston, W., Rawlings, W., Gimblett, R. and MacFarlane, J., *The Seabound Coast: The Official History of the Royal Canadian Navy, 1867–1939*, Toronto, Dundurn Press, 2010.

Jones, E., *John Lingard and the Pursuit of Historical Truth*, Brighton, Sussex Academic Press, 2001.

Jordan, J. and Caresse, P., *French Armoured Cruisers, 1887–1932*, Barnsley, Seaforth, 2019.

Jordanova, L., *History in Practice*, London, Arnold, 2000.

Kemp, P. (ed.), *The Papers of Admiral Sir John Fisher*, 2 vols, London, Navy Records Society, 1960 & 1964.

Kennedy, P.M., *The Rise and Fall of the Anglo-German Antagonism, 1860–1914*, London, Allen Lane, 1980.

Kerr, M., *Prince Louis of Battenberg: Admiral of the Fleet*, London, Longman, 1934.

Keyes, R., *The Naval Memoirs of Admiral of the Fleet Sir Roger Keyes*, 2 vols, London, Thornton, 1934–5.

Kochanski, H., *Sir Garnet Wolseley: Victorian Hero*, London, Hambleden Press, 1999.

Koss, S., *Lord Haldane: Scapegoat for Liberalism*, New York, Columbia UP, 1969.

Kuhle, A., 'Putting Theory into Practice: Ludwig von Wolzogen and the Russian Campaign of 1812', *War in History* 27, 2020, pp. 156–78.

Lambert, A.D., *The Foundations of Naval History: John Knox Laughton, the Royal Navy and the Historical Profession*, London, Chatham Press, 1998.

Lambert, A.D., 'Wirtschaftliche Macht, technologischer Vorsprung und Imperiale Stärke: GrossBritannien als einzigartige globale Macht: 1860 bis 1890', in M. Epkenhans and G.P. Gross (eds), *Das Militär und der Aufbruch die Moderne 1860 bis 1890*, Munich, Verlag, 2003, pp. 243–68.

Lambert, A.D., ' "This is All We Want": Great Britain and the Baltic Approaches 1815–1914', in J. Sevaldsen (ed.), *Britain and Denmark: Political, Economic and Cultural Relations in the 19th and 20th Centuries*, Copenhagen, Museum Tusculanum Press, 2003, pp. 147–69.

Lambert, A.D., *Nelson: Britannia's God of War*, London, Faber, 2004.

Lambert, A.D., *Admirals*, London, Faber, 2007.

Lambert, A.D., ' "The Possibility of Ultimate Action in the Baltic": Die Royal Navy im Krieg, 1914–1916', in M. Epkenhans, J. Hillman and F. Nägler (eds), *Skagerrakschlact: Voergeschichte – Ereignis – Verarbeitung*, Munich, R. Oldenbourg Verlag, 2009, pp. 73–112.

Lambert, A.D., *The Crimean War: British Grand Strategy against Russia, 1854–1856*, Manchester, Manchester UP, 1990; 2nd edn Farnham, Ashgate, 2011.

Lambert, A.D., *The Challenge: Britain versus America in the Naval War of 1812*, London, Faber, 2012.

Lambert, A.D., 'Sir Julian Corbett and the *Naval Review*', in P. Hore (ed.), *Dreadnought to Daring: 100 Years of Comment, Controversy and Debate in the* Naval Review, London, Chatham, 2012, pp. 37–52.

Lambert A.D., ' "The Army is a Projectile to be Fired by the Navy": Securing the Empire 1815–1914', in P. Dennis (ed.), *Armies and Maritime Strategy: 2013 Chief of Army History Conference*, Canberra, Big Sky Publishing, 2014, pp. 29–47.

Lambert, A.D., *Crusoe's Island*, London, Faber, 2016.

Lambert, A.D. (ed.), *Twenty-first-century Corbett*, Annapolis, MD, USNIP, 2017.

Lambert, A.D., ' "Doctrine – The Soul of Warfare": Teaching Strategy in the Royal Navy before 1914', in D.E. Delaney, R. Engen and M. Fitzpatrick (eds), *Military Education and the British Empire*, Vancouver, University of British Columbia Press, 2018, pp. 48–68.

Lambert, A.D., *Seapower States*, New Haven, CT, and London, Yale UP, 2018.

Lambert, N., *Sir John Fisher's Naval Revolution*, Columbia, SC, University of South Carolina Press, 1999.

Lambert, N., 'False Prophet? The Maritime Theory of Julian Corbett and Professional Military Education', Review Essay, *Journal of Military History* 77, 2013, pp. 1055–78.

Lang, C. (ed.), *The Letters of Matthew Arnold*, Charlotte, VA, University of Virginia Press, vol. II, 1997.

Laughton, Sir John Knox: for a full bibliography of Laughton's works, see A.D. Lambert, *The Foundations of Naval History: John Knox Laughton, the Royal Navy and the Historical Profession*, London, Chatham Press, 1998.

Laurvik, J.N. and Morison, M. (eds), *Letters of Henrik Ibsen*, New York, Fox, Duffield & Co., 1905.

Lawrence, T.E., 'Three Unsigned Articles in *The Times* of 26–28 Nov. 1918', in M. Brown (ed.), *T.E. Lawrence in War and Peace: An Anthology of the Military Writings of Lawrence of Arabia*, London, Greenhill Books, 2005, pp. 221–31.

Lecky, W.E.H., *A History of England in the Eighteenth Century*, 8 vols, London, Longman, 1878–90.

Liddell Hart, B.H., 'Economic Pressure or Continental Victories', *Journal of the Royal United Services Institute for Defence Studies* 76, 1931, pp. 486–503.

Loreburn, Earl, *Capture at Sea*, London, Methuen, 1905; 2nd edn 1913.

Luvaas, J., 'The First British Official Historians', *Military Affairs* 26(2), 1962, pp. 49–58.

Luvaas, J., *The Education of an Army: British Military Thought 1815–1940*, London, Cassell, 1964

MacCarron, D., *Letters from an Early Bird: The Life and Letters of Denys Corbett Wilson 1882–1915*, Barnsley, Pen & Sword, 2006.

MacCarthy, F., *William Morris: A Life for our Times*, London, Faber, 1994.

MacCarthy, F., *The Last Pre-Raphaelite: Edward Burne-Jones and the Victorian Imagination*, London, Faber, 2011.

McCartney, D., *W.E.H. Lecky: Historian and Politician*, Dublin, Lilliput Press, 1994.

Macartney, I., *Jutland: The Archaeology of a Naval Battlefield*, London, Bloomsbury, 2016.

Macaulay, T.B., *History of England*, 6 vols, ed. C. Firth, London, Macmillan, 1913–16.

McGeach, H.F. and Sturgess, H.A.C., *Register of Admissions to the Honourable Society of the Middle Temple: From the Fifteenth Century to the Year 1944*, London, Butterworth, vol. II, 1959.

Mackay, R., *Fisher of Kilverstone*, Oxford, Oxford UP, 1974.

Mackay, R., *Arthur Balfour: Intellectual Statesman*, Oxford, Oxford UP, 1985.

Mackenzie, N. (ed.), *The Letters of Sidney and Beatrice Webb*, vol. II: *Partnership, 1892–1912*, Cambridge, Cambridge UP, 1978.

McKitterick, D., *A History of Cambridge University Press*, vol. III: *New Worlds for Learning, 1873–1972*, Cambridge, Cambridge UP, 2004.

Macmillan, M., *The Peacemakers: The Paris Peace Conference 1919*, London, Murray, 2018.

Mahan, A.T., *The Influence of Sea Power upon History, 1660–1783*, Boston, MA, Little, Brown, 1890.

Mahan, A.T., *The Influence of Sea Power upon the French Revolution and Empire, 1793–1812*, 2 vols, London, Sampson Low, 1892.

Mahan, A.T., *Types of Naval Officer, Drawn from the History of the British Navy*, London, Sampson Low, 1902.

Mahan, A.T., 'Reflections Historic and Others, Suggested by the Battle of the Japan Sea', *United States Naval Institute Proceedings*, June 1906, pp. 447–71, reprinted in *RUSI*, November 1906, pp. 1327–46.

Mahan, A.T., *Some Neglected Aspects of War*, Boston, MA, Little, Brown, 1907.

Mahan, A.T., *Naval Strategy*, Boston, MA, Little, Brown, 1911.

Maltzahn, Baron K. von, *Naval Warfare: Its Historical Development from the Age of the Great Geographical Discoveries to the Present Time*, trans. J.C. Miller, London, Longman, 1908.

Marder, A.J., *The Anatomy of British Sea Power*, London, Putnam, 1940.

Marder A.J., *Portrait of an Admiral: The Life and Papers of Sir Herbert Richmond*, London, Cape, 1952.

Marder, A.J. (ed.), *Fear God and Dread Nought*, 3 vols, London, Cape, 1952–8.

Marder, A.J., *From the Dreadnought to Scapa Flow*, 5 vols, Oxford, Oxford UP, 1960–70.

Marsden, R.G. (ed.), *Documents Relating to the Law and Custom of the Sea*, 2 vols, London, NRS, 1915.

Martel, G., *Imperial Diplomacy: Rosebery and the Failure of Foreign Policy*, Kingston, ON, McGill-Queen's, 1986.

Matthew, H.C.G., *The Liberal Imperialists: The Ideas and Politics of a Post-Gladstonian Elite*, Oxford, Oxford UP, 1973.

Mattingly, G., *The Defeat of the Spanish Armada*, London, Cape, 1959.

Maurice, E., *Sir Frederick Maurice: A Record of his Work and Opinions, with Eight Essays of Discipline and National Efficiency*, London, Edward Arnold, 1913.

Maurice, J.F., *The Balance of Military Power in Europe: An Examination of the War Resources of Great Britain and the Continental States*, London, Blackwood, 1888.

Maurice, J.F., 'Mahan's Testimony to England's Power', *United Services Magazine*, 1893, pp. 792–98.

Messinger, G.M., *British Propaganda and the State in the First World War*, Manchester, Manchester UP, 1992.

Middleton, R., *The Bells of Victory: The Pitt–Newcastle Ministry and the Conduct of the Seven Years' War, 1757–1762*, Cambridge, Cambridge UP, 1983.

Morgan, C., *The House of Macmillan (1843–1943)*, London, Macmillan, 1944.

Morgan-Owen, D.G., 'Cooked Up in the Dinner Hour? Sir Arthur Wilson's War Plan Reconsidered', *EHR* 130, 2015, pp. 865–906.

Morgan-Owen, D.G., *The Fear of Invasion: Strategy, Politics and British War Planning, 1880–1914*, Oxford, Oxford UP, 2017.

Morgan-Owen, D., 'War as it Might Have Been: British Sea Power and the First World War', *Journal of Military History* 83, 2019, pp. 1095–131.

Morley, J., *The Life of Richard Cobden*, London, Fisher Unwin, 1883.

Morris, A.J., *The Scaremongers: The Advocacy of War and Rearmament, 1896–1914*, London, Routledge, 1984.

Murfett, M. (ed.), *The First Sea Lords: From Fisher to Mountbatten*, Westport, CT, Praeger, 1995.

Nelles, H.V., *The Art of Nation-building: Pageantry and Spectacle at Quebec's Tercentenary*, Toronto, University of Toronto Press, 1999.

Newton, A.P. (ed.), *The Sea Commonwealth and other Essays*, London, Dent, 1919.

Nicholls, M. and Williams, P., *Sir Walter Raleigh in Life and Legend*, London, Continuum, 2011.

Novick, P., *That Noble Dream: The 'Objectivity Question' and the American Historical Profession*, Cambridge, Cambridge UP, 1998.

O'Connor, D.P., *Between Peace and War: British Defence and the Royal United Services Institute, 1831–2010*, London, RUSI, 2011.

Offer, A., *The First World War: An Agrarian Interpretation*, Oxford, Oxford UP, 1989.

Oppenheim, M., *A History of the Administration of the Royal Navy, 1509–1660*, London, Bodley Head, 1896.

Otte, T.G. (ed.), *An Historian in Peace and War: The Diaries of Harold Temperley*, Abingdon, Routledge, 2016 (first published Farnham, Ashgate, 2014).

Otte, T.G. (ed.), *The Age of Anniversaries: The Cult of Commemoration, 1895–1925*, Abingdon, Routledge, 2018.

Otte, T.G., *Statesmen of Europe: A Life of Sir Edward Grey*, London, Allen Lane, 2020.

Owen, D., *Ocean Trade and Shipping*, Cambridge, Cambridge UP, 'Naval and Military Series', 1914.

Pares, R., *War and Trade in the West Indies, 1739–1763*, Oxford, Oxford UP, 1936.

Paret, P., *Clausewitz and the State*, Oxford, Oxford UP. 1976.

Parker, W.H., *Mackinder: Geography as an Aid to Statecraft*, Oxford, Oxford UP, 1982.

Pearce, G., *Carpenter to Cabinet: Thirty-seven Years of Parliament*, Melbourne, Hutchinson, 1951.

Pearce-Higgins, A., *Defensively Armed Merchant Ships and Submarine Warfare*, London, Stevens, 1917.

Perrin, W.G., *British Flags*, Cambridge, Cambridge UP, 1922.

Philpott, W., 'The General Staff and the Paradoxes of Continental War', in D. French and B. Holden Reid (eds), *The British General Staff: Reform and Innovation, 1890–1939*, London, Cass, 2002, pp. 95–111.

Pollard, A.F., *The Claims of Historical Research*, pamphlet, London, London UP, 1920.

Porter, B., *Absent-minded Imperialists: What the British Really Thought about Empire*, Oxford, Oxford UP, 2004.

Poulson, C., *Morris, Burne-Jones and the Quest of the Holy Grail*, Kelmscott Lecture 1998, London, William Morris Society, 2001.

Proceedings of the British Academy 1913–1914, London, British Academy, 1914.

Ranft, B.M. (ed.), *The Beatty Papers*, 2 vols, London, NRS, 1989–93.

Rawley, J.A. (ed.), *The American Civil War: An English View. The Writings of Field Marshal Viscount Wolseley*, Mechanicsburg, PA, Stackpole, 2002.

Repington, C., *Imperial Strategy by the Military Correspondent of The Times*, London, John Murray, 1906.

Repington, C., *Vestigia*, London, Constable, 1919.

Reynolds, S., *Sir William Blake Richmond*, Norwich, Michael Russell, 1995.

Richards, T., *The Imperial Archive: Knowledge and the Fantasy of Empire*, London, Verso, 1993.

Richmond, H., *The Navy in the War of 1739–48*, 3 vols, Cambridge, Cambridge UP, 1920.

Richmond, H., 'National Policy and Naval Strength, 16th to 20th Century', *Proceedings of the British Academy* 8, 1922.

Richmond, H., Corbett Obituary, *Naval Review*, February 1923, p. 18.

Richmond, H., *Statesmen and Seapower*, Oxford, Oxford UP, 1946.

Robb-Webb, J., 'Corbett and *The Campaign of Trafalgar*: Naval Operations in their Strategic Context', *Defence Studies* 8(22), 2008, pp. 157–89.

Rodger, N.A.M., *The Safeguard of the Sea: A Naval History of Britain*, vol. I: *660–1649*, London, Harper Collins, 1997.

Rohl, J.G.C., *The Kaiser and his Court: Wilhelm II and the Government of Germany*, Cambridge, Cambridge UP, 1995.

Rohlfs, F.G., *Adventures in Morocco: Journeys through the Oases of Draa and Tafilet*, London, Sampson Low, 1874.

Røksund, A., *The Jeune École: The Strategy of the Weak*, Oslo, University of Oslo, 2005.

Rose, J.H. (ed.), *Select Dispatches Relating to the Third Coalition against France, 1804–5*, London, Camden Society, 1904.

Rose, J.H. and Broadley, A.M., *Dumouriez and the Defence of England against Napoleon*, London, Bodley Head, 1909.

Roskill, S.W., 'The Navy at Cambridge, 1919–23', *Mariner's Mirror* 49, 1963, pp. 178–91.

Roskill, S.W., *Naval Policy between the Wars*, vol. I: *The Period of Anglo-American Antagonism, 1919–1929*, London, Collins, 1968.

Roskill, S.W., *Hankey: Man of Secrets*, 2 vols, London, Collins, 1970, 1972.

Roskill, S.W. *Admiral of the Fleet Earl Beatty: The Last Naval Hero: An Intimate Biography*, London, Collins, 1980.

Rüger, J., *The Great Naval Game: Britain and Germany in the Age of Empire*, Cambridge, Cambridge UP, 2007.

Russell, B., *Prize Courts and U-Boat: International Law at Sea and Economic Warfare during the First World War*, Dordrecht, Republic of Letters, 2009.

Sargent, L.T. (ed.), *British and American Utopian Literature, 1516–1985*, New York, Garland, 1988.

Scheer, R., *Germany's High Seas Fleet in the World War*, London, Cassell, 1920.

Schleihauf, W. and McLaughlin, S. (eds), *Jutland: The Naval Staff Appreciation*, Barnsley, Seaforth, 2016.

Schurman, D.M., *The Education of a Navy: The Development of British Naval Strategic Thought 1867–1914*, London, Cassell, 1965.

Schurman, D.M., *Julian S. Corbett, 1854–1922: Historian of British Maritime Policy from Drake to Jellicoe*, London, Royal Historical Society, 1981.

Seager II, R. and Maguire, D. (eds), *Letters and Papers of Alfred Thayer Mahan*, 3 vols, Annapolis, MD, USNIP, 1975.

Seeley, J.R., *The Expansion of England*, London, Macmillan, 1883.

Seeley, J.R., *The Growth of English Policy: An Historical Essay*, 2 vols, Cambridge, Cambridge UP, 1895.

Seeley, J.R., 'War and the British Empire', *Journal of the Military Service of the United States* 10, September 1889, pp. 488–500.

Seligmann, M., *Spies in Uniform*, Oxford, Oxford UP, 2006.

Seligmann, M. (ed.), *Naval Intelligence from Germany*, Aldershot, NRS, 2007.

Seligmann, M., '"Failing to Prepare for the Great War": The Absence of Grand Strategy in British War Planning before 1914', *War in History* 20(4), 2017, pp. 414–37.

Semmel, B., *Liberalism and Naval Strategy: Ideology, Interest and Sea Power during the Pax Britannica*, London, Allen & Unwin, 1986.

Siegel, J., *Endgame: Britain, Russia and the Final Struggle for Central Asia*, London, I.B. Tauris, 2002.

Simms, B., *Three Victories and a Defeat: The Rise and Fall of the First British Empire, 1714–1783*, London, Allen Lane, 2007.

Slater, M., *The National Debt: A Short History*, London, Hurst, 2018.

Soffer, R.N., *Discipline and Power: The University, History and the Making of an English Elite, 1870–1930*, Stanford, CA, Stanford UP, 1994.

Squiers, J.D., *British Propaganda at Home and in the United States from 1914 to 1917*, Cambridge, MA, Harvard UP, 1935.

Stephens, W.R.W., *Life and Letters of Edward A. Freeman*, 2 vols, London, Macmillan, 1895.

Stibbe, M., *German Anglophobia and the Great War, 1914–1918*, Cambridge, Cambridge UP, 2006.

Still Jr, W., *Victory without Peace: The United States Navy in European Waters, 1919–1924*, Annapolis, MD, USNIP, 2018.

Stone, J., 'The Influence of Clausewitz on G.F.R. Henderson's Military Histories', in S. Berger, P. Lambert and P. Schumann (eds), *Historikerdialoge: Geschichte, Mythos und Gedächtnis im deutsche-britischen kulturellen Austausch 1750–2000*, Göttingen, Vandenhoeck & Ruprecht, 2003, pp. 197–218.

Strachan, H., *The First World War*, vol. I: *To Arms*, Oxford, Oxford UP, 2000.

Strachan, H., *The Direction of War: Contemporary Strategy in Historical Perspective*, Cambridge, Cambridge UP, 2013.

Sugden, J., *Sir Francis Drake*, London, Barrie & Jenkins, 1990.

Survey of London, vol. XIII: *St Margaret, Westminster*, Part II: *Whitehall*, I, London, Batsford, 1930.

Sylvest, C., *British Liberal Internationalism, 1880–1930: Making Progress?* Manchester, Manchester UP, 2009.

Temple Patterson, A. (ed.), *The Jellicoe Papers*, 2 vols, London, NRS, 1966–8.

Thursfield, J., *Naval Warfare*, Cambridge, Cambridge UP, 1913.

Tirpitz, A., *My Memoirs*, London, Hurst & Blackett, 1919.

Tooze, A., *The Deluge: The Great War and the Remaking of Global Order, 1916–1931*, London, Allen Lane, 2014.

Trask, D.F., *Captains and Cabinets: Anglo-American Naval Relations, 1917–1918*, Columbus, MO, Missouri UP, 1972.

Trevelyan, G.M., *England under Queen Anne*, 3 vols, London, Longman, 1930.

Trevor-Roper, H., 'Jacob Burckhardt', Master-mind Lecture, *Proceedings of the British Academy* 70, 1984, pp. 359–378.

Tunstall, W.C.B., *Naval Warfare in the Age of Sail: The Evolution of Fighting Tactics 1860–1815*, ed. N. Tracey, London, Conway, 1991.

Tupper, R., *Reminiscences*, London, Jarrolds, n.d.

Turner F.M., *The Greek Heritage in Victorian Britain*, New Haven, CT, and London, Yale UP, 1981.

Tyler, J.E., *The British Army and the Continent, 1904–1914*, London, Arnold, 1914.

Venn, J.A., *Alumni Cantabrigiensis, 1752–1900*, Cambridge, Cambridge UP, vol. II, 1944.

Vetch, R., *General Sir Andrew Clarke*, London, Murray, 1905.

Walworth, A., *Wilson and his Peacemakers: American Diplomacy at the Paris Peace Conference, 1919*, New York, Norton, 1986.

Wathen, B., *Sir Francis Drake: The Construction of a Hero*, Woodbridge, Brewer, 2009.

Wawn, A., *The Vikings and the Victorians: Inventing the Old North in 19th Century Britain*, Woodbridge, Brewer, 2000.

Wemyss, Lady, *The Life and Letters of Lord Wester Wemyss*, London, Eyre & Spottiswoode, 1935.

Wemyss, Lord Wester, *The Navy in the Dardanelles Campaign*, London, Hodder & Stoughton, 1924.

Wernham, R.B., *Before the Armada: The Growth of English Foreign Policy 1485–1588*, London, Cape, 1966.

Wernham, R.B., *After the Armada: Elizabethan England and the Struggle for Western Europe, 1588–1595*, Oxford, Oxford UP, 1984.

Wernham, R.B., *The Return of the Armadas: The Last Years of the Elizabethan War against Spain, 1595–1603*, Oxford, Oxford UP, 1994.

Why We Are at War with Germany: Great Britain's Case, Oxford, Clarendon Press, 1914.

Widen, J.J., *Theorist of Maritime Strategy: Sir Julian Corbett and his Contribution to Military and Naval Thought*, Farnham, Ashgate, 2012.

Williams, B., *Stanhope: A Study in Eighteenth-century War and Diplomacy*, Oxford, Oxford UP, 1932.

Williams, R., *Defending the Empire: The Conservative Party and British Defence Policy, 1899–1915*, New Haven, CT, and London, Yale UP, 1991.

Wilson, K., *Channel Tunnel Visions 1850–1945*, London, Hambleden, 1994.

Winfield, R., *British Warships in the Age of Sail: 1817–1863. Design, Construction, Careers and Fates*, Barnsley, Seaforth, 2014.

Wolseley, Lady, *Some of the Smaller Manor Houses of Sussex*, London, Medici Society, 1925.

Wolseley, Viscount, *The Story of a Soldier's Life*, London, Constable, vol. II, 1905.

Wood, C., *Olympian Dreamers: Victorian Classical Painters, 1860–1914*, London, Constable, 1983.

Wormell, D., *Sir John Seeley and the Uses of History*, Cambridge, Cambridge UP, 1980.

Yearwood, P.J., *Guarantee of Peace: The League of Nations in British Policy, 1914–1925*, Oxford, Oxford UP, 2009.

Unpublished PhD theses

Alan Anderson, 'The Laws of War and Naval Strategy in Great Britain and the United States, 1899–1909', King's College London, 2016.

Online resources

History of Parliament
Oxford Dictionary of National Biography
Among the wealth of searchable online journals the *Athenaeum, Edinburgh Review, Quarterly Review, Spectator* and *The Times* were especially useful, but the *Fishing Gazette*, 26, 1893, may stand in for many others which provided useful insight.

ACKNOWLEDGEMENTS

This book has a long history. My interest in Corbett can be traced back more than forty years, prompted by my friend and tutor Professor Bryan Ranft, the last Professor of History at the Royal Naval College, Greenwich, and the first Professor of Naval History in the Department of War Studies at King's College London. Bryan wrote the introduction to the first post-1945 edition of *Some Principles*, to ensure the Royal Navy understood the critical role of the sea in national strategy. He emphasised the depth and sophistication of Corbett's work, work that helped shape the strategic focus and methods of my PhD and the book that followed. The discovery that Corbett was also engaged with the use of British power in the Baltic, and had begun to study the Crimean War, helped frame my research (published as *The Crimean War: British Grand Strategy against Russia, 1854–1856*, Manchester University Press, 1990; 2nd edn, Ashgate, 2011). While researching the career of Professor Sir John Laughton (see *The Foundations of Naval History: John Knox Laughton, the Royal Navy and the Historical Profession*, Chatham Press, 1998) it became apparent that I would have to write about Corbett. The two lives were linked by shared agendas and personal empathy. That work began in desultory fashion, examining aspects of a complex career, only becoming a serious attempt to assess Corbett's intellectual life after the belated rediscovery of most of his diaries, the single most important source for any attempt to unravel his complex relationship with the Navy, history, strategy and much else.

In the intervening years I have discussed aspects of Corbett's career and his wider context with many scholars, beginning with the late Don Schurman, his first biographer and greatest advocate, and the late Eric Grove, who edited his key text and promoted his ideas in the Royal Navy of another era, as well as Dan Baugh, Michael Clemmesen, Michael Epkenhans, John Ferris, James Goldrick, Richard Harding, John Hattendorf, Beatrice

Heuser, Thomas Otte and Matthew Seligman; their expertise has been a source and sounding board across two decades. I have been fortunate to work with several outstanding research students on aspects of the Corbett era, including Alan Anderson, John Brooks, Tim Dougall, Richard Dunley, Shawn Grimes. David Kohnen, Robert Mullins and James Ulry. My colleague David Morgan Owen has done much to widen my understanding of the context in Corbett operated, while Jake Widen has developed the analysis of Corbett's theory. Doug Delaney and Peter Dennis provided valuable opportunities to examine Corbett's role in the Commonwealth context, while Norman Friedman offered fresh perspectives on the ships and technologies of the Fisher era. Many more scholars, students, colleagues and friends have engaged with this project: their support is greatly appreciated.

The Department of War Studies at King's College London remains the ideal location for those who study history and strategy, and I like to think that Corbett, who knew the college and lectured within its walls, would have approved of what we are doing. He believed the constant interaction of academic and professional education – founded on history, but extending across strategic theory, law and other critical contexts – was the only way to think about conflict, and prepare for the future.

The main sources for this work have been Corbett's papers and diaries at the National Maritime Museum in Greenwich, complemented by additional material in the Liddell Hart Military Archive Centre at King's College London, the Liddle Collection at Leeds University, Churchill College, Cambridge, the Records of Cambridge University and the University Press, the Bodleian Library at Oxford and the British Library, along with the Admiralty, Official History, and Cabinet and Foreign Office Records at the National Archives at Kew. The standard of support provided by archives and libraries has been so high that there was a danger we might take them for granted. The Covid pandemic made me appreciate the luxury of archival access and library shelves, and above all the dedicated people who make them accessible and agreeable places to work. When the pandemic began I thought research for the book was complete: lockdown exposed the absurdity of such notions.

I cannot close without expressing my appreciation for the outstanding team at the London office of Yale University Press. This book became a reality when my longtime editor Julian Loose asked what was next. His support, understanding and commitment exemplify the very best traditions of the profession. Between any author and their public stands an impressive production team; the quality of their work is best appreciated by the author, who knows what a catalogue of errors and oversights has been rectified. I had the good fortune to work with a great production team, Rachael Lonsdale, Lucy Buchan and Percie Edgeler; copy-editor Sophie Richmond found her grandfather on the first page, and corrected a related error: it was not the last to require her attention. Jessica Cuthbert-Smith proofread the text with commendable rigour, and I have to thank Amanda Speake for the excellent index.

Finally I can only apologise for taking so long to wrap up a project that began so long ago. My debt to Freddie, Michael, Nola, Tama and Zohra is different: no family could have endured the presence of such an all-consuming project with greater tolerance and understanding. I wish I could say it won't happen again.

INDEX